EUROPEAN CONTRACT LAW

# EUROPEAN CONTRACT LAW

Michael Stürner

INTERSENTIA
LEFEBVRE GROUP

Intersentia
Lefebvre Belgium SA
Avenue Jean Monnet 4
1348 Louvain-la-Neuve
Belgium
Email: contact@larcier-intersentia.com

*Distribution for the UK, Ireland and*
*Rest of the World (excl. France, Belgium and Luxembourg)*
Ingram Publisher Services UK
1 Deltic Avenue, Rooksley
Milton Keynes MK13 8LD
United Kingdom
Tel: +44 1752 202 301 | Fax: +44 1752 202 331
Email: ipsuk.customercare@ingramcontent.com

*Distribution for France and Rest of the World (excl. Ireland and the UK)*
Interforum Editis
92 avenue de France
75013 Paris
France

*Distribution for Belgium and Luxembourg*
Larcier-Intersentia
Avenue Jean Monnet 4
1348 Louvain-la-Neuve
Belgium



ISBN 978-1-83970-540-3
D/2025/06040/0383
NUR 822

British Library Cataloguing in Publication Data. A catalogue record for this book is available from the British Library.

# PREFACE

One may rightly say that the private law of the European Union is in a profound identity crisis. After many years of progressive integration, the development towards ever closer harmonisation, which was outlined in the founding treaties and also emphasised later on a political level, has now lost much of its momentum. Only a little more than ten years ago, following an impressive number of sectoral legal instruments, it was still possible, albeit with considerable effort, to adopt the Consumer Rights Directive, the aim of which was cross-cutting, or horizontal, harmonisation. However, this could only be achieved politically by leaving out the area of sales law, which is so central to private law, as well as the tricky field of standard terms. A little after that, the proposal for a Common European Sales Law (CESL), whose optionality seemed to offer a supposedly elegant alternative to the legal-political tightrope walk of fully harmonising legislation, came to a rather inglorious end. The years that followed were marked by a certain struggle to find a proper form in which the failed CESL proposal could be moulded. In the framework of the EU Commission's Digital Agenda, a special regime for contracts for the provision of digital content and services was finally introduced. A second proposal, initially primarily dedicated to the online trade in goods, is now little more than a cautious evolution of the Consumer Sales Directive, even though it does bring a few innovations in terms of content. In the past years, sustainability issues have become increasingly important also for private law. The 2024 Right to Repair Directive bears witness to the difficulties in marrying this policy goal with the traditional postulate of consumer protection. EU private law can therefore still be characterised as the often-cited patchwork quilt – or more optimistically: as a pointillistic painting.

Legal scholarship has accompanied these developments throughout Europe critically, but also constructively. Over the decades, is has been increasingly departing from a purely dogmatic view of national law, opening up to a comparative perspective. A truly European legal academia will prepare the ground for better legislation at the level of the EU. It is one of the aims of this volume to contribute to this endeavour. Initially published in German under the title *Europäisches Vertragsrecht. Institutionelle und methodische Grundlagen, materielles Recht, Kollisionsrecht* (Berlin/Boston: De Gruyter, 2021), the present work strives at being more than a mere translation. Its content has been adapted to a readership more interested in a primarily European perspective, and less keen on learning details about the subtleties of integrating the content of EU directives into the German civil law system and the fine-tuning connected to it.

Moreover, it has been brought up to date, e.g. with a new chapter on the right to the repair of goods. Readers may still note that, throughout the volume, German law and literature are very visible. This is partly due to the fact that German academia is notoriously thorough and exhaustive when it comes to new legislation and case law. At the same time, of course, it reflects the academic environment in which the original version of this book was made.

Preparing a translation – or, more accurately: a second edition in English language – is a painstaking enterprise. My team at the University of Konstanz – Carolin Dedek, Julia Linhart, Olivia Radlmayr, and Eva Winkelmann – have done their best to make the task as easy as possible. A special thanks goes to Dr Adrian Hemler, LLM (Cantab), who has not only coordinated the work on the manuscript, but also provided me with an excellent textual basis for the overhaul. At Intersentia, Nicolas Cassart has always been very supportive towards the project, and Sophie Joiris has done a marvellous job at copy-editing the voluminous manuscript. Readers are welcome to share their comments and thoughts on European contract law with me at michael.stuerner@uni-konstanz.de.

Konstanz, May 2025
Michael Stürner

# CONTENTS

*PART TWO. SUBSTANTIVE CONTRACT LAW*

# TABLE OF ABBREVIATIONS

| | |
|---|---|
| A.C./AC | Law Reports, Appeal Cases (Third Series) |
| AcP | Archiv für die civilistische Praxis |
| ACQP | Acquis Principles |
| ADR | Alternative Dispute Resolution |
| AG | Aktiengesellschaft; Amtsgericht |
| AG | Attorney General |
| AL | Ad Legendum (journal) |
| All ER | All England Law Reports |
| Am.J.Comp.L. | American Journal of Comparative Law |
| AnwBl | Anwaltsblatt (journal) |
| AöR | Archiv des öffentlichen Rechts (journal) |
| Art. | Article |
| B2B | Business-to-Business |
| B2C | Business-to-Consumer |
| BAG | Bundesarbeitsgericht (German Federal Labour Court) |
| BAGE | Official collection of decisions of the German Federal Labour Court |
| BauR | Zeitschrift für das gesamte öffentliche und zivile Baurecht (journal) |
| BB | Betriebs-Berater (journal) |
| BeckOGK | Beck'scher online Großkommentar zum BGB |
| BeckRS | Beck Rechtssache |
| BFH | Bundesfinanzhof (German Federal Revenue Court) |
| BG | Bundesgericht (Swiss Supreme Court) |
| BGB | Bürgerliches Gesetzbuch (German Civil Code) |
| BGBl. | Bundesgesetzblatt (Official Journal, Germany) |

| | |
|---|---|
| BGE | Sammlung der Entscheidungen des Schweizerischen Bundesgerichts (Official collection of decisions of the Swiss Supreme Court |
| BGH | Bundesgerichtshof (German Federal Court of Justice) |
| BGHZ | Sammlung der Entscheidungen des Bundesgerichtshofs in Zivilsachen (Official collection of decisions of the German Federal Court of Justice) |
| BKR | Zeitschrift für Bank- und Kapitalmarktrecht (journal) |
| BLJ | Bucerius Law Journal |
| BR-Drucks. | Bundesrats-Drucksache (German Parliamentary Documents) |
| BT-Drucks. | Bundestags-Drucksache (German Parliamentary Documents) |
| BVerfG | Bundesverfassungsgericht (German Federal Constitutional Court) |
| BVerfGE | Sammlung der Entscheidungen des Bundesverfassungsgerichts (Official collection of decisions of the German Federal Constitutional Court) |
| BVerwG | Bundesverwaltungsgericht (German Federal Administrative Court) |
| BVerwGE | Sammlung der Entscheidungen des Bundesverwaltungsgerichts (Official collection of decisions of the German Federal Administrative Court) |
| C. A. | Court of Appeal |
| c.c. | Codice Civile (Italy) |
| c.i.c. | culpa in contrahendo |
| C2C | Consumer-to-Consumer |
| Cal. L. Rev. | California Law Review |
| CEFL | Commission on European Family Law |
| CESL | Common European Sales Law |
| CFR | Charter of Fundamental Rights |
| Ch. | Law Reports, Chancery Division |
| ChD | Chancery Division |

| | |
|---|---|
| CISG | United Nations Convention on Contracts for the International Sale of Goods |
| civ | civil |
| CJEU | Court of Justice of the European Union |
| CJQ | Civil Justice Quarterly |
| Clev. St. L. Rev. | Cleveland State Law Review |
| CML Rev. | Common Market Law Review |
| CMR | Convention relative au contrat de transport international de marchandises par route |
| COM | Commission documents (European Commission) |
| CoPECL | Common Principles of European Contract Law |
| Cornell Int'l L.J. | Cornell International Law Journal |
| CPR | Civil Procedure Rules (England) |
| CR | Computer und Recht (journal) |
| DAO | Decentralised Autonomous Organisation |
| DAR | Deutsches Autorecht (journal) |
| DB | Der Betrieb (journal) |
| DCFR | Draft Common Frame of Reference |
| DGVZ | Deutsche Gerichtsvollzieher Zeitung (journal) |
| DNotZ | Deutsche Notarzeitschrift (journal) |
| DRiZ | Deutsche Richterzeitschrift (journal) |
| DVBl | Deutsches Verwaltungsblatt (journal) |
| e.a. | et alii |
| EBLR | European Business Law Review |
| ECHR | European Court of Human Rights |
| ECLI | European Case Law Identifier |
| EGBGB | Einführungsgesetz zum Bürgerlichen Gesetzbuch (German Introductory Act to the Civil Code) |
| Einl. | Einleitung (introduction) |
| EJCCL | European Journal of Commercial Contract Law |
| ELI | European Law Institute |

| | |
|---|---|
| EnzEuR | Enzyklopädie des Europarechts |
| EPRS | European Parliamentary Research Service |
| ERCL | European Review of Contract Law |
| ERPL | European Review of Private Law |
| etc. | et cetera |
| EU | European Union |
| EuCML | Journal of European Consumer and Market Law (journal) |
| EuGRZ | Europäische Grundrechte-Zeitschrift (journal) |
| EULA | End User Licence Agreement |
| EuR | Zeitschrift für Europarecht (journal) |
| Europa dir. priv. | Europa e Diritto Privato (journal) |
| euvr | Zeitschrift für Europäisches Unternehmens- und Verbraucherrecht (journal) |
| EuZA | Europäische Zeitschrift für Arbeitsrecht (journal) |
| EuZW | Europäische Zeitschrift für Wirtschaftsrecht (journal) |
| EWHC | Decisions of the High Court of London |
| EWS | Europäisches Wirtschafts- und Steuerrecht (journal) |
| FamRZ | Zeitschrift für das gesamte Familienrecht (journal) |
| ff. | following |
| FS | Festschrift |
| GDP | gross domestic product |
| GDPR | General Data Protection Regulation |
| GG | Grundgesetz (German Constitution) |
| GmbHR | GmbH-Rundschau (journal) |
| GPR | Zeitschrift für das Privatrecht der Europäischen Union (journal) |
| GRUR Int | Gewerblicher Rechtsschutz und Urheberrecht Internationaler Teil (journal) |
| GRUR RR | Gewerblicher Rechtsschutz und Urheberrecht Rechtsprechungs-Report (journal) |

| | |
|---|---|
| GRUR | Gewerblicher Rechtsschutz und Urheberrecht (journal) |
| GRUR-Prax | Gewerblicher Rechtsschutz und Urheberrecht, Praxis im Immaterialgüter- und Wettbewerbsrecht (journal) |
| GS | Gedächtnisschrift |
| GTC | general terms and condititions |
| H. L./HL | House of Lords |
| HRR | Höchstrichterliche Rechtsprechung (Zeitschrift) |
| ICANN | International Corporation for Assigned Names and Numbers |
| ICLQ | International and Comparative Law Quarterly |
| IHR | Internationales Handelsrecht (journal) |
| IMCO | Committee on the Internal Market and Consumer Protection (European Parliament) |
| Ind. J. Global L. Stud. | Indiana Journal of Global Legal Studies |
| int. | international |
| IPRax | Praxis des internationalen Privat- und Verfahrensrechts (journal) |
| IPRG | Bundesgesetz über das Internationale Privatrecht (Swiss Act on Private International Law) |
| IPRspr | Die deutsche Rechtsprechung auf dem Gebiete des Internationalen Privatrechts |
| IWRZ | Zeitschrift für Internationales Wirtschaftsrecht (journal) |
| JbItalR | Jahrbuch für Italienisches Recht (journal) |
| JPrivIntL | Journal of Private International Law |
| JURA (JK) | JURA-Kartei (journal) |
| JURA | Juristische Ausbildung (journal) |
| JURI | Committee on Legal Affairs (European Parliament) |
| JuS | Juristische Schulung (journal) |
| JZ | Juristenzeitung (journal) |
| K&R | Kommunikation und Recht (journal) |
| KG | Kammergericht; Kommanditgesellschaft |

| | |
|---|---|
| KTS | Zeitschrift für Insolvenzrecht (journal) |
| L.J. | Law Journal |
| LG | Landgericht (German Regional Court) |
| LMK | Kommentierte BGH-Rechtsprechung Lindenmaier Möhring (journal) |
| Ltd. | Limited |
| MDR | Monatsschrift für deutsches Recht (journal) |
| MEP | Member of the European Parliament |
| Mich. L. Rev. | Michigan Law Review |
| MLR | Modern Law Review |
| MMR | Multimedia und Recht (journal) |
| MüKo | Münchener Kommentar zum BGB (commentary on the German civil code) |
| NIPR | Nederlands internationaal privaatrecht (journal) |
| NJ | Neue Justiz (journal) |
| NJOZ | Neue Juristische Online Zeitschrift (journal) |
| NJW | Neue Juristische Wochenschrift (journal) |
| NJW-aktuell | Neue Juristische Wochenschrift aktuell (journal) |
| NJW-RR | Neue Juristische Wochenschrift Rechtsprechungsreport (journal) |
| NVersZ | Neue Zeitschrift für Versicherung und Recht (journal) |
| NZA | Neue Zeitschrift für Arbeitsrecht (journal) |
| NZG | Neue Zeitschrift für Gesellschaftsrecht (journal) |
| NZM | Neue Zeitschrift für Mietrecht (journal) |
| NZV | Neue Zeitschrift für Verkehrsrecht (journal) |
| ODR | Online Dispute Resolution |
| OGH | Oberster Gerichtshof (Austrian Supreme Court) |
| Ohio St. J. Disp. Res. | Ohio State Journal on Dispute Resolution |
| ÖJZ | Österreichische Juristen-Zeitung (journal) |
| OLG | Oberlandesgericht (Higher Regional Court, Germany) |

| | |
|---|---|
| PECL | Principles of European Contract Law |
| PICC | Principles of International Commercial Contracts |
| PIL | Private International Law |
| PWW | Prütting/Wegen/Weinreich (commentary on the German civil code) |
| QB | Law Reports Queen's Bench Division |
| RabelsZ | Rabels Zeitschrift für ausländisches und internationales Privatrecht (journal) |
| Rass. dir. civ. | Rassegna di diritto civile (journal) |
| RdA | Recht der Arbeit (journal) |
| Rev. crit. DIP | Revue critique de droit international privé (journal) |
| Rev. trim. dr. civ. | Revue trimestrielle de droit civil (journal) |
| RGZ | Entscheidungen des Reichsgerichts in Zivilsachen (Official collection of decisions of the German Imperial Court) |
| Riv. dir. civ. | Rivista di diritto civile (journal) |
| RIW | Recht der Internationalen Wirtschaft (journal) |
| RRa | Reiserecht aktuell (journal) |
| SCE | Societas Cooperativa Europaea |
| SchiedsVZ | Neue Zeitschrift für Schiedsverfahren (journal) |
| SE | Societas Europaea |
| sec. | section |
| SME | Small and Medium Enterprise |
| TFEU | Treaty on the Functioning of the European Union |
| UN | United Nations |
| UNCITRAL | United Nations Commission On International Trade Law |
| UNIDROIT | Institut international pour l'unification du droit privé |
| Unif. L. Rev. | Uniform Law Review |
| UNSDG | United Nations Sustainable Development Goals |
| US | United States |
| v. | versus |
| VersR | Versicherungsrecht (journal) |

| | |
|---|---|
| VuR | Verbraucher und Recht (journal) |
| Wash.U.L.Rev. | Washington University Law Review |
| WLR | Weekly Law Reports |
| WM | Wertpapiermitteilungen (journal) |
| WRP | Wettbewerb in Recht und Praxis (journal) |
| Yale L.J. | Yale Law Journal |
| ZEuP | Zeitschrift für Europäisches Privatrecht (journal) |
| ZEuS | Zeitschrift für europarechtliche Studien (journal) |
| ZfPW | Zeitschrift für die gesamte Privatrechtswissenschaft (journal) |
| ZfRV | Zeitschrift für Rechtsvergleichung, internationales Privatrecht und Europarecht (journal) |
| ZGB | Zivilgesetzbuch (Swiss Civil Code) |
| ZGR | Zeitschrift für Gesellschaftsrecht (journal) |
| ZGS | Zeitschrift für das gesamte Schuldrecht (journal) |
| ZHR | Zeitschrift für das gesamte Handels- und Wirtschaftsrecht (journal) |
| ZIP | Zeitschrift für Wirtschaftsrecht (journal) |
| ZJS | Zeitschrift für das juristische Studium (journal) |
| ZKM | Zeitschrift für Konfliktmanagement (journal) |
| ZLW | Zeitschrift für Luft- und Weltraumrecht (journal) |
| ZPO | Zivilprozessordnung (German Code of Civil Procedure) |
| ZRP | Zeitschrift für Rechtspolitik (journal) |
| ZSR | Zeitschrift für Schweizerisches Recht (journal) |
| ZUM | Zeitschrift für Urheber- und Medienrecht (journal) |
| ZVertriebsR | Zeitschrift für Vertriebsrecht (journal) |
| ZVglRWiss | Zeitschrift für vergleichende Rechtswissenschaft (journal) |
| ZZP | Zeitschrift für Zivilprozess (journal) |
| ZZPInt | Zeitschrift für Zivilprozess International (journal) |

# MATERIALS

## 1. Cases, Materials and Text Compilations


- Grolimund, P./Mosimann, N., *Internationales Privat- und Zivilverfahrensrecht der Europäischen Union*, 2nd ed., Dike-Verlag, Zürich/St. Gallen 2015
- Grundmann, S./Riesenhuber, K., *Textsammlung Europäisches Privatrecht. Vertrags- und Schuldrecht, Arbeitsrecht, Gesellschaftsrecht*, 3rd ed., De Gruyter, Berlin/New York 2020
- Hartkamp, A./Sieburgh, C./Devroe, W., *Cases, Materials and Text on European Law and Private Law*, Hart Publishing, Oxford 2017
- Jayme, E./Hausmann, R., *Internationales Privat- und Verfahrensrecht – Textausgabe*, 21st ed., C.H. Beck, Munich 2022
- Schulze, R./Zimmermann, R., *Europäisches Privatrecht – Basistexte*, 6th ed., Nomos, Baden-Baden 2020


## 2. Academic Model Rules


- von Bar, C./Clive, E./Schulte-Nölke, H. (eds.), *Principles, Definitions and Model Rules of European Private Law. Draft Common Frame of Reference (DCFR)*, Full Edition, Sellier, Munich 2009
- Beale, H./Lando, O., *The Principles of European Contract Law, Part I, Performance, Non-Performance and Remedies*, Prepared by the Commission on European Contract Law, Dordrecht 1995
- Gandolfi, G. (ed.), *Code Européen des Contrats, Avant-projet*, Livre Premier, Mailand 2001
- Jansen, N./Zimmermann, R. (eds.), *Commentaries on European Contract Laws*, Oxford University Press, Oxford 2018
- Lando, O./Beale, H. (eds.), *Principles of European Contract Law*, Parts I and II, Den Haag 2000
- Lando, O./Clive, E./Prüm, A./Zimmermann, R. (eds.), *Principles of European Contract Law*, Part III, Den Haag 2003


## 3. Textbooks

### a) On European Private Law


- Heiderhoff, B., *Europäisches Privatrecht*, 6th ed., C.F. Müller, Heidelberg 2023

- Herresthal, C., '§2: Vertragsrecht', in K. Langenbucher (ed.), *Europäisches Privat- und Wirtschaftsrecht*, 5th ed., Nomos, Baden-Baden 2022
- Langenbucher, K./Donath, P.B., '§1: Europarechtliche Methodenlehre', in K. Langenbucher (ed.), *Europäisches Privat- und Wirtschaftsrecht*, 5th ed., Nomos, Baden-Baden 2022
- Ranieri, F., *Europäisches Obligationenrecht – Ein Handbuch mit Texten und Materialien*, 3rd ed., Springer, Vienna 2009
- Riesenhuber, K., *EU-Vertragsrecht*, Mohr Siebeck, Tübingen 2013
- Schulze, R./Zoll, F., *European Contract Law*, 3rd ed., C.H. Beck/Hart/Nomos, Baden-Baden 2021
- Weatherill, S., *Contract Law of the Internal Market*, Intersentia, Cambridge 2016

**b) On European Private International Law**

- von Bar, C./Mankowski, P., *Internationales Privatrecht*, Volume 2: Besonderer Teil, 2nd ed., C.H. Beck, Munich 2019
- van Calster, G., *European Private International Law*, 4rd ed., Hart Publishing, Oxford/Portland 2024
- Junker, A., *Internationales Privatrecht*, 5th ed., C.H. Beck, Munich 2022
- Rauscher, Thomas, *Internationales Privatrecht. Mit internationalem Verfahrensrecht*, 5th ed., C.F. Müller, Heidelberg 2017
- Rogerson, P., *Collier's Conflict of Laws*, 4th ed., Cambridge University Press, Cambridge 2013
- Stone, P., Stone on *Private International Law in the European Union*, 4th ed., Edward Elgar Publishing, Cheltenham 2018
- Torremans, P. (ed.), *Cheshire, North & Fawcett, Private International Law*, 15th ed., Oxford University Press, Oxford 2017
- Stürner, M., '§8: Internationales Privatrecht', in Langenbucher (ed.), *Europäisches Privat- und Wirtschaftsrecht*, 5th ed., Nomos, Baden-Baden 2022

**5. Monographs, Handbooks, Collective Volumes**
**a) On European Private Law**

- Alpa, G./Andenæs, M., *Grundlagen des Europäischen Privatrechts*, Springer, Berlin 2010
- Andenæs, M./Baasch Anderson, C., *Theory and Practice of Harmonization*, Edward Elgar Publishing, Cheltenham 2012
- Arnold, S. (ed.), *Grundlagen eines europäischen Vertragsrechts*, Sellier, Munich 2014

- Baldus, C./Müller-Graff, P.-C. (eds.), *Die Generalklausel im Europäischen Privatrecht. Zur Leistungsfähigkeit der deutschen Wissenschaft aus romanischer Perspektive*, Munich 2006
- Basedow, J., *EU Private Law. Anatomy of a Growing Legal Order*, Intersentia, Cambridge 2021
- Basedow, J./Hopt, K./Zimmermann, R. (eds.) *Max Planck Encyclopedia of European Private Law*, Oxford University Press, Oxford 2012
- Cauffman, C./Smits, J.M. (eds.), *The Citizen in European Private Law: Norm-setting, Enforcement and Choice*, Intersentia, Cambridge 2016
- Collins, H. (ed.), *The EU Charter of Fundamental Rights and European Contract Law*, Intersentia, Cambridge 2017
- Dannemann, G./Vogenauer, S. (eds.), *The Common European Sales Law in Context: Interactions with English and German Law*, Oxford University Press, Oxford 2013
- De Cristofaro, G./de Franceschi, A. (eds.), *Consumer Sales Law in Europe – After the Implementation of the Consumer Sales Directive*, Intersentia, Cambridge 2016
- Ebers, M., *Rechte, Rechtsbehelfe und Sanktionen im Unionsprivatrecht*, Mohr Siebeck, Tübingen 2016
- Eidenmüller, H./Faust, F./Grigoleit, C./Jansen, N./Wagner, G./Zimmermann, R., *Revision des Verbraucher-acquis*, Mohr Siebeck, Tübingen 2011
- Fornasier, M./Stanzione, M.G. (eds.), *The European Convention on Human Rights and its Impact on National Private Law. A Comparative Perspective*, Intersentia, Cambridge 2023
- Gardiner, C., *Unfair Contract Terms in the Digital Age. The Challenge of Protecting European Consumers in the Online Marketplace*, Edward Elgar Publishing, Cheltenham 2022
- Gebauer, M., *Grundfragen der Europäisierung des Privatrechts. Eine Untersuchung nationaler Ansätze unter Berücksichtigung des italienischen und des deutschen Rechts*, C. Winter, Heidelberg 1998
- Gebauer, M./Teichmann, C. (eds.), *Enzyklopädie Europarecht Volume 6: Europäisches Privat- und Unternehmensrecht*, 2nd ed., Nomos, Baden-Baden 2022
- Gebauer, M./Wiedmann, T. (eds.), *Europäisches Zivilrecht*, 3rd ed., C.H. Beck, Munich 2021
- Goanţă, C., *Convergence in European Consumer Sales Law. A Comparative and Numerical Approach*, Intersentia, Cambridge 2016
- Grundmann, S. (ed.), *Systembildung und Systemlücken in Kerngebieten des Europäischen Privatrechts – Gesellschaftsrecht, Arbeitsrecht, Schuldvertragsrecht*, Mohr Siebeck, Tübingen 2000
- Grundmann, S. (ed.), *European Contract Law in the Digital Age*, Intersentia, Cambridge 2018

- Grundmann, S./Grochowski, M., *European Contract Law and the Creation of Norms*, Intersentia, Cambridge 2021
- Gsell, B./Herresthal, C. (eds.), *Vollharmonisierung im Privatrecht – Die Konzeption der Richtlinie am Scheideweg?*, Mohr Siebeck, Tübingen 2010
- Gutman, K., *The Constitutional Foundations of European Contract Law: A Comparative Analysis*, Oxford University Press, Oxford 2014
- Hartkamp, A., *European Law and National Private Law*, 2nd ed., Hart Publishing, Oxford 2016
- Heiderhoff, B./Lohsse, S./Schulze, R. (eds.), *EU-Grundrechte und Privatrecht*, Nomos, Baden-Baden 2016
- Helleringer, G./Purnhagen, K. (eds.), *Towards a European Legal Culture*, C.H. Beck/Hart/Nomos, Baden-Baden 2014
- Hesselink, M.W., *Justifying Contract in Europe. Political Philosophies of European Contract Law*, Oxford University Press, Oxford 2021
- Janssen, A./Lehmann, M./Schulze, R. (eds.), *The Future of European Private Law*, Nomos, Baden-Baden 2023
- Jud, B./Wendehorst, C. (eds.), *Neuordnung des Verbraucherprivatrechts in Europa? Zum Vorschlag einer Richtlinie über Rechte der Verbraucher*, Manz, Vienna 2009
- Letto-Vanamo, P./Smits, J. (eds.), *Coherence and Fragmentation in European Private Law*, Sellier, Munich 2012
- van Leeuwen, B., *European Standardisation of Services and its Impact on Private Law. Paradoxes of Convergence*, Hart Publishing, Oxford 2017
- von Leuken, R., *Private Law and the Internal Market. Direct Horizontal Effect of the Treaty Provisions on Free Movement*, Intersentia, Cambridge 2017
- Lohse, E.J., *Rechtsangleichungsprozesse in der Europäischen Union. Instrumente, Funktionsmechanismen und Wirkparameter effektiver Harmonisierung*, Mohr Siebeck, Tübingen 2017
- Lurger, B., *Grundfragen der Vereinheitlichung des Vertragsrechts in der Europäischen Union*, Springer, Vienna 2002
- Lüttringhaus, J.D., *Vertragsfreiheit und ihre Materialisierung im Europäischen Binnenmarkt – Die Verbürgung und Materialisierung unionaler Vertragsfreiheit im Zusammenspiel von EU-Privatrecht, BGB und ZPO*, Mohr Siebeck, Tübingen 2018
- Martens, S., *Methodenlehre des Unionsrechts*, Mohr Siebeck, Tübingen 2013
- Metzger, A., *Extra legem, intra ius. Allgemeine Rechtsgrundsätze im europäischen Privatrecht*, Mohr Siebeck, Tübingen 2009
- Micklitz, H.W./Sieburgh, C. (eds.), *Primary EU Law and Private Law Concepts*, Intersentia, Cambridge 2017
- Miller, L., *The Emergence of EU Contract Law – Exploring Europeanization*, Oxford University Press, Oxford 2011

- Mittwoch, A.-C., *Vollharmonisierung und Europäisches Privatrecht – Methode, Implikationen und Durchführung*, De Gruyter, Berlin 2013
- Mörsdorf, O., *Ungleichbehandlung als Norm. Eine dogmatische Analyse des unional determinierten Antidiskriminierungsrechts in Deutschland*, Mohr Siebeck, Tübingen 2018
- Müller-Graff, P.-C. (ed.), *Gemeinsames Privatrecht in der Europäischen Gemeinschaft*, 2nd ed., Nomos, Baden-Baden 1999
- Niglia, L., *The Struggle for European Private Law. A Critique of Codification*, Hart Publishing, Oxford 2017
- Niglia, L., *The Structural Transformation of European Private Law. A Critique of Juridical Hermeneutics*, Hart Publishing, Oxford 2024
- Perner, S., *Grundfreiheiten, Grundrechte-Charta und Privatrecht*, Mohr Siebeck, Tübingen 2013
- Reich, N., *General Principles of EU Civil Law*, Intersentia, Cambridge 2013
- Remien, O., *Zwingendes Vertragsrecht und Grundfreiheiten des EG-Vertrags*, Mohr Siebeck, Tübingen 2003
- Riesenhuber, K. (ed.), *European Legal Methodology*, 2nd ed., Intersentia, Cambridge 2021
- Riesenhuber, K., *System und Prinzipien des Europäischen Vertragsrechts*, De Gruyter, Berlin 2003
- Rutgers, J./Sirena, P. (eds.), *Rules and Principles in European Contract Law*, Intersentia, Cambridge 2015
- van Schagen, E., *The Development of European Private Law in a Multilevel Legal Order*, Intersentia, Cambridge 2016
- Schmidt-Kessel, M. (ed.), *Der Gemeinsame Referenzrahmen, Entstehung, Inhalte, Anwendung*, Sellier, Munich 2009
- Schmidt-Kessel, M. (ed.), *Ein einheitliches europäisches Kaufrecht? Eine Analyse des Vorschlags der Kommission*, Sellier, Munich 2012
- Schulte-Nölke, H./Zoll, F./Jansen, N./Schulze, R. (eds.), *Der Entwurf für ein optionales europäisches Kaufrecht*, Sellier, Munich 2012
- Schulze, R./Staudenmayer, D. (eds.), *Digital Revolution: Challenges for Contract Law in Practice*, Nomos, Baden-Baden 2016
- Schulze, Reiner/Staudenmayer, Dirk (eds.), *EU Digital Law: Article-by-Article Commentary*, Nomos, Baden-Baden 2020
- Schulze, R./von Bar, C./Schulte-Nölke, H. (eds.), *Der akademische Entwurf für einen Gemeinsamen Referenzrahmen*, Mohr Siebeck, Tübingen 2008
- Smits, J.M./Husa, J./Valcke, C./Narciso, M. (eds.), *Elgar Encyclopedia of Comparative Law*, Edward Elgar Publishing, Cheltenham 2023
- Stürner, M. (ed.), *Vollharmonisierung im europäischen Verbraucherrecht?*, Munich 2010
- Twigg-Flesner, C. (ed.), *Research Handbook on EU Consumer and Contract Law*, Edward Elgar Publishing, Chelthenham 2016

- Twigg-Flesner, C. (ed.), *The Cambridge Companion to European Union Private Law*, Cambridge University Press, Cambridge 2010

### b) On European Private International Law

- Arnold (ed.), *Grundfragen des Europäischen Kollisionsrechts*, Mohr Siebeck, Tübingen 2016
- Basedow, J./Rühl, G./Ferrari, F./de Miguel Asensio, P. (eds.), *Encyclopedia of Private International Law*, Edward Elgar Publshing, Cheltenham 2017
- Fallon, M./Lagarde, P./Poillot-Peruzzetto, S., *Quelle architecture pour un code européen de droit international privé?*, P. Lang, Brussels 2011
- Guinchard, E. (ed.), *Rome I and Rome II in Practice*, Intersentia, Cambridge 2020
- von Hein, Jan/Rühl, G. (eds.), *Kohärenz im Internationalen Privat- und Verfahrensrecht der Europäischen Union*, Mohr Siebeck, Tübingen 2016
- von Hein, J./Kieninger, E.-M./Rühl, G (eds.), *How European is European Private International Law? Sources, Court Practice, Academic Discourse*, Intersentia, Cambridge 2019
- Leible S./Unberath, H. (eds.), *Brauchen wir eine Rom 0-Verordnung?*, JWV, Jena 2013
- Stone, P./Farah, Y. (eds.), *Research Handbook on EU Private International Law*, Edward Elgar Publishing, Cheltenham 2015
- Trüten, D., *Die Entwicklungen des Internationalen Privatrechts in der Europäischen Union. Auf dem Weg zu einem europäischen IPR-Gesetz*, Nomos/Stämpfli, Baden-Baden/Basel 2015
- Wilke, F.M., *A Conceptual Analysis of European Private International Law. The General Issues in the EU and its Member States*, Intersentia, Cambridge 2019

## 6. Journals

- Common Market Law Review (CMLRev)
- Contratto e impresa / Europa
- Europäisches Wirtschafts- und Steuerrecht (EWR)
- European Review of Contract Law (ERCL)
- European Review of Private Law (ERPL)
- Europäische Zeitschrift für Wirtschaftsrecht (EuZW)
- Praxis des Internationalen Privat- und Verfahrensrechts (IPRax)
- Journal of European Consumer and Market Law (EuCML) (previously: Zeitschrift für Europäisches Unternehmens- und Verbraucherrecht, euvr)
- Journal of Private International Law
- Rabels Zeitschrift für ausländisches und internationales Privatrecht (RabelsZ)

- Revue des contrats
- Yearbook of Private International Law
- Zeitschrift für das Privatrecht der Europäischen Union (GPR) (previously: Zeitschrift für Gemeinschaftsprivatrecht)
- Zeitschrift für Europäisches Privatrecht (ZEuP)
- Zeitschrift für Europäisches Wirtschaftsrecht (EuZW)

# PART ONE

# INSTITUTIONAL AND METHODOLOGICAL FOUNDATIONS

# CHAPTER 1

# FUNDAMENTAL CONCEPTS AND BASIC TERMINOLOGY

## §1. FUNCTION AND OBJECTIVES OF PRIVATE LAW HARMONISATION

CONTENTS



References: A. Beckers/H.-W. Micklitz/R. Vallejo/P. Letto-Vanamo (eds.), *The Foundations of European Transnational Private Law* (London: Bloomsbury Publishing, 2024); W. Hallstein, 'Angleichung des Privat- und Prozeßrechts in der Europäischen Wirtschaftsgemeinschaft', *RabelsZ* 28 (1964), 211; T. Wilhelmsson, *Free Movement of Legal Ideas. Towards a Dynamic Europeanisation of Private Law* (London: Bloomsbury Publishing, 2024).

## I. REALISATION OF THE EUROPEAN INTERNAL MARKET

1. One of the EU's main objectives is to implement an internal market (Article 3(3) TEU), i.e. an area without internal borders in which the free movement of goods, persons, services and capital is guaranteed. The EU can adopt the measures necessary for this purpose (Article 26(1) TFEU). Private law, particularly contract law, is essential for exercising the above-mentioned fundamental freedoms since contracts are the primary legal devices to cater for,

and enable, the exchange of goods and services in a market economy. Therefore, its regulation lies at the heart of any legal policy approach that aims to ensure the functioning of the internal market.

**2.** This was not always the case. In the first decades after the founding of the European Economic Community (EEC) on 25 March 1957, the main concern was to remove direct obstacles to fundamental freedoms through protectionist legislation in the Member States. While the harmonisation of private law had already been foreseen in the mid-1960s by the then-president of the Commission, Walter Hallstein,[1] the first directives directly related to private law did not follow until the 1980s.[2] Today, large areas of contract law, especially consumer law, are subject to strong European influence. This harmonisation essentially pursues two goals: (1) the standardisation of the level of protection on the demand side in the internal market to strengthen confidence in the internal market and (2) the standardisation of the conditions of competition for businesses to create a 'level playing field' for all market participants. Both perspectives show that the harmonisation of European contract law aims to standardise general market conditions.

## 1. HARMONISATION OF CONSUMER PROTECTION LEVELS

References: M.W. De Hoon/V. Mak, 'Consumer Empowerment Strategies – A Rights-Oriented Approach Versus a Needs-Oriented Approach', *ZEuP* 2011, 518; H.-W. Micklitz, 'Europäisches Regulierungsprivatrecht: Plädoyer für ein neues Denken', *GPR* 2009, 254 and *GPR* 2010, 2; M. Stürner, 'Grundstrukturen des Verbrauchervertrags', *JURA* 2015, 30; C. Wendehorst, 'Regulierungsprivatrecht. Verhaltenssteuerung durch Privatrecht am Beispiel des europäischen Verbrauchervertragsrechts', in E. Schumann (ed.), *Das erziehende Gesetz* (Berlin: de Gruyter, 2014), p. 113.

**3.** The primary objective of the legal acts related to European contract law is to achieve a high level of consumer protection in all Member States. Hence, European contract law also realises a principle of primary EU law since Article 169 TFEU demands the promotion of the interests of consumers. According to an established view, this objective was to be achieved by establishing a minimum degree of harmonisation.[3] In justifying its legislative action, the EU Commission often emphasised the furthering of the internal market: Differing legal frameworks for concluding contracts might obstruct the functioning of the internal market, given that they could deter consumers from cross-border

---

1 Hallstein, *RabelsZ* 28 (1964), 211.
2 On the history of private law harmonisation in Europe, see §3.
3 On the concept of minimum harmonisation, see paras. 75–77 below.

purchases of products and services.[4] However, if consumers found a harmonised level of protection in all Member States, they appeared much more likely to benefit from the internal market. At the same time, the concept of minimum harmonisation allowed Member States to introduce or maintain national regulations that were more favourable to consumers overall.[5] Thus, this body of law may be called regulatory private law.[6]

**4.** Keeping in mind that Article 6 of the Rome I Regulation, which is usually applicable to cross-border contracts between businesses and consumers,[7] calls for the application of the law of the consumer's domicile, this could even be seen as an incentive for the Member States to establish a comparably high level of consumer protection in order to make the legal framework as favourable as possible for their own consumers in cross-border legal transactions. However, such considerations remained largely theoretical: Since an increase in the level of consumer protection will also affect purely domestic cases and given that these represent the vast majority of consumer contracts, at least in large Member States, the argument of protecting one's own consumers against foreign providers usually carries little weight. This is mainly due to the fact that domestic entrepreneurs would also have to adjust to said higher level of consumer protection. While a different treatment of the domestic and internal market, i.e. discrimination against domestic citizens, remains possible under EU law,[8] this would usually need justification under the principle of equality in domestic constitutional law and is usually unacceptable in terms of legal policy. Hence, the incentives that the concept of minimum harmonisation can exert to increase consumer protection are quite limited.

**5.** From the point of view of the Member States, the concept of minimum harmonisation causes a comparatively minor interference with national contract law. However, since it does not aim to realise full harmonisation, the legal rules above the minimum protection standards are usually inconsistent again, meaning that legal fragmentation continues to exist, albeit at a higher level. Therefore, the more recent legal acts within EU private law typically follow the concept of full harmonisation.[9]

---

4 Recitals 2–6 Unfair Terms Directive; Recitals 3–5 CSD.

5 Examples: Article 8 Doorstep Selling Directive, Article 8 Unfair Terms Directive, Article 8(2) CSD, Article 14 Distance Selling Directive.

6 Namely Micklitz, *GPR* 2009, 254, *GPR* 2010, 2.

7 See paras. 1188–1200 below for more details, including the concept of directing the business activity to the consumer's country of residence.

8 See A. Epiney, *Umgekehrte Diskriminierungen* (Cologne: Carl Heymanns, 1994).

9 Namely the Second Consumer Credit Directive, the Second Timeshare Directive, the CRD, the Sale of Goods Directive and the Digital Content Directive. In detail, see paras. 78–83 below.

## 2. HARMONISATION OF COMPETITION CONDITIONS FOR BUSINESSES

**6.** With the harmonisation of consumer law, the competition conditions for corporations operating in the internal market are also assimilated. Consumer law can, therefore, also be seen as 'external' legal framework for businesses.[10] In this respect, every increase in the level of consumer protection simultaneously entails a change in the market conditions for businesses on the supply side. For example, the introduction of duties of information for consumer contracts[11] forces businesses to adapt the modalities regarding the conclusion of the contract. Similarly, establishing rights of withdrawal for consumer contracts[12] causes costs that are likely to increase the product's price.[13]

**7.** However, the internal market does not only open the possibility of conducting cross-border business with consumers. EU regulation also covers trade between businesses (B2B). Most important in this respect are the regulations against unfair competition, particularly the Unfair Commercial Practices Directive,[14] the regulations in the area of antitrust law (which are partly based on primary law)[15] and the Product Liability Directive.[16] This field can be described as market-opening and competition law.[17] Contract law, in the classical sense, has only been regulated in a piecemeal manner. One example is the law on commercial agents, where the Commercial Agents Directive[18] has introduced a series of regulations concerning the parties' contractual obligations, commission, termination of the contract or the right to compensation.[19]

**8.** However, a more far-reaching unification of commercial law is still pending – a quite astonishing finding in light of this subject-matter's central importance for the internal market. For some time now, a Franco-German initiative aims

---

10 S. Grundmann, *Europäisches Schuldvertragsrecht* (Berlin: De Gruyter, 1999), pp. 12 ff.

11 In particular through the CRD, for more on this, see §11.

12 Examples: CRD, Second Consumer Credit Directive, Second Timeshare Directive. Cf. below at paras. 557–609.

13 On this point Eidenmüller, *AcP* 210 (2010), 67, 71 ff.

14 Directive 2005/29/EC of the European Parliament and of the Council of 11 May 2005 concerning unfair business-to-consumer commercial practices in the internal market.

15 See the provisions in Articles 101, 102 TFEU.

16 Council Directive 85/374/EEC of 25 July 1985 on the approximation of the laws, regulations and administrative provisions of the Member States concerning liability for defective products.

17 This is the title of the work of the same name by P. Behrens, *Europäisches Marktöffnungs- und Wettbewerbsrecht* (Heidelberg: C.F. Müller, 2017).

18 Council Directive 86/653/EEC of 18 December 1986 on the coordination of the laws of the Member States relating to self-employed commercial agents.

19 See in more detail below paras. 1050–1057.

to create models rules of a European Commercial Code.[20] This working group, supported by the *Fondation pour le droit continental* and the *Association Henri Capitant*, aims to submit specific harmonisation proposals in different areas of commercial and economic law.[21] As things stand, however, the law of commercial contracts will not be part of it. In its White Paper on the Future of Europe, the EU Commission has at least mentioned the scenario of a commercial code for those Member States that want to participate.[22]

### 3. HARMONISATION OF GENERAL MARKET CONDITIONS

**9.** It makes sense in the process of harmonisation of laws in the internal market to consider all market participants' interests. Contract law, in particular, represents the legal framework for participation in the internal market for consumers and businesses alike. This could also be called 'market participant law' since it contains mandatory and non-mandatory rules for economic agents within the internal market.

## II. SINGLE AREA OF JUSTICE

**10.** The numerous regulations enacted at the European level over the past decades have created a single area of justice. However, this does not amount to more than the fact that certain standards and rules apply within the internal market. Under no circumstances can the EU be compared with the uniform legal area of a state or federation. In many cases, there are only fragmentary EU regulations or none at all. Sometimes, the metaphors of the 'patchwork quilt', the 'pointillistic painting', or the 'islands in the sea' were used to illustrate this.[23] Approaches to a more overarching harmonisation have hardly been successful so far.[24] However, more and more general legal principles are emerging which may reduce the urge to implement extensive legal harmonisation within the internal market. In this respect, a central role is played by the CJEU's extensive case law, which has contributed to the development of an *acquis communautaire* of legal

---

20 On this Lehmann, *ZHR* 181 (2017), 9; Lehmann, *GPR* 2017, 262; Riesenhuber, *GPR* 2017, 270; Dupichot, *ZEuP* 2017, 145.

21 See also paras. 202–205 below.

22 White Paper on the Future of Europe – Reflections and scenarios for the EU27 by 2025, 1 March 2017, COM(2017) 2025, p. 12. It reads: 'A group of countries works together and agree on a common "Business Law Code" unifying corporate, commercial and related domains of law, helping businesses of all sizes to easily operate across borders.' On the resulting perspectives Lehmann, *ERPL* 2020, 73.

23 See also paras. 1293–1298 below.

24 More on the development see at paras. 1299–1317 below.

principles which have also proven to be tremendously significant for the area of contract law.

## III. THE ROLE OF CONTRACT LAW IN THE INTERNAL MARKET

**11.** European contract law has a double significance in the internal market: On the one hand, it is the basis for the economic activity of market participants. No goods, services, or capital exchange is conceivable without contract law. Contract law thus directly helps serve the realisation of the fundamental EU freedoms. On the other hand, the rules of contract law, at least when they are mandatory, might also obstruct the internal market: Non-harmonised law creates disparities between the Member States' legal systems, which can create obstacles to cross-border trade. This tension must be resolved by legislation, courts, and legal academics alike.

# §2. CONCEPT AND SUBJECT MATTER OF EUROPEAN CONTRACT LAW

## CONTENTS

References: J. Basedow, 'Grundlagen des europäischen Privatrechts', in E.-M. Kieninger/O. Remien (eds.), *Privat- und Wirtschaftsrecht im Zeichen der Europäischen Integration* (Baden-Baden: Nomos, 2004), p. 101; M. Cannarsa, '(Re)Shaping European Private Law – The Role of Core Legal Areas: Contract Law and Tort Law', in A. Janssen/M. Lehmann/R. Schulze (eds.), *The Future of European Private Law* (Baden-Baden: Nomos, 2023), p. 245; M. Gebauer, *Grundfragen der Europäisierung des Privatrechts* (Heidelberg: C. Winter, 1998), §§7–11; B. Gsell, 'Zivilrechtsanwendung im Europäischen Mehrebenensystem', *AcP* 214 (2014), 99; C. Herresthal, 'Vertragsrecht', in K. Langenbucher, *Europäisches Privat- und Wirtschaftsrecht* (Baden-Baden: Nomos, 2022), §2; P.-C. Müller-Graff (ed.), *Privatrecht und Europäisches Gemeinschaftsrecht – Gemeinschaftsprivatrecht*, 2nd ed. (Baden-Baden: Nomos, 1991); L. Niglia, *The Structural Transformation of European Private Law. A Critique of Juridical Hermeneutics* (London: Bloomsbury Publishing, 2023); K. Riesenhuber, *EU-Vertragsrecht* (Tübingen: Mohr Siebeck, 2013), §2; R. Schulze, *European Private Law – Current Status and Perspectives* (Munich: Sellier, 2011); M. Stürner, 'Das Privatrecht der Europäischen Union', *JURA* 2016, 1133; A. Zaccaria, 'Il Diritto privato europeo nell'epoca del postmodernismo', in *Mélanges Fritz Sturm*, Volume II, (Liège: Éditions juridiques de l'Université de Liège, 1999), p. 1311.

# I. EUROPEAN CONTRACT LAW AS PART OF EU PRIVATE LAW

**12.** European contract law forms a subset of the rules of European private law. There is little terminological clarity as both terms are not used consistently.[1] Primarily, this concerns the question of when a private law rule might qualify as 'European'. The ideas about what belongs to private law also diverge, sometimes considerably, between different Member States.

## 1. EUROPEAN UNION PRIVATE LAW

**13.** In the narrower or formal sense, European private law refers to laws enacted by the EU that contain private law. This refers, in particular, to secondary law. The terms EU private law, or formerly Community private law, or *ius communitatis*, are also commonly used. Furthermore, primary law may also have private law content. This applies first and foremost to the prohibition of cartels in Article 101 TFEU, but also to the fundamental freedoms, which can require or prohibit certain forms of private law as overriding principles.[2] Rules and principles developed by CJEU case law may also be considered EU private law. However, strictly speaking, this is already a borderline case given that the CJEU's decisions also emerge based on a comparative legal overview of the Member States' legal systems and not only by way of interpretation and further development of EU law. In this respect, using the term EU private law is not self-evident.

## 2. COMMON EUROPEAN PRIVATE LAW OR *IUS COMMUNE*

**14.** In contrast to the term EU private law, which is oriented towards positive law, the term common European private law (or *ius commune*) refers to the sum of all legal principles that are, from a historical and comparative perspective, shared by EU Member States.[3] Admittedly, a precise definition appears to be impossible, both with regard to the question of what is European (only EU states or also Switzerland, for example)[4] and the criteria of what is required for the

---

1 See also Gsell, *AcP* 214 (2014), 99, 102.

2 For the legal sources, see below paras. 210–216.

3 Gebauer, *Grundfragen der Europäisierung des Privatrechts*, 1998, p. 62 ff.; Riesenhuber, System und Prinzipien des Europäischen Vertragsrechts, 2003, p. 44 ff. The work of Kötz, *European Contract Law*, 2nd ed. 2017, is based on a comparative law approach including common principles of European private law.

4 However, the UNIDROIT Principles of International Commercial Contracts (PICC), for example, would not be part of common European private law, as they are not fed solely by European legal principles. See para. 105 below for more information.

commonality of a legal principle. Some approaches to this issue can be found in European harmonisation projects that various groups of legal scholars have created, for example, the Principles of European Contract Law (PECL) or the Draft Common Frame of Reference (DCFR),[5] which, according to the intention of their authors, are supposed to reflect the state of common European private law within the areas they relate to.[6] The sum of these legal principles may also be called European private law in a broader or substantive sense. Their significance sometimes goes beyond that of purely academic texts – for example, the DCFR has been drafted with the perspective of a possible legislative initiative in mind.[7]

**15.** The vagueness of the concept of common European private law becomes particularly apparent if, following a widespread view, one would also like to include national legal principles insofar as they are common to the European legal systems.[8] This only promises to be possible with regard to a few principles, such as the principle of *pacta sunt servanda*, whereas it will be much more challenging to reach a consensus on the principle of good faith or the prohibition of abuse of rights.[9] This shows that this set of rules belongs first and foremost to the domain of comparative law.

## 3. EUROPEAN PRIVATE LAW AS A GENERIC TERM

**16.** The term European private law (*droit privé européen; Europäisches Privatrecht; diritto privato europeo* etc) is also used widely in the academic discourse.[10] In principle, it is based on the formal concept of EU private law as described above, i.e. the entire body of those private law rules that the EU legislator has enacted. At the same time, however, it includes a substantive dimension (without a primarily comparative perspective) which relates to the common European roots of private law. Only this more comprehensive view appropriately reflects the significant interdependency of the various levels within European private law.

---

5 See paras. 120–129 below.

6 See more on this and other unification projects below paras.160–208.

7 See below paras. 120–129.

8 According to Flessner, *JZ* 2002, 14, 15 on the other hand, all provisions of national private law belong to the concept of European private law. However, the classification thus becomes contourless; it does not show clearly enough that European private law is a legal system still in the process of formation.

9 See Stürner, *Der Grundsatz der Verhältnismäßigkeit im Schuldvertragsrecht*, 2010, pp. 414 ff. and paras. 409–476 below.

10 See e.g. Heiderhoff, *Europäisches Privatrecht*, para. 1.

**17.** Given that the main part of European private law consists of directives requiring implementation in the respective Member State's law,[11] the reality of the existence of European private law is ultimately and predominantly reflected in national law. Consequently, national implementation standards cannot be ignored when considering the European *acquis communautaire*. This book is therefore based on a broad understanding of European private law.[12] However, a clear distinction from EU private law in the formal sense perspective appears neither necessary nor meaningful.[13] European private law is a dynamic subject. Matters that related to individual Member States yesterday may belong to the *acquis communautaire* tomorrow. This is, for example, illustrated by the standardisation of the legal treatment of digital content, which is increasingly finding its way into EU private law, especially because some Member States had created explicit regulations in this regard while others did not.[14]

## II. EUROPEAN CONTRACT LAW

References: G. Alpa, 'Conceptions and Definitions of Contract. Some Thoughts on the Differences in English and German Law', *IWRZ* 2019, 51; P. Benson, *Justice in transactions: a theory of contract law* (Cambridge (MA), Harvard University Press, 2019); A.W. Dnes/N. Garoupa, 'Efficient Breach and Ex-post Disgorgement of the Defendant's Gain: A Comparative Contract Law and Economics Perspective', *ERCL* 2022, 32; T. Gutmann, 'Gibt es ein Konzept des Vertrags im europäischen Vertragsrecht?', in S. Arnold (ed.), *Grundlagen eines europäischen Vertragsrechts* (Munich: Sellier, 2014), p. 19; M.W. Hesselink, 'Progress in EU Contract Law', *ERCL* 2022, 281; L. Kähler, 'Zum Vertragsbegriff im Europarecht', in S. Arnold (ed.), *Grundlagen eines europäischen Vertragsrechts* (Munich: Sellier, 2014), p. 79; E.-M. Kieninger, 'Europäische Vertragsrechtsvereinheitlichung aus rechtsökonomischer Sicht', in *Festschrift für Hans-Bernd Schäfer* (Wiesbaden: Gabler, 2008), p. 353.

### 1. STARTING POINT

**18.** Following this terminological framework, it is now necessary to narrow the focus to European contract law. In a formal sense, this is the positive contract law that can be traced back to EU law. However, due to the above-mentioned clarifications, it also seems indispensable to include Member State law, at least

[11] More on this below paras. 308–400.

[12] See also on the term formation Jansen, Entry 'Europäisches Privatrecht', in *Handwörterbuch des Europäischen Privatrechts* (Tübingen: Mohr Siebeck, 2009), 2009; Zaccaria, in *Mélanges Fritz Sturm*, vol. II, 1999, p. 1311.

[13] Franzen (*GPR* 2020, 280) describes the term 'European private law' as 'iridescent'.

[14] See paras. 929–1003 below.

insofar as it serves to implement EU law or has another connection to the EU. Looking at our topic more specifically, contract law may be defined as that part of private law which deals with the formation, validity and content of contracts. The question of what exactly a contract is can be answered differently; however, this discussion shall not be held in-depth here. At least during the emergence of EU private law, there was no debate on the concept of contract as such. Until today, there is no overarching definition.[15] Thus, for the time being, one may confidently state: 'The answer to the question of whether there is a concept of contract in European contract law is: no.'[16]

## 2. DIFFERENT APPROACHES TO THE CONCEPT OF THE CONTRACT

### a) *A Legal Philosophical Point of View*

**19.** The contract is a means provided by the legal system in order to regulate private matters. In a market economy, the principle of private autonomy is of utmost importance.[17] It is a direct consequence of the recognition of every legal subject as a person and is based on the philosophical idea of respecting fellow human beings as autonomous subjects.[18] A characteristic feature of a contract is the self-binding effect brought about by its conclusion. The French Code civil contains the classic expression: 'Contracts which are lawfully formed have the binding force of legislation for those who have made them.' ('*Les conventions légalement formées tiennent lieu de loi à ceux qui les ont faites.*' – Article 1103 Code civil).[19] In general, this is also recognised in EU law, albeit tacitly. In this respect, the legal philosophical reappraisal of the concept of contract is primarily left to academia.[20]

---

15 On the diversity of contract definitions in EU private law Kähler, in Arnold, *Grundlagen eines europäischen Vertragsrechts*, 2014, p. 79. See below paras. 107–159.

16 Gutmann, in Arnold, Grundlagen eines europäischen Vertragsrechts, 2014, p. 19.

17 See paras. 409–418 below.

18 This is also the position of the German Constitutional Court, cf. BVerfGE 49, 286, 298: 'Article 1(1) of the German Constitution protects the dignity of man as he understands himself in his individuality and becomes aware of himself. This includes that man can dispose of himself and shape his destiny on his own responsibility.' The ongoing discussion about the philosophical foundations of contract law cannot be unfolded here. See e.g. the seminal work by Benson, *Justice in transactions: a theory of contract law*, 2019 and the comments by Cherednychenko, Hoffmann, Rödl, Gutmann, Fabre-Magnan, Oman, Kreitner, Hesselink, and Bagchi in *ERCL* 17 (2021), Vol. 2 (pp. 127-255) and the reply by Benson, *ERCL* 2021, 256.

19 On the validity of the principle pacta sunt servanda in European Union law, see below paras. 412–418.

20 See Arnold, in Arnold, *Grundlagen eines europäischen Vertragsrechts*, 2014, pp. 1, 13 ff.

### b) *An Economic Point of View*

**20.** One can also approach the concept of the contract from an economic perspective. The economic analysis of contract law[21] looks at the consequences that a contract and its implementation have from a perspective primarily focused on efficiency. In principle, this can be done independently of the actual content of the applicable contract law. For example, from an economic point of view, it can be enquired under which conditions the breach of a contractual obligation is efficient (efficient breach).[22] Conversely, the law can also be shaped in a way that promotes economically desirable effects. In theory, the exchange of goods works best when the parties are as free as possible to conclude contracts. From a neoclassical perspective, this furthers the collective welfare of society.[23] Accordingly, it is up to each market participant to decide for themselves what is beneficial for them. Concerning contract law, the economic analysis of law takes a liberal stance by assuming a functioning market; for market participants, the contract involves an optimal balance of interests between the (rational, utility-maximising) parties since they themselves are best able to represent their interests.[24]

**21.** The classic economic analysis of law assumes that individual market participants act both rationally and in accordance with their self-interest; the purpose of the law, then, is to control this behaviour in order to achieve an efficient allocation of scarce resources.[25] Transaction costs are usually ignored. In general, different ways of determining the efficiency of legal rules are proposed, but each is based on the assumption that all market participants are informed and act rationally as well as in a utility-maximising manner.[26] Incarnations of this theory can be found, for example, in the informational duties of businesses vis-à-vis consumers within European contract law.[27]

---

21 Some scholars have raised fundamental criticism of the premises and the claim to validity of the economic analysis of law, cf. Horn, *AcP* 176 (1976), 307; Fezer, *JZ* 1986, 817, 821 ff.; *id.*, *JZ* 1988, 223; Rittner, *JZ* 2005, 668.

22 In addition paras. 757–758 below.

23 Summary of arguments in Kötz, *JuS* 2003, 209.

24 Cf. S.A. Smith, *Contract Theory* (Oxford: Oxford University Press, 2004), p. 110; H. Unberath, *Die Vertragsverletzung* (Tübingen: Mohr Siebeck, 2007), pp. 136 f.; E. Posner, 112 *Yale L.J.* 829, 863 (2003); Dnes/Garoupa, *ERCL* 2022, 32.

25 Cf. S.A. Smith, *Contract Theory* (Oxford: Oxford University Press, 2004), p. 119 ff.; H.B. Schäfer/C. Ott, *Lehrbuch der ökonomischen Analyse des Zivilrechts*, 4th ed. (Berlin/Heidelberg: Springer, 2005), pp. 3 ff.; Taupitz, *AcP* 196 (1996), 114, 117 f.

26 For some time now, a behaviourist approach has been discussed in particular, which modifies the model of homo oeconomicus according to cognitive-psychological insights, see Korobkin/Ulen, 88 *Cal. L. Rev.* 1053 (2000); Eidenmüller, *JZ* 2005, 216; Lurger, in Arnold, *Grundlagen eines europäischen Vertragsrechts*, 2014, pp. 101, 118 ff.

27 See below paras. 477–498.

### c) *Functional Definition: Contract as a Voluntarily Accepted Obligation*

**22.** The above-mentioned approaches primarily mark different perspectives; they are not necessarily contradictory. The CJEU's definition of the contract is much more technical. The court defines the contract in the context of the jurisdiction of the place of performance in Article 7(1)(a) Brussels I*bis* Regulation simply as an 'obligation freely assumed by one party towards another'.[28] This relatively broad concept suffices within the domains of private international law and procedural law.[29]

**23.** This does also not mean that there must be a uniform understanding of the contract within EU law.[30] Given that the starting point for each secondary legal act lies in its regulatory purpose, this may require a different interpretation of seemingly similar or identical legal terms.[31] Concerning the term of the contract in the directives and regulations of substantive EU private law, there is not necessarily a need to develop overarching terms because of the fragmentary regulatory approach still pursued.[32] For example, the Consumer Rights Directive (CRD) restricts itself to a description of individual types of contracts (sales contracts, service contracts, distance and off-premises contracts and so on, Article 2 nos. 5–8 CRD) without elucidating the core of the contract concept itself.

**24.** Overall, the term of the contract in EU law hardly differs from that of most European legal orders. There, the contract is understood as an autonomous legal agreement through a legal transaction based on the concurring declaration of intent of at least two parties.[33] The Draft Common Frame of Reference (DCFR), which was created based on comparative law studies,[34] contains the following provision in its Article II.-1:101: '(1) A contract is an agreement which is intended to give rise to a binding legal relationship or to have some other legal effect. It is a bilateral or multilateral juridical act.' Since EU private law remains fragmented, it can perhaps be said that the term of the contract remains somewhat incomplete compared to the respective definitions in national legal systems. In this respect, there is probably a tendency towards greater terminological openness, as the doctrinal framework is far less strict. However,

---

[28] CJEU, 17 June 1992, Case C-26/91, *Handte*, ECLI:EU:C:1992:268, para. 15; since then settled case law.

[29] See also paras. 1146–1150 and 1447–1461 below; on the distinction from non-contractual obligations see paras. 25–27 below.

[30] In addition see paras. 1335–1338 below.

[31] On the term consumer below paras. 28–39.

[32] See paras. 1292–1298.

[33] This is the classic formulation in W. Flume, *Allgemeiner Teil des Bürgerlichen Rechts*, Volume II: Das Rechtsgeschäft, 4th ed. (Berlin: Springer, 1992), §33, 2 (p. 602).

[34] In addition cf. paras. 120–129.

EU law approaches novel phenomena such as contracts involving third parties (for example, online intermediary platforms) more from a regulatory point of view and less from a perspective focused on contract law.[35] This does not represent a new approach to contract law, as advocated, for example, by the doctrine of contractual networks.[36]

## 3. DELIMITATION TO TORT LAW

References: M. Martín-Casals (ed.), *The Borderlines of Tort Law: Interactions with Contract Law* (Cambridge: Intersentia, 2019); T. Riehm, Gesetzliche Schuldverhältnisse, in K. Langenbucher, *Europäisches Privat- und Wirtschaftsrecht* (Baden-Baden: Nomos), §3 paras. 35 ff.

**25.** The difference between contract and tort law has long been a permanent focus of private law scholarship.[37] It plays a vital role whenever one sub-system imposes different liability requirements than the other. This is particularly evident in the German Civil Code: Here, in contrast to contract law, tortious liability for pure economic loss is limited to particular cases that require, for example, intent (in sec. 826 German Civil Code) or an exceptional quality of the interference (for example, in the case of a violation of the right to an established and exercised business in sec. 823(1) German Civil Code). Therefore, in some cases it appears necessary to mitigate these perceived gaps in the liability system in other ways, for example, by means of a contract with protective effects for third parties or by extending an existing contractual liability to pre-contractual conduct (*culpa in contrahendo*).

**26.** Given that a fragmentary approach to regulation still prevails in European private law, a general distinction between contract and tort is, therefore, neither necessary nor possible. In the area of non-contractual obligations, there are only a few regulations anyway (in this respect, the Product Liability Directive may be mentioned).[38] Delimitation issues, therefore, rarely arise between the doctrinal macro-categories of contract and tort but instead regarding the factual scope of application of particular provisions within secondary law.

---

35 See also paras. 989–996.

36 On this topic see M. Rohe, *Netzverträge - Rechtsprobleme komplexer Vertragsverbindungen* (Tübingen: Mohr Siebeck, 1998); Eberl-Borges, *AcP* 203 (2003), 633; Grundmann, *AcP* 207 (2007), 718; from a conflict-of-laws perspective *Grušić, ICLQ* 65 (2016), 581.

37 See, for example, Kegel, *Vertrag und Delikt* (Cologne: Carl Heymanns, 2002).

38 Council Directive 85/374/EEC of 25 July 1985 on the approximation of the laws, regulations and administrative provisions of the Member States concerning liability for defective products, OJ 1985 L 210/29. For further examples see Riehm, in Langenbucher, *Europäisches Privat- und Wirtschaftsrecht*, §3 para. 39.

**27.** However, things are different in the area of private international law and procedural law. There, the Rome I and Rome II Regulations, as well as the Brussels Ibis Regulation, offer comprehensive sets of rules, each containing special conflict-of-laws rules for contractual and tortious obligations, so that a general demarcation becomes necessary. This will be discussed in greater detail later.[39] It has already been mentioned that the CJEU defines the contract as an obligation freely assumed by one party towards another;[40] consequentially, the court considers those obligations to be non-contractual that do not fall under this definition of contract.[41]

## 4. CONSUMERS AND TRADERS IN THE INTERNAL MARKET

References: J. Basedow, *EU Private Law. Anatomy of a Growing Legal Order* (Cambridge: Intersentia, 2021), p. 136; B. Gsell, 'Verbraucherrealitäten und Verbraucherrecht im Wandel', *JZ* 2012, 809; I. Hoffmann, *Die Verbraucherrolle. Zur Frage nach den maßgeblichen Kriterien im materiellen Recht und im Prozessrecht* (Tübingen: Mohr Siebeck, 2019); *Micklitz*, in *Verhandlungen des 69. Deutschen Juristentages*, Volume I: Gutachten A: Brauchen Konsumenten und Unternehmen eine neue Architektur des Verbraucherrechts? (Munich: C.H. Beck, 2012); E. van Schagen/S. Weatherill (eds.), *Better Regulation in EU Contract Law. The Fitness Check and the New Deal for Consumers* (Oxford: Hart Publishing, 2019); H. Schulte-Nölke, 'The Brave New World of EU Consumer Law – Without Consumers, or Even Without Law?', *EuCML* 2015, 135.

**28.** European contract law is, to a significant extent, consumer (protection) law. It remains true that the principle of contractual freedom, i.e. 'the individual's self-determination of legal relationships according to their will',[42] continues to apply in private law. However, it has been recognised for a long time that this formal perspective on contractual justice fails to reflect economic and social reality. Therefore, nowadays, the law often intervenes in the contractual structure through mandatory or semi-mandatory rules. In particular, this applies to labour law, tenancy law and, for some time now, consumer law.

### *a) The Consumer's Need for Protection*

**29.** The decisive impetus to strengthen consumer protection came from Brussels. As one of the first consumer protection directives, Directive 85/577/EEC,[43]

---

39 See paras. 1146–1150 and 1447–1461 below.

40 CJEU, 17 June 1992, Case C-26/91, *Handte*, ECLI:EU:C:1992:268, para. 15; since then settled case law.

41 CJEU, 27 September 1988, Case 189/87, *Kalfelis*, ECLI:EU:C:1988:459, para. 17; CJEU, 13 March 2014, Case C-548/12, *Brogsitter*, ECLI:EU:C:2014:148, para. 20.

42 W. Flume, *Allgemeiner Teil des Bürgerlichen Rechts*, Volume II: Das Rechtsgeschäft, 4th ed. (Berlin: Springer, 1992), §1, 1 und 5 (pp. 1, 6); likewise Canaris, *AcP* 200 (2000), 273, 277.

43 Council Directive 85/577/EEC of 20 December 1985 to protect the consumer in respect of contracts negotiated away from business premises.

usually referred to as the Doorstep Selling Directive, introduced a right of withdrawal for consumers concerning contracts concluded in so-called doorstep situations. Numerous other acts followed. From a European perspective, the harmonisation of consumer protection regulations serves the realisation of the internal market; Article 38 of the Charter of Fundamental Rights even awards the goal of a high level of consumer protection constitutional status.[44] The central aim is to strengthen the confidence of European consumers in the internal market.[45] Nowadays, contractual consumer protection has become a keystone of any modern legal system; this is illustrated best by Directive 2011/83/EU on consumer rights, which is intended to fully harmonise some central areas of consumer protection law and thus serve as a 'horizontal legal instrument'.[46]

**30.** Nevertheless, there is no consensus on the doctrinal justification of consumer protection law. Traditionally, it has been said that businesses are in a position of power vis-à-vis the consumer and must therefore be protected; hence, socio-political objectives dominate.[47] Economic models see information asymmetries and justify legislative intervention on the grounds of alleged market failure.[48] For the EU legislator, consumer protection relates primarily to its importance for the internal market. This is codified in Article 38 of the Charter of Fundamental Rights. Furthermore, it also results from the primary law requirements in Article 169(1) TFEU and Article 114(3) TFEU, according to which a high level of consumer protection must be ensured in all legal initiatives within the framework of the internal market.

### *b) The Term 'Consumer'*

**31.** The term 'consumer' is of utmost importance. Numerous EU acts contain definitions of this notion. Article 2 no. 2 of the Sale of Goods Directive defines a consumer as 'any natural person who, in relation to contracts covered by this Directive, is acting for purposes which are outside that person's trade, business, craft or profession'. These two conditions – only natural persons; no professional or commercial purpose – can be found in all relevant directives.

**32.** The situation is different concerning natural persons who collaborate, without any further legal capacity, as a group: If the other requirements are

44 See also the provision in Articles 12 and 169 TFEU.

45 See in more detail below paras. 78–83.

46 OJ 2011 L 304/64.

47 In this regard, B. Heiderhoff, *Grundstrukturen des nationalen und europäischen Verbrauchervertragsrechts* (Munich: Sellier, 2004), pp. 257 ff. On the protection of the weaker party in European contract law, see below paras. 434–447.

48 Cf. B. Dauner-Lieb, *Verbraucherschutz durch Ausbildung eines Sonderprivatrechts für Verbraucher* (Berlin: Duncker & Humblot, 1983).

met, they are to be regarded as consumers. Thus, for example, communities of co-owners and civil unions, marital communities of property or communities of heirs, as they may exist under some national laws, can benefit from consumer protection provisions.[49] Consequently, this protection ends where the legal capacity and, therefore, the independence of a legal person begins.

**33.** The applicability of consumer protection laws thus depends on the situation at hand:[50] A shopkeeper might be a consumer when they buy furniture for their own home; likewise, a lawyer is subject to the protection of consumer law when they take out a loan intended for personal use.[51]

**34.** The decisive point in time is the consumer's declaration of intent to conclude the contract since the information to be provided according to the relevant directives must have reached the consumer by then, or at least by the time of the conclusion of the contract. From a purely formal point of view, start-ups could thus be regarded as consumers. However, the CJEU rejected this in a case pertaining to procedural law; here, the decisive factor was the connection with the envisaged professional or commercial activity, even if this was merely planned in the future.[52] Although this is not per se binding for the area of substantive law, more recent directives show similar trends: The Sale of Goods Directive, for example, leaves it up to the Member States to include business start-ups in the national transposition measures' scope of protection (Recital 21 Sale of Goods Directive). Hence, it seems likely that the Directive does not intend to cover them.

**35.** The question of whether a loss of the consumer status can occur after the conclusion of the contract is also disputed. First and foremost, this plays a role in the case of continuing obligations such as in contracts relating to platforms or to social media. It can also turn out to be critical, for example, in the case of a purchase if a privately acquired laptop is now used professionally after setting up a business and if a defect occurs at this time. Once again within a case relating to procedural law, the CJEU affirmed the possibility of a loss of the consumer status in principle[53] by referring to the requirement of a narrow interpretation of Article 17–19 Brussels Ibis Regulation. Notwithstanding this case law, the

---

49 Cf. for German law, G. Bachmann, in *Münchener Kommentar zum BGB*, 10th ed. (Munich: C.H. Beck, 2025), §13 paras. 91 ff.

50 Micklitz, in Verhandlungen des 69. Deutschen Juristentages, 2012, pp. 36 ff., 104 ff. with the plea for a 'dynamic system' with different types of consumers. Critical appraisal by Gsell, *JZ* 2012, 809, 816.

51 In that sense on the Unfair Terms Directive CJEU, 3 September 2015, Case C-110/14, *Volksbank România*, ECLI:EU:C:2015:538, paras. 14 ff.

52 CJEU, 3 July 1997, Case C-269/95, *Benincasa*, ECLI:EU:C:1997:337, para. 17.

53 CJEU, 25 January 2018, Case C-498/16, *Schrems/Facebook*, ECLI:EU:C:2018:37, para. 37.

term 'consumer' 'is distinct from the knowledge and information that the person concerned actually possesses', so that 'neither the expertise which that person may acquire in the field covered by those services nor his assurances given for the purposes of representing the rights and interests of the users of those services can deprive him of the status of a "consumer" [...]'.[54] This seems to warrant the opposite conclusion, i.e. a static view based solely on the consumer status at the time of the conclusion of the contract. Only such a view seems preferable – beyond instances of an abuse of rights – not only for procedural law issues but for all areas of consumer law.

**36.** Finally, so-called dual-use contracts pose difficulties, such as the purchase of a laptop by a lawyer, which is to be used for business appointments away from home as well as for private correspondence. If the CJEU's case law on the concept of the consumer in the area of international procedural law were taken as a starting point, the relevant provisions would only apply if the professional purpose only played a very subordinate and secondary role in the overall context of the respective transaction.[55] In contrast, the CRD, which is often decisive in contract law contexts, considers it sufficient if the commercial purpose is not dominant.[56] This also shows that a uniform understanding of the term 'consumer' does not exist in European secondary law. Ultimately, the specific contract and its respective context under EU law are always decisive.

### c) *Scope of Protection*

**37.** Consumer protection in contract law is by no means all-encompassing; it only extends to individual contract types or contents and certain modalities of a contract's conclusion. This again shows the primarily selective regulatory approach by way of sector-specific directive law.

**38.** The group of regulations relating to contract types includes, in particular, consumer goods sales contracts (Consumer Sales Directive), timeshare contracts (Timeshare Directive), loan contracts and financing aids (Consumer Credit Directive), instalment supply contracts (CRD), and loan brokerage contracts (Consumer Credit Directive and Mortgage Credit Directive). Finally, the Unfair Terms Directive fulfils a distinct role since it applies primarily, but not exclusively, to contracts between businesses and consumers. The set of rules on the modalities of the conclusion of a contract mainly relates to distance contracts and off-premises contracts, both of which are found within the CRD.

---

[54] CJEU, 25 January 2018, Case C-498/16, *Schrems/Facebook*, ECLI:EU:C:2018:37, para. 39.

[55] CJEU, 20 January 2005, Case C-464/01, *Gruber*, ECLI:EU:C:2005:32, paras. 32 f.

[56] Recital 17 CRD.

### d) *Protective Mechanisms*

**39.** Contractual consumer protection works in very different ways. The trader's information obligations and the consumer's right of withdrawal are of central importance.[57] Furthermore, the passing-on of costs to the consumer is prevented by other provisions if this is conceived as unreasonable. In addition, consumer protection also plays a significant role within private international law (Article 6 Rome I Regulation[58]), international procedural law (Articles 17 et seq. Brussels I*bis* Regulation as well as Injunctions Directive[59]) and alternative dispute resolution mechanisms (ADR Directive and ODR Regulation[60]).

## 5. SUPRA-INDIVIDUAL OBJECTIVES IN CONTRACT LAW

References: S. Arnold, *Vertrag und Verteilung. Die Bedeutung der iustitia distributiva im Vertragsrecht* (Tübingen: Mohr Siebeck, 2014); A. Beckers, 'Three Concepts of European Private Law and the Transnational Markets', in A. Beckers/H.-W. Micklitz/R. Vallejo/P. Letto-Vanamo (eds.), *The Foundations of European Transnational Private Law* (Oxford: Hart Publishing, 2024), p. 27; A. Halfmeier, 'Nachhaltiges Privatrecht', *AcP* 216 (2016), 717; A. Hellgardt, *Regulierung und Privatrecht. Staatliche Verhaltenssteuerung mittels Privatrecht und ihre Bedeutung für Rechtswissenschaft, Gesetzgebung und Rechtsanwendung* (Tübingen: Mohr Siebeck, 2016); M.W. Hesselink, 'Progress in EU Contract Law', *ERCL* 2022, 281; P. Jaffey, *Justice in Private Law* (London: Bloomsbury Publishing, 2023); B. Keirsbilck/E. Terryn (eds.), *Consumer Protection in a Circular Economy* (Cambridge: Intersentia, 2019); B. Lurger, 'Gerechtigkeitskonzepte für ein europäisches Vertragsrecht und Instrumente zu ihrer Umsetzung', in S. Arnold, *Grundlagen eines europäischen Vertragsrechts* (Munich: Sellier, 2014), p. 101; V. Mak/E. Lujinovic, 'Towards a Circular Economy in EU Consumer Markets – Legal Possibilities and Legal Challenges and the Dutch Example', *EuCML* 2019, 4; H.W. Micklitz, 'Squaring the Circle? Reconciling Consumer Law and the Circular Economy', *EuCML* 2019, 229; C. Wendehorst, 'Regulierungsprivatrecht. Verhaltenssteuerung durch Privatrecht am Beispiel des europäischen Verbrauchervertragsrechts', in E. Schumann (ed.), *Das erziehende Gesetz* (Berlin: De Gruyter, 2014), p. 113.

### a) *Elements of Distributive Justice*

**40.** According to the classical view, contract law merely serves to enable a fair and interest-based exchange of services. Increasingly, however, the idea that private law should also be employed to achieve supra-individual purposes is gaining support. This is, in essence, a question of distributive justice, i.e. the

[57] See paras. 477–498 below.
[58] See paras. 1181–1200 below.
[59] See paras. 1413, 1440–1446 below.
[60] On this Stürner, *GPR* 2014, 122 as well as paras. 1496–1520 below.

justification of distributive elements in contract law. In principle, it is accepted that public law, such as tax law, must take on distributive tasks. This is because distributive justice potentially collides with the freedom to conclude contracts: In this respect, it needs to be borne in mind that a market participant does not have to behave purposively; they can also act irrationally and choose their contractual partners freely. The legal system must respect this.[61] Consequently, any attempt to use contract law as a tool to implement elements of distributive justice will have to pay a certain price, namely to restrict contractual freedom to some extent.

**41.** Nevertheless, more and more exceptions to this basic rule have recently been introduced.[62] These provisions introduce political considerations into the contractual relationship, for example, in the area of employee protection, consumer protection or anti-discrimination legislation.[63] The DCFR also considers itself an instrument of commutative justice (*iustitia commutativa*),[64] but accepts distributive elements, especially when they are necessary to protect the consumer.[65] A private law system based on private autonomy and competition (thus promoting commutative justice) contributes significantly to achieving distributive justice by allowing citizens easy access to goods and services. The insertion of distributive elements into private law must therefore remain exceptional.[66]

*b) Sustainability*

**42.** With the adoption of the 17 Sustainable Development Goals by the UN in 2015 at the latest, sustainability has made its appearance as a legal principle.

---

61 Decidedly H. Honsell, in *Festschrift für Mayer-Maly* (Cologne: Böhlau, 2002), pp. 287, 294 ff.; likewise in principle also C.-W. Canaris, *Die Bedeutung der iustitia distributiva im deutschen Vertragsrecht* (Munich: Bayerische Akademie der Wissenschaften, 1997), pp. 13 ff., 33, 73. On the term contractual justice in European private law *Lurger*, in Arnold, *Grundlagen eines europäischen Vertragsrechts*, 2014, pp. 101, 103 ff.

62 For a fundamental discussion see Arnold, *Vertrag und Verteilung. Die Bedeutung der iustitia distributiva im Vertragsrecht*, 2014, p. 263 ff., 297 ff.

63 For more details see below paras. 424–433, as well as paras. 777–790 and 791–809.

64 In addition cf. para. 430.

65 C. von Bar/E. Clive/H. Schulte-Nölke, *DCFR 2008 Interim Edition* (Munich: Sellier, 2008), Introduction No 24. Critically Eidenmüller/Faust/Grigoleit/Jansen/Wagner/Zimmermann, *JZ* 2008, 529, 534 f.

66 C.-W. Canaris, *Die Bedeutung der iustitia distributiva im deutschen Vertragsrecht* (Munich: Bayerische Akademie der Wissenschaften, 1997), pp. 35 ff., mentions majority decisions in company law, monopoly or market-dominant companies and labour law as possible areas of application. On the unsuitability of contract law as a distribution mechanism, see H. Eidenmüller, *Effizienz als Rechtsprinzip*, 4th ed. (Tübingen: Mohr Siebeck, 2015), pp. 273 ff., 283 ff. On the corresponding debate on the function of contract law in the Anglo-American area Zumbansen, 14 *Ind. J. Global L. Stud.* 191 (2007); on contract governance from a German perspective S. Grundmann/F. Möslein/K. Riesenhuber (eds.), *Contract governance: dimensions in law and interdisciplinary research* (Oxford: Oxford University Press, 2015); Lurger, in Arnold, *Grundlagen eines europäischen Vertragsrechts*, 2014, pp. 101, 115 ff.

Sustainability is not originally a legal term; it was used in forestry, for example, where it meant that no more wood should be cut down than could grow back.[67] In the modern context, it serves as a catch-all term for all goals of responsible politics and economics understood as good and right. Understood this way, 'sustainable contract law' cannot be more than an umbrella term. When analysing its content, individual facets of sustainability must be addressed.[68]

**43.** The EU is committed to the 17 United Nations Sustainable Development Goals (UNSDG) of 2015, which aim to transform economies towards more sustainable development in the social, environmental and economic fields by 2030.[69] Such developments can influence contract law in many ways. Assuming that the EU's previous strategy might have always put the functioning of the internal market first, a contrary development may have been initiated nowadays, even if the EU Commission repeatedly emphasises that economic growth and sustainable development are not contradictory.

**44.** In this respect, things differ from the above-discussed consumer protection law: Its prominent role since the 1990s should not obscure the fact that it was always intended to strengthen the internal market, which is already evident from the respective provision on the EU's legislative power in Article 169 TFEU that also refers to the general internal market clause of Article 114 TFEU.[70] Thus, a constant effort can be observed to intertwine the guiding stars of the internal market and consumer protection with the idea of sustainable growth. Recital 32 of the Sale of Goods Directive, for example, states: 'Ensuring longer durability of goods is important for achieving more sustainable consumption patterns and a circular economy'. The consumer's right to remedy a material defect is not only justified by the contract but also legitimised by sustainability considerations: 'Enabling consumers to require repair should encourage sustainable consumption and could contribute to greater durability of products.' (Recital 48 of the Sale of Goods Directive)[71]

---

67 One may make reference here to Hans Carl von Carlowitz (1645-1714), a Chief Mining Commissioner from Saxony, who published 'Sylvicultura Oeconomica, oder Haußwirtschaftliche Nachricht und Naturgemäße Anweisung zur Wilden Baum-Zucht' (1713). In this work, he speaks of 'sustainable utilisation of the forests' and pleads for '… a cultivation of the wood so that there is a continuous, consistent and sustainable use'.

68 Cf. Halfmeier, *AcP* 216 (2016), 717. On transnational private regulation of environmental sustainability through commercial contracts, cf. Cafaggi, *ERCL* 2024, 25.

69 More information can be found at https://sustainabledevelopment.un.org/.

70 More see below para. 224.

71 For a consumer law oriented towards sustainability considerations Micklitz, *EuCML* 2019, 229.

**45.** It is not difficult to see potential conflicts between consumer protection on the one hand, and sustainable development goals on the other, as the following examples may demonstrate:

For distance contracts and off-premises contracts, Article 9(1) CRD establishes a right of withdrawal for the consumer. During the withdrawal period, the consumer may exercise this right through a simple declaration (Article 11(1) CRD). A particular justification for the withdrawal is not required. Even though returns of the goods delivered cause carbon dioxide emissions, this is not a relevant factor in the exercise of this right. Likewise, the fact that some goods, especially clothes, are sometimes destroyed following the return as they cannot be sold as new anymore,[72] does not play any role. A solution may consist in making withdrawal more expensive by charging the consumer not only for the costs of returning the goods (Article 14(1) CRD), but also for the costs of sending them to the consumer (unlike the current version of Article 13(2) CRD). However, this would lower the level of consumer protection. The EU legislator has – so far – chosen a different approach: under Article 25 Ecodesign Regulation 2024/1781,[73] unsold goods may only be destroyed if this is necessary for safety or health reasons. It remains to be seen and discussed, whether this solution under public law will bear any repercussions on private law.

**46.** Likewise, the primacy of consumer choice under the law as it currently stands within the EU, in case of non-conformity, is in potential conflict with sustainability concerns: Pursuant to Article 13(2) SDG, the consumer may choose between repair and replacement. The seller may either object impossibility or that the remedy chosen would cause disproportionately high costs compared to the other. In determining this, it is no relevant factor whether, e.g. repair would cause much less carbon dioxide emissions compared to replacement. Moreover, should the consumer choose replacement, goods which might be easy to repair will probably be destroyed. A solution might imply to limit the consumer's right to choose between repair and replacement, which would again lower the level of consumer protection. Such a step seems to be, despite the political vow towards sustainability, unviable. By contrast, in its Action Plan for the Circular Economy of 11 March 2020,[74] the EU Commission had proposed to establish a

---

72 For Germany, a 2019 Study carried out by the University of Bamberg has revealed that 4% of all returned goods are being destroyed, cf. https://www.bmuv.de/faqs/warenvernichtung.

73 Regulation (EU) 2024/1781 of the European Parliament and of the Council of 13 June 2024 establishing a framework for the setting of ecodesign requirements for sustainable products, amending Directive (EU) 2020/1828 and Regulation (EU) 2023/1542 and repealing Directive 2009/125/EC, OJ 2024 L, 2024/1781.

74 A new action plan for the circular economy. Towards a cleaner and more competitive Europe, COM(2020) 98 final.

'right to repair'.[75] After political and parliamentary debates, on 13 June 2024, the European Parliament and the Council have adopted Directive (EU) 2024/1799 on common rules promoting the repair of goods.[76] This Directive introduces a right to repair with respect to certain goods against the manufacturer (but not against the seller), which operates outside the existing contract between consumer and trader. The seller of the good is not under any obligation to repair the good sold unless there is a non-conformity of the good with the requirements.[77]

**47.** The idea of sustainability has recently also been used affirmatively, without being the primary regulatory objective: In Germany, an Act on fair consumer contracts introduced, among other things, the elimination of sec. 476(2) German Civil Code, according to which a contractual reduction of the limitation period up to one year was possible for the purchase of used goods. According to the case law of the CJEU, this violated the provisions of the Consumer Sales Directive.[78] Since interpreting the law in conformity with the Directive was quite challenging, the legislator had to take action. The draft bill, however, did not fail to point out that the proposed changes, 'in the interest of sustainable consumption, among other things, promote the marketability of second-hand goods', which is in line with objective 12 of the UNSDG.

## 6. THE ROLE OF HARMONISATION PROJECTS

**48.** The importance of academic harmonisation projects as part of common European private law has already been mentioned.[79] European scholarship has dealt with contract law particularly intensively. This can be explained, on the one hand, by the central importance of the institution of the contract within private law. On the other hand, contract law is also far more accessible to a comparative analysis than other areas such as property law,[80] family law[81] or inheritance law,[82] in which either a strong connection with institutional circumstances, such as the existence of

---

75 COM(2020) 98 final, p. 6. See e.g. E. Terryn, in Keirsbilck/Terryn, *Consumer Protection in a Circular Economy*, 2019, p. 127; Kieninger, *ZEuP* 2020, 264, 274 ff.

76 Directive (EU) 2024/1799 of the European Parliament and of the Council of 13 June 2024 on common rules promoting the repair of goods and amending Regulation (EU) 2017/2394 and Directives (EU) 2019/771 and (EU) 2020/1828, OJ 2024 L 2024/1799.

77 For a detailed discussion see below at paras. 120–129.

78 CJEU, 13 July 2017, Case C-133/16, *Ferenschild*, ECLI:EU:C:2017:541.

79 See above at para. 14.

80 See C. von Bar, *Gemeineuropäisches Sachenrecht Volume I: Grundlagen, Gegenstände sachenrechtlichen Rechtsschutzes, Arten und Erscheinungsformen subjektiver Sachenrechte* (Munich: C.H. Beck, 2015); id., *Gemeineuropäisches Sachenrecht Volume 2: Besitz, Erwerb und Schutz subjektiver Sachenrechte* (Munich: C.H. Beck, 2019).

81 Here, the work of the Commission on European Family Law (CEFL) should be mentioned, in more detail https://ceflonline.net/.

82 Cf. namely K.G.C. Reid/M.J. de Waal/R. Zimmermann (eds.), *Comparative Succession Law I: Testamentary Formalities* (Oxford: Oxford University Press, 2011); *id.*, *Comparative Succession*

registers, as in property law, or legal cultural peculiarities of the respective systems, as in family law and also inheritance law, make such analyses difficult.

**49.** Ultimately, however, one reason may also be found in the fact that the political intent to harmonise contract law in particular was much more vigorous at the European level than in other areas: As early as in 1989, the European Parliament had called for the harmonisation of private law systems in a 'Resolution on action to bring into line the private law of the Member States',[83] as well as for the 'necessary preparatory work for the drafting of a harmonised European code of private law'. The Commission acted rather cautiously at first, but then devoted itself intensively to the harmonisation of contract law at the beginning of the new century, starting with the Communication on European contract law of 11 July 2001,[84] which led to the drafting of the DCFR.[85]

**50.** Pioneering work in this respect was done by the Commission on European Contract Law, also known after its initiator, the Danish law professor Ole Lando, as the Lando Group, which was constituted in the early 1980s. One major result of this group were the Principles of European Contract Law, which were published in three parts.[86] They exerted significant influence, especially on legislative activity in the EU's new Eastern European Member States. Above all, this interweaving with positive law makes a study of the academic drafts, even in the context of a book that deals primarily with current European contract law, sensible and worthwhile.[87]

## III. TWO AREAS OF EUROPEAN CONTRACT LAW

**51.** European contract law is divided into two sub-areas: On the one hand, it is constituted by European contract law in the narrower sense as the sum of all substantive legal norms, and on the other hand, it consists of European international contract law, i.e. the totality of those rules which determine the (substantive) law applicable to cross-border contracts.

---

*Law II: Intestate Succession* (Oxford: Oxford University Press, 2015); *id.*, *Comparative Succession Law III: Mandatory Family Protection* (Oxford: Oxford University Press, 2020).

83 Of 26 May 1989, O.J. 1989, C 158/400.

84 Communication from the Commission of the European Communities to the Council and the European Parliament on European Contract Law, 11 July 2001, COM(2001) 398 final.

85 On this in detail see below paras. 160–208.

86 H. Beale/O. Lando, *The Principles of European Contract Law, Part I, Performance, Non Performance and Remedies*, 1995; O. Lando/H. Beale, *Principles of European Contract Law, Parts I and II*, 2000; O. Lando/E. Clive/A. Prüm/R. Zimmermann, *Principles of European Contract Law, Part III*, 2003.

87 More on those endeavours below at paras. 160–208.

## 1. SUBSTANTIVE EUROPEAN CONTRACT LAW

**52.** Substantive contract law includes those provisions that give rise to the rights and obligations of the parties. This includes directives with private law content, even though they merely constitute rights and obligations in an indirect manner, i.e. after their implementation in the Member States' law.

## 2. INTERNATIONAL CONTRACT LAW

**53.** In contrast, the rules of international contract law do not deal with the existence and content of contractual rights and obligations;[88] they intervene at a preliminary stage by resolving the 'conflict' between different legal jurisdictions in situations with a cross-border context. They do so by referring to one (or more) applicable substantive legal systems. At the outset, each state establishes such conflict-of-laws rules autonomously. This can lead to diverging connecting factors and might indirectly create different starting positions for the actors within the internal market. The harmonisation of the internal market consequently also covers conflict-of-laws rules. The Rome Convention on the law applicable to contractual obligations of 1980 (Rome Convention),[89] which was created as an international treaty through intergovernmental cooperation due to the lack of EC jurisdiction, pioneered the harmonisation of conflict-of-laws rules.

**54.** With the Treaty of Amsterdam, the EC gained far-reaching legislative powers for judicial cooperation, which also included private international law (Article 81(2)(c) TFEU). After intense preparatory works, the Rome I Regulation on the law applicable to contractual obligations entered into force on 17 December 2009.[90] It is based on the Rome Convention and developed it further in a rather cautious manner.[91]

**55.** The Rome II Regulation on the law applicable to non-contractual obligations also needs to be considered,[92] given that it governs the legal institution of *culpa in contrahendo*, which is classified as a non-contractual obligation at the European level (Articles 2(1), 12 Rome II Regulation). The Regulation is

---

88 For more details, see paras. 1080–1105 below.

89 Rome Convention on the Law Applicable to Contractual Obligations of 19 June 1980, entered into force on 1 April 1991.

90 Regulation (EC) no 593/2008 of the European Parliament and of the Council of 17 June 2008 on the law applicable to contractual obligations (Rome I), OJ 2008 L 177/6.

91 See paras. 1143–1291 below.

92 Regulation (EC) no 864/2007 of the European Parliament and of the Council of 11 July 2007 on the law applicable to non-contractual obligations ('Rome II'), OJ 2007 L 199/40.

grounded in the CJEU case law on jurisdiction in tort claims (Article 5 no. 3 Brussels I Regulation, today: Article 7 no. 2 Brussels Ibis Regulation), which qualified the claim arising *from culpa in contrahendo* as tortious if the contract has not been concluded.[93] However, Article 12(1) Rome II Regulation provides for an accessory reference to the (hypothetical) contract statute. Tort law applies only if this cannot be determined (Article 12(2) Rome II Regulation).[94]

## IV. LEGAL APPROXIMATION AND HARMONISATION IN THE EUROPEAN UNION

References: M. Andenas/C. Baasch/T. Andersen (eds.), *Theory and Practice of Harmonisation* (Cheltenham: Edward Elgar Publishing, 2011); J. Basedow, *EU Private Law. Anatomy of a Growing Legal Order* (Cambridge: Intersentia, 2021), p. 75; O.O. Cherednychenko, 'The Relationship between European and National Private Law: Lessons for EU-Law Making and Enforcement', in A. Janssen/M. Lehmann/R. Schulze (eds.), *The Future of European Private Law* (Baden-Baden: Nomos, 2023), p. 455; T. von Danwitz, 'Die Aufgabe des Gerichtshofes bei der Entfaltung des europäischen Zivil- und Zivilverfahrensrechts', *ZEuP* 2010, 463; S. Grundmann, 'Europäisches Vertragsrecht – Quo vadis?', *JZ* 2005, 860; M. Fornasier, 'Harmonisation through the back door? The Impact of the European Convention on Human Rights on National Private Law', in M. Fornasier/M.G. Stanzione (eds.), *The European Convention on Human Rights and its Impact on National Private Law. A Comparative Perspective* (Cambridge: Intersentia, 2023), p. 305; B. Gsell/C. Herresthal (eds.), *Vollharmonisierung im Privatrecht: Die Konzeption der Richtlinie am Scheideweg?* (Tübingen: Mohr Siebeck, 2010); B. Jud/C. Wendehorst (eds.), *Neuordnung des Verbraucherprivatrechts in Europa? Zum Vorschlag einer Richtlinie über Rechte der Verbraucher* (Vienna: Manz, 2009); E.J. Lohse, *Rechtsangleichungsprozesse in der Europäischen Union* (Tübingen: Mohr Siebeck, 2017); M.B.M. Loos, Harmonization of Private Law in the 2020s: Targeted Full Harmonization 2.0?, in A. Janssen/M. Lehmann/R. Schulze (eds.), *The Future of European Private Law* (Baden-Baden: Nomos, 2023), p. 403; K. Riesenhuber, 'Auf dem Weg zu einem europäischen Privatrecht', in K.J. Hopt/D. Tzouganatos (eds.), *Das Europäische Wirtschaftsrecht vor neuen Herausforderungen* (Tübingen: Mohr Siebeck, 2014), p. 183; E. Sanchez Lasaballett, 'Conceptualizing harmonization: the case for contract law', *Unif. L. Rev.*, Vol. 24, 2019, 73; E. van Schagen, *The Development of European Private Law in a Multilevel Legal Order* (Cambridge: Intersentia, 2016); M. Stürner (ed.), *Vollharmonisierung im Europäischen Verbraucherrecht?* (Munich: Sellier, 2010); S. Weatherill, *Contract Law of the Internal Market* (Cambridge: Intersentia, 2016), Ch. 5.

93 CJEU, 17 September 2002, Case C-334/00, *Tacconi*, ECLI:EU:C:2002:499.
94 More below paras. 1231–1235.

## 1. HARMONISATION OBJECTIVES

**56.** The harmonisation of private law regulation is a central concern in the European Union. According to Article 26(1) TFEU, the EU 'shall adopt measures with the aim of establishing or ensuring the functioning of the internal market […]'. The fundamental pillar of the internal market is the abolition of all internal borders in order to ensure the free movement of goods, persons, services and capital (Article 26(2) TFEU). Legal regulations can also present obstacles to the internal market. In private law, the need to eliminate legal fragmentation in the internal market, which constitutes a potential obstacle to the fundamental freedoms, is generally referred to as a justificatory reason for legal acts.[95] For this purpose, regulations and directives are available as regulatory instruments to advance complete or partial harmonisation.[96]

## 2. WAYS OF HARMONISATION

**57.** There are two structurally different ways of overcoming legal differences in the internal market: The harmonisation of private international law on the one hand and the approximation of substantive law on the other. For the establishment of harmonised conflict-of-laws provisions, Article 81(2)(c) TFEU provides the EU with legislative powers. Concerning the harmonisation of substantive law, on the other hand, the legislative jurisdiction does not exist for contract law as a whole but only fragmentary, in particular for the area of consumer protection in Articles 114, 169(2)(a) TFEU.

### *a) Harmonisation of Conflict-of-Laws Rules*

**58.** The advantages of a (mere) harmonisation of conflict-of-laws rules are obvious: Since the substantive law systems of the Member States remain untouched, the interference in the national private law systems is relatively small. The diversity of legal systems and national legal cultures is thus preserved to a great extent. At the same time, the necessary uniformity of the application of the law is conserved, given that the same substantive law is always invoked for any identical set of facts, irrespective of potentially different rules on jurisdiction. This is even more true where the harmonisation of conflict-of-laws rules is

---

95 For example, the Explanatory Memorandum of the Commission's proposal of 8 October 2008 for a Directive on Consumer Rights, COM(2008) 614 final, p. 3.

96 In some cases, the accusation is made that harmonisation as a theoretical concept has not been sufficiently researched or defined, see Sanchez Lasaballett, *Unif. L. Rev.*, Vol. 24 (2019), 73, 75 ff. This can only be pursued selectively, for example with regard to the question of whether fully harmonising directives are more likely to promote the internal market than minimum-harmonising ones, see paras. 74–86 below.

accompanied by a uniform set of rules on jurisdiction. In this way, the potential for innovation is also preserved, which is fostered by the diversity of legal systems in the first place: Especially in an internal market, the Member States are in competition with each other, which becomes visible not only with regard to economic and tax systems but also concerning their legal systems.[97] In the area of contract law, this can be seen, for example, in the area of digital goods. Here, individual Member States had already adopted regulations, thereby setting standards with tangible effects on the legislative behaviour of other jurisdictions in this rapidly growing economic area. The EU Commission has taken this as an opportunity to propose harmonisation measures for its part,[98] which have recently been adopted after an extensive legislative process.[99]

**59.** However, this also comes with disadvantages: A pure harmonisation of conflict-of-laws rules retains the differences in the substantive law area and thus only partially resolves the legal uncertainty of market participants. Furthermore, the coordination of applicable substantive law brought about by harmonised conflict-of-laws provisions remains theoretical insofar as it presupposes uniformity in the application of conflict-of-laws provisions by all Member States' courts. The choice of law also entails risks, on the one hand, in purely forensic terms, and on the other hand, because the choice of law cannot remain unlimited, especially in the relationship between businesses and consumers.[100] Therefore, a harmonised contract law for all transactions remains an illusion for a business operating in the internal market. Harmonising the conflict-of-laws rules in the EU would, thus, ultimately be unable to remove all potential obstacles to the internal market.

### *b) Harmonisation of Substantive Law*

**60.** A complete harmonisation of substantive law would at least on a theoretic level make conflict-of-laws rules in the area of the internal market unnecessary:[101] They lose their practical justification whenever harmonised

---

[97] This becomes visible, for example, in the area of dispute resolution, see Duve/Rösch, *ZVglRWiss* 114 (2015), 387; G. Wagner, *Rechtsstandort Deutschland im Wettbewerb – Impulse für Justiz und Schiedsgerichtsbarkeit* (Munich: C.H. Beck, 2017), pp. 183 ff.; Stürner, *JZ* 2019, 1122.

[98] Proposal for a Directive of the European Parliament and of the Council on certain aspects of contract law relating to the provision of digital content, COM(2015) 634 final.

[99] Directive (EU) 2019/770 of the European Parliament and of the Council of 20 May 2019 on certain aspects of contract law relating to the provision of digital content and digital services, OJ 2019 L 136/1. See paras. 942–988 below.

[100] See paras. 1194–1200 below.

[101] It is not necessary to clarify here whether conflict-of-laws rules only have a justification to exist if and insofar as there are different substantive law systems, see G. Kegel/K. Schurig, *Internationales Privatrecht*, 9th ed. (Munich: Beck, 2004), §1 III.

substantive law applies to the states in question.[102] However, beyond the question of whether such a complete harmonisation of even contract law alone would be desirable at all, there is, in any case, currently no corresponding legislative power of the EU. The limited transfer of legislative powers from the Member States to the EU engenders to the principle that the EU can only act within the powers conferred to it. Contract law as such does not feature among the relevant provisions of the TFEU which confer legislative competencies on the EU. Hence, full harmonisation would only be possible within the framework of the existing legislative powers, which concerns consumer law in particular.[103]

### c) *The Mixed System of the Current Law and its Partial Deficits*

**61.** For these reasons, it is hardly surprising that the EU legislator is pursuing an approach of combined harmonisation: On the one hand, the harmonisation of conflict-of-laws rules is pushed forward very intensively. In this regard, Article 81(2)(c) TFEU contains a far-reaching provision on the EU's jurisdiction. This has led to the private international law of contractual and non-contractual obligations being almost fully harmonised by the Rome I and Rome II Regulations. Even in other areas of private law, such as maintenance law, divorce law, matrimonial property law and inheritance law, there are now harmonised conflict-of-laws provisions, even if some of the relevant regulations in the area of family law could only be implemented by way of enhanced cooperation and thus do not apply to all Member States.[104]

**62.** At the same time, the EU legislator is pursuing the harmonisation of substantive law, mainly through directives. The two approaches are not necessarily coordinated, neither timewise nor in terms of the content they refer to. Older directives, in particular, contain conflict-of-laws provisions that have not been integrated into the new regulations. Central terms such as those of the contract or consumer are not necessarily used consistently or congruently.[105]

**63.** Both harmonisation methods seem to compete with each other. For example, in the draft Directive on Consumer Rights, the Commission attested that the Rome I Regulation, which had entered into force shortly before, was unsuitable for eliminating the internal market's legal fragmentation.[106] In some cases, conflict-of-laws provisions even stand in the way of the harmonisation of

---

[102] On this and the boundaries see below para. 1080.

[103] For more details on the existing competences in the area of private and contract law see below paras. 217–227.

[104] More see below paras. 1118–1142.

[105] See paras. 1328–1337. below.

[106] COM(2008) 614 final., p. 2.

substantive law, especially in the case of the proposal for a Common European Sales Law, whose relationship to the conflict-of-laws provision on consumer law of Article 6 Rome I Regulation was highly controversial.[107]

## 3. LEVEL OF HARMONISATION

**64.** Whereas in conflict of laws, at least since the communitarisation of the corresponding legislative power, harmonisation has been carried out exclusively through regulations, different approaches can be found in the area of substantive law. Usually, a distinction is made between harmonisation on the one hand and approximation on the other.[108] While harmonisation refers to the establishment or existence of uniform legal norms, approximation is also aimed at eliminating differences between legal systems but does not intend complete harmonisation.

**65.** The term harmonisation is used inconsistently and sometimes serves as an overarching term for both the harmonisation and approximation of laws. This is shown by the terms full and minimum harmonisation: The former refers to a standardisation of law using a directive, which leaves the Member States no possibility to deviate from the given standard. Conversely, the latter gives the Member States leeway to adopt deviating provisions if necessary. Harmonisation can take place in various ways: It can be carried out by higher-ranking law ('top-down approach'), i.e. in particular by European or international law, or by way of autonomous harmonisation without such binding requirements ('bottom-up approach').

### *a) Approximation of Laws: Regulation through Directives*

**66.** The approximation of substantive law in the internal market is pursued by directive law. Directives only prescribe the end result bindingly but give leeway as to how this result is achieved (Article 288(3) TFEU). In the area of substantive law, this is by far the preferred approach to harmonisation. Here too, however, a further distinction between minimum or full harmonising directives must be made, as directives sometimes leave the Member States more and sometimes less margin of manoeuvre regarding their implementation.[109]

---

107 See M. Gebauer (ed.), *Gemeinsames Europäisches Kaufrecht – Anwendungsbereich und kollisionsrechtliche Einbettung* (Munich: Sellier, 2013); see also Stürner, *GPR* 2011, 236; Busch, *EuZW* 2011, 655; Fornasier, *RabelsZ* 76 (2012), 401; Stadler, *AcP* 212 (2012), 473, 475 ff. For more on this question, see below para. 1154.

108 On the terminology already J. Kropholler, *Internationales Einheitsrecht* (Tübingen: Mohr Siebeck, 1975), pp. 17 ff.; see also Sanchez Lasaballett, *Unif. L. Rev.*, Vol. 24 (2019), 73, 95 ff.

109 See paras. 74–84 below.

### b) *Harmonisation: Regulatory Law, Primary Law and Convention Law*

**67.** Legal harmonisation, on the other hand, sets binding standards and leaves the Member States no leeway. Regarding the legal instrument used, regulations, which have direct and immediate effect and, therefore, unlike the directive, do not require any implementation (Article 288(2) TFEU), are usually chosen. Regulations are the dominant tool to achieve harmonisation within the area of conflict of laws. In the area of substantive law, on the other hand, the jurisdictional powers are being limited by the subsidiarity and, above all, the proportionality principle and, therefore, curtail harmonisation possibilities through regulations. Thus, this is where directive law is found predominantly;[110] however, this can still come quite close to regulation approaches through full harmonisation.

**68.** Legal harmonisation – understood in a loose way – can also be advanced by optional regulations.[111] These do not leave any room for implementation but are designed as opt-in instruments whose application remains at the discretion of the contracting parties. Such an approach was pursued, for example, with the Common European Sales Law, which, however, is currently no longer on the political agenda.

**69.** Harmonisation can also be realised by EU primary law, although private law provisions are rarely to be found here. One example is the prohibition of cartels in Article 101 TFEU.

**70.** Private law within state treaties can also lead to a unification of the law. However, unlike EU regulations, international conventions do not directly and immediately affect the legal systems of the Member States. Even if they bind the contracting states in their external relations with the other contracting states (Article 26 Vienna Convention on the Law of Treaties), in many systems they must first be transformed into domestic law.[112] Nevertheless, there is no room for manoeuvre regarding their implementation; deviations from the requirements of a convention generally constitute violations of international law.[113] It should be noted, however, that such violations usually remain unpunished.[114] In many

---

110 A notable exception is the Air Passenger Regulation, see paras. 1058–1079 below.

111 More on this at paras. 89–91 below.

112 On the relationship between international law and national law, see Articles 25 and 59(2) of the German Basic Law; this expresses a moderately dualistic basic view, see the decision of the German Constitutional Court in the *Görgülü* case, BVerfGE 111, 307, 318.

113 These so-called treaty overrides constitute violations of the principle pacta sunt servanda enshrined in Articles 26 and 27 of the Vienna Convention on the Law of Treaties.

114 Article 60(1) of the Vienna Convention on the Law of Treaties gives the other party the right to suspend or terminate a bilateral treaty in the event of a material breach.

cases, there are also possibilities for reservations, such as in Article 22 of the Rome Convention.

## 4. METHODS AND TECHNIQUES OF HARMONISATION

**71.** Enacting positive laws is only one possibility of harmonisation. Different methods and techniques of harmonisation must be distinguished.[115]

### *a) Positive and Negative Harmonisation*

**72.** The dichotomy of positive and negative harmonisation is not intended to express any evaluation of successful or disapproved legislative acts. Instead, positive harmonisation aims to designate the law that the EU has enacted. The area of negative harmonisation, on the other hand, includes all requirements for a Member State's law that exist beyond these positively set, rule-based harmonisation steps.[116] This concerns primarily the influence of primary law on the law of the Member States, for example, by means of the fundamental freedoms, the prohibition of discrimination and the Charter of Fundamental Rights. Above all, the CJEU, as the much-cited 'driving force behind harmonisation', has decisively advanced negative harmonisation through an integration-friendly interpretation of the legal principles mentioned – and has been criticised numerous times in the process.[117]

### *b) Legislative and Judicial Harmonisation*

**73.** Similarly, a distinction depending on which institution provides the impetus, i.e. between legislative and judicial harmonisation, can be made.[118] Judicial harmonisation does not only encompass the narrow area of case law[119] but also the determination of the content of directives and regulations as a result

115 Sanchez Lasaballett, *Unif. L. Rev.*, Vol. 24 (2019), 73, 83 ff. identifies three different ways in which harmonisation can be achieved: through new laws, through general principles of law and through model laws.

116 On the distinction Gebauer, *Grundfragen der Europäisierung des Privatrechts*, 1998, pp. 84 f.; Franzen, *Privatrechtsangleichung durch die Europäische Gemeinschaft*, 1999, p. 10 f.; *Lohse, Rechtsangleichungsprozesse in der Europäischen Union*, pp. 60 ff.

117 For example CJEU, 22 November 2005, Case C-144/04, *Mangold*, ECLI:EU:C:2005:709 and on this the fundamental critique by Gerken/Rieble/Roth/Stein/Streinz, *'Mangold' als ausbrechender Rechtsakt*, 2009.

118 Sanchez Lasaballett, *Unif. L. Rev.*, Vol. 24 (2019), 73, 80 ff. differentiates between four drivers: the market, public policy, jurisprudence and legal practice.

119 On its admissibility and significance in European private law, see paras. 234–307 below.

of interpretation by the CJEU as well as the resulting changes in the Member States' private laws.[120]

### c) *Minimum and Full Harmonisation*

**74.** Concerning the level of harmonisation, a distinction can be made between minimum harmonisation on the one hand and full harmonisation on the other. In between both modalities is the mixed form called targeted full harmonisation.

#### aa) Minimum Harmonisation

**75.** For a long time, directives followed the principle of minimum harmonisation. The directive only sets a minimum standard, which the Member States can exceed within their transposition laws. The extent to which it is possible to go beyond the minimum standard is determined by the directive's purpose and is usually regulated explicitly. In the case of consumer protection directives, minimum harmonisation allows for a higher level of consumer protection.

**76.** This approach has the advantage of leaving the Member States a reasonably large scope for implementation. This allows them to maintain coherence within their legal systems, for example, by structuring the temporal limits for the exercise of contractual rights such as rescission or withdrawal uniformly, both regarding harmonised or non-harmonised areas. At the same time, their own legal policy goals, such as exceptionally high levels of consumer protection, can be pursued this way. As a side effect, minimum harmonisation fuels the above-mentioned competition between legal systems by making certain standards binding without limiting them 'upwards'.

**77.** Nevertheless, this form of harmonisation usually does not lead to the creation of a level playing field; instead, legal fragmentation as such remains.[121] If one equates private law with market regulation law, such a state of affairs is unsatisfying since, depending on the Member State to which a market participant seeks access, the legal framework conditions may well be different. From the Commission's point of view, the Member States' leeway associated with minimum harmonisation, which makes it possible to introduce stricter protective provisions in favour of consumers, has led to the creation of a legal panorama that is confusing for consumers and businesses alike and that continues to obstruct cross-border trade.

---

[120] On this Franzen, *Privatrechtsangleichung durch die Europäische Gemeinschaft*, 1999, pp. 12 ff., 291 ff.

[121] On this Riesenhuber, in Hopt/Tzouganatos, *Das Europäische Wirtschaftsrecht vor neuen Herausforderungen*, 2014, pp. 183, 199 ff.

### bb) Full Harmonisation

**78.** With the proposal for a so-called horizontal Directive on Consumer Rights, the Commission has, therefore, steered towards full harmonisation in the area of consumer law.[122] In this proposal, the four central legal acts in the field of consumer contract law – the Doorstep Selling Directive, the Distance Selling Directive, the Unfair Terms Directive and the Consumer Sales Directive – were to be combined and modernised.[123] In the end, however, this plan could only be implemented rudimentarily.[124] Nevertheless, full harmonisation has now become the standard model for substantive law. With full harmonisation, Member States cannot over-fulfil the protection requirements. In this way, the directive comes closer to the regulation, even though the fully harmonising directive continues to require an act of implementation.[125]

**79.** At the same time, the change from minimum to full harmonisation within a substantive field of the law threatens to render the common justification of improving the internal market, which was initially used to support minimum harmonisation (see above), absurd. In the case of the Consumer Sales Directive, for example, it was argued that the encroachment on the legal systems of the Member States brought about by minimum harmonisation was comparatively minor;[126] moreover, consumer confidence in the internal market was strengthened precisely by the fact that the Member States could provide for a higher level of protection.[127]

**80.** In favour of full harmonisation, however, it is generally argued that it creates a level playing field for all market participants within the internal market;[128] but this is only correct to a certain extent: On the one hand, the directive's harmonisation technique leaves the Member States a certain amount of discretion regarding its implementation. In Germany, for example, the

---

122 COM(2008) 614 final.

123 On the development M. Stürner, in M. Stürner (ed.), *Vollharmonisierung im Verbraucherrecht?* (Munich: Sellier, 2010), p. 3.

124 By Directive 2011/83/EU of 25 October 2011 on consumer rights.

125 On the implementation of fully harmonising directives T. Riehm, in M. Zimmermann/C. Kopp/C. Busch/M.R. McGuire (eds.), *Europäische Methodik: Konvergenz und Diskrepanz nationalen und europäischen Privatrechts*, Jahrbuch junger Zivilrechtswissenschaftler 2009 (Stuttgart: Boorberg, 2010), p. 159.

126 Thus, with reference to the principle of subsidiarity, the explanatory memorandum to the Commission proposal for a Directive of the European Parliament and of the Council on the sale of consumer goods and associated guarantees of 18 June 1996, COM(95) 520 final, p. 11.

127 See Recital 5 on the CSD: 'Whereas the creation of a common set of minimum rules of consumer law, valid no matter where goods are purchased within the Community, will strengthen consumer confidence and enable consumers to make the most of the internal market.'

128 Recitals 8 and 9 of the proposal of the Distance Selling Directive; Recital 7 of the CRD.

fully harmonising Consumer Rights Directive was essentially integrated into general contract law (sec. 312 et seq., 355 et seq. German Civil Code), whereas in other Member States, it is found in special consumer codes (France, Italy, partly also Austria) or is regulated entirely independently (as in the pre-Brexit UK). Nevertheless, this may still be seen as a structural aspect without any far-reaching effects on the content. On the other hand, and more importantly, due to the limited material scope of application of fully harmonising directives, regulations of general contract law also apply in many cases (e.g. concerning the conclusion of contracts, vitiated consent, representation or the existence of claims for damages), which for the most part have not been harmonised. In this respect, there is no 'level playing field'.

**81.** Leaving these aspects aside, creating a level playing field through full harmonisation does have one major disadvantage: it harbours the danger of legal petrification by de facto preventing competition between the Member States for the best consumer law. The example of sales law illustrates this perfectly: In the course of the implementation of the minimum harmonising Consumer Sales Directive, this regulatory technique led to the enactment of regulations in the Member States' legal systems that were, in some cases, significantly more consumer-friendly than the directive's requirements, for example in terms of the consumer's free choice of a remedy or an extended limitation period.[129] The new, fully harmonising version of the directive will now establish a uniform level of consumer protection for the foreseeable future.[130] This led to the consequence that consumers in some of these Member States are legally worse off than before since exceptionally consumer-friendly regulations are no longer permitted. The Commission was well aware of this,[131] but considered it less important than creating harmonised market conditions. However, the Commission's assumption that full harmonisation creates welfare gains is at least questionable.[132]

**82.** The concept of full harmonisation is by no means new: The oldest fully harmonising directive in the field of private law dates back to the Product Liability Directive of 1985.[133] However, we have only been aware of its fully harmonising nature since 2002: In that year, the CJEU had to decide on the conformity of French and Greek law with the Directive; both national laws provided for the

---

129 See the examples in the Commission proposal, COM(2015) 635 final, pp. 6 f.

130 On the Sale of Goods Directive, see para. 826 below.

131 Commission proposal, COM(2015) 635 final, p. 12. See also the comment by Riesenhuber, in Hopt/Tzouganatos, *Das Europäische Wirtschaftsrecht vor neuen Herausforderungen*, 2014, pp. 183, 199: It is easier to agree on lower standards than on higher ones.

132 On this see Mittwoch, *Vollharmonisierung und Europäisches Privatrecht*, 2013, pp. 177 ff.

133 Council Directive 85/374/EEC of 25 July 1985 on the approximation of the laws, regulations and administrative provisions of the Member States concerning liability for defective products, OJ 1985 L 210/29.

manufacturer's liability for damages caused by a defect to objects other than the product itself, even without the flat deduction of € 500[134] that the directive mandated.[135] Even though the relevant provisions of national law were more favourable to the injured party than those provided for by the directive, the CJEU found an infringement on the grounds that the Product Liability Directive was fully harmonising. The CJEU relied, among other things, on a comparison with the Unfair Terms Directive, which, in contrast to the Product Liability Directive, contains an explicit statement on its goal of minimum harmonisation.[136]

**83.** Directives that explicitly state their fully harmonising character are, on the other hand, all comparably recent. In the area of private law, these are, in particular, the recast Consumer Credit Directive,[137] the revised Timeshare Directive,[138] the Unfair Commercial Practices Directive[139] and, with restrictions, the Payment Services Directive.[140] The justification used is as stereotypical as it is identical among all mentioned directives. Take Recital 3 to the Timeshare Directive as an example, where further harmonisation of laws is called for in order to improve legal certainty and to realise the internal market. The need for full harmonisation is directly derived from these postulates.[141] Whether this rationale can be applied to consumer law as a whole seems questionable in view

---

134 Article 9(1)(b) of Directive 85/374/EEC provides for a deductible of 500 euros.

135 CJEU, 25 April 2002, Case C-52/00, *Commission/France*, ECLI:EU:C:2002:252; CJEU, 25 April 2002, Case C-154/00, *Commission/Greece*, ECLI:EU:C:2002:254. See also the further decision CJEU, 25 April 2002, Case C-183/00, *González Sánchez*, ECLI:EU:C:2002:255.

136 This is somewhat contradicted by the decision of the CJEU, 4 June 2009, Case C-285/08, *Moteurs Leroy Somer*, ECLI:EU:C:2009:351. In this case, a provision of French law, which, in contrast to Article 9(b) Product Liability Directive, also provides for a claim for compensation for commercially used goods, was held to be in conformity with the Directive. This was justified by the consumer protection objective of the Directive, which did not exclude the inclusion of commercially used objects.

137 Directive 2008/48/EC of the European Parliament and of the Council of 23 April 2008 on credit agreements for consumers and repealing Council Directive 87/102/EEC, OJ 2008 L 133/66.

138 Directive 2008/122/EC of the European Parliament and of the Council of 14 January 2009 on the protection of consumers in respect of certain aspects of timeshare, long-term holiday product, resale and exchange contracts, OJ 2008 L 33/10.

139 Directive 2005/29/EC of the European Parliament and of the Council of 11 May 2005 concerning unfair business-to-consumer commercial practices in the internal market and amending Council Directive 84/450/EEC, Directives 97/7/EC, 98/27/EC and 2002/65/EC of the European Parliament and of the Council and Regulation (EC) no 2006/2004 of the European Parliament and of the Council (Unfair Commercial Practices Directive), OJ 2005 L 149/22.

140 Directive 2007/64/EC of the European Parliament and of the Council of 13 November 2007 on payment services in the internal market amending Directives 97/7/EC, 2002/65/EC, 2005/60/EC and 2006/48/EC and repealing Directive 97/5/EC, OJ 2007 L 319/1.

141 Recital 3 of the Timeshare Directive 2008/122/EC; comparable Recitals 7-9 of the Consumer Credit Directive 2008/48/EC and Recitals 4, 11-13 of the Fair Trading Directive 2005/29/EC; but cf. also the exemption provision in Recital 34 of the Payment Services Directive 2007/64/EC.

of the respective sectoral limitations of the directives mentioned above: There, friction with non-harmonised areas is to be feared less.[142] However, similar justifications for the necessity of full harmonisation are also given for all recent directives in the area of consumer law.[143]

### cc) Targeted Full Harmonisation

**84.** A combined form of minimum and full harmonisation is the so-called 'targeted full harmonisation'. Here, deviation from an otherwise prescribed level of harmonisation is permitted in relation to individual subject areas through option clauses. More recent directives mostly follow this approach. Here, the Member States have greater leeway compared to regular full harmonisation: This follows, on the one hand, from the limited scope of the directives and, on the other hand, and most importantly, from option clauses that give the Member States the possibility to deviate from the prescribed standard in some areas. With regard to the remaining regulatory leeway of Member States, it is, therefore, essential to distinguish whether an area of regulation is outside or within the scope of application of the directive. In the former case, the Member States have unrestricted legislative powers, and in the latter, they can legislate only insofar as the directive's provisions do not have a blocking effect.[144] The situation gets considerably more complicated as these directives deviate from their 'pure' form by means of generous opening clauses. In some sense, it seems contradictory to justify full harmonisation with the existing legal fragmentation while also – and counterintuitively – excluding large areas of the directive using option clauses.[145] It probably must be conceded that the regulatory technique of targeted full harmonisation is likely unavoidable due to the compromise culture in Brussels. This should not obscure the fact that for individual sub-areas, full harmonisation seems to make perfect sense in practice, especially concerning more technical questions such as the right of withdrawal or the statute of limitations.[146]

### *d) Harmonisation at Different Speeds*

**85.** Inherent to the internal market's purpose, one might think, is always the endeavour to harmonise the law of *all* Member States. This seems to contrast

---

[142] On this point Obergfell, in M. Stürner (ed.), *Vollharmonisierung im Verbraucherrecht?* (Munich: Sellier, 2010), p. 159.

[143] See, for example, Recital 3 of the Sale of Goods Directive.

[144] In-depth analysis of the distinction Riehm, in Gsell/Herresthal (eds.), *Vollharmonisierung im Privatrecht*, 2009, pp. 83, 90 ff, 100 ff.

[145] On this Loos, in M. Stürner (ed.), *Vollharmonisierung im Verbraucherrecht?* (Munich: Sellier, 2010), p. 47.

[146] On this see Oehler, in M. Stürner (ed.), *Vollharmonisierung im Verbraucherrecht?* (Munich: Sellier, 2010), p. 99.

strongly with the idea of a 'two-speed Europe', which has been advocated for some time now due to the increasing difficulties in separating factual issues from national political interests in the decision-making process.

**86.** At the same time, the EU, having 27 Member States after Brexit, has reached a size that risks making every legal act, no matter how insignificant, an ordeal. While some Member States significantly withdrew their participation in the area of judicial cooperation, others were willing to integrate more; hence, the EU faced the difficult task of enabling closer cooperation for only some of its Member States. The Treaty of Amsterdam had already attempted to achieve this with the instrument of enhanced cooperation (now Articles 20 TEU, 326 et seq. TFEU). According to this instrument, individual Member States – at least nine (Article 20(2) TEU) – may be authorised by the Council to implement further measures, but only if 'the objectives of such cooperation cannot be attained within a reasonable period by the Union as a whole' (Article 20(2) TEU).

**87.** Enhanced cooperation is thus subsidiary to the standard process of integration. The Rome III Regulation on the conflict of laws in divorce matters is the first example of the failure of EU-wide harmonisation in the field of private law.[147] The proposal for a regulation submitted by the Commission in 2006 ultimately failed after lengthy discussions in 2008 mainly due to Sweden's opposition. As a result, ten Member States applied for enhanced cooperation.[148] After initial hesitation, the Commission finally agreed to the project in March 2010; the adoption of the Regulation by the Council then took place shortly before Christmas 2010.[149] Since the Regulation entered into force on 21 June 2012,[150] a total of 17 Member States now have a uniform regime on the conflict of laws regarding divorce and legal separation.[151]

**88.** Is enhanced cooperation a blessing or a curse for European judicial cooperation? Many commentators are cautiously optimistic: Although it leads to a regionalisation of European harmonisation, this is always preferable to a standstill in the harmonisation process.[152] Gradual or differentiated

---

147 The European Matrimonial Property Regime Regulation and the European Property of Registered Partnerships Regime Regulation should also be mentioned.

148 On the procedure Fiorini, *ICLQ* 59 (2010), 1143.

149 Cf. Article 3(1) Rome III Regulation in conjunction with Council Decision 2010/405/EU of 12 July 2010 authorising enhanced cooperation in the area of the law applicable to divorce and legal separation, OJ 2010 L 189/12.

150 Cf. in detail Article 18 Rome III Regulation.

151 Participating Member States were then: Belgium, Bulgaria, Germany, Spain, France, Italy, Latvia, Luxembourg, Hungary, Malta, Austria, Portugal, Romania and Slovenia. Subsequently, Lithuania, Greece and Estonia have also declared participation.

152 Mansel/Thorn/Wagner, *IPRax* 2011, 1, 2, 30.

integration[153] does indeed offer a way out of a legal impasse from which one could otherwise only escape through more compromises which eventually might endanger the actual regulatory goal altogether. In this respect, it should be noted that differentiated integration has long been a reality outside of judicial cooperation anyway; take, for example, the European Monetary Union or the Schengen Agreement.

### e) *Optional Harmonisation*

References: C. von Bar, 'Privatrecht europäisch denken!', *JZ* 2014, 473; M. Stürner, 'Der deutsch-französische Wahlgüterstand als Modell für die europäische Rechtsvereinheitlichung', *JZ* 2011, 545.

**89.** Differentiated integration can also take place outside of formally binding EU law. The EU legislator increasingly relies on regulatory instruments that do not lead to a binding standardisation or harmonisation of law. Instead, they are available to the parties as so-called optional instruments. In company law, for example, supranational forms of corporate entities have been created, such as the European Economic Interest Grouping (EEIG), the Societas Europaea (European Company, EC) and the Societas Cooperativa Europaea (European Cooperative Company, EEC) These do not affect the validity of the traditional legal persons at the Member State level, i.e. they do not create a binding uniform law on corporate entities.[154] However, in the case of the EC, for example, any public limited company with a registered office in the EU is free to use such a legal entity. The fact that the associated appearance of internationality may be quite appealing is proven by the fact that several large corporations have changed their holding companies' legal personality to an SE.

**90.** Similar developments can also be observed in the area of judicial cooperation. For some time now, it has been possible to enforce cross-border claims using the so-called European Payment Order procedure or, up to a disputed amount of (currently) EUR 5000, with the European small claims procedure. These types of proceedings also do not affect the law of the Member States, but – and this is entirely intentional – they compete with, for example, an order for

[153] This is the programmatic title of the conference volume by P. Jung/C. Baldus (eds.), *Differenzierte Integration im Gemeinschaftsprivatrecht* (Munich: Sellier, 2007).

[154] The proposal for a Regulation on the Statute for a European Private Company for Small and Medium-sized Enterprises – SPE, COM(2008) 396 did not succeed; it gave rise to the idea of a Societas Unius Personae (SUP), a type of single-member company with its own legal capacity, COM(2014) 212. However, this proposal has now also been withdrawn by the Commission, see OJ 2018 C 233/7. Also withdrawn was the proposal for a Regulation on the Statute for a European Foundation (FE), COM(2012) 35, see OJ 2015 C 80/21.

payment procedure or small claims tracks within the laws of some Member States.

**91.** The unifying idea behind these optional instruments is that by providing supranational legal standards, parties are provided with uniform rules for their economic activity in the internal market, which presents them, of course, with a valuable advantage. At the same time, the regulatory scope of the Member States is not directly restricted by these instruments. However, a certain pressure to adapt is exerted insofar as the competing national laws are pressured to justify themselves due to the increasing acceptance of an optional instrument by the 'legal consumer', i.e. the participants in economic transactions.[155]

## 5. DELIMITATION TO LEGAL HARMONISATION OUTSIDE EU LAW

### a) *Harmonisation in the Narrow Sense*

#### aa) UN Sale of Goods Convention

**92.** The UN Sale of Goods Convention (CISG)[156] has been in force since 1 January 1988 and is now applicable in 97 countries worldwide.[157] Once transposed, the Convention is part of the relevant legal system and *ipso iure* applicable as soon as the prerequisites of Article 1(1)(a) CISG are met, i.e. without any requirement of a separate choice of law.[158] According to the latter provision, it is only necessary that the parties to a cross-border sale of goods are residents of different contracting states. In addition, the UN Sale of Goods Convention is also applicable if the conflict-of-laws rules of the *forum* refer to the law of a contracting state, either because it accepts a choice of law by the parties or because it is most significantly connected to the respective set of facts, Article 1(1)(b) CISG.[159]

---

155 In addition see paras. 1305–1309 below.

156 United Nations Convention on Contracts for the International Sale of Goods of 11 April 1980.

157 As of March 2024. A list of all treaty countries can be found at https://uncitral.un.org/en/texts/salegoods/conventions/sale_of_goods/cisg/status.

158 Cf. for Germany Federal Court of Justice, BGHZ 134, 201, 206; Ferrari, in Schlechtriem/Schwenzer/Schroeter, *Kommentar zum Einheitlichen UN-Kaufrecht*, 7th ed. 2019, vor Arts. 1–6 para. 34. This is apparently not the case in French case law, according to which negotiations of the parties on the non-uniform French law were regarded as an exclusion of the CISG, cf. the decision of the Cour de Cassation of 26 June 2001, CISG-online nos. 598 and 600.

159 Cf. OLG Düsseldorf IHR 2005, 24; OLG Karlsruhe IHR 2004, 62. Some contracting states (among others the USA and China) have declared reservations against the application of Article 1(1)(b) CISG according to Article 95 CISG.

**93.** In view of these requirements and the ratification process progressing worldwide, one might expect that the importance of the UN Sale of Goods Convention for the international sale of goods would continue to increase.[160] In legal practice, however, this is not always the case.[161] In cross-border legal transactions, the possibility to exclude the UN Sale of Goods Convention under Article 6 CISG is employed regularly;[162] for a long time, it could be said that the UN Sale of Goods Convention would only apply if the parties – for whatever reason – did not successfully opt-out.[163] However, for example, in Germany, the modernisation of the law of obligations in 2002 brought about some notable changes in this respect[164] since, now, there is a great degree of convergence between the German Civil Code and CISG.[165]

#### bb) Other Conventions on the Law of Obligations

**94.** In addition to the CISG, the Convention on the Contract for the International Carriage of Goods by Road (CMR) may be mentioned as an important conventional regulatory instrument within the area of contract law. It entered into force on 2 July 1961 and currently applies to 58 contracting states.[166]

### *b) Harmonisation through Soft Law*

#### aa) Defining the Notion

**95.** The term soft law is a somewhat iridescent legal term. It is generally used as a catch-all term for all rules besides the formally binding law, which can be described as hard law in this respect. Even after centuries of legal-academic and

160 The CISG has already been described as 'the most significant harmonising private law convention to date', cf. Magnus, in Staudinger, *BGB Kommentar* (Berlin: Sellier/De Gruyter, 2018), Einl. zum CISG para. 1; similarly Meyer, *RabelsZ* 69 (2005), 457, 458 ('one of the most successful projects of legal harmonisation') as well as *Janssen*, ERPL 13 (2005), 463.

161 Cf. the empirical study carried through by Meyer, *RabelsZ* 69 (2005), 457, 466 ff., 472: according to the author, about two thirds of the 479 lawyers participating in the survey stated that they regularly exclude UN sales law. About one third expressly or tacitly include UN sales law.

162 If one does not want to understand the CISG itself as a separate legal system in this sense, this norm thus represents an exception to the principle of conflict of laws that a legal system can only be chosen or waived as a whole.

163 Cf. Schillo, *IHR* 2003, 257, 259; Regula/Kannowski, *IHR* 2004, 45; Meyer, *RabelsZ* 69 (2005), 457, 462 in note 24, 473.

164 Thus, the model GTC of many interest groups no longer provide for a general deselection of the CISG, see P. Schlechtriem/U.G. Schroeter, *Internationales UN-Kaufrecht*, 6th ed. (Tübingen: Mohr Siebeck, 2016), para. 16.

165 On this see Grundmann, *AcP* 202 (2002), 40.

166 As of March 2024, see https://treaties.un.org/pages/ViewDetails.aspx?src=TREATY&mtdsg_no=XI-B-11&chapter=11&clang=_en.

philosophical research, no consensus could be reached on what law – soft or hard – actually is. At the end of the 18th century, Emmanuel Kant famously asserted that 'Jurists are still searching for a definition of their concept of law',[167] which is probably just as true today. One can look at it in an ultra-realist fashion like Oliver Wendell Holmes, who spoke of law as the accurate prediction of what the courts will decide.[168] One can focus on enforceability like Kelsen, who saw the decisive criterion in the moment of coercion,[169] on the positivist approach advocated by H.L.A. Hart,[170] or on a principle-based theory as forcefully elaborated namely by Dworkin.[171]

**96.** One can go as far as postmodernism, whose supporters advocate for a non-hierarchical coexistence of different legal systems or legal traditions within a social system. Such approaches can be traced back to Eugen Ehrlich.[172] The multi-ethnic composition of his homeland, the Duchy of Bukovina, with its different legal traditions and customs, led Ehrlich to focus on legal reality, or, as he called it, 'living law'. The phenomenon of globalisation has given rise to the idea of legal pluralism.[173] Among others, it has found fertile ground with representatives of postmodern theory,[174] legal anthropology[175] and systems theory;[176] in this respect, Teubner famously coined the term 'Global Bukovina'.[177]

**97.** In terms of its content, the debate about soft law is particularly concerned with considering and ranking non-state regulations, i.e. those of indigenous or religious origin, as well as normative structures set by private regulators. In this respect, central questions relate to the control and order of the diverse legal sources. If one takes note of the diversity of law not only as an actual phenomenon but also asks about its normative implications, it is necessary to define the requirements, whatever they may be, for the applicability of each rule.

---

167 Kant, *Kritik der Reinen Vernunft*, B 759 Anmerkung.

168 Oliver Wendell Holmes, *The Path of the Law*, Volume X, 1897, p. 460.

169 H. Kelsen, *Reine Rechtslehre* (Vienna: Franz Deuticke, 1960), pp. 34 ff.

170 H. Hart, *The Concept of Law* (Oxford: Oxford University Press, 1961).

171 R. Dworkin, *Taking Rights Seriously* (Cambridge (MA): Harvard University Press, 1977).

172 *Grundlegung der Soziologie des Rechtes*, 1913.

173 In summary Michaels, *Annual Review of Law and Social Science* 5 (2009), 243; Berman, 80 *Southern California Law Review* 1155 (2007).

174 Santos, 14 *Journal of Law and Society* 293 (1987); cf. also E. Jayme, 'Identité culturelle et intégration: le droit international privé postmoderne' in *Cours général de droit international privé, Recueil des cours*, tome 251 (Leiden: Martinus Nijhoff, 1995), p. 9.

175 Riles, 56 *American Journal of Comparative Law* 605 (2008).

176 Teubner, 5 *Cardozo Law Rev.*, 1443 (1992).

177 G. Teubner, *Global Law Without a State* (Dartmouth, 1997), p. 3.

**98.** The lack of enforceability or non-sanctionability of its norms is often referred to as a criterion for discerning soft law from hard law.[178] However, this is not a clear-cut criterion: A number of regulations that one would easily classify as hard law also do not trigger any enforceable obligations, for example, in some legal systems, certain obligations regarding gambling, betting or marriage brokerage. Conversely, violating soft law standards of conduct might, in fact, trigger civil law liability.[179]

**99.** Thus, it may be possible to agree on a pragmatic working definition of law, which considers it the totality of all applicable norms, i.e. such rules enacted by a legislator and/or applied by the courts.[180] Below the so-understood 'hard law', 'soft law' begins. However, concerning the 'norms' gathered under the umbrella of soft law, it is often even debatable whether they are 'law' at all given that they might include instruments that originate from private or semi-private authorship.[181] This applies, for example, to model laws or rules such as the UNCITRAL Model Law on International Commercial Arbitration of 1985 (which has served 90 states or 123 jurisdictions worldwide[182] as a model for their arbitration law), the UNIDROIT Principles of International Commercial Contracts (PICC), the Principles of European Contract Law (PECL), the ELI/UNIDROIT European Rules of Civil Procedure, or to largely unwritten commercial customs such as the *lex mercatoria* or private standards such as the International Financial Reporting Standards (IFRS). Ultimately, each case has to be considered separately.

**100.** Soft law instruments seem to enjoy great popularity today. If one asks for the reasons, it is unnecessary to go so far as to claim that the vague, imprecise and non-binding nature of soft law represents the hallmark of a time in which postmodern arbitrariness seems to prevail in many places. However, it certainly seems to correspond to the creeping deconstruction of the post-war order – with only a few superpowers and clear divisions between East and West – and clear tendencies away from multilateralism that makes international rule-making increasingly difficult; it seems like, quite often, compromises can perhaps only be reached if they do not lead to binding commitments.

---

178 K.F. Röhl/H.C. Röhl, *Allgemeine Rechtslehre*, 3rd ed. (Cologne: Carl Heymanns, 2008), p. 222 (soft law as law without sanctions?); see also Schwarze, *EuR* 2011, 3.

179 See below at para. 1114 ff. for a conflict-of-laws perspective.

180 In that sense B. Rüthers/C. Fischer/A. Birk, *Rechtstheorie mit Juristischer Methodenlehre*, 12th ed. (Munich: C.H. Beck, 2021), para. 53.

181 K. Nowrot, in C. Tietje/K. Nowrot (eds.), *Internationales Wirtschaftsrecht*, 3nd ed. (Berlin: De Gruyter, 2021), §2 paras. 77 ff.: no soft law.

182 As of March 2024, see https://uncitral.un.org/en/texts/arbitration/modellaw/commercial_arbitration/status.

**101.** On a somewhat different level, soft law is used to escalate rule-making, i.e. as a preliminary stage of 'real' rule-making with an announcement or – depending on the perspective – warning function. This can be observed in EU law, for example, where green or white papers or even action plans are first published in an area that has been identified as a field in need of regulation, possibly followed by a recommendation from the Commission, which as such is non-binding and can thus be counted as soft law according to the above working definition. The real rule-making in the form of directives or regulations then regularly follows a few years later; in these cases, it no longer comes as a surprise and is easier to enforce.

**102.** Finally, soft law can also prove to be a possibility of participatory rule-making. It leads to the delegation of quasi-legislative powers to experts without a recognisable political agenda. This increases the authority of the envisaged hard law rules and possibly facilitates the political enforceability of the regulatory desideratum behind it.

#### bb) Autonomous Harmonisation through Soft Law

**103.** For a Member State legislator, the impetus for harmonisation will regularly come 'from above', especially in the form of an EU directive. However, this does not exclude the possibility that harmonisation may also be pursued for autonomous motives. Possible reasons for this could lie, above all, in the desire to provide a modern and internationally competitive legal system. This is intended to strengthen the attractiveness of domestic law, which is being put under pressure by the multitude of legal options.[183] This goes so far that Western industrialised countries are actively promoting the quality of their own law, for example, through a consortium of professional associations, judges' associations and the business community with the support of the Federal Ministry of Justice and Consumer Protection for 'Law Made in Germany'. The French -*Fondation pour le droit continental*' follows a similar approach.[184] Here, the law is openly regarded as a product that the law-seeking public chooses if the price-performance ratio appears favourable.[185]

**104.** However, such initiatives regularly concern international trade. In other areas of private law, especially where consumers are involved, autonomous

[183] This is especially true if party autonomy also refers to the choice of the place of jurisdiction, as is the case for the EU in Article 25 Brussels I*bis* Regulation. The same applies to the possibility of derogating state courts from the outset by way of an arbitration agreement, cf. for example sec. 1029, 1032 (1) ZPO.

[184] On both see Vogenauer, *ERPL* 2013, 30; U. Kischel, *Rechtsvergleichung* (Munich: C.H. Beck, 2015), pp. 144 ff.

[185] Eidenmüller, *JZ* 2009, 641; Basedow, 62 *American Journal of Comparative Law*, 821 (2014).

harmonisation will often arise due to the harmonisation of law through EU directives. For example, since the recodification of many ancillary laws during the modernisation of the law of obligations in 2001, the German legislator has implemented a whole series of such directives in an 'overshooting' manner, meaning that the transposition of the EU law requirements went far beyond their intended scope.[186] This usually follows from the demands of the principles of internal uniformity and freedom from systematic contradictions.

### cc) UNIDROIT Principles

References: E. Brödermann, *UNIDROIT Principles of International Commercial Contracts – An Article-by-Article Commentary* (Alphen aan den Rijn: Kluwer Law International, 2018); S. Vogenauer (ed.), *Commentary on the UNIDROIT Principles of International Commercial Contracts (PICC)*, 2nd ed. (Oxford: Oxford University Press, 2015); K. Erler/M. Schmidt-Kessel, 'The Use of the UPICC in Order to Interpret or Supplement German Contract Law', in M. Schmidt-Kessel (ed.), *German National Reports on the 20th International Congress of Comparative Law* (Tübingen: Mohr Siebeck, 2018), p. 39.

**105.** The UNIDROIT Principles of International Commercial Contracts (PICC) were first published in 1994; the current version dates to 2016. The PICC are also soft law; they have not been enacted by a democratically legitimised legislator. Designating the PICC by means of a choice of law agreement is, therefore, not viable.[187] Nevertheless, the Principles enjoy some popularity, both in the area of international contract drafting[188] and with regard to the creation of new laws, such as the novel Estonian Code of Obligations.[189] However, the PICC has, so far, seldomly been used as a frame of reference for the interpretation of contracts in German jurisprudence (for example, they are taken into account within the framework of the customs and practices applicable in commercial transactions, cf. sec. 346 German Commercial Code).[190]

### dd) PECL and DCFR

References: A. Stadler, 'Struktur, Stil und Regelungstechnik des DCFR', in *Festschrift für Schwenzer* (Bern: Stämpfli Verlag, 2011), p. 1605.

---

186 In this regard Habersack/Mayer, in Riesenhuber, *European Legal Methodology*, §14.

187 See para. 1156 below.

188 Decidedly Brödermann, *IWRZ* 2019, 7.

189 See I. Kull/M. Torga, in I. Kull (ed.). Development of Estonian Contract and Company Law in the Context of Harmonized EU Law (Tartu: Univ.Press, 2010), p. 43.

190 Fore more details see Erler/Schmidt-Kessel, in Schmidt-Kessel (ed.), *German National Reports on the 20th International Congress of Comparative Law*, 2018, p. 39, with further references to the existing legal literature.

**106.** Attempts to create a similar regulatory framework for European private law have been largely unsuccessful. The Draft Common Frame of Reference (DCFR[191]), promoted by the EU Commission and based on the Principles of European Contract Law (PECL),[192] was intended to achieve more coherent legislation at the EU level. However, this approach has, so far, not found its way into EU legislation or legal policy. Thus, the DCFR remains an academic model code, which could, however, serve as a blueprint for smaller Member States that aim to modernise their private law systems.[193] Here, too, Estonia can serve as an example since it has drawn on various sources of inspiration, including those of soft law origin such as PECL and PICC, in the reorganisation of its Code of Obligations.[194]

---

191 See von Bar/Clive/Schulte-Nölke, *Principles, Definitions and Model Rules of European Private Law. Draft Common Frame of Reference (DCFR)*, Full Edition, 2009.

192 On both below paras. 160–172 and 120.

193 See for example Jung, in Schmidt-Kessel (ed.), *Der Gemeinsame Referenzrahmen*, 2009, pp. 255, 258 ff.

194 On this see I. Kull, *Juridica International* 1999, 147; *id.*, *Juridica International* 2004, 32.

# §3. THE HISTORIC EVOLUTION OF EUROPEAN CONTRACT LAW

CONTENTS

References: J. Basedow, *EU Private Law. Anatomy of a Growing Legal Order* (Cambridge: Intersentia, 2021), p. 60; H. Beale, 'The story of EU contract law – from 2001 to 2014', in C. Twigg-Flesner (ed.), *Research Handbook on EU Consumer and Contract Law* (Cheltenham; Edward Elgar Publishing, 2016), p. 431; M. Gebauer, *Grundfragen der Europäisierung des Privatrechts* (Heidelberg: C. Winter, 1998); F. Gómez, 'The Harmonization of Contract Law through European Rules: a Law and Economics Perspective', *ERCL* 2008, 89; S. Grundmann, 'Europäisches Vertragsrecht – Quo vadis?', *JZ* 2005, 860; S. Grundmann/M. Grochowski, The Creation of Norms: An Evolutionary View on European Contract Law, in S. Grundmann/M. Grochowski (ed.), *European Contract Law and the Creation of Norms* (Cambridge: Intersentia, 2021), p. 3; G. Hamza, 'Bemerkungen zur Angleichung des Privatrechts in Europa', in *Festschrift für Müller-Graff* (Baden-Baden: Nomos, 2015), p. 59; M.W. Hesselink, *Justifying Contract in Europe. Political Philosophies of European Contract Law* (Oxford: Oxford University Press, 2021), p. 16; M.W. Hesselink, 'Progress in EU Contract Law', *Eur. Rev. Contract Law* 2022, 281; H. Honsell, 'Die Erosion des Privatrechts durch das Europarecht', *ZIP* 2008, 621; H. Kötz, *European Contract Law*, 2nd ed. (Oxford: Oxford University Press, 2017), §1; E.A. Kramer, 'Internationale, europäische und schweizerische Perspektiven des Vertragsrechts', *JBl* 2012, 750; S. Leutheusser-Schnarrenberger, 'Europäisches Zivilrecht – die nächsten Etappen', *ZEuP* 2011, 451; J. Mance, 'The Common Frame of Reference', *ZEuP* 2010, 457; U. Magnus, 'EU Private Law: A Zeitgeist-Idea from the Past?', in A. Janssen/M. Lehmann/R. Schulze (eds.), *The Future of European Private Law* (Baden-Baden: Nomos, 2023), p. 89; A.-C. Mittwoch, 'Die Vereinheitlichung des Privatrechts in Europa – auf dem Weg zu einem Europäischen Zivilgesetzbuch?', *JuS* 2010, 767; L. Niglia, The Struggle for European Private Law. A Critique of Codification (Oxford: Hart Publishing, 2017); L. Niglia, *The Structural Transformation of European Private Law. A Critique of Juridical Hermeneutics* (London: Bloomsbury Publishing, 2024); P. Pichonnaz, 'A Bird's-Eye View: The Oscilliation between Ius Commune and National Law', in A. Janssen/M. Lehmann/R. Schulze (eds.), *The Future of European Private Law* (Baden-Baden: Nomos, 2023), p. 43; H. Schulte-Nölke, 'EU Private Law: Classic Values and Purposes of National Private Law and Their Entanglement with the Purposes of the EU', in A. Janssen/M. Lehmann/R. Schulze (eds.), *The Future of European Private Law* (Baden-Baden: Nomos, 2023), p. 75; S. Vogenauer/S. Weatherill, 'Eine empirische Untersuchung zur Angleichung des Vertragsrechts in der EG', *JZ* 2005, 870.

## I. THE *IUS COMMUNE* AS A PRECURSOR OF EUROPEAN PRIVATE LAW

References: A. Bürge, 'Das römische Recht als Grundlage für das Zivilrecht im künftigen Europa', in F. Ranieri (ed.), *Die Europäisierung der Rechtswissenschaft* (Baden-Baden: Nomos, 2002-, p. 19; H. Coing, *Von Bologna bis Brüssel – Europäische Gemeinsamkeiten in Vergangenheit, Gegenwart und Zukunft* (Cologne: Bergisch Gladbach, 1989); H. Coing,

*Die ursprüngliche Einheit der europäischen Rechtswissenschaft* (Wiesbaden: Steiner, 1968); H. Coing, *Europäisches Privatrecht I* (Munich; C.H. Beck, 1985); H. Coing, *Europäisches Privatrecht II* (Munich: C.H. Beck, 1989); M. Gebauer, *Grundfragen der Europäisierung des Privatrechts* (Heidelberg: C. Winter, 1998), §§1–6; R. Zimmermann, 'Das römisch-kanonische ius commune als Grundlage europäischer Rechtseinheit', *JZ* 1992, 8; R. Zimmermann, *The Law of Obligations. Roman Foundations of the Civilian Tradition* (Oxford: Oxford University Press, 1996); R. Zimmermann, 'Römisches Recht und europäische Kultur', *JZ* 2007, 1.

## 1. THE DEVELOPMENT OF A 'COMMON EUROPEAN LAW'

**107.** From the 11th and 12th centuries, a 'common European law' (*ius commune*) had already emerged from the reception of Roman and canon law. Its basis was the *corpus iuris civilis*, a collection of laws compiled by Emperor Justinian in the 6th century, and various collections of canonical sources. The *ius commune* was a 'substitute legal system' for the patchy local laws. The development was characterised by a predominantly uniform legal education throughout Europe, the Europe-wide acceptance of Latin as the language of the sciences, and the fact that jurists were often appointed to key positions in administration. They often tended to apply the *ius commune*, which was familiar to them, instead of local law. The comparably high mobility of academics also contributed to the spread of the *ius commune*.[1] The revival of the *ius commune* began in the newly founded universities of Upper Italy, above all in Bologna in the 11th and 12th centuries, and from the 13th century also in Padua and Naples.[2] In this sense, a 'European' private law already existed in the Middle Ages.

**108.** Note that England was not left untouched by this development: Only Roman law was taught at the only two English universities until the 19th century, Oxford and Cambridge. Common law was essentially regarded as a purely practical matter. However, the need for a renaissance of the *ius commune* was not as strong as on the continent since the common law was a quite mature legal system compared to, for example, the laws in force in the German states, given that the Kingdom of England (or, later on, of Great Britain) provided a comparably high degree of historical continuity and legal unity.[3] In Scotland, on the other hand, there is evidence of a reception of the *ius commune* since the 16th century.[4]

1 Examples are given in Zimmermann, *JZ* 1992, 8, 11.
2 Overview in Zimmermann, *JZ* 1992, 8.
3 On the historical connections between common law and civil law Zimmermann, *ZEuP* 1993, 4; *id.*, *JZ* 2007, 1, 11 f.
4 See Zimmermann/MacLeod, Entry 'Schottisches Privatrecht', in *Handwörterbuch des Europäischen Privatrechts*, 2009.

## 2. NATIONALISATION OF PRIVATE LAW SYSTEMS THROUGH CODIFICATIONS

**109.** From the late 17th century onwards, there was a renewed focus on local laws; also, legal education were carried through in the respective national language. This was accompanied by increasing trends towards nationalisation in the 18th century. The Enlightenment, the French Revolution and the creation of the French Code civil in 1804 marked a decisive departure from a jurisprudence that until then could undoubtedly be described as European. Now, this idea was replaced by the codification idea and the idea of the nation-state.[5] The Codex Maximilianeus Bavaricus civilis of 1756 and the Prussian General Land Law of 1794 could already be categorised as codifications of natural law; later, they were followed by the Austrian Civil Code of 1812. These codifications embodied the ideal of the bourgeois state, i.e. a legal code that regulates the rights and duties of all citizens and thus embodies the civil constitution. Even today, the French Code civil is occasionally referred to as 'the true political constitution of France'.[6] The contract and freedom of contract are of central importance,[7] as they allow citizens to shape their legal interests freely.[8] Law and jurisprudence were primarily oriented nationally; the European dimension of jurisprudence began to fade away.

## 3. HISTORICAL OBSERVATION AS A MEANS OF UNDERSTANDING THE PRESENT

**110.** A widespread trend in European private law scholarship, especially in Germany, relies on the historical understanding of the development of law in Europe in order to derive three main tenets from it. The first one is the idea that, in doing so, a justification for the European harmonisation of law can be established: What has already been a lived legal reality for centuries might again form the basis for today's European legal unity. Thus, according to Reinhard Zimmermann, the current stage can be understood 'as a mere transitory stage

---

5 On this epoch Gebauer, *Grundfragen der Europäisierung des Privatrechts*, 1998, pp. 48 ff.

6 J. Carbonnier, 'Le Code civil', in P. Nora (ed.), *Les lieux de mémoire, Volume 2* (Paris: Gallimard, 1986), p. 309 (code civil as 'la véritable constitution politique de la France'). Critically Cabrillac, 'Le Code civil est-il la véritable constitution de la France?', (2005) 39 *Revue juridique Thémis*, 245.

7 In the opera Rheingold (1869), for example, Richard Wagner lets the giant Fasolt exclaim towards Wotan: 'Contracts keep faith! What you are, you are only through contracts […].' Even if the content of this contract was hardly to be condoned – Wotan had promised the 'cession' of the goddess Freia to Fafner and Fasolt as payment for the construction of the turnkey castle of the gods – the utterance at least reflects the spirit of the times.

8 On the importance of the contract for society M. Weber, *Wirtschaft und Gesellschaft* (Tübingen: Mohr, 1922), pp. 412 ff.

on the way to a renewed *usus modernus pandectarum*'.[9] Secondly, however, this historical approach opposes a primarily neutral and technical approach to harmonisation with an exclusive orientation towards the internal market, which essentially represents the approach of the EU Commission. It calls for greater penetration of the substance of European law beyond its superficial divisions. This leads, thirdly, to a demand for a specific aim towards long-term goals; major projects such as the DCFR, which have been driven to publication in only a few years, tend to create some scepticism.[10]

**111.** A reminiscence of the emergence of the above-mentioned medieval universities and the remarkable level of academic exchange of that time can be seen in the so-called Bologna Process: It was initiated by a declaration of the EU Ministers of Education on 19 June 1999 in Bologna; here, the intention was declared to create a uniform higher education area in Europe by 2010 through the introduction of comparable higher education degrees and mutual recognition of academic achievements, the switch to a tiered system of Bachelor's and Master's degrees, increased mobility of students and teachers as well as the development of a European dimension of higher education.[11] These innovations, which remain far-reaching for the universities, cannot be discussed in detail here.[12]

## II. THE LONG-TERM GOAL: CODIFICATION OF EUROPEAN PRIVATE LAW

References: K. Gutman, *The Constitutional Foundations of European Contract Law: A Comparative Analysis* (Oxford: Oxford University Press, 2014), p. 156; N. Jansen/L. Rademacher, European Civil Code, in J.M. Smits/J. Husa/C. Valcke/M. Narciso (eds.), *Elgar Encyclopedia of Comparative Law* (Cheltenham: Edward Elgar Publishing, 2023), p. 47; O. Lando, 'Does the European Union need a Civil Code?', *RIW* 2003, 1; M. Lehmann, 'Braucht Europa ein Handelsgesetzbuch?', *ZHR* 181 (2017), 9; M. Lehmann, 'EU Law-Making 2.0: The Prospect of a European Business Code', *ERPL* 2020, 73; L. Niglia, *The Struggle for European Private Law. A Critique of Codification* (Oxford: Har Publishing, 2017); K. Riesenhuber, 'Und jetzt ein Europäisches Wirtschaftsgesetzbuch?', *GPR* 2017, 270; A. Zaccaria, 'Il futuro del diritto privato europeo', *Studium Iuris* 2007, 1299; P. Pichonnaz, 'Europäisches Privatrecht: Eine Vereinheitlichung beginnt im Geiste', in *Gedächtnisschrift für Huguenin* (Zürich/St. Gallen: Dike Verlag, 2018), p. 325

9 Zimmermann, *JZ* 1992, 8, 20; similarly Coing, *NJW* 1990, 937, 940 with the plea for the development of a European jurisprudence according to the historical model.

10 In addition paras. 120–129 below.

11 For example Jeep, *JZ* 2006, 459.

12 Cf. the country reports in C. Jamin/W. van Caenegem (eds.), *The Internationalisation of Legal Education* (Cham: Springer, 2016).

## 1. CODIFICATION AND THE INTERNAL MARKET

**112.** In a certain sense, it would lie within the historical logic of the internal market's development to move towards a codification in the area of private property law. The arguments that favour full harmonisation[13] – such as avoiding legal fragmentation, legal certainty, and reduction of transaction costs – would apply even more to a comprehensive harmonisation of the private law systems.

**113.** Legal scholars, however, hold very different views on this. On the one hand, there are those authors who consider the recognition and protection of legal cultural differences within the EU essential; in this respect, it is often stated that these should not fall victim to legislative measures.[14] It has also been questioned whether or not the EU would have legislative powers for such a project.[15] The opposing view points to the unifying power of the major codifications in the past and wants to revive this idea in the European legal area.[16] Especially from around the mid-1990s until the publication of the DCFR in 2008, a somewhat optimistic mood prevailed in this respect. Numerous conferences and anthologies on the subject of European harmonisation of private law bear witness to this.[17] A number of treaties, namely from Germany and Austria, dealt with the foundations of the Europeanisation of private law;[18] countless dissertations considered specific aspects.[19] A quote from Winfried Tilman – 'Europe, show what you can do!' – illustrates this optimism perfectly.[20]

**114.** However, the recent past has shown that there would currently be no political majority for such an ambitious project as a European Civil Code.

---

13 See paras. 78–83 above.

14 Cf. generally, for example, Schulze, *ZEuP* 1993, 442, 473; Collins, *ERPL* 1995, 353; Sandrock, *JZ* 1996, 1, 6 ff.; Markesinis, *ERPL* 1997, 519; Berger, *ERPL* 2001, 21, 24 ff.; Luther, *RabelsZ* 45 (1981), 253 (on matrimonial law); cf. in a different context also Flume, *ZIP* 2000, 1427, 1429 (German Civil Code as a 'cultural monument'). Radically against any unification of law Legrand, 60 *MLR* 1997, 44.

15 See paras. 224–227 below.

16 Cf. e.g. Basedow, (1996) 33 *CMLR* 1169, 1181 ff.; *id.*, *ERPL* 2001, 35, 40 ff.; Lando, *ERPL* 1997, 525, 531 f.; *Drobnig*, in D. Martiny/N. Witzleb (eds.), *Auf dem Wege zu einem Europäischen Zivilgesetzbuch* (Berlin/Heidelberg: Springer, 1999), pp. 109, 116 ff.

17 The seminal work is Müller-Graff (ed.), *Gemeinsames Privatrecht in der Europäischen Gemeinschaft*, 2nd ed. 1999; cf. also Martiny/Witzleb (eds.), n. 16 above.

18 For example Franzen, *Privatrechtsangleichung durch die Europäische Gemeinschaft*, 1999; Leible, *Wege zu einem Europäischen Privatrecht*, Habil. 2001; Lurger, *Grundfragen der Vereinheitlichung des Vertragsrechts in der Europäischen Union*, 2002; Riesenhuber, *System und Prinzipien des Europäischen Vertragsrechts*, 2003.

19 Fundamental approach in particular in Gebauer, *Grundfragen der Europäisierung des Privatrechts*, 1998.

20 Tilman, *ZEuP* 1997, 595, 598.

Nevertheless, several academic initiatives continue to deal with the systematic compilation or synthesis of legal rules of European provenance.[21]

**115.** More optimism seems to be warranted in the area of commercial law.[22] In the White Paper 'The Future of Europe' of 1 March 2017,[23] a codification was explicitly conceived as a possible scenario, albeit only in the context of tiered integration ('Those who want more, do more'). It reads: 'A group of countries works together and agree on a common "Business Law Code" unifying corporate, commercial and related domains of law, helping businesses of all sizes to easily operate across borders.'[24]

## 2. THE 1989 RESOLUTION OF THE EUROPEAN PARLIAMENT

**116.** As early as 1989, in a 'Resolution on action to bring into line the private law of the Member States',[25] the European Parliament had called for the harmonisation of private law systems pending the start of the 'necessary preparatory work for the drafting of a uniform European code of private law'. Since the sole right of initiative for legislative measures lies with the Commission, this appeal remained unheard for some time; no definite proposals were made.

## 3. THE COMMISSION'S ACTION PLAN AND SUBSEQUENT COMMUNICATIONS

**117.** The Parliament's plea was only acted on by the Commission's Communication on European Contract Law of 11 July 2001,[26] in which the Commission presented various options for further harmonisation of European contract law, ranging from refraining from further action to adopting new legislation at the EC level.[27]

**118.** Taking into account the numerous reactions to the Communication, the Commission presented in its 'A more coherent European contract law –

---

21 See paras. 160–208 below.

22 Lehmann, *ZHR* 181 (2017), 9; Lehmann, *GPR* 2017, 262.

23 COM(2017) 2025 final.

24 White paper, COM(2017) 2025, p. 12. On the Franco-German initiative underlying this passage, see below paras. 202–205.

25 Of 26 May 1989, OJ 1989 C 158/400.

26 Communication from the Commission of the European Communities to the Council and the European Parliament on European Contract Law of 11 July 2001, COM(2001) 398 final.

27 COM(2001) 398, pp. 14 ff.

An action plan'[28] of 15 March 2003 a model which, in order to unify contract law, envisaged, on the one hand, the revision and consolidation of the existing *acquis communautaire* and, on the other hand, the creation of a 'Common Frame of Reference' which would lay down common principles and concepts in the field of European contract law and be addressed primarily to the EC institutions. This frame of reference was also supposed to serve as the basis for an 'optional instrument', i.e. a set of rules that could be chosen by the parties.[29] In a Communication of 11 October 2004, the Commission specified this approach.[30]

**119.** The Joint Network on European Private Law (CoPECL) was entrusted with the development of a 'Draft Common Frame of Reference' (DCFR), funded by the 6th EU Research Framework Programme.[31] The work of the CoPECL network has found its way into several progress reports by the Commission.[32] The leading members of the CoPECL network were the Study Group on a European Civil Code, which, as the successor group to the Commission of European Contract Law, continued and expanded the work on the PECL,[33] and the European Research Group on Existing EC Private Law (Acquis Group), which is aimed at summarising existing Community private law in a coherent form.[34] Both groups and their working methods are described later.[35]

28 COM(2003) 68 final.

29 COM(2003) 68 final, pp. 27 f.

30 Communication from the Commission to the European Parliament and the Council. European contract law and the revision of the acquis – the way forward, COM(2004) 651 final.

31 On the functioning of the network, inter alia, partly critically, Lando, ERCL 2007, 245; R. Schulze, in R. Schulze, *Common Frame of Reference and Existing EC Contract Law* (Munich: Sellier, 2009), p. 3; Hirsch, *ZIP* 2007, 937, 939 f.; Mance, *EBLR* 2007, 77, 92 ff. In an exaggerated manner against any harmonisation of law Legrand, *Journal of Comparative Law* 1 (2006), 13.

32 First Annual Progress Report on European Contract Law and the Review of the Acquis communautaire, 23 September 2005, COM(2005) 456 final; Second Progress Report on the Common Frame of Reference, 25 July 2007, COM(2007) 447 final; cf. also European Parliament resolution on European contract law and the revision of the *acquis communautaire* of 23 March 2006, 2005/2022(INI), P6_TA(2006)0109; European Parliament resolution on European contract law of 7 September 2006, 2006/2603(RSP), P6_TA(2006)0352; European Parliament Resolution on European Contract Law of 12 December 2007, P6_TA(2007)0615; European Parliament Resolution on the Common Frame of Reference for European Contract Law of 3 September 2008, P6_TA-PROV(2008)0397.

33 On the work of the Study Group, for example von Bar, in *Festschrift für Henrich* (Bielefeld: E. und W. Gieseking, 2000), p. 1; McGuire, *ZfRV* 2006, 163; Schmidt-Kessel, Entry 'Study Group on a European Civil Code', in *Handwörterbuch des Europäischen Privatrechts*, Volume II, pp. 1453 ff.

34 On this point Schulte-Nölke, *ZGS* 2002, 261; Grigoleit/Tomasic, Entry 'Acquis Principles', in *Handwörterbuch des Europäischen Privatrechts*, Volume I, 2009, pp. 12 ff.

35 See paras. 180–186 and 187–193 below.

# III. THE FAILURE OF THE GRAND SCHEME: THE DRAFT COMMON FRAME OF REFERENCE (DCFR)

References: J. Basedow, 'Kodifikationsrausch und kollidierende Konzepte', *ZEuP* 2008, 673; H. Eidenmüller/F. Faust/H.C. Grigoleit/N. Jansen/G. Wagner/R. Zimmermann, 'Der Gemeinsame Referenzrahmen für das Europäische Privatrecht - Wertungsfragen und Kodifikationsprobleme', *JZ* 2008, 529; W. Ernst, 'Der "Common Frame of Reference" aus juristischer Sicht', *AcP* 208 (2008), 248; N. Jansen/R. Zimmermann, '"A European Civil Code in all but name": discussing the nature and purposes of the draft common frame of reference', (2010) 69 *Cambridge Law Journal* 98; J. Mance, 'Is Europe Aiming to Civilise the Common Law?', (2007) *European Business Law Review* 18, 77; T. Pfeiffer, 'Von den Principles of European Contract Law zum Draft Common Frame of Reference', *ZEuP* 2008, 679; R. Schulze/C. von Bar/H. Schulte-Nölke (eds.), *Der akademische Entwurf für einen Gemeinsamen Referenzrahmen* (Tübingen: Mohr Siebeck, 2008); A. Stadler, 'Struktur, Stil und Regelungstechnik des DCFR', in *Festschrift für Schwenzer* (Bern: Stämpfli, 2011), p. 1605.

## 1. CONTENT

**120.** The Draft Common Frame of Reference (DCFR) sees itself as a model for a European codification of private law, which is why it was generally perceived as 'a European civil code in all but name'.[36] Whereas the PECL was a purely academic project that was primarily committed to the elaboration of common European legal principles, the DCFR has reached a new stage of legal harmonisation at the European level insofar as, for the first time, the deciding impetus for the harmonisation of contract law came from the EC institutions.

**121.** The Draft Common Frame of Reference contains rules far beyond contract law; it basically covers the entire private law (without family law and law of succession).[37] It consists of two main sources:[38] On the one hand, the PECL, in the version revised and substantially expanded by the Study Group,[39]

---

36 Jansen/Zimmermann, (2010) 69 *Cambridge Law Journal* 98.

37 On this, for example, Eidenmüller/Faust/Grigoleit/Jansen/Wagner/Zimmermann, *JZ* 2008, 529; Pfeiffer, *AcP* 208 (2008), 227; Ernst, *AcP* 208 (2008), 248; Gómez, *ERCL* 2008, 89; Schulze/Wilhelmsson, *ERCL* 2008, 154; Zimmermann, Entry 'Common Frame of Reference', in *Handwörterbuch des Europäischen Privatrechts*, Volume I, 2009, p. 276 ff. Previously, for example, Beale, *ERCL* 2007, 257.

38 Cf. also Eidenmüller/Faust/Grigoleit/Jansen/Wagner/Zimmermann, *JZ* 2008, 529, 532 f.

39 In parallel to the drafting of the DCFR, but within the CoPECL network, a group of French scholars has endeavoured to revise the PECL and to elaborate terminological commonalities in European contract law: Association Henri Capitant/Société de législation comparée (eds.), *Projet de Cadre commun de référence - Terminologie contractuelle commune*, as well as *Principes contractuels communs*, both published in 2008.

serve as the basis of the DCFR;[40] on the other hand, the *acquis communautaire* as it was presented based on the work of the Acquis Group was integrated.[41] In its final version, the so-called Full Edition, which was published in October 2009, the DCFR contains comments and comparative law notes on the individual provisions in the style of the PECL. According to the intention of its authors, it should form the basis for a possible 'political CFR'[42] but serve as an independent academic reference model ('academic CFR') independent of how the Community institutions implement it.[43]

## 2. POSSIBLE AREAS OF APPLICATION

**122.** Initially, it remained open in what form the DCFR would be implemented or used by the Community institutions. After the Commission had promoted the work on the DCFR under the 6th Research Framework Programme, there were, at first, many indications that the model law would be used quickly to create a European contract law instrument. However, in the years that followed, the Commission seemed to turn away from this project. Given that the long-term goal of a European Contract Law Code had not been formulated officially[44] since the first progress report of 23 September 2005,[45] and due to the fact that the Commission concentrated on a revision of the consumer acquis, it had to be considered unlikely even before the publication of the DCFR that there could be a comprehensive 'political CFR'.[46] The Commission seemed to see the

40 On similarities and differences Pfeiffer, *ZEuP* 2008, 679.

41 On this point Schulte-Nölke, in Schulze/von Bar/Schulte-Nölke, *Der akademische Entwurf für einen Gemeinsamen Referenzrahmen*, 2008, p. 47. It is noteworthy that both Study Group and Acquis Group have published their work in self-standing publications independently of the preparation of the Common Frame of Reference, cf. von Bar/Clive/Schulte-Nölke, *DCFR 2008 Interim Edition*, Introduction Nos. 55 ff. On the Acquis Principles critically Jansen/Zimmermann, *JZ* 2007, 1113.

42 Von Bar/Clive/Schulte-Nölke, *DCFR 2008 Interim Edition*, Introduction Nos. 6, 60 ff.; von Bar/Clive, *DCFR 2009 FE*, Introduction No. 6.

43 On this von Bar, in Schmidt-Kessel, *Der Gemeinsame Referenzrahmen*, 2009, p. 23; Schulze, in Schulze/von Bar/Schulte-Nölke, *Der akademische Entwurf für einen Gemeinsamen Referenzrahmen*, 2008, p. 1; Schulte-Nölke, in Schulze, *Common Frame of Reference and Existing EC Contract Law*, 2009, p. 47.

44 On the development Schmidt-Kessel, Entry 'European Civil Code', in *Handwörterbuch des Europäischen Privatrechts*, Volume I, 2009, pp. 553 f.

45 COM(2005) 456 final.

46 Green Paper on the Consumer Acquis from 8 February 2007, COM(2006) 744 final. On 8 October 2008, the Commission presented a proposal for a Directive on Consumer Rights, which combines four central consumer protection directives (Doorstep Selling Directive, Terms Directive, Distance Selling Directive and Consumer Sales Directive) and modifies them in the sense of full harmonisation, COM(2008) 614 final. See, inter alia, Smits, *ERPL* 2010, 5; Hondius, *ERPL* 2010, 103 as well as various conference proceedings, such as Jud/Wendehorst, *Neuordnung des Verbraucherprivatrechts in Europa?*;

(political) CFR exclusively as an internal tool for private law directives and not as an independent reference model.[47] Similarly, the European Council's position in the Stockholm Programme was that the CFR should be 'a non-binding set of fundamental principles, definitions and model rules to be used by the lawmakers at Union level to ensure greater coherence and quality in the lawmaking process'.[48]

**123.** It was proposed to use parts of the DCFR as a model for the revision and systematic connection ('horizontal approach') of a total of eight of the consumer protection directives already adopted,[49] which would have underlined its function as a 'toolbox'.[50] Admittedly, the image of a toolbox may not be entirely appropriate since the DCFR is conceived more as a reservoir of building blocks for legal instruments and thus has the function of a repository of standards.[51]

**124.** Independent of this, a finalised CFR such as the PECL could have served in practice as a reference point for the identification of common legal principles of EU law: If the existing EU private law does not contain a straightforward solution to a specific problem, the interpretation of the instrument in question might have been supported by comparing it with the corresponding regulation in the CFR. This approach can be found in various Advocate Generals' Opinions since 2008.[52] Thus, Advocate General Trstenjak, for example, referred to Article III.-3:708(1) DCFR with regard to the question of the accruing of interest

---

Gsell/Herresthal, *Vollharmonisierung im Privatrecht*; Stürner, *Vollharmonisierung im Europäischen Verbraucherrecht?*, 2010. On the fate of the proposal below paras. 127–129.

47 Thus Commissioner Kuneva in a plenary session of the European Parliament on 1 September 2008 in response to an oral question by MEP Lehne, cf. the corresponding communication in *NJW* 2008, issue 41, p. XXIV.

48 10 and 11 December 2009 (Doc. No 17024/09, p. 33).

49 Ernst, *AcP* 208 (2008), 248, 275.

50 Von Bar/Clive/Schulte-Nölke, *DCFR 2008 Interim Edition*, Introduction No. 76.

51 Ernst, *AcP* 208 (2008), 248, 277; in a similar sense Herresthal, in Langenbucher, *Europäisches Privat- und Wirtschaftsrecht*, §2 para. 4.

52 See, in addition to those mentioned in the footnotes below (without claiming to be exhaustive), for example, CJEU, Opinion of AG Trstenjak of 7 May 2009, Case C-227/08, *Martín*, ECLI:EU:C:2009:295, para. 51 (on the nullity and voidability of contracts); CJEU, Opinion of AG Trstenjak of 4 September 2008, Case C-445/06, *Danske Slagterier*, ECLI:EU:C:2008:464, para. 94 with note 57 (on the three-year limitation period); CJEU, Opinion of AG Trstenjak of 8 September 2009, Case C-215/08, *Friz*, ECLI:EU:C:2009:522, para. 69 with note 62 (reversal after consumer withdrawal); CJEU, Opinion of AG Trstenjak of 24 March 2010, Case C-540/08, *Mediaprint*, ECLI:EU:C:2010:161, para. 33 with note 7 (for taking into account the 'requirements' of the DCFR in the reform of fair trading and contract law in the EU); CJEU, Opinion of AG Cruz Villalón of 15 November 2012, Case C-103/11 P, *Systran*, ECLI:EU:C:2012:714, para. 72 with note 24 (on contract interpretation); CJEU, Opinion of AG Kokott of 24 October 2013, Case C-396/12, *van der Ham*, ECLI:EU:C:2013:698, para. 77 with note 39 (on attribution of fault to a third party); CJEU, Opinion of AG Saugmandsgaard Øe of 7 April 2016, Case C-149/15, *Wathelet*, ECLI:EU:C:2016:217, para. 29 with note 6, para. 32 with notes 9, 10 and para. 51 with note 22 (intermediary may be regarded as seller from

to the principal claim.[53] However, this was done to indicate that the DCFR was currently not part of the applicable EU law.[54] Another Opinion dealt with the requirements for the conclusion of a contract; here, Advocate General Trstenjak referred to the 'Draft Common Frame of Reference' and added, probably to increase its authority, that it 'may in the future be the starting point for a uniform system of European private law'.[55]

**125.** However, since the DCFR is designed as a soft law model only, the fear has been expressed that recourse to the CFR in the interpretation of EU law, for example, by the CJEU, could be hasty and result-oriented, without sufficient consideration of the existing legal requirements contained in formal EU law.[56] Overall, it seems like this has not proven to be the case; the references in the Opinion have remained isolated occurrences and do not regard the DCFR or PECL as a formal source of law. With these caveats in mind, the DCFR is a valuable source for the academic study of European contract law and can provide comparative law scholars with information on the state of the *ius commune europaeum*.[57]

**126.** Under no circumstances, however, may the EU legislator, for example, using a reference in the recitals of a directive, confer on the (D)CFR normative authority. This is due to the fact that it lacks democratic legitimacy.[58] Thus, if reference is made to the 'academic "Draft Common Frame of Reference"' in Recital 28 of the Late Payments Directive 2011/7/EU[59] this does not endow the corresponding provisions with normative validity. This is true all the more given that the recitals are not part of the enacting terms of the respective secondary legislation anyway, which is why their significance for interpreting individual provisions is thus quite limited.[60]

consumer's perspective). Further references can be found in Basedow, *AcP* 210 (2010), 157, 185 note 103.

53 Opinion of 11 June 2008, Case C-275/07, *Commission/Italy*, ECLI:EU:C:2008:334, para. 90.

54 See Trstenjak, in Schmidt-Kessel, *Der Gemeinsame Referenzrahmen*, 2009, p. 235.

55 CJEU, Opinion of AG Trstenjak of 11 September 2008, Case C-180/06, *Ilsinger*, ECLI:EU:C:2008:483, para. 49.

56 Ernst, *AcP* 208 (2008), 248, 260 f. speaks of a possible introduction of the DCFR 'by the back door'; critically also Zaccaria, *GPR* 2011, 277.

57 In that sense also Pfeiffer, *ZEuP* 2008, 679, 704 ff.

58 In this direction however Purnhagen, *EuR* 2011, 690, 698 referring to CJEU, 1 March 2011, Case C-236/09, *Test-Achats*, ECLI:EU:C:2011:100, para. 17, where the reference was to the Charter of Fundamental Rights, which was not yet in force at the time, found in the Recitals of the 4th Equality Directive 2004/113/EC. For more details, see paras. 788–790 below.

59 On this cf. paras. 762–767 below.

60 See paras. 330–333 below.

## 3. THE DCFR AS A REPOSITORY OF STANDARDS

**127.** Finally, the 'Green Paper on the Review of the Consumer Acquis' presented by the Commission in 2007[61] indicated that the priority would be shifted to a revision of the existing consumer law. This thesis was confirmed by the fact that the Commission apparently did not consider the DCFR,[62] which was already known at that time, at any point during the work on the draft Directive on Consumer Rights.[63]

**128.** However, the Consumer Rights Directive project and especially the approach of full harmonisation pursued therein has arguably proved to be too ambitious. Council and Parliament have shown little sympathy for the Commission's approach in their Opinions on the draft.[64] The Commission's Green Paper 'on policy options for progress towards a European Contract Law for consumers and businesses', published on 1 July 2010,[65] states in a somewhat resigned tone that '[in the] two years of intensive negotiations in the European Parliament and Council [it has been] highlighted that there are limits to an approach based on full harmonisation'.[66]

**129.** Thus, the Commission subsequently focused on alternatives. The then Commissioner for Justice, Fundamental Rights and Citizenship, Viviane Reding, announced further steps towards a European contract law for the first half of her term of office.[67] The Common Frame of Reference was to be completed and enter into force in the form of a legal act.[68] This project was expected to rank equally with the adoption of the planned Consumer Rights Directive. In the Communication 'EUROPE 2020: A strategy for smart, sustainable and inclusive growth', published in March 2010,[69] the Commission announced that, in parallel to harmonising consumer protection rules, it

---

61 'Green Paper on the Review of the Consumer Acquis' of 8 February 2007, COM(2006) 744 final.

62 Jud/Wendehorst, *GPR* 2009, 68; Schmidt-Kessel, in Jud/Wendehorst (eds.), *Neuordnung des Verbraucherprivatrechts in Europa?*, 2009, pp. 21, 38 f.

63 COM(2008) 614 final.

64 On this see Stürner, in Stürner (ed.), *Vollharmonisierung im Europäischen Verbraucherrecht?*, 2010, pp. 3, 9 ff.

65 COM(2010) 348 final.

66 COM(2010) 348 final, p. 5.

67 Speech of 15 March 2010 at the Consumer Days in Madrid, see Reding, SPEECH/10/91; likewise already the Commissioner's position at a hearing before the European Parliament on 7 January 2010, CM\800797EN.doc, PE431.139v02-00.

68 Reding, CM\800797EN.doc, PE431.139v02-00, p. 7: 'I want to make substantial progress in the work towards a European contract law [...]. I therefore intend to complete – with the help of academic expertise from across Europe – the work on the common frame of reference in the course of 2010, and to include it thereafter into a well-publicised legal instrument.'

69 COM(2010) 2020 final.

would also engage in 'by making progress towards an optional European Contract Law'.[70] That there might be such an optional instrument at the end of this process was indicated by the establishment of an expert group by a Commission Decision of 26 April 2010,[71] whose task was to assist the Commission in the elaboration of a common frame of reference in the area of European contract law, and this explicitly related to both consumer and commercial contract law.[72] The expert group was to have completed its work within a year.[73] It could be expected that the role of the DCFR as a legislative toolbox would be taken literally, i.e. that substantial parts of it would be transferred into the optional instrument.

## IV. TAKING THE BULL BY THE HORNS: THE PROPOSAL FOR A COMMON EUROPEAN SALES LAW (CESL)

References: Y. Adar/P. Sirena, 'Principles and Rules in the Emerging European Contract Law: From the PECL to the CESL, and Beyond', *ERCL* 2013, 1; Y. Adar/P. Sirena, 'Principles versus Rules in the Emerging European Contract Law', in J. Rutgers/P. Sirena (eds.), *Rules and Principles in European Contract Law* (Cambridge: Intersentia, 2015), p. 7; G. Alpa/G. Conte/U. Perfetti/F. Graf von Westphalen (eds), *The Proposed Common European Sales Law – the Lawyers' View* (Munich: Sellier, 2013); S. Balthasar, 'Das Gemeinsame Europäische needs it?', Kaufrecht – eine Analyse aus unternehmerischer Sicht', *RIW* 2012, 361; J. Basedow, 'Fakultatives Unionsprivatrecht oder: Grundlagen des 28. Modells', in *Festschrift für Säcker* (Munich: C.H. Beck, 2011), p. 29; M. Blüm, *Das Gemeinsame Europäische Kaufrecht als wesentlicher Zwischenschritt zu einem kodifizierten Europäischen Vertragsrecht?* (Jena: JWV, 2015); C. Busch, 'From European Sales Law to Online Contract Law: The CESL in the European Parliament', *euvr* 2013, 33; C. Busch/R. Domröse, 'From a Horizontal Instrument to a Common European Sales Law', *euvr* 2012, 48; D. Caruso, 'The Baby and the Bath Water: The American Critique of European Contract Law', (2013) 61 *American Journal of Comparative Law* 479; I. Claeys/

[70] COM(2010) 2020 final, p. 21: 'The Commission will propose action to tackle bottlenecks in the single market by: [...] Making it easier and less costly for businesses and consumers to conclude contracts with partners in other EU countries, notably by offering harmonised solutions for consumer contracts, EU model contract clauses and by making progress towards an optional European Contract Law.' The Action Plan prepared by the Commission to implement the Council's Stockholm Programme, 'An area of freedom, security and justice for Europe's citizens – Action Plan Implementing the Stockholm Programme', COM(2010) 171 final, formulates this less clearly but is comparable in content.

[71] Commission Decision of 26 April 2010 establishing an expert group on a common frame of reference in the area of European contract law (2010/233/EU) and press release of 21 May 2010, IP/10/595.

[72] Article 2 Decision 2010/233/EU.

[73] The term of office of the expert group was two years (Article 4(5) Decision 2010/233/EU). Nevertheless, a draft was apparently already expected for May 2011, cf. the press release of 21 May 2010, IP/10/595.

R. Feltkamp, *The Draft Common European Sales Law: Towards an Alternative Sales Law? A Belgian Perspective* (Cambridge: Intersentia, 2013); G. Dannemann/S. Vogenauer (eds.), *The Common European Sales Law in Context. Interactions with English and German Law* (Oxford; Oxford University Press, 2013); W. Doralt, 'Strukturelle Schwächen in der Europäisierung des Privatrechts', *RabelsZ* 75 (2011), 260; H. Eidenmüller, 'What can be wrong with an option? An optional Common European Sales Law as a regulatory tool', (2013) 50 *Common Market Law Review*, 69; H. Eidenmüller/N. Jansen/E.-M. Kieninger/G. Wagner/R. Zimmermann, 'Der Vorschlag für eine Verordnung über ein Gemeinsames Europäisches Kaufrecht. Defizite der neuesten Textstufe des europäischen Vertragsrechts', *JZ* 2012, 269; H. Fleischer, 'Optionales europäisches Privatrecht (28. Modell)', *RabelsZ* 76 (2012), 235; M. Gebauer (ed.), *Gemeinsames Europäisches Kaufrecht - Anwendungsbereich und kollisionsrechtliche Einbettung* (Munich: Sellier, 2013); S. Grundmann, 'Kosten und Nutzen eines optionalen Europäischen Kaufrechts', *AcP* 212 (2012), 502; J.-U. Hahn (ed.), *Gemeinsames Europäisches Kaufrecht - Moderner Ansatz oder praxisferne Vision?* (Munich; C.H. Beck, 2012); P. Hellwege, 'UN-Kaufrecht oder Gemeinsames Europäisches Kaufrecht?', *IHR* 2012, 221; C. Herresthal, 'Ein europäisches Vertragsrecht als Optionales Instrument', *EuZW* 2011, 7; C. Herresthal, 'Das geplante europäische Vertragsrecht: Die optionale Ausgestaltung des sog. Optionalen Instruments', *ZIP* 2011, 1347; C. Herresthal, 'Der Entwurf für ein Gemeinsames Europäisches Kaufrecht - Chancen, Risiken, Strukturdefizite', *WiVerw* 2012, 140; N. Konecny, *Der Verordnungsentwurf über ein Gemeinsames Europäisches Kaufrecht - Meilenstein der europäischen Integration oder Irrlicht der europäischen Politik?* (Frankfurt am Main: Peter Lang, 2014); J.-J. Kuipers, 'The Legal Basis for a European Optional Instrument', *European Review of Private Law (ERPL)* 2011, 545; M. Lehmann (ed.), *Common European Sales Law Meets Reality* (Munich: Sellier, 2014); E. Łętowska, 'Is the Optional Instrument (the Common European Sales Law) consistent with the principle of subsidiarity (Article 5 TEU)?', *euvr* 2013, 28; M.B.M. Loos/I. Samoy (eds.), *The Position of Small and Medium-Sized Enterprises in European Contract Law* (Cambridge: Intersentia, 2014); P. Mankowski, 'Der Vorschlag für ein Gemeinsames Europäisches Kaufrecht (CESL)', *IHR* 2012, 1; P. Mankowski, 'CESL - who *IHR* 2012, 45; H.-P. Mansel, 'Der Verordnungsvorschlag für ein Gemeinsames Europäisches Kaufrecht', WM 2012, 1253 and 1309; Max Planck Institute, Policy Options for Progress Towards a European Contract Law. Comments on the issues raised in the Green Paper from the Commission of 1 July 2010, COM(2010) 348 final, *RabelsZ* 75 (2011), 371; L. Moccia (ed.), *The Making of European Private Law: Why, How, What, Who* (Munich: Sellier, 2013); T. Pfeiffer, 'How innovative is the CESL - The CESL and the new German law of obligations', *Contratto e impresa/Europa* 2013, 548; J. Pisuliński, 'Die Entwicklung des europäischen Zivilrechts - Gedanken namentlich zum Entwurf eines Gemeinsamen Europäischen Kaufrechts', *GPR* 2013, 254; E.A. Posner, 'The Questionable Basis of the Common European Sales Law: The Role of an Optional Instrument in Jurisdictional Competition', (2013) 50 *Common Market Law Review* 261; V. Reding, 'Warum Europa ein optionales Europäisches Vertragsrecht benötigt', *ZEuP* 2011, 1; O. Remien/S. Herrler/P. Limmer (eds.), *Gemeinsames Europäisches Kaufrecht für die EU? Analyse des Vorschlags der Europäischen Kommission für ein optionales Europäisches Vertragsrecht vom 11. Oktober 2011* (Munich: C.H. Beck, 2012); N. Reich, 'Variationen des Verbraucherkaufrechts in der EU', *EuZW* 2011, 736; K. Riesenhuber, 'Der Vorschlag für eine Verordnung über ein "Gemeinsames Europäisches Kaufrecht" - Kompetenz, Subsidiarität, Verhältnismäßigkeit', *EWS* 2012, 7; G. Rühl, 'The Common European Sales Law: 28th Regime, 2nd Regime or 1st Regime?', (2012) *Maastricht Journal of European and Comparative Law* 19, 148; M. Schmidt-Kessel (ed.), *Ein einheitliches europäisches Kaufrecht? Eine Analyse des Vorschlags der Kommission* (Munich: Sellier, 2012); M. Schmidt-Kessel (ed), *Der Entwurf für ein Gemeinsames Europäisches Kaufrecht* (Munich: Sellier, 2014); H. Schulte-Nölke/F. Zoll/N. Jansen/R. Schulze (eds.), *Der Entwurf für ein optionales europäisches Kaufrecht* (Munich: Seller, 2012); R. Schulze (ed.), *Common European Sales Law - Commentary* (Munich: C.H. Beck, 2012); A. Stadler, 'Anwendungsvoraussetzungen und Anwendungsbereich des Common European Sales Law', *AcP* 212 (2012), 473; D. Staudenmayer, 'Der Kommissionsvorschlag für eine Verordnung zum Gemeinsamen Europäischen Kaufrecht', *NJW* 2011, 3491; C. Wendehorst/B. Zöchling-Jud (eds.), *Am Vorabend eines Gemeinsamen Europäischen Kaufrechts. Zum Verordnungsentwurf der Europäischen Kommission vom 11.10.2011* (Vienna, Manz 2012); Whittaker, '"General Principles" and "Underlying Principles" in the Proposed Common European Sales Law and their Role in its Interpretation', in J. Rutgers/P. Sirena (eds.), *Rules and Principles in European Contract Law* (Cambridge: Intersentia, 2015), p. 69; A.J. Wulf, *Institutional Competition between Optional Codes in European Contract Law: A Theoretical and Empirical Analysis* (Wiesbaden: Springer, 2014); R. Zimmermann, 'Perspektiven des künftigen österreichischen und europäischen Zivilrechts. Zum Verordnungsvorschlag über ein Gemeinsames Europäisches Kaufrecht', *Juristische Blätter* 2012, 2.

## 1. SUBJECT-MATTER OF REGULATION AND BASIS OF COMPETENCE

**130.** On 11 October 2011, the EU Commission presented a proposal for a Regulation on a Common European Sales Law.[74] The draft regulation itself (CESL Regulation) consists of only a few articles; it regulates, in particular, the scope and conditions of application of the Common European Sales Law.[75] The actual substantive regulations are contained in Annex I to the CESL Regulation, which is also referred to as Common European Sales Law (CESL). In addition to sales contracts, the proposal also covers the provision of digital content and related services. It contains rules for contracts between businesses (B2B) and for contracts between businesses and consumers (B2C). The Common European Sales Law is designed as an optional instrument. It is, therefore, only applicable if the parties expressly choose it. Thus, in principle, it does not affect the validity of other European legal acts or the respective autonomous national sales law.

---

[74] COM(2011) 635 final. See on the following already Stürner, in C. Reithmann/D. Martiny, *Internationales Vertragsrecht*, 8th ed. (Cologne: Otto Schmidt, 2015), paras. 6.187 ff.

[75] See also paras. 136–140 below.

### a) *Promotion of the Internal Market*

**131.** The starting point for the Commission's proposal for a regulation was the finding that the still-existing differences between the contract law systems of the Member States are considered trade barriers and are thus likely to hinder the smooth functioning of the internal market.[76] In particular, it was argued that small and medium-sized enterprises (SME) would be prevented from doing cross-border business because of the incurring transaction costs. The CESL aims to mitigate this since a cross-border sales contract subject to the CESL creates the same conditions and standards for both parties. The transaction costs that might otherwise be necessary to determine applicable foreign law would be eliminated. Overall, this could lead to cheaper products in the internal market. The Commission expected growth potential in the range of double-digit billions through the provision of a uniform contract law regime.[77] Similarly, it was argued that the CESL would be suitable to encourage consumers to conclude cross-border sales contracts, given that, due to the uncertainty about the applicable law and its level of protection in other Member States, they currently only buy in their home market.[78]

### b) *Genesis of the Proposal*

**132.** It should be emphasised once again that the various textual stages of the European Sales Law have appeared with increasing rapidity.[79] The first stage, the PECL drafted by the Lando Commission, were created between 1980 and 2002. Their subject matter is contract law, including general principles on legal transactions. The DCFR is based on them. The CoPECL network was then commissioned by the EU Commission to draft the DCFR in 2004. The text version was published in 2008, and an additional annotated version in six volumes in 2009.[80] In April 2010, the EU Commission set up a working group with the task 'to assist the Commission in the preparation of a proposal for a Common Frame of Reference in the area of European contract law, including consumer and business contract law [...]'.[81] On 3 May 2011, the expert group

---

76 COM(2011) 635 final, pp. 2 ff.; see also Reding, *ZEuP* 2011, 1, 2 f.

77 COM(2011) 635 final, p. 4.

78 COM(2011) 635 final, p. 4.

79 In-depth on the genesis Schulte-Nölke, in Schulte-Nölke/Zoll/Jansen/Schulze, *Der Entwurf für ein optionales europäisches Kaufrecht*, 2012, p. 1. See also Mansel, *WM* 2012, 1253, 1254 f.; Eidenmüller/Jansen/Kieninger/Wagner/Zimmermann, *JZ* 2012, 269, 270 f.

80 Von Bar/Clive (eds.), *Principles, Definitions and Model Rules of European Private Law. Draft Common Frame of Reference (DCFR)*, Full Edition, 2009.

81 Article 2 of the Commission Decision of 26 April 2010 setting up the Expert Group on a Common Frame of Reference in the area of European contract law (2010/233/EU); see also the press release of 21 May 2010 (IP/10/595).

presented a so-called 'Feasibility Study', which was published again in revised form on 19 August 2011 and took into account more than 100 comments received from the interested public.[82] The Commission's proposal of October 2011 adopted the Feasibility Study in almost all essential points.

### c) *Legislative Power*

**133.** The question of the EU's legislative powers to adopt such an optional instrument remains controversial.[83] The principle of limited conferral of power applies (Article 5(2) TEU) so that the EU can only adopt legal acts if and to the extent that primary law contains explicit authorisation to do so. The Commission based its proposal on Article 114 TFEU, the general legislative power relating to the establishment of the internal market. This provision concerns measures for the approximation of the laws and regulations of the Member States that aim to contribute to the establishment and functioning of the internal market.[84]

**134.** Concerning the CESL, it already seems doubtful whether such a set of rules – at least in the form of the Commission's proposal – can realise the removal of trade barriers. This presupposes that a reduction in transaction costs could be achieved at all.[85] When assessing this, one has to grant the Commission a certain leeway regarding their prognosis (despite all the criticism on details).[86] More serious is the fact that the Common Sales Law is optional, i.e. it does not directly lead to any approximation of the rights of the Member States but only adds a second layer of uniform law. From a formal point of view, Article 114 TFEU would thus not be fulfilled from the outset.[87] However, it could be argued that, from a teleological point of view, Article 114 TFEU must cover an optional

---

[82] See in detail Lehmann, *GPR* 2011, 218 and (in comparative perspective) Reich, *EuZW* 2011, 736.

[83] For more details on the competence of the EU to harmonise private law cf. Streinz, in Stürner, *Vollharmonisierung im Europäischen Verbraucherrecht?*, 2010, p. 23; on the competence regarding the CESL also Blüm, *Das Gemeinsame Europäische Kaufrecht als wesentlicher Zwischenschritt zu einem kodifizierten Europäischen Vertragsrecht?*, 2015, Chapter 2.

[84] For more details see below at paras. 220 ff.

[85] This point will be taken up later, cf. para. 221.

[86] However, considering this to be exceeded Grigoleit, in Remien/Herrler/Limmer, *Gemeinsames Europäisches Kaufrecht für die EU?*, 2012, pp. 67, 80.

[87] Against this, therefore e.g. Basedow, in *Festschrift für Säcker*, 2011, pp. 29, 38 ff., Kuipers, *ERPL* 2011, 545; Mansel, *WM* 2012, 1309, 1315 f.; Stadler, *AcP* 212 (2012), 473, 483 f.; Müller-Graff, in Schulte-Nölke/Zoll/Jansen/Schulze, *Der Entwurf für ein optionales europäisches Kaufrecht*, 2012, pp. 21, 35; Grigoleit, in Remien/Herrler/Limmer, *Gemeinsames Europäisches Kaufrecht für die EU?*, 2012, pp. 67, 75 ff.; Eidenmüller/Jansen/Kieninger/Wagner/Zimmermann, *JZ* 2012, 269, 274; Herresthal, *EuZW* 2011, 7, 9; MPI, *RabelsZ* 75 (2011), 371, 393 f.; Riesenhuber, *EWS* 2012, 7; W.-H. Roth, *EWS* 2012, 12. Positive in contrast Staudenmayer, *NJW* 2011, 3491, 3495 f.; Graf von Westphalen, *ZIP* 2011, 1985; Moser, in Remien/Herrler/Limmer, *Gemeinsames Europäisches Kaufrecht für die EU?*, 2012, pp. 7, 10 f.; Wojcik, in Gebauer, *Gemeinsames Europäisches Kaufrecht – Anwendungsbereich und*

legal act since the latter cannot affect the Member States' legal systems, meaning it interferes far less with their existence than a directive or regulation. Contrary to this assumption, the CJEU has clarified within the context of the Regulation on the European Cooperative Company (ECC), which introduced an optional corporate body, that such an additional legal person does not bring about any approximation of laws and is thus not covered by Article 114 TFEU.[88] If this view were transferred to the Commission's proposal, the CESL would lack legislative powers under Article 114 TFEU.[89]

**135.** Since the legislative powers for judicial cooperation under Article 81 TFEU can already be ruled out because the CESL can neither be regarded as a procedural legal act nor a body of conflict-of-laws rules, the 'rounding-off clause' of Article 352 TFEU might be a last resort. According to this provision, the EU has legislative powers if 'action by the Union should prove necessary, within the framework of the policies defined in the Treaties, to attain one of the objectives set out in the Treaties, and the Treaties have not provided the necessary powers'. Since this provision has outstanding potential to weaken the principle of limited conferral of powers, it requires a unanimous decision in the Council, thus raising considerable obstacles. It was probably for this reason that the Commission persistently excluded this particular legislative power. Formally, the provision also contains a third paragraph, which explicitly stipulates that no regular legislative power – in this case, this would be Article 114 TFEU – may be circumvented. If one would argue that this provision would not be fulfilled already, Article 352 TFEU only requires that the measure is necessary to achieve one of the objectives of the Treaties. If the general objective of achieving the internal market (Article 26 TFEU) is interpreted broadly, the CESL would probably fall under the rounding-off clause, but at the price of the necessity of a unanimous Council decision.[90]

### d) *Reactions from Academia and Legal Practice, and Further Developments*

**136.** The proposal's publication triggered a sometimes heated debate. In academic circles, a rather critical and dismissive tone prevailed in the development

---

*kollisionsrechtliche Einbettung*, 2013, p. 51, 61 ff.; Micklitz/Reich, in Moccia, *The Making of European Private Law*, 2013, pp. 21, 23 ff.

88 CJEU, 2 May 2006, Case C-436/03, *Parliament/Council*, ECLI:EU:C:2006:277, paras. 40 ff.

89 Following a recommendation of the Legal Affairs Committee (BT-Drucks. 17/8000), the German Bundestag lodged a subsidiarity complaint against the draft regulation on 1 December 2011. However, the quorum of one third of the parliaments of all Member States required under Article 7(2) of Protocol no. 2 on the application of the principles of subsidiarity and proportionality was not reached.

90 On closer examination, however, problems also arise here, which will be examined in more detail elsewhere (see below para. 1315).

phase already,[91] although positive voices could be heard occasionally,[92] but mostly only on the ground of the premise that the optional instrument mostly consisted of dispositive legal provisions.[93] The proposal of the CESL itself was widely considered unacceptable.[94] The criticism did not only refer to the proposal itself but also to how it was developed since political ambitions appear to have been placed above the content's maturity.[95] Businesses feared disadvantages due to legal uncertainty, which is, however, always to be expected with the dawn of an entirely new regulatory instrument.[96] Consumer associations warned against the CESL because although its overall level of consumer protection was higher than the existing *acquis communautaire*, it may fall short compared to the higher level of protection existing in some Member States, so that consumers – unlike previously, cf. Article 6(2) Rome I Regulation – could not be sure that the choice of a law other than the law of the consumer's domicile might not lead to any disadvantages.[97] However, members of the legal profession, in particular, welcomed the initiative in principle.[98] The European Law Institute also issued a detailed Opinion on the Commission's proposal.[99]

**137.** The Polish Council Presidency, which fell into the second half of 2011, strongly supported the idea of a Common European Sales Law. The Commission's proposal was discussed in the Justice and Home Affairs Council in December 2011, about two months after publication.[100] It already became clear that several points still needed thorough discussion. The question of the EU's legislative power, which was considered particularly problematic,[101] was put on the back burner; first, clarity had to be gained on essential points regarding the content and economic effects of a Common Sales Law.[102] During another meeting of the Justice and Home Affairs Council in June 2012, the proposal was discussed again. In summary, the conclusions were not very optimistic: It was determined that both the need for such an instrument and fundamental legal issues had not yet been sufficiently clarified.

---

91 See for example Doralt, *AcP* 211 (2011), 1, 32 f.

92 Leible, *BB* 2008, 1469; Lehmann, *European Journal of Commercial Contract Law* 1 (2009), 173.

93 Thus inter alia. Herresthal, *EuZW* 2011, 7; MPI, *RabelsZ* 75 (2011), 371.

94 Cf. e.g. Eidenmüller/Jansen/Kieninger/Wagner/Zimmermann, *JZ* 2012, 269.

95 See Riesenhuber, *JZ* 2011, 537; Doralt, *RabelsZ* 75 (2011), 260; Mansel, *WM* 2012, 1253, 1255.

96 See Balthasar, *RIW* 2012, 361, 364.

97 See, for example, German Consumer Association (*Verbraucherzentrale Bundesverband*), press release of 13 January 2012. On the relationship to (consumer) conflict of laws, see below para. 1154.

98 For example, the German Bar Association in its statement 3/2011 of January 2011.

99 The document of 7 September 2012 together with an amendment of 28 February 2014 is available at https://www.europeanlawinstitute.eu/projects-publications/publications.

100 See the report: Council document 18353/11 of 8 December 2011.

101 See supra para. 133.

102 Council document 18353/11, para. 10.

**138.** The European Parliament also recommended improving several points[103] – while maintaining a thoroughly optimistic attitude.[104] The parliament's Committee on Economic and Monetary Affairs (ECON) dealt with the CESL first and approved the proposal as such in general. It was suggested, for example, that regulations on the transfer of title should be included.[105] However, the Legal Affairs Committee (JURI) and the Internal Market and Consumer Protection Committee (IMCO) were ultimately responsible for the Commission proposal.[106] Both committees expressed different ideas on how to proceed: In the IMCO, a narrow majority favoured the transformation of the CESL to a minimum harmonising directive, excluding those subjects already contained in the CRD.[107] However, a clear majority in the lead committee on legal affairs was in favour of reducing the material scope of application of the CESL to distance contracts, particularly online contracts, and retaining the optional character of the CESL. In terms of its content, numerous amendments were proposed.[108] On 26 February 2014, the plenary of the European Parliament approved the version adopted by the Legal Affairs Committee in the first reading.[109] The new elections of the European Parliament in May 2014 signified a certain disruption, so it was unclear when the second reading would take place. Given the general scepticism towards the CESL, which was clearly visible in some fractions of the Council, it was expected that the topic would not be on the agenda again until the second half of 2015.[110]

**139.** However, even this did not materialise. In the face of the political headwinds for the CESL, the Juncker Commission made a turnaround even before 2015. In its 'Work Programme 2015 – A New Start',[111] the Commission announced that it no longer wanted to maintain the proposal in its current form. Thus, Annex II at no. 60 which concerning the CESL states: 'Modified proposal in order to fully unleash the potential of e-commerce in the Digital

---

103 For more details, see Mayer/Lindemann, *ZEuP* 2014, 1.

104 European Parliament resolution of 8 June 2011 on options for the introduction of a European Contract Law for consumers and businesses, P7_TA(2011)0262.

105 Report of the Economic and Monetary Affairs Committee of 4 June 2012, rapporteur: Marianne Thyssen, PE491.011v01-00; PA\903823DE.doc.

106 On the exact division of responsibilities between the two committees Mayer/Lindemann, *ZEuP* 2014, 1, 2 f.

107 Report of 11 July 2013 (A7-0301/2013, at p. 134), Rapporteurs Evelyne Gebhardt and Hans-Peter Mayer.

108 See the Report on the proposal for a regulation of the European Parliament and of the Council on a Common European Sales Law of 24 September 2013, A7-0301/2013 (Rapporteurs: Klaus-Heiner Lehne and Luigi Berlinguer). The report also takes into account proposed amendments submitted by the European Law Institute in the above-mentioned opinion.

109 European Parliament, Legislative Resolution of 26 February 2014 on the proposal for a regulation of the European Parliament and of the Council on a Common European Sales Law, Oral P7_TA-PROV(2014)0159.

110 Mayer/Lindemann, *ZEuP* 2014, 1, 6.

111 COM(2014) 910 final.

Single Market.' The 'Digital Single Market Strategy for Europe', presented by the Commission on 6 May 2015,[112] now advocated for a further extension of the fully harmonising rules on online transactions; in particular, it wanted to allow sellers to fall back on their domestic law. Also in 2015, the Commission announced 'legislative proposals for simple and effective cross-border contract rules for consumers and businesses'.[113] On 9 December 2015, the Commission then presented two proposals for fully harmonising directives: one on the provision of digital content[114] and the other on online commerce.[115]

**140.** At present, it seems highly unlikely that the CESL proposal will gain political support again. However, this cannot be ruled out entirely. Due to its importance for the development of contract law in Europe, especially with regard to the directives that follow in time and are related in content, the CESL proposal will be presented in the following section.

## 2. REGULATION TECHNIQUE AND CHARACTERISTICS OF THE CESL

### a) *Structure*

**141.** The Commission proposal consists of several parts. The actual regulation, the CESL Regulation (also called chapeau rules), consists of only 16 articles. It contains definitions and prescribes the Regulation's material and personal scope of application and the requirements for an opt-in.

**142.** The actual CESL, which is attached to the CESL Regulation as Annex I, consists of eight parts.[116] Unlike the DCFR, the CESL does not contain a complete General Part; in this respect, the structure is more similar to the UN Sales Convention. The main reason given for this is increased user-friendliness.[117] From a linguistic point of view, the drafters of the CESL tried to use less technical language,[118] which led to some redundancies.[119] The structure of the

---

112 COM(2015) 192 final.

113 COM(2015) 192 final, p. 20.

114 COM(2015) 634, final.

115 COM(2015) 635, final; on both see in more detail below paras. 148–152.

116 The report of the Committee on Legal Affairs (Report on the proposal for a regulation of the European Parliament and of the Council on a Common European Sales Law of 24 September 2013, A7-0301/2013) proposes a merger of both parts in view of the criticism expressed against the division into two parts (p. 128).

117 Staudenmayer, *NJW* 2011, 3491, 3496; see also Lehmann, *GPR* 2011, 218, 219 f.

118 See Lehmann, *GPR* 2011, 218, 220.

119 Eidenmüller/Jansen/Kieninger/Wagner/Zimmermann, *JZ* 2012, 269, 272; Herresthal, in Schulte-Nölke/Zoll/Jansen/Schulze, *Der Entwurf für ein optionales europäisches Kaufrecht*,

CESL largely follows the 'life cycle of the sales contract' (cf. Recital 6 of the CESL Regulation).

**143.** The introductory part contains some general principles such as freedom of contract (Article 1 CESL), freedom of form (Article 6 CESL), the principle of good faith (Article 2 CESL), the duty to cooperate (Article 3 CESL) and, in addition, definitions (Article 5, 7-9 CESL) as well as rules relating to interpretation and application (Article 4, 10, 11 CESL). In some cases, existing legal principles are used. For example, it is generally recognised that the EU legislator has so far subscribed to the principle of the freedom to contract.[120]

**144.** Finally, Annex II to the CESL Regulation contains the standard information sheet on the CESL, which the trader must provide to the consumer before the opt-in to the CESL can take place.

### *b) Optionality*

**145.** A characteristic feature of the CESL is its optional character (Article 3 CESL Regulation).[121] This distinguishes the proposal from other uniform sets of rules, such as the UN Sales Convention, which is based on an opt-out approach (Article 6 CISG). In essence, the provisions of the CESL are, therefore, substantive uniform law. However, this term is avoided in the Commission proposal in favour of *Common* Sales Law. This reflects the fact that it is not intended to be a legal system that displaces the respective conflict-of-laws rules, but one that only becomes valid when the applicable conflict-of-laws rules refer to the law of a Member State. According to the conception of the Commission's proposal, the CESL is a 'second regime' alongside the national contract law systems.[122] This means that the respective national sales law continues to exist and that the regulations of the CESL only displace them as soon as the CESL has been chosen. Doctrinally, this construction presupposes that an EU regulation can be national law simultaneously.[123] Keeping the different legislative origins in mind, this only appears to be accurate due to the Regulation's direct applicability brought about by Article 288(2) TFEU.[124]

---

2012, pp. 85, 137 ff.

120 See, for example, Recitals 8 and 9 of the CSD; further references paras. 409–418 below.

121 On the economic implications of this optionality, in particular Grundmann, *AcP* 212 (2012), 502; Eidenmüller, (2013) 50 *Common Market Law Review* 69; E.A. Posner, (2013) 50 *Common Market Law Review* 261.

122 On the implications of conflict of laws, see para. 1154 below.

123 Thus explicitly Amendment 2 to Recital 9 of the European Parliament Legislative Resolution of 26 February 2014, P7_TA-PROV(2014)0159: 'This directly applicable second regime should be an integral part of the legal order applicable in the territory of the Member States.'

124 Cf. Mansel, *WM* 2012, 1253, 1262.

#### c) *The Consumer-Protective Character of the CESL*

**146.** The CESL is primarily designed as an instrument for legal transactions between traders and consumers and is therefore intended to provide a high level of consumer protection. This is stated explicitly in Article 1(3) of the CESL Regulation.[125] If the CESL is chosen, it supersedes the respective consumer protection provisions of the respective Member State's national law from whose legal system the opt-in was made.[126] To avoid undermining the current level of consumer protection in the EU, which would already be problematic due to Article 169 TFEU,[127] the respective level in the CESL must be equally high. This is all the more true since the recently adopted Consumer Rights Directive has a fully harmonising effect, as the need for yet another instrument of harmonisation is hard to advocate. In summary, it can be stated that in the CESL, the level of protection of the previous consumer acquis is at least maintained but often exceeded.[128]

**147.** However, because the directives issued so far in European consumer law have predominantly followed the principle of minimum harmonisation, meaning that the Member States could provide for a higher level of protection in favour of consumers when transposing the directive, there are several protection requirements in the law of the individual Member States that deviate, in part significantly, from the minimum level of the directive acquis. The choice of the CESL could therefore result in a lower level of consumer protection, depending on the consumer's country of residence.[129] However, the Commission's proposal did not take the highest level of protection in all Member States as a benchmark and merely oriented itself towards the existing *acquis communautaire*.

## V. FURTHER DEVELOPMENTS: CONTRACT LAW IN THE DIGITAL SINGLE MARKET

References: M. Artz/B. Gsell (eds.), *Verbrauchervertragsrecht und digitaler Binnenmarkt – Die Richtlinienvorschläge zum Fernabsatz von Waren und zur Bereitstellung digitaler Inhalte* (Tübingen: Mohr Siebeck, 2018); A. De Franceschi, 'The EU Digital Single Market Strategy in the Light of the Consumer Rights Directive: The "Button Solution" for Internet Cost Traps and the Need for a More Systematic Approach', *EuCML* 2015, 144; J. Kindl/ T. Arroyo Vendrell/B. Gsell (eds.), *Verträge über digitale Inhalte und digitale Dienstleistungen*

[125] As a purely programmatic phrase, this sentence would be superfluous, see also Recital 11 of the CESL Regulation.

[126] For possible exceptions (e.g. overriding mandatory norms or public policy exception).

[127] However, Article 169 TFEU does not contain an absolute bar to any lowering the level of consumer protection once achieved by the acquis, see para. 230 below.

[128] This is explicitly stated at the end of Recital 11 of the CESL Regulation.

[129] See the criticism to this effect from the consumer's point of view (supra paras. 136–140).

(Baden-Baden: Nomos, 2018); F. Maultzsch, 'Der Entwurf für eine EU-Richtlinie über den Online-Warenhandel und andere Formen des Fernabsatzes von Waren', *JZ* 2016, 236; M. Schmidt-Kessel/K. Erler/A. Grimm/M. Kramme, 'Die Richtlinienvorschläge der Kommission zu Digitalen Inhalten und Online-Handel', *GPR* 2016, 2 and 54; R. Schulze, 'The New Shape of European Contract Law', *EuCML* 2015, 139; G. Spindler, 'Verträge über digitale Inhalte – Anwendungsbereich und Ansätze', *MMR* 2016, 147; M. Wendland, 'GEK 2.0? Ein europäischer Rechtsrahmen für den Digitalen Binnenmarkt', *GPR* 2016, 8.

## 1. FOCUSSING ON THE DIGITAL SINGLE MARKET

**148.** In the 'Digital Single Market Strategy for Europe', which the Commission presented on 6 May 2015,[130] an extension of fully harmonising regulations on online transactions was announced. On 9 December 2015, the Commission finally presented two proposals for fully harmonising directives: firstly, concerning the provision of digital content (hereinafter: draft Digital Content Directive),[131] and secondly, with regard to the online trade of goods (hereinafter: draft Distance Selling Directive).[132] Both initiatives have generated an intense response in the academic literature.[133]

## 2. THE STEP BACK TOWARDS FULL HARMONISATION

**149.** The two proposals for directives methodically implement a fully harmonising approach (Article 3 draft Distance Selling Directive; Article 4 draft Digital Content Directive). This approach differs fundamentally from the optional approach pursued in the CESL: The private law systems of the Member States must integrate the requirements fully – no 'second sales law' is created; instead, the law of the Member States must adapt.

## 3. THE POLITICAL DECISION-MAKING PROCESS

**150.** Initially, the proposal for a Digital Content Directive was a priority in the political decision-making process. In the first half of 2016, the Dutch Council Presidency pushed the dossier forward quickly. Then, the Brexit vote

130 COM(2015) 192 final.

131 Proposal for a Directive of the European Parliament and of the Council on certain aspects concerning contracts for the supply of digital content, COM(2015) 634 final.

132 Proposal for a Directive of the European Parliament and of the Council on certain aspects concerning contracts for the online and other distance sales of goods, COM(2015) 635 final.

133 See e.g. Schmidt-Kessel/Erler/Grimm/Kramme, *GPR* 2016, 2 and 54; Wendland, *EuZW* 2016, 126; Maultzsch, *JZ* 2016, 236.

of 23 June 2016 seemed to have reoriented the focus to other issues.[134] At least a Council working group subsequently dealt with the proposal intensively.[135] However, it took several years until the proposal was coordinated in Parliament and Council in such a way that nothing stood in the way of its adoption. The Parliament then approved the proposal at first reading on 26 March 2019;[136] the Council adopted it on 15 April 2019,[137] thus issuing Directive (EU) 2019/770 of the European Parliament and of the Council of 20 May 2019 on certain aspects of contract law relating to the provision of digital content and digital services.[138]

**151.** The parallel proposal for the Distance Selling Directive was effectively put on ice for a long time. That dossier was to be resumed only after the Consumer Sales Directive ('REFIT') evaluation was completed.[139] This seemed sensible, as the privileged treatment of distance selling transactions vis-a-vis offline sales contracts, which was pursued in many respects in the proposal for a directive, was driven by the policy-goal to promote online sale rather than by an inherent need for consumer protection. On 31 October 2017, the Commission presented a new version of the proposal[140] that eliminated this distinction and henceforth covered the entire material scope of the Consumer Sales Directive, thus making it obsolete. After further intensive discussion in the so-called trilogue procedure,[141] the Parliament approved the proposal in its first reading on 26 March 2019;[142] the Council eventually adopted it on 15 April 2019.[143] Thus, Directive (EU) 2019/771 of the European Parliament and of the Council of 20 May 2019 on certain aspects concerning contracts for the sale of goods, which also amended Regulation (EU) 2017/2394 and Directive 2009/22/EC and repealed Directive 1999/44/EC was adopted.[144]

**152.** Both directives were to be implemented by the Member States by 1 July 2021; the corresponding provisions apply since 1 January 2022 (Article 24 Directive (EU) 2019/770 and Article 24 Directive (EU) 2019/771).

---

134 The legislative development can be followed here: http://eur-lex.europa.eu/legal-content/en/HIS/?uri=CELEX%3A52015PC0634.

135 See the relevant Council document of 1 December 2016, ST_14827_2016_INIT.

136 P8_TA(2019)0232.

137 ST 8614 2019 INIT.

138 OJ 2019 L 136/1. More on the content see below paras. 942–988.

139 For the results, see SWD(2017) 209 final.

140 Amended proposal for a Directive of the European Parliament and of the Council on certain aspects of contract law relating to trade in goods, amending Regulation (EC) No 2006/2004 of the European Parliament and of the Council and Directive 2009/22/EC of the European Parliament and of the Council and repealing Directive 1999/44/EC of the European Parliament and of the Council, COM(2017) 637 final.

141 This is an informal voting procedure between the Commission, Parliament and Council.

142 P8_TA(2019)0233.

143 ST 8615 2019 INIT.

144 OJ 2019 L 136/28. More on the content see below paras. 826–827.

# VI. THE IMPLICATIONS OF BREXIT

References: J. Basedow, 'Brexit und das Privat- und Wirtschaftsrecht', *ZEuP* 2016, 567; A. Briggs, 'Brexit and Private International Law: An English Perspective', *Rivista di diritto internazionale privato e processuale* 2019, 261; A. Dickinson, 'Close the Door on Your Way Out', *ZEuP* 2017, 539; M. *Dougan (ed.): The UK after Brexit. Legal and Policy Challenges* (Cambridge: Intersentia, 2017); W. Ernst, '"RETAINED EU-LAW" Probleme einer neuen Rechtserscheinung', *ZfPW* 2018, 369; B. Hess, 'Back to the Past: BREXIT und das europäische internationale Privat- und Verfahrensrecht', *IPRax* 2016, 409; M. Kramme, 'Consequences of Brexit in the Area of Consumer Protection', *GPR* 2017, 210; M. Lehmann/D. Zetzsche, 'Die Auswirkungen des Brexit auf das Zivil- und Wirtschaftsrecht', *JZ* 2017, 62; J. Mohamed, 'Effekte des Brexit aus europäisch gesellschaftsrechtlicher Perspektive – de lege lata über lege ferenda', *ZVglRWiss* 117 (2018) 189; G. Rühl, 'Die Wahl englischen Rechts und englischer Gerichte nach dem Brexit', *JZ* 2017, 72; M. Schmidt-Kessel, 'Grundfragen des Brexit-Austrittsabkommens', *GPR* 2018, 119; M. Sonnentag, Die Konsequenzen des Brexits für das Internationale Privat- und Zivilverfahrensrecht (Tübingen: Mohr Siebeck, 2017); J. Ungerer, 'Consequences of Brexit for European Private International Law', (2019) 4 *European Papers* 395; J. Ungerer, 'Brexit von Brüssel und den anderen EU-Verordnungen zum Internationalen Zivilverfahrens- und Privatrecht', in M. Kramme/C. Baldus/M. Schmidt-Kessel (eds.), *Brexit. Privat- und wirtschaftsrechtliche Folgen*, 2nd ed. (Baden-Baden: Nomos, 2020), p. 605; S. Vogenauer, '"Taking Back Control of our Laws?" Zur Weitergeltung europäischen Rechts im Vereinigten Königreich nach dem Brexit', *JZ* 2024, 209; M.-P. Weller/C. Thomale/S. Zwierlein, 'Brexit: Statutenwechsel und Acquis communautaire', *ZEuP* 2018, 892.

## 1. THE WITHDRAWAL OF THE UNITED KINGDOM FROM THE EU

**153.** On 23 June 2016, a referendum was held in the United Kingdom on whether the country should remain in the EU. A narrow majority of the votes cast favoured leaving the Union, the so-called Brexit. On 29 March 2017, the United Kingdom submitted its application to leave the EU under Article 50 TEU. After turbulent political disputes and multiple postponements, the UK finally left the EU on 31 January 2020 at midnight CET. The legal relations between the UK and the EU are – for the time being – regulated by the withdrawal agreement signed on 24 January 2020. This provided for a transitional phase until 31 December 2020, during which the previous legal rules relating to the single market continued to apply for the most part. The political intention – ultimately on both sides – was to negotiate a framework that allowed for further political and economic coexistence during this period.[145] However, the COVID-19 pandemic, which affected nearly all EU states by March 2020 onwards, slowed down this process.

[145] See the comment by MacPherson, *ZEuP* 2020, 529.

## 2. THE ADOPTION OF EU LAW IN THE UNITED KINGDOM ('RETAINED EU LAW')

**154.** With the withdrawal of the United Kingdom, EU secondary legislation was no longer valid on the grounds of Article 288 TFEU. The British Parliament was, therefore, free to amend or abolish laws that transposed directives or served to implement regulations. The European Union (Withdrawal) Act 2018 first repealed the European Communities Act 1972, meaning that from now on, the fact that EU law was no longer formally binding was also reflected at the domestic level. At the same time, some degree of continuity had to be established. Therefore, sec. 2(1) of the European Union (Withdrawal) Act 2018 provides that transposition law continues to apply subject to several exceptions in sec. 5: 'EU-derived domestic legislation, as it has effect in domestic law immediately before exit day, continues to have effect in domestic law on and after exit day.' Directly applicable EU law, in particular EU regulations, are transformed into domestic law immediately according to sec. 3(1): 'Direct EU legislation, so far as operative immediately before exit day, forms part of domestic law on and after exit day'. These laws are called 'Retained EU Law'.[146] CJEU decisions do not embody any kind of formal authority for the interpretation of these rules, but courts are free to take them into account (sec. 6(1) and (2) European Union (Withdrawal) Act 2018). In particular, the Supreme Court and, in certain circumstances, the High Court are not bound by retained EU law and may depart from it; the same conditions apply for any departure from a precedent (sec. 6(4) and (5) European Union (Withdrawal) Act 2018). This allows for a gradual 're-anglicisation' of the adopted EU law by the courts. Of course, retained EU law can also be amended by national legislation at any time (sec. 7 European Union (Withdrawal) Act 2018).[147]

## 3. REVIVAL OF INTERNATIONAL LAW?

**155.** Given that the Rome I Regulation expired for the United Kingdom, it has been discussed if the Rome Convention on the law applicable to contractual obligations[148] could become applicable again.[149] In other areas of private international law, such state treaties do not exist, meaning that, from the UK's point of view, autonomous national conflict-of-laws rules would have to be applied or created. However, the

---

146 For more details, see Ernst, *ZfPW* 2018, 369; Vogenauer, *JZ* 2024, 209.

147 Specifically on consumer law cf. Freeman, *EuCML* 2020, 1.

148 In addition cf. para. 13 above.

149 In favour Dickinson, *JPrivIntL* 12 (2016), 195, 204; Ungerer, in Kramme/Baldus/Schmidt-Kessel (eds.), *Brexit. Privat- und wirtschaftsrechtliche Folgen*, 2nd ed. 2020, pp. 605, 608 ff.; Lehmann/Zetzsche, *JZ* 2017, 62, 64 f.; in contrast Hess, *IPRax* 2016, 409, 417; Rühl, *JZ* 2017, 72, 74 f., each with further references.

above-mentioned European Union (Withdrawal) Act 2018 also ensures that the Rome I Regulation is kept as retained EU law. Hence, legal practice will not have to change radically for the foreseeable future. From the EU Member States' point of view, the EU conflict-of-laws rules, which are applicable universally,[150] continue to apply to the United Kingdom as a third country.

**156.** In the area of international procedural law, which is probably more important in practical terms, the main concern from the British point of view is to safeguard London's position as an international forum. Its attractiveness for an international audience could be in danger if the judgments pronounced there were no longer recognised throughout the EU:[151] The fact that the Brussels Ibis Regulation continues to apply as retained EU law does not give the judgments of British courts the desired effects of recognition and enforceability inside the EU. Here, too, it was discussed whether the Brussels *Ibis* Regulation could be revived in the relationship between the remaining 27 EU Member States and the United Kingdom after Brexit.[152] On the British side, there has been a discussion of acceding to the 2007 Lugano Convention. The application filed with the Contracting States, however, has been rejected by the EU Commission on 4 May 2021.[153]

## 4. BREXIT AND THE LEGAL CULTURE OF EU LAW

References: H. Eidenmüller, 'Collateral Damage. Brexit's Negative Effects on Regulatory Competition and Legal Innovation in Private Law', *ZEuP* 2018, 868; M. Flohr, *Rechtsdogmatik in England* (Tübingen: Mohr Siebeck, 2017); S. Worthington, 'The Unique Charm of the Common Law', *ERPL* 2011, 345

**157.** On the face of it, the UK's withdrawal from the EU could appear to make lawmaking easier by removing a common law country with a unique and cherished legal culture and some marked differences to continental European legal thinking. In this respect, it should suffice to recall the UK's peculiar role within the framework of judicial cooperation: Contrary to most other Member States, the UK was allowed to declare its participation in every

150 On the principle of universality below paras. 1260–1261.

151 See on the discussion on the creation of Commercial Courts as a reaction to this Stürner, *JZ* 2019, 1122.

152 In favour Dickinson, *JPrivIntL* 12 (2016), 195, 205; Lehmann/Zetzsche, *JZ* 2017, 62, 70; in contrast Hess, *IPRax* 2016, 409, 413; Rühl, *JZ* 2017, 72, 77.

153 COM(2021) 222 final. On possible ways of future cooperation, cf. Dittrich, Ensuring Efficient Cooperation with the UK in civil law matters, JURI Study, IPOL_STU(2023)743340_EN, March 2023. For the UK perspective, cf. The Windsor Framework: a new way forward, February 2023.

single legal act. The potential for disruption to the legislative process should be obvious. There were also many content-related 'red lines' of British origin, for example, regarding overriding mandatory provisions of foreign states (cf. Article 9(3) Rome I Regulation[154]), concerning the conflicts of laws of the liability for infringements of personality rights (cf. Article 1(2)(g) Rome II Regulation) or in many areas within family and succession law (for example in the EU Maintenance Regulation, the EU Succession Regulation or the European Matrimonial Property Regime Regulation).

**158.** However, it should not be forgotten that Ireland, Malta and Cyprus, i.e. countries with a common law tradition, are still EU Member States. It remains crucial that their voices are not marginalised in the EU's law-making process.[155] It would be short-sighted to believe that, as most Member States belong to the continental civil law tradition, better legislation will now be possible. The remaining 27 EU Member States do not share a homogeneous view of what EU law should look like, even if only the 24 countries with a continental tradition are considered. In the medium term, repression of ideas from the common law tradition would also do more harm than good to EU law: It is precisely the merging of both worlds that has characterised European law in the past. Additionally, the relationship with third countries will be more successful if EU law itself remains pluralistic.

**159.** Conversely, it would be unfortunate if, after the UK's withdrawal, a significant step was taken back in the UK to the traditional common law in the form of a 'roll-back'. In many respects, this would counter the development of recent decades, which has brought about a mutually beneficial convergence of the two approaches.[156] In global trade, common law is dominant anyway; this applies, for example, to international contract practice or dispute settlement. EU law cannot and must not ignore this.[157] The efforts of individual Member States to establish commercial courts in competition with London, the leading institution in this respect, are emblematic of this.[158]

---

[154] See paras. 1274–1282 below.

[155] In this direction also Hess, *IPRax* 2016, 409, 418.

[156] See 1343–1358 below.

[157] For example, the EU Parliament has discussed the question of whether a European Commercial Court should be established, see Rühl, 'Building Competence in Commercial Law in the Member States, Study for the JURI Committee of the European Parliament', September 2018, pp. 58 ff. (available at http://www.europarl.europa.eu/RegData/etudes/STUD/2018/604980/IPOL_STU(2018)604980_EN.pdf).

[158] See the contributions in X.E. Kramer/J. Sorabji (eds.), *International Business Courts: A European and Global Perspective* (The Hague: Eleven International Publishing, 2019), and in Zucconi Galli Fonseca/Henke/Torsello (eds.), *International Commercial Courts: A paradigm for the future of adjudication?* (Naples, Edizioni scientifiche italiane, 2024).

# §4. THE CONTRIBUTION OF ACADEMIC ENDEAVOURS IN THE FIELD OF EUROPEAN PRIVATE LAW

## CONTENTS



References: K. Gutman, *The Constitutional Foundations of European Contract Law: A Comparative Analysis* (Oxford: Oxford University Press, 2014), pp. 148–156; A. Metzger, *Extra legem, intra ius: Allgemeine Rechtsgrundsätze im Europäischen Privatrecht* (Tübingen:

Mohr Siebeck, 2009), pp. 221 ff.; R. Michaels, 'Privatautonomie und Privatkodifikation. Zur Anwendbarkeit und Geltung allgemeiner Vertragsrechtsprinzipien', *RabelsZ* 62 (1998), 580; H.W. Micklitz, '(Selbst-) Reflektionen über die wissenschaftlichen Ansätze zur Vorbereitung einer europäischen Vertragsrechtskodifikation', *GPR* 2007, 2; K. Riedl, *Vereinheitlichung des Privatrechts in Europa: Wissenschaftliche Initiativen im Europäisierungsprozeß* (Baden-Baden: Nomos), 2004; P. Sirena, 'Die Rolle wissenschaftlicher Entwürfe im europäischen Privatrecht', *ZEuP* 2018, 838; W. Wurmnest, 'Common Core, Grundregeln, Kodifikationsentwürfe, Acquis-Grundsätze – Ansätze internationaler Wissenschaftlergruppen zur Privatrechtsvereinheitlichung in Europa', *ZEuP* 2003, 714; R. Zimmermann, 'Die Rolle der wissenschaftlichen Entwürfe im europäischen Privatrecht', *ZEuP* 2018, 862.

**160.** It has already been explained that this book is based on a broad understanding of European private law, i.e. one that is not limited to positive EU law.[1] From this perspective, it is necessary to include academic projects in the field, as they contribute significantly to the contouring and further development of the law. It is true that this is not hard law – according to some definitions, it is not even soft law[2] but merely 'legal language organised in rules'.[3] However, their importance for the understanding of EU private law can hardly be underestimated. The following section, therefore, provides an overview of the most important academic projects and institutions and their work.

## I. THE COMMISSION ON EUROPEAN CONTRACT LAW (LANDO COMMISSION)

References: M. Durovic, '(Re)Drafting the Principles of European Contract Law (PECL)?', in A. Janssen/M. Lehmann/R. Schulze (eds.), *The Future of European Private Law* (Baden-Baden: Nomos, 2023-, p. 489; R. Zimmermann, 'Die Principles of European Contract Law als Ausdruck und Gegenstand europäischer Rechtswissenschaft', *JURA* 2005, 289 (Teil I) and 441 (Teil II).

### 1. ORIGINS

**161.** The Principles of European Contract Law (PECL), which have been drawn up by the Commission on European Contract Law (also known as the Lando Group after its founder and chairman, the Danish law professor Ole Lando) since 1982, follow the same spirit as the Vienna Convention on

1 See para. 16 above.
2 See paras. 95–106 above for the relevant terminology.
3 In that sense Schmidt-Kessel, Entry 'Study Group on a European Civil Code', in *Handwörterbuch des Europäischen Privatrechts*, 2009. On the nature and functions of these texts Sirena, *ZEuP* 2018, 838, 848 ff.

Contracts for the International Sale of Goods (CISG) that was adopted shortly before. The progress of this private working group received a significant impetus from the European Parliament's resolution on efforts to harmonise the Member States' private laws.[4] The Lando Group considered European contract law a central issue that had to be addressed with high priority. It did not have an official mandate, even though it partially received financial support from the EU.[5]

**162.** Part I of the PECL was first published in English in 1995;[6] a consolidated version appeared together with Part II in 2000.[7] Part III finally followed in 2003.[8] Although the PECL are non-binding (strictly speaking, they are not even a restatement of the contract law principles applicable in the various European legal systems), they nevertheless serve as a vital point of reference for the private law-related legal principles common to all Member States.

## 2. LAW-MAKING TECHNIQUE

### a) *Principles or Rules?*

**163.** Despite their designation as 'principles' or 'basic rules', the PECL have almost always been formulated in a rule-based manner that makes a case-based application of the law conceivable. For example, according to Article 1:101(2) PECL, the principles are applicable if the parties have chosen them.

### b) *Choice of Law*

**164.** However, under the Rome I Regulation (and contrary to Article 3(2) of its original draft),[9] choosing the PECL by means of a choice of law is impossible. A choice of the PECL would hence only affect the applicable substantive law since only state law can be chosen under current conflict-of-laws rules.[10]

---

4 Of 26 May 1989, OJ 1989 C 158/400. See para. 107 above.

5 At least, this is what the Wikipedia entry (keyword 'History') suggests: https://en.wikipedia.org/wiki/Principles_of_European_Contract_Law. See also Zimmermann, Entry 'Principles of European Contract Law', in *Handwörterbuch des Europäischen Privatrechts*, 2009.

6 Beale/Lando, *The Principles of European Contract Law, Part I, Performance, Non Performance and Remedies*, 1995.

7 Lando/Beale, Principles of European Contract Law, Parts I and II, 2000.

8 Lando/Clive/Prüm/Zimmermann, Principles of European Contract Law, Part III, 2003.

9 COM(2005) 650 final.

10 For example, Magnus, *IPRax* 2010, 27, 33. For more details, see para. 1156 below.

### c) *Indeterminate Legal Terms: 'Reasonable'*

**165.** In international regulatory instruments such as the UN Sales Convention, the Consumer Sales Directive, the PECL or the DCFR, the term 'reasonableness' is used quite frequently; in the case of the DCFR it is almost used excessively.[11] In Article 1:302 PECL, reasonableness is defined as follows:

> 'Under these Principles reasonableness is to be judged by what persons acting in good faith and in the same situation as the parties would consider to be reasonable. In particular, in assessing what is reasonable the nature and purpose of the contract, the circumstances of the case, and the usages and practices of the trades or professions involved should be taken into account.'

**166.** This definition seems to have been kept deliberately fuzzy in order to allow the judge to take into account all the circumstances of the individual case.[12] According to the authors of the PECL, the concept of reasonableness and its synonyms 'belong to the common core of the legal systems',[13] even though the various European legal systems, with few exceptions, do not contain such definitions.[14] It is undoubtedly true that every legal system uses open terminology in order to be able to achieve just results in individual cases. However, the drafters of the DCFR, in particular, appear to have elevated this legislative technique to a system of its own.[15] The frequent use of reasonableness expresses, on the one hand, the compromise character that a set of rules with a transnational claim to validity must necessarily bear: It might appear sensible to steer clear of divergent value judgements and to resort to the seemingly objective criterion of reasonableness. On the other hand, this complies with the practical requirement of using terms that are not already doctrinally occupied by the Member States' legal systems since they might be interpreted according to a specific national pre-understanding. Considering this background, the criterion of reasonableness appears sensible.

---

11 A full text search in the 'Interim Outline Edition' for the words '(un)reasonable' and 'reasonably' yielded over 400 hits. In the PECL (although much more limited in scope), the search yielded a good 80 hits.

12 Cf. comment B on Article 1:302 PECL. The DCFR contains a slightly different description of 'reasonable' in the preceding definitions: 'What is "reasonable" is to be objectively ascertained, having regard to the nature and purpose of what is being done, to the circumstances of the case and to any relevant usages and practices.'

13 Comment on Article 1:302 PECL. Critical therefore J. Schmidt, in *Festschrift für Großfeld* (Heidelberg: Recht und Wirtschaft, 1999), pp. 1017, 1022.

14 An example (albeit narrowly limited in its factual scope) is the English Unfair Contract Terms Act 1977, see Stürner, *Der Grundsatz der Verhältnismäßigkeit im Schuldvertragsrecht*, 2010, pp. 141 ff.

15 Cf. the criticism by Eidenmüller/Faust/Grigoleit/Jansen/Wagner/Zimmermann, JZ 2008, 529, 536 f.

**167.** Therefore, what is to be understood by reasonableness depends on the respective normative context and the possibly conflicting fundamental values behind it; those aspects have to be reconciled by the legal interpreter in each given case.[16] This makes sense, given that a uniform concept of 'reasonableness' does not exist in Europe. There is no clear-cut German translation for the term. This can be seen, for example, in the UN Sales Convention. In the (unofficial[17]) German translation, the term 'reasonable' is sometimes also translated as appropriate, proportionate or even as unreasonable.[18] One might wonder if this was done for purely practical reasons, such as the desire to use familiar terms, or if the diversity in translation reflects an opportunity to introduce a new regulatory concept.

**168.** The concept of reasonableness, as used in the PECL, DCFR and CISG, primarily aims to embody specific standards of conduct that relate to a person.[19] It denotes an objective standard of care, which can be shown, for example, by how long a period of time is to be measured when it comes to prescription etc,[20] how a declaration of intent is to be understood (for example, in Article 8(2) CISG[21]), whether or not a contracting party could have foreseen the disadvantage caused to the other party by a breach of contract (Article 25 CISG)[22] or what quality the consumer may expect with regard to a sold item in light of respective public statements made by the seller or the producer, provided that the seller was not aware of it on reasonable grounds (according to Article 2(2)(d) and (3) CSD respectively).

---

16 The authors of the DCFR explicitly point this out in the introduction: von Bar/Clive, *DCFR 2009 Final Edition*, Introduction No 22.

17 Only the Arabic, Chinese, English, French, Russian and Spanish versions are authentic, cf. the final formula to the United Nations Convention on Contracts for the International Sale of Goods of 11 April 1980.

18 Cf. J. Schmidt, in *Festschrift für Großfeld*, 1999, p. 1017, 1027. Critically, Troiano, in Schulze, *New Features in Contract Law*, 2007, pp. 375, 377.

19 This is shown by the definition in Article 1:302 PECL; the reference to persons is less clear in Article I.-1:104 DCFR. In terms of content, however, no change is intended, cf. commentary on Article I.-1:104 DCFR.

20 Cf.the lists in J. Schmidt, in *Festschrift für Großfeld*, 1999, pp. 1017, 1019 (on the PECL) and in *Troiano*, in Schulze, New Features in Contract Law, 2007, pp 375, 396 (on the CISG).

21 Under the UN Sale of Goods Convention, a declaration of intent is to be interpreted as a reasonable person would have understood it. Cf. the further examples in Troiano, in Schulze, *New Features in Contract Law*, 2007, pp. 375, 389 ff.

22 This traditionally seems to be the largest area of application of reasonableness: Liability (especially non-contractual) is limited to that which could have been avoided by the application of reasonable care. Fundamental to English law is the products liability case *Donoghue* v. *Stevenson* [1932] AC 562, 599, HL (Lord Atkin).

**169.** In addition, the term reasonableness is also used in other ways. While the reasonable person[23] in the cases described can be understood as a substitute for one of the contracting parties who sets the standard for a 'reasonable' decision, reasonableness also assesses questions of contractual balance as a neutral third party might.[24] For example, the already discussed Article 9:102(2)(b) PECL limits a claim for performance in kind if this would signify an 'unreasonable expense or effort'.

## 3. SIGNIFICANCE AND RECEPTION

**170.** Of all the model sets of rules, the PECL had the most significant influence to date. This applies not only to jurisprudence but also to jurisdiction: Even though the CJEU only cites its own judgments (following the French tradition) in addition to the applicable law, the PECL are nevertheless occasionally mentioned in more recent Opinions of the Advocates General.[25]

**171.** In this context, reference to the PECL typically only provides argumentative support for a result already found based on positive law, but it does at least serve to affirm the existence of a legal principle common to all European legal systems.

**172.** In addition, the PECL serve as a model for national legislators; for example, Estonia[26] relied, among other things, on the PECL as a model legal system for the reform of the Code of Obligations.[27] The reform of the French

23 In classical English cases, of course, reference is frequently made to the 'reasonable man', cf. for example *Donoghue* v. *Stevenson* [1932] AC 562, 619 f., HL (Lord Macmillan).

24 On these cases also Troiano, in Schulze, *New Features in Contract Law*, 2007, pp. 375, 398 f., 410 ff. According to *Troiano*, reasonableness is an 'equilibrium component' within the concepts of good faith and diligence, namely as an 'intersection between colliding interests'. Reasonableness, however, almost completely coincides with the concept of *equità* (equity).

25 For example, in the Opinion of GA Trstenjak of 15 November 2007, Case C-404/06, *Quelle*, ECLI:EU:C:2007:682, para. 44 (reference to Article 9:102(1) PECL), in the Opinion of 6 March 2007, Case C-1/06, *Bonn Fleisch*, ECLI:EU:C:2007:137, para. 68 (on the interpretation of declarations of intent in Chapter 5 PECL), ECLI:EU:C:2007:137, para. 68 (on the interpretation of declarations of intent in Chapter 5 PECL); in the Opinion of 18 February 2009, Case C-489/07, *Messner/Krüger*, ECLI:EU:C:2009:98, paras. 85, 94 (reference to the regulation of the consumer's liability when exercising the right of withdrawal in the DCFR) as well as in the Opinion of GA Poiares Maduro of 21 November 2007, Case C-412/06, *Hamilton*, ECLI:EU:C:2007:695, para. 24 (with reference to the principles of limitation regulated in Chapter 14 PECL).

26 In addition, the German Civil Code, the Swiss Code of Obligations, the CISG and the UNIDROIT Principles were also consulted: cf. Kull, *Juridica International* 1999, 147; Kull, *Juridica International* 2004, 32.

27 The commission set up to reform the Hungarian Civil Code also cites the PECL, among others, as a model for legislative work, cf. Vékás, *ZEuP* 2009, 536, 540; on this also Z. Csehi, in

Code of Obligations, the so-called *avant-projet Catala* (*avant-projet de réforme du droit des obligations et de la prescription*) was also partly inspired by the PECL model.[28] Traces can still be found in the reform, which was realised on 1 October 2016.[29]

## II. THE ACCADEMIA DEI GIUSPRIVATISTI EUROPEI (GANDOLFI GROUP)

References: G. Gandolfi, 'Pour un code européen des contrats', *Rev. trim. dr. civ.*, 1992, 707; G. Gandolfi, 'Der Vorentwurf eines europäischen Vertragsgesetzbuchs', *ZEuP* 2002, 1; G. Gandolfi, 'Das Zweite Buch (über "Einzelne Verträge") des europäischen Vertragsgesetzbuchs - einige Vorbemerkungen', in *Festschrift für Canaris*, Volume 2 (Munich: C.H. Beck, 2007), p. 585; G. Gandolfi, 'Europäisches Vertragsgesetzbuch Vorentwurf - Zweiter Buch - Erster Titel', *ZEuP* 2009, 628; S. Patti, 'Kritische Anmerkungen zum Entwurf eines europäischen Vertragsgesetzbuches', *ZEuP* 2004, 118; M.L. Ruffini Gandolfi, 'Le Code européen des contrats - Livre I, à l'Institut de France (et les travaux préparatoires du Livre II, à l'Université de Pavie)', *R.I.D.C.* 3-2006, 953; J.H. Sonnenberger, 'Der Entwurf eines Europäischen Vertragsgesetzbuchs der Akademie Europäischer Privatrechtswissenschaftler - ein Meilenstein', *RIW* 2001, 409; F. Sturm, 'Bemühungen um ein einheitliches europäisches Vertragsrecht', *JZ* 1991, 555; F. Sturm, 'Der Entwurf eines Europäischen Vertragsgesetzbuch', *JZ* 2001, 1097; R. Zimmermann, 'Der "Codice Gandolfi" als Modell eines einheitlichen Vertragsrechts für Europa? - Überlegungen zur Regelung der Aufrechnung (Art. 132)', in *Festschrift für Jayme* (Munich: Sellier, 2004), p. 1401.

### 1. THE ACCADEMIA DEI GIUSPRIVATISTI EUROPEI

**173.** The *Accademia dei giusprivatisti europei* was founded in Pavia in 1992;[30] its *spiritus rector* and promoter was the Italian law professor Giuseppe Gandolfi, which is why the name Gandolfi Group is often used as well. Their aim was not to create basic principles of contract law but rather to formulate a complete code

W.Heun/V. Lipp, *Europäisierung des Rechts* (Göttingen: Universitätsverlag Göttingen, 2008), pp. 59, 71 ff.

28 Cf. P. Catala, 'Avant-projet de réforme du droit des obligations et de la prescription'. On the draft, see, inter alia, Ancel, in *Schuldrechtsmodernisierung und Europäisches Vertragsrecht*, p. 45; Sonnenberger, *ZEuP* 2007, 421; Fauvarque-Cosson, ZEuP 2007, 428; Fauvarque-Cosson/Mazeaud, Unif. L. Rev. 2006, 103; Lorenz, *Revue des contrats* 2007, 57; Lehmann, *Revue des contrats* 2007, 1427.

29 On this point, Babusiaux/Witz, *JZ* 2017, 496.

30 Gandolfi, *ERA Forum* 2/2003, 99, 121; Wurmnest, *ZEuP* 2003, 714, 735; Sonnenberger, *RIW* 2001, 409. See http://www.accademiagiusprivatistieuropei.it.

in the field of contract law[31] that all Member States would consider acceptable.[32] The European Parliament's resolution of 1989[33] certainly played a significant role in the creation of the *Accademia*.[34]

**174.** In 1998, a preliminary draft of the first book of European contract law on the law of contracts of obligations was published.[35] In 2001, the preliminary draft of the first book was then published in French,[36] including a report by the coordinator Gandolfi.[37] A second, revised and corrected edition of the draft with translations into German, English, Spanish and Italian was published in 2002, and a further revised and corrected edition was published in 2004.[38] In 2006, this was followed by the official presentation of the preliminary draft of the first title of the second book, which deals with the sale of movable property.[39] Only the sale of movable goods is incorporated since, from the authors' point of view, the Common Law's rules on the sale of immovable goods differed too much from those of the Civil Law and, moreover, Community Law leaves the regulations on property in the Member States largely unaffected.[40] The work continues until today; the group are currently drafting the second book of the draft on individual contracts.[41]

## 2. DRAFTING TECHNIQUES

**175.** The Italian Codice civile was of central importance to the Gandolfi group's work.[42] It is widely considered a sound synthesis between German and French

[31] Patti, *ZEuP* 2004, 118; Zimmermann, in *Festschrift für Jayme*, 2004, p. 1401; Gandolfi, *ERA Forum* 2/2003, 99, 122; Ruffini Gandolfi, R.I.D.C. 3-2006, 953; Sonnenberger, RIW 2001, 409 f.; Metzger, *Extra legem, intra ius: Allgemeine Rechtsgrundsätze im Europäischen Privatrecht*, 2009, p. 230; Gandolfi, in *Festschrift für Canaris*, 2007, pp. 585, 587.

[32] Gandolfi, *ERA Forum* 2/2003, 99, 122 f.; Gandolfi, in *Festschrift für Canaris*, 2007, pp. 585, 589.

[33] See para. 116 above.

[34] Sturm, *JZ* 1991, 555; Olzen, in Staudinger, *BGB Kommentar* (2024), Einleitung zum Schuldrecht, para. 302.

[35] Olzen, in Staudinger, *BGB Kommentar* (2024), Einleitung zum Schuldrecht, para. 302; Zimmermann, in *Festschrift für Jayme*, 2004, p. 1401, 1406; Gandolfi, in *Festschrift für Canaris*, 2007, pp. 585, 586.

[36] Sturm, *JZ* 2001, 1097; Patti, *ZEuP* 2004, 118.

[37] Zimmermann, in *Festschrift für Jayme*, 2004, pp. 1401, 1405.

[38] See http://www.accademiagiusprivatistieuropei.it.

[39] Olzen, in Staudinger, *BGB Kommentar* (2024), Einleitung zum Schuldrecht, para. 302; Metzger, Extra legem, intra ius: Allgemeine Rechtsgrundsätze im Europäischen Privatrecht, 2009, p. 231; Gandolfi, in *Festschrift für Canaris*, 2007, pp. 585, 586.

[40] Gandolfi, in *Festschrift für Canaris*, 2007, pp. 585, 592.

[41] See http://www.accademiagiusprivatistieuropei.it.

[42] Olzen, in Staudinger, *BGB Kommentar* (2024), Einleitung zum Schuldrecht, para. 302; Wurmnest, *ZEuP* 2003, 714, 736; Zimmermann, in *Festschrift für Jayme*, 2004, pp. 1401, 1405.

law[43] that also did not contain any contradictions to common law principles.[44] Furthermore, McGregor's draft Contract Code,[45] which unified English and Scottish contract law, was also taken into account.[46] Gandolfi himself bore the main burden of the work. There were no thematically limited working groups; instead, the group members discussed individual factual points (partly based on questionnaires sent to national subgroups or individual scholars).[47] The editorial work was carried out solely by Gandolfi.[48]

**176.** Like the PECL, the Gandolfi Group's drafts are purely academic; they do not have binding force. The principle of *pacta sunt servanda* is of central importance, and the regulations intend to ensure legal clarity and rapid implementation of contracts. The grammatical interpretation of contractual agreements is, therefore, seen to take priority.[49] Mandatory law is avoided wherever possible; the same is true for severe legal consequences such as validity/nullity or performance/non-performance. The drafts also avoid legal concepts that carry a different meaning in some Member States (e.g. the terms *Rechtsgeschäft* [juridical act], obligation or consideration).[50]

## 3. SIGNIFICANCE AND RECEPTION

**177.** In academic literature, the richness of the Gandolfi Group's normative concepts, which also take into account the preliminary work of other private initiatives and the CISG, is often emphasised, particularly regarding the first preliminary draft.[51] In addition, the deeper density of regulations compared to the PECL and the inclusion of comparably extensive legal areas are usually highlighted.[52]

---

43 Patti, *ZEuP* 2004, 118, 119 f.; Wurmnest, *ZEuP* 2003, 714, 736; Ruffini Gandolfi, *R.I.D.C.* 3-2006, 953, 955; Sonnenberger, RIW 2001, 409, 410; Metzger, *Extra legem, intra ius: Allgemeine Rechtsgrundsätze im Europäischen Privatrecht*, 2009, p. 230.

44 Sturm, *JZ* 1991, 555.

45 H. McGregor, Contract Code drawn up on behalf of the English Law Commission (Milan: Giuffrè, 1993).

46 Sonnenberger, *RIW* 2001, 409, 410; Patti, *ZEuP* 2004, 118, 120; Wurmnest, *ZEuP* 2003, 714, 736; Zimmermann, in *Festschrift für Jayme*, 2004, p. 1401, 1405; Ruffini Gandolfi, *R.I.D.C.* 3-2006, 953, 955; Metzger, *Extra legem, intra ius: Allgemeine Rechtsgrundsätze im Europäischen Privatrecht*, 2009, p. 230.

47 Patti, *ZEuP* 2004, 118, 120.

48 Zimmermann, in *Festschrift für Jayme*, 2004, pp. 1401, 1403 f.

49 Gandolfi, *ERA Forum* 2/2003, 99, 124; Gandolfi, *ZEuP* 2001, 1, 3.

50 Gandolfi, *ERA Forum* 2/2003, 99, 122; Gandolfi, in *Festschrift für Canaris*, 2007, pp. 585, 588 f.; Gandolfi, *ZEuP* 2002, 1, 4.

51 Sonnenberger, *RIW* 2001, 410, 416; Troiano, *IHR* 2008, 221, 234.

52 Wurmnest, *ZEuP* 2003, 714, 737.

**178.** Ultimately, however, a critical reception seems to dominate. Some scholars primarily criticised the methodological approach of the *Accademia*, which on the one hand, based its work on only two normative sources, the Codice civile and the McGregor draft, and on the other hand, placed the overall responsibility for the content and design of the drafts in the hands of its coordinator Gandolfi only.[53] Regarding its content, the form of codification chosen by the *Accademia* is sometimes described as 'not very elastic and adaptable'.[54] The preliminary drafts also did not consider the legislative developments at the European level, which led to the creation of a significant amount of mandatory contract law. Finally, the blanket and open clauses that were extensively used did not necessarily facilitate the harmonisation of law, as they are understood differently by the European legal systems.[55]

**179.** In any case, both the Parliament and the Commission have taken note of the preliminary draft;[56] the work has also been mentioned in various opinions of the CJEU's Advocates General.[57]

## III. THE STUDY GROUP ON A EUROPEAN CIVIL CODE

References: C. von Bar, 'Die Study Group on a European Civil Code', in *Festschrift für Henrich* (Bielefeld: E. und W. Gieseking, 2000), p. 1; C. von Bar, 'Konturen des Deliktsrechtskonzeptes der Study Group on a European Civil Code – Ein Werkstattbericht', *ZEuP* 2001, 515; M.-R. McGuire, 'Ziel und Methode der Study Group on a European Civil Code', *ZfRV* 2006, 163; H.W. Micklitz, '(Selbst-) Reflektionen über die wissenschaftlichen Ansätze zur Vorbereitung einer europäischen Vertragsrechtskodifikation', *GPR* 2007, 2; M. Prisching, 'Der Gemeinsame Referenzrahmen (GRR) – ein Begriff in aller Munde', *ZfRV* 2007, 12; M. Schmidt-Kessel, 'Stichwort "Study Group on a European Civil Code"', in *Handwörterbuch des Europäischen Privatrechts* (Tübingen: Mohr Siebeck, 2009); H. Schulte-Nölke, 'Ziele und Arbeitsweisen von Study Group und Acquis Group bei der Vorbereitung des DCFR', in M. Schmidt-Kessel (ed.), *Der gemeinsame Referenzrahmen. Entstehung, Inhalte, Anwendung* (Munch: Sellier, 2009), p. 9.

---

53 Wurmnest, *ZEuP* 2003, 714, 738; Metzger, *Extra legem, intra ius: Allgemeine Rechtsgrundsätze im Europäischen Privatrecht*, 2009, p. 230.

54 Patti, *ZEuP* 2004, 118, 119.

55 Patti, *ZEuP* 2004, 118, 130.

56 Gandolfi, *ERA Forum* 2/2003, 99, 122.

57 CJEU, Opinion of Advocate General Poiares Maduro of 21 November 2007, Case C-412/06, *Hamilton*, ECLI:EU:C:2007:695, para. 24 (prescription as a generally accepted principle of law); CJEU, Opinion of Advocate General Trstenjak of 11 September 2008, Case C-180/06, *Ilsinger*, ECLI:EU:C:2008:483, para. 50 (offer and acceptance as a constituent element of the contract in all European legal systems).

## 1. THE STUDY GROUP

**180.** The Study Group on a European Civil Code was founded in 1998 and started its activities in 1999 in order to continue the Lando Group's work.[58] The impetus came from some members of the Lando Group; its figurehead was the German law professor Christian von Bar.[59] In the long term, the aim was to draft a European civil code in the area of property law, including the law of movable property.[60] This intended to serve the European legislator as an aid in the adoption of new Community private law and provide assistance to the CJEU in the development of general principles of law. Contracting parties should also be able to refer to the rules of the European Civil Code in cross-border legal transactions.[61]

**181.** The Study Group was supported by various national research organisations (particularly by the German Research Foundation [DFG], since 2000).[62] Under the 6th EU Framework Programme for Research and Technological Development, a consortium led by the Study Group and the Acquis Group[63] was awarded a three-year grant starting in May 2005 to develop a Common Frame of Reference for European Contract Law.[64]

**182.** This resulted in various publications, most notably the Interim Outline Edition of the Draft Common Frame of Reference in 2008,[65] followed shortly by

---

58 E.H. Hondius, 'Towards a European Civil Code', in A.S. Hartkamp e.a. (eds.), *Towards a European Civil Code*, 4th ed. (Nijmegen: Kluwer Law International, 2011), pp. 3, 13; von Bar, in *Festschrift für Henrich*, 2000, p. 1, 2; *McGuire*, ZfRV 2006, 163, 166; Schmidt-Kessel, Entry 'Study Group on a European Civil Code', in *Handwörterbuch des Europäischen Privatrechts*, 2009; Metzger, *Extra legem, intra ius: Allgemeine Rechtsgrundsätze im Europäischen Privatrecht*, 2009, p. 226.

59 Von Bar, in *Festschrift für Henrich*, 2000, p. 1, 3.

60 Gutman, *The Constitutional Foundations of European Contract Law*, 2014, p. 152; Wurmnest, *ZEuP* 2003, 714, 732; von Bar, in *Festschrift für Henrich*, 2000, pp. 1, 3 f.; Metzger, *Extra legem, intra ius: Allgemeine Rechtsgrundsätze im Europäischen Privatrecht*, 2009, p. 227.

61 Weighing up different approaches in von Bar, in *Festschrift für Henrich*, 2000, p. 1, 5 ff.; see also Wurmnest, *ZEuP* 2003, 714, 732 f.; McGuire, *ZfRV* 2006, 163, 167 ff.

62 Von Bar, in *Festschrift für Henrich*, 2000, pp. 1, 3; Schmidt-Kessel, Entry 'Study Group on a European Civil Code', in *Handwörterbuch des Europäischen Privatrechts*, 2009.

63 On this see below paras. 187–193.

64 Joint Network on European Private Law (CoPECL: Common Principles of European Contract Law), Network of Excellence under the 6th EU Framework Programme for Research and Technological Development, Priority 7 -FP6-2002-CITIZENS- 3, Contract N8513351. See also Prisching, ZfRV 2007, 12, 14; Metzger, *Extra legem, intra ius: Allgemeine Rechtsgrundsätze im Europäischen Privatrecht*, 2009, p. 226.

65 Von Bar/Clive/Schulte-Nölke (eds.), Principles, Definitions and Model Rules of European Private Law. Draft Common Frame of Reference (DCFR), Interim Outline Edition, 2008.

the Outline Edition.[66] Finally, in October 2009, the Full Edition was published. It consisted of six volumes in which the provisions of the Draft Common Frame of Reference are both annotated and supplemented with comparative remarks.[67]

**183.** In addition, the group has developed the Principles of European Law (PEL), which have been published in separate volumes.[68] So far, works have been published on the sale of goods,[69] the lease of goods,[70] the provision of services,[71] distribution contracts,[72] personal securities,[73] the agency of necessity,[74] tort law,[75] the law of enrichment,[76] mandate contracts,[77] movable goods[78] and proprietary securities.[79] Volumes on gifts and trusts were planned as well.[80] In 2008, the Study Group concluded its content-related work.[81]

## 2. DRAFTING TECHNIQUES

**184.** Following the Lando Group, the Study Group also intended to develop tangible regulatory proposals. The work was based on a functional comparative law approach,[82] which deliberately dropped traditional doctrinal frameworks of

66 Von Bar/Clive/Schulte-Nölke (eds.), Principles, Definitions and Model Rules of European Private Law. Draft Common Frame of Reference (DCFR), Outline Edition, 2009.

67 Von Bar/Clive/Schulte-Nölke, Principles, Definitions and Model Rules of European Private Law. Draft Common Frame of Reference (DCFR), Full Edition, 2009.

68 Schmidt-Kessel, Entry 'Study Group on a European Civil Code', in *Handwörterbuch des Europäischen Privatrechts*, 2009.

69 E. Hondius/V. Heutger/C. Jeloschek/H. Sivesand/A. Wiewiorowska, *Sales* (Munich: Sellier, 2008).

70 K. Lilleholt/A. Victorin/A. Fötschl/B.-E. Konow/A. Meidell/A. Bjoranger-Torum, *Lease of Goods* (Munich: Sellier, 2008).

71 M. Barendrecht/C. Jansen/M. Loos/A. Pinna/R. Cascao/S. van Gulijk, *Service Contracts* (Munich: Sellier, 2007).

72 M. Hesselink/J. Rutgers/O. Bueno Diaz/M. Scotton/M. Veldman, *Commercial Agency, Franchise and Distribution Contracts* (Munich: Sellier, 2006).

73 U. Drobnig, *Personal Security* (Munich: Sellier, 2007).

74 C. von Bar, Benevolent Intervention in Another's Affairs (Munich: Sellier, 2006).

75 C. von Bar, Non-Contractual Liability Arising out of Damage Caused to Another (Munich: Sellier, 2009).

76 S. Swann/C. von Bar, *Unjustified Enrichment* (Munich: Sellier, 2010).

77 O. Bueno Díaz/M.B.M. Loos, *Mandate Contracts* (Munich: De Gruyter, 2013).

78 B. Lurger/W. Faber, Acquisition and Loss of Ownership of Goods (Munich: Sellier, 2011).

79 U. Drobnig/O. Böger, *Proprietary Security in Movable Assets* (Munich: Sellier, 2015).

80 See the corresponding reference in Schmidt-Kessel, Entry 'Study Group on a European Civil Code', in *Handwörterbuch des Europäischen Privatrechts*, 2009.

81 Schmidt-Kessel, Entry 'Study Group on a European Civil Code', in *Handwörterbuch des Europäischen Privatrechts*, 2009.

82 Micklitz, *GPR* 2007, 2, 8; McGuire, *ZfRV* 2006, 163, 170.

individual legal systems in order to create internationally acceptable solutions.[83] In doing so, it was focused on the law of the current as well as the (then) future Member States.[84]

**185.** Contrary to the Gandolfi Group, the drafting of individual sub-sections was usually carried out in a decentralised manner. Individual working groups of about ten academic staff members and one team leader[85] were tasked to produce drafts on various private law areas.[86] An advisory team supported them[87] to prevent one-sided national views.[88] The steering committee, chaired by von Bar, was responsible for organisation and management.[89] The Coordinating Committee,[90] composed of national project leaders and additional experts, discussed[91] and voted on the working group's proposals.[92]

### 3. SIGNIFICANCE AND RECEPTION

**186.** The most significant work of the Study Group has been the Draft Common Frame of Reference, which has already been discussed.[93] The other results of the work, which are independent of this, have found little resonance.

## IV. THE EUROPEAN RESEARCH GROUP ON THE EXISTING EC PRIVATE LAW (ACQUIS GROUP)

References: H.C. Grigoleit/L. Tomasic, 'Acquis Principles', in *Handwörterbuch des Europäischen Privatrechts* (Tübingen: Mohr Siebeck, 2009); N. Jansen/R. Zimmermann, 'Grundregeln des bestehenden Gemeinschaftsprivatrechts?', *JZ* 2007, 1113; H.W. Micklitz, '(Selbst-)Reflektionen über die wissenschaftlichen Ansätze zur Vorbereitung einer europäischen Vertragsrechtskodifikation', *GPR* 2007, 2; H. Schulte-Nölke, 'Europäische

83 Jansen, *ZEuP* 2002, 641, 643.
84 An exception was made by the project group on insurance contract law, which took into account the law of Switzerland, which is important for the insurance market, and Australian law as a model for a modern common-law country, see Wurmnest, *ZEuP* 2003, 714, 733.
85 Wurmnest, *ZEuP* 2003, 714, 733.
86 Prisching, *ZfRV* 2007, 12, 14.
87 Wurmnest, *ZEuP* 2003, 714, 733.
88 Von Bar, in *Festschrift für Henrich*, 2000, p. 1, 2 f.; McGuire, *ZfRV* 2006, 163, 171.
89 Wurmnest, *ZEuP* 2003, 714, 733; von Bar, in *Festschrift für Henrich*, 2000, pp. 1, 2.
90 Von Bar, in Festschrift für Henrich, pp. 1, 2.
91 Prisching, *ZfRV* 2007, 12, 14; McGuire, *ZfRV* 2006, 163, 171.
92 Wurmnest, *ZEuP* 2003, 714, 733.
93 See paras. 120–129 above.

Forschergruppe zum geltenden Gemeinschaftsprivatrecht ("Acquis Gruppe") gegründet', *ZEuP* 2002, 893; H. Schulte-Nölke, 'Arbeiten an einem europäischen Vertragsrecht – Fakten und populäre Irrtümer', *NJW* 2009, 2161; H. Schulte-Nölke, 'Ziele und Arbeitsweisen von Study Group und Acquis Group bei der Vorbereitung des DCFR', in M. Schmidt-Kessel (ed.), *Der gemeinsame Referenzrahmen. Entstehung, Inhalte, Anwendung* (Munch: Sellier, 2009), p. 9; R. Schulze, 'Die Acquis-Grundregeln und der gemeinsame Referenzrahmen', *ZEuP* 2007, 731; C. Twigg-Flesner,' The Acquis Principles: An Insider's Critical Reflections on the Drafting Process', *GPR* 2011, 54; F. Zoll, 'Die Grundregeln der Acquis-Gruppe im Spannungsverhältnis zwischen acquis commun und acquis communautaire', *GPR* 2008, 106.

## 1. THE ACQUIS GROUP

**187.** The European Research Group on the Existing EC Private Law, known as the Acquis Group, was founded in May 2002.[94] Its coordinator is the German law professor Hans Schulte-Nölke, and its spokesperson is the Italian law professor Gianmaria Ajani.[95] The foundation of the Acquis Group is directly related to the Commission's Communication on European Contract Law of 11 July 2001[96] and the subsequent Action Plan 'A more coherent European contract law'.[97] The Acquis Group aimed to prepare the existing acquis communautaire in the style of restatements along the lines of the American Law Institute. In this respect, no independent draft law in the style of a better law was to be created but (only) an aid for the interpretation, further development and implementation of Community private law.[98] The Acquis Group was also a founding member of the Joint Network on European Private Law, which was tasked to develop a Common Frame of Reference.[99]

**188.** The Acquis Principles (ACQP) were originally intended to consist of three annotated parts with comparative law explanations. The first part was supposed to deal with general principles of European contract law, the second

94 Jansen/Zimmermann, *JZ* 2007, 1113, 1114; Olzen, in Staudinger, *BGB Kommentar* (2024), Einleitung zum Schuldrecht, para. 303; Wurmnest, *ZEuP* 2003, 714, 740; Twigg-Flesner, *GPR* 2011, 54, 55.

95 Gutman, *The Constitutional Foundations of European Contract Law*, 2014, p. 154.

96 Communication from the Commission of the European Communities to the Council and the European Parliament on European Contract Law, 11 July 2001, COM(2001) 398 final.

97 COM(2003) 68 final. On both, cf. already above paras. 117–119.

98 Schulte-Nölke, *ZEuP* 2002, 893; Wurmnest, *ZEuP* 2003, 714, 741; Schulte-Nölke, *NJW* 2009, 2161, 2163.

99 Grigoleit/Tomasic, Entry 'Acquis Principles', in *Handwörterbuch des Europäischen Privatrechts*, Volume I, 2009, p. 12 ff.; Schmidt-Kessel, *GPR* 2004, 298.

with definitions of the most important legal terms and the third with the body of rules of general and special contract law.[100]

**189.** A first study on the private law *acquis communautaire* in the area of information duties and the conclusion of contracts was presented in 2003.[101] In 2007, the most important content of the third part of the ACQP was published in a commented draft version.[102] This concerned pre-contractual obligations, the conclusion of contracts, the content of contracts, and essential rules of general contract law. Further parts were published shortly afterwards.[103]

## 2. DRAFTING TECHNIQUES

**190.** Due to their character as a restatement, the ACQP are intended to put together the rules and principles of contract law which were already harmonised within the EC (Article 1:102(2) ACQP).[104] This aspect refers to Options III and IV[105] of the Commission Communication on European Contract Law of 2001,[106] i.e. the goal to 'improve the quality of legislation already in place' and 'adopt new comprehensive legislation at EC level'. The existing acquis, particularly secondary private law and respective court judgements, but also other sets of rules such as the CISG or PECL,[107] was to be summarised coherently and, at the same time, revised and improved.[108] The decisive question of whether a rule or a legal principle belongs to the acquis was to be determined by means of

---

100 Schulte-Nölke, *ZEuP* 2002, 893; Grigoleit/Tomasic, Entry 'Acquis Principles', in *Handwörterbuch des Europäischen Privatrechts*, Volume I, 2009, pp. 12 ff.

101 R. Schulze/M. Ebers/H.C. Grigoleit (eds.), *Informationspflichten und Vertragsschluss im Acquis communautaire* (Tübingen: Mohr Siebeck, 2003).

102 Research Group on the Existing EC Private Law (Acquis Group), Contract I. Pre-contractual Obligations, Conclusions of Contract, Unfair Terms, 2007. See for example Schulze, *ZEuP* 2007, 731.

103 Research Group on the Existing EC Private Law (Acquis Group), Contract II. General Provisions. Delivery of Goods. Package Travel and Payment Services, 2009; Contract III. General Provisions, Delivery of Goods, Package Travel, Payment Services, Consumer Credit and Commercial Agency Contracts, 2014.

104 Schulte-Nölke, *NJW* 2009, 2161, 2163.

105 Schulte-Nölke, *ZEuP* 2002, 893; Wurmnest, *ZEuP* 2003, 714, 741.

106 Communication from the Commission of the European Communities to the Council and the European Parliament on European Contract Law, 11 July 2001, COM(2001) 398 final. On this already above para. 117.

107 Jansen/Zimmermann, *JZ* 2007, 1113, 1115, 1117; Schulte-Nölke, *ZEuP* 2002, 893; Schulte-Nölke, *NJW* 2009, 2161, 2163; Twigg-Flesner, *GPR* 2011, 54, 56; Ernst, *AcP* 208 (2008), 248, 254.

108 Grigoleit/Tomasic, Entry 'Acquis Principles', in *Handwörterbuch des Europäischen Privatrechts*, Volume I, 2009, pp. 12 ff.

interpretation according to the provisions' purposes and the *effet utile*. Disputed points were to be clarified normatively and explained within the respective sections.[109]

**191.** Similar to the Study Group, the Acquis Group also consisted of various sub-groups (drafting teams), which analysed the *acquis communautaire* with regard to specific topics and submitted drafts.[110] After preparation by the Redaction Committee and the Terminology Group, the drafts were discussed in the Plenary Assembly, modified if necessary and adopted.[111]

## 3. SIGNIFICANCE AND RECEPTION

**192.** The responses to the drafts of the acquis group were quite varied. While the aim of creating a transparent European body of rules was generally praised,[112] the primarily descriptive approach of the restatement technique was criticised. Thus, the sometimes relatively narrow framework of directive law was abandoned in order to extend the acquis rules to related subject areas, for example, in the area of pre-contractual information duties.[113] The underlying political decision in favour of a specific model was also not always sufficiently disclosed.[114] Ultimately, it must be conceded that an opportunity had been missed to subject the acquis to a critical evaluation.[115]

**193.** The work of the Acquis Group must also be compared with the impact of the Draft Common Frame of Reference.[116] In this respect, it can be observed that (solely) individual opinions of the CJEU Advocates General refer to the Acquis Principles.[117] The other individual works produced by the Acquis

109 Jansen/Zimmermann, *JZ* 2007, 1113, 1117; Ernst, *AcP* 208 (2008), 248, 254.

110 Grigoleit/Tomasic, Entry 'Acquis Principles', in *Handwörterbuch des Europäischen Privatrechts*, Volume I, 2009, pp. 12 ff.

111 Grigoleit/Tomasic, Entry 'Acquis Principles', in *Handwörterbuch des Europäischen Privatrechts*, Volume I, 2009, pp. 12 ff.; Twigg-Flesner, *GPR* 2011, 54, 58 f.

112 Grigoleit/Tomasic, Entry 'Acquis Principles', in *Handwörterbuch des Europäischen Privatrechts*, Volume I, 2009, pp. 12 ff.

113 Jansen/Zimmermann, *JZ* 2007, 1113, 1119 ff.; Grigoleit/Tomasic, Entry 'Acquis Principles', in *Handwörterbuch des Europäischen Privatrechts*, Volume I, 2009, p. 12.; on a positive note, however, Zoll, *GPR* 2008, 106, 110 ff.

114 Jansen/Zimmermann, *JZ* 2007, 1113, 1121.

115 Grigoleit/Tomasic, Entry 'Acquis Principles', in *Handwörterbuch des Europäischen Privatrechts*, Volume I, 2009, p. 12 ff.; Jansen/Zimmermann, *JZ* 2007, 1113, 1126; from an empirical point of view also Micklitz, *GPR* 2009, 254, 255.

116 See paras. 120–129 above.

117 CJEU, Opinion of AG Poiares Maduro of 21 November 2007, Case C-412/06, *Hamilton*, ECLI:EU:C:2007:695, para. 24 with note 8 (limitation period as a generally accepted legal

Group members were probably perceived less as the group's work and more as monographs.[118]

## V. COMMON CORE OF EUROPEAN PRIVATE LAW (TRENTO GROUP)

References: J. Cartwright, 'The Common Core of European Private Law', *ZEuP* 1999, 989; F. Fiorentini, 'A Report on the 2001 and 2002 "Common Core of European Private Law" Meetings', *ZEuP* 2003, 444; R. Sacco, Legal Formants: A Dynamic Approach to Comparative Law, The American Journal of Comparative Law, Vol. 39 (Cheltenham: Edward Elgar Publishing, 1991), 1 and 343.

### 1. THE TRENTO GROUP

**194.** The Trento Group, named after its place of foundation, was founded in 1993 by the Italian law professors Mauro Bussani and Ugo Mattei.[119] Like the Acquis Group, it did not plan to create new law but rather to create a basic set of common legal principles from the legal systems of the EC Member States.[120] The group is not pursuing a legal policy objective.[121] The aim is to create the grounds for the development of a uniform European civil law based on a common European legal culture.[122]

**195.** Therefore, the Trento Group sees itself primarily as an academic working group that enables and promotes basic research in comparative law within a rather broad framework. The group has successfully produced a whole series of works on diverse topics.[123]

---

principle); CJEU, Opinion of AG Trstenjak *of* 18 February 2009, Case C-489/07, *Messner/Krüger*, ECLI:EU:C:2009:98, para. 85 (value replacement in case of withdrawal).

118 This seems to be the departing point for Schulze/Ebers/Grigoleit (eds.), n. 101 above.

119 Wurmnest, *ZEuP* 2003, 714, 716; Fiorentini, *ZEuP* 2003, 444; Cartwright, *ZEuP* 1999, 989; Olzen, in Staudinger, *BGB Kommentar* (2024), Einleitung zum Schuldrecht, para. 300.

120 Cf. Olzen, in Staudinger, *BGB Kommentar* (2024), Einleitung zum Schuldrecht, para. 300.

121 Wurmnest, *ZEuP* 2003, 714, 716; Fiorentini, *ZEuP* 2003, 444 f.

122 Wurmnest, *ZEuP* 2003, 714, 716; Olzen, in Staudinger, *BGB Kommentar* (2024), Einleitung zum Schuldrecht, para. 300.

123 R. Zimmermann/S. Whittaker (eds.), *Good Faith in European Contract Law* (Cambridge: Cambridge University Press, 2000); J. Gordley (ed.) *The Enforceability of Promises in European Contract Law* (Cambridge: Cambridge University Press, 2001); M. Bussani/V.V. Palmer (eds.), *Pure Economic Loss in Europe* (Cambridge: Cambridge University Press, 2003).

### 2. MODE OF OPERATION

**196.** The Trento Group is committed to the comparative law tradition of the so-called Cornell Project by Rudolf Schlesinger and Rodolfo Sacco.[124] This approach is based on the idea that a legal system is not only characterised by positive law but by many sources, the so-called legal formants.[125] These are 'any legal proposition that affects the solution of a legal problem'.[126] In principle, at least from a comparative law perspective, these legal formants are not ranked. This explains the research objective of the Trento Group, which is to establish common legal principles based on a comparative analysis of hypothetical cases.[127] The procedure consists of two stages: First, using a questionnaire, country rapporteurs solve these cases based on their legal system; then, they classify and explain this solution further.[128] Second, these solutions are brought together and condensed in order to identify any common denominators.[129]

### 3. SIGNIFICANCE AND RECEPTION

**197.** Given that the Trento project, unlike the working groups discussed so far, does not pursue the goal of drafting regulatory proposals, it is not easy to assess its relevance for the development of European contract law. The comparative law approach is undoubtedly most welcome; also, the long-term goal of convergence through the identification of commonalities is, in principle, preferable to hasty rulemaking. However, it is difficult to assess the research results produced by the Trento Group as a whole; in the end, one is limited to look at individual works.[130]

## VI. THE EUROPEAN LAW INSTITUTE (ELI)

<u>References:</u> F. Graf von Westphalen, 'European Law Institute – dem amerikanischen Beispiel verpflichtet', *ZIP* 2011, 1555; I. Griss, 'Das European Law Institute – eine gemeinsame Initiative', *ZEuP* 2011, 231; I. Griss/R. Zimmermann,' Towards a European Law Institute: A Joint Initiative', *ZEuP* 2011, 432; 'Vienna Memorandum', ZEuP 2011,

124 Cf. the seminal work by R.B. Schlesinger, *Formation of Contracts: A Study of the Common Core of Legal Systems*, Volume I, (Dobbs Ferry (NY): Oceana, 1968).

125 Sacco, *Am.J.Comp.L.*, 39 (1991), 1, 21 ff.

126 Mattei, *Comparative Law and Economics*, 1997, p. 104.

127 Wurmnest, ZEuP 2003, 714, 717; Metzger, *Extra legem, intra ius: Allgemeine Rechtsgrundsätze im Europäischen Privatrecht*, 2009, p. 234.

128 Wurmnest, *ZEuP* 2003, 714, 717; Fiorentini, *ZEuP* 2003, 445.

129 Wurmnest, *ZEuP* 2003, 714, 717.

130 In that sense also Wurmnest, *ZEuP* 2003, 714, 717.

433; H. Wicke, 'Das European Law Institute – Institution zur Qualitätsverbesserung europäischen Rechts', *DNotZ* 2011, 803; R. Zimmerman, 'Challenges for the European Law Institute', (2012) 16 *Edinburgh L. Rev.* 5, 5.

**198.** The European Law Institute (ELI) was founded in Vienna on 1 June 2011.[131] It is an economically and politically independent non-profit organisation[132] which joins other initiatives and working groups but does not replace them.[133] It is intended to provide an umbrella for research initiatives and projects dealing with European law as well as a discussion forum. At the same time, it aims to assist the EU institutions, in particular during legislative processes.[134] Science and practice are to be involved equally.[135] As the name already shows, the American Law Institute has a model function, despite all the differences.[136]

**199.** In the area of European contract law, the ELI working group on the proposal for a Common European Sales Law (CESL), which the EU Commission presented on 10 November 2011, should also be mentioned.[137] An ELI Opinion on that proposal was already published in September 2012.[138] Its importance is illustrated by the fact that the draft report of the Legal Affairs Committee of the European Parliament (JURI) of 18 February 2013 took up many of the ELI's suggestions. Subsequently, the ELI working group published a first supplement to the Opinion in 2014,[139] which essentially deals with a possible imitation of the CESL contract to distance contracts and legal aspects on cloud computing and digital content. Following the Commission's announcement that it would no longer pursue the project of a Common European Sales Law, the ELI working group presented detailed proposals for a general concept for a new legislative draft in a second supplement to the Opinion.[140]

---

131 Looschelders, in Staudinger, *BGB Kommentar* (2024), Einleitung IPR, para. 436.

132 See Article 2 of the ELI's Articles of Association. The ELI is established as an international non-profit association (Association internationale sans but lucratif, AISBL) under Belgian law, see Article 1(2) of the Articles of Association.

133 Vienna Memorandum, *ZEuP* 2011, 433 (point III); see also Wicke, *DNotZ* 2011, 803, 804 ff.

134 Vienna Memorandum, *ZEuP* 2011, 433 (point I) and Article 3 of the ELI Articles of Association.

135 Wicke, *DNotZ* 2011, 803, 806.

136 Looschelders, in Staudinger, *BGB Kommentar* (2024), Einleitung IPR, para. 436; Wicke, *DNotZ* 2011, 803; Schmidt-Kessel/Meyer, *GPR* 2011, 320.

137 COM(2011) 635, see paras. 130–147 above.

138 Available at https://www.europeanlawinstitute.eu/fileadmin/user_upload/p_eli/Publications/S-2-2012_Statement_on_the_Proposal_for_a_Regulation_on__a_Common_European_Sales_Law.pdf.

139 Available at https://www.europeanlawinstitute.eu/fileadmin/user_upload/p_eli/Publications/CESL_1st_Supplement.pdf.

140 Available at https://www.europeanlawinstitute.eu/fileadmin/user_upload/p_eli/Publications/Unlocking_the_Digital_Single_Market.pdf.

**200.** A follow-up project dealt with the Commission's proposal for a directive on certain aspects of contract law relating to the provision of digital content of 9 December 2015;[141] here, too, an extensive Opinion followed promptly.[142]

**201.** An ongoing project is dedicated to the platform economy. The goal is to create model rules for online intermediary platforms.[143] Another project deals with the topic of 'Blockchain Technology and Smart Contracts'.[144]

## VII. THE PROJET DE CODE EUROPÉEN DES AFFAIRES

References: L. d'Avout, 'Das erstaunliche Projekt eines europäischen Wirtschaftsgesetzbuches', *ZEuP* 2019, 653; P. Dupichot, 'Vom Brexit zum Europäischen Wirtschaftsgesetzbuch', *ZEuP* 2017, 245; M. Lehmann, 'Braucht Europa ein Handelsgesetzbuch?', *ZHR* 181 (2017), 9; M. Lehmann, 'Das Europäische Wirtschaftsgesetzbuch - Eine Projektskizze', *GPR* 2017, 262; M. Lehmann, 'Editorial - Der Aachener Vertrag - "Peu d'ambitions" oder Anbruch einer neuen Epoche deutsch-französischer Zusammenarbeit?', *GPR* 2019, 49; M. Lehmann, 'EU Law-Making 2.0: The Prospect of a European Business Code', *ERPL* 2020, 73; M. Lehmann/J. Schmidt/R. Schulze, 'Das Projekt eines Europäischen Wirtschaftsgesetzbuchs', *ZRP* 2017, 225; S. Özfirat, 'Großer Wurf statt schleichender Optimierung im Detail - Für ein Europäisches Wirtschaftsgesetzbuch', *NJOZ* 2019, 689; K. Riesenhuber, 'Und jetzt ein Europäisches Wirtschaftsgesetzbuch?', *GPR* 2017, 270; J. Schmidt, 'Ein Europäisches Wirtschaftsgesetzbuch?!', *GmbHR* 2016, R369; K. Scholl, 'Der Vertrag von Aachen - auf dem Weg zu einem Europäischen Wirtschaftsgesetzbuch?', *ZEuP* 2019, 441.

**202.** Since 2017, the Fondation pour le droit continental has been working together with the Association Henri Capitant to draft a European Business Code ('*Code européen des affaires*').[145] Shortly before, the Association Henri Capitant had presented an 'inventory',[146] which outlined the European acquis in commercial and economic law.[147] On these grounds, a group of lawyers, mainly

141 COM(2015) 634 final; see paras. 942–988 below for more details.

142 Available at https://www.europeanlawinstitute.eu/fileadmin/user_upload/p_eli/Publications/ELI_Statement_on_DCD.pdf.

143 On this, C. Busch, in U. Blaurock/M. Schmidt-Kessel/K. Erler (eds.), *Plattformen: Geschäftsmodell und Verträge* (Baden-Baden: Nomos, 2018), p. 38; Busch/Dannemann/Schulte-Nölke/Wiewiórowska-Domagalska/Zoll, *EuCML* 2020, 61. On the Platform Regulation, see paras. 989–996 below.

144 See https://www.europeanlawinstitute.eu/projects-publications/current-projects-feasibility-studies-and-other-activities/current-projects/blockchains.

145 See http://www.codeeuropeendesaffaires.eu. It should be noted here that the author is actively involved in the project as co-rapporteur of the Voies d'exécution working group.

146 Association Henri Capitant, La construction européenne en droit des affaires: Acquis et perspectives (Issy-les-Moulineaux: LGDJ, 2016).

147 On this point, Lehmann/Schmidt/Schulze, *ZRP* 2017, 225, 228; Lehmann, *GPR* 2017, 262, 265; Dupichot, *ZEuP* 2017, 245 246.

from France and Germany, attempted to summarise and organise the current economic law of the EU.[148] With the UK being on the eve of Brexit, this was at least partly intended to serve as a signal in favour of the cohesion of the EU-27. At the same time, it was hoped to promote the internal market.[149]

**203.** The project was partly financed by the French state[150] and by private donations.[151] Funding by the EU Commission was deliberately not sought to preserve greater freedom with regard to the project's content.[152] The spokespersons are the law professors Philippe Dupichot (Paris) and Matthias Lehmann (Vienna).

**204.** So far, twelve working groups have been constituted: Market law (competition and distribution law), e-commerce law, company law, credit securities, enforcement law, insolvency law, banking law, capital market law, insurance law, intellectual property law, labour law and tax law.[153] The starting point is primarily the acquis, which is to be ordered, consolidated and, if necessary, simplified.[154] A style change is encouraged where possible: Rules ought to be formulated less bureaucratically in order to achieve greater comprehensibility, acceptance and enforcement in practice.[155] An introductory chapter will define basic terms.[156] The sub-area of e-commerce is at least related to contract law. The commercial contract was deliberately omitted to avoid any reminiscences of the failed CESL.[157]

**205.** The European Commission has welcomed the initiative and highlighted the possibility of a Business Law Code[158] in its White Paper on the Future of Europe of 1 March 2017.[159] The project is also mentioned in the Treaty

---

148 Lehmann, *GPR* 2017, 262, 265 f.

149 Riesenhuber, *GPR* 2017, 270, 271. Critical of the d'Avout project, *ZEuP* 2019, 653, 656 ff. (dubbing it as 'dangerous' and 'unrealisable').

150 Lehmann, *GPR* 2017, 262, 265; Dupichot, *ZEuP* 2017, 245, 249.

151 Paul Bayzelon, an entrepreneur and former advisor to the French Minister of Economy Edmond Alphandéry, should be mentioned here in particular, see Lehmann, *GPR* 2017, 262, 264.

152 Lehmann, *GPR* 2017, 262, 267.

153 Lehmann, *GPR* 2017, 262, 266.

154 Lehmann, *GPR* 2017, 262, 266; Lehmann/Schmidt/Schulze, *ZRP* 2017, 225, 228.

155 Lehmann, *GPR* 2017, 262, 266.

156 Lehmann, *GPR* 2017, 262, 266.

157 Lehmann, *GPR* 2017, 262, 268.

158 The White Paper states at p. 12 under the scenario 'Those who want more do more': 'A group of countries works together and agree on a common "Business Law Code" unifying corporate, commercial and related domains of law, helping businesses of all sizes to easily operate across borders.'

159 White Paper on the Future of Europe – Reflections and scenarios for the EU-27 by 2025, COM(2017) 2025.

of Aachen of 22 January 2019, the successor instrument to the 1963 Elysée Treaty.[160] The German Bundestag and the French *Assemblée nationale* signed a Franco-German parliamentary agreement on 25 March 2019, which seeks to adopt joint legislation in the field of commercial law to promote cross-border cooperation.[161] Whether political support beyond such declarations of intent can be realised, for example, within a future Franco-German economic area,[162] remains to be seen.[163]

## VIII. THE COMMENTARIES ON EUROPEAN CONTRACT LAWS

References: N. Jansen/R. Zimmermann (eds.), *Commentaries on European Contract Laws* (Oxford: Oxford University Press, 2018); N. Jansen, 'Commenting upon European Contract Law', *GPR* 2015, 2.

**206.** A binding legal code that covers all of European contract law is hardly to be expected at present. Instead, it is necessary to keep an eye on a multitude of reference texts that reflect the state of the legal field in different ways and with different authority; particularly after the failure of the CESL, European private law scholarship is once again thrown back to the often labour-intensive research into the genesis of pertinent legal texts.[164] This finding marks the starting point for the Commentaries on European Contract Laws.[165] They were created by a total of four editors and 18 contributors, most of them with current or former affiliations to the Max Planck Institute for Comparative and International Private Law in Hamburg. The Commentaries are intended to provide a genetical synopsis of the various textual stages of European contract law. They differ from the above-mentioned undertakings insofar as the working group does not have an 'official' name: Only the results count.

160 Scholl, *ZEuP* 2019, 441.

161 Article 14(1) of the parliamentary agreement reads: 'They further undertake to promote the development of cross-border cooperation by harmonising and simplifying the applicable law. If legal obstacles to the implementation of joint cross-border projects cannot be overcome by other means, the German Bundestag and the Assemblée nationale shall seek the adoption of legislation allowing derogations from national legal regulations.'

162 See, for example, the book authored by C. Lebrecht, *Richterliche Vertragsgerechtigkeitskontrolle im unternehmerischen Geschäftsverkehr* (Tübingen: Mohr Siebeck, 2020), p. 3, who takes the idea of a Franco-German economic area as a foil against which he develops uniform standards for contract and clause effectiveness review in Franco-German commercial transactions.

163 On this from the perspective of legal policy Scholl, *ZEuP* 2019, 441; Özfirat, *NJOZ* 2019, 689.

164 In addition, see paras. 328–343 and 1339–1366 below.

165 Jansen/Zimmermann (eds.), *Commentaries on European Contract Laws*, 2018.

**207.** The editors do not intend to comment on *one specific* legal act since such a codification does not exist in European contract law. Instead, the aim is to provide explanations of European legal texts. The work's title, a homage to Blackstone's Commentaries on the Laws of England,[166] reflects this approach.[167] The Principles of European Contract Law (PECL), one of the oldest relevant model codes, serve as main reference and starting point to the historical-genealogical text analysis, which namely Reinhard Zimmermann has promoted within the field of European private law.[168] While the PECL were almost exclusively compiled based on classical comparative law, the approach pursued in the Commentaries also includes the *acquis communautaire.*

**208.** This leads to a partial departure from the approach taken in the PECL. The editors' aim is to generate a synthesis regarding each of the PECL provisions that reflects the '"most appropriate" text in terms of the critical, historical, and comparative analysis'.[169] However, this does not amount to a claim to regulatory authority: 'We have not regarded it as our task to formulate our own rules, i.e. new texts, which we, for one reason or another, regard as desirable, but have limited ourselves to making a reasoned choice between the available texts, drafted by the various international working groups.'[170] What sounds like matter-of-factly work and purposeless academic rationality is, in fact, much more: If the Commentaries create a completely renewed version of the PECL that reflects the state of European contract law post-CESL, this can hardly be detached from the claim to present the most up-to-date and thoroughly researched reference text. Ultimately, the Commentaries add a new textual level to European contract law.[171] In this respect, the self-limitation formulated by the editors is perhaps overly modest.[172] The Commentaries will continue to retain their academic significance. In a certain sense, they are a placeholder for a discussion on the harmonisation of European contract law, which may one day re-emerge.

---

166 Jansen/Zimmermann, *Commentaries on European Contract Laws*, 2018, 'General Introduction', para. 30.

167 See already Jansen, *GPR* 2015, 2.

168 Zimmermann, *EuZW* 2009, 319, 322.

169 Jansen/Zimmermann, *Commentaries on European Contract Laws*, 2018, 'General Introduction', para. 33.

170 Jansen/Zimmermann, *Commentaries on European Contract Laws*, 2018, 'General Introduction', para. 34.

171 On this, with examples, Stürner, *GPR* 2018, 301.

172 This modesty may be related to the accusation made by the editors of the Commentaries more than ten years ago against the authors of the Acquis Principles, that under the flag of a mere restatement they were in fact introducing new model rules based on insufficiently disclosed political evaluations, see Jansen/Zimmermann, *JZ* 2007, 1113.

# §5. LEGAL SOURCES AND LEGAL BASES OF EUROPEAN INTERNAL MARKET LAW

## CONTENTS



References: J. Basedow, *EU Private Law. Anatomy of a Growing Legal Order* (Cambridge: Intersentia, 2021), p. 163; M. Franzen, *Privatrechtsangleichung durch die Europäische Gemeinschaft* (Berlin: De Gruyter, 1999); O. Remien, 'Europäisches Privatrecht als Verfassungsfrage', *EuR* 2005, 699; M. Stürner, 'Die Einwirkungen des EU-Primärrechts auf das nationale Privatrecht', *JURA* 2017, 26.

**209.** The following part deals with EU private law legislation, i.e. with the emergence of positive European private law.[1] In this respect, the principle of

[1] For a definition of the term cf. above paras. 12–17.

conferred powers is of central importance: The EU may only legislate to the extent that corresponding legislative powers have been conferred to it. Since there is no explicit jurisdictional provision for the area of private law, corresponding legal acts must be based on other heads of competence.

# I. LEGAL SOURCES

## 1. PRIMARY LAW

**210.** From a functional point of view, EU primary law – in particular, the TEU, the TFEU and the Charter of Fundamental Rights – is essentially constitutional law, meaning it regulates the organisation and structure of the Union.[2] It also contains legislative powers for the area of private law. However, there are also other reasons why primary law is relevant concerning private law: On the one hand, it directly contains provisions regulating legal relationships between private law subjects, such as the prohibition of cartels in Article 101 TFEU. On the other hand, the primacy of application of EU law influences national private law.[3]

## 2. SECONDARY LAW

**211.** The EU has at its disposal the legislative instruments regulated in Article 288 TFEU.[4] Rules based on these are referred to as secondary legislation since they are derived from legislative powers within the primary law.[5]

### *a) Regulation*

**212.** The Regulation has general application (Article 288(2) TFEU). It realises a harmonisation of the law without any leeway for the Member States. In the typical fields of private law, the legal instrument of regulation is used very little.[6] On the one hand, this is due to the principle of proportionality.[7] On the other hand, it is due to the fact that the harmonisation of laws by means of directives gives the Member States greater room for manoeuvre in

2 For example, C. Calliess, in C. Calliess/M. Ruffert, *EUV/AEUV*, 6th ed. (Munich: C.H. Beck, 2022,) Art. 1 TEU para. 64; R. Streinz, *Europarecht*, 12th ed. (Heidelberg: C.F. Müller, 2023), paras. 141 ff.

3 See Stürner, *JURA* 2017, 26.

4 In external relations, Article 216 TFEU applies.

5 M. Herdegen, *Europarecht*, 24th ed. (Munich: C.H. Beck, 2023), §8 para. 43.

6 Overview in Heiderhoff, *Europäisches Privatrecht*, pp. 311 ff.

7 In addition, see para. 229 below.

order to coherently embed EU law within their national private law systems.[8] Important private law regulations exist in the area of air traffic, where the Air Passenger Rights Regulation[9] provides, among other things, a right to compensation in the case of overbooking and delay, or regarding cross-border payments in Euros.[10] Also, in the area of company law, new legal persons such as the EEIG or the European Company were created through regulation law. Finally, regulations are of particular importance in private international law and procedural law, including mutual legal assistance, where a whole series of legal acts have been adopted based on Article 81 TFEU.[11] These regulations can be mandatory insofar as they are always applied if the respective conditions are met. For example, the liability regime of the Air Passenger Rights Regulation is not at the parties' disposal. Other regulations are optional, meaning that their application depends on a corresponding act of will by the parties. This can amount to a bilateral consensus, as in the case of the CESL proposal,[12] or a unilateral option, as in the case of several regulations on (international) procedural law.[13]

### b) *Directive*

**213.** The directive is the main legislative instrument in the field of private law.[14] It aims to approximate the Member States' laws; a national act of implementation is always required. The directive formulates binding objectives but leaves it to the Member States how to achieve them (Article 288(3) TFEU). Thus, the directive's requirements can be fulfilled, for example, by either integrating them into an existing codification or by adopting a special act. Directives can follow the principle of minimum harmonisation by setting only a minimum standard that the Member States can exceed within their transposition laws, or they can harmonise the law fully, where this is not possible.[15]

---

8 Cf. Heiderhoff, *Europäisches Privatrecht*, para. 11.

9 Regulation (EC) no 261/2004 of the European Parliament and of the Council of 11 February 2004 establishing common rules on compensation and assistance to passengers in the event of denied boarding and of cancellation or long delay of flights, and repealing Regulation (EEC) no 295/91, OJ 2004 L 46/1. The legal basis is Article 100(2) TFEU (ex Article 80(2) EC).

10 Regulation (EC) no 2560/2001 of the European Parliament and of the Council of 19 December 2001 on cross-border payments in euro, OJ 2001 L 344/13.

11 On this point, Stürner, *JURA* 2015, 813.

12 For more details, see paras. 130–147 above.

13 Examples are the European Enforcement Order Regulation, the European Order for Payment Regulation or the European Small Claims Regulation.

14 Overview in Heiderhoff, *Europäisches Privatrecht*, pp. 311 ff.

15 Heiderhoff, *Europäisches Privatrecht*, paras. 21 ff. A mixed form is the so-called targeted full harmonisation, in which the level of harmonisation is allowed to be exceeded with regard to individual areas. Cf. already at paras. 74–84 above.

### c) *Decision*

**214.** The decision (Article 288(4) TFEU) of an EU institution regulates individual cases in a binding manner. It represents a vital instrument in commercial law, for example, in antitrust law or merger control; it is not used to regulate private law in general.[16]

### d) *Recommendation and Opinion*

**215.** Recommendations and Opinions are non-binding legal acts (Article 288(5) TFEU). They are usually not used in the private law area.[17]

## 3. GENERAL PRINCIPLES OF LAW

**216.** In addition to these formal sources of law, the existence of general principles of EU law is recognised.[18] Due to the fragmentary character of the EU's legal system (which is caused by the principle of limited conferral, see below), legal acts cannot achieve comprehensive, horizontal harmonisation. Therefore, the CJEU sometimes also draws on the Member States' legal systems to fill gaps with generally accepted principles.[19] The result can be an unwritten legal principle of EU law. Thus, even before the Charter of Fundamental Rights and the relevant provision of Article 21 CFR came into force, the CJEU derived, for example, an unwritten principle of the prohibition of age discrimination from primary law.[20] The prohibition of an abuse of rights also belongs to the general legal principles of EU law.[21] Principles relating to contract law will be discussed in greater detail later.[22]

---

16 Langenbucher/Donath, in Langenbucher, *Europäisches Privat- und Wirtschaftsrecht*, §1 para. 57.

17 Langenbucher/Donath, in Langenbucher, *Europäisches Privat- und Wirtschaftsrecht*, §1 para. 57.

18 R. Streinz, *Europarecht*, 12th ed. (Heidelberg: C.F. Müller, 2023), para. 456; M. Haag/M. Kotzur, in R. Bieber/A. Epiney/M. Haag/M. Kotzur, *Die Europäische Union*, 13th ed. (Baden-Baden/Basel: Nomos Helbing Lichtenhahn, 2019), §6 para. 16; M. Herdegen, *Europarecht*, 24th ed. (Munich: C.H. Beck, 2023), §8 para. 15; W. Schroeder, in R. Streinz, *EUV/AEUV*, 3rd ed. (Munich: C.H. Beck, 2018), Article 288 TFEU para. 18; C. Calliess, in C. Calliess/M. Ruffert, *EUV/AEUV*, 6th ed. (Munich: C.H. Beck, 2022,) Art. 1 TFEU para. 10. On the unclear methodological basis of the emergence of such principles C. Mak, *ERPL* 2012, 323.

19 On historical parallels Knütel, *JuS* 1996, 768.

20 CJEU, 22 November 2005, Case C-144/04, *Mangold*, ECLI:EU:C:2005:709; see paras. 244–303 below.

21 See for instance CJEU, 6 February 2018, Case C-359/16, *Altun*, ECLI:EU:C:2018:63, para. 49.

22 See below paras. 456–459.

# II. FUNDAMENTAL LEGAL ASPECTS

References: C.M. Bron, *Rechtsangleichung des Privatrechts auf Ebene der Europäischen Union* (Baden-Baden: Nomos, 2011), M. Schmidt-Kessel, 'Binnenmarkt im Gleichgewicht – Folgen der Akzentverschiebung für den Verbraucherschutz', in *Festschrift für Müller-Graff* (Baden-Baden: Nomos, 2015), p. 163; S. Weatherill, *Contract Law of the Internal Market* (Cambridge: Intersentia, 2016), Ch. 3 and 5.

## 1. COMPETENCES

### *a) Principle of Conferral*

**217.** According to Article 5(2) TEU, the European Union is not automatically competent to legislate, but only if provisions of primary law authorise it explicitly. This is known as the principle of limited conferral:[23] Given that the EU is a supranational organisation, sovereignty from the Member States may only be transferred to a precisely defined extent.[24] Several previously unwritten jurisdictional powers, which have been developed in the jurisdiction of the CJEU according to the doctrine of implied powers under public international law,[25] are now laid down in Articles 3(2), 216 TFEU.

**218.** The legislative powers of the EU are, in principle, shared with the Member States (Article 4(1) TFEU):[26] The Member States are competent until the EU takes action; from that point on, the legislative power is passed on to the EU (Article 2(2) TFEU). In the area of private law[27] there are (shared) competences for consumer protection (Article 169 in conjunction with Article 114 TFEU), to a limited extent for labour law (Article 153 TFEU), company law (Article 50(2)(g) TFEU[28]) and private international law and procedural law (Article 81 TFEU). The competence of Article 19 TFEU, on which various directives in civil and

---

23 Cf. R. Streinz, *Europarecht*, 12th ed. (Heidelberg: C.F. Müller, 2023), para. 544.

24 Cf. C. Calliess, in C. Calliess/M. Ruffert, *EUV/AEUV*, 6th ed. (Munich: C.H. Beck, 2022,) Art. 1 TEU para. 68.

25 *CJEU*, 31 March 1971, Case 22/70, *AETR*, ECLI:EU:C:1971:32, paras. 15/19 ff.; CJEU, 14 July 1976, 3, Cases 4 and 6/76, *Kramer*, ECLI:EU:C:1976:114, paras. 30–31.

26 The EU has exclusive competence, for example, to lay down the competition rules necessary for the functioning of the internal market (Article 3(1)(b) TFEU).

27 See Heiderhoff, *Europäisches Privatrecht*, paras. 13 ff. and – with a focus on contract law – Riesenhuber, *EU-Vertragsrecht*, 2013, §3.

28 Overview of the directives adopted on this basis in P.-C. Müller-Graff, in R. Streinz, *EUV/AEUV*, 3rd ed. (Munich: C.H. Beck, 2018), Art. 50 TFEU para. 18.

labour law on equal treatment were based, is also indirectly relevant to private law.[29]

**219.** Finally, the so-called flexibility clause in Article 352 TFEU was occasionally used to create new forms of private law, such as the European Economic Interest Grouping (EEIG),[30] the European Company (EC)[31] or the Community Trademark.[32] This jurisdictional provision, which certainly challenges the principle of limited conferral because of its extensive scope of application, requires unanimity in the Council. However, in a strict sense, the legal acts based on Article 352 TFEU were not harmonisation measures but the introduction of new legal forms.[33] This was particularly important with regard to the proposal for a Common European Sales Law (CESL).[34]

### *b) The General Competence from Article 114 TFEU*

#### aa) History

**220.** The final title of competence for the internal market was introduced by the Single European Act in 1986:[35] Legal acts can be adopted if they pursue the objectives set out in Article 26(1) TFEU, i.e. if they aim to realise the internal market or ensure its functioning. It is not always easy to judge ex-ante when a legal provision can bring about the necessary facilitation of intra-European trade. The Commission tends towards a broad interpretation, according to which the mere harmonisation of the Member States' law is sufficient to meet this requirement.[36] In favour of this, it can be argued that, under Article 114(1) TFEU, the harmonisation of laws as such already has the functioning of the internal market as 'its objective'.[37] However, if the internal market clause does intend uncurbed legislative powers, which seems evident in light of the principle of limited conferral, legislation must go beyond mere approximation; it must

---

29 On this cf. R. Streinz, in R. Streinz, *Europarecht*, 12th ed. (Heidelberg: C.F. Müller, 2023), Art. 19 TFEU para. 24.

30 Council Regulation (EEC) no 2137/85 of 25 July 1985 on the European Economic Interest Grouping (EEIG), OJ 1985 L 199/1.

31 Council Regulation (EC) no 2157/2001 of 8 October 2001 on the Statute for a European company (EC), OJ 2001 L 294/1.

32 Council Regulation (EC) no 207/2009 of 26 February 2009 on the Community trade mark, OJ 2009 L 78/1.

33 In this regard, M. Rossi, in C. Calliess/M. Ruffert, *EUV/AEUV*, 6th ed. (Munich: C.H. Beck, 2022,) Art. 352 TFEU paras. 58 ff.

34 See paras. 133–147 above.

35 OJ 1986 L 169/7.

36 On preventive legal harmonisation Seidel, *EuR* 2006, 26.

37 Heiderhoff, *Europäisches Privatrecht*, para. 14.

pursue the objective of a noticeable improvement of the functioning of the internal market in a tangible and economic way.[38]

bb) The CJEU's Tobacco Cases

**221.** In the so-called tobacco cases, the CJEU specified the goal to improve the internal market to the effect that, from an objective point of view, an actual, recognisable elimination of trade barriers must be achieved. At the same time, the legal act must also aim to improve the conditions for the establishment and functioning of the internal market.[39] In the case concerning the annulment of the first Tobacco Products Directive, the legal problem was the admissibility of the ban on all forms of advertising and sponsorship in favour of regulated tobacco products therein.[40] The Commission had argued that the Member States' legal systems had, so far, differed in the intensity of the prohibition, which led to trade barriers for press products containing tobacco advertising. The CJEU, however, argued that a recognisable improvement of the internal market was necessary; this had to go beyond mere harmonisation, for example, by reducing trade barriers and competition distortions. In the case of the tobacco advertising ban, the focus was clearly on health protection, which could not be harmonised according to Article 152(4)(c) EC.

**222.** However, dismantling trade barriers does not have to be the sole objective of a directive. Thus, it could be considered irrelevant if the Tobacco Products Directive protected health, which, on a side note, also represents an objective of the Community in Article 152(1) EC.[41] Therefore, the ban on the sale of certain types of chewing tobacco was also considered unproblematic. In particular, the ban was not disproportionate, as the Community was granted a wide margin of discretion concerning health protection.[42] Regarding the revised Tobacco Products Directive, the CJEU also no longer saw any issues relating to the EC's legislative power:[43] In substance, a jurisdictional title under Article 114 TFEU always exists if the directive reacts to differences in the Member States' laws and realises a corresponding harmonisation of laws which, according

---

[38] With reference to the CJEU decision on the tobacco advertising ban: Heiderhoff, *Europäisches Privatrecht*, para. 15; cf. also Schröder, in R. Streinz, *EUV/AEUV*, 3rd ed. (Munich: C.H. Beck, 2018), Art. 114 TFEU para. 19.

[39] CJEU, *5 October 2000, Case C-376/98, Germany/Parliament and Council*, ECLI:EU:C:2000:544, para. 83 (tobacco advertising ban).

[40] CJEU, *5 October 2000, Case C-376/98, Germany/Parliament and Council*, ECLI:EU:C:2000:544, para. 83 (tobacco advertising ban).

[41] CJEU, 10 December 2002, Case C-491/01, *British American Tobacco*, ECLI:EU:C:2002:741.

[42] CJEU, 14 December 2004, Case C-210/03, *Swedish Match*, ECLI:EU:C:2004:802.

[43] CJEU, 12 December 2006, Case C-380/03, *Germany/Parliament and Council*, ECLI:EU:C:2006:772.

to the Commission's prerogative of assessment, is suitable to bring about an improvement of the internal market's functioning.

### c) *Concurrent Legislative Competence*

**223.** However, the internal market clause does not result in an exclusive legislative competence but only a concurrent one.[44] This is also sufficient to achieve Article 26 TFEU's objective since the EU has the prerogative to act: As soon as it takes legislative action, the corresponding legislative powers of the Member States expire; only then does the EU's competence become exclusive.

### d) *Competence for Consumer Law*

**224.** Article 169 TFEU provides a specific legislative competence for consumer law. According to para. 1, 'in order to promote the interests of consumers and to ensure a high level of consumer protection, the Union shall contribute to protecting the health, safety and economic interests of consumers, as well as to promoting their right to information, education and to organise themselves in order to safeguard their interests'. To achieve this, the EU adopts measures based on the internal market clause of Article 114 TFEU. This is widely perceived as a concurrent competence since the EU is only supposed to 'contribute' to consumer protection. Moreover, Article 169 TFEU does not create an independent competence but merely refers to the general internal market clause (Article 169(2)(a) TFEU).[45]

### e) *The Legislative Power to Regulate EU Contract Law*

**225.** While for many years, the introduction of a codification-like EU contract law was at least seen as a distant goal on the horizon of legal policy, this issue has been settled for the foreseeable future with the failure of a Common Frame of Reference.[46] Whether the EU might have the legislative powers to introduce such a legal act, in whatever form, has been discussed controversially.[47] Ultimately,

---

44 Cf. CJEU, 10 December 2002, Case C-491/01, *British American Tobacco*, ECLI:EU:C:2002:741; similarly CJEU, 14 December 2004, Case C-210/03, *Swedish Match*, ECLI:EU:C:2004:802.

45 B. Lurger, in R. Streinz, *EUV/AEUV*, 3rd ed. (Munich: C.H. Beck, 2018), Art. 169 TFEU para. 17; C. Stumpf, in J. Schwarze, *EU-Kommentar*, 4th ed. (Baden-Baden/Vienna/Basel: Nomos/Facultas/Helbing Lichtenhahn, 2019), Art. 169 TFEU para. 31; S. Krebber, in C. Calliess/M. Ruffert, *EUV/AEUV*, 6th ed. (Munich: C.H. Beck, 2022,) Art. 169 TFEU para. 10 with further references.

46 On this see already above paras. 120–129.

47 In favour of this Heiderhoff, *Europäisches Privatrecht*, para. 25 ff.; Basedow, *AcP* 200 (2000), 445, 474 ff., 482 ff.; *Sturm*, JZ 2001, 1097, 1102. With doubts: Bangemann, *ZEuP* 1994,

from the perspective of Article 114 TFEU, it depends on the extent to which such an instrument could promote the internal market. Prima facie, it would follow the logic of progressive integration that the efforts to harmonise laws would culminate in this project. It can be argued that only the possible improvement of the functioning of the internal market matters, which seems to follow from the explanatory memorandum of the Commission's proposal, and not empirical evidence.[48] However, even if the tobacco jurisdiction's criteria were fulfilled, the subsidiarity and proportionality limitations to the EU's legislative powers would need to be taken into account: it could certainly be argued that the functioning of cross-border private legal transactions has already been ensured through a uniform conflict-of-laws system as well as the harmonisation of international civil procedural law.[49]

**226.** It is highly controversial whether it might make a difference if EU contract law was realised as an optional instrument. After all, it could be argued that such a legislative project would not demonstrate the necessity of harmonising the Member States' legal systems. However, this could be countered by an *argumentum a fortiori*: If one takes the view that such a measure would, in principle, be covered by Article 114 TFEU, it would seem contradictory if the alternative of optional harmonisation, which intervenes less intensely in the legal systems of the Member States, was no longer covered by this legislative title. Moreover, an optional legal act would provide a uniform regulatory regime throughout the EU so that the harmonisation objective could ultimately be justified plausibly.

**227.** The CJEU's boundaries between the competencies of Article 114 and 352 TFEU appear to have greater impact overall.[50] If an optional legal act such as the proposal for a Common European Sales Law was regarded as a new legal instrument, then only Article 352 TFEU would be available; any recourse to Article 114 TFEU would be excluded, meaning that unanimity in the Council would be required.[51]

---

377, 378; C. Schmid, *JZ* 2001, 674, 676 ff. In contrast Ernst, *AcP* 208 (2008), 248, 251, 259; Eidenmüller/Faust/Grigoleit/Jansen/Wagner/Zimmermann, *JZ* 2008, 529, 530 (who describe the rejectionist attitude as far predominant). See also Ludwigs, *EuR* 2006, 370; summarising Schmidt-Kessel, Entry 'Europäisches Zivilgesetzbuch', in *Handwörterbuch des Europäischen Privatrechts*, Volume I, 2009, p. 554.

48 In that sense Heiderhoff, *Europäisches Privatrecht*, para. 26.

49 Cf. Herresthal, in Langenbucher, *Europäisches Privat- und Wirtschaftsrecht*, §2 para. 20 with further references.

50 See para. 134 above.

51 For example, Riesenhuber, *EU-Vertragsrecht*, 2013, §3, para. 42. See paras. 148–152 above.

## 2. RESTRICTING LEGISLATIVE POWERS: SUBSIDIARITY AND PROPORTIONALITY

### a) *Subsidiarity, Article 5(3) TEU*

References: M. Lehmann, 'Subsidiariätsprinzip und Europäisches Privatrecht', in *Festschrift für Müller-Graff* (Baden-Baden: Nomos, 2015), p. 91.

**228.** If the EU has legislative powers, it may nevertheless, due to the principle of subsidiarity, only legislate insofar as the individual Member States cannot sufficiently promote the objectives to be achieved, and therefore, EU-wide regulation becomes necessary.[52] Two criteria have emerged: On the one hand, it must be established that the Member States were unable to promote this objective sufficiently (test of comparative efficiency).[53] On the other hand, its realisation must be more successful at the Union level.[54] The EU institutions have a certain margin of discretion here.[55] Particularly with regard to Article 114 TFEU, it should be clear from the outset that the realisation of the internal market can be better achieved at the EU level.[56] However, the specific legislative act has to be considered individually; no general rules exist.[57] For example, criticism of the subsidiarity principle has been levelled against the CESL proposal.[58] However, it is difficult to justify to what extent the Member States would be able to introduce a uniform, optional sales law valid within the internal market.[59] If, on the other hand, one broadens the focus and asks about the necessity of a uniform private law system for the functioning of an integrated market, numerous counter-examples, both from a historical and a comparative perspective, will come to mind.[60] In this respect, the subsidiarity clause would definitely be affected.

---

52 With reference to private law Lehmann, in *Festschrift für Müller-Graff*, 2015, p. 91.

53 C. Calliess, in C. Calliess/M. Ruffert, *EUV/AEUV*, 6th ed. (Munich: C.H. Beck, 2022,) Art. 5 TEU para. 33.

54 Cf. R. Bieber/M. Kotzur, in R. Bieber/A. Epiney/M. Haag/M. Kotzur, *Die Europäische Union*, 13th ed. (Baden-Baden/Basel: Nomos Helbing Lichtenhahn, 2019), §3 para. 31; in detail Calliess, in C. Calliess/M. Ruffert, *EUV/AEUV*, 6th ed. (Munich: C.H. Beck, 2022,) Art. 5 TEU paras. 30 ff.

55 Cf. R. Bieber/M. Kotzur, in R. Bieber/A. Epiney/M. Haag/M. Kotzur, *Die Europäische Union*, 13th ed. (Baden-Baden/Basel: Nomos Helbing Lichtenhahn, 2019), §3 para. 32.

56 On the validity of the subsidiarity principle in the context of Article 114 TFEU Heiderhoff, *Europäisches Privatrecht*, para. 19.

57 Lehmann, in *Festschrift für Müller-Graff*, 2015, pp. 91, 95 ff.

58 Riesenhuber, *EWS* 2012, 7; Suhr, in *Festschrift für Rüßmann* (Saarbrücken: JURIS, 2013), p. 1053; different opinion for instance Łętowska, **euvr 2013, 28, 30**. On 1 December 2011, the German Bundestag raised a subsidiarity complaint against the draft CESL Regulation. See para. 134 above.

59 Therefore, according to Heiderhoff, *Europäisches Privatrecht*, para. 27, the subsidiarity principle was not affected here.

60 Lehmann, in *Festschrift für Müller-Graff*, 2015, pp. 91, 95 ff.

### b) *Proportionality, Article 5(4) TEU*

References: J. Saurer, 'Der kompetenzrechtliche Verhältnismäßigkeitsgrundsatz im Recht der Europäischen Union', *JZ* 2014, 281.

**229.** In addition to subsidiarity, the principle of proportionality must be observed whenever the EU exercises its legislative powers.[61] Hereafter, legislation must be shaped in a way so that the intervention with the least intensity is always chosen. In practice, this can mean that, in order to improve the internal market, the legal form of a directive must be selected instead of a regulation:[62] While the latter is directly and immediately applicable in all Member States according to Article 288(2) TFEU, the former comes with a margin of implementation (Article 288(3) TFEU). Compliance with the principle of proportionality is fully justiciable;[63] however, the EU has vast political discretion. Therefore, the CJEU's scrutiny is restricted to obvious violations.[64]

## 3. LIMITATIONS ON COMPETENCE STEMMING FROM FUNDAMENTAL FREEDOMS

References: C. Herresthal, 'Die Ablehnung einer primärrechtlichen Perpetuierung des sekundärrechtlichen Verbraucherschutzniveaus', *EuZW* 2011, 328.

**230.** It is sometimes assumed that the level of protection achieved in the consumer acquis is enshrined in primary law, which, therefore, would limit future legal acts.[65] However, this cannot be assumed.[66] From the primary law's point of view, the EU would not be prevented from creating, for example, an optional sales law that does not achieve the previous acquis' level of consumer protection. However, the EU's objective of ensuring a high level of consumer protection (Articles 114(3), 169(1) TFEU as well as Article 38 CFR) speaks in favour of a non-disposable core area to which, for example, the right of withdrawal in distance contracts should belong. However, there would be no proviso concerning a selective reduction. For example, the buyer's right to

---

61 Saurer, *JZ* 2014, 281.

62 On the 'hierarchy of means' C. Calliess, in C. Calliess/M. Ruffert, *EUV/AEUV*, 6th ed. (Munich: C.H. Beck, 2022,) Art. 5 TEU para. 53.

63 Cf. R. Streinz, in R. Streinz, *Europarecht*, 12th ed. (Heidelberg: C.F. Müller, 2023), Art. 5 EUV para. 50 with further references.

64 See, for example, CJEU, 13 May 1997, Case C-233/94, *Germany/Parliament and Council*, ECLI:EU:C:1997:231, para. 56 (on the Deposit Guarantee Directive); CJEU, 12 November 1996, Case C-84/94, *United Kingdom/Council*, ECLI:EU:C:1996:431, para. 57 (on the Working Time Directive).

65 For example Reich, *ZEuP* 1994, 381, 394; *Tamm*, EuZW 2007, 756, 758.

66 In this regard, Herresthal, *EuZW* 2011, 328, 329 ff.

choose between subsequent delivery and repair (Article 13(2) of the Sale of Goods Directive) could, in the future, also be transferred to the seller.[67]

## III. AREAS COVERED

### 1. LAW OF CONTRACTUAL OBLIGATIONS

**231.** In the core area of private law – the law of obligations – three central directives have existed for some time now: The Consumer Rights Directive,[68] the Consumer Sales Directive[69] and the Unfair Terms Directive.[70] These are joined by the new Digital Content and Services Directive[71] and the reformed Sale of Goods Directive,[72] which has replaced the Consumer Sales Directive. All these directives aim to promote the internal market by reducing competition distortions caused by differing legal provisions. They also aim to strengthen consumer confidence by harmonising legal standards. In some systems, the implementation of these directives has led to some fundamental innovations: For example, the Consumer Sales Directive provided the external impetus for the large-scale modernisation of the German law of obligations in 2001.

### 2. OTHER PRIVATE LAW AREAS WITH RELEVANCE FOR CONTRACT LAW

**232.** EU legislation has also created rules in many other areas of private law. In some cases, this has led to the introduction of new contract types, such as

---

67 This is advocated by G. Wagner, *ZEuP* 2007, 180, 202 ff. However, the draft of the CESL also left the consumer's right to choose, see Article 111(1) CESL.

68 Directive 2011/83/EU of the European Parliament and of the Council of 25 October 2011 on consumer rights etc., OJ 2011 L 304/64.

69 Directive 1999/44/EC of the European Parliament and of the Council of 25 May 1999 on certain aspects of the sale of consumer goods and associated guarantees, OJ 1999 L 171/12. For more details see below paras. 826–827.

70 Council Directive 93/13/EEC of 5 April 1993 on unfair terms in consumer contracts, OJ 1993 L 95/29. For more details see below paras. 626–632.

71 Directive (EU) 2019/770 of the European Parliament and of the Council of 20 May 2019 on certain aspects of contract law relating to the provision of digital content and digital services, OJ 2019 L 136/1. For more details see below paras. 942–988.

72 Directive (EU) 2019/771 of the European Parliament and of the Council of 20 May 2019 on certain aspects of the sale of goods under contract law, amending Regulation (EU) 2017/2394 and Directive 2009/22/EC and repealing Directive 1999/44/EC, OJ 2019 L 136/28. For more details see below paras. 826–827.

the timeshare[73] or package travel contract.[74] Elsewhere, EU directives, such as the Consumer Credit Directive[75] or the Payment Services Directive,[76] made modifications to existing types of contracts necessary.

**233.** An overview of adopted and planned legal acts can be found at the beginning of Part Two.[77]

---

73 Directive 2008/122/EC of the European Parliament and of the Council of 14 January 2009 on the protection of consumers in respect of certain aspects of timeshare, long-term holiday product, resale and exchange contracts, OJ 2009 L 33/10. For more details see paras. 1041–1049 below.

74 Council Directive of 13 June 1990 on package travel, package holidays and package tours (90/314/EEC), OJ 1990 L 158/59. It is replaced by Directive (EU) 2015/2302 of the European Parliament and of the Council of 25 November 2015 on package travel, package holidays and linked travel arrangements amending Regulation (EC) no 2006/2004 and Directive 2011/83/EU of the European Parliament and of the Council and repealing Council Directive 90/314/EEC, OJ 2015 L 326/1. For more details see paras. 1023–1040 below.

75 Directive 2008/48/EC of the European Parliament and of the Council of 23 April 2008 on credit agreements for consumers and repealing Council Directive 87/102/EEC, OJ 2008 L 133/66. For more details see below paras. 1004–1022.

76 Directive 2007/64/EC of the European Parliament and of the Council of 13 November 2007 on payment services in the internal market amending Directives 97/7/EC, 2002/65/EC, 2005/60/EC and 2006/48/EC and repealing Directive 97/5/EC, OJ 2007 L 319/1.

77 See below para. 401.

# CHAPTER 2

# EFFECTS OF EU LAW ON NATIONAL PRIVATE LAW

## §6. EU LAW AS A (SECOND) META-ORDER FOR NATIONAL CONTRACT LAW

CONTENTS

References: C. Busch, 'Europäischer Grundrechtsschutz im Privatrecht nach Lissabon: Die EU-Grundrechtecharta als neuer Prüfungsmaßstab für Umsetzungsgesetze', *DRiZ* 2010, 63; L. Gerken/V. Rieble/G.H. Roth/T. Stein/R. Streinz, *'Mangold' als ausbrechender Rechtsakt* (Munich: Sellier, 2009); O. Mörsdorf, 'Private enforcement im sekundären Unionsprivatrecht: (k)eine klare Sache?', *RabelsZ* 83 (2019), 797.

## I. SUPREMACY OF HIGHER-RANKING PROVISIONS

**234.** At least in systems that provide for formal supremacy of the constitution, private law, and thus also contract law, must fulfil the requirements of national constitutional law. For example, the German Federal Constitutional Court's case law on the interpretation of the German Civil Code is of utmost importance. This is a consequence of the German constitution's supremacy over all the other laws (Article 20(3) German Basic Law). The Constitution can thus be described as a meta-order for private law. However, EU law also enjoys primacy over the Member States' national laws. It thus acts as a second meta-order for national private law, which is why its requirements must be taken into account directly or indirectly during every application of the law.

# II. PRIMACY OF EUROPEAN UNION LAW

## 1. PRINCIPLE

**235.** It is undisputed that EU law takes precedence over national law. This was less evident during the time of the European Communities' foundation. Since the EEC was designed for lasting and progressive integration, the law created by the EEC Treaty was described by the CJEU as 'a new legal order of international law'[1] or 'law stemming from [...] an independent source of law'.[2] However, this supremacy can be formulated or accentuated differently depending on whether one takes the CJEU's perspective or that of national law, particularly that of the national constitutional courts.

### *a) The Perspective of EU Law*

**236.** In the landmark decision *Costa/E.N.E.L.*,[3] the CJEU clearly stated what is now generally accepted: Community law supersedes divergent or conflicting national law. This also includes any interpretation of EU law and even any further development of EU law by the CJEU. However, this does not result in the nullity of the respective national provisions but only in the primacy of application of EU law within its scope of application: For a purely national situation or a situation relating to a third country without any connection to the internal market, a provision contrary to EU law can continue to be applicable. This primacy of application also relates to the fundamental rights of the national legal systems; they do not occupy any unique position.

### *b) The Perspective of the Member States*

**237.** Some constitutional courts of the Member States see the latter differently. The German constitutional court initially doubted whether the European standard of protection of fundamental rights could be considered sufficient. Consequently, the court reserved the right to review EC legal acts regarding their compliance with domestic fundamental rights. In the 'Solange I Decision' of 29 May 1974, the court argued as follows:[4]

> 'As long as the integration process has not progressed so far that Community law receives a catalogue of fundamental rights decided on by a parliament and of settled

[1] CJEU, 5 February 1963, Case 26/62, *van Gend en Loos*, ECLI:EU:C:1963:1.

[2] CJEU, 15 July 1964, Case 6/64, *Costa/E.N.E.L.*, ECLI:EU:C:1964:66. Cf. also the German Constitutional Court, BVerfGE 22, 293, 296; BVerfGE 31, 145, 173 ff.

[3] CJEU, 15 July 1964, Case 6/64, *Costa/E.N.E.L.*, ECLI:EU:C:1964:66, settled jurisdiction.

[4] BVerfGE 37, 271, 285. Translations are courtesy of https://law.utexas.edu/.

> validity, which is adequate in comparison with the catalogue of fundamental rights contained in the [German] Basic Law, a reference by a court of the Federal Republic of Germany to the Federal Constitutional Court in judicial review proceedings, following the obtaining of a ruling of the European Court under Article 177 of the Treaty, is admissible and necessary if the German court regards the rule of Community law which is relevant to its decision as inapplicable in the interpretation given by the European Court, because and in so far as it conflicts with one of the fundamental rights of the Basic Law.'

**238.** More than ten years later, an opposite assessment was reached: In the 'Solange II Decision', the German Constitutional Court now held that the standard of protection had generally increased under CJEU's case law in such a way that intervention by the Federal Constitution Court was not necessary anymore. The decision of 22 October 1986 therefore stated:[5]

> 'As long as the European Communities, in particular European Court case law, generally ensure effective protection of fundamental rights as against the sovereign powers of the Communities which is to be regarded as substantially similar to the protection of fundamental rights required unconditionally by the Constitution, and in so far as they generally safeguard the essential content of fundamental rights, the Federal Constitutional Court will no longer exercise its jurisdiction to decide on the applicability of secondary Community legislation cited as the legal basis for any acts of German courts or authorities within the sovereign jurisdiction of the Federal Republic of Germany, and it will no longer review such legislation by the standard of the fundamental rights contained in the Basic Law; references to the Court under Article 100(1) Basic Law for those purpose are therefore inadmissible.'

**239.** In these and other decisions, the German Constitutional Court shaped the image of a 'cooperative relationship' between the two courts where the CJEU is responsible for the protection of fundamental rights in European cases and the Federal Constitutional Court in German cases.[6] Thus, prima facie, there seems to be little potential for conflict. However, several decisions show that the Federal Constitutional Court is quite prepared to defend the principle of democracy in particular, for example, in the Lisbon ruling;[7] however, in this decision, the German Basic Law's friendliness towards EU law was emphasised as well. The Federal Constitutional Court reiterated that it considers itself entitled to intervene where legislative powers are violated, i.e. where the EU leaves the framework of the sovereign state rights conferred

5 BVerfGE 73, 339, 387; confirmed in BVerfGE 89, 155, 174 f. (Maastricht) and BVerfGE 102, 147, 162 ff. (banana market regulation).

6 BVerfGE 89, 155, 175.

7 BVerfGE 123, 267.

to it under Article 23 German Basic Law. Such so-called *ultra vires* acts can be subjected to constitutional scrutiny.[8] But here, too, a pro-European view must be taken.[9] In the area of private law, this is unlikely to become relevant even once.[10] Even the 'formal transfer control' postulated by the Federal Constitutional Court, which led to the nullity of the law on the Agreement of 19 February 2013 on a Unified Patent Court,[11] is unlikely significantly affect the area of contract law.[12]

**240.** The same ultimately applies to the ruling on the European Central Bank (ECB) of 5 May 2020.[13] In this ruling, the Federal Constitutional Court held that the CJEU's judicial mandate arising from Article 19(1) TEU ends 'where an interpretation of the Treaties is no longer comprehensible and is therefore objectively arbitrary'. If the Court of Justice exceeds this limit, this decision 'lacks, at least for Germany, the minimum degree of democratic legitimacy required under Article 23(1) sentence 2, Article 20(1) and (2) and Article 79(3) of the Basic Law'.[14] Admittedly, it cannot be ruled out that a private law-related judgment might also be considered *ultra vires* in this sense. However, in a politically sensitive context such as the ECB's government bond purchase programme, the probability seems significantly higher than in the more technical and neutral area of private law.

## 2. APPLICATION OF NATIONAL LAW IN CONFORMITY WITH EU LAW

**241.** Keeping the supremacy of all directly applicable EU acts in mind, it still needs to be discussed what consequences contradictions between national law and not directly applicable EU law have. This area is particularly interesting with regard to private law, as this primarily concerns the relationship of EU directives to the Member States' private laws. Due to its considerable doctrinal and practical significance, this will be discussed later.[15]

---

8 BVerfGE 126, 286, 302 (Honeywell) with reference to previous case law.
9 BVerfGE 123, 267, 354; BVerfGE 126, 286, 303 ff.
10 On a possible example from the area of the Brussels I Regulation, Wudarski/Stürner, *IPRax* 2013, 278.
11 BVerfG EuZW 2020, 324.
12 See paras. 12–17 above.
13 BVerfG NJW 2020, 1647.
14 BVerfG NJW 2020, 1647.
15 See paras. 308–400 below.

# III. PRIMARY EUROPEAN UNION LAW AND NATIONAL LAW

References: A.S. Hartkamp, 'The Effect of the EC Treaty in Private Law: On Direct and Indirect Horizontal Effects of Primary Community Law', *ERPL* 2010, 527; A.S. Hartkamp, 'The General Principles of EU Law and Private Law', *RabelsZ* 75 (2011), 241; C. Herresthal, 'Grundrechtecharta und Privatrecht', *ZEuP* 2014, 238; T. Körber, *Grundfreiheiten und Privatrecht* (Tübingen: Mohr Siebeck, 2004); S. Leible/R. Domröse, 'Interpretation in Conformity with Primary Law', in K. Riesenhuber (ed.), *European Legal Methodology* (Cambridge: Intersentia, 2021), §8; S. Perner, *Grundfreiheiten, Grundrechte-Charta und Privatrecht* (Tübingen: Mohr Siebeck, 2013), pp. 84 ff.; M. Safjan/P. Mikłaszewicz, 'Horizontal Effect of the General Principles of EU Law in the Sphere of Private Law', *ERPL* 2010, 475; M. Stürner, 'Die Einwirkungen des EU-Primärrechts auf das nationale Privatrecht', *JURA* 2017, 26.

## 1. GENERAL PROHIBITION OF DISCRIMINATION

**242.** Private law provisions almost never tie rights or duties to nationality, which is why instances of a violation of the general prohibition of discrimination (Article 18 TFEU) can be found only very rarely. However, indirect violations also suffice: They occur when there is no direct link to nationality but to other characteristics, provided that they affect foreigners predominantly. This is usually the case if the criterion is habitual residence in one particular country, as foreigners will generally not have such residence in the respective state. Those rules violate the prohibition of discrimination. For example, the CJEU held that a provision of the German Code of Civil Procedure, according to which plaintiffs domiciled abroad had to provide security for litigation costs at the defendant's request, was contrary to the prohibition of discrimination in primary EU law.[16] Such provisions must be interpreted in conformity with primary law to the effect that 'domestic' is to be read as 'having a domicile in the EU'.

## 2. FUNDAMENTAL FREEDOMS AS PROHIBITIONS OF RESTRICTIONS

References: G.T. Davies, 'Freedom of Movement, Horizontal Effect, and Freedom of Contract', *ERPL* 2012, 805; L. Gerken/V. Rieble/G.H. Roth/T. Stein/R. Streinz,

[16] Sec. 110 Code of Civil Procedure (old version), see CJEU, 1 July 1993, Case C-20/92, *Hubbard*, ECLI:EU:C:1993:280. However, the prohibition of discrimination does not apply to third-country nationals; here, national procedural law may provide for the lodging of a security for procedural costs, see CJEU, 7 April 2011, Case C-291/09, *Guarnieri*, ECLI:EU:C:2011:217 (for plaintiffs from Monaco).

*'Mangold' als ausbrechender Rechtsakt* (Munich: Sellier, 2009); A. Metzger, 'Allgemeine Rechtsgrundsätze in Europa – dargestellt am Beispiel des Gleichbehandlungsgrundsatzes', *RabelsZ* 75 (2011), 845.

### a) *Fundamentals*

**243.** A prohibition of restrictions also follows from the fundamental freedoms: Even such regulations that do not have a formally discriminatory effect can violate the fundamental freedoms if they do not amount to direct or indirect discrimination but unjustifiably restrict the exercise of the fundamental freedoms in some way. This question arises in particular in the case of private law provisions: Here, the issue is whether a regulation actually makes cross-border traffic worse than domestic traffic. In this respect, a distinction between private and public law is not essential; even the legal systems of most Member States draw this distinction in a very blurry manner. The way in which the restriction of fundamental freedoms is carried out (either a prohibition under public law, which leads to the nullity of the contract, e.g. via public policy clauses, or a direct prohibition under private law) is irrelevant from the EU law's perspective.

### b) *Approaches of the CJEU*

**244.** The EU is based on the pursuit of a progressive realisation of the internal market (Article 3(3) TEU). To reach this goal, trade barriers have gradually been dismantled. The foundations of this process are the four fundamental freedoms (Article 26(2) TFEU), which, in principle, not only prohibit the Member States from discriminatory but also restrictive action. For private law, the free movement of goods (Article 34 TFEU) has proven to be the most important. According to the CJEU's extensive interpretation in the *Dassonville* case, 'all trading rules enacted by Member States which are capable of hindering, directly or indirectly, actually or potentially, intra-Community trade' are prohibited.[17] This also applies to non-discriminatory law.[18] However, the free movement of goods is not affected by 'provisions restricting or prohibiting certain selling arrangements [...], so long as those provisions apply to all relevant traders operating within the national territory and so long as they affect in the same manner, in law and in fact, the marketing of domestic products and those from other Member States'.[19] The CJEU thus distinguishes between exempt sales modalities, at least with regard to non-discriminatory state action, and product-related rules, for which the free movement of goods fully applies. The *Dassonville* principle also applies to other fundamental freedoms.

---

17 CJEU, 11 July 1974, Case 8/74, *Dassonville*, ECLI:EU:C:1974:82.

18 CJEU, 20 February 1979, Case 120/78, *Cassis de Dijon*, ECLI:EU:C:1979:42.

19 CJEU, 24 November 1993, Case C-267/91, *Keck*, ECLI:EU:C:1993:905.

### c) *Intensity of Control in the Area of Private Law: The* CMC Motorradcenter *Case*

**245.** Hence, infringements of fundamental freedoms are also conceivable in the area of private-law provisions. For example, the provisions of social tenancy law could obstruct the free movement of capital to the extent that they make the purchase of residential property in other Member States more difficult; mandatory sales laws could hinder the free movement of goods; mandatory employee protection laws might restrict investments. However, such national restrictions of fundamental freedoms will rarely have a decisive effect in the case of non-discriminatory domestic regulations. This is illustrated by the CJEU case '*CMC Motorradcenter GmbH/Pelin Baskiciogullari*':[20]

**246.** The CMC motorbike dealership in Augsburg purchased a Yamaha motorbike from a German importer, who had bought it from a French authorised dealer. At the time of that purchase, the German importer was promised that the final purchasers could claim warranty at any authorised Yamaha dealer. Subsequently, CMC resold the motorbike to Ms Baskiciogullari (B). CMC knew that German authorised dealers usually refuse to carry out warranty repairs on 'grey' imported motorbikes; however, they did not inform B. After B got aware of this, she refused to accept the motorbike and pay the purchase price. CMC, however, insisted on the fulfilment of the contract. Also, it was true that 'grey' importers profited from the lower net prices in France. In any case, CMC claimed that the freedom to import would be restricted if customers had to be informed about such matters as the warranty conditions of authorised dealers; every buyer had to see for themselves how to protect their rights.

#### aa) Existence of the Claim under German Law

**247.** The grounds for the respective claim was sec. 433(2) German Civil Code. A valid purchase contract was concluded; thus, CMC could, in principle, also demand performance, i.e. payment, according to sec. 433(2) German Civil Code. However, the claim might have been subject to a limitation in time.

**248.** Also, a challenge due to fraudulent misrepresentation under sec. 123, 142(1) German Civil Code appeared possible. This required a duty of disclosure on the part of CMC. Such an obligation does not always exist regarding circumstances that are obviously relevant to the contracting party's decision, but only if the contracting party, based on the situation at hand, could expect in good faith and, according to common practice, to be informed about such

[20] CJEU, 13 October 1993, Case C-93/92, *CMC Motorradcenter*, ECLI:EU:C:1993:838. See also CJEU, 27 January 2000, Case C-190/98, *Graf*, ECLI:EU:C:2000:49.

circumstances that are of decisive importance to them.[21] This could be assumed here: The scope of the warranty or guarantee is of considerable significance, particularly in the case of motorbikes, since a warranty case may occur far away from the seller's residence. In this respect, it could be presumed that, had B known about the breach of the duty of disclosure, she would not have concluded the contract.

**249.** In any case, the claim could also be opposed by other means: B could have a claim for cancellation of the contract based on *culpa in contrahendo*, sec. 311(2), 280(1), 249(1) German Civil Code. Again, the violation of a duty of disclosure is a prerequisite. The legal consequence would be a compensation claim, which in this case would be to relieve B from the effects of the undesired contract. The contract cancellation claim can be held against the demand for performance under the principle of good faith (sec. 242 German Civil Code) according to the principle of *dolo agit qui petit quod statim redditurus est.*

bb) Violation of EU Law Standards?

**250.** However, denying the claim to perform the contract resulting (indirectly) from the (violation of the) duty to provide information could be seen as a violation of the free movement of goods under Article 34 TFEU. The scope of protection of the free movement of goods is extensive; also, there are no specific EU rules covering the subject matter. Moreover, the case was of cross-border nature, and motorbikes can be classified as commercial goods as provided by Article 34 TFEU. It is questionable whether the pre-contractual obligation of a 'grey importer' to inform the buyer of the fact that some authorised dealerships might not service it under warranty impairs the free movement of goods.

**251.** The present case does not involve a quantitative import restriction in the sense of Article 34 TFEU, as importing motorbikes is not generally prohibited by the obligation to provide information. However, the obligation to provide information could represent a 'measure having equivalent effect' according to Article 34 TFEU. Under the *Dassonville* principle, measures having equivalent effects are all trade regulations that are capable of hindering, directly or indirectly, actually or potentially, intra-Community trade.[22] This could be the case in the present case because, in the context of the pre-contractual duty of information, CMC, being a 'grey importer', has information obligations that do not apply to dealers who sell motorbikes that were imported directly from Japan or dealers who import such motorbikes from other EU Member States

21 BGH NJW 2010, 3362.

22 CJEU, 11 July 1974, Case 8/74, *Dassonville*, ECLI:EU:C:1974:82.

via 'official' distribution channels. Requiring a dealership to explicitly state that certain other dealers do not carry out warranty repairs (even if they are legally obliged to do so) could deter some buyers. Since this duty of disclosure only applies to 'grey' imports and not to those imported through 'official' distribution channels, this could pose an obstacle to trade.

**252.** However, this argument does not hold up to scrutiny. This is because the pre-contractual duty to provide information applies, at least in the case of products from the EU, to all contractual relationships subject to this law. It is not intended to regulate commercial transactions only. Thus, there is no elevated danger to the free movement of goods. On the contrary, possible obstacles are not caused by the obligation to provide information but by the fact that some of the authorised dealers refuse to carry out warranty work on 'grey' imports.[23]

**253.** Accordingly, the restrictive effects which the obligation to provide information might have on the free movement of goods are too uncertain and too indirect for that obligation to be regarded as capable of hindering trade between Member States.[24] Consequently, Article 34 TFEU does not preclude a rule established in a Member State's law which prescribes an obligation to provide information in the pre-contractual stage.

#### d) *Further Examples*

**254.** Several other decisions of the CJEU also deal with the relationship of fundamental freedoms to private law provisions. Overall, a direct violation of a prohibition of restrictions was never found.

**255.** One example is the *Graf* decision.[25] An Austrian employer had refused to pay the German employee Graf severance pay, which under Austrian law is only owed in cases of termination by the employer. In this case, however, the employee Graf had cancelled the contract himself. He now argued that the corresponding provision of Austrian law violated the freedom of movement: From his point of view, this provision was likely to deter employees from terminating employment contracts for the purpose of taking up employment in another Member State. The CJEU, however, did not see a violation of fundamental freedoms if the national law did not provide for severance pay in the case of an employee quitting on their own volition. First, domestic and foreign employees were treated indiscriminately.[26] Moreover, the case concerned a question of access to

[23] CJEU, 13 October 1993, Case C-93/92, *CMC Motorradcenter*, ECLI:EU:C:1993:838, para. 11.
[24] CJEU, 13 October 1993, Case C-93/92, *CMC Motorradcenter*, ECLI:EU:C:1993:838, para. 12.
[25] CJEU, 27 January 2000, Case C-190/98, *Graf*, ECLI:EU:C:2000:49.
[26] CJEU, 27 January 2000, Case C-190/98, *Graf*, ECLI:EU:C:2000:49, paras. 15 ff.

another Member State's labour market, not of leaving it.[27] Uncertain and indirect impairments, such as the prospect of severance pay, were considered insufficient to constitute a violation of fundamental freedoms.[28]

**256.** Further decisions concerning labour law related to age discrimination in particular.[29] The salient issue here is less about fundamental freedoms and more about the prohibition of age discrimination, which has now been codified in Article 21 CFR. This will be discussed below.[30] Areas of private regulatory law relevant to fundamental freedoms are national rules on fees for lawyers[31] or architects:[32] Although such fee scales represent potential encroachments on the freedom to provide services, they can be justified, both with regard to minimum prices (in this respect, quality standards, consumer protection or construction safety might play a role) and concerning maximum prices (for example, due to consumer protection, transparency or the prevention of price-related competition).[33]

### e) *Private Law as a Mere Modality of Sale (in the Sense of* Dassonville*)?*

**257.** Even if there was no infringement in the *CMC Motorradcenter* case and others found, it still remains to be clarified which position private laws occupy within the CJEU's doctrinal concept of fundamental freedoms. The occasionally held belief that private law could be exempt from scrutiny under fundamental freedoms seems too far-reaching.[34] In this respect, the market economy principle (cf. Article 120 TFEU) can serve as justification since private law helps to realise the internal market. A restriction might then only follow from the principle of proportionality.[35] In general, EU law does not differentiate categorically between public and private law, so assuming an extensive exemption for all private law would be far-fetched for this reason alone. The law's hierarchical structure also

---

27 CJEU, 27 January 2000, Case C-190/98, *Graf*, ECLI:EU:C:2000:49, para. 23.

28 CJEU, 27 January 2000, Case C-190/98, *Graf*, ECLI:EU:C:2000:49, para. 25.

29 CJEU, 22 November 2005, Case C-144/04, *Mangold*, ECLI:EU:C:2005:709 or CJEU, 19 January 2010, Case C-555/07, *Kücükdeveci*, ECLI:EU:C:2010:21.

30 In addition, see paras. 265–277 below.

31 CJEU, 5 December 2006, Joined Cases C-94/04 and C-202/04, *Cipolla*, ECLI:EU:C:2006:758, paras. 55 ff.

32 CJEU, 4 July 2019, Case C-377/17, *Commission/Germany*, ECLI:EU:C:2019:562, paras. 56 ff. There, however, it was argued not so much with the freedom to provide services, but with the relevant provisions of the Services Directive.

33 On this in detail CJEU, 5 December 2006, Joined Cases C-94/04 and C-202/04, *Cipolla*, ECLI:EU:C:2006:758, paras. 61 ff.; CJEU, 4 July 2019, Cases C-377/17, *Commission/Germany*, ECLI:EU:C:2019:562, paras. 70 ff.

34 E. Steindorff, *EG-Vertrag und Privatrecht* (Baden-Baden: Nomos, 1996), p. 268.

35 Cf. Schwintowski, in Grundmann, Systembildung und Systemlücken, 2000, pp. 457, 469. This point of view is shared in Heiderhoff, *Europäisches Privatrecht*, para. 67.

generally speaks against excluding certain parts of lower-ranking law from scrutiny.

**258.** According to the *Dassonville* principle, any mandatory provisions of private law can, at least prima facie, constitute a potential infringement on fundamental freedoms since they appear to be at least potentially capable of acting as a barrier to market access.[36] For example, tenant protection regulations could prevent investors from acquiring flats and thus restrict the free movement of capital; the same could be argued for employee protection. Mandatory consumer protection regulations could be seen as another restriction to the free movement of goods and the freedom to provide services. Indeed, the CJEU has found a limitation of the free movement of capital in the so-called Volkswagen Act, which granted special rights to the shareholding German Federal State of Lower Saxony ('golden shares').[37] However, the case is somewhat different since the public sector was involved. This opens up reasonably far-reaching scrutiny regarding fundamental freedoms; however, in other cases, it will also often be found that social purposes legitimise an encroachment.

**259.** If one adheres to CJEU's doctrinal framework, private law provisions could be considered mere sales modalities so that, in principle, there would be no conflict with the fundamental freedoms in the sense of the *Keck* case.[38] Here too, however, a review of a possible violation of fundamental freedoms is not excluded from the outset.[39] Irrespective of this, it is not always easy to draw the line between this issue and product-related rules. It always depends on whether or not the regulation in question imposes a barrier to the internal market. This will rarely be the case with non-mandatory private law.[40]

## 3. THIRD-PARTY EFFECTS OF THE FUNDAMENTAL FREEDOMS?

**260.** A distinction must be made between this and the extent to which the fundamental freedoms have a horizontal effect, i.e. if they cover the relationship

---

36 See E. Steindorff, *EG-Vertrag und Privatrecht* (Baden-Baden: Nomos, 1996), p. 48; see also O. Remien, *Zwingendes Vertragsrecht und Grundfreiheiten des EG-Vertrages* (Tübingen: Mohr Siebeck, 2003), pp. 178 ff.

37 CJEU, 23 October 2007, Case C-112/05, *Commission/Germany*, ECLI:EU:C:2007:623.

38 O. Remien, *Zwingendes Vertragsrecht und Grundfreiheiten des EG-Vertrages* (Tübingen: Mohr Siebeck, 2003), pp. 193 ff.

39 See, for example, CJEU, 10 May 1995, Case C-384/93, *Alpine Investments*, ECLI:EU:C:1995:126, paras. 23 ff. (prohibition of cold calling).

40 Herresthal, in Langenbucher, *Europäisches Privat- und Wirtschaftsrecht*, §2 paras. 66 ff.; Riesenhuber, *EU-Vertragsrecht*, 2013, §2 para. 35; Heiderhoff, *Europäisches Privatrecht*, paras. 57 ff.

between subjects of private law. This is not a question of rank. Instead, this problem is well known from national constitutional law, where this is called the problem of (indirect) third-party effects of fundamental rights. At the outset, it seems like this question has to be answered negatively: If the fundamental freedoms are prohibitions on restrictions related to market access, they cannot cover the behaviour of private parties. After all, unfair behaviour of private actors is regulated by antitrust and competition law. In many cases, therefore, a direct third-party effect of the fundamental freedoms must be rejected.[41] The CJEU, however, follows a much more generous approach. A paradigm for this is the *Bosman* ruling, according to which the obligation to pay compensation for (professional) football training sessions in the event of a change of club, which is laid down in association statutes, impedes the free movement of persons.[42] Here and in other decisions, however, there was usually a situation in which an association or a similar larger organisation acted on one side. In this respect, it seems difficult to draw general conclusions.

## 4. CHARTER OF FUNDAMENTAL RIGHTS AND NATIONAL LAW

References: C. Baldus/T. Raff, 'Good news, bad news zu horizontaler Direktwirkung und europäischer Methodenlehre: Weitere Konstitutionalisierung des unionalen und nationalen Privatrechts?', *GPR* 2018, 175; H. Collins, 'The Rule of Law and the Charter of Fundamental Rights as a Source of European Private Law', in S. Grundmann/ M. Grochowski (eds.), *European Contract Law and the Creation of Norms* (Cambridge: Intersentia, 2021), p. 73; M. Fornasier, 'The Impact of EU Fundamental Rights on Private Relationships: Direct or Indirect Effect?', *ERPL* 2015, 29; E. Frantziou, '(Most of) the Charter of Fundamental Rights is Horizontally Applicable', (2019) *European Constitutional Law Review*, 306; C. Herresthal, 'Die Bedeutung der Charta der Grundrechte für das europäische und das nationale Privatrecht', *ZEuP* 2014, 238; H.D. Jarass, 'Die Bedeutung der Unionsgrundrechte unter Privaten', *ZEuP* 2017, 310; O. Mörsdorf, 'Die Auswirkungen des neuen "Grundrechts auf Verbraucherschutz" gemäß Art. 38 GR-Ch auf das nationale Privatrecht', *JZ* 2010, 759; O. Mörsdorf, 'Europäisierung des Privatrechts durch die Hintertür? – Einige Gedanken zum Einfluss der Grundrechte-Charta auf das nationale Privatrecht in der jüngeren Rechtsprechung des EuGH (Egenberger, Bauer, CCOO u.a.)', *JZ* 2019, 1066; S. Perner, *Grundfreiheiten, Grundrechte-Charta und Privatrecht* (Tübingen: Mohr Siebeck, 2013), pp. 141 ff.; C. Poncibò, 'A More Coherent EU Contract Law? Fundamental Rights Come First', in A. Janssen/M. Lehmann/R. Schulze (eds.), *The Future of European Private Law* (Baden-Baden: Nomos, 2023), p. 429; M. Stürner, 'How autonomous should private law be? – Elements of a private law constitution', in H. Collins (ed.), *The EU Charter of Fundamental Rights and European Contract Law* (Cambridge:

41 Bachmann, *AcP* 210 (2010), 424.

42 CJEU, 15 December 1995, Case C-415/93, *Bosman*, ECLI:EU:C:1995:463.

Intersentia, 2017), p. 33; D. Wielsch, 'The Function of Fundamental Rights in EU Private Law – Perspectives for the Common European Sales Law', *ERCL* 2014, 365.

**261.** With the Charter of Fundamental Rights entering into force through the Treaty of Lisbon, there is now another source of primary law (Article 6(1) TEU), which thus enjoys supremacy over national law. This raises the question of the Charter's relationship to national private law.[43]

### a) *The Scope of Application of the Charter of Fundamental Rights*

**262.** The Charter of Fundamental Rights is directed both to EU institutions and to the Member States; it applies only within the scope of application of the treaties (Article 51 CFR). For the provisions of private law, no special exceptions apply: They may not be designed in a way that restrict Charter rights without sufficient justification. Here, too, the question of third-party effects must be discussed.

### b) *The Operation of the Charter of Fundamental Rights in Private Law*

#### aa) Private Law Directives

**263.** Of course, the supremacy of primary law also applies within EU law: Secondary legislation, such as regulations or directives under private law, may not violate the provisions of the TEU, the TFEU and the Charter of Fundamental Rights. Thus, due to the prohibition of gender discrimination in Articles 21 and 23 CFR, the CJEU considered the gender-specific tariffs in the area of insurance law (cf. Article 5(2) of the 4th Equal Treatment Directive[44]), which considered it permissible to take actuarial assessments into account, invalid.[45] Violations of this kind are also conceivable in other areas of private law.[46]

#### bb) Charter Rights and National Private Law

**264.** Here, too, the question of the relationship to Member State private law arises.[47] For a long time, the CJEU has avoided taking a clear stance. The

---

[43] Herresthal, *ZEuP* 2014, 238; Fornasier, *ERPL* 2015, 29.

[44] Council Directive 2004/113/EC of 13 December 2004 implementing the principle of equal treatment between men and women in the access to and supply of goods and services, OJ 2004 L 373/37.

[45] CJEU, 1 March 2011, Case C-236/09, *Test-Achats*, ECLI:EU:C:2011:100. See below paras. 788–790.

[46] See Herresthal, *ZEuP* 2014, 238, 258 ff.; for the Consumer Rights Directive in particular Wendehorst, *GPR* 2015, 55.

[47] Herresthal, *ZEuP* 2014, 238; Fornasier, *ERPL* 2015, 29.

development is not necessarily linear; in the following, it will be presented based on several important decisions which primarily originate in labour law.

### (1) Prior to the Charter of Fundamental Rights: Unwritten Fundamental Rights

**265.** Even before the Charter of Fundamental Rights and the relevant provision of Article 21 CFR came into force, the CJEU deduced an unwritten principle of the prohibition of age discrimination from primary law. Take the *Kücükdeveci* case.[48]

**266.** Ms K was born on 12 February 1978. She had been employed by S, a German business, since 4 June 1996, i.e. since the age of 18. In a letter dated 19 December 2006, S gave notice of termination, effective from 31 January 2007 and in line with the statutory notice period. Ms K challenged the termination before the labour court. She argued that according to sec. 622(2) German Civil Code, a four-month notice period, corresponding to ten years of service, should have been given from 31 December 2006 to 30 April 2007. In Ms K's opinion, the then-applicable version of sec. 622(2) German Civil Code, which did not take into account periods of service before the employee's 25th birthday, constituted discrimination on the grounds of age, so it was in breach of EU law and, therefore, had to remain inapplicable.

**267.** The employment relationship between S and K had already existed for more than ten years when S gave notice of termination. According to sec. 622(2), first sentence, of the German Civil Code, a notice period of four months to the end of a calendar month applies to the termination of such an employment relationship. According to this provision, S could have terminated K's employment in December 2006 only at the end of 30 April 2007. However, according to the then-applicable sec. 622(2), second sentence, of the German Civil Code,[49] only the periods of employment completed after the employee reached the age of 25 were considered when calculating the notice periods. According to this provision, only the period after K's 25th birthday on 12 February 2003 was considered to calculate the employment period. From this point in time, K's employment relationship until the notice of termination on 19 December 2006 lasted no more than ten, but only more than three years. According to sec. 622(2) German Civil Code, the employment relationship could, therefore, have been terminated by the employer with one month's notice to the end of a calendar month and thus

48 After CJEU, 19 January 2010, Case C-555/07, *Kücükdeveci*, ECLI:EU:C:2010:21; see also CJEU, 22 November 2005, Case C-144/04, *Mangold*, ECLI:EU:C:2005:709.

49 The provision was repealed with effect from 1 January 2019.

to 31 January 2007. Under the then-applicable sec. 622(2) German Civil Code, the notice period used by S was therefore correct.

**268.** However, the calculation of the notice period by applying the then-applicable sec. 622(2) German Civil Code might be seen as a violation of the requirements of EU law, particularly the prohibition of age discrimination under European law. Since sec. 622(2) German Civil Code regulated the conditions for the dismissal of an employee, the provision fell under the scope of application of the General Equal Treatment Directive 2000/78/EC (according to Article 3(1)(c) of the Directive 2000/78/EC). It is irrelevant that the then-applicable sec. 622(2) German Civil Code did not serve to implement the Directive but existed long before.

**269.** Sec. 622(2) German Civil Code generally discriminated against young employees compared to more senior ones, as the former could be excluded from the advantage of the gradual extension of the notice periods under sec. 622(2) German Civil Code despite having been with the company for several years, while older employees with a comparable length of employment benefited from it. The then-applicable sec. 622(2) German Civil Code thus prescribed an age-based unequal treatment.

**270.** However, a different treatment on the grounds of age may be justified under Article 6(1) of Directive 2000/78/EC. According to this provision, an age-based distinction does not constitute discrimination if it is objective, proportionate and justified by a legitimate aim under national law, which includes, in particular, legitimate objectives relating to employment, the labour market and vocational training. Furthermore, the means of achieving that aim must be appropriate and necessary.

**271.** The objective of the then-applicable sec. 622(2) German Civil Code was to provide the employer with greater flexibility in personnel management by reducing their troubles concerning the dismissal of younger employees who can be expected to have greater professional and personal mobility. This objective is part of employment and labour market policy under Article 6(1) of Directive 2000/78/EC. However, sec. 622(2) German Civil Code applied irrespective of how old the employee was at the time of the notice of termination. If an employee had entered the employment relationship 'young', the provision still had an adverse effect on them even if their employment relationship was to be terminated only after a long period of service and they were already 'old' at that time. The then-applicable sec. 622(2) German Civil Code was, therefore, not an appropriate measure regarding the stated objective; hence, the unequal treatment based on age was not justified.

**272.** The prohibition of discrimination on the grounds of age constitutes a fundamental right of the EU under Article 21(1) CFR.[50] Directive 2000/78/EC only substantiates this right. Consequently, the then-applicable sec. 622(2) German Civil Code violated the prohibition of age discrimination.

**273.** According to Article 288(3) TFEU, a European directive binds only the Member States. Therefore, it does not apply to private law entities, so a direct third-party effect between private individuals does not exist.[51] Consequently, an EU citizen cannot directly invoke European directive laws in a legal dispute against another private actor.[52] K could, therefore, not rely directly on the right to non-discriminatory treatment under Directive 2000/78/EC.[53]

**274.** According to the requirement of an interpretation in conformity with the Directive,[54] a national court had to interpret the then-applicable sec. 622(2) German Civil Code in the light of with Directive 2000/78/EC in order to achieve the Directive's objective. Due to the unambiguous wording of sec. 622(2) German Civil Code (old version), which was therefore not open to further interpretation, it was impossible to interpret the German provision in conformity with the Directive.[55]

**275.** Therefore, further development of the law in conformity with the directive had to be considered. In fact this would mean to ignore the entire provision in sec. 622(2) German Civil Code (old version). However, there are several methodological caveats in this respect: A legal loophole, which is necessary for such a methodological operation according to German legal doctrine, might have already been non-existent since the then-applicable sec. 622(2) German Civil Code did not serve to transpose a directive and, therefore, a reference to the legislator's general intention of transposing EU law in a correct way appeared problematic. However, this could be considered irrelevant if the requirements of EU law could be taken into account in a different way.

**276.** As explained, there also was a violation of the primary law prohibition of age discrimination. Therefore, the national court that had to decide on the

---

50 This also applies before the entry into force of the Charter of Fundamental Rights, as primary law contains an unwritten prohibition of age discrimination according to the interpretation by the CJEU, see CJEU, 22 November 2005, Case C-144/04, *Mangold*, ECLI:EU:C:2005:709, para. 75.

51 On this point, Stürner, *JURA* 2017, 394.

52 CJEU, 19 January 2010, Case C-555/07, *Kücükdeveci*, ECLI:EU:C:2010:21, para. 46.

53 However, the *Mangold* decision of the CJEU could be understood differently, CJEU, 22 November 2005, Case C-144/04, *Mangold*, ECLI:EU:C:2005:709, paras. 77, 79.

54 More on this below paras. 346–354.

55 Such was the decision of the Federal Labour Court: BAG NJW 2011, 1626.

case at hand was obliged (in this case as concretised by Directive 2000/78/EC) to ensure, within the framework of its competencies, the remedies afforded to individuals under EU law and to guarantee the full effectiveness of Union law by not applying, if necessary, any provision of national law contrary to that prohibition.[56]

**277.** Consequently, the then-applicable sec. 622(2) German Civil Code was not to be applied in the legal relationship between K and S. The notice period was calculated according to sec. 622(2) German Civil Code and could not expire before 30 April 2007.

### (2) (At Least) Indirect Third-Party Effect of the Charter Rights

**278.** In the *Dominguez* case,[57] it had to be clarified whether the right to paid annual leave under Article 31(2) CFR had a direct third-party effect. The opinion of Advocate General Trstenjak[58] contained lengthy comments on this issue. However, the CJEU did not address this and concentrated on the more formal question of whether the employer was to be regarded as a public authority since this would already lead to a horizontal effect of the relevant Directive.[59] In the *Association de médiation sociale* case,[60] it was Advocate General Cruz Villalón who argued in favour of a direct effect of the right of employees to information and consultation under Article 27 CFR,[61] but the CJEU again did not address this.[62] Both cases may also serve to exemplify that the question of indirect or direct third-party effect is of more doctrinal than practical interest. This is because the validity of the corresponding Charter law can regularly be justified already through means of indirect influence on the respective national rule.

### (3) Direct Third-Party Effect?

**279.** The discussion around the direct third-party effect of the Charter of Fundamental Rights has recently been reignited by some recent decisions of the CJEU. In these cases, the Court had to abandon its reluctant position and take

---

56 CJEU, 19 January 2010, Case C-555/07, *Kücükdeveci*, ECLI:EU:C:2010:21, paras. 49 ff.

57 CJEU, 24 January 2012, Case C-282/10, *Dominguez*, ECLI:EU:C:2012:33.

58 Opinion of 8 September 2011, Case C-282/10, ECLI:EU:C:2011:559, paras. 75–77.

59 Directive 2003/88/EC of the European Parliament and of the Council of 4 November 2003 concerning certain aspects of the organisation of working time, OJ 2003 L 299/9.

60 CJEU, 15 January 2014, Case C-176/12, *Association de médiation sociale*, ECLI:EU:C:2014:2.

61 Opinion of 18 July 2013, Case C-176/12, ECLI:EU:C:2013:491, paras. 28–41.

62 See, for example, B. Gsell, in *Festschrift für Köhler* (Munich: C.H. Beck, 2014), p. 197. The European Court of Human Rights also denies a direct third-party effect of the Convention rights with reference to Article 1 ECHR, cf. J. Meyer-Ladewig, *Europäische Menschenrechtskonvention*, 3rd ed. (Baden-Baden: Nomos, 2011), Art. 1 para. 10.

a stand since, unlike before, it was impossible to refer to the duty to interpret national laws in conformity with the directives.

**280.** The CJEU's new line of reasoning was initiated in April 2018 by the *Egenberger* case[63] (after submission by the German Federal Labour Court.[64] Ms Egenberger (E), who did not belong to any community of faith, had applied for a temporary position advertised by the Protestant church. It is not without a certain irony that the application's primary purpose was to prepare a report on eliminating all forms of (in particular, racist) discrimination. Although her application had initially remained in the selection process, E was not invited for an interview. The applicant who was finally hired had stated that he was an 'evangelical Christian socialised in the Berlin regional church'. Assuming that her application had been unsuccessful due to her lack of a denomination, E sued all the way to the German Federal Labour Court for appropriate compensation under sec. 15(2) German General Equal Treatment Act. The German Federal Labour Court submitted three questions to the CJEU. The second question is of particular importance for the problem of third-party effects: The German Federal Labour Court believed that sec. 9 German General Equal Treatment Act, which justifies a different, employment-related treatment based on religion by religious communities, could not be reconciled with Article 4(2) of Directive 2000/78 without a *contra legem* interpretation.[65] In this respect, according to the German Federal Labour Court, it was a question of whether the prohibition of discrimination laid down in Article 21 CFR 'confers on individuals a subjective right which they may assert in legal proceedings between private parties and which obliges the courts to refrain from applying conflicting national provisions', in this case, sec. 9 German General Equal Treatment Act.[66] In other words, the question was whether Article 21 CFR had a direct third-party effect.

**281.** The CJEU answered this question in the affirmative: 'Article 21 CFR is sufficient in itself to confer on individuals a right which they may rely on as such in disputes between them in a field covered by EU law.'[67] Article 21 of the Charter, like the other relevant provisions of primary law, prohibited various forms of discrimination even if they resulted from contracts between private individuals.[68] In addition, the CJEU referred to the mandatory character of Article 21 CFR and emphasised that, due to its definiteness, the rule did

63 CJEU, 17 April 2018, Case C-414/16, *Egenberger*, ECLI:EU:C:2018:257.
64 BAGE 154, 285.
65 BAGE 154, 285, para. 51.
66 BAGE 154, 285, para. 54.
67 CJEU, 17 April 2018, Case C-414/16, *Egenberger*, ECLI:EU:C:2018:257, para. 76.
68 CJEU, 17 April 2018, Case C-414/16, *Egenberger*, ECLI:EU:C:2018:257, para. 77 referring inter alia to CJEU, 8 April 1976, Case 43/75, *Defrenne*, ECLI:EU:C:1976:56, para. 39 and CJEU, 6 June 2000, Case C-281/98, *Angonese*, ECLI:EU:C:2000:296, paras. 33–36.

not require any specification by national law.[69] However, it was the task of the national court to establish a proportionate balance between the various fundamental rights.[70] This explicated what the CJEU had already indicated in the *Association de médiation sociale* case: There, the court rejected the direct third-party effect of the Article 27 CFR in question, but at the same time pointed out that, in contrast, Article 21 CFR, which was not relevant in the case, did confer a subjective right on the individual, which they could assert as such in a private law dispute.[71] What is decisive, however, is the consequence of this case law: The national court must not apply a provision of national law that cannot be reconciled with a correctly interpreted provision of primary law.[72] Taken in isolation, this has nothing to do with direct third-party effects: Rather, it is about the higher rank that primary law has compared to national law. The fact that a private individual in a civil law dispute can 'assert as such' a right that follows from the Charter of Fundamental Rights does not appear to be a revolutionary statement in light of the principle *iura novit curia*.

**282.** This reasoning was confirmed and expanded in the cases *Bauer* and *Broßonn*,[73] which were decided a short time later. The plaintiffs, Bauer and Broßonn, each claimed compensation for residual leave entitlements of their deceased husbands after the employment relationship of the deceased had been terminated by their deaths and compensation claims had not yet arisen. The German Federal Labour Court ultimately dealt with the case and turned to the CJEU with two questions for a preliminary ruling.[74] First, the German Federal Labour Court wanted to know whether Article 7 of Directive 2003/88[75] or Article 31(2) CFR granted the heirs a direct claim to financial compensation for the remaining annual leave, even though this was precluded under German law.[76] According to German law, the employee's entitlement to paid annual leave under sec. 7(4) German Federal Paid Leave Act in conjunction with sec. 1922 German Civil Code lapses upon death and does not become part of the inheritance.[77] According to the German Federal Labour Court, any other interpretation of German law would be *contra legem* and thus inadmissible.[78]

---

69 CJEU, 17 April 2018, Case C-414/16, *Egenberger*, ECLI:EU:C:2018:257, paras. 76 and 78.

70 CJEU, 17 April 2018, Case C-414/16, *Egenberger*, ECLI:EU:C:2018:257, paras. 79–81.

71 CJEU, 15 January 2014, Case C-176/12, *Association de médiation sociale*, ECLI:EU:C:2014:2, para. 47.

72 CJEU, 17 April 2018, Case C-414/16, *Egenberger*, ECLI:EU:C:2018:257, paras. 79, 82.

73 CJEU, 6 November 2018, Joined Cases C-569/16 and C-570/16, *Bauer and Broßonn*, ECLI:EU:C:2018:871.

74 BAG ErbR 2017, 85 (*Bauer*); BAG NZA 2017, 207 (*Broßonn*).

75 Directive 2003/88/EC concerning certain aspects of the organisation of working time, OJ 2003 *L 299/9*.

76 BAG NZA 2017, 207, para. 18.

77 BAG NZA 2017, 207, para. 15.

78 BAG NZA 2017, 207, para. 16.

A claim could, therefore, only follow directly from the corresponding Directive or the Charter of Fundamental Rights.

**283.** The second question referred to the CJEU, which only concerns the *Broßonn* case, is of utmost importance.[79] While in the *Bauer* case, the former employer was a public law entity (the city of Wuppertal), Ms Broßonn's former employer was a private corporation, the Willmeroth company. Thus, the question arose whether a direct application of charter rights was also possible in the case of an employment relationship between two private individuals. As in the *Egenberger* case, the CJEU argued for a direct effect of the Charter between private individuals as well.[80] The court first argued that Article 31(2) CFR was mandatory and not subject to further conditions since the Charter did not need to be substantiated by Union or national law.[81] The concerns about the applicability of the Charter between private parties based on Article 51(1) CFR – according to which the Charter applies only to the institutions, bodies, offices and agencies of the Union and to the Member States when they are implementing Union law – were discarded quite pragmatically: According to the CJEU, Article 51 of the Charter does not regulate whether private persons may be (directly, if applicable) obliged to comply with individual provisions of the Charter; the provision can therefore not be interpreted as a categorical exclusion.[82] The CJEU thus agreed with the statements of Advocate General Bot, who also argued in favour of a direct effect of the Charter between private individuals, without Article 51(1) of the Charter being an obstacle to this interpretation.[83] Arguing on a legal theoretical level, the CJEU went on to say that the right to paid annual leave contained in Article 31(2) CFR 'entails, by its very nature, a corresponding obligation on the employer, which is to grant such periods of paid leave leave'.[84] Of course, this 'mirror approach' is only convincing if one follows the CJEU's reasoning that Article 31(2) CFR has direct relevance to private law. But what follows from all this? The CJEU's answer follows an established line of reasoning: The national court must not apply the provisions

---

79 BAG NZA 2017, 207, para. 22.

80 CJEU, 6 November 2018, Joined Cases C-569/16 and C-570/16, *Bauer and Broßonn*, ECLI:EU:C:2018:871, paras. 79 ff.

81 CJEU, 6 November 2018, Joined Cases C-569/16 and C-570/16, *Bauer and Broßonn*, ECLI:EU:C:2018:871, para. 85. This distinguishes Article 31(2) CFR from the right to information and consultation under Article 27 CFR, which refers to 'cases and [...] conditions provided for by Union law and national laws and practices', see CJEU, 15 January 2014, Case C-176/12, *Association de médiation sociale*, ECLI:EU:C:2014:2.

82 CJEU, 6 November 2018, Joined Cases C-569/16 and C-570/16, *Bauer and Broßonn*, ECLI:EU:C:2018:871, para. 87.

83 Opinion of 29 May 2018, Joined Cases C-569/17 and C-570/16, ECLI:EU:C:1999:583, para. 78.

84 CJEU, 6 November 2018, Joined Cases C-569/16 and C-570/16, *Bauer and Broßonn*, ECLI:EU:C:2018:871, para. 90.

that conflict with EU law if they cannot be interpreted in a way that secures conformity.[85] Therefore, the German labour courts would have to refrain from applying sec. 7(4) of the German Federal Paid Leave Act in conjunction with sec. 1922 German Civil Code. But was Ms Broßonn then able to claim residual leave entitlements of her deceased husband? Since a direct horizontal effect of the Directive is still out of the question, the labour court would have to rely on Article 31(2) CFR directly. This consequence, however, is not clearly stated by the CJEU. The German Federal Labour Court has taken a different direction: It has abandoned its previous line of reasoning and now regards the entitlement to compensation for annual leave as inheritable by applying domestic law in conformity with the Directive.[86] Therefore, the question of the private law effects of Article 31(2) CFR was no longer relevant.[87]

**284.** In German legal literature, the decision was significantly more discussed than the *Egenberger* case.[88] The Court's reasoning was often criticised:[89] The fact that Article 51(1) of the Charter does not explicitly exclude a horizontal effect is not necessarily an argument for this being true for individual Charter rights.[90] The drafting history instead suggests the opposite conclusion, namely that Article 51 of the Charter should be understood as conclusive in the sense that only states are concerned.[91] Moreover, contrary to the CJEU's view, Article 31(2) CFR is not sufficiently specific:[92] While Article 21(1) CFR states an explicit prohibition, Article 31(2) CFR merely contains a rather nonspecific right: In particular, it does not specify the minimum duration of the leave or the amount of entitlement.

**285.** Subsequently, the CJEU confirmed its jurisdiction in other cases. In the cases *Max-Planck-Gesellschaft*[93] and *Hein*,[94] as in *Bauer/Broßonn*, the issue was the direct third-party effect of Article 31(2) CFR; in *Cresco Investigation*[95] and

---

85 CJEU, 6 November 2018, Joined Cases C-569/16 and C-570/16, *Bauer and Broßonn*, ECLI:EU:C:2018:871, para. 91.

86 BAG NJW 2019, 2046, paras. 10, 19 ff. as well as BAG NJW 2019, 2052 paras. 18, 27 ff.

87 BAG NJW 2019, 2046, para. 19.

88 Cf. Wutte, *EuZA* 2019, 222; Sura, *EuZA* 2019, 350, 359 f.; Mehrens/Witschen, *EuZA* 2019, 326, 330 f. with further references.

89 B. Hüpers/B. Reese, in J. Meyer/S. Hölscheidt, *Charta der Grundrechte der europäischen Union*, 5th ed. (Baden-Baden/Bern/Vienna: Nomos/Stämpfli/Verlag facultas, 2019), Art. 38 para. 38 with further references; Mehrens/Witschen, *EuZA* 2019, 326, 331.

90 Sura, *EuZA* 2019, 350, 359; Mehrens/Witschen, *EuZA* 2019, 326, 331.

91 Cf. the explanations of the Praesidium of the Convention on the drafting of the Charter on Article 51 CFR, which are to be taken into account in the interpretation of the Charter pursuant to Article 52(7) CFR; cf. also Höpfner, *RdA* 2013, 16, 21; Mehrens/Witschen, *EuZA* 2019, 326, 331.

92 Sura, *EuZA* 2019, 350, 360 with further references; Mehrens/Witschen, *EuZA* 2019, 326, 331; Höpfner, *RdA* 2013, 16, 19; Wutte, *EuZA* 2019, 222, 230.

93 CJEU, 6 November 2018, Case C-684/16, *Max-Planck-Gesellschaft*, ECLI:EU:C:2018:874, paras. 49–55 and 69 ff.

94 CJEU, 13 December 2018, Case C-385/17, *Hein*, ECLI:EU:C:2018:1018, para. 52 f.

95 CJEU, 22 January 2019, Case C-193/17, *Cresco Investigation*, ECLI:EU:C:2019:43, paras. 76–85.

*IR*,[96] as in *Egenberger*, the problem was the direct third-party effect of Article 21 CFR. Further reasoning did not follow in these judgments either; in each case, the court only referred to the *Egenberger* and *Bauer/Broßonn* cases.

(4) Consequences

**286.** All these cases have one aspect in common: A directive was transposed incorrectly, and the national norm cannot be applied in conformity with the directive without being interpreted *contra legem*. In order not to break with the doctrine of the prohibition of the horizontal direct effect of directives, the inapplicability of the national provision is based on a Charter right. In this way, the ascertained content of the directive is ultimately projected into another category of legal rules. Structurally, this line of reasoning is comparable to the *Dominguez*[97] and *Kucükdeveci* cases.[98] In these cases, the incorrectly transposed directives were ultimately given effect by recourse to a general legal principle of EU law. Hence, all directives, at least to the extent that they specify a fundamental Charter right – which is likely to apply to every directive to a certain extent – could be given horizontal effect via these primary law 'detours'; however, this would lead to the differentiation between directives and regulations provided for in Article 288(2) and (3) TFEU being rendered almost meaningless and the doctrine of the prohibition of the horizontal effect of directives, which the CJEU still postulates, would be undermined.[99]

**287.** First of all, it can be stated that the decisions examined come almost exclusively from the area of labour law. The horizontal effect of fundamental rights is probably easier to justify here, at least at a higher level of abstraction, given the need to protect employees. However, the question arises as to whether the CJEU's line of reasoning can be applied to all fundamental Charter rights.[100] Even a superficial analysis shows that a differentiated view is necessary: In qualitative terms, the provision in question must be mandatory and not require complementary measures.[101] The fact that the CJEU takes its own criteria seriously is already shown by the decision *Association de médiation sociale*: Here, the direct third-party effect of Article 27 CFR was rejected, as it

96 CJEU, 11 September 2018, Case C-68/17, *IR/JQ*, ECLI:EU:C:2018:696, para. 69 f.

97 CJEU, 19 January 2010, Case C-555/07, *Kücükdeveci*, ECLI:EU:C:2010:21.

98 CJEU, 24 January 2012, Case C-282/10, *Dominguez*, ECLI:EU:C:2012:33.

99 Cf. Sura, *EuZA* 2019, 350, 360; Wutte, *EuZA* 2019, 222, 230; see before that already Höpfner, *RdA* 2013, 16, 21.

100 In summary, Frantziou, *European Constitutional Law Review* 2019, 306, 319 ff.

101 CJEU, 17 April 2018, Case C-414/16, *Egenberger*, ECLI:EU:C:2018:257, para. 78; CJEU, 6 November 2018, Joined Cases C-569/16 and C-570/16, *Bauer and Broßonn*, ECLI:EU:C:2018:871, para. 85; AG Bot, Opinion of 29 May 2018, Joined Cases C-569/17 and C-570/16, ECLI:EU:C:1999:583, paras. 80–83.

had to be specified by provisions of Union or national law.[102] With regard to Article 31(2) CFR, the CJEU found that it was sufficiently specific. However, it has already been stated that there are considerable doubts as to whether the Charter provisions can actually be regarded as 'self-executing': In any case, their application would require a significant amount of concretion. Technically, the CJEU would be competent to do so. It is expected that, in the end, it would be the relevant directive's task to fill the gaps. On the other hand, the decisions discussed also suggest that the CJEU considers the national courts responsible for handling the necessary transposition. This approach would be somewhat comparable to the concretisation of open and general clauses within directives: Here, too, the CJEU regularly considers the Member State's courts responsible and competent to specify these rules further since EU law itself lacks the methodological standards to specify such rules.[103]

**288.** The CJEU's approach could lead to a far-reaching competence shift from the Member States to the EU. In particular in the states where the national legal methodology does not allow for a directive-compliant application of the law *contra legem*,[104] it would become necessary to refer to the Charter of Fundamental Rights (which may have to be specified accordingly) directly. This approach differs decisively from the conventional one: According to this latter approach, the claimant is left only with a claim for state liability due to inadequate implementation of the directive.[105] The normative quality of the corresponding fundamental rights of the Charter changes as well: From a functional point of view, the rights of the Charter that the CJEU endows with direct horizontal effects are being transformed into private law provisions since they regulate rights and obligations between private actors. Their unique feature is that they are of a higher rank than other private law provisions. They can therefore be called constitutional private law.[106] These tendencies should be viewed very critically. Constitutional courts such as the CJEU decide individual questions on the interpretation of EU law; they bear no responsibility for the private law systems of the Member States. The more far-reaching constitutional private law becomes, the less the national private laws can guarantee their internal

102 CJEU, 15 January 2014, Case C-176/12, *Association de médiation sociale*, ECLI:EU:C:2014:2, para. 45; reference to this in CJEU, 6 November 2018, Joined Cases C-569/16 and C-570/16, *Bauer and Broßonn*, ECLI:EU:C:2018:871, para. 84. Cf. also Frantziou, *European Constitutional Law Review* 2019, 306, 315.

103 See paras. 317–321 below on this problem area using the example of the Unfair Terms Directive.

104 On the question of the application of national law in conformity with the Directive, see below paras. 346–354.

105 See paras. 1476–1481 below.

106 Stürner, in Collins, *The EU Charter of Fundamental Rights and European Contract Law*, 2017, p. 33; similarly for German law Ipsen, *JZ* 2014, 157.

systematic coherence and, thus, also the predictability of legal regulations for private actors.[107]

### c) *Individual Fundamental Rights Relevant to Contract Law*

**289.** The following is an overview of the Charter's fundamental rights relevant to contract law. These are primarily the freedom to conduct a business (Article 16 CFR) and consumer protection (Article 38 CFR). For labour law, Article 21 CFR (prohibition of discrimination) and Article 31 CFR (appropriate working conditions/occupational health and safety) are particularly relevant.

#### aa) The Freedom to Conduct a Business, Article 16 CFR

**290.** The freedom to conduct a business is a fundamental legal principle and, besides the freedom to choose an occupation (Article 15 CFR) and the guarantee of property (Article 17 CFR), constitutes the central fundamental economic right.[108] The fundamental right of Article 16 CFR is based on the CJEU's case law, which can also be found in the explanations to the Charter, and includes the freedom to pursue an economic or business activity, free competition and, in particular, the (entrepreneurial) freedom to contract.[109] Thus, with the freedom of economic activity, Article 16 CFR contains an essential component of private autonomy, which is also protected by EU law. The other economically relevant aspects of private autonomy are also grounded in the fundamental freedoms of primary law. The freedom of contract contained therein includes, among other things, the free choice of a business partner and the freedom to set the price for a service.[110] Entrepreneurial freedom also includes the freedom of opinion and information of businesses.[111]

**291.** Functionally, Article 16 CFR contains a right of defence.[112] It is disputed to what extent it also has a positive dimension, i.e. if it allows the right-holder to demand information and benefits.[113] In any case, it is recognised that Article 16

---

107 Piekenbrock, *GPR* 2019, 93, 95 f. speaks of a de-dogmatisation and de-systematisation of civil law.

108 H.D. Jarass, *Charta der Grundrechte der EU*, 4th ed. (Munich: C.H. Beck, 2021), Art. 16 para. 2.

109 Charter Explanations, OJ 2007 C 303/23; CJEU, 22 January 2013, Case C-283/11, *Sky Österreich*, ECLI:EU:C:2013:28, para. 42 f.

110 CJEU, 22 January 2013, Case C-283/11, *Sky Österreich*, ECLI:EU:C:2013:28, para. 43 with further references.

111 CJEU, 17 December 2015, Case C-157/14, *Neptune*, ECLI:EU:C:2015:823.

112 H.D. Jarass, *Charta der Grundrechte der EU*, 4th ed. (Munich: C.H. Beck, 2021), Art. 16 para. 2; F. Wollenschläger, in H. von der Groeben/J. Schwarze/A. Hatje, *Europäisches Unionsrecht*, 7th ed. (Baden-Baden: Nomos, 2015), Art. 16 CFR para. 9 (or even claims for economic promotion).

113 See Tettinger, *NJW* 2001, 1014.

CFR contains an enforceable right and is not a mere Charter principle within the meaning of Article 52(5) CFR. This goes back to the CJEU's case law, to which reference is made in the Charter Explanations.[114] The CJEU had already recognised the full justiciability of the freedom of occupation for self-employed workers before the Charter entered into force.[115] The same must now remain true under Article 16 CFR.[116] All the more, this raises the question of any direct third-party effects of Article 16 CFR, which has already been introduced above. In the legal literature, such an effect is usually rejected;[117] it is generally claimed that Article 16 CFR cannot establish obligations for private individuals. The question could be raised again in light of the recent CJEU case law. However, the direct third-party effect of Article 16 CFR must also be rejected under the criteria set out by the CJEU: The court had only affirmed the direct effect of the Charter right in question on the condition that it did not have to be specified any further by provisions of EU or national law.[118] Consequently, the principles laid down in *Association de médiation sociale* were not abandoned.[119] The wording of Article 16 CFR is very similar to that of Article 27 CFR, with both provisions referring to EU law, national law and legal practice. The two fundamental rights thus already provide for some degree of specification. According to the newly established criteria of the CJEU, Article 16 CFR cannot be applied directly in legal disputes between private parties.[120]

**292.** Nevertheless, the fundamental right remains important among private parties. For example, the freedom to conduct a business may be restricted if a private broadcaster holding exclusive transmission rights is unable to decide which TV station receives the right to short news coverage (and at what price).[121] Regulations of executive remunerations or further specifications of minimum or maximum working conditions also restrict the freedom to conduct a business.[122] Another prominent example regarding the private law effect of Article 16 CFR

---

114 Charter Explanations, OJ 2007 C 303/23.

115 H.D. Jarass, *Charta der Grundrechte der EU*, 4th ed. (Munich: C.H. Beck, 2021), Art. 16 para. 2 with further references; CJEU, 10 July 1991, Joindes Cases C-90/90 and 91/90, *Neu*, ECLI:EU:C:1991:303; CJEU, 22 January 2013, Case C-283/11, *Sky Österreich*, ECLI:EU:C:2013:28 as well as CJEU, 18 July 2013, Case C-426/11, *Alemo-Herron*, ECLI:EU:C:2013:521.

116 See CJEU, 22 January 2013, Case C-283/11, *Sky Österreich*, ECLI:EU:C:2013:28 as well as CJEU, 18 July 2013, Case C-426/11, *Alemo-Herron*, ECLI:EU:C:2013:521.

117 H.D. Jarass, *Charta der Grundrechte der EU*, 4th ed. (Munich: C.H. Beck, 2021), Art. 16 para. 2.

118 CJEU, 17 April 2018, Case C-414/16, *Egenberger*, ECLI:EU:C:2018:257, para. 78; CJEU, 6 November 2018, Joined Cases C-569/16 and C-570/16, *Bauer and Broßonn*, ECLI:EU:C:2018:871, para. 85.

119 Cf. Frantziou, *European Constitutional Law Review* 2019, 306, 315.

120 See also Frantziou, *European Constitutional Law Review* 2019, 306, 320.

121 CJEU, 22 January 2013, Case C-283/11, *Sky Österreich*, ECLI:EU:C:2013:28, para. 43.

122 Gundel, *ZHR* 180 (2016), 323, 351.

is the CJEU's *Alemo-Herron* case.[123] In this case, a division of a corporation was sold. The buyer and the seller were both private companies. Furthermore, the buyer also took over the employees. The CJEU had to deal with the question of whether the union rate (which provided for a wage increase) also bound the buyer. In its decision, the CJEU first stated that Article 3 of Directive 2001/23 had to be interpreted in the light of Article 16 CFR. Accordingly, the buyer 'must be able to assert its interests effectively in a contractual process to which it is party and to negotiate the aspects determining changes in the working conditions of its employees with a view to its future economic activity'.[124] As the buyer was prevented from participating in the collective agreement in question, he could neither assert his interests nor negotiate the factors determining the development of his employees' working conditions with respect to future economic activities. In these circumstances, the contractual freedom of the buyer was, in the view of the CJEU, limited to the extent that such a restriction could affect the core of his right to freedom to conduct a business.[125] The Court thus ruled that a contractual clause providing the union rate cannot be invoked against the buyer in the event of a transfer of a business if the buyer was unable to participate in the collective labour agreement. This shows that the court considers contractual freedom highly valuable.

**293.** The freedom to conduct a business also covers the freedom of expression and information.[126] Accordingly, both informatory communication and warnings of both the state and private actors are to be regarded as encroachments on the freedom to conduct a business. However, this will likely become particularly important in administrative law and less so in private law.

#### bb) Consumer Protection, Article 38 CFR

**294.** Another fundamental right relevant to private law is found in Article 38 CFR, which aims to 'ensure a high level of consumer protection' and therefore refers to Article 169 TFEU.[127] Furthermore, Article 38 CFR guarantees the so-called 'fundamental right to consumer protection'.[128] The aim is to protect citizens, who typically are in a weaker position – both regarding knowledge and bargaining power – vis-à-vis private corporations.

---

[123] CJEU, 18 July 2013, Case C-426/11, *Alemo-Herron*, ECLI:EU:C:2013:521.

[124] CJEU, 18 July 2013, Case C-426/11, *Alemo-Herron*, ECLI:EU:C:2013:521, para. 33.

[125] CJEU, 18 July 2013, Case C-426/11, *Alemo-Herron*, ECLI:EU:C:2013:521, para. 35.

[126] CJEU, 17 December 2015, Case C-157/14, *Neptune*, ECLI:EU:C:2015:823.

[127] H.D. Jarass, *Charta der Grundrechte der EU*, 4th ed. (Munich: C.H. Beck, 2021), Art. 38 para. 2; CJEU, 31 January 2013, Case C-12/11, *McDonagh*, ECLI:EU:C:2013:43, para. 63.

[128] K.-O. Knops, in H. von der Groeben/J. Schwarze/A. Hatje, *Europäisches Unionsrecht*, 7th ed. (Baden-Baden: Nomos, 2015), Art. 38 GRC para. 1.

**295.** In contrast to Article 16 CFR, Article 38 CFR does not provide an enforceable right[129] since its provisions are too vague. Accordingly, it is only a principle within the meaning of Article 52(5) CFR. Article 38 CFR must first be substantiated by further provisions of EU law or national law to be fully effective.[130] A direct third-party effect of Article 38 CFR must therefore be rejected.[131] Nevertheless, Article 38 CFR can have an effect on private law, in particular through (partly fully harmonising) directives and their implementing acts. Furthermore, Article 38 CFR must be considered in interpreting the relevant secondary law and (if EU law is implemented) in the interpretation of national law.[132] Consumer protection law concerns, in particular, areas such as travel law, financial services, brokerage contracts, building contracts, product liability and protection against unfair competition. It also focuses on the situational protection of consumers when concluding contracts in off-premises and distance selling transactions such as e-commerce.[133] The special regulations on the sale of consumer goods are vital as well. Furthermore, consumer protection can be described as a 'general legal principle inherent in the law of obligations'.[134]

### cc) Prohibition of Discrimination, Article 21 CFR

**296.** Article 21 CFR is also of considerable importance among private individuals. Article 21(1) CFR prohibits discrimination concerning characteristics which are immutably attached to a person or can only be changed with difficulty; furthermore, it concerns properties to the presence or absence of which they

---

129 B. Giesecke, in J. Meyer/S. Hölscheidt, *Charta der Grundrechte der europäischen Union*, 5th ed. (Baden-Baden/Bern/Vienna: Nomos/Stämpfli/Verlag facultas, 2019), Art. 38 para. 14; H.D. Jarass, *Charta der Grundrechte der EU*, 4th ed. (Munich: C.H. Beck, 2021), Art. 38 para. 3 with further references; C. Stumpf, in J. Schwarze, *EU-Kommentar*, 4th ed. (Baden-Baden/Vienna/Basel: Nomos/Facultas/Helbing Lichtenhahn, 2019), Art. 38 CFR para. 1; a different opinion can be found in K.-O. Knops, in H. von der Groeben/J. Schwarze/A. Hatje, *Europäisches Unionsrecht*, 7th ed. (Baden-Baden: Nomos, 2015), Art. 38 CFR para. 36 f.

130 H.D. Jarass, *Charta der Grundrechte der EU*, 4th ed. (Munich: C.H. Beck, 2021), Art. 38 para. 3; CJEU, 22 May 2014, Case C-356/12, *Glatzel*, ECLI:EU:C:2014:350 (the judgment was given on Article 26 CFR, which, however, also contains a principle within the meaning of Article 52(5) CFR).

131 By the same token H.D. Jarass, *Charta der Grundrechte der EU*, 4th ed. (Munich: C.H. Beck, 2021), Art. 38 para. 4.

132 H.D. Jarass, *Charta der Grundrechte der EU*, 4th ed. (Munich: C.H. Beck, 2021), Art. 38 para. 4.

133 K.-O. Knops, in H. von der Groeben/J. Schwarze/A. Hatje, *Europäisches Unionsrecht*, 7th ed. (Baden-Baden: Nomos, 2015), Art. 38 CFR para. 4 with numerous further examples.

134 Grüneberg, in Grüneberg, *BGB Kommentar*, 84th ed. (Munich: C.H. Beck, 2025), Einl. para. 1; K.-O. Knops, in H. von der Groeben/J. Schwarze/A. Hatje, *Europäisches Unionsrecht*, 7th ed. (Baden-Baden: Nomos, 2015), Art. 38 CFR para. 5.

only have limited influence.[135] Paragraph 1 thus deals with the prohibition of discrimination based on personal characteristics. Here, unequal treatment is particularly severe. Paragraph 2 prohibits discrimination based on nationality and thus repeats Article 18(1) TFEU. Article 21 CFR, like Article 16 CFR, contains an enforceable right and not a mere principle in the sense of Article 52(5) CFR.[136]

**297.** Article 21 CFR can also become relevant for private actors.[137] For example, private law provisions are inapplicable if they violate Article 21 CFR. An example of this is the *Kücükdeveci* case already described.[138] In such a constellation, Article 21 CFR has an indirect effect: The fundamental right plays its role as it is specified further by the directive. The facts of the case are subsequently decided according to national law but without taking into consideration the provision that violates the Charter (or the specifying directive). This can, of course, lead to the opposite result considering the facts of the relevant case: In the *Kücükdeveci* case, the termination at the intended (earlier) date was invalid. If the then-applicable sec. 622(2) German Civil Code had been applied, the termination of the contract would already have been effective at the end of the following month. The CJEU's *Mangold* decision can serve as an additional example:[139] In this case, sec. 14(3) of the German Part-time and Fixed-term Employment Act, which provided for the possibility of a fixed-term employment contract for older employees without reason, was considered inapplicable by the CJEU. Here, the court relied on the unwritten principle of age discrimination, which is now codified in Article 21 CFR.

**298.** A second case relevant to private law is the *interpretation* of a private law provision in conformity with fundamental rights[140] – as opposed to their *inapplicability* discussed above. The prerequisite is that the provisions fall within the scope of application of the Charter of Fundamental Rights.

135 H.D. Jarass, *Charta der Grundrechte der EU*, 4th ed. (Munich: C.H. Beck, 2021), Art. 21 para. 2.

136 CJEU, 15 January 2014, Case C-176/12, *Association de médiation sociale*, ECLI:EU:C:2014:2, para. 43 ff.; H.D. Jarass, *Charta der Grundrechte der EU*, 4th ed. (Munich: C.H. Beck, 2021), Art. 21 para. 3 with further references.

137 H.D. Jarass, *Charta der Grundrechte der EU*, 4th ed. (Munich: C.H. Beck, 2021), Art. 38 para. 4 names four constellations.

138 CJEU, 19 January 2010, Case C-555/07, *Kücükdeveci*, ECLI:EU:C:2010:21, para. 51, 53.

139 CJEU, 22 November 2005, Case C-144/04, *Mangold*, ECLI:EU:C:2005:709.

140 Exemplary CJEU, 3 September 2014, Case C-201/13, *Deckmyn*, ECLI:EU:C:2014:2132, para. 30; H.D. Jarass, *Charta der Grundrechte der EU*, 4th ed. (Munich: C.H. Beck, 2021), Art. 21 para. 4.

**299.** Finally, the question of direct third-party effects also arises concerning Article 21 CFR. However, most commentators reject such a direct obligation of private actors.[141] As detailed above, the CJEU has taken a different path and established the direct third-party effect of Article 21 CFR.[142] According to the CJEU, Article 21 CFR has a mandatory character and does not have to be substantiated by provisions of EU or national law.[143] Consequently, the prohibition 'laid down in Article 21(1) of the Charter, is sufficient in itself to confer on individuals a right which they may rely on as such in disputes between them in a field covered by EU law'.[144] However, there is no direct third-party effect where the territorial scope of primary law is applicable.[145]

#### dd) Fair and Just Working Conditions, Article 31 CFR

**300.** The content of Article 31 CFR also refers to legal relations between private actors.[146] The provision covers four areas of application.[147] Paragraph 1 guarantees the right to healthy and safe working conditions and thus ensures workplace safety. Paragraph 1 also contains the right to working conditions that respect the workers' dignity, thus aiming at a working environment free of harassment.[148] Paragraph 2 regulates labour protection through maximum working hours, daily and weekly rest periods and paid annual leave. Due to

---

[141] H.D. Jarass, *Charta der Grundrechte der EU*, 4th ed. (Munich: C.H. Beck, 2021), Art. 21 para. 4 with further references.

[142] CJEU, 22 January 2019, Case C-193/17, *Cresco Investigation*, ECLI:EU:C:2019:43, paras. 76–85; CJEU, 11 September 2018, Case C-68/17, *IR/JQ*, ECLI:EU:C:2018:696, para. 69 f.; CJEU, 17 April 2018, Case C-414/16, *Egenberger*, ECLI:EU:C:2018:257, paras. 76–79.

[143] CJEU, 17 April 2018, Case C-414/16, *Egenberger*, ECLI:EU:C:2018:257, para. 78.

[144] CJEU, 17 April 2018, Case C-414/16, *Egenberger*, ECLI:EU:C:2018:257, para. 76.

[145] In that sense concerning Article 18(1) TFEU cf. CJEU, 11 June 2020, Case C-581/18, *TÜV Rheinland*, ECLI:EU:C:2020:453, para. 31 ff. In the case, in the context of the liability case concerning defective breast implants of the French manufacturer PIP, the question was whether Article 18(1) TFEU precluded the limitation of an obligation to insure liability for the use of medical devices to the territory of a Member State. The referring Higher Regional Court of Frankfurt (*NJW* 2019, 525) raised the question of a direct effect of the prohibition of discrimination, which, however, the CJEU did not answer in substance, as is evident.

[146] Hence, employment contracts between private individuals, cf. H.D. Jarass, *Charta der Grundrechte der EU*, 4th ed. (Munich: C.H. Beck, 2021), Art. 31 para. 3.

[147] B. Hüpers/B. Reese, in J. Meyer/S. Hölscheidt, *Charta der Grundrechte der europäischen Union*, 5th ed. (Baden-Baden/Bern/Vienna: Nomos/Stämpfli/Verlag facultas, 2019), Art. 31 para. 25.

[148] B. Hüpers/B. Reese, in J. Meyer/S. Hölscheidt, *Charta der Grundrechte der europäischen Union*, 5th ed. (Baden-Baden/Bern/Vienna: Nomos/Stämpfli/Verlag facultas, 2019), Art. 31 para. 25 with reference to the Explanations to the Charter.

the heading 'fair and just working conditions', questions of remuneration are sometimes considered to be covered as well.[149]

**301.** Article 31 CFR embodies an enforceable right and not a mere principle in the sense of Article 52(5) CFR.[150] It is primarily addressed to the EU and the Member States, but once again, the question arises as to whether it also creates obligations for private actors. In a manner comparable to its case law regarding Article 21 CFR, the CJEU has ruled that a private party (here: employer) can be directly obliged by Article 31(2) CFR.[151] In the respective cases, the employees (or, as in *Bauer* and *Broßonn*, the legal successors) could thus directly derive rights from the Charter. For example, in the *Broßonn* case discussed above, a claim for compensation for holiday entitlement was granted based on Article 31(2) CFR.[152]

**302.** Most of the legal commentators continue to reject an obligation of private parties based on Article 31(2) CFR for several reasons:[153] On the one hand, contrary to the CJEU's view, Article 31(2) CFR does not appear to be sufficiently precise in its wording, and on the other hand, Article 51(1) CFR, which according to this view conclusively defines the scope of application of the Charter, already precludes an obligation of private actors. Nevertheless, even

[149] However, in view of differently formulated preliminary drafts (cf. CHARTE 4192/00 CONVENT 18 of 27 March 2000), the history of origins does not clearly prove this in any case; for more details, see B. Hüpers/B. Reese, in J. Meyer/S. Hölscheidt, *Charta der Grundrechte der europäischen Union*, 5th ed. (Baden-Baden/Bern/Vienna: Nomos/Stämpfli/Verlag facultas, 2019), Art. 31 para. 14 f., 25, 61.

[150] H.D. Jarass, *Charta der Grundrechte der EU*, 4th ed. (Munich: C.H. Beck, 2021), Art. 31 para. 2.

[151] CJEU, 6 November 2018, Joined Cases C-569/16 and C-570/16, *Bauer and Broßonn*, ECLI:EU:C:2018:871, para. 79 ff., 85; CJEU, 6 November 2018, Case C-684/16, *Max-Planck-Gesellschaft*, ECLI:EU:C:2018:874, para. 49-55 and 69 ff.; CJEU, 13 December 2018, Case C-385/17, *Hein*, ECLI:EU:C:2018:1018, para. 52 ff.

[152] This is also discussed for the question of the recording of working time, even though the CJEU has not yet answered this question, see CJEU, 14 May 2019, Case C-55/18, *CCOO*, ECLI:EU:C:2019:402: The questions referred there only related to Spain's possible obligations. However, AG Pitruzella, Opinion on CJEU, Case C-55/18, *CCOO*, ECLI:EU:C:2019:87, para. 93 ff.

[153] B. Hüpers/B. Reese, in J. Meyer/S. Hölscheidt, *Charta der Grundrechte der europäischen Union*, 5th ed. (Baden-Baden/Bern/Vienna: Nomos/Stämpfli/Verlag facultas, 2019), Art. 31 para. 38 in the end; *Sura*, EuZA 2019, 350, 360 with further references; Mehrens/Witschen, *EuZA* 2019, 326, 331; Wutte, *EuZA* 2019, 222, 230. Previously already S. Lembke, in H. von der Groeben/J. Schwarze/A. Hatje, *Europäisches Unionsrecht*, 7th ed. (Baden-Baden: Nomos, 2015), Art. 31 CFR para. 10 with further references; H.D. Jarass, *Charta der Grundrechte der EU*, 4th ed. (Munich: C.H. Beck, 2021), Art. 31 para. 3; *Höpfner*, RdA 2013, 16, 19 ff.; AG *Trstenjak*, 8 September 2011, C-282/10, ECLI:EU:C:2011:559, para. 83.

according to this approach, the fundamental rights are of utmost importance between private actors. Hence, an indirect effect of fundamental rights is not disputed.[154] Private law rules that violate Article 31 CFR must remain inapplicable.[155] Furthermore, private individuals can be bound by regulations that prescribe positive obligations.[156] Finally, private law regulations must be interpreted in conformity with fundamental rights.[157]

#### ee) Other Fundamental Rights Relevant to Private Law

**303.** Further fundamental rights of particular importance to private law include Article 7 CFR (respect for private and family life), Article 11 CFR (freedom of expression) and Article 17 CFR (right to property), as well as, for labour law, Article 15 CFR (freedom to choose an occupation and the right to work), Article 23 CFR (equality between men and women), Article 30 CFR (protection against unfair dismissal) and Article 32 CFR (protection of children and young people).[158] Again, all these fundamental rights contain enforceable rights.[159] Private law rules that violate Charter rights are not applied. Also, private law rules must be interpreted in conformity with fundamental rights.[160] Finally, private individuals can be bound by regulations that promote the positive enforcement of Charter rights.[161]

## IV. REGULATORY LAW AND NATIONAL LAW

### 1. DIRECTLY BINDING LAW

**304.** According to Article 288(2) TFEU, regulations have general application; they are binding in their entirety and directly applicable in all Member States.

---

154 S. Lembke, in H. von der Groeben/J. Schwarze/A. Hatje, *Europäisches Unionsrecht*, 7th ed. (Baden-Baden: Nomos, 2015), Art. 31 CFR para. 10 with further references.

155 H.D. Jarass, *Charta der Grundrechte der EU*, 4th ed. (Munich: C.H. Beck, 2021), Art. 31 para. 3.

156 H.D. Jarass, *Charta der Grundrechte der EU*, 4th ed. (Munich: C.H. Beck, 2021), Art. 31 para. 3.

157 AG Trstenjak, 8 September 2011, Case C-282/10, ECLI:EU:C:2011:559, para. 83; H.D. Jarass, *Charta der Grundrechte der EU*, 4th ed. (Munich: C.H. Beck, 2021), Art. 31 para. 3.

158 Herresthal, *ZEuP* 2014, 238, 253 f.

159 Cf. on the individual fundamental rights the references in H.D. Jarass, *Charta der Grundrechte der EU*, 4th ed. (Munich: C.H. Beck, 2021), Art. 7 para. 7, Art. 11 para. 6, Art. 15 para. 2, Art. 17 para. 2, Art. 23 para. 3, Art. 30 para. 2, Art. 32 para. 2.

160 Cf. in each case the references in H.D. Jarass, *Charta der Grundrechte der EU*, 4th ed. (Munich: C.H. Beck, 2021), Art. 7 para. 8, Art. 11 para. 7, Art. 15 para. 3, Art. 17 para. 3, Art. 23 para. 5, Art. 30 para. 3, Art. 32 para. 3.

161 However, this only applies to Articles 11, 15, 30 and 32, cf. in each case the references in H.D. Jarass, *Charta der Grundrechte der EU*, 4th ed. (Munich: C.H. Beck, 2021), Art. 11 paras. 7, 24, Art. 15 paras. 3, 12, Art. 30 paras. 3, 9, Art. 32 paras. 3, 11.

Accordingly, implementation is not required. In contrast to directives, including fully harmonising directives,[162] the Member States no longer have any room for manoeuvre. However, the Member States sometimes issue national rules implementing the regulations.[163] On the one hand, these aim to fill regulatory gaps in regulations; on the other hand, they serve as an intermediary between EU legislation and the Member States' autonomous legal systems. In private law, regulations are chosen rarely. The directive offers greater flexibility in rulemaking and tends to fulfil the requirements of the principle of proportionality to a greater extent.[164]

### 2. EFFECTS ON NATIONAL LAW

**305.** Provisions adopted by a Member State concerning requirements of EU regulations may be called 'regulation-induced' law.[165] The nature of such national rules that originate in EU law must be considered when interpreting and applying them.[166]

## V. DIRECTIVES AND NATIONAL LAW

**306.** The relationship between European directives and national law is of great importance in the domain of European contract law. This will be discussed in detail below.[167]

## VI. STATE LIABILITY

**307.** Since national laws that violate EU law are not rendered void (sometimes, they are not even superseded), there may be cases where the EU law's supremacy does not materialise in practice. In the area of private law, this is particularly relevant in cases where EU directives have not or inadequately been transposed into national law.[168] If such behaviour remained without consequences, this would indeed lead to EU law having a dispositive nature. Moreover, the

162 For this purpose see paras. 78–83 above.

163 For example, with regard to judicial cooperation in the European Union, the provisions of the 11th Book of the German Code of Civil Procedure (sec. 1067–1120 ZPO).

164 On this already see above para. 229.

165 Nordmeier, *GPR* 2011, 158.

166 In this regard, Nordmeier, *GPR* 2011, 158, 162 ff. using the example of sec. 338 ZPO old version.

167 See below paras.308–400.

168 For more details see below paras. 385–399.

individual subjects of the law affected by the incorrect or omitted transposition would not be protected adequately. Therefore, in order to realise the supremacy of EU law comprehensively, the legal demand to apply national transpositions in conformity with the directives is accompanied by a state liability claim. This claim can be directed against the EU itself, but above all, against the Member State concerned. This will be considered in greater detail in §35 below.[169]

[169] See below paras. 1462–1495.

# §7. HARMONISATION OF PRIVATE LAW THROUGH DIRECTIVES

## CONTENTS

References: S. Pötters/R. Christensen, 'Richtlinienkonforme Rechtsfortbildung und Wortlautgrenze', *JZ* 2011, 387; B. Schinkels, 'Unbegrenzte richtlinienkonforme Rechtsfortbildung als Haftung Privater für Legislativunrecht? – Für ein subjektives Recht auf Transparenz', *JZ* 2011, 394; M. Stürner, 'Privatrechtsangleichung durch EU-Richtlinien', *JURA* 2017, 394; M. Stürner, 'Die richtlinienkonforme Rechtsanwendung im Privatrecht, Teil I – Methodische Grundlagen', *JURA* 2017, 777, 'Teil II – Anwendungsbeispiele', *JURA* 2017, 1163.

## I. THE TRANSPOSITION OF DIRECTIVES

**308.** The directive is the most important legislative instrument, at least in the core area of EU private law. An overview of the relevant legal acts can be found at the beginning of the Second Part of this work.[1] The directive does not aim at a complete harmonisation but only an approximation of laws. Unlike a regulation, which has a direct effect in all Member States, directives require an act of transposition by the Member States.[2]

---

1 See below para. 401. Overview also in Heiderhoff, *Europäisches Privatrecht*, pp. 319 ff.; see also already Stürner, *JURA* 2016, 1133, 1135.

2 For possible exceptions see below paras. 317–321 and 386–399.

## 1. LEEWAY DURING TRANSPOSITION

**309.** Article 288(3) TFEU leaves the Member States some leeway when transposing directives: It is binding only with regard to the legislative objective but not concerning the means. The Member States also remain free regarding the legislative form and technique (e.g. law, ordinance, federal, national, regional). This relative autonomy is restricted to the extent that rules of national law may not be less favourable than those on similar national matters (principle of equivalence); furthermore, the states must not render the exercise of the rights conferred onto the EU practically impossible or excessively difficult (principle of effectiveness).[3] Moreover, the principle of transparency applies.[4] Hence, the legal consequences of incomplete or defective transpositions are of practical importance.[5]

**310.** The more detailed a directive is, the less room for leeway remains. The dividing line between mere approximation and partial or complete harmonisation (e.g. through fully harmonising directives) or even regulations, is almost fluid.

## 2. CODIFICATION OR SPECIAL LAW?

**311.** Hence, the Member States are free to fulfil the directive's requirements by way of integration into an already existing codification or to pass a special law for this purpose only. The German legislator initially tended to follow the latter approach. The modernisation of the law of obligations in 2001 marked a turning point: A whole series of ancillary national private acts were recodified during the transposition of the Sale of Goods Directive. Even though the legislator still adheres to this principle in consumer law, there have been repeated calls to 'outsource' the transposition legislation to a dedicated codification on consumer protection law, following the example of other Member States, such as France or Italy.[6]

**312.** However, this is likely to bring about advantages only at first sight. It would result in an increasing divergence between consumer protection and general private law, which could lead to a loss of importance of the latter because of the dynamics of the former. Regarding the law's content, it is crucial that both areas remain intertwined. Furthermore, an exclusive application of such a hypothetical

[3] See, for example, CJEU, 18 December 2014, Case C-449/13, *CA Consumer Finance*, ECLI:EU:C:2014:2464, para. 23; CJEU, 5 March 2020, Case C-679/18, *OPR-Finance*, ECLI:EU:C:2020:167, para. 32.

[4] See the example of control of standard terms, below at paras. 317–321.

[5] More on this see below at paras. 385–399.

[6] A 'liberating blow' was called for by Wendehorst, *NJW* 2011, 2551, 2555; Wendehorst, *ZEuP* 2011, 263, 286 f.

Code on consumer protection law would possibly be in opposition to the *effet utile* principle: It would hardly be justifiable if consumers were better protected under general private law than the specific provisions of consumer protection law. Italian law, for example, provides the consumer with a choice between rules on warranty and liability from the Codice civile and specific consumer rights from the Codice del consumo.[7] However, such free competition between the two systems can lead to the consumer not proceeding according to the Codice del consumo but only according to the Codice civile – for example, in the case of a contract's termination, which is impossible in the case of non-performance (Article 1453 Codice civile), whereas Article 130(5), (7)(b) Codice del consumo, following the Consumer Sales Directive, prioritises the consumer's claim for subsequent performance and allows the contract to be terminated only after the expiry of a reasonable period of time.[8] Creating special legislation for consumers would, therefore, not lead to any advantages in terms of transparency.

## II. NATIONAL LEGISLATIVE FREEDOM

**313.** Outside of a directive's scope, the national legislator may continue to legislate freely; however, the *effet utile* principle remains applicable.

### 1. MATERIAL SCOPE

#### a) *Internal Matters*

**314.** As a general rule, directives in the area of private law also apply to purely domestic matters. Cross-border transactions are no prerequisite since the aim is to create a level playing field in all Member States. The legislative powers from Article 169, 114 TFEU thus differ from Article 81 TFEU, where a cross-border element is explicitly required for legal acts in the area of judicial cooperation.[9]

---

7 Article 135 Codice del consumo. The parallel provision in the Codice civile, Article 1469-bis Codice civile, provides that the rules on contracts in general (Articles 1321 ff. Codice civile) also apply to consumer contracts, unless these contain more specific rules or rules that are more favourable to the consumer. On the relationship between the two regimes, Dalla Massara, *Riv. dir. civ.*, 2007, II, 123 ff.; see also Gebauer, *JbItalR* 20 (2007), pp. 3, 13 ff. in summary.

8 The possibility of immediate termination of the contract according to Article 1453 Codice civile in case of non-performance should nevertheless be in conformity with the Directive, since a higher level of consumer protection is permissible according to Article 8(2) CSD. In this sense also Mansel, *AcP* 204 (2004), 396, 435. On the legal situation under the fully harmonising Sales of Goods Directive see below paras. 374–384.

9 For more details see M. Stürner, in *Frankfurter Kommentar zu EUV, GRC, AEUV*, 2nd ed. (Tübingen: Mohr Siebeck, 2023), Art. 81 AEUV paras. 17 f.

A Member State's legislator is thus not free to create a special regime for purely domestic matters that is not based on the applicable directive's requirements. It would only be possible to differentiate between domestic and internal market situations in the case of minimally harmonising consumer protection directives if the level of protection for the latter were higher than for purely domestic situations. However, under domestic (constitutional) law, such unequal treatment could hardly be justified in the end.[10]

### b) *Internal Market Matters*

**315.** Private law directives thus generally cover internal market matters; as stated above, this term also includes purely internal matters.

### c) *Non-EU States*

**316.** In principle, directives also cover situations involving a non-EU ('third') country. This is true at least insofar as the pertinent national law transposing the directive is applicable in the given situation under the relevant conflict-of-laws rules. In principle, a categorical exception for consumer contracts with traders domiciled in third countries would not be a relevant obstruction to market access. However, harmonisation through directives is precisely about establishing a uniform level of protection.

## 2. TRANSPOSITION OF DIRECTIVES THROUGH GENERAL CLAUSES

References: M. Siems, 'Effektivität und Legitimität einer Richtlinienumsetzung durch Generalklauseln', *ZEuP* 2002, 747.

**317.** The binding objective of the directive limits the Member States' room for manoeuvre in transposing directives. In particular, the principle of effectiveness and transparency of EU law must be obeyed: Individuals must be able to identify rights under the directive clearly. Therefore, a Member State cannot claim that transposition is unnecessary because corresponding principles can be derived from an existing general rule of national law. This can violate the transparency requirement since it is not sufficiently clear to what extent the domestic rule in question transposes EU law requirements. This is illustrated by the case *Commission v. Netherlands*:[11]

---

10 See already above para. 3.

11 Cf. CJEU, 10 May 2001, Case C-144/99, *Commission/Netherlands*, ECLI:EU:C:2001:257.

**318.** When the transposition deadline for Directive 93/13/EEC on unfair terms in consumer contracts[12] expired in 1994, the Netherlands had not taken any legislative measures in this respect. In particular, Article 4(2) and (5) of the Directive, according to which terms in consumer contracts must be drafted clearly and intelligibly, were not transposed. In its transposition report submitted to the EU Commission, the Dutch government pointed out that the Hoge Raad, the country's highest private law court, had developed a well-established case law on unfair terms under the general rule of Article 6:233 Burgerlijk Wetboek (Dutch Civil Code), which already complied with the directive's requirement. A separate transposition law was therefore considered unnecessary.

**319.** The Commission then initiated infringement proceedings against the Netherlands under Article 258 TFEU.[13] The CJEU found that the Netherlands had breached the requirement of transparent transposition.[14] Although the obligation to transpose a directive does not necessarily always require action by the legislature, it is 'essential for national law to guarantee that the national authorities will effectively apply the directive in full, that the legal position under national law should be sufficiently precise and clear and that individuals are made fully aware of their rights and, where appropriate, may rely on them before the national courts'.[15] The fact that the objectives pursued by the Directive could (possibly) also be achieved by a systematic interpretation of the Dutch provisions, taking into account the relevant case law,[16] was considered insufficient.[17]

**320.** As much as the transparency argument appears plausible on the grounds of a protective purpose-oriented interpretation, it entails a considerable encroachment on the Member States' legislative autonomy. General and open rules, being necessary tools in any legal system for new legal developments, are devalued to a certain extent since they are not considered suitable as such to serve the implementation of directive requirements. This also applies to already existing general rules. The transparency argument is also likely to have few practical benefits: The right-holders under the directive are unlikely to be informed of their rights only based on the transposition law. Further communication and information are typically required, e.g. by news outlets or other associations. These are likely to reflect the scope of the rights correctly.

---

12 Council Directive 93/13/EEC of 5 April 1993 on unfair terms in consumer contracts, OJ 1993 L 95/29 (so-called Unfair Terms Directive).

13 At that time Article 169 ECT, later Article 226 EC.

14 CJEU, 10 May 2001, Case C-144/99, *Commission/Netherlands*, ECLI:EU:C:2001:257.

15 CJEU, 10 May 2001, Case C-144/99, *Commission/Netherlands*, ECLI:EU:C:2001:257, para. 17.

16 This is the argumentation of the Dutch government; against this, the Opinion of Advocate General Tizzano, ECLI:EU:C:2001:50, paras. 26 ff.

17 CJEU, 10 May 2001, Case C-144/99, *Commission/Netherlands*, ECLI:EU:C:2001:257, para. 19, referring to the Opinion of Advocate General Tizzano, ECLI:EU:C:2001:50, paras. 26 ff.

**321.** It is true that existing case law on domestic general rules may be incomplete or change in the future. The latter, however, is only the case in unique situations, even in systems where a doctrine of precedent does not exist. In the words of the German Federal Supreme Court: 'A departure from the continuity of case-law can only be accepted as an exception if there are clearly overriding or even absolutely compelling reasons for doing so.'[18] Whether, on the other hand, an incomplete case law amounts to enough uncertainty regarding the directive's legal scope would have to be determined in each individual case; a general exclusion of this transposition technique would go too far.[19] However, it should be noted that the more recent directives are far more detailed than, for example, the Unfair Terms Directive, so the problem of transposition through existing general clauses is unlikely to arise again.

### 3. 'EXCESSIVE' TRANSPOSITION, OR GOLD-PLATING

**322.** Some further issues arise in the case of so-called excessive transpositions, also called gold-plating. Those occur when the Member States deviate from the directive's requirements during transposition, e.g. by giving it a broader material scope of application. This transposition technique is particularly relevant in Member States which (like Germany) aim to integrate private law directives into their general private law codifications. The resulting problems will be discussed separately.[20]

## III. FURTHER EFFECTS OF DIRECTIVES

### 1. DIRECT THIRD-PARTY EFFECT

**323.** The so-called direct third-party effect of a directive can, on the one hand, refer to the relationship of a private individual to the state. If an individual can derive rights from the directive vis-à-vis a Member State that has not transposed it or has not transposed it fully, one can call this a direct vertical third-party effect.[21] If, on the other hand, the effects of a directive that has not or inadequately been transposed are at issue in the relationship between two private actors, this is called a direct horizontal third-party effect. This will be discussed further in

18 BGHZ 85, 64, 66. For detailed information on the content and limits of the doctrine of binding precedent see K. Langenbucher, *Die Entwicklung und Auslegung von Richterrecht* (Munich: Beck, 1996), pp. 106 ff., 126 ff. and Krebs, *AcP* 195 (1995), 171, 182 ff.

19 Along these lines also Siems, *ZEuP* 2002, 747, 750 ff.

20 See paras. 366–373 below.

21 More on this see below para. 386-399.

the section on the consequences of transposition deficiencies.[22] It should already be noted that the CJEU has consistently rejected the idea of private parties being bound by directives.[23]

## 2. INDIRECT THIRD-PARTY EFFECT

**324.** Nevertheless, a directive has an indirect third-party effect, at least to the extent that a Member State's entire national legal system must be interpreted so that the directive's objectives are achieved. The main addressees of this demand are the courts of the Member States. The content of the directive thus enters the private law relationship via methodological diversions.[24]

## 3. PRE-EMPTIVE EFFECT OF DIRECTIVES

**325.** The CJEU attributes a pre-emptive effect to directives even before the transposition deadline has expired.[25] However, this only amounts to a prohibition of frustration, which does not fundamentally prevent the national legislator from enacting conflicting national provisions.[26]

# IV. THE INTERPRETATION OF DIRECTIVES

References: K. Riesenhuber, 'Interpretation of EU Secondary Law', in K. Riesenhuber (ed.), *European Legal Methodology* (Cambridge: Intersentia, 2021), §10; M. Stürner, 'Privatrechtsangleichung durch EU-Richtlinien', *JURA* 2017, 394.

## 1. THE CJEU AS THE ULTIMATE AUTHORITY ON INTERPRETATION OF EU LAW

**326.** EU law is primarily applied by the courts and other bodies of the Member States. However, not least due to the different legal traditions in the EU, differences can arise, which would again endanger the harmonisation of the law. To avoid this, primary law grants the CJEU a monopoly on interpretation: According to Article 267 TFEU, the CJEU alone is responsible for the authoritative

22 More on this see below paras. 392–397.
23 Since CJEU, 14 July 1994, Case C-91/92, *Faccini Dori*, ECLI:EU:C:1994:292, paras. 19 ff.
24 More on this see below paras. 346–354.
25 CJEU, 14 June 2007, Case C-422/05, *Commission/Belgium*, ECLI:EU:C:2007:342.
26 Hofmann, in Riesenhuber, *European Legal Methodology*, §15.

interpretation of EU law. This aims to promote uniform application of EU law and avoid legal fragmentation. Unlike many other acts of uniform law (e.g. the UN Sales Convention), EU law thus has a central authority that decides on the interpretation of all legal acts of the EU in a binding manner.

**327.** To ensure that this uniform interpretation is realised, it must be ensured that the CJEU is permitted to rule on all cases involving EU law. In theory, a separate EU court system could achieve this. The US legal system could serve as a role model: Here, all federal states have fully developed state courts. At the same time, however, there is also an independent system of federal courts with their own jurisdiction and appeal system.[27] The EU has not followed this approach. Instead, EU law is enforced decentrally by the courts and institutions of the Member States.

## 2. METHODS OF INTERPRETING EUROPEAN UNION LAW

References: C. Buck, *Über die Auslegungsmethoden des Gerichtshofs der Europäischen Gemeinschaften* (Frankfurt am Main: Lang, 1998).

**328.** In principle, the interpretation of EU law is autonomous, i.e. detached from the principles of the Member States' legal systems and based solely on primary and secondary Union law. The reason is the principle of uniform application of EU law in all Member States.[28]

### *a) Literal Interpretation*

**329.** First and foremost, the CJEU approaches the meaning of a secondary legal act through its wording. In this respect, it is essential to note that EU law is multilingual, and all official languages are equally authoritative (Article 55(1) TEU). As a general rule, however, only the most common language versions, i.e. English, French, German, Italian and Spanish, are considered.

### *b) Systematic-Teleological Interpretation*

**330.** The CJEU interprets a rule of secondary law in a teleological way to accompany or clarify contradictions between the language versions.[29] The

---

27 H. Schack, *Einführung in das US-amerikanische Zivilprozessrecht*, 4th ed. (Munich: C.H. Beck, 2010), paras. 4 ff.

28 CJEU, 20 January 2005, Case C-464/01, *Gruber*, ECLI:EU:C:2005:32, para. 31.

29 Cf. Grundmann/Riesenhuber, *JuS* 2001, 529, 530. In general on systematic and teleological interpretation in Union law Riesenhuber, in Riesenhuber, *European Legal Methodology*, §10

regulation's practical effectiveness (*effet utile*) usually plays a distinct role. This usually results in a line of reasoning in favour of further integration. In consumer protection law, in particular, this approach has led to a series of judgments that have virtually turned upside down the traditional approaches of the Member States' legal systems. Examples include the *Quelle* decision,[30] which postulated a general inadmissibility of compensation for use in the case of a demand for subsequent performance, or the *Weber/Putz* decision,[31] from which it follows that the trader is obliged to bear the costs for the removal of the defective item and the installation of the new, defect-free item. Both judgments opposed the previously dominant view of German law and forced the legislator to act. The reasoning in each case is based on the consumer's right to free restoration of the contractual condition according to Article 3(2) of the CSD; according to the CJEU, this right would not be fully effective if interpreted differently.[32]

**331.** This approach includes systematic arguments, albeit to a lesser extent that this would be done in some Member States' systems. Since European private law is currently still structured in a rather fragmentary manner, the idea of the legal order's unity, which is, for example, the guiding star of systematic interpretation within the German legal system, can only be employed to a limited extent. Instead, a kind of 'internal systematic interpretation' that considers the regulatory approaches within the same regulation or directive is used. The two decisions mentioned above also illustrate this.[33]

**332.** The CJEU often refers to the recitals, which always precede secondary legislation. It is doubtful whether these should carry much weight since they are not normatively binding.[34] In many cases, the recitals are simply repetitions or paraphrases of the legal texts, which generally diminishes their practical significance.[35] If, however, they contain substantive clarifications capable of influencing the result of interpretation concerning a specific provision, the

---

paras. 22 ff.; C. Höpfner, *Die systemkonforme Auslegung* (Tübingen: Mohr Siebeck, 2008), pp. 99 ff., 108 f.; Höpfner/Rüthers, *AcP* 209 (2009), 1, 12 f.

30 CJEU, 17 April 2008, Case C-404/06, *Quelle*, ECLI:EU:C:2008:231; for details see below at paras. 348–354.

31 CJEU, 16 June 2011, Joined Cases C-65/09 and C-87/09, *Weber* and *Putz*, ECLI:EU:C:2011:396.

32 CJEU, 17 April 2008, Case C-404/06, *Quelle*, ECLI:EU:C:2008:231, paras. 34–36; CJEU, 16 June 2011, Joined Cases C-65/09 and C-87/09, *Weber* and *Putz*, ECLI:EU:C:2011:396, paras. 46, 52–55.

33 CJEU, 17 April 2008, Case C-404/06, *Quelle*, ECLI:EU:C:2008:231, paras. 34–36; CJEU, 16 June 2011, Joined Cases C-65/09 and C-87/09, *Weber* and *Putz*, ECLI:EU:C:2011:396, paras. 46, 52–55.

34 See on this from the perspective of conflict of laws Requejo Isidro, in *Festschrift für Kohler* (Bielefeld: Gieseking, 2018), pp. 425, 434 ff.

35 Cf. Langenbucher/Donath, in Langenbucher, *Europäisches Privat- und Wirtschaftsrecht*, §1 para. 17.

question arises as to how to assess the fact that the European legislator has not included this in the legal act. The CJEU seems to take a result-oriented stance here. In its view, the 'operative part of an [Community] act is [in this respect] indissociably linked to the statement of reasons for it, so that, when it has to be interpreted, account must be taken of the reasons which led to its adoption'.[36] Referring to this, the CJEU has, for example, extended the claim for compensation arising in the case of flight cancellations (Article 7 of Regulation 261/2004) to delays, although Article 6 of Regulation 261/2004 does not provide for this; in this respect, a connection between cancellation and delay highlighted in Recital 15 of Regulation 261/2004 served as justification.[37]

**333.** However, the CJEU draws a red line when the recitals would substantively change the meaning of legal provisions: The recitals of an EU legal act have 'no binding legal force and cannot be relied on either as a ground for derogating from the actual provisions of the act in question or for interpreting those provisions in a manner clearly contrary to their wording'.[38] The CJEU also refers to the guidelines published by the Commission as practical guidance for certain legal acts as 'useful tools for interpreting'.[39] However, the ends sometimes justify the means to the extent that such guidelines are sometimes disregarded if they do not support the result of the interpretation.[40]

### c) *Interpretation across Several Legal Acts*

**334.** According to the CJEU's case law, 'each provision of Community law must be placed in its context and interpreted in the light of the provisions of Community law as a whole [...]'.[41] However, the intensity of the systematic interpretation thus

---

36 CJEU, 29 April 2004, Case C-298/00 P, *Italy/Commission*, ECLI:EU:C:2004:240, para. 97, with references.

37 CJEU, 19 November 2009, Joined Cases C-402/07 and C-432/07, *Sturgeon and Böck*, ECLI:EU:C:2009:716, paras. 42 ff.

38 Cf. CJEU, 19 November 1998, Case C-162/97, *Nilsson*, ECLI:EU:C:1998:554, para. 54; CJEU, 25 November 1998, Case C-308/97, *Manfredi*, ECLI:EU:C:1998:566, para. 30; CJEU, 24 November 2005, Case C-136/04, *Deutsches Milch-Kontor*, ECLI:EU:C:2005:716, para. 32; CJEU, 19 June 2014, Case C-345/13, *Karen Millen Fashions*, ECLI:EU:C:2014:2013, para. 31; CJEU, 13 September 2018, C-287/17, *Česká pojišťovna*, ECLI:EU:C:2018:707, para. 33; CJEU, 19 April 2019, Case C-131/18, *Gambietz/Ziegler*, ECLI:EU:C:2019:306, para. 28.

39 CJEU, 8 May 2019, Case C-631/17, *Inspecteur van de Belastingdienst*, ECLI:EU:C:2019:381, para. 41.

40 For example, in the case CJEU, 27 March 2019, Case C-681/17, *slewo*, ECLI:EU:C:2019:255, where no reference is made to the existing guide to the CRD. In his Opinion of 19 December 2018, Case C-681/17, ECLI:EU:C:2018:1041, para. 37, AG Saugmandsgaard Oe had mentioned the Guide but rejected the result arising from it. On the case in more detail see below para. 347.

41 CJEU, 6 October 1982, Case 283/81, *CILFIT*, ECLI:EU:C:1982:335, para. 20; CJEU, 23 March 2000, Case C-208/98, *Berliner Kindl*, ECLI:EU:C:2000:152, paras. 24–26.

addressed depends on the degree of harmonisation in the relevant area of law. The harmonisation of law in the internal market has so far been sector-specific; hence, the EU legislator has also pursued different regulatory objectives in the various legal acts or has not always coordinated the individual legal acts sufficiently.[42]

**335.** The attempt to create a common frame of reference for European contract law has to be considered a failure.[43] This would have created a horizontal reference point for systematic interpretation. Realising the proposal for a Common European Sales Law would also have achieved a similar effect.[44]

**336.** A special form of interpretation across legal acts is the interpretation in conformity with primary law: Secondary legal acts must always be considered in the light of primary law and interpreted in such a way that no contradiction with the treaties arises.[45] This applies, in particular, to the Charter of Fundamental Rights. However, the focus is primarily on resolving conflicts of rank and, thus, on a type of systematic interpretation that follows very unique rules. The aspects relevant to private law have already been considered above.[46]

**337.** Overall, systematic thinking is not yet very strong in European private law.[47] For each individual legal field, it must be examined to what extent parallels exist between existing legal acts. The more dense the regulatory network, the more possible and necessary it is to interpret legal acts coherently.[48] The related question of the existence of an internal system and the resulting consequences for the systematic interpretation of EU private law will be considered later.[49]

### d) *Comparative Law Interpretation*

**338.** Secondary legislation is often incomplete. To fill such gaps, the CJEU sometimes resorts to Member State law.[50] In some cases, the CJEU refers to comparative law to identify common principles of EU law. For example, the

---

42 In European labour law, for example, approaches to an internal system formation are observed, cf. K. Riesenhuber, *European Employment Law*, 2nd ed. (Cambridge: Intersentia, 2021), §1 para. 44. This is a minimum requirement for a systematic interpretation refering to other sources of secondary law.

43 See paras. 120–129 above.

44 In addition, see paras. 1310–1317 below.

45 For an example cf. CJEU, 1 October 2015, Case C-340/14, *Trijber*, ECLI:EU:C:2015:641.

46 See paras. 243–259 above.

47 See Langenbucher/Donath, in Langenbucher, *Europäisches Privat- und Wirtschaftsrecht*, §1 para. 11. On the idea of coherence in European private law see below paras. 1292–1366.

48 Riesenhuber, *System und Prinzipien des Europäischen Vertragsrechts*, 2003, p. 62, referring to CJEU, 7 March 1996, Case C-192/94, *El Corte Inglés*, ECLI:EU:C:1996:88, paras. 18 ff.

49 See below paras. 1318–1338.

50 CJEU, 22 November 2012, Case C-139/11, *Cuadrench Moré*, ECLI:EU:C:2012:741, paras. 25 ff.

general prohibition of abuse of rights is derived from the common principles of the Member States' legal systems.[51] This does not contradict the principle of autonomous interpretation because directives were themselves created based on comparative law considerations.[52] In that sense, an interaction between EU law and national law can be observed: EU law is no completely detached legal system; harmonisation also requires consideration of existing legal principles.

**339.** However, in the CJEU judgments, which are relatively concise overall (following the 'French decision style'), more detailed comparative law considerations are rarely found since the reasons for the judgments generally contain references to own case law exclusively. The Opinions of the Advocates General, on the other hand, are different; they often contain extensive comparative legal reasoning. Comparative law arguments are also sometimes used in the deliberations of the CJEU.[53] In many cases, the decisions of the CJEU contain references to the Opinions so that the common tradition of the Member States' legal systems is taken into account.

### *e) Further Development of the Law*

**340.** It has already become clear that the dividing line between interpretation and further development of law (to translate the German term *Rechtsfortbildung*) cannot be drawn sharply. The teleological interpretation often used by the CJEU may sometimes be called daring; its legitimacy would then lie in the court's power to progressively develop the law. From the outset, one should act somewhat cautiously in EU law in this respect: The principle of conferral applies;[54] any further development of the law expands the material scope of application of the secondary legislation and thus shifts the existing structure of competences in favour of the EU. The admissibility of arguments by analogy must be assessed similarly; here, too, a cautious approach must be taken.[55]

### *f) Economic Analysis and Legal Interpretation*

**341.** It has already been shown that the economic analysis of law concerns the economic efficiency of legal transactions.[56] An economic view of contract

51 CJEU, 12 May 1998, Case C-367/96, *Kefalas*, ECLI:EU:C:1998:222, para. 20.

52 E.g. CJEU, 14 December 1996, Case C-104/95, *Kontogeorgas/Kartonpark*, ECLI:EU:C:1996:492, para. 28. Further example on the interpretation of the term 'consumer': CJEU, 14 March 1991, Case C-361/89, *Di Pinto*, ECLI:EU:C:1991:118, para. 22.

53 Franzen, *Privatrechtsangleichung durch die Europäische Gemeinschaft*, 1999, pp. 454 f., 465 ff., showing scepticism as to the use of comparative arguments.

54 See paras. 217–227 above.

55 For example, see CJEU, 20 February 1975, Case 64/74, *Reich*, ECLI:EU:C:1975:27, para. 3; CJEU, 12 December 1985, Case 165/84, *Krohn*, ECLI:EU:C:1985:507, para. 14.

56 Above at paras. 20–21.

law may, however, contradict the values of the applicable law, as the example of the efficient breach of a contract shows.[57] It is controversial to what extent the principles of the economic analysis of law can also be used to interpret applicable provisions. According to this approach, the question is whether a certain regulation generates efficient results; normatively, an efficient interpretation can be demanded. The economic analysis of the law is not, at least according to the predominant view in continental Europe, a method equivalent to traditional means of legal interpretation: The interpretation of a provision under the aspect of efficiency can only be considered in exceptional cases, usually only when this corresponds to its purpose.[58] Only in rare cases will this be the law's primary objective. The German Environmental Liability Act may serve as an example: Here, the legislator explicitly aimed to efficiently allocate resources by introducing strict liabilities for damages caused by the environmental impacts of certain devices or buildings.[59] If this is not the case, economic analysis is limited to its function as a theory on legislation that can assist in creating standards by considering economic consequences.[60]

**342.** Regarding some central provisions of the law of obligations, an economic purpose is sometimes said to be at least intended by the legislator: For example, the modernised German law of obligations is based on the Consumer Sales Directive. The reform legislator has made the directive's regulatory concept, which is per se limited to consumer sales, a model for all contracts. The directive, in turn, aims to harmonise consumer sales law in the internal market. This implies the regulatory goal of improving efficiency.[61] If this market-oriented background were already sufficient for applying economic criteria in interpretation,[62] then the entire law of obligations would be accessible to economic analysis.[63]

---

57 See below at paras. 757–758.

58 In this regard, H. Eidenmüller, *Effizienz als Rechtsprinzip*, 4th ed. (Tübingen: Mohr Siebeck, 2015), pp. 463 ff.; Taupitz, *AcP* 196 (1996), 114, 127 f., 135 f.; Grundmann, *RabelsZ* 61 (1997), 423, 430 ff.; for the community private law context Grundmann/Riesenhuber, *JuS* 2001, 529, 532 f.

59 See the explanatory memorandum in BT-Drucks. 11/6454, p. 13; on this H. Eidenmüller, *Effizienz als Rechtsprinzip*, 4th ed. (Tübingen: Mohr Siebeck, 2015), pp. 453 f.; Taupitz, *AcP* 196 (1996), 114, 146 ff. with further references. It should be mentioned in passing that the German Civil Code legislator has also already made extensive economic considerations, for example in the area of liability for game damage; however, this cannot lead to interpreting the entire liability law according to efficiency criteria.

60 On this again H. Eidenmüller, *Effizienz als Rechtsprinzip*, 4th ed. (Tübingen: Mohr Siebeck, 2015), pp. 414 ff., 452 ff. ('Efficiency as a policy of the law'); Taupitz, *AcP* 196 (1996), 114, 122 f.; likewise U. Huber, *Leistungsstörungen*, Volume I (Tübingen: Mohr Siebeck, 1999), § 2 V 5 (pp. 54 ff.).

61 See on the importance of economic reasoning in Union private law Franck, in Riesenhuber (ed.), *European Legal Methodology*, §5.

62 Fundamental to such an approach Posner/Rosenfield (1977) 6 *Journal of Legal Studies* 83.

63 In this spirit Grundmann/Riesenhuber, *JuS* 2001, 529, 532 f.

**343.** However, such a view overstates the economic regulatory purpose of the Consumer Sales Directive. The main purpose of the harmonisation of laws intended by the directive is to strengthen consumer confidence in cross-border trade in goods and services. According to Recital 3 CSD, harmonisation serves to avoid distortions of competition that may arise from the Member States' inconsistent laws in the area of consumer sales. However, this does not imply an efficiency-oriented objective of the regulations contained therein; the wording is instead to be understood as an indication that the Directive fulfils the requirements of Article 95 TEC (now Article 114 TFEU). This is insufficient to account for the general permissibility of an efficiency-oriented interpretation. Instead, what is required is that a specific rule, or at least the regulatory context,[64] has the efficient allocation of resources as its object according to the intention of EU legislator.

## V. THE ROLE OF NATIONAL COURTS IN THE INTERPRETATION OF DIRECTIVES

References: T. Henninger, *Europäisches Privatrecht und Methode* (Tübingen: Mohr Siebeck, 2009); C. Herresthal, *Richterliche Rechtsfortbildung im europäischen Bezugsrahmen* (Munich: C.H. Beck, 2006); C. Herresthal, 'Voraussetzungen und Grenzen der gemeinschaftsrechtskonformen Rechtsfortbildung', *EuZW* 2007, 396; C. Herresthal, 'Die Grenzen der richtlienkonformen Rechtsfortbildung im Kaufrecht', *WM* 2007, 1354; F. Kainer, 'Privatrecht zwischen Richtlinien und Grundrechten – Zu den Grenzen richtlinienkonformer Auslegung und horzontalen Richtlinienwirkungen', *GPR* 2016, 262; E.A. Kramer, 'Die Methode bestimmt den Inhalt: eine weiterhin offene Grundsatzfrage des Unionsrechts', *GPR* 2015, 262; E.A. Kramer, 'Replik zu Riesenhuber, Methodendivergenzen ertragen', *GPR* 2016, 210; P. Reimer, 'Richtlinienkonforme Rechtsanwendung: Spielräume und Bindungen mitgliedstaatlichen Rechts', *JZ* 2015, 910; K. Riesenhuber, 'Methodendivergenzen ertragen!', *GPR* 2016, 158; K. Riesenhuber/R. Domröse, 'Richtlinienkonforme Rechtsfindung und nationale Methodenlehre', *RIW* 2005, 47; J. Schürnbrand, 'Die Grenzen richtlinienkonformer Rechtsfortbildung im Privatrecht', *JZ* 2007, 910; H. Unberath, 'Die richtlinienkonforme Auslegung am Beispiel der Kaufrechtsrichtlinie', *ZEuP* 2005, 5.

### 1. BASICS

**344.** Directives do not lead to complete harmonisation but only to an approximation of laws. For the respective Member State, this generally results in a transposition obligation. In the area of private law, this has the advantage

64 Cf. Taupitz, *AcP* 196 (1996), 114, 127 f.

that a certain leeway remains as to how the objective set by the directive can be achieved in a binding manner (Article 288(3) TFEU): The national legislator can fit the European requirements more smoothly into the regulatory framework and the systematics of the private law system compared to a regulation, which has direct and immediate effect (Article 288(2) TFEU). Admittedly, the transformation does not always succeed completely. This is partly due to omissions in the transposition process, but also partly because the provisions of the directives are sometimes not entirely clear, and in some cases, the provision's content is only clarified later by the CJEU.[65] Moreover, the increasing shift from minimum to full harmonisation in recent years, especially in consumer law, has once again significantly limited the remaining freedom of the Member States. If this increases the risk of incorrect transposition, because the Member States are denied the safe path of overfulfilment of minimum requirements, or gold-plating, the question of the consequences of such deficiencies is of increased importance. On the one hand, a direct effect of the directive might appear to be a suitable solution; however, according to the still valid case law of the CJEU, this is out of the question, at least in horizontal relationships.[66] On the other hand, the individual who suffers legal disadvantages due to the incorrect transposition must be compensated. This is done through an EU state liability claim.[67]

**345.** However, there is a third possible consequence of transposition deficiencies: Applying the law in conformity with the directive. If this succeeds, this makes the further steps of horizontal effect and even more so of state liability superfluous. The responsibility for this lies primarily with the judiciary. The interpretation of national law in conformity with directives is comparatively unproblematic. This applies to a much lesser extent to the further development of law in accordance with directives, which raises several fundamental methodological problems. In this respect, the observance of the directive's requirements in the case of excessive transposition is particularly important.

## 2. INTERPRETATION OF NATIONAL LAW IN CONFORMITY WITH THE DIRECTIVE

### a) *Doctrinal Justification*

**346.** German private law is generally unfamiliar with any written rules on methodology. From a comparative law perspective, this is by no means

---

65 On this point, Leenen, *JURA* 2012, 753; Stürner, *JURA* 2017, 394, 399 ff.

66 Since CJEU, 14 July 1994, Case C-91/92, *Faccini Dori*, ECLI:EU:C:1994:292, paras. 19 ff.; on this field see below paras. 392–397.

67 More on this see below paras. 1470–1495.

self-evident.[68] However, the four traditional canons of interpreting a provision according to its wording, history of origins, systematics, as well as meaning and purpose, which can all be traced back to Savigny,[69] are well established.[70] They take into account the fact that hardly any legislator will succeed in regulating all circumstances of life comprehensively and without contradiction. Legal practice – and thus, ultimately, the courts – is responsible for the correct and consistent interpretation of the law. Observing methodological guidelines ensures a uniform and consistent approach. In the European multi-level system, however, the methodological standards of EU law must also be considered. According to the case law of the CJEU, 'the Member States' obligation arising from a directive to achieve the result envisaged by that directive and their duty to take all appropriate measures, whether general or particular, to ensure the fulfilment of that obligation are binding on all the authorities of the Member States including, for matters within their jurisdiction, the courts'.[71] The primacy of application of EU law must thus be observed by the courts across the entire spectrum of national law. This applies to primary law as well as to secondary law: National law must therefore be interpreted in conformity with EU law in the event of friction.[72]

**347.** This obligation to apply national law in conformity with EU law thus follows primarily from Union law itself, namely from Article 288(3) TFEU. In some cases, the Member States' loyalty to the EU (Article 4(3) TEU) is also taken into account.[73] Article 291(1) TFEU clearly states: 'Member States shall adopt all measures of national law necessary to implement legally binding Union acts.' With regard to EU directives, the principle of *effet utile* and the practical effectiveness of Union law is also of particular importance. The CJEU considers this topic highly significant when interpreting directives. The Court also argues for the greatest possible consideration of the requirements of EU law during the interpretation of national law.

*b) Content*

**348.** According to the case law of the CJEU, it follows from all this that the courts of the Member States are under an obligation to interpret national law in

[68] For more details see Wendehorst, *RabelsZ* 75 (2011), 730.

[69] See F. von Savigny, *System des heutigen römischen Rechts*, Volume I, 1840, p. 213.

[70] Detailed presentation in E.A. Kramer/R. Arnet, *Juristische Methodenlehre*, 7th ed. (Stämpfli, Manz, C.H. Beck, 2024), paras. 63 ff.

[71] CJEU, 19 January 2010, Case C-555/07, *Kücükdeveci*, ECLI:EU:C:2010:21, para. 47 with references to previous case law.

[72] Langenbucher/Donath, in Langenbucher, *Europäisches Privat- und Wirtschaftsrecht*, §1 paras. 85 ff.

[73] CJEU, 13 November 1990, Case C-106/89, *Marleasing*, ECLI:EU:C:1990:395, para. 8.

the light, as far as possible, of the wording and purpose of the directive, making full use of the margin of appreciation conferred on them by national law, in order to achieve the directive's objective.[74] This duty is not restricted to the interpretation of the transposed law but 'requires the national court to consider national law as a whole in order to assess to what extent it may be applied so as not to produce a result contrary to that sought by the directive'.[75] One may see such interpretation in conformity with the directive as a sub-type of systematic interpretation since not only the transposing law itself but the entire legal order must observe the requirements of Union law.[76]

**349.** The effects are illustrated by the facts on which the *Quelle* decision of the CJEU was based: Ms A purchased a cooker set from Quelle AG. After about one year of use, she noticed that the coating on the cooker tops was beginning to flake off. Quelle AG then provided A with a new cooker set but demanded compensation of 150 euros for the duration of use.[77]

#### aa) Compensation for Use in Case of Subsequent Performance: New and Old Law

**350.** Under current German law, this case does not present any problems: Claims by Quelle AG for compensation for use (sec. 439(4), 346(1), (2) no 1 German Civil Code) are subject to the exclusion provision of sec. 475(3) German Civil Code, as are any claims for enrichment. This provision was only inserted at the end of 2008.[78] The reason for the amendment was the above-mentioned case.

**351.** Under German law as it then stood, the questions arose as to whether the claim for compensation for use, which did exist per se, whether there was a violation of the requirements of the Consumer Sales Directive. In essence, the

---

74 CJEU, 10 April 1984, Case 14/83, *von Colson and Kamann*, ECLI:EU:C:1984:153, paras. 26, 28; CJEU, 5 October 2004, Joined Cases C-397/01 to C-403/01, *Pfeiffer*, ECLI:EU:C:2004:584, para. 113.

75 CJEU, 5 October 2004, Joined Cases C-397/01 to C-403/01, *Pfeiffer*, ECLI:EU:C:2004:584, para. 115.

76 B. Rüthers/C. Fischer/A. Birk, *Rechtstheorie mit Juristischer Methodenlehre*, 12th ed. (Munich: C.H. Beck, 2021), paras. 766 ff. (who further differentiate between systematic interpretation and system-conform application of the law, para. 762a); K.F. Röhl/H.C. Röhl, *Allgemeine Rechtslehre*, 3rd ed. (Cologne: Carl Heymanns, 2008), §78 VI (p. 623); Grüneberg, in Grüneberg, *BGB Kommentar*, 84th ed. (Munich: C.H. Beck, 2025), Einl. paras. 42 f. Likewise, this affects the teleological interpretation when it comes to the interpretation of a norm that directly serves the implementation of a directive.

77 CJEU, 17 April 2008, Case C-404/06, *Quelle*, ECLI:EU:C:2008:231; cf. also BGHZ 179, 27.

78 By Article 5 of the Act Implementing the Convention of 30 October 2007 on Jurisdiction and the Recognition and Enforcement of Judgments in Civil and Commercial Matters and Amending the Civil Code, BGBl. I, p. 2399; in force since 16 December 2008 (originally as sec. 474(2) German Civil Code, later as sec. 474(5) German Civil Code).

issue was, first of all, the scope of the obligation to grant restitution under the then-applicable sec. 439(4) German Civil Code (today: sec. 439(5) German Civil Code), which had to be determined by interpretation.

**352.** In addition to the return of the object of performance received, sec. 346(1) German Civil Code provides for the obligation to surrender the benefits derived in rescission, including the benefits of use according to sec. 100 German Civil Code. According to sec. 346(2) German Civil Code, the person liable for restitution must compensate the creditor accordingly. The wording of the reference in sec. 439(5) German Civil Code thus also includes the claim for restitution of the benefits or compensation for their value. This is based on the legislator's assessment that the buyer, who receives a new item with the subsequent delivery, was able to use the item to be returned free of charge in the previous period and would therefore benefit from the defectiveness if they were not obliged to pay compensation for use. Thus, the buyer, to whom the seller has to deliver a new item and who has to return the initially delivered defective item, owes compensation for use according to sec. 439(5), 346(1) German Civil Code.[79] This also appears to be systematically consistent: According to sec. 446 German Civil Code, the buyer is entitled to use the object of sale from the beginning. Unlike rescission, in the case of a replacement delivery, the purchase price remains with the seller, including the benefits derived therefrom. If one wanted to oblige only the buyer to surrender the benefits unilaterally, this would amount to an unjustified better position for the poorly performing seller.[80]

#### bb) The Requirements of the Consumer Sales Directive

**353.** However, it appeared questionable whether this legal situation aligned with the requirements of the Consumer Sales Directive (CSD). According to the *Quelle* decision of the CJEU, this was not the case: According to Article 3(2), (3) and (4) CSD, the European legislator intended to make the seller's obligation to restore the consumer goods to their contractual condition free of charge an essential element of consumer protection as guaranteed by the Directive.[81] This duty to bring the goods into conformity with the contract free of charge is intended to protect the consumer against the threat of financial burdens which might deter them from exercising their rights. This means that any monetary claim by the seller in the context of the performance of their obligation to bring the consumer good into conformity with the contract is excluded.[82] The consumer is not enriched unjustly by obtaining a new consumer good to replace

---

79 BT-Drucks. 14/6040, pp. 232 f.

80 In that sense BGH NJW 2006, 3200 para. 11 (order for reference).

81 CJEU, 17 April 2008, Case C-404/06, *Quelle*, ECLI:EU:C:2008:231, para. 33.

82 CJEU, 17 April 2008, Case C-404/06, *Quelle*, ECLI:EU:C:2008:231, para. 34.

the non-conforming item. They merely belatedly receive a consumer good that complies with the terms of the contract, as they should have received it at the beginning.[83]

cc) Implementation of the Requirements by Way of Interpretation

**354.** The question now was whether these binding requirements could be implemented in German law through an interpretation in conformity with the Directive. According to the orthodox German view, the limit of any interpretation is the provision's wording.[84] Sec. 439(5) German Civil Code refers to sec. 346 to 348 German Civil Code in the case of a replacement delivery. There is no evidence that this only regulates the return of the defective item itself and cannot grant the seller a claim for restitution of the benefits derived by the buyer because then, at least the reference to sec. 347 German Civil Code would be meaningless since this provision exclusively regulates the question of uses and usages. A restrictive interpretation of sec. 439(5) German Civil Code to the effect that the reference to the rescission provisions does not also establish a claim of the seller to compensation for use would thus contradict the legislator's wording and clearly stated intention. Such an interpretation, therefore, does not seem permissible according to the German methodology, even if the requirements of the CSD actually demand this. However, further development of the law in conformity with the Directive was possible. The prerequisites for this are to be clarified in the following.

## 3. JUDICIAL DEVELOPMENT OF NATIONAL LAW IN CONFORMITY WITH THE DIRECTIVE

*a) Basics*

**355.** According to a widespread view in German scholarship, the above-described limits of literal interpretation mark the dividing line between the mere interpretation of a provision and the judicial development of the law. Even if the transitions are fluid and the justification for the separation has often been questioned with good reasons, it is at least justified in that the wording of a provision marks the legislative intent and, thus, the extent to which the law binds the judiciary within the meaning of the principle of the rule of law (Article 20(3)

---

83 CJEU, 17 April 2008, Case C-404/06, *Quelle*, ECLI:EU:C:2008:231, para. 41.

84 On that point, cf. K. Larenz/C.-W. Canaris, *Methodenlehre der Rechtswissenschaft*, 3rd ed. (Berlin: Springer, 1995), p. 143; E.A. Kramer/R. Arnet, *Juristische Methodenlehre*, 7th ed. (Stämpfli, Manz, C.H. Beck, 2024), pp. 67 ff.

German Basic Law).[85] Beyond this limit, there is an increased need to legitimise judicial law-making. But what are the requirements here? Swiss private law takes an unequivocal position, with Article 1(2) of the Civil Code paradigmatically stating:

> 'In the absence of a provision, the court shall decide in accordance with customary law and, in the absence of customary law, in accordance with the rule that it would make as legislator.'

**356.** Such a rule is missing in German law. Nevertheless, the admissibility of judicial development of the law is recognised; it is also expressed in the fact that Article 20(3) German Basic Law binds the judge 'to law *and justice*'. According to the case law of the Federal Constitutional Court, the power of the courts to develop the law is also recognised; the primacy of the law laid down in Article 20(3) German Basic Law does not prohibit the courts from closing existing gaps through further judicial development of the law.[86] The content and limits of this power have always been disputed; the respective discussion cannot be presented here.[87] In the following, only specific EU law issues will be dealt with. Here, it is essential to distinguish between two perspectives: That of EU law, from which the primacy of application follows, and that of Member State law, whose methodology must react to the EU law requirements.

*b) The Perspective of EU Law*

**357.** According to the CJEU's case law, EU law respects national methodological doctrines. If, under the law of a Member State, the wording of a provision forms the absolute limit of interpretation and, thus, judicial development of the law is considered inadmissible, this is to be accepted under EU law. Union law does not require modification of the national array of methods. This has generally been the case since the decision in the *Marleasing* case.[88] Here the CJEU stated:

---

85 On the constitutional implications of the choice of method from a German perspective, B. Rüthers/C. Fischer/A. Birk, *Rechtstheorie mit Juristischer Methodenlehre*, 12th ed. (Munich: C.H. Beck, 2021), paras. 704 ff.

86 BVerfGE 82, 6, 11 f.; BVerfGE 111, 54, 82; on the limits BVerfG NJW 2012, 669.

87 See, for example, K.F. Röhl/H.C. Röhl, *Allgemeine Rechtslehre*, 3rd ed. (Cologne: Carl Heymanns, 2008), § 80 (pp. 633 ff.); B. Rüthers/C. Fischer/A. Birk, *Rechtstheorie mit Juristischer Methodenlehre*, 12th ed. (Munich: C.H. Beck, 2021), paras. 822 ff., 936 ff.; E.A. Kramer/R. Arnet, *Juristische Methodenlehre*, 7th ed. (Stämpfli, Manz, C.H. Beck, 2024), pp. 205 ff., 267 ff.

88 CJEU, 13 November 1990, Case C-106/89, *Marleasing*, ECLI:EU:C:1990:395. For a summary of the principles established by the CJEU, see e.g. CJEU, 5 March 2020, Case C-679/18, *OPR-Finance*, ECLI:EU:C:2020:167, paras. 41–45.

'It follows that, in applying national law, whether the provisions in question were adopted before or after the directive, the national court called upon to interpret it is required to do so, *as far as possible*, in the light of the wording and the purpose of the directive in order to achieve the result pursued by the latter and thereby comply with the third paragraph of Article 189 of the Treaty.'[89]

**358.** This restriction ('as far as possible') is usually understood as follows: Union law does not require an extension of the national methods of interpretation; instead, the states may proceed using their existing methodological principles. Later, the CJEU further clarified this, stating that 'national courts [are required] to do whatever lies within their jurisdiction, taking the whole body of domestic law into consideration and applying the *interpretative methods recognised by domestic law*, with a view to ensuring that the directive in question is fully effective and achieving an outcome consistent with the objective pursued by it'.[90] This may also require, where appropriate, the modification of established national case laws if they are based on an interpretation of national laws that is incompatible with a directive's objectives.[91]

**359.** However, the obligation to apply the law in conformity with the directive must not serve as a basis for an interpretation *contra legem*.[92] Therefore, the limits of applying the law in conformity with the directive lie in the national methodological doctrines. This results in freedom for the national legislator.[93] At the same time, respect for the Member States' regulatory autonomy prevents the de facto introduction of a horizontal direct effect of directives, which, as is well known, the CJEU continues to reject.[94]

---

89 CJEU, 13 November 1990, Case C-106/89, *Marleasing*, ECLI:EU:C:1990:395, para. 8 (emphasis added by the *author*). – Article 189(3) of the EEC Treaty corresponds today to Article 288(3) TFEU.

90 CJEU, 24 January 2012, Case C-282/10, *Dominguez*, ECLI:EU:C:2012:33, para. 27 (emphasis added by the *author*); see also CJEU, 5 October 2004, Joined Cases C-397/01 to C-403/01, *Pfeiffer*, ECLI:EU:C:2004:584, para. 116; CJEU, 23 May 2019, Case C-52/18, *Fülla*, ECLI:EU:C:2019:447, para. 47; CJEU, 8 May 2019, Case C-486/18, *Praxair*, ECLI:EU:C:2019:379, para. 37; CJEU, 11 September 2019, Case C-143/18, *Romano*, ECLI:EU:C:2019:701, para. 37.

91 CJEU, 5 September 2019, Case C-331/18, *Pohotovosť*, ECLI:EU:C:2019:665, para. 56; CJEU, 5 March 2020, Case C-679/18, *OPR-Finance*, ECLI:EU:C:2020:167, para. 43.

92 CJEU, 16 July 2009, Case C-12/08, *Mono Car Styling*, ECLI:EU:C:2009:466, para. 61; CJEU, 15 January 2014, C-176/12, *Association de médiation sociale*, ECLI:EU:C:2014:2, para. 39; CJEU, 8 May 2019, Case C-566/17, *Związek Gmin Zagłębia Miedziowego*, EU:C:2019:390, para. 49; CJEU, 11 September 2019, Case C-143/18, *Romano*, ECLI:EU:C:2019:701, para. 38; CJEU, 5 March 2020, Case C-679/18, *OPR-Finance*, ECLI:EU:C:2020:167, para. 45.

93 Applauding this: Hatje/Mankowski, *EuR* 2014, 155, 166 ff.

94 CJEU, 14 July 1994, Case C-91/92, *Faccini Dori*, ECLI:EU:C:1994:292, paras. 19 ff.; see also paras. 392–397 below.

**360.** On the other hand, this creates a certain degree of inequality with regard to the practical effectiveness of Union law in the Member States: While a deficient transposition in one Member State can possibly be remedied by the judiciary by way of further development of the law in conformity with the directive, this possibility is ruled out in other Member States because, here, a strict *contra legem* barrier applies,[95] so that the legal situation contrary to Union law will continue to exist without legislative intervention.[96] In the latter case, the affected party would only have a state liability claim under EU law, which, given its factual requirements and litigation risks, will only rarely be a practicable possibility. There are good reasons to criticise this state of affairs. Thus, *Kramer* has called for the elaboration of a 'common European minimum methodological consensus' by the CJEU, which could at least prevent some extreme methodological outliers within the Member States' legal systems.[97]

**361.** Advocate General *Bot*'s approach in the Opinion of 25 November 2015 on the *Dansk Industri* case shares this general tendency.[98] A Member State's court may not sneak out of its responsibility for the effective implementation of a directive by referring to the prohibition of the application of the law in conformity with the directive *contra legem*. Instead, it is up to the CJEU to determine the limits of this *contra legem* boundary that it has set itself. Thus, it is precisely in the spirit of cooperation with the courts of the Member States as well as the *effet utile* principle to 'indicate to the national court how it should proceed, in order to avoid improper reliance on the limit on the obligation of consistent interpretation represented by the *contra legem* interpretation of national law'.[99] This rather far-reaching proposal[100] was nevertheless rejected by the CJEU in its subsequent decision.[101] Nonetheless, the court emphasised that the prohibition of *contra legem* does not cover the case of established case laws: Those must be

95 See the country reports in Riesenhuber (ed.), *European Legal Methodology*, §§24–28.

96 See the comparative law study by J. Suhr, Richtlinienkonforme Auslegung im Privatrecht und nationale Auslegungsmethodik (Baden-Baden: Nomos, 2011).

97 Kramer, *GPR* 2015, 262; rejoinder by Riesenhuber, *GPR* 2016, 158; conclusion by Kramer, *GPR* 2016, 210. On the development of a common European methodology also Brenncke, *EuR* 2015, 440, 445 ff.

98 Opinion of 25 November 2015, Case C-441/14, *Dansk Industri* v. *Rasmussen*, ECLI:EU:C:2015:776.

99 Opinion of 25 November 2015, Case C-441/14, *Dansk Industri v Rasmussen*, ECLI:EU:C:2015:776, para. 53.

100 Critically, Baldus/Raff, *GPR* 2016, 71; Kainer, *GPR* 2016, 262, 264 ff.

101 CJEU, 19 April 2016, Case C-441/14, *Dansk Industri/Rasmussen*, ECLI:EU:C:2016:278, para. 32; also CJEU, 17 April 2018, Case C-414/16, *Egenberger*, ECLI:EU:C:2018:257, para. 71; CJEU, 7 August 2018, Case C-122/17, *Smith/Meade*, ECLI:EU:C:2018:631, para. 40; CJEU, 6 November 2018, Joined Cases C-569/16 and C-570/16, *Bauer and Broßonn*, ECLI:EU:C:2018:871, para. 26; CJEU, 27 March 2019, Case C-545/17, *Pawlak*, ECLI:EU:C:2019:260, para. 85.

changed if they are based on an interpretation of national law incompatible with a directive's objectives.[102]

**362.** Ultimately, a perspective of general restraint is probably the preferable solution.[103] How should the CJEU decide when a solution in conformity with the directive is *contra legem* and when it is not, without necessarily including national law? The latter is beyond the court's competence. However, the further the boundary is pushed in favour of the practical effectiveness of Union law, the closer one gets to the horizontal direct effect of directives. Borderline cases can probably be dealt with in a different way: If a Member State drew the *contra legem* line so restrictive that the effectiveness requirement would be violated, there would be the possibility of initiating infringement proceedings to enforce EU law. In this respect, the question of the content of a *contra legem* under EU law is certainly justified; normatively, this would relate to Article 288(3) TFEU. It arises in a similar way, for example, in the case of the specification of the conflict-of-laws rule on the public policy exception: Here, too, it is up to the Member States to determine the content of the public policy exception based on what they consider to be fundamental legal provisions and principles, but the CJEU ensures that this does not impair the practical effectiveness of the respective EU regulations.[104] Moreover, even the seemingly autonomy-preserving solution of the CJEU is not unproblematic for those Member States in which precedents are formally binding, so a deviation, at least by lower-instance courts, would eventually also be *contra legem*.[105]

### c) *The Perspective of German Law*

**363.** From the perspective of German law, the problem of the EU law's necessity to further develop the law does not arise to the same extent as in other Member States. This is because, as explained, the judiciary has the task and legitimisation to act *praeter* or even *contra legem* to develop the law further if there are gaps in the written law.[106] The *Quelle* case described above illustrates the consequences of this. If the further development of the law in conformity with the directive were methodologically impermissible, the result would have to remain that A owes compensation for use, although it is clear that the CSD is opposed to this.

---

102 CJEU, 19 April 2016, Case C-441/14, *Dansk Industri/Rasmussen*, ECLI:EU:C:2016:278, para. 33 referring to CJEU, 13 July 2000, Case C-456/98, *Centrosteel*, ECLI:EU:C:2000:402, para. 17; similarly, CJEU, 17 April 2018, Case C-414/16, *Egenberger*, ECLI:EU:C:2018:257, para. 72.

103 Along these lines also Baldus/Raff, *GPR* 2016, 71, 75 f.; Kainer, *GPR* 2016, 262, 264 ff.

104 See paras. 1283–1291 below.

105 Accurately Kainer, *GPR* 2016, 262, 267.

106 On the question of when a gap exists Baldus/Raff, *GPR* 2017, 158.

A would be referred to the EU law's state liability claim against the German state. In any case, it would have to be proven that there was a sufficiently serious breach of EU law in the chosen transposition, i.e. that the German legislator manifestly and significantly exceeded the limits set by EU law. This is unlikely to succeed, as the explanatory memorandum to the law at least gives justifiable reasons for the obligation to pay compensation for use in the case of subsequent performance.[107]

**364.** However, further development of the law in conformity with the Directive was possible under German law. Sec. 439(5) German Civil Code could therefore be teleologically reduced to the effect that in cases of the sale of consumer goods (sec. 474(1) German Civil Code) the provisions on rescission only apply to the return of the defective item itself, but do not lead to a claim of the seller for the surrender of the benefits derived or for compensation for the use of the defective item. There would first have to be an unplanned regulatory gap for this to be the case. In its preliminary reference of 16 August 2006, the German Federal Supreme Court denied this by referring to a 'clearly declared intention of the legislator'.[108] However, the gap in the present case could be justified by the fact that the legislator, on the one hand, wanted to establish a claim for the seller's compensation, but on the other hand, also wanted to create a regulation in conformity with the Directive. Thus, the law proves to be incomplete, contrary to the legislator's intent. There is a hidden legal loophole because the reference in sec. 439(5) German Civil Code does not contain any restriction for the scope of application of the Directive and is therefore not in conformity with it. The incomplete transposition of the directive stems from the fact that the legislator explicitly stated in the explanatory memorandum that it intended to create a provision in conformity with the directive, especially concerning compensation for previous use. It can therefore be ruled out that the legislator would have enacted the provision in the same way if it had known that it was not in conformity with the directive.[109] This loophole is to be closed through further judicial development of the law.[110] The German Federal Supreme Court eventually achieved the same result by further developing the law in conformity with the Directive, which the legislature had already set in motion with the above-mentioned reform law.[111]

---

107 Cf. above para. 351.

108 BGH NJW 2006, 3200, paras. 14 f.

109 BGHZ 201, 101 para. 23 with further references; also BVerwGE 157, 249; see Baldus/Raff, *GPR* 2017, 158.

110 BGHZ 179, 27, paras. 24 f.

111 Cf. note 1470–1495 below.

# VI. THE IMPACT OF DIRECTIVES ON NATIONAL LAW BEYOND ITS SCOPE OF APPLICATION

References: A. C. Kümpers, *Das Gold-Plating europäischer Richtlinien. Zum Vergleich der Umsetzungspraxis in Deutschland und Frankreich* (Tübingen: Mohr Siebeck, 2023); M. Habersack/C. Mayer, 'Gold-Plating: The Implementation of Directives Through National Provisions with a Wider Scope of Application', in K. Riesenhuber (ed.), *European Legal Methodology* (Cambridge: Intersentia, 2021), §14; T. Jäger, *Überschießende Richtlinienumsetzung im Privatrecht* (Baden-Baden: Nomos, 2006); C. Mayer/J. Schürnbrand, 'Einheitlich oder gespalten? – Zur Auslegung nationalen Rechts bei überschießender Umsetzung von Richtlinien', *JZ* 2004, 545; T. Riehm, 'Die überschießende Umsetzung vollharmonisierender EG-Richtlinien im Privatrecht', *JZ* 2006, 1035; M. Stürner, 'Die Bedeutung des EU-Rechts für das nicht-harmonisierte Privatrecht', *JURA* 2018, 35.

**365.** It should be recalled that a directive only binds the Member States concerning the result, not regarding the means of how it is achieved.[112] Member States can use this leeway to varying degrees. Beyond the directive's requirements, their regulatory autonomy remains, in principle, unrestricted. Some Member States use the transposition process as a stepping stone to harmonise non-directive law in the light of the directive's content. In this respect, one may speak of an 'excessive' transposition of a directive, or gold-plating.

## 1. EXCESSIVE TRANSPOSITION OF DIRECTIVES, OR GOLD-PLATING

### a) *Admissibility*

**366.** First of all, it must be clarified whether an excessive transposition is permissible under EU law at all.[113] This depends on the degree of harmonisation pursued by the respective legal act. While many private law directives since the beginning of the harmonisation of private laws in the 1980s were only designed to achieve a minimum degree of harmonisation, today, the EU legislator almost exclusively pursues the principle of full harmonisation: Hence, Member States may neither fall short nor exceed the requirements of the directive. In many cases, however, more recent directives contain opening clauses that give Member States room for manoeuvre in certain areas. This technique is called targeted full

[112] See paras. 308–312 above.

[113] Cf. Habersack/Mayer, *JZ* 1999, 913; Mayer/Schürnbrand, *JZ* 2004, 545; Jäger, *Überschießende Richtlinienumsetzung im Privatrecht*, 2006; Riehm, *JZ* 2006, 1035.

harmonisation.[114] For example, Article 4 CRD stipulates the following regarding the degree of harmonisation: 'Member States shall not maintain or introduce, in their national law, provisions diverging from those laid down in this Directive, including more or less stringent provisions to ensure a different level of consumer protection, unless otherwise provided for in this Directive.'

**367.** Therefore, each legal act must clarify which objective is being pursued and where regulatory autonomy remains. If it is a consumer protection directive that follows the principle of minimum harmonisation, the Member States are free to strive for a higher level of protection than provided for in the directive. This is exactly what many Member States have done, especially concerning the Consumer Sales Directive.[115] Other purposes are, of course, conceivable, for example, the Late Payments Directive[116] pursues the protection of creditors and, in this respect and to this extent, allows the level of protection to be exceeded.[117] Fully harmonising directives, on the other hand, also serve to achieve a uniform level of competition ('level playing field'); deviations would be detrimental to this goal. Therefore, whether an excessive implementation of fully harmonising directives is permissible must be clarified through a teleological interpretation of this legal act. On the one hand, a distinction must be made concerning the objective of the overshooting transposition between an extension of the territorial, factual, personal and temporal scope of application of the directive.[118] On the other hand, cases of substantive excessive transposition are also conceivable.[119] Both constellations are explained below.

### *b) Extensive Transposition*

**368.** Extensive transpositions of directives are pretty common. The most prominent example is the German legislator's transposition of the Consumer Sales Directive in 2001. The Directive itself only applies to contracts between consumers and commercially active sellers (Article 1, Article 2(1) CSD). Based on an extension of the personal scope of application of the Directive, the provisions were implemented by the German Act to Modernise the Law of Obligations,

114 See already above at para. 84.

115 See the examples in the Proposal for a Directive of the European Parliament and of the Council on certain aspects of contract law applicable to online sales of goods and other forms of distance selling, COM(2015) 635 final, pp. 6 f.

116 Directive 2011/7/EU of the European Parliament and of the Council of 16 February 2011 on combating late payment in commercial transactions, OJ 2011 L 48/1.

117 Article 12(3) Late Payment Directive.

118 On this already Drexl, in *Festschrift für Heldrich* (Munich: C.H. Beck, 2005), pp. 67, 70 ff.

119 Distinction made in Habersack/Mayer, in Riesenhuber, *European Legal Methodology*, §14 paras. 5 ff.; on the inconsistent terminology Mittwoch, *Vollharmonisierung und Europäisches Privatrecht*, 2013, pp. 157 ff.

at least in part, for all sales contracts. Moreover, the transposition also went beyond the directive's scope insofar as the directive's system was adopted for the general law on breach of contract and essentially also for the law on contracts for work and services. The scope of application of various consumer protection directives was also extended in terms of persons by sec. 13 German Civil Code, which now also applies to persons who act in the context of a dependent but professional activity. Some recent directives explicitly address the question of whether the legal act in question also has a blocking effect outside its scope of application. Recital 13 of the Consumer Rights Directive, for example, allows for an excessive transposition of the Directive into Member State law[120] and mentions the extension of the Directive's provisions to newly established or small and medium-sized enterprises as an example.

**369.** An extension in geographical terms may exist if the provisions of the Directive only apply to cross-border situations, but the national legislator also extends it to purely domestic constellations.[121]

**370.** From a temporal point of view, it is conceivable that the effect of the directive is brought forward, i.e. that the requirements are transposed before the specified deadline, as well as that the transposition standards remain in force after the expiry of a directive. In practice, both will only occur in exceptionally rare cases, at least in the area of private law. Transposition before the usually two-year deadline expires regularly fails due to domestic legislative procedures. And the temporal after-effect has no relevance because the expiry of directives is typically linked to their transformation into new legal acts.[122] It should be noted that, according to the CJEU's case law, directives already have a prior effect (after entry into force but before the transposition deadline), which is, however, limited to a kind of frustration prohibition.[123]

### c) *Excessive Transposition Regarding Content ('Over-Fulfilment')*

**371.** The cases of substantive over-fulfilment differ from the constellations just described insofar as the Member State remains within the directive's scope but merely over-fulfils its requirements. This happens quite frequently in the

[120] Where this is not the case, the question must be clarified by way of interpretation, see on the likewise fully harmonising Consumer Credit Directive 2008 CJEU, 12 July 2012, Case C-602/10, *Volksbank România*, ECLI:EU:C:2015:538, para. 40.

[121] For a – no longer current – example from the law of payment services Habersack/Mayer, in Riesenhuber, *European Legal Methodology*, §14 para. 9.

[122] For example, with regard to the transfer of the Distance Selling Directive and the Doorstep Selling Directive into the Consumer Rights Directive.

[123] For further details, cf. Hofmann, in Riesenhuber, *European Legal Methodology*, §15 paras. 7 ff.

case of minimum harmonising directives. For example, the old Doorstep Selling Directive provided for a seven-day withdrawal period in Article 5(1); Article 6(1) of the Distance Selling Directive was designed similarly. During the implementation of that Directive, the German legislator prescribed a uniform withdrawal period of fourteen days in both cases.[124] The legislator was free to do so because both directives allowed for the introduction of more consumer-friendly provisions in domestic law.

372. However, such modifications are more difficult to assess regarding fully harmonising directives.[125] Here, the above-mentioned criteria apply: For each legal act, it must be clarified by interpretation whether and to what extent it allows for an over-fulfilment of the requirements. In some cases, such areas are defined within the framework of 'targeted' full harmonisation. For example, Article 8(6) CRD allows the introduction of a mandatory confirmation for distance contracts concluded by telephone.[126]

373. In other cases, there is great uncertainty in this regard. For example, during the transposition of the Product Liability Directive, France had included in Article 3 of Law No. 98-389 of 19 May 1998 on liability for defective products, among other things, damages below 500 euros. However, Article 9(b) of the Directive provides for a deductible of 500 euros. The Commission then initiated infringement proceedings against France.[127] In this respect, it was of decisive importance whether the deductible standardised in the Directive was mandatory. This depended on the objective pursued by the legal act: If the primary aim is to protect legal transactions from defective products, then, from a teleological point of view, an over-fulfilment of the directive's requirements would not be problematic. There would then be good reasons for the directive to follow the principle of minimum harmonisation, as this is basically more in line with the subsidiarity principle than full harmonisation.[128] If, however, the Product Liability Directive primarily pursues market-steering objectives, the over-fulfilment of the requirements by the French transposition law could lead to unequal conditions in the internal market: Businesses within the scope of the French transposition law[129] would be disadvantaged, as they would be fully liable, while in all other cases, the deductible would apply. The CJEU

124 By the Act on Distance Contracts and Other Issues of Consumer Law and on the Conversion of Regulations to the Euro of 27 June 2000, BGBl. I, p. 897.
125 In detail Riehm, *JZ* 2006, 1035.
126 Similarly, Article 9(3) CRD; further examples in Mittwoch, *Vollharmonisierung und Europäisches Privatrecht*, 2013, pp. 33 ff.
127 Cf. CJEU, 25 April 2002, Case C-52/00, *Commission/France*, ECLI:EU:C:2002:252.
128 See above at para. 325.
129 The conflict-of-laws problems inherent in this area cannot be discussed here, see Article 5 Rome II Regulation.

agreed with the latter.[130] The fact that the Directive did not contain an explicit minimum harmonisation clause meant it was exhaustive and mandatory. Its primary purpose was also to create uniform rules and to guarantee undistorted competition. For these teleological reasons, over-fulfilment, too, was not permissible.

## 2. INTERPRETATION OF EXCESSIVELY TRANSPOSING PARTS OF NATIONAL LAW

**374.** The duty to observe and enforce the requirements of Union law (Article 291(1) TFEU) applies not only to the legislator but to all state bodies. Thus, the courts must also ensure that Member State law is interpreted and applied in conformity with EU law as far as methodologically possible.[131] However, this leads to the question of how the judiciary should deal with legal matters not based on direct requirements of Union law. From the perspective of EU law, there is no obligation to interpret the excessively transposed parts in conformity with the directives (cf. Article 288(3) TFEU, Article 4(3) TEU). However, the CJEU has repeatedly stated that the EU has a clear interest in ensuring that the provisions and concepts adopted from Community law are interpreted uniformly, irrespective of the conditions under which they are to be applied, in order to prevent future differences in interpretation.[132] Hence, the origin of the provision in EU law can and must be considered in any case and in accordance with the national rules of interpretation.

**375.** Thus, it may be advisable to observe the directive's provisions for the excessively transposed part if this appears necessary to prevent contradictions and legal fragmentation in national law. This is supported by the intention of the legislator, who deliberately chose the regulatory context of the directive as a model for its national law. Therefore, compliance with the directive is probably mandatory. However, each individual case may be different, as the following examples show.

**376.** First, consider the problems arising from the CJEU's *Quelle* decision[133] without consumer involvement ('B2B'), as illustrated by the following example case: Albert runs a restaurant. He buys a professional cooker set from Quelle Co. Ltd.

---

130 CJEU, 25 April 2002, Case C-52/00, *Commission/France*, ECLI:EU:C:2002:252, paras. 16 ff.

131 CJEU, 5 October 2004, Joined Cases C-397/01 to C-403/01, *Pfeiffer*, ECLI:EU:C:2004:584, para. 115.

132 CJEU, 17 July 1997, Case C-28/95, *Leur-Bloem*, ECLI:EU:C:1997:369, paras. 27, 32; CJEU, 17 October 2013, Case C-184/12, *Unamar*, ECLI:EU:C:2013:663, para. 31; for further references cf. below at paras. 1394–1396.

133 CJEU, 17 April 2008, Case C-404/06, *Quelle*, ECLI:EU:C:2008:231.

After about one year of use, he notices that the coating on the cooker tops is beginning to flake off. Quelle then provides Albert with a new cooker set but demands compensation of 1000 euros for the duration of use.

**377.** The question is whether Quelle is entitled to compensation for use under sec. 439(5), 346(1), (2) no. 1 German Civil Code. The factual requirements are met. Albert is also, undoubtedly, not a consumer, so the restrictions that exist for consumer purchases in sec. 475(3) German Civil Code do not apply here, at least at first glance.[134] However, the legislative background of the regulations of the law on sales could justify a different assessment. The aforementioned provision was introduced as a reaction to the *Quelle* decision of the CJEU of 17 April 2008. In a hypothetical consideration without the provision, it would have to be asked whether the principles established there – no compensation for use in the case of subsequent performance due to a defect of the sold item in consumer contracts – also apply to other contracts.

**378.** Since the legislator modernising the law of obligations has implemented the Consumer Sales Directive in an overshooting (expanding) manner, namely also including B2B transactions and deliberately transferring the systematics of the Directive to all sales contracts, a split interpretation would initially appear to contradict the chosen system, and, therefore, not be intended by the legislator. Teleological arguments also speak against this, particularly the legal idea of sec. 446 German Civil Code, according to which the benefits should remain with the buyer after the risk transfer. On the other hand, the legislator has clarified through sec. 475(3) German Civil Code that a separation between consumer and entrepreneur purchase is, indeed, intended. This clearly speaks for a split interpretation.

**379.** Consider another variant of the *Quelle* case:[135] Suppose a consumer has bought a used car from a trader. After they have driven it for some time, it turns out that the car has already run 100,000 km more than stated on the meter. The buyer then rescinds the contract and demands repayment of the purchase price. In return, the trader asserts claims for compensation for use since the consumer has driven 5000 km with the car. Rightly so?

**380.** The trader could be entitled to compensation for the value of use under sec. 437 no. 2, 440, 323, 346(1), (2) no. 1 German Civil Code because of the benefits of use (sec. 100 German Civil Code) of the vehicle during the period of possession. While the factual prerequisites are undoubtedly met, the CJEU's

---

[134] See paras. 348–354 above for the solution to this case in the B2C constellation.

[135] Cf. BGHZ 182, 241.

*Quelle* case law might stand in the way of this. However, this would require the Consumer Sales Directive to cover the present case. The *Quelle* ruling only applies to the question of compensation for use in the case of subsequent performance. In the present case, however, the issue is the rescission of the sales contract, in which the buyer receives back the purchase price (including interest). Recital 15 CSD explicitly allows Member States to consider the use of the non-conforming goods in the event of contract termination.[136]

**381.** From the perspective of German law, too, the idea of systematic coherence does not require equal treatment of rescission and subsequent performance, which is now also supported by the new version of sec. 475(3) German Civil Code: With this particular provision, the legislator has indicated that it wishes to differentiate between the various categories of warranty law under the law of sales. In light of the different effects of rescission and subsequent performance, an analogy cannot be made: Whereas the former leads to a complete reversal of the transaction, in which the buyer also receives back the performance rendered by them (purchase price) together with the benefits (interest), the compensation for use burdens the buyer unilaterally.

**382.** According to the CJEU's *Weber/Putz* decision,[137] the seller is obliged to pay for removal and installation in the context of subsequent performance. In this respect, the question needs to be raised whether this can be applied to B2B transactions. In its referral to the CJEU, the German Federal Supreme Court basically stated that the claim for subsequent performance under sec. 439(1) German Civil Code only concerns the buyer's interest in contractual equivalence. In contrast, the costs of removal and installation affect the buyer's interests in integrity and would thus only be subject to a claim for damages.[138] The contrary view of the CJEU then led to a – methodically dubious – interpretation of sec. 439(1) German Civil Code in the subsequent judgement of the German Federal Supreme Court:[139] In the absence of a special provision for removal of the defective item and further installation costs in consumer contracts along the lines of sec. 474(5) German Civil Code, there were good reasons for a uniform interpretation of sec. 439(1) German Civil Code. The legislator embedded this solution in German sales law on 1 January 2018: The newly appended sec. 439(3) German Civil Code now follows the CJEU case law by clearly stating a duty of the seller to pay compensation, even for contracts other than consumer

136 In this sense also CJEU, 17 April 2008, Case C-404/06, *Quelle*, ECLI:EU:C:2008:231, paras. 38 f.

137 CJEU, 16 June 2011, Joined Cases C-65/09 and C-87/09, *Weber* and *Putz*, ECLI:EU:C:2011:396; see paras. 355–356 above.

138 BGH NJW 2009, 1660 paras. 11 f.

139 BGHZ 192, 148, para. 26.

contracts.[140] According to the revised sec. 439(3) German Civil Code, the claim was only excluded if the buyer was in bad faith concerning the defect at the time of installation or attachment. Note that now the law has changed again following the transposition of the Sale of Goods Directive. The replacement of the defective item itself, however, is not owed by the seller.

**383.** Nevertheless, the German Federal Supreme Court has rightly positioned itself in favour of a uniform interpretation concerning the concept of the 'consumer' used in sec. 13 German Civil Code:[141] The German follow-up decisions to the CJEU decisions in the *Quelle* and *Weber/Putz* cases are valid not only for the consumer concept of the Consumer Sales Directive but also for sec. 13 German Civil Code, which, as explained,[142] is somewhat broader than the directive's understanding. In this respect, no further differentiations, such as special regulations for persons who act in the context of a dependent but professional activity, exist, so this intention of uniformity must remain a decisive interpretation guideline.

**384.** Further examples – in both directions – can be found easily.[143] Therefore, it is impossible to presume a uniform interpretation generally.[144] Instead, the decisive factor must be how important it was to the legislator whether the constellations of cases within and outside the directive's scope are treated equally.[145] This can be decided first and foremost by reference to the legislator's regulatory framework. If, for example, special rules were introduced (as in sec. 474 ff. German Civil Code), it is not easy to justify uniformity of interpretation.

## VII. DEFICIENCIES OF IMPLEMENTATION AND THEIR CONSEQUENCES

References: C. Baldus, 'Horizontale Direktwirkung von Richtlinien: Auf des Luxemburger Lieferwagens Ladefläche?', *GPR* 2018, 55; O. Mörsdorf, 'Unmittelbare Anwendung von EG-Richtlinien zwischen Privaten', *EuR* 2009, 219.

140 By the Act on the Reform of Construction Contract Law, on the Amendment of Liability for Defects under the Law on the Sale of Goods, etc. of 28 April 2017, BGBl. I, p. 969.

141 BGHZ 192, 148 para. 44; also already BGHZ 179, 27 para. 27.

142 Cf. para. 230.

143 For example, on the freedom of form of agreements on the quality of the good in BGH NJW 2015, 1815, on this Baldus/Raff, *GPR* 2017, 71 ('prime example of divided interpretation'); see further Kuhn, *EuR* 2015, 216, 229 ff.; U. Kornblum/M. Stürner, *Fälle zum Allgemeinen Schuldrecht*, 9th ed. (Munich: C.H. Beck, 2022), Fall 20; Jäger, *Überschießende Richtlinienumsetzung im Privatrecht*, 2006, pp. 83 ff.

144 Habersack/Mayer, in Riesenhuber, *European Legal Methodology*, §14 paras. 41 ff. but immediately putting this into perspective.

145 Kuhn, *EuR* 2015, 216, 235 ff.

## 1. STARTING POINT

**385.** Article 4(3) TEU and Article 288(3) TFEU oblige the Member States to transpose a directive correctly and in due time. Concerning the effectiveness of this obligation, the extent to which its non-fulfilment or insufficient fulfilment entails tangible consequences is of decisive importance.

## 2. DEFICIENCIES OF IMPLEMENTATION

**386.** The most obvious solution to transposition deficiencies would be to allow direct effects of the directive. This would mean that private actors could directly invoke the directive, although only the Member States are the intended recipients. Ultimately, transposition deficiencies would become irrelevant. However, this would contradict Article 288(3) TFEU, which requires an act of transposition. However, the practical effectiveness (*effet utile*) of EU law would be diminished if transposition in this sense was ultimately left to the discretion of the Member States. A Member State would also be behaving contradictorily and disloyal if, on the one hand, it violated its obligations under EU law and, on the other hand, defended itself against corresponding lawsuits by citizens with precisely this implementation failure. Finally, the failed implementation of the Member State in question would possibly be detrimental to the citizens, who, in many cases, are to be granted legal positions through directives.

**387.** The CJEU had to deal with this issue in the *Van Duyn* case, for example.[146] In the underlying dispute, Ms van Duyn, a Dutch national, wanted to work in the UK as a secretary for the Church of Scientology, relying on the freedom of movement for workers. Directive 64/221/EEC,[147] which specifies this fundamental freedom, stipulated in Article 3(1): 'Measures taken on grounds of public policy or of public security shall be based exclusively on the personal conduct of the individual concerned.' This provision had not been implemented in the UK; hence, Ms van Duyn had been refused entry because of her affiliation with the Church of Scientology. The issue now was whether Ms van Duyn could rely directly on the Directive and the provision favourable to her. The CJEU answered this question in the affirmative and relied above all on the principle of practical effectiveness (*effet utile*): In each individual case, it had to be examined whether the relevant provision was suitable in terms of its legal nature, system and wording to give rise to direct legal effects between an individual and a

146 CJEU, 4 December 1974, Case 1/74, *van Duyn*, ECLI:EU:C:1974:133.

147 Directive 64/221/EEC of 25 February 1964 on the co-ordination of special measures concerning the movement and residence of foreign nationals which are justified on grounds of public policy, public security or public health, OJ 1964 56/850.

Member State.[148] For the aforementioned Article 3(1) of Directive 64/221/EEC, the CJEU affirmed this.[149]

**388.** The following prerequisites for the vertical direct effect of a directive in the relationship between the state and a private person have emerged in the meantime in established case law:[150]

- Expiry of the implementation period[151]
- No implementation or at least not a full implementation of the Directive[152]
- The content of the relevant provision of the directive must be unconditional and sufficiently precise ('self-executing')[153]

**389.** It is not entirely clear whether the provision in question must be suitable for granting rights to the individual. The CJEU's earlier case law[154] seemed to favour this approach, however, the court did not explicitly repeat this criterion later on.[155] In private law, subjective rights are not of decisive importance anyway.

**390.** This vertical direct effect applies to the state, its administrative bodies and other decentralised authorities and agencies.[156] However, other state-related institutions are also covered. The rights from a directive, according to the criteria above, may also be invoked against organisations and bodies sufficiently close to the state, either because they are legal persons under public law, or because they are subject to the state or its supervision, or because they are entrusted with the performance of a task in the public interest and are thus endowed with special rights which go beyond those which apply under the rules governing relations between private individuals.[157]

---

148 CJEU, 4 December 1974, Case 1/74, *van Duyn*, ECLI:EU:C:1974:133, para. 12.

149 CJEU, 4 December 1974, Case 1/74, *van Duyn*, ECLI:EU:C:1974:133, paras. 13–15; see also CJEU, 5 April 1979, Case 148/78, *Ratti*, ECLI:EU:C:1979:110, para. 22.

150 An overview of the relevant decisions can also be found in BGH RIW 2020, 297 para. 26.

151 On the pre-emptive effect of directives already above para. 325.

152 CJEU, 26 February 1986, Case 152/84, *Marshall I*, ECLI:EU:C:1986:84, para. 46.

153 CJEU, 5 April 1979, Case 148/78, *Ratti*, ECLI:EU:C:1979:110, para. 23.

154 Cf. CJEU, 19 January 1982, Case 8/81, *Becker*, ECLI:EU:C:1982:7, para. 25: 'Thus, wherever the provisions of a directive appear, as far as their subject-matter is concerned, to be unconditional and sufficiently precise, those provisions may, in the absence of implementing measures adopted within the prescribed period, be relied upon as against any national provision which is incompatible with the directive or in so far as the provisions define rights which individuals are able to assert against the State.'

155 On the development M. Ruffert, in C. Calliess/M. Ruffert, *EUV/AEUV*, 6th ed. (Munich: C.H. Beck, 2022), Art. 288 TFEU paras. 66 ff.

156 Cf. e.g. CJEU, 7 August 2018, Case C-122/17, *Smith/Meade*, ECLI:EU:C:2018:63, para. 45; CJEU, 6 November 2018, Joined Cases C-569/16 and C-570/16, *Bauer and Broßonn*, ECLI:EU:C:2018:871, para. 71.

157 The leading case is CJEU, 12 July 1990, Case C-188/89, *Foster*, ECLI:EU:C:1990:313, paras. 18 ff.; see further CJEU 19 April 2007, Case C-356/05, *Farrell I*, ECLI:EU:C:2007:229,

**391.** However, direct application of provisions of directives containing obligations of private persons is not possible:[158] If this were true, someone would be held liable who bears no responsibility for the failure to transpose or for the incorrect transposition. This applies, above all, if the state wanted to rely on a directive right vis-a-vis a citizen directly. The aforementioned prohibition of contradictory conduct applies here in particular.

## 3. NO HORIZONTAL DIRECT EFFECT

**392.** This leads to the question of the validity of provisions of directives between private persons (so-called horizontal direct effect or third-party effect).[159] In principle, following the *Faccini Dori* case law, the CJEU still rejects this.[160]

**393.** Ms Faccini Dori was approached at Milan Central Station by a representative of the company Lingua Franca to ask if she would like to learn English and signed a contract for an English course by distance learning. Later she cancelled the contract by registered letter. Lingua Franca nevertheless demanded performance and initiated dunning proceedings. The competent Italian peace judge (*giudice conciliatore*) referred the question as to whether a right of withdrawal followed from the Doorstep Selling Directive to the CJEU. However, the directive had not yet been transposed in Italy, despite the expiry of the transposition deadline.

**394.** In its arguments against a horizontal direct effect, the CJEU relied primarily on the wording of Article 288(3) TFEU, which is explicitly addressed to the Member States and does not contain any obligations for private parties.[161] Moreover, the accusation of unfairness, which seemed to speak in favour of a vertical direct effect, did not apply since only private persons were affected.[162] Finally, an obligation of private parties can only be brought about by the regulation.[163] The opposing voices repeatedly expressed in the legal literature, however, refer to the *effet utile* principle; it is argued that this must result in a horizontal direct effect in favour of consumers, especially in the case of consumer

---

para. 40; CJEU, 24 January 2012, Case C-282/10, *Dominguez*, ECLI:EU:C:2012:33, para. 39; CJEU, 10 October 2017, Case C-413/15, *Farrell II*, ECLI:EU:C:2017:745, para. 33; CJEU, 7 August 2018, Case C-122/17, *Smith/Meade*, ECLI:EU:C:2018:63, para. 45; CJEU, 6 September 2018, Case C-17/17, *Hampshire*, ECLI:EU:C:2018:674, paras. 54 f.

158 CJEU, 26 February 1986, Case 152/84, *Marshall I*, ECLI:EU:C:1986:84, para. 48.

159 See above at para. 323.

160 Cf. CJEU, 14 July 1994, Case C-91/92, *Faccini Dori*, ECLI:EU:C:1994:292, paras. 19 ff.

161 CJEU, 14 July 1994, Case C-91/92, *Faccini Dori*, ECLI:EU:C:1994:292, para. 22.

162 CJEU, 14 July 1994, Case C-91/92, *Faccini Dori*, ECLI:EU:C:1994:292, para. 23.

163 CJEU, 14 July 1994, Case C-91/92, *Faccini Dori*, ECLI:EU:C:1994:292, para. 24. Likewise the German Federal Court of Justice, cf. e.g. BGH RIW 2020, 297 para. 24.

protection directives.[164] It must be conceded that the persons disadvantaged by the non-implemented or inadequately implemented directive would indeed only be left with a state liability[165] claim if the horizontal direct effect were denied. This is exactly the burden that the CJEU wanted to avoid for private actors. If the horizontal effect was used to assign the risk of a claim to businesses, then these would be referred to state liability claims – it seems like the inherent litigation risk is better located there than on the side of the consumers.

**395.** The CJEU probably also sees it the latter way, even if the court prescribed a different methodological approach: Formally, the CJEU still upholds the prohibition of a horizontal direct effect.[166] In fact, however, similar results are achieved through the obligation of the Member States to apply the law in accordance with the directive.[167] The essential difference, however, is that the respective Member State law decides, within the framework of its methodology, to what extent, in particular, further development of its law in compliance with the directive is possible.[168] It may occur that the directive is not transposed correctly because the national law does not allow for a methodical solution in conformity with the directive. In the case of horizontal direct effect, however, the directive would always prevail. This is shown, for example, by the CJEU's decision in the *Heininger* case:[169]

**396.** The Heininger family living in Germany concluded a real estate loan contract at home with a representative of the B-Bank. Years later, they revoked the declaration of intent to conclude the contract. However, the legal basis of a possible revocation was questionable: The right of revocation contained in the German Consumer Credit Act in force at the time did not apply to real estate loan agreements.[170] This was in line with EU law requirements, as the (first) Consumer Credit Directive did not prescribe a right of withdrawal but only recommended it.[171] As the contract had been concluded in a doorstep

---

164 Cf. M. Ruffert, in C. Calliess/M. Ruffert, *EUV/AEUV*, 6th ed. (Munich: C.H. Beck, 2022), Art. 288 AEUV para. 60.

165 Cf. also below at paras. 1470–1495.

166 CJEU, 5 October 2004, Joined Cases C-397/01 to C-403/01, *Pfeiffer*, ECLI:EU:C:2004:584, para. 109; CJEU, 24 January 2012, C-282/10, *Dominguez*, ECLI:EU:C:2012:33, para. 42; CJEU, 15 January 2014, Case C-176/12, *Association de médiation sociale*, ECLI:EU:C:2014:2, para. 36; CJEU, 7 August 2018, Case C-122/17, *Smith/Meade*, ECLI:EU:C:2018:63, paras. 42 ff.

167 CJEU, 22 November 2005, Case C-144/04, *Mangold*, ECLI:EU:C:2005:709 as well as CJEU, 19 January 2010, Case C-555/07, *Kücükdeveci*, ECLI:EU:C:2010:21.

168 In consideration of the recent tendencies to grant horizontal direct effect to individual provisions of the Charter of Fundamental Rights, one can also speak of direct third-party effect of directives through the back door in this regard, cf. above at paras. 279–288.

169 Cf. CJEU, 13 December 2001, Case C-481/99, *Heininger*, ECLI:EU:C:2001:684.

170 The provision has been moved to sec. 495 German Civil Code.

171 But see the Article 14 of the revised Consumer Credit Directive 2008/48/EC.

situation,[172] a right of withdrawal under the German Doorstep Selling Act's old version appeared, prima facie, possible. However, this was excluded in the scope of application of the German Consumer Credit Act (sec. 5(2) German Doorstep Selling Act (old version)), as the German legislator considered the Consumer Credit Directive *lex specialis* to the Doorstep Selling Directive. As a result, there was no right of withdrawal under German law. However, from the perspective of Community law at the time, it was doubtful whether the provisions of the Doorstep Selling Directive had thus been implemented correctly. The CJEU held that this Directive was applicable based on teleological considerations, even though the contract in question was a real estate credit agreement: 'The fact that the credit agreement is secured by a charge on immovable property does not render any less necessary the protection which is accorded to the consumer who has entered into such an agreement away from the trader's business premises.'[173] The CJEU found no normative evidence for any priority of the Consumer Credit Directive over the Doorstep Selling Directive.[174] Hence, the Heininger couple should have been entitled to a right of withdrawal under Community law. However, implementing these provisions in German law was problematic:[175] A horizontal direct effect of the Doorstep Selling Directive and thus, a right of withdrawal derived from it was out of the question given the established CJEU case law. However, since Community law demanded precisely this result, the German Federal Court of Justice methodically resorted to a directive-compliant interpretation of the subsidiarity clause of sec. 5(2) German Doorstep Selling Act's (old version).[176] The fact that their wording was relatively unambiguous and required a teleological reduction did not pose any obstacles in the view of the Court. Even if the result was the same: A horizontal direct effect of the Doorstep Selling Directive was not justified.

**397.** Given that the further development of the law in conformity with the directive is relatively distant from the German Federal Court of Justice's general case law and since the result is often hardly foreseeable by the affected parties, it was proposed to grant the disadvantaged contracting party a state liability claim if the content of the national provision changed by the interpretation could not have been foreseen without knowledge of the EU Directive.[177] This

[172] Today, the right of withdrawal exists for all off-premises contracts, sec. 312b, 312g German Civil Code. On this form of distribution of goods and services in the law as it stands today cf. below at paras. 519–539.

[173] CJEU, 13 December 2001, Case C-481/99, *Heininger*, ECLI:EU:C:2001:684, para. 34.

[174] CJEU, 13 December 2001, Case C-481/99, *Heininger*, ECLI:EU:C:2001:684, paras. 38 ff.

[175] BGH NJW 2002, 1881.

[176] BGH NJW 2002, 1881, 1882 ff.

[177] Schinkels, *JZ* 2011, 394, 398; for a critical appraisal of this approach, cf. Heiderhoff, *Europäisches Privatrecht*, para. 98.

is contradictory because the EU Directive, being EU law, is part of the national legal order, and its ignorance cannot, therefore, be a sufficient basis for liability.

## 4. DIRECTIVE IMPLEMENTATION THROUGH CONFLICT OF LAWS?

**398.** Since the entire legal system must conform to EU law, the question arises whether a directive can or must be enforced in the case of implementation deficiencies – possibly by employing the public policy exception. Is the forum state whose conflict-of-laws rules refer to a legal system that has not transposed a relevant directive, or has transposed it inadequately, obliged to enforce EU law, at least after the transposition deadline has expired? This problem became practically significant in the so-called Gran Canaria cases, which had occupied numerous German courts, especially in the 1990s: German tourists concluded contracts for the sale of goods at sales events in Spain. The usefulness of the purchased items turned out to be doubtful after the tourists returned to Germany. In the contracts, which were set up in German language, it was agreed that Spanish law would apply; the deliveries were to be handled by a company based in Germany. At the time, consumers could not withdraw from contracts in Spanish law because the Doorstep Selling Directive had not yet been transposed.

**399.** Hence, the courts were faced with the problem that they had to apply a law chosen by the parties contrary to Community law due to the non-implementation of the Directive. Accordingly, very different solutions were developed to achieve the intended goal of protecting the consumer by a right of withdrawal. These spanned from a direct application of the Directive, which is problematic due to the conflicting case law of the CJEU, to the interpretation of the chosen law in conformity with the Directive, to more complex solutions under conflict of laws.[178] The now-applicable Article 6 Rome I Regulation extends the scope of consumer protection law further than under old law by encompassing any countries to which the professional 'directed' their activities.[179] This should now do away with the cases discussed at that time. The consequence of this is that the Gran Canaria cases are now essentially a thing of the past, as German law would generally be applicable in all comparable cases.[180] Besides, Spanish law has by now of course established a right to withdrawal.

---

178 See the references in Coester-Waltjen, in *Festschrift für W. Lorenz* (Tübingen: Mohr Siebeck, 1991), pp. 297, 310 at note 85.

179 Cf. below at paras. 1181–1200.

180 On the question of whether the content of EU directives is part of the public policy exception, below at paras. 1285–1287.

## VIII. DAMAGES FOR NON-IMPLEMENTED DIRECTIVES?

**400.** Since there may be cases in which failed or inadequate implementation of a directive does not entail any third-party effect, the question of further consequences arises. These can be found in the already mentioned claim for state liability under EU law: The individual who suffers disadvantages due to the failure to comply with the transposition obligation under Article 288(3) TFEU may be entitled to a claim for compensation against the respective Member State. The corresponding prerequisites are discussed later.[181]

[181] Cf. below at paras. 1470–1495.

# PART TWO

# SUBSTANTIVE CONTRACT LAW

# §8. OVERVIEW AND CATEGORIES

## CONTENTS



## I. OVERVIEW OF EXISTING AND PLANNED DIRECTIVES AND REGULATIONS

References: B. Heiderhoff, *Europäisches Privatrecht*, 6th ed. (Heidelberg: C.F. Müller, 2023), Annex (pp. 311 ff.); K. Riesenhuber, *EU-Vertragsrecht* (Tübingen: Mohr Siebeck, 2013), §1 paras. 24 ff.

### 1. LEGISLATIVE INSTRUMENTS IN FORCE

**401.** The large number of existing legal acts relevant to contract law makes it necessary to compile them in chronological order first. The following list includes all regulations and directives in the area of private law, including those in the domain of conflict of laws and anti-discrimination. Legal acts in copyright and patent law, general labour law, family and inheritance law and procedural law are not included. A systematisation can be found at paras. 403 ff.[1]

- Equal Pay Directive[2] (replaced by Equal Treatment Directive in Employment and Occupation, see below)
- Equal Treatment Directive (working conditions)[3] (replaced by Equal Treatment Directive in Employment and Occupation, see below)
- Product Liability Directive[4] (replaced by Product Liability Directive II, see below)

1 Cf. below at para. 403.
2 Directive 75/117/EEC, OJ 1975 L 45/19.
3 Directive 76/207/EEC, OJ 1976 L 39/40.
4 Directive 85/374/EEC, OJ 1985 L 210/29.

- Doorstep Selling Directive[5] (replaced by Consumer Rights Directive, see below)
- Commercial Agents Directive[6]
- Consumer Credit Directive[7] (replaced by Consumer Credit Directive II, see below)
- Package Travel Directive[8] (replaced by Package Travel Directive II, see below)
- Air Passenger Rights Regulation[9] (replaced by Air Passenger Rights Regulation II, see below)
- Unfair Terms Directive[10]
- Timeshare Directive[11] (replaced by Timeshare Directive II, see below)
- Equal Treatment Directive (Social Security)[12] (replaced by Equal Treatment Directive in Employment and Occupation, see below)
- Distance Selling Directive[13] (replaced by Consumer Rights Directive, see below)
- Regulation on air carrier liability in the event of accidents[14]
- Injunctions Directive[15] (replaced by Injunctions Directive II, see below)
- Consumer Sales Directive[16] (CSD) (replaced by the Sale of Goods Directive, see below).
- Signatures Directive[17] (replaced by eIDAS Regulation, see below)
- E-Commerce Directive[18]
- Late Payment Directive[19] (replaced by Late Payment Directive II, see below)
- Racial Equality Directive[20]
- Equality Framework Directive (employment and occupation)[21]
- Regulation on cross-border payments in euro[22] (replaced by Regulation on cross-border payments in the Community, see below)

5 Directive 85/577/EEC, OJ 1985 L 372/31.
6 Directive 86/653/EEC, OJ 1986 L 382/17.
7 Directive 87/102/EEC, OJ 1987 L 42/48.
8 Directive 90/314/EEC, OJ 1990 L 158/59.
9 Regulation (EEC) No 295/91, OJ 1991 L 36/5.
10 Directive 93/13/EEC, OJ 1993 L 95/29.
11 Directive 94/47/EC, OJ 1994 L 280/83.
12 Directive 96/97/EC, OJ 1997 L 46/20.
13 Directive 97/7/EC, OJ 1997 L 144/19.
14 Regulation (EC) No 2027/97, OJ 1997 No L 285/1.
15 Directive 98/27/EC, OJ 1998 L 166/51.
16 Directive 1999/44/EC, OJ 1999 L 171/12.
17 Directive 1999/93/EC, OJ 1999 L 13/12.
18 Directive 2000/31/EC, OJ 2000 L 178/1.
19 Directive 2000/35/EC, OJ 2000 L 200/35.
20 Directive 2000/43/EC, OJ 2000 L 180/22.
21 Directive 2000/78/EC, OJ 2000 L 303/16.
22 Regulation (EC) No 2560/2001, OJ 2001 L 344/13.

- Distance Marketing of Consumer Financial Services Directive[23]
- Life Assurance Directive[24] (replaced by Solvency II Directive, see below)
- Insurance Mediation Directive[25] (replaced by Insurance Distribution Directive, see below)
- Air Passenger Rights Regulation (Recast)[26]
- Equal Treatment Directive (gender)[27]
- Unfair Commercial Practices Directive[28]
- Air Passenger Rights Regulation (reduced mobility)[29]
- Equal Treatment Directive in Employment and Occupation[30]
- Services Directive[31]
- Rome II Regulation[32]
- Rail Passenger Rights Regulation[33]
- Payment Services Directive[34] (replaced by Payment Services Directive II, see below)
- Consumer Credit Directive II[35] (replaced by Consumer Credit Directive III, see below)
- Rome I Regulation[36]
- Timeshare Directive II[37]
- Injunctions Directive II (replaced by the Representative Actions Directive, see below)[38]
- Regulation on cross-border payments in the Community[39]
- Solvency II Directive[40]
- Late Payments Directive II[41]
- Consumer Rights Directive (CRD)[42]

23 Directive 2002/65/EC, OJ 2002 L 271/16.
24 Directive 2002/83/EC, OJ 2002 L 345/1.
25 Directive 2002/92/EC, OJ 2003 L 9/3.
26 Regulation (EC) No 261/2004, OJ 2004 L 46/1.
27 Directive 2004/113/EC, OJ 2004 L 373/37.
28 Directive 2005/29/EC, OJ 2005 L 149/22.
29 Regulation (EC) No 1107/2006, OJ 2006 L 204/1.
30 Directive 2006/54/EC, OJ 2006 L 204/23.
31 Directive 2006/123/EC, OJ 2006 L 376/36.
32 Regulation (EC) No 864/2007, OJ 2007 L 199/40.
33 Regulation (EC) No 1371/2007, OJ 2007 L 315/14.
34 Directive 2007/64/EC, OJ 2007 L 319/1.
35 Directive 2008/48/EC, OJ 2008 L 133/66.
36 Regulation (EC) No 593/2008, OJ 2008 L 177/6.
37 Directive 2008/122/EC, OJ 2009 L 33/10.
38 Directive 2009/22/EC, OJ 2009 L 110/30.
39 Regulation (EC) No 924/2009, OJ 2009 L 266/11.
40 Directive 2009/138/EC, OJ 2009 L 335/1.
41 Directive 2011/7/EU, OJ 2011 L 48/1.
42 Directive 2011/83/EU, OJ 2011 L 304/64.

- Credit Rating Agencies Regulation (CRA)[43]
- Mortgage Credit Directive[44]
- eIDAS Regulation[45]
- PRIIPs Regulation[46]
- Package Travel Directive II[47]
- Payment Services Directive II[48]
- Insurance Distribution Directive[49]
- General Data Protection Regulation (GDPR)[50]
- Geo-blocking Regulation[51]
- Electronic Communications Code Directive[52]
- Digital Content Directive[53]
- Sale of Goods Directive[54]
- Platform Regulation[55]
- Directive on Better Enforcement and Modernisation of Union Consumer Protection Rules[56]
- Representative Actions Directive[57]
- Consumer Credit Directive III[58]
- Corporate Sustainability Due Diligence Directive ('CS3D')[59]
- Repair of Goods Directive[60]
- Product Liability Directive II[61]

43 Regulation (EU) No 462/2013, OJ 2013 L 146/1.

44 Directive 2014/17/, OJ 2014 L 60/34.

45 Regulation (EU) No 910/2014, OJ 2014 L 257/73.

46 Regulation (EU) No 1286/2014, OJ 2014 L 352/1.

47 Directive (EU) 2015/2302, OJ 2015 L 326/1.

48 Directive (EU) 2015/2366, OJ 2015 L 337/35.

49 Directive (EU) 2016/97, OJ 2016 L 26/19.

50 Regulation (EU) No 2016/679, OJ 2016, L 119/1, L 314/72 and OJ 2018 L 127/2.

51 Regulation (EU) No 2018/302, OJ 2018 L 601/1.

52 Directive (EU) 2018/1972, OJ 2018 L 321/36.

53 Directive (EU) 2019/770, OJ 2019 L 136/1.

54 Directive (EU) 2019/771, OJ 2019 L 136/28.

55 Regulation (EU) 2019/1150, OJ 2019 L 186/57.

56 Directive (EU) 2019/2161, OJ 2019 L 328/7.

57 Directive (EU) 2020/1828, OJ 2020 L 409/1.

58 Directive (EU) 2023/2225 of the European Parliament and of the Council of 18 October 2023 on credit agreements for consumers and repealing Directive 2008/48/EC, OJ 2023 L 2023/2225.

59 Directive (EU) 2024/1760 of the European Parliament and of the Council of 13 June 2024 on corporate sustainability due diligence and amending Directive (EU) 2019/1937 and Regulation (EU) 2023/2859, OJ L, 2024/1760.

60 Directive (EU) 2024/1799 of the European Parliament and of the Council of 13 June 2024 on common rules promoting the repair of goods and amending Regulation (EU) 2017/2394 and Directives (EU) 2019/771 and (EU) 2020/1828, OJ L 2024/1799.

61 Directive (EU) 2024/2853 of the European Parliament and of the Council of 23 October 2024 on liability for defective products and repealing Council Directive 85/374/EEC, OJ L 2024/2853.

### 2. PROPOSALS

**402.** The following Legislative Proposals were, or still are, under discussion:

- Proposal for a Council Directive on implementing the principle of equal treatment between persons irrespective of religion or belief, disability, age or sexual orientation (withdrawn)[62]
- Proposal for a Regulation on a Common European Sales Law[63] (currently not being pursued further[64])
- Proposal for a Regulation on the safety of consumer products[65]
- Proposal for a Regulation on the conflict-of-laws effects of the assignment of claims for third parties (withdrawn)[66]
- Proposal for a Directive on adapting non-contractual civil liability rules to artificial intelligence (AI Liability Directive)[67]
- Proposal for a Directive amending Directive (EU) 2015/2302 to make the protection of travellers more effective and to simplify and clarify certain aspects of the Directive[68]

## II. CATEGORISATION OF SECONDARY LEGISLATION

**403.** If one attempts to bring this diversity into a more transparent form, a categorisation according to the content or addressee of the legal act appears suitable.[69]

### 1. GENERAL AND OVERARCHING PROVISIONS

**404.** The sectoral approach to harmonisation that has prevailed so far means that EU contract law knows few overarching provisions. An attempt at

62 COM(2008) 426 final. As there was no foreseeable agreement, the Proposal was withdrawn, cf. Commission Work Programme 2025, COM(2025) 45 final, Annex IV no. 26.

63 COM(2011) 635 final.

64 Commission Work Programme 2015 – A New Start, COM(2014) 910 final: the Proposal features on the list of withdrawals or modifications of pending proposals in Annex II, No 60.

65 COM(2013) 78 final.

66 COM(2018) 96 final. Meanwhile, as there was no foreseeable agreement, the Proposal was withdrawn, cf. Commission Work Programme 2025, COM(2025) 45 final, Annex IV no. 31.

67 COM(2022) 496 final. As there was no foreseeable agreement, the Commission will assess whether another proposal should be tabled or another type of approach should be chosen, cf. Commission Work Programme 2025, COM(2025) 45 final, Annex IV no. 32.

68 COM(2023) 905 final.

69 In Schulze/Zoll, *European Contract Law*, 3rd ed. 2021, pp. 18 ff., the systematisation is as follows: consumer protection, SMEs, e-commerce, payment services, non-discrimination, insurance contracts, other regulatory areas.

'horizontal' grouping in the area of consumer law through the 2008 proposal for a Directive on Consumer Rights has only been partially successful.[70] However, the Consumer Rights Directive, which was finally adopted, contains quite general rules on pre-contractual information, the conclusion of the contract and rights of withdrawal that apply to all consumer contracts.[71] The E-Commerce Directive can also be mentioned in this respect. Lastly, the various Equal Treatment Directives also form cross-cutting issues that apply to general contract law and labour law.

## 2. CONTRACTS WITH END-USERS (CONSUMER PROTECTION)

**405.** Many secondary acts regulate legal aspects of contracts with end users. Typically, these are consumers. In this respect, the law on the sales of goods is of utmost importance, particularly the Consumer Sales Directive and its replacement, the Sale of Goods Directive.[72] Further relevant contracts are consumer credit, timeshare, and package travel contracts. The various directives from the area of insurance law must also be mentioned in this respect.

## 3. COMMERCIAL CONTRACTS

**406.** Outside of consumer law, regulations exist, in particular, in the area of commercial agency contracts.[73] The Late Payments Directive also regulates legal relationships without any involvement of consumers.

## 4. PAYMENT SERVICES

**407.** Payment services are usually based on a contract of agency between the customer and the bank. The Payment Services Directive is not a consumer protection directive in the narrower sense, but it does cover in-person actors and small and medium-sized businesses (Recital 53 Payment Services Directive). It aims to facilitate cross-border payment transactions and thus promote the internal market (Recital 5 Payment Services Directive).

---

70 See above at paras. 127–129.

71 See below at paras. 480–488, 519–539 and 563–576.

72 See below at paras. 818–903.

73 See below at paras. 1050–1057.

## 5. FURTHER RELATED AREAS OF PRIVATE LAW

**408.** There are also numerous European regulations in the field of labour law,[74] insurance law,[75] corporate law,[76] and capital markets law,[77] as well as in general business and competition law[78] which cannot be dealt with in detail in this volume.

---

74 On this topic K. Riesenhuber, *European Employment Law*, 2nd ed. (Cambridge: Intersentia, 2021).

75 On the topic G. Rühl, Obliegenheiten im Versicherungsvertragsrecht. Auf dem Weg zum Europäischen Binnenmarkt für Versicherungen (Tübingen: Mohr Siebeck, 2004).

76 Cf. S. Grundmann, *Europäisches Gesellschaftsrecht*, 2nd ed. (Heidelberg: C.F. Müller, 2011).

77 On this topic M. Lutter/W. Bayer/J. Schmidt, *Europäisches Unternehmens- und Kapitalmarktrecht*, 6th ed. (Berlin: De Gruyter, 2017); R. Veil (ed.), *Europäisches und deutsches Kapitalmarktrecht*, 3rd ed. (Tübingen: Mohr Siebeck, 2022).

78 Cf. P. Behrens, *Europäisches Marktöffnungs- und Wettbewerbsrecht* (Heidelberg: C.F. Müller, 2017).

# CHAPTER 1

# GENERAL PRINCIPLES OF CONTRACT LAW

## §9. FREEDOM OF CONTRACT AND CONTRACTUAL OBLIGATION

CONTENTS




References: R. Babayev, *Private Autonomy in EU Internal Market Law. Parameters of its Protection and Limitation* (London: Hart Publishing, 2024); J. Basedow, *EU Private Law. Anatomy of a Growing Legal Order* (Cambridge: Intersentia, 2021), p. 405; M. Giancaspro, *Consideration in Contract Law. Historic and Contemporary Principles and Perspectives* (Cheltenham: Edward Elgar Publishing, 2024); M. Grochowski, 'Default Rules Beyond a State: Special Purpose Lawmakers in the Platform Economy', in S. Grundmann/M. Grochowski (eds.), *European Contract Law and the Creation of Norms* (Cambridge: Intersentia, 2021), p. 250; M.W. Hesselink, *Justifying Contract in Europe. Political Philosophies of European Contract in Europe* (Oxford: Oxford University Press, 2021), p. 336; L. Leuschner, 'Grenzen der Vertragsfreiheit im Rechtsvergleich', *ZEuP* 2017, 335; H.-W. Micklitz, 'Contract Law under Regulatory Siege – Revival of Contract Law? Standardisation, Regulation and Consent', in S. Grundmann/M. Grochowski (eds.), *European Contract Law and the Creation of Norms* (Cambridge: Intersentia, 2021), p. 199; F. Möslein, 'Ambiguities of Self-Regulation: Some Illustrative Examples of "Good" Companies' Certification', in S. Grundmann/M. Grochowski (eds.), *European Contract Law and the Creation of Norms* (Cambridge: Intersentia, 2021), p. 175; S. Patti, 'Contractual Autonomy and European Private Law', in J. Rutgers/P. Sirena (eds.), *Rules and Principles in European Contract Law* (Cambridge: Intersentia, 2015), p. 123; K. Riesenhuber, 'Privatautonomie – Rechtsprinzip oder "mystifizierendes Leuchtfeuer"', *ZfPW* 2018, 352.

# I. THE IMPORTANCE OF FREEDOM OF CONTRACT

**409.** According to Flume, private autonomy and, thus, the freedom to contract includes 'the principle of the self-determination of legal relationships by the individual according to their will'.[1] The constitutionally guaranteed freedom to contract[2] includes, in particular, the freedom to conclude contracts and the freedom of contractual content:[3] Every legal entity is free to choose their contractual partner and formulate the contractual agreement as they wish.[4]

**410.** The freedom to contract is an essential prerequisite for the internal market, which is committed to the (social) market economy according to Article 3(2) TEU.[5] However, it is not explicitly mentioned in primary law or the Charter of Fundamental Rights; the EU legislator, however, naturally assumes its validity, as is proven, for example, by Recitals 8 and 9 of the Consumer Sales Directive.[6] Article 16 CFR guarantees the freedom to conduct a business and, thus, also the freedom to contract.[7] Article II.-1:102(1) DCFR also stated this clearly: 'Parties are free to make a contract or other judicial act and to determine its contents, subject to the rules of good faith and fair dealing and any other applicable mandatory rules.' Consequently, on may safely assume that the freedom to contract is an integral part of EU law.

**411.** In principle, this also applies to the freedom of contractual content. However, the increased focus on consumer protection leads to ever-more mandatory laws (for example, the detailed prescription of the seller's

1 W. Flume, Allgemeiner Teil des Bürgerlichen Rechts, Volume II: Das Rechtsgeschäft, 4th ed. (Berlin: Springer, 1992), §1, 1 and 5 (pp. 1, 6); likewise Canaris, *AcP* 200 (2000), 273, 277.

2 For Germany cf. BVerfGE 8, 274, 328; BVerfGE 70, 115, 123; BVerfGE 72, 155, 179.

3 Cf. W. Höfling, *Vertragsfreiheit. Eine grundrechtsdogmatische Studie* (Heidelberg: C.F. Müller, 1991), p. 3; in detail also M. Cornils, *Die Ausgestaltung der Grundrechte* (Tübingen: Mohr Siebeck, 2005), pp. 165 ff.; S. Lorenz, *Der Schutz vor dem unerwünschten Vertrag* (Munich: Beck, 1997), pp. 18 ff.

4 If the so-called 'social' approaches regard freedom of contract 'on precise inspection' as 'a dream castle, a utopia and not a reality' (cf. Zweigert, in *Festschrift für Rheinstein*, Volume II (Tübingen: Mohr Siebeck, 1969, pp. 493, 503; K. Zweigert/H. Kötz, *Rechtsvergleichung*, Volume II, 2nd ed. (Tübingen: Mohr, 1984), p. 10) because it assumes an equality of legal subjects that does not exist in reality, they fail to realise that freedom of contract as understood e.g. by the German Civil Code does not presuppose formal equality. See in summary Bruns, *JZ* 2007, 385, 387.

5 Cf. amply Babayev, *Private Autonomy in EU Internal Market Law*. Parameters of its Protection and Limitation, 2024.

6 Cf. Reich, *General Principles of EU Civil Law*, 2014, pp. 17 ff.; Riesenhuber, *EU-Vertragsrecht*, 2013, para. 897 at note 15.

7 For references to the case law of the CJEU cf. R. Streinz, in R. Streinz, EUV/AEUV, 3rd ed. (Munich: C.H. Beck, 2018), Art. 16 GR-Charta para. 6. See already the discussion above at paras. 290–303.

performance obligations in the Consumer Sales Directive). EU law primarily aims to promote cross-border trade and less the material freedom to conclude contracts. Therefore, consumer confidence in the cross-border conclusion of contracts needs to be strengthened. For example, Recital 2 to the Consumer Sales Directive states: 'Consumers resident in one Member State should be free to purchase goods in the territory of another Member State on the basis of a uniform minimum set of fair rules governing the sale of consumer goods.' The solution lies in providing information on the one hand and the possibility of the contract's dissolution (e.g through rights of withdrawal) on the other. Only an informed conclusion of a contract is protected; in the case of information deficits, a right of withdrawal arises, or the limitation in time for its exercise is extended.[8]

## II. *PACTA SUNT SERVANDA*

**412.** The freedom to contract's flip side is the principle of contractual obligation or *pacta sunt servanda*.[9] What the parties have agreed on is endowed by the legal system with a command of validity and is, therefore, enforceable before state courts. Without this binding force, freedom to contract would not be completely meaningless[10] since legal systems are conceivable that do not recognise obligatory contracts as binding but only acts of disposal.[11] However, the commitment to the contract must be considered an essential characteristic of a contract law system based on private autonomy.[12] Like the freedom to contract, it is explained by the free self-determination of the individual which includes the freedom to bind oneself legally.[13]

---

8 On the information model cf. below at paras. 477–479.

9 For references cf. M.-P. Weller, *Die Vertragstreue* (Tübingen: Mohr Siebeck, 2009), pp. 37 f.

10 In that sense however Bruns, *JZ* 2007, 385, 386 (Freedom of contract not conceivable without pacta sunt servanda).

11 Cf. F. Bydlinski, *Privatautonomie und objektive Grundlagen des verpflichtenden Rechtsgeschäfts* (Vienna: Springer, 1967), pp. 67 f.; Stathopoulos, *AcP* 194 (1994), 543, 545 f. with the example of early Greek (especially Attic) law, according to which apparently actionable rights existed only in the event of the occurrence of a pecuniary loss; this in turn was affirmed only in the event of the breach of a contract of disposition, but not in the event of an obligatory contract.

12 Cf. M.-P. Weller, *Die Vertragstreue* (Tübingen: Mohr Siebeck, 2009), pp. 41, 274 ff.; H. Unberath, *Die Vertragsverletzung* (Tübingen: Mohr Siebeck, 2007), pp. 46 ff.; Remien, *Zwingendes Vertragsrecht und Grundfreiheiten des EG-Vertrags*, 2003, pp. 311 ff.; F. Bydlinski, ibid., pp. 109 ff.; Bruns, *JZ* 2007, 385, 386. Historical and comparative account in A. Supiot, *Homo Juridicus. On the Anthropological Function of the Law* (Londo: Verso, 2007), pp. 78 ff.

13 Cf. K. Larenz, *Richtiges Recht. Grundzüge einer Rechtsethik* (Munich: Beck, 1979), p. 57; for a detailed account cf. M.-P. Weller, *Die Vertragstreue* (Tübingen: Mohr Siebeck, 2009), pp. 156 ff.

**413.** The principle of contractual obligation is not a self-evident legal consequence, even if corresponding promises exist. Classical Roman law still held the opposite view by declaring a *nudum pactum* (today, one would speak of a moral obligation) unenforceable and recognising a binding obligation only if a contract was in writing.[14] This rule was broken more and more often, and finally, the principle was accepted in the Middle Ages: '*Pacta quantumque nuda servanda sunt*'; however, it needs to be noted that this statement is contained in the Corpus Juris Canonici, which is, as such, not of Roman legal origin.[15] Even today, English law assumes that an informal promise is only binding if the recipient engages in a counter-performance, even if only symbolic, 'in consideration of the offer'.[16]

**414.** The binding force of a validly concluded contract lies in the legitimising effect of a party's legal will. If, from the legal system's point of view, the contractual agreement came about through a faultless will-forming process, i.e. without any relevant error, deception or threat, then the contract is endowed with formal validity.[17] The content of the agreement and the rights and obligations resulting from it are generally accepted by the legal system. Only if a legal transaction violates a statutory prohibition, good morals or public policy is it denied validity.[18] If these outer limits of contractual freedom have not been exceeded, the legal system, in principle, assumes that the concurring will of the contracting parties to shape their legal obligations is sufficient to create an acceptable balance of interests. The necessity of corresponding wills in the form of a consensus also leads, as a general rule, to the assumption that the interests of both contracting parties are equally satisfied by the contract. This assumption is the basis for freedom of content, i.e. the principle that contracts with any content can be concluded within the limits described above.[19]

**415.** In the context of EU private law, the (cross-border) contract is primarily considered an institution for exercising fundamental freedoms, which thus

---

14 'Nuda pactio obligationem non parit, sed parit exceptionem' (Ulp. D. 2, 14, 7, 4). For the historical development of the principle of pacta sunt servanda cf. M.-P. Weller, *Die Vertragstreue* (Tübingen: Mohr Siebeck, 2009), pp. 58 ff.

15 On the point this R. Zimmermann, *The Law of Obligations. Roman Foundations of the Civilian Tradition* (Oxford: Oxford University Press, 1996), pp. 508 ff., 542 ff.

16 On the doctrine of consideration S.A. Smith, *Atiyah's Introduction to the Law of Contract*, 6th ed. (Oxford: Clarendon Press, 2005), pp. 106 ff.

17 At this point it can be left open whether this is a state-induced order or whether the binding effect is, as it were, preexisting by natural law. See below on the principle of specific performance paras. 719–776.

18 There may also be restrictions concerning market-dominant companies.

19 On the limits of freedom of content within this external framework, see also K. Larenz, *Richtiges Recht. Grundzüge einer Rechtsethik* (Munich: Beck, 1979), pp. 65 ff.

serves the realisation of the internal market. However, explicit mention of party autonomy is nowhere to be found. In part, there are indirect regulations, for example, in Article 2 no. 5 Package Travel Directive I, where the contract is defined as an 'agreement linking the consumer to the organizer and/or the retailer'. Nevertheless, EU private law recognises the fundamental elements of the contract law systems of the Member States, such as the principle of contractual obligation. Thus, the CJEU stated:[20] 'The rules invoked by Racke form an exception to the *pacta sunt servanda* principle, which constitutes a fundamental principle of any legal order and, in particular, the international legal order.'[21] The freedom of content of contractual agreements can also be regarded as a general legal principle of EU law.[22]

**416.** Whether the right of withdrawal, which can often be found in EU consumer protection directives,[23] constitutes a restriction or precisely a confirmation of the principle *pacta sunt servanda* is disputed.[24] Any answer to this issue must first address the purpose that the directives follow in each case; a one-size-fits-all approach is out of the question.[25] Wherever the right of withdrawal can be seen as a reaction to a deficit in the mechanisms regarding the contract's conclusion, it can be understood – analogous to defects of will, deception or threat – as a reaction to an imperfect conclusion of the contract, and thus as a confirmation of the principle *pacta sunt servanda*: The binding of the contract only appears to be justified where it was sufficiently ensured that the conclusion of the contract was based on self-determined and informed wills of both parties.

## III. A DUTY TO CONCLUDE A CONTRACT?

**417.** In a legal order which subscribes to the ideal of freedom of contract, it is hard to imagine circumstances under which a person is under a duty to conclude a contract. However, even in the most liberal systems, such freedom may be restricted if other principles require so. For instance, where a trader has a dominating market position, it may be abusive not to conclude contracts with

---

20 CJEU, 16 June 1998, Case C-162/96, *Racke*, ECLI:EU:C:1998:293, para. 49.

21 Court of First Instance, 25 May 2004, Case T-154/01, *Distilleria Palma/Kommission*, ECLI:EU:T:2004:154, para. 45; cf. also the Opinion of the Advocate General Trstenjak, 30 June 2009, Case C-101/08, *Audiolux*, ECLI:EU:C:2009:410.

22 See below at paras. 557–609.

23 See below at para. 561.

24 Cf., on the one hand, Eidenmüller, *AcP* 210 (2010), 67 ff. and M.-P. Weller, *Die Vertragstreue* (Tübingen: Mohr Siebeck, 2009), pp. 294 ff., on the other.

25 For more details see below at para. 561.

customers-to-be. Moreover, when it comes to the provision of services of general interest, such as compulsory insurances or basic banking services, traders may be under an obligation to contract.

**418.** As will be explained in more detail later,[26] the Right to Repair Directive introduces under certain circumstances an obligation of the manufacturer of a good to conclude a repair contract with a consumer. The manufacturer may fulfil this obligation by subcontracting repair, but there is no way simply to reject justified requests of consumers for repair of a good falling within the scope of Article 5 of the Directive.

26 Cf. below at §22.

# §10. SUBSTANTIVE CONTRACTUAL JUSTICE

## CONTENTS



References: Y. Adar/P. Sirena, 'Principles versus Rules in the Emerging European Contract Law', in J. Rutgers/P. Sirena (eds.), *Rules and Principles in European Contract Law* (Cambridge: Intersentia, 2015), p. 7; S. Grundmann/M. Grochowski, 'The Creation of Norms: An Evolutionary View on European Contract Law', in S. Grundmann/M. Grochowski (eds.), *European Contract Law and the Creation of*

*Norms* (Cambridge: Intersentia, 2021), p. 3; A.S. Hartkamp, 'The General Principles of EU Law and Private Law', *RabelsZ* 75 (2011), 241; B. Lurger, 'Gerechtigkeitskonzepte für ein europäisches Vertragsrecht und Instrumente zu ihrer Umsetzung', in S. Arnold, Grundlagen eines europäischen Vertragsrechts (Munich: Sellier, 2014), p. 101; C. Mak, 'Hedgehogs in Luxembourg? A Dworkinian Reading of the CJEU's Case Law on Principles of Private Law and Some Doubts of the Fox', *ERPL* 2012, 323; P. Morvan, 'What's a Principle?', *ERPL* 2012, 313; E. Poillot, 'The CJEU and General Principles Derived from the Acquis Communautaire', in J. Rutgers/P. Sirena (eds.), *Rules and Principles in European Contract Law* (Cambridge: Intersentia, 2015), p. 33; N. Reich, *General Principles of EU Civil Law* (Cambridge: Intersentia, 2014); C. Sieburgh, 'Principles in Private Law: From Luxury to Necessity - Multi-layered Legal Systems and the Generative Force of Principles', *ERPL* 2012, 295.

# I. MATERIALISATION OF CONTRACT LAW

## 1. PRESUMPTION OF EQUIVALENCE AND 'CHANCE OF CORRECTNESS'

**419.** The contracting parties are also free to enter high-risk transactions and commit themselves to services that can only be provided under favourable circumstances.[1] German law, like many other legal systems, is based on the premise that the contract's binding force is not questioned if a freely entered obligation subsequently proves undesirable. In this context, following Schmidt-Rimpler, there is widespread discussion around a 'guarantee of correctness'[2] or at least a 'chance of correctness'[3] that the 'contract mechanism' is supposed to safeguard. This results from the fact that the necessity to agree on the content of the contract includes a mutually beneficial compulsion; the resulting consideration of the interests of both parties usually leads to the presumption that what is agreed is also correct or objectively fair in terms of its content.[4]

1 Such is at least the position of the German Federal Court of Justice: BGHZ 107, 92, 98.

2 Schmidt-Rimpler, *AcP* 147 (1941), 130, 149 ff. Case law has also taken up Schmidt-Rimpler's approach, cf. for example BVerfGE 81, 242, 254; BVerfG NJW 2006, 596, 598; BGHZ 101, 350.

3 The term was coined by M. Wolf, Rechtsgeschäftliche Entscheidungsfreiheit und vertraglicher Interessenausgleich (Tübingen: Mohr Siebeck, 1970), pp. 74, 81 f. Similar in essence C.-W. Canaris, *Die Bedeutung der iustitia distributiva im deutschen Vertragsrecht* (Munich: Bayerische Akademie der Wissenschaften, 1997), p. 49 (critical, however, of the meaningfulness of this term, as most contracts are not freely negotiated); Looschelders/Olzen, in Staudinger, BGB Kommentar (2024), §242 para. 458; L. Fastrich, Richterliche Inhaltskontrolle im Privatrecht (Munich: C.H. Beck, 1992), pp. 51 ff.

4 Schmidt-Rimpler, in his oft-quoted article, nevertheless does not assume that the contract represents the realisation of private autonomy (*AcP* 147 (1941), 130, 159). The background to the treatise was the renewal of contract law in the context of the work on the Nazi 'People's Code'. The 'correctness' of the agreement under private law is understood in this not as the result of the creative power of private autonomy, but as 'justice' as well as 'the expediency

**420.** Schmidt-Rimpler's concept is criticised because of the use of the term 'correctness': It cannot be determined when a contract is 'right' or 'wrong'; the term 'rightness' already implies a value-judgement that should not be made for any self-determined agreement.[5] *Flume*, in particular, advocated for such aa formal view of the freedom to contract underlying the German Civil Code. There certainly is a presumption that the contractual agreement fairly represents both parties' interests in a mutually beneficial exchange (which is not necessarily fair in a material sense – this assessment is beyond any outsider's competence); in other words, it can be assumed that the contractual performances are in balance, even if this is only the case from the subjective perspectives of the parties: *Stat pro ratione voluntas*.[6]

**421.** As a starting point, this purely formal view may be justified. However, it cannot adequately explain why, especially in contract law, more and more mechanisms have been created that pursue a detailed review of the contractual agreement's content, such as the control of general terms and conditions, the recognition of the frustration of the contract's basis (rebus sic stantibus) or specific interest thresholds to avoid predatory loans. This process has sometimes been dubbed a materialisation of contractual justice.[7] The legal system's task is to ensure that the conclusion of a contract is designed so that the individual's self-determination is guaranteed both formally and materially. In this respect, one may speak of a formal understanding of justice, as it is also expressed in the sentence *volenti non fit iniuria*.[8]

---

seen by the community' (*AcP* 147 (1941), 130, 132). According to Schmidt-Rimpler, the risk of the agreement being incorrect must be accepted, since the only alternative is a sovereign arrangement, which is consistently more disadvantageous (*AcP* 147 (1941), 130, 165 ff.). Later Schmidt-Rimpler (in: *Festschrift für Raiser* (Tübingen: Mohr Siebeck, 1974), p. 3, 15) clarified this approach to the effect that the term 'correctness' covers not only the contract mechanism as such, but also the subjective evaluations of the parties. Cf. on the importance of Schmidt-Rimpler's approach also (critical) R. Singer, *Selbstbestimmung und Verkehrsschutz im Recht der Willenserklärungen* (Munich: C.H. Beck, 1995), pp. 9 ff.; M. Auer, *Materialisierung, Flexibilisierung, Richterfreiheit. Generalklauseln im Spiegel der Antinomien des Privatrechtsdenkens* (Tübingen: Mohr Siebeck, 2005), pp. 36 ff.

5 Decidedly W. Flume, Allgemeiner Teil des Bürgerlichen Rechts, Volume II: Das Rechtsgeschäft, 4th ed. (Berlin: Springer, 1992), §1, 6 (pp. 7 f.).

6 Cf. W. Flume, ibid., §1, 5 (p. 6). Likewise in principle also C.-W. Canaris, *Die Bedeutung der iustitia distributiva im deutschen Vertragsrecht* (Munich: Bayerische Akademie der Wissenschaften, 1997), pp. 44 ff. The origin of this parromy is, of course, probably not primarily a legal one. 'Hoc volo, sic iubeo, stat pro ratione voluntas', the Roman satirist Iuvenal writes (Satires VI, 223). With these words, a woman demands of her husband the immediate execution of a slave without investigating his guilt. On the origin of this sentence also Mayer-Maly, in *Festschrift für Kramer* (Basel: Helbing & Lichtenhahn, 2004), pp. 21, 26.

7 Canaris, *AcP* 200 (2000), 273, 282 ff.

8 In detail Canaris, C.-W. Canaris, *Die Bedeutung der iustitia distributiva im deutschen Vertragsrecht* (Munich: Bayerische Akademie der Wissenschaften, 1997), pp. 46 ff.; Canaris, *AcP* 200 (2000), 273, 277 ff., 294 (who calls this sentence a 'basic value for the procedural

**422.** The formal link between performance and consideration is usually described as the subjective equivalence principle.[9] Primarily, this refers to primary contractual obligations, which typically relates to one party's specific performance and the other party's corresponding remuneration. In a broad understanding, however, the term also covers ancillary contractual conditions.[10] The law considers the subjective principle of equivalence in various ways, for example, by respecting the consensual equilibrium – outside violation of good morals and public policy – not only at the time of the conclusion of the contract but also by evaluating the subsequent fate of performance and counter-performance against the standard of equivalence at the beginning (e.g., in the case of the defence of reduction of price, where the counter-performance is to be reduced proportionally according to the impairment caused by the defect). In the case of a subsequent and fundamental change of essential circumstances, the principle of equivalence also requires further action: In this case, sec. 313(1) of the German Civil Code does not provide for a proportional reduction but for a different adjustment of the contract depending on the circumstances. Furthermore, the equivalence principle is affected if the legal system sets requirements for appropriate remuneration without considering the parties' volition.[11]

## 2. CATEGORISATION OF MATERIAL CONTRACTUAL JUSTICE

**423.** The materialisation of contract law can be categorised in different ways. Reich, for example, lists the following guiding principles:[12] (1) framed autonomy; (2) protection of weaker parties; (3) non-discrimination; (4) effectiveness; (5) balancing; (6) proportionality; and (7) good faith. This largely coincides with the classification in this book, even though the following description does not consider itself conclusive and ultimately only wants to propose some form of a topical framework – it may still be a long way from the current state of affairs to the formation of guiding principles. It is doubtful whether it is possible or even

---

view of contractual justice'). On the various aspects of this sentence A. Ohly, '*Volenti non fit iniuria*'. *Die Einwilligung im Privatrecht* (Tübingen: Mohr Siebeck, 2002), pp. 11 ff., 63 ff. On the antinomy of freedom of contract and material justice in detail M. Auer, *Materialisierung, Flexibilisierung, Richterfreiheit. Generalklauseln im Spiegel der Antinomien des Privatrechtsdenkens* (Tübingen: Mohr Siebeck, 2005), pp. 28 ff.

9 According to the idea of balancing justice, a contract should ideally lead to a result that does equal justice to the interests of the contracting parties, cf. Olzen, in Staudinger, *BGB Kommentar* (2024), Einleitung zum Schuldrecht para. 66; F. Wieacker, *Privatrechtsgeschichte der Neuzeit*, 2nd ed. (Göttingen: Vandenhoeck & Ruprecht 1967), pp. 295 f., 482, 520.

10 Cf. P. Härle, *Die Äquivalenzstörung. Ein Beitrag zur Lehre von der Geschäftsgrundlage* (Bern: Lang, 1995), pp. 9 ff. (who himself, however, only uses the narrow concept of equivalence).

11 Cf. Canaris, *AcP* 200 (2000), 273, 283.

12 Reich, General Principles of EU Civil Law, 2014, pp. 1 ff.

necessary to approach this matter with a fixed list of principles.[13] Nevertheless, the following categories prove to be particularly significant for European contract law: (1) equal treatment; (2) protection of weaker parties; (3) good faith; (4) prohibition of abuse of rights; and (5) proportionality. In addition, there are the principles of freedom to contract and the principle of contractual obligation, which have already been discussed.[14]

## II. EQUAL TREATMENT

References: J. Basedow, *EU Private Law. Anatomy of a Growing Legal Order* (Cambridge: Intersentia, 2021), p. 452; M. Grünberger, *Personale Gleichheit. Der Grundsatz der Gleichbehandlung im Zivilrecht* (Baden-Baden: Nomos, 2013); P. Jaffey, *Justice in Private Law* (London: Bloomsbury Publishing, 2023); A. Metzger, 'Allgemeine Rechtsgrundsätze in Europa – dargestellt am Beispiel des Gleichbehandlungsgrundsatzes', *RabelsZ* 75 (2011), 845; N. Reich, *General Principles of EU Civil Law* (Cambridge: Intersentia, 2014), pp. 59 ff.

**424.** The validity of a prohibition of discrimination or even a requirement of equal treatment is not self-evident in private law. The liberal spirit of the 19th century almost universally prioritised the freedom to contract. This also included contractual arbitrariness, meaning that the conclusion of a contract could be refused for extraneous reasons, such as the gender, ethnic origin or sexual orientation of the potential contracting party. Freedom of contract, in this sense, is thus precisely the opposite of equality. However, Aristotle already showed that aspects of equality can also play a role between private actors. Concerning general justice (*iustitia universalis*), Aristotle differentiated between distributive justice (*iustitia distributiva*) and compensatory justice (*iustitia commutativa*).[15] Both forms of justice aim to preserve equality, but in different relations.

### 1. *IUSTITIA DISTRIBUTIVA*: EQUALITY IN DISTRIBUTION

**425.** The *iustitia distributiva* governs the distribution of what we would nowadays refer to as public goods.[16] It requires equal treatment, but only

[13] Cf. F. Bydlinski, *System und Prinzipien des Privatrechts* (Vienna: Springer, 1996), citing no less than 131 principles.

[14] Cf. above at paras. 409–418.

[15] Aristotle, *Nicomachean Ethics*, Book V 5, 1130b-1131a. The term first appeared in the Middle Ages and goes back to Thomas Aquinas. Sometimes the term iustitia correctiva is used, cf. Honsell, in *Festschrift für Mayer-Maly* (Cologne: Böhlau, 2002), pp. 287, 289.

[16] On this point, cf. H. Coing, *Grundzüge der Rechtsphilosophie*, 5th ed. (Berlin: De Gruyter, 1993), pp. 193 ff.

between equals: When the state distributes goods, not every citizen must receive the same amount, but only to the extent that their 'worth' is comparable. Those who are less worthy also receive correspondingly less. Thus, distributive justice is proportional justice; Aristotle calls it geometric proportion.[17] To determine equality between the beneficiaries of the distribution, an external and interchangeable criterion is required, which Aristotle described as follows:

> 'For what is just in distributions must appear according to a certain worthiness; in this all agree. But precisely by this appropriateness not all understand the same thing: the advocates of the democratic principle mean freedom, those of the oligarchic mean wealth or the nobility of birth, and the aristocrats mean high manhood.'[18]

**426.** Ulpian's general tenet '*ius suum cuique tribuere*' also illustrates how the idea of *iustitia distributiva* also greatly influenced Roman law.

**427.** The principles of *iustitia distributiva* are applied not only to goods of the state but wherever benefits and burdens are to be distributed among group members.[19] Here too, if the members are equally 'worthy', there is also an equal right to a share and, conversely, an equal obligation to carry burdens. This proportionality principle was implemented, for example, by sec. 734 of the German Civil Code (old version)[20] for a simple company concerning the distribution of a surplus, usually in the event of the company's dissolution: The 'worthiness' of the members and thus the amount of their right of participation is determined according to the ratio of their shares.[21]

**428.** As a starting point, contract law thus does not belong to the domain of *iustitita distributiva*.[22] This is already very clear in Aristotle's writings, given that he considers 'in the sphere of contractual relations of man to man, voluntary and involuntary', the so-called *iustitia commutativa* the decisive form of justice.[23] The *iustitia commutativa* was, therefore, aptly described as 'justice without consideration of the person'.[24] Whether distributive elements can or should nevertheless play a role in contract law is the subject of current debate. In principle, it is agreed that distributive tasks must be carried out by public law, in particular, for example, by tax law. This is because distributive justice potentially

17 Aristotle, *Nicomachean Ethics*, Book V 7, 1131b.

18 Aristotle, *Nicomachean Ethics*, Book V 6, 1131a.

19 H. Coing, *Grundzüge der Rechtsphilosophie*, 4th ed. (Berlin: De Gruyter, 1985), p. 218.

20 Sec. 736d(6) German Civil Code as of 1 January 2024.

21 Cf. K. Larenz, *Richtiges Recht. Grundzüge einer Rechtsethik* (Munich: Beck, 1979), pp. 124 ff.

22 Honsell, in *Festschrift für Mayer-Maly* (Cologne: Böhlau, 2002), pp. 287, 291 ff., 295 ff.

23 Aristotle, *Nicomachean Ethics, Book* V 7, 1131b.

24 Cf. C.-W. Canaris, *Die Bedeutung der iustitia distributiva im deutschen Vertragsrecht* (Munich: Bayerische Akademie der Wissenschaften, 1997), p. 11 with further references; approvingly Honsell, in *Festschrift für Mayer-Maly* (Cologne: Böhlau, 2002), pp. 287, 294.

collides with the freedom to contract: A market participant does not necessarily need to behave in a purposive and rational manner; they can also act irrationally and choose their contractual partners as they choose. The legal system must respect this.[25]

**429.** Nevertheless, more and more exceptions to those general principles have been created recently, especially at the level of EU private law. Those rules introduce policy considerations into the contractual relationship, for example, in the area of employee protection,[26] consumer protection[27] or, increasingly, non-discrimination.[28] The DCFR also considers itself an instrument of *iustitia commutativa* but accepts distributive elements, especially when they are necessary to protect the consumer. The promotion of a private law system oriented towards party autonomy and competition (which thus promotes commutative justice) contributes significantly to the achievement of distributive justice by providing citizens with easy access to goods and services. Therefore, the insertion of distributive elements into private law must have an exceptional character.[29]

## 2. *IUSTITIA COMMUTATIVA*: EQUALITY AMONG EQUALS

**430.** Thus, legal relations between equals are subject to the principle of *iustitia commutativa*. In this respect, Aristotle further distinguished between voluntary and involuntary relations:[30] As an example of the first, he mentioned purchase,

---

25 Decidedly Honsell, in *Festschrift für Mayer-Maly* (Cologne: Böhlau, 2002), pp. 287, 294 ff.; Canaris, ibid., pp. 13 ff., 33, 73; C.-W. Canaris, in L.E. Kotsiris, *Law at the Turn of the 20th Century* (Thessaloniki: Sakkoulas, 1994), p. 281, who, however, makes the case for individual exceptions.

26 C.-W. Canaris, *Die Bedeutung der iustitia distributiva im deutschen Vertragsrecht* (Munich: Bayerische Akademie der Wissenschaften, 1997), pp. 35 ff., 63 ff., 78 ff.

27 Against this in principle G. Wagner, *ZEuP* 2007, 180, 200 ff., 208 ff. (contract law is unsuitable for redistribution, since every corresponding measure has the effect of correspondingly higher prices and the goal is therefore reversed); positive, on the other hand Hesselink, *ERCL* 2005, 44, 52.

28 Cf. below at paras. 791–809.

29 C.-W. Canaris, *Die Bedeutung der iustitia distributiva im deutschen Vertragsrecht* (Munich: Bayerische Akademie der Wissenschaften, 1997), pp. 35 ff., mentions majority decisions in company law, monopoly or dominant companies and labour law as possible areas of application. On the unsuitability of contract law as a distribution mechanism in detail H. Eidenmüller, *Effizienz als Rechtsprinzip*, 4th ed. (Tübingen: Mohr Siebeck, 2015), pp. 273 ff., 283 ff. On the corresponding debate on the function of contract law in the Anglo-American world Zumbansen, 14 *Ind. J. Global L. Stud.* 191 (2007); on contract governance from a German perspective Möslein, *JZ* 2010, 72; S. Grundmann/F. Möslein/K. Riesenhuber (eds.), *Contract governance: dimensions in law and interdisciplinary research* (Oxford: Oxford University Press, 2015).

30 Aristotle, *Nicomachean Ethics*, Book V 5, 1131a.

surety, rent, deposit, etc., and thus outlined the core area of what is today called the law of contractual obligations; overall, Aristotle considered the mutual free will of the parties essential in this respect. Involuntary relationships, on the other hand, arise from theft, adultery, poison mixing or even abuse, deprivation of liberty and manslaughter, i.e. from tortious acts.[31] *Iustitia commutativa*'s task is to compensate for the inequality created by (voluntary or involuntary) action; the result to be achieved was labelled arithmetical proportionality by Aristotle.[32] In contrast to *iustitia distributiva*, which considers the respective personal quality of the recipient the criterion for allocating resources, compensatory justice demands the establishment of equality *without* any consideration of the affected person. Whether a poor person has killed a rich person or a rich person has killed a poor person: The compensation must be the same in both cases. Overall, Aristotle understands money to be the standard means of remuneration.[33]

**431.** In contract law, the (subjective) equivalence principle reflects the significance of the maxim of *iustitia commutativa*.[34] It neither demands the objective equality of performance and remuneration nor requires a fair price.[35] If equivalence means equality between the parties' performances, then proportionality can serve to describe permitted deviations from these standards. The simplest case is the institute of *laesio enormis*, which rigidly specifies the permissible amount of inequality – or disproportionality – to the effect that it is always made up of twice the fair value of the object of purchase.[36]

---

31 A distinction between (public) criminal law and private law was not known at the time.

32 Aristotle, *Nicomachean Ethics*, Book V 7, 1132a.

33 Aristotle, *Nicomachean Ethics*, Book V 8, 1133a-1133b. Against this backdrop, the cases of structural imbalance are difficult to interpret as examples of the application of iustitia commutativa, since an imbalance (of power) between the parties does not play a role from the outset according to the concept.

34 Cf. Wieacker, in *Festschrift für R. Fischer* (Berlin: De Gruyter, 1979), pp. 867, 877, who sees the iustitia commutativa in the sense of a 'justice of exchange' and thus focuses on the material equivalence principle.

35 Critical of the concept of exchange justice C.-W. Canaris, *Die Bedeutung der iustitia distributiva im deutschen Vertragsrecht* (Munich: Bayerische Akademie der Wissenschaften, 1997), p. 11 at note 10 (claiming that this notion had engendered the misinterpretation, already to be found in Thomas Aquinas, that Aristotle had been concerned with a just price).

36 The medieval doctrine of *iustum pretium* was based on the idea that every good had its own value in the sense of an appropriate price in the objective sense. Accordingly, it was not *laesio enormis* that marked the limit of what was offensive, but any deviation from iustum pretium. In this extreme position, proportionality means nothing other than equality. In this direction even today Gordley, (1981) 69 *California Law Review* 1587, 1625, who sees any deviation from the market price as a violation of the *iustitia commutativa*. Critically C.-W. Canaris, *Die Bedeutung der iustitia distributiva im deutschen Vertragsrecht* (Munich: Bayerische Akademie der Wissenschaften, 1997), p. 18 with notes 15, 57 ff.; on Gordleys approach cf. also H. Unberath, *Die Vertragsverletzung* (Tübingen: Mohr Siebeck, 2007), pp. 89 ff.

**432.** The prohibition of usury e.g. in sec. 138 of the German Civil Code refines this further by standardising gross disproportion and linking it to the objective standard of good morals. In this context, it is still a comparatively modern idea that subsequent changes in the contractual circumstances can entitle one party to cancel or depart from the contract by means of the *clausula rebus sic stantibus* and its various descendants.

**433.** The idea of *iustitita commutativa* can also be applied to ancillary contractual obligations.[37] This is necessary because considering the principal obligations alone cannot determine the contractual exchange's fairness alone. However, an unequal distribution of rights and obligations is more challenging to determine in this area compared to principal obligations. In this respect, it must be noted that in determining the voidability of standard terms, Article 3(1) of the Unfair Terms Directive uses the notion of an unreasonable disadvantage to the contractual partner induced by the standard term under scrutiny.

## III. PROTECTION OF THE WEAKER PARTY

References: J. Basedow, *EU Private Law. Anatomy of a Growing Legal Order* (Cambridge: Intersentia, 2021), pp. 499, 507; M.W. Hesselink, *Justifying Contract in Europe. Political Philosophies of European Contract in Europe* (Oxford: Oxford University Press, 2021), p. 272; G. Howells, 'The Contribution of Consumer Law to the (Re)shaping of European Private Law', in A. Janssen/M. Lehmann/R. Schulze (eds.), *The Future of European Private Law* (Baden-Baden: Nomos, 2023), p. 267; N. Reich, *General Principles of EU Civil Law* (Cambridge: Intersentia, 2014), pp. 37 ff.; H. Rösler, 'Schutz des Schwächeren im Europäischen Vertragsrecht. Typisierte und individuelle Unterlegenheit im Mehrebenenprivatrecht', *RabelsZ* 73 (2009), 889; A. Somma, 'Der Schutz der schwächeren Vertragspartei – rechtshistorische und rechtspolitische Aspekte', in R. Schulze (ed.), *New Features in Contract Law* (Munich: Sellier, 2007), p. 25.

**434.** The idea of weaker party protection is closely connected to the principle of equal treatment: If one can and must only treat equals equally, to what extent may unequal parties treated unequally?

### 1. HOW MUCH INEQUALITY IS ALLOWED?

**435.** It has been shown that contract law is primarily the domain of *iustitia commutativa* and that, in this respect, it is the principle of equivalence that

[37] Cf. also H. Hanau, *Der Grundsatz der Verhältnismäßigkeit als Schranke privater Gestaltungsmacht* (Tübingen: Mohr Siebeck, 2004), pp. 123 f.

establishes equality, while proportionality, in turn, serves as a yardstick for any deviations from the latter. But how shall cases be classified in which the equivalence of performance and remuneration, as well as of contractual rights and obligations, appears to exist from the outset, but one party interferes with the interests of the other by asserting a contractual right? *Iustitia commutativa* does not seem to demand compensation here since it is primarily based on the original and formally equivalent contractual exchange relationship. Coing, in particular, has coined a third form of justice to deal with these cases, the *iustitia protectiva*.[38] This approach aims to limit power over other people, which, by its nature, tends to be abused, by reference to the purpose for which the power exercised is justified. This applies not only in the relationship between states and citizens but wherever 'power relationships enter the field of law'.[39] The principle of proportionality limits the exercise of power to the extent that its original purpose must still cover it.[40]

**436.** This concept should also apply whenever a contracting party can unilaterally intervene in another party's sphere of interest by exercising a contractual right.[41] Particularly where the concerned person's consent no longer legitimises the interference, the principle of overriding interests applies, placing the justificatory burden on the interfering party to show that the right in question remains appropriate.[42] As welcome as this approach to limit power even when exercised between private parties appears, it remains challenging to determine when a contractual right can be regarded as an exercise of power.[43]

## 2. CONSUMER PROTECTION AS A PARADIGM OF WEAKER PARTY PROTECTION?

**437.** The principle of protecting the weaker party seems to emerge particularly clearly in the area of consumer contracts: In contracts between businesses and consumers, the latter are granted special rights that aim to reflect their perceived

---

38 Cf. H. Coing, *Die obersten Grundsätze des Rechts. Ein Versuch zur Neugründung des Naturrechts* (Heidelberg: Schneider, 1947), p. 48; H. Coing, *Grundzüge der Rechtsphilosophie*, 4th ed. (Berlin: De Gruyter, 1985), pp. 220 ff.; H. Henkel, *Einführung in die Rechtsphilosophie*, 2nd ed. (Munich: C.H. Beck, 1977), p. 408.

39 H. Coing, *Grundzüge der Rechtsphilosophie*, 4th ed. (Berlin: De Gruyter, 1985), p. 223. For private law, Coing mentions the relationship between monopolist and contracting party, as well as the relationship between association and individual member.

40 H. Coing, ibid., p. 221.

41 H. Hanau, *Der Grundsatz der Verhältnismäßigkeit als Schranke privater Gestaltungsmacht* (Tübingen: Mohr Siebeck, 2004), pp. 102 f.

42 H. Hanau, ibid., pp. 107 f.

43 Cf. M. Bieder, *Das ungeschriebene Verhältnismäßigkeitsprinzip als Schranke privater Rechtsausübung* (Munich: Beck, 2007), p. 108 note 469.

inferior legal and/or factual position. However, it has already been explained that the paradigm of consumer protection as an embodiment of a principle regarding the protection of weaker parties cannot be maintained in this generality. Nevertheless, individual groups of cases can be identified where consumers are granted situational protection, for example, because formal contractual justice cannot be assumed due to the trader's superior knowledge.

### a) *Information and Disclosure Obligations*

**438.** The relevant EU directives are based on the premise that there is an information deficit to the detriment of consumers, which must be compensated by corresponding information and disclosure obligations on the part of the businesses.[44] It is assumed that a consumer who is informed in this way will make a deliberate decision regarding the contract's conclusion, as the contract's content will then be more likely to meet their legitimate expectations. In the CJEU's own words:[45]

> 'The information provided, before a contract is concluded, on the terms of the contract and the consequences of concluding it, is of fundamental importance for a consumer [...]. It is on the basis of that information that the consumer decides whether he wishes to be contractually bound to the trader.'

**439.** However, the information model reaches practical limits because consumers are generally neither willing nor able to absorb the information they receive, let alone channel it into a rational decision.[46] Nevertheless, the EU continues to follow it – probably for lack of a better model.

**440.** Accordingly, the Consumer Rights Directive contains numerous information and disclosure obligations, all of which are addressed towards businesses. For example, in the case of telephone calls initiated by businesses, they must explicitly disclose their identity, i.e. their or their corporation's name and, if applicable, of the caller (e.g. if it is an agency commissioned by the entrepreneur), and the business-related purpose of the contact (Article 5(1)(b) and Article 8(5) CRD). This enables the consumer not to talk further about an unwelcome subject or with an unwanted person. Furthermore, the entrepreneur has to inform the consumer about a range of other points, such as the essential characteristics of the advertised goods, their total price or, if applicable, terms of payment, delivery and performance (Articles 5(1) and 6(1)

44 H. Fleischer, *Informationsasymmetrie im Vertragsrecht* (Munich: C.H. Beck, 2001).
45 Cf. CJEU, 23 January 2019, Case C-430/17, *Walbusch*, ECLI:EU:C:2019:47, para. 36.
46 Cf. Eidenmüller, *JZ* 2005, 216, 221.

of the Consumer Rights Directive). The legal consequences of breaches of such duties of information do not arise directly from EU law. It is for domestic law to assert protection, e.g. by way of injunctive relief or claims for damages.

*b) Rights of Withdrawal*

**441.** In the case of certain types of contracts or forms of conclusion, the consumer has a right of withdrawal after the conclusion of the contract. Its legal nature and doctrinal classification were disputed for a long time. The exercise of the right of withdrawal allows the consumer to dissolve the contract unilaterally. Reasons do not have to be stated. The right of withdrawal is subject to a limitation in time (this is, therefore, also referred to as a cooling-off period). The business must inform the consumer of the possibility of withdrawal due to the information duties described above. If they fail to do so or the information given is incomplete, the cooling-off period does not begin. This could also be interpreted as a reaction to the typically inferior position of the consumer.[47]

*c) Arrangements Regarding the Payment of Fees*

**442.** The protective mechanisms in favour of the consumer are also clearly evident concerning contractual fee regulations outside of the primary obligation's scope. Often, consumers only focus on the business's primary obligations, only to be surprised to find out later that additional fees need to be paid. Contesting the corresponding declaration of intent will often not be possible or successful since the consumer's misconception relates only to a minor additional payment obligation (such as a fee for a certain method of payment). In these cases, the consumer's misconception did likely not cause the declaration of intent. Hence, Article 22 CRD therefore requires that the consumer explicitly expresses their intention in a declaration concerning the payable fees; implied consent of the consumer is just as insufficient as a corresponding, separate agreement in standard terms.

**443.** Hidden ancillary costs can also arise in the context of payment methods. According to Recital 54 of the CRD, efficient means of payment should be promoted. So businesses must permit at least one common and reasonable means of payment free of charge (such as direct debit, credit transfer, credit card payment and other mobile or electronic payments). Moreover, the business may only pass on costs to the consumer that were actually caused by the use of the respective means of payment (Article 19 CRD). These regulations are intended to counteract the tendency, especially in online trade, for means of payment

[47] Cf. below at paras. 582 ff.

(especially credit card payments) to be offered at excessive prices without any corresponding costs on the part of the business.[48]

**444.** Finally, Article 21 CRD prohibits businesses from charging additional fees for hotlines that exceed costs relating to the provision of the phone call itself. This covers, for example, calls by consumers to obtain information about the contract's content, to assert warranty rights or to complain about an invoice. Notably, this prohibition has a third-party effect vis-à-vis the telecommunication service provider: The latter has no claims against the consumer. Instead, the provider can demand payment for the mere use of telecommunication services from the business. If a fee agreement has not become part of the contract according to the principles just described or if it is invalid, the rest of the contract remains valid. This aims to prevent a situation where the consumer might end up without any contractual claims at all if the business has not fulfilled some of its legal obligations.

## 3. NO GENERAL LEGAL PRINCIPLE OF PROTECTION OF THE WEAKER PARTY

**445.** Does a general maxim of protection of the weaker party follow from this? For German law, the case law of the German Federal Constitutional Court on 'structural imbalances' could provide a foundation for such considerations.[49] On closer inspection, however, the idea appears problematic.[50] Even though the legislator has justified legislative action with imbalances of power, which exist in many cases but are difficult to grasp in normative terms (this is particularly evident in labour law, tenancy law or consumer law), this cannot conceal the fact that private law, in principle, assumes formal equality of all legal subjects and does not generally presuppose structural weakness of any party. In German law, this is proven in particular by sec. 138(2) of the German Civil Code, which assumes situational imbalance, but additionally requires exploitation of this situation by the contracting party and, moreover, a conspicuous disproportion between performance and consideration. It follows (only) from this that the validity of certain legal transactions is denied altogether if a position of power is used for the unilateral enforcement of interests. Comparative law also shows that the existence of an imbalance between the contracting parties is repeatedly used

---

48 BT-Drucks. 17/12637, p. 52.

49 The decision in BVerfGE 89, 214 is particularly lucid. On the historical development of the protection of the 'weaker party' in contract law Somma, in Schulze, *New Features in Contract Law*, 2007, p. 25.

50 On this M. Bieder, *Das ungeschriebene Verhältnismäßigkeitsprinzip als Schranke privater Rechtsausübung* (Munich: Beck, 2007), pp. 120 ff.

as a starting point for further scrutiny.[51] However, no sustainable justification for the general protection of weaker parties can be derived from this.[52]

## 4. PROTECTION OF LEGITIMATE EXPECTATIONS

References: B. Heiderhoff, *Europäisches Privatrecht*, 6th ed. (Heidelberg: C.F. Müller, 2023), paras. 273 ff.; S. Osmola, 'Fixing Reasonable Expectations in European Contract Law', *ERCL* 2023, 136.

**446.** Finally, the topic of justified consumer expectations can also be mentioned in the context of consumer protection. In this respect, the focus is not on the inferior position of a potential contracting party. Instead, one party is granted a protected legal position, which results from their trust in the future occurrence of certain circumstances for which the other party bears responsibility. As a normative starting point, Recitals 8 and 17 CSD may be mentioned: The consumer may reasonably expect that the object of sale will remain free of defects for two years. Therefore, the limitation in time of the warranty claim is set to a minimum of two years in Article 5(1) of the CSD. Also, in Article 7(1)(c) and (d) and (3)(a) of the Sale of Goods Directive, the objective contractual standards are based on the (reasonable) expectations of consumers; the same applies to the Digital Content Directive.[53] A similar regulation can be found in Article 6 of the Product Liability Directive.

**447.** However, whether this already gives rise to a principle of legitimate expectations is highly questionable.[54] This is mainly due to the fact that none of the corresponding approaches have been consistently implemented: For example, the proposal to assume the unfairness of general terms and conditions if they 'caus[e] the performance of the contract to be significantly different from what the consumer could legitimately expect' was not realised.[55] Instead, the protection of legitimate expectations can be embedded in the general principles of contract law, namely the binding force of the contractual obligation. Overall, it is about setting objective contractual standards from the perspective of

[51] Cf. Stürner, *Der Grundsatz der Verhältnismäßigkeit im Schuldvertragsrecht*, 2010, pp. 64 ff.

[52] In this direction, however, *Reich*, General Principles of EU Civil Law, 2014, pp. 56 ff.

[53] Article 8(1)(b) and (c) and (2)(b). See further, e.g., Article 16(2) of the Sale of Goods Directive.

[54] For example Micklitz, *ZEuP* 1998, 253, 264; H. Rösler, *Europäisches Konsumentenvertragsrecht* (Munich: Beck, 2004), pp. 190 ff.; against that Roth, *JZ* 2000, 529, 534; Riesenhuber, *System und Prinzipien des Europäischen Vertragsrechts*, 2003, pp. 571 f. Cf. also Heiderhoff, *Europäisches Privatrecht*, paras. 273 ff.; Heiderhoff, *ZEuP* 2003, 769. For a constructive approach to the interpretation of the term, cf. Osmola, *ERCL* 2023, 136.

[55] This is the wording of Article 2(1) of the Commission proposal of 3 September 1990 for a Council Directive on Unfair Terms in Consumer Contracts, COM(90) 322 final.

a reasonable third party. Ultimately, this view mirrors the perspective of a reasonable consumer. It should not, however, have any content beyond that in the area of consumer protection.

## IV. GOOD FAITH

References: J. Basedow, *EU Private Law. Anatomy of a Growing Legal Order* (Cambridge: Intersentia, 2021), p. 476; W.T. Dajczak, '"Treu und Glauben" im System des Gemeinsamen Referenzrahmens und die Idee einer "organisch vollzogenen" Privatangleichung in Europa', GPR 2009, 63; E. Navaretta, 'Good Faith and Reasonableness in European Contract Law', in J. Rutgers/P. Sirena (eds.), *Rules and Principles in European Contract Law* (Cambridge: Intersentia, 2015), p. 135; C. Perry, *Good Faith in Contract Law* (Cheltenham: Edward Elgar Publishing), 2024; N. Reich, *General Principles of EU Civil Law* (Cambridge: Intersentia, 2014), pp. 189 ff.; C. Stempel, *Treu und Glauben im Unionsprivatrecht* (Tübingen: Mohr Siebeck, 2016).

### 1. THE *ACQUIS COMMUNAUTAIRE*

**448.** European secondary law contains only isolated references to the principle of good faith. This is not surprising due to the fragmentary nature of harmonisation in the area of private law. In the core area of consumer contract law, the Unfair Terms Directive applies the principle of good faith to the question of whether a contractual form clause is unreasonable. According to Recital 16 of the Unfair Terms Directive, this must essentially be understood as the duty to consider the consumer's interests and to act loyally and fairly.[56]

**449.** In addition, the Commercial Agents Directive[57] contains in its Articles 3(1) and 4(1) the obligation for the parties to the commercial agency contract to act in good faith.[58] In contrast to the Unfair Terms Directive, both parties are equally subject to this standard of conduct. The specifications of the mutual duties of good faith in Articles 3(2) and 4(2) of the Commercial Agents Directive provide information on the content of the contractual duties of both parties but hardly establish any further obligations. The agency contract is characterised by the commercial agent's commitment to broker and conclude the transactions entrusted to them (Article 3(2) of the Commercial Agents Directive). The fact that the commercial agent only has to 'make proper efforts', that they only have to follow 'reasonable instructions' of the principal, is to be

[56] More on the standard of clause control below at paras. 656 ff.

[57] Directive 86/653/EEC, OJ 1986 L 382/17.

[58] In more detail with further examples Riesenhuber, *System und Prinzipien des Europäischen Vertragsrechts*, 2003, pp. 401 ff.

seen as an expression of the principle of proportionality;[59] ultimately, this also amounts to protection of the weaker party. It proves that the requirement to balance interests is inherent in the principle of good faith.

**450.** The 'Green Paper on the Review of the Consumer Acquis',[60] which was published in early 2007, states that consumer protection law does not contain a general obligation to act in good faith or in accordance with the principle of fairness. The Commission advocates for introducing such a provision on good faith in order to close unexpected gaps in consumer protection; this also illustrates the tendency towards a unilateral good faith obligation of businesses only.[61] The Commission's proposal for a Directive on Consumer Rights[62] submitted in October 2008, however, did not contain such a general clause but merely repeated, *mutatis mutandis*, the content of Article 3(1) Unfair Terms Directive. This shows that, while the principle of good faith has been developed in secondary law, it exhibits different contents depending on the regulatory context and, therefore, cannot be considered a general principle yet.

**451.** The case law of the CJEU confirms this: The Court continuously regards the principle of good faith as a self-evident part of the common legal principles of the Member States. This is shown in the decision *Messner/Krüger*.[63] The question here was whether Article 6 of the Distance Selling Directive,[64] which has since been repealed by the Consumer Rights Directive, precludes provisions of national law that expose the consumer to claims for compensation for the use of the purchased item when exercising the right of withdrawal to which they are entitled under the Directive. The CJEU affirmed this[65] but simultaneously made clear that the scope of protection of the Distance Selling Directive does not go 'beyond what is necessary to allow him effectively to exercise his right of withdrawal'.[66] From this, the court concluded that the Directive does not prohibit the Member States from imposing an obligation to compensate the consumer for use if they have used the purchased item 'in a manner incompatible with the principles of civil law, such as those of good faith or unjust enrichment'.[67] However, this does not transform the principle of good faith, as it has been

59 Cf. Riesenhuber, *System und Prinzipien des Europäischen Vertragsrechts*, 2003, p. 404.

60 COM(2006) 744 final.

61 COM(2006) 744 final, pp. 19 f. (at para. 4.3). This contradicts the concept of good faith as a standard for the conduct of *both* parties. The Commercial Agents Directive also assumes a mutual commitment.

62 COM(2008) 614.

63 CJEU, 3 September 2009, Case C-489/07, *Messner*, ECLI:EU:C:2009:502, para. 26.

64 Directive 97/7/EC, OJ 1997 L 144/19.

65 CJEU, 3 September 2009, Case C-489/07, *Messner*, ECLI:EU:C:2009:502, paras. 22 ff.

66 CJEU, 3 September 2009, Case C-489/07, *Messner*, ECLI:EU:C:2009:502, para. 25.

67 CJEU, 3 September 2009, Case C-489/07, *Messner*, ECLI:EU:C:2009:502, para. 26.

developed in German case law based on sec. 242 of the German Civil Code, to an overarching principle of EU law.[68] Rather, the CJEU accepts that core principles of Member States' law such as the good faith principle may be relied on even if this may lead to a restriction of a legal position conferred on a party by EU law.

**452.** The EU Platform Regulation[69] also refers to the principle of good faith. However, first and foremost, this relates to the Regulation's market-regulating function and does not primarily concern contract law. It follows from the observation that the providers of online intermediary services[70] often have greater bargaining power than the businesses using these platforms. This creates the risk of unfair behaviour, for example, by unilaterally imposing practices on commercial users that grossly deviate from good business practices or violate the requirements of good faith and fair dealing (cf. Recital 2 of the Platform Regulation). To respond to the imbalance of bargaining power in certain cases, the Regulation, therefore, seeks to ensure that contractual relationships are structured in good faith and based on fair commercial practices (Recital 32 Platform Regulation). This primarily concerns the design of the general terms and conditions of online intermediary services and, in this respect, in particular, the areas mentioned in Article 8 of the Platform Regulation, i.e. the inadmissibility of retroactive changes to disadvantageous general terms, information on the possibility of terminating the contract and information on the content to which the intermediary service still has access after the termination of the contract.[71] All three points appear quite specific and do not require further justification by the overriding principle of good faith. However, their frequent mention in the regulation, also in connection with the imbalance principle, especially the unilateral use of bargaining power and unfair behaviour, indeed exhibits a starting point for a doctrinal generalisation.

## 2. RECOGNITION IN THE *ACQUIS COMMUN*

**453.** In Article 1:102 PECL, the PECL make freedom of contract subject to the requirements of good faith and fair dealing. In Article 1:201 PECL, the duty of the parties to 'act in accordance with good faith and fair dealing' is prescribed as well.[72] This general rule, which exhibits numerous individual manifestations in the PECL, is accompanied by Article 1:202 PECL, which postulates the contracting parties' duty to cooperate to give full effect to the contract. The

---

68 On this point Heiderhoff, *Europäisches Privatrecht*, paras. 300 ff.
69 See para. 989 below.
70 A definition can be found in Article 2 no. 2 and 3 Platform Regulation.
71 For clause control also para. 692 below.
72 Likewise Article 1.7 UNIDROIT Principles.

principle of good faith is conceptualised as an overarching principle for all constellations falling within the scope of the PECL; it is intended to assist in the enforcement of 'generally recognised standards of decency, fairness and reasonableness' in business transactions.[73] Clearly, this has to be seen as standing in the tradition of the well-established case law on the basis of sec. 242 of the German Civil Code.

**454.** The DCFR maintains the principle of good faith's key role.[74] Article II.-1:102(1) DCFR revisits the inherent restriction of the freedom of contract contained in Article 1:102 PECL through the principles of good faith and fair dealing.[75] Article III.-1:103(1) DCFR specifies the duty of the parties to observe the maxims of good faith and fair dealing within all contractual stages, i.e. from the performance or the request for performance to the assertion or defence of a remedy for non-performance until the exercise of a right to terminate the contract. For the area of contract negotiations, Article II.-3:201(2) DCFR contains an independent standardisation of the principle of good faith. This establishes an objective standard of conduct for the contracting parties.[76] Article III.-1:103(3) DCFR,[77] which has no precursor in the PECL, also states that acting contrary to good faith does not give rise to immediate claims for non-performance but only deprives the party acting in bad faith of a claim, remedy or defence.[78]

## 3. POSSIBLE FUTURE DEVELOPMENTS

**455.** In the future, the principle of good faith could emerge as a central concept of EU law on contractual obligations. The Unfair Terms Directive, in particular, prescribes a uniform standard of good faith regarding the control of general terms and conditions. Beyond these and other individual manifestations, the

---

73 Thus explicitly comment B on Article 1:201 PECL. Cf. Castronovo, *Europa dir. priv.*, 2005, 589, 598.

74 On this point cf. also Mekki/Kloepfer-Pelèse, *ERCL* 2008, 338; Dajczak, *GPR* 2009, 63.

75 Very critical of this Eidenmüller/Faust/Grigoleit/Jansen/Wagner/Zimmermann, *JZ* 2008, 529, 538, who see in the provision a possible gateway (probably not intended by the authors of the DCFR) for a general judicial price control. Also critical Dajczak, *GPR* 2009, 63, 65 f.

76 Cf. the corresponding definition of 'good faith and fair dealing' in Article I.-1:103 Abs. 1 DCFR.

77 The provision reads: 'Breach of the duty does not give rise directly to the remedies for nonperformance of an obligation but may preclude the person in breach from exercising or relying on a right, remedy or defence which that person would otherwise have.'

78 Hesselink, *ERCL* 2008, 248, 267 f. fears that this would curtail the enabling function inherent in the principle of good faith. In contrast, this norm only seems to address the barrier function, not the (possible) power of the courts to create new obligations. Such an authorisation is in any case likely to be based on the more general norm of Article II.-1:102(1) DCFR.

foundation for the principle of good faith in the European model codes lies in its more or less visible roots in the separate European legal systems. It cannot be ruled out that Brexit will accelerate this development:[79] Even though the differences between civil law and common law do not appear to be insurmountable[80] in terms of its content, the legal concept of 'good faith' as such already triggered fundamental defensive reactions from the UK.[81] Overall, one should not use good faith as an omnipresent loophole wherever a codified solution does not exist. The aspiration for individual justice embodied in this instrument must not displace legislative value judgements: Otherwise, these would be delegated to the courts of the Member States, and legal uncertainty would increase. It should also be noted that not all Member States' legal cultures grant their judiciaries such broad methodological powers as in Germany.

## V. PROHIBITION OF ABUSE OF RIGHTS

References: J. Basedow, *EU Private Law. Anatomy of a Growing Legal Order* (Cambridge: Intersentia, 2021), p. 369; P. Eichenhofer, *Rechtsmissbrauch. Zu Geschichte und Theorie einer Figur des Europäischen Privatrechts* (Tübingen: Mohr Siebeck, 2019); H. Fleischer, 'Der Rechtsmißbrauch zwischen Gemeineuropäischem Privatrecht und Gemeinschaftsprivatrecht', *JZ* 2003, 865; F. Ranieri, 'Die Anwendung des Europäischen Gemeinschaftsprivatrechts und das Verbot der treuwidrigen und mißbräuchlichen Rechtsausübung. Spannungen zwischen nationalem Recht und Gemeinschaftsrecht?', in F. Ranieri (ed.), *Die Europäisierung der Rechtswissenschaft* (Baden-Baden: Nomos, 2002), p. 129; M. Schmidt-Kessel, 'Rechtsmißbrauch im Gemeinschaftsprivatrecht: Folgerungen aus den Rechtssachen Kefalas und Diamantis', in B. Jud/T. Bachner/R. Bollenberger (eds.), *Prinzipien des Privatrechts und Rechtsvereinheitlichung, Jahrbuch junger Zivilrechtswissenschaftler 2000* (Stuttgart: Boorberg, 2001), p. 61; C. Stempel, *Treu und Glauben im Unionsprivatrecht* (Tübingen: Mohr Siebeck, 2016), pp. 202 ff.

**456.** The prohibition of abuse of rights is closely related to the principle of good faith. It states that a right-holder or duty-bearer may not derive any advantage from their position if this only serves to cause harm to others. EU private law knows only very isolated positive legal expressions of this principle. However, the

---

79 See above at para. 157.

80 It is remarkable that there is a fairly strong consensus in the European legal systems with regard to the resolution of 'hard cases', as the comparative study by Zimmermann/Whittaker (Good Faith in European Contract Law, 2000) clearly shows: Good faith is not always invoked, but the results are very similar.

81 The following dictum is quoted time and again, cf. *Interfoto Picture Library Ltd.* v. *Stiletto Visual Programmes Ltd.* [1989] QB 433, 439, CA (Bingham LJ): 'English law has, characteristically, committed itself to no such overriding principle [that in making and carrying out contracts parties should act in good faith] but has developed piecemeal solutions in response to demonstrated problems of unfairness.'

validity of the prohibition of abuse of rights is recognised in the case law of the CJEU.[82] The *Kefalas* and *Diamantis* cases were ground-breaking in this respect.[83] In both cases, the question arose to what extent a shareholder action against a capital increase by the Greek Institution for the Reorganisation of Enterprises, which had taken place contrary to Article 25(1) of the Directive 77/91/EEC[84] and grants this right to the general meeting alone, could be considered an abuse of rights under Greek law. The Greek court considered the abuse of rights under Article 281 of the Greek Civil Code to be based on the fact that the plaintiffs had not suffered any disadvantage due to the capital increase because their economic interests had been protected. The CJEU ruled that a provision of Community law may be interpreted restrictively by a national court if the assertion of a right would otherwise be abusive. The CJEU explicitly stated that the prohibition of abuse of rights must be considered a general legal principle of the Community.[85] This should not, however, restrict the practical effectiveness (*effet utile*) of the relevant provision of Community law.[86] In particular, the application of the prohibition of abuse of rights by a national court must not lead to the purpose of the provision under Community law being frustrated. However, this was the case in the *Kefalas* case: According to the interpretation of the CJEU, Article 25(1) of the Directive also includes the right of the general meeting to decide on the capital increase (precisely during an economic crisis of the company).

**457.** However, this provision does not specify the legal consequences of a violation. Consequently, the respective national law decides on the type and manner of possible sanctions. Community law does not preclude a national rule which prohibits a sanction as being an abuse of rights if the shareholder 'of the remedies available for a situation that has arisen in breach of that provision, […] has chosen a remedy that will cause such serious damage to the legitimate interests of others that it appears manifestly disproportionate'.[87] Under these conditions, the *effet utile* of Community law is not impaired.

**458.** The CJEU did not justify an independent prohibition of abuse of rights but considered it self-evident that national legal systems apply it – notwithstanding the threshold of the *effet utile* – to provisions of Community law. For example, according to the CJEU, the right of withdrawal under the Distance Selling

82 Cf. CJEU, 6 February 2018, Case C-359/16, *Altun*, ECLI:EU:C:2018:63, para. 49.

83 Of fundamental importance are the decisions in CJEU, 12 May 1998, Case C-367/96, *Kefalas*, ECLI:EU:C:1998:222, paras. 20 f. and in CJEU, 23 March 2000, Case C-373/97, *Diamantis*, ECLI:EU:C:2000:150, paras. 33 ff.

84 Directive 77/91/EEC, OJ 1977 L 26/1.

85 CJEU, 12 May 1998, Case C-367/96, *Kefalas*, ECLI:EU:C:1998:222, para. 20.

86 CJEU, 23 March 2000, Case C-373/97, *Diamantis*, ECLI:EU:C:2000:150, para. 34.

87 CJEU, 23 March 2000, Case C-373/97, *Diamantis*, ECLI:EU:C:2000:150, para. 43.

Directive would be impaired 'if the amount of compensation [...] were to appear disproportionate in relation to the purchase price of the goods at issue'.[88]

**459.** Another topical issue, which has often been tested before the German Federal Court of Justice, relates to the forfeiture of the right to withdraw from consumer contracts. If consumer behaviour amounts to an abuse of rights, such possible forfeiture appears to be accepted in the CJEU's case law. Similar considerations may be made in labour law, where 'discrimination hopping', i.e. a systematic application for jobs with essentially the sole purpose of making a claim for compensation on the grounds of discrimination in the event of rejection, may also be classified as an abuse of rights from the perspective of Union law.[89]

## VI. PROPORTIONALITY

References: J. Basedow, *EU Private Law. Anatomy of a Growing Legal Order* (Cambridge: Intersentia, 2021), p. 341; C. Caufman, 'The Principle of Proportionality and European Contract Law', in J. Rutgers/P. Sirena (eds.), *Rules and Principles in European Contract Law* (Cambridge: Intersentia, 2015), p. 69; L. Kähler, 'Raum für Maßlosigkeit. Zu den Grenzen des Verhältnismäßigkeitsgrundsatzes im Privatrecht', in M. Jestaedt/O. Lepsius (eds.), *Verhältnismäßigkeit. Zur Tragfähigkeit eines verfassungsrechtlichen Schlüsselkonzepts* (Tübingen: Mohr Siebeck, 2015), p. 210; N. Reich, *General Principles of EU Civil Law* (Cambridge: Intersentia, 2014), pp. 155 ff.; M. Stürner, *Der Grundsatz der Verhältnismäßigkeit im Schuldvertragsrecht* (Tübingen: Mohr Siebeck, 2010); A. Tischbirek, *Die Verhältnismäßigkeitsprüfung. Methodenmigration zwischen öffentlichem Recht und Privatrecht* (Tübingen: Mohr Siebeck, 2017); A. Tischbirek, 'Fächerdichotomie und Verhältnismäßigkeit', *JZ* 2018, 421.

**460.** The principle of proportionality is rarely addressed as an independent principle of EU private law.[90] However, its importance can hardly be overestimated.[91]

### 1. PROPORTIONALITY AS A LEGAL PRINCIPLE

**461.** The principle of proportionality is a general legal principle that also applies in private law. It is a formal principle that resolves the collision of

88 CJEU, 3 September 2009, Case C-489/07, *Messner*, ECLI:EU:C:2009:502, para. 27.
89 CJEU, 28 July 2016, Case C-423/15, *Kratzer*, ECLI:EU:C:2016:604.
90 On its significance for the union's legislative competence already para. 229 above.
91 The following arguments are based on Stürner, *Der Grundsatz der Verhältnismäßigkeit im Schuldvertragsrecht*, 2010, pp. 442 ff.

different legal interests and values whenever a solution is not already included in a specific substantive provision.[92] However, by seeking to balance conflicting interests, the principle of proportionality can ultimately be traced back to the idea of the appropriateness of legal measures and, in this way, aims to establish (material) justice. From this perspective, the principle of proportionality can be described as an instrument of procedural justice: It provides a procedure aimed at achieving substantively correct results without prescribing evaluative judgements as such.[93] However, this formal character of the principle of proportionality does not exclude the goal of (individual) justice. In this sense, every procedural theory can be understood as a material theory insofar as it is directed towards achieving a just result.[94]

**462.** On such a level of abstraction, the principle of proportionality can be considered to be a general, structure-forming legal principle. As such, it serves as a guideline for establishing structures of legal rules; in other words, it is a basic pattern of the contractual balancing of interests. Contract law is governed by the principle of subjective equivalence: There is a presumption that the respective rights and obligations of the contracting parties are equivalent.[95] The principle of proportionality complements the principle of equivalence insofar as it aims to describe permissible deviations from the equality of contractual performances.[96]

**463.** From this perspective, every rule of private law and every regulatory context can be considered a manifestation of the principle of proportionality. Thus, for example, the remedies of the law on interference with the performance of contractual duties in the Consumer Sales Directive, the Sale of Goods Directive or the Digital Content Directive are a system of gradual, and therefore proportionate, reactions to the debtor's misconduct.[97] This hierarchy, with the debtor's right to a second tender at the top and the dissolution of the contract as a last resort, reflects the idea of (exchange) justice and, thus, correspondingly, the principle of proportionality.

---

92 Stürner, ibid., pp. 330 ff.

93 C. Heinrich, *Formale Freiheit und materiale Gerechtigkeit* (Tübigen: Mohr Siebeck, 2000), pp. 473 ff.; Stürner, ibid., pp. 383 f.; L. Hirschberg, *Der Grundsatz der Verhältnismäßigkeit* (Göttigen: Schwartz, 1981), p. 86; Spendel, in *Festschrift für Radbruch* (Heidelberg: Adolf Rausch Verlag, 1948), pp. 68, 88.

94 This distinguishes them from purely formal theories that consider the outcome irrelevant, cf. *Auer*, Materialisierung, Flexibilisierung, Richterfreiheit. Generalklauseln im Spiegel der Antinomien des Privatrechtsdenkens, 2005, pp. 33 ff.

95 See para. 419 above.

96 See para. 431 above.

97 See para. 759 below.

## 2. PROPORTIONALITY AS A BALANCING EXERCISE

**464.** Those cases where the legislator openly prescribes a proportionality test must be separated from proportionality as a structure-forming principle.[98] In the former, a decision is not made abstractly by specifying fixed legal consequences but rather by a judicial determination during an evaluation of the individual case. The principle of proportionate application of a legal rule is thereby specified by the judge in each individual case. This reference to individual issues inherent in these rules gives the principle of proportionality a certain multidimensionality. On these grounds, it has often been stated that there is no single principle of proportionality but rather only many different manifestations of it.[99] It is true that the effect of the principle of proportionality in contract law cannot be described in a uniform manner but that it must instead be considered separately and in accordance with its different regulatory contexts: In particular, the principle of proportionality has very different effects depending on whether it is applied in the area of primary obligations, secondary obligations or only concerning a specific contract.[100]

**465.** Notwithstanding these differences, all forms of proportionality have one aspect in common: They require weighing the interests of both contracting parties. This balancing task is structurally comparable to other evaluative processes that aim to achieve some sort of equilibrium, such as the judicial assessment of evidence or the exercise of discretion by public authorities.[101]

**466.** The terminology used by the legislator is irrelevant: The terms appropriateness, disproportionality, unreasonableness or reasonableness express semantic variations at best. Ultimately, all of them are expressions of the proportionality principle since they require an evaluative comparison of different interests.[102]

**467.** Finally, efficiency considerations can undoubtedly play a role in the proportionality test. However, the balancing cannot always be reduced to a cost-benefit analysis. This is only possible when efficiency is firmly established as the law's purpose.[103]

---

98 Similar distinction to be found in Medicus, *AcP* 192 (1992), 35, 37.

99 L. Hirschberg, *Der Grundsatz der Verhältnismäßigkeit* (Göttigen: Schwartz, 1981), p. 94; U. Preis, *Prinzipien des Kündigungsrechts bei Arbeitsverhältnissen* (Munich: C.H. Beck, 1987), p. 281; Merten, in *Festschrift für Schambeck* (Berlin: Duncker & Humblot, 1994), pp. 349, 365; Canaris, *ZHR* 143 (1979), 113, 128 ff.

100 Stürner, *Der Grundsatz der Verhältnismäßigkeit im Schuldvertragsrecht*, 2010, pp. 384 ff.

101 T. Riehm, *Abwägungsentscheidungen in der praktischen Rechtsanwendung* (Munich: Beck, 2006); Stürner, ibid., pp. 347 ff.

102 For examples cf. Stürner, ibid., pp. 336 ff.

103 Stürner, ibid., pp. 367 ff.

## 3. THE PRINCIPLE OF PROPORTIONALITY IN PUBLIC LAW AND PRIVATE LAW

**468.** The principle of proportionality plays a dominant role in public law, especially constitutional law. It serves to connect the actions of the state to legitimate purposes. Regarding the doctrine of fundamental rights, the principle of proportionality regulates sovereign interventions in the citizens' freedoms: It helps realise the balancing with countervailing legal positions and interests. In this respect, its application already follows from the fundamental rights themselves.[104] However, if one also considers the principle of proportionality as an embodiment of the pursuit of material justice (as described above), its roots also lie in the rule of law principle.

**469.** The principle of proportionality in the broader sense, as it is applied in public and especially constitutional law, has a different mode of operation than in private and, in particular, contract law. The interests at play – the relationship of subordination and the state's commitment to the common good versus (formal) equality and private autonomy – differ fundamentally in both areas so that a transfer of the principle of proportionality as it is understood in public law (with the test of appropriateness, necessity and proportionality) to private law does not appear to be very sensible.[105] With regard to contractual obligations, a standard other than that expressed in public law doctrine must prevail: Any reference to a power imbalance between private law subjects as a general trigger for a proportionality test must also formulate tangible criteria for one side's alleged excess of power. Any simple transfer of the doctrine of the public law principle of proportionality is thus out of the question.

**470.** From a comparative and private law perspective, a private law doctrine of the principle of proportionality detached from public law also appears preferable given that the influence of constitutional law on private law is considered far less dominant in other legal systems. However, the structure of the proportionality test in public and private law exhibits common features insofar as it serves to regulate the restriction of legal positions in both cases: Proportionality usually describes a relationship of an exception to a rule, where the exercise of a right is the rule and its restriction can only be justified as an exception to said rule,

104 Stürner, ibid., pp. 294 ff.

105 In that sense, however, e.g. M. Bieder, *Das ungeschriebene Verhältnismäßigkeitsprinzip als Schranke privater Rechtsausübung* (Munich: Beck, 2007), pp. 5 ff., 15 ff. and Preis, in *Festschrift für Dieterich* (Munich: C.H. Beck, 1999), pp. 429, 431, 435; against this Stürner, *Der Grundsatz der Verhältnismäßigkeit im Schuldvertragsrecht*, 2010, pp. 288 ff. The term 'migration of methods' is also used by Tischbirek, *Die Verhältnismäßigkeitsprüfung. Methodenmigration zwischen öffentlichem Recht und Privatrecht*, 2017.

typically whenever strongly overriding interests exist. In this context, the exception is dynamic insofar as it does not relate to firmly defined areas but instead makes the repression of the rule's interest dependent on a higher ranking of the interests of the person affected by the right's exercise.[106]

## 4. PARTICULARITIES OF PROPORTIONALITY IN THE LAW OF CONTRACTUAL OBLIGATIONS

**471.** The principle of proportionality works as a limiting and balancing factor in the law of contractual obligations.[107] However, the test of appropriateness and necessity, which in public law are part of the principle of proportionality in the broader sense, cannot claim general application in private law – particularly in the law of contractual obligations. They are based on assessing the relationship between the ends and means in actions taken by public authorities and presuppose the existence of several alternative courses of action. Potential and alternative actions in a contractual relationship, however, are based on an autonomous agreement between private actors. Although this agreement obliges the parties to consider the other party's interests, it does not contain any requirements to always choose the least burdensome means for the other party. Therefore, only the principle of proportionality's consideration requirement is intrinsic to private law.[108] Its background, at least according to the German doctrine, is the principle of good faith, which dominates all private law and results in an inherent barrier to every legal position.[109] Due to the paramount importance of the principle of contractual obligation in any contract law system, its breach is only permitted above this threshold of unfairness.

**472.** Any exercise of private rights is abusive due to its disproportionality if it proves to be an excessive reaction to a minor misconduct of the contractual partner. From a perspective focusing on the fairness of the exchange, breaches of contractual duties may also be sanctioned. Thus, the sanction has the character of a rule, whereas the restriction is the exception to this – it is subject to the proviso of insignificance.[110] Thus, according to Article 3(6) CSD, the consumer does not have the right to terminate the contract in the case of a minor lack of conformity of the promised performance. This makes the strongest warranty right leading to termination of the contractual relationship subject to the proviso

106 *Stürner*, ibid., pp. 330 ff.

107 *Stürner*, ibid., pp. 285 ff.

108 *Stürner*, ibid., pp. 318 ff.

109 See para. 448 above.

110 Among these so-called 'de minimis' cases Stürner, *Der Grundsatz der Verhältnismäßigkeit im Schuldvertragsrecht*, 2010, pp. 236 ff., 394 ff.

that a certain *de minimis* threshold is exceeded. This reflects, on the one hand, the *favor contractus* underlying the Consumer Sales Directive,[111] but also, on the other hand, the principle of proportionality (as the Council explicitly stated in its Common Position on the Directive) as justification for the exclusion of a contract's termination due to minor breaches.[112]

**473.** Comparative law analysis shows that the proportionality test has many functional equivalents. Still, compared to German law, the role of the principle of proportionality is much more limited in Italian law and even more so in English law. This is essentially due to the far less dominant role of the principle of good faith in these legal systems.[113] The developments in European contract law, however, show how both the principles of good faith and proportionality occupy important doctrinal positions.[114]

## 5. PROPORTIONALITY AS 'SEEKING MIDDLE GROUND'

**474.** Throughout Europe, the tendency can be identified to seek 'middle ground' solutions both at the legislative and judicial levels and to enable fair compensation in individual cases by referring to open formulations such as proportionality, equity or reasonableness.[115] This 'pursuit of the middle' corresponds almost paradigmatically to the idea of proportionality. Due to its interest-balancing nature, it is also designed to develop compromises.[116] This is particularly evident in the DCFR, which, through the frequent use of terms such as reasonable or similar, has – admittedly, with some degree of exaggeration – virtually transformed the weighing of individual cases into a system of its own.[117] This is also associated with a loss of legal certainty.[118] The more case-by-case decisions a law contains, the fewer clear normative judgements exist; the tools to clearly ascertain the law diminish, especially in the context of proportionality

111 Cf. C.M. Bianca, in S. Grundmann/C.M. Bianca, *EU-Kaufrechts-Richtlinie*, 2002, Art. 3 para. 36. See para. 770 below as well as para. 873.

112 Cf. the explanations on Article 3 in the Council's Common Position No 51/98, OJ 1998 C 333/46, p. 53.

113 Stürner, *Der Grundsatz der Verhältnismäßigkeit im Schuldvertragsrecht*, 2010, pp. 410 ff.

114 See para. 448 above.

115 Similar Perlingieri, *Rass. dir. civ.*, 2001, 334, 353. Cf. also Bydlinski, *AcP* 204 (2004), 309. According to Esser (in: summum ius, summa iniuria, 1963, pp. 22, 31 f.) this is possibly a consequence of the change in consciousness brought about by the Enlightenment, namely that the law must serve the individual and not vice versa.

116 Critically also W. Leisner, *Der Abwägungsstaat. Verhältnismäßigkeit als Gerechtigkeit?* (Berlin: Duncker & Humblot, 1997), pp. 235 ff.

117 Critically also Eidenmüller/Faust/Grigoleit/Jansen/Wagner/Zimmermann, *JZ* 2008, 529, 537; Weller, *JZ* 2008, 764, 772; Lorenz, *JbItalR* 21 (2008), pp. 43, 59.

118 On the 'price of equity' Gernhuber, in summum ius, summa iniuria, 1963, p. 205.

tests. To put it bluntly: What is proportionate does not result from the principle of proportionality. Moreover, the ever-stronger legal anchoring of proportionality has resulted in delegating decision-making power from the legislator to the judge, which can affect the principle of separation of powers in extreme cases.[119]

**475.** In terms of legal policy, it is, therefore, essential to meaningfully combine a fixed set of rule-based guidelines with openness in the form of general provisions. The principle of proportionality seems to occupy a kind of middle position between the two extremes in that, on the one hand, it regularly prescribes the aspects to be taken into account and thus tries to stipulate a certain amount of clear-cut preconditions, but on the other hand, it allows for a different weighting of the relevant factors in individual cases and thus contains an extensive, general clause-like decision-making framework.[120] The attractiveness of the principle of proportionality, which lies in its almost universal applicability, also gives rise to its most essential weakness: The loss of legal certainty due to the pursuit of case-by-case justice.

**476.** Wherever rights are subject to provisos relating to their fair exercise, i.e. where the principle of good faith acts as a barrier, the principle of proportionality also applies: The necessity of taking into account the interests of the contracting party requires a weighing of interests before exercising the respective contractual right. In this respect, one can already speak of the principle of proportionality being a legal principle accepted throughout Europe.[121]

---

119 Against the background of the domination of more and more parts of the legal system by the principle of proportionality, Hirschberg already made the (resignating?) prognosis in 1979 with regard to the further development, especially for private law: 'It comes as it comes'. (L. Hirschberg, *Der Grundsatz der Verhältnismäßigkeit* (Göttigen: Schwartz, 1981), p. 186).

120 Cf. C.-W. Canaris, *Systemdenken und Systembegriff in der Jurisprudenz*, 2nd ed. (Berlin: Duncker & Humblot, 1983), pp. 80 ff. with regard to the 'movable system' (*bewegliches System*), which he sees as a middle solution between a rigid legal taxonomy and general clauses.

121 In that sense Canivet, *ERPL* 11 (2003), 50, 57. Riesenhuber also seems to take this approach, describing the principle of proportionality as a 'fundamental value' of European contract law and linking it closely to the principle of good faith: Riesenhuber, *Europäisches Vertragsrecht*, 2nd ed. 2006, paras. 649 and 938 ff.

# CHAPTER 2
# CONCLUSION OF CONTRACT

## §11. DUTIES OF INFORMATION

CONTENTS



References: C. Busch, 'The future of pre-contractual information duties: from behavioral insights into big data', in C. Twigg-Flesner (ed.), *Research Handbook on EU Consumer and Contract Law* (Cheltenham: Edward Elgar Publishing, 2016), p. 221; H. Fleischer, 'Vertragsabschlußbezogene Informationspflichten im Gemeinschaftsprivatrecht', *ZEuP* 2000, 773; H. Fleischer, *Informationsasymmetrie im Vertragsrecht* (Munich: C.H. Beck, 2001); M. Piers, 'Pre-contractual Information Duties in the CESL', *ZEUP* 2012, 867; K. Riesenhuber, *EU-Vertragsrecht* (Tübingen: Mohr Siebeck, 2013), §7 paras. 16 ff.; B. Schinkels, 'Duties of information and Disinformation of Consumers: German Law Report', in M. Schmidt-Kessel (ed.), *German National Reports on the 20th International Congress of Comparative Law* (Tübingen: Mohr Siebeck, 2018), p. 183; I.M. Zuloaga, *Reliance in the Breaking-Off of Contractual Negotiations. Trust and Expectation in a Comparative Perspective* (Cambridge: Intersentia, 2019).

# I. THE INFORMATION MODEL IN CONSUMER LAW

**477.** The socio-political justification of special private laws for consumers is often seen in a structural imbalance in relation to businesses. The consumer's structural inferiority is also based to a certain extent on the fact that they often lack sufficient knowledge of the possibly complex subject matter of the contract – in distance selling contracts, for example, this is, among other things, due to the fact that the object of purchase cannot be checked before the purchase. Consumer law often aims to compensate for this lack of information. In this respect, the law is based on the ideal of a 'responsible consumer';[1] it assumes that, after correcting the information asymmetry, the consumer will make a well-considered decision regarding the conclusion of the contract.

**478.** However, things are usually not that simple. In many cases, the average consumer will be neither willing, nor able, to absorb the high amount of information received, let alone channel it into a rational decision.[2] From the consumer's point of view, therefore, the secondary consequences that the law attaches to omitted or incomplete information are particularly interesting, especially their influence on the withdrawal period, but also, where applicable, the creation of obligations to pay damages.

**479.** First, Article 5 CRD contains general information duties for all consumer contracts. These are accompanied or superseded by special information duties for special types of contracts, forms of distribution or conclusion situations, such as consumer credit contracts, e-commerce contracts, off-premises contracts or distance contracts. For the latter two types, Article 6 CRD provides for specific information duties. Following the pre-contractual information duties, the business is also obliged under Articles 7(2) and 8(7) of the CRD to provide the consumer with copies and confirmations of the concluded contract.

# II. INFORMATION REQUIREMENTS FOR SPECIAL FORMS OF DISTRIBUTION

**480.** The information to be given to the consumer is intended to enable the consumer to assess the offered service and to decide on the transaction in a fully informed manner.[3] Some Member States, like Germany, have chosen

1 Cf. F. Klinck/K. Riesenhuber (eds.), Verbraucherleitbilder – Interdisziplinäre und Europäische Perspektiven (Berlin: De Gruyter, 2015).

2 Cf. Eidenmüller, *JZ* 2005, 216, 221; Grigoleit, in Eidenmüller/Faust/Grigoleit/Jansen/Wagner/Zimmermann, *Revision des Verbraucher-acquis*, 2011, pp. 223, 247 ff.

3 Cf. Recital No 21 Directive 2002/65/EC.

to transpose some of those information duties in an excessive manner. This approach is permissible even though the CRD pursues full harmonisation: Since the CRD repealed the former Doorstep Selling Directive, which also covered contracts on financial services, but given that the CRD itself does not refer to financial services, the legislator is not (longer) bound by directives in this area. Finally, the Distance Marketing of Consumer Financial Services Directive does not prevent any extension to other areas. For businesses, this approach has the practical advantage that they can use identical information templates to fulfil their duties of information for contracts on financial services – irrespective of the form of distribution chosen in the individual case.[4]

## 1. CONTENT

### *a) Informing the Consumer*

**481.** The information duties listed e.g. in Articles 6, 7 and 8 CRD concern, for example, the essential characteristics and the total price of the goods or services, the identity of the entrepreneur, the terms of payment and delivery and the scope of the statutory warranty for material defects. These obligations are waived in the case of off-premises contracts for repair and maintenance work if the performance occurs immediately and if the payment consumer's payment does not exceed 200 euros, provided the consumer has expressly requested the entrepreneur's services (Article 7(4) CRD). The same applies to distance contracts to be concluded utilizing distance communication means that offer only limited space or time for the information to be given to the consumer (Article 8(4) CRD). This includes, for example, advertising spots on radio or television. The entrepreneur must always provide the consumer with the necessary information in a clear and comprehensible manner before the consumer makes their contractual declaration (requirement of clarity or transparency, Article 6(1) CRD).[5]

**482.** A transposition of Article 6(1)(c) of the CRD in domestic law which requires an entrepreneur to always provide their telephone number before concluding a distance or off-premises contract with a consumer[6] violates EU law. Nor is there any obligation on the entrepreneur to set up a new telephone or fax connection or an e-mail account so that consumers can contact them. It only obliges the entrepreneur to provide the telephone or fax number or their e-mail address if they already have these means of communication with consumers.

4 BT-Drucks. 17/12637, p. 54.

5 Cf. e.g. the German case in BGH NJW 2006, 211.

6 Such as Article 246a sec. 1(1) Introductory Act to the German Civil Code.

Finally, the entrepreneur may also provide other means of communication than those mentioned in Article 6(1)(c) CRD.[7]

### b) *Duties of Information as an Integral Part of the Contract*

**483.** In the case of contracts concluded away from business premises and distance contracts that do not include financial services, the information requirements set out in the relevant provisions of domestic law become an integral part of the contract, as is specified e.g. in sec. 312d (1) of the German Civil Code. This is due to Article 6(5) CRD; it had to be transposed into national law due to the requirement of full harmonisation underlying the CRD. Other provisions only apply if the parties have explicitly agreed otherwise.

**484.** If, for example, the business sends the consumer GTC containing different information after the information has already been provided, the original information will only be changed if the consumer has expressly agreed to the GTC; tacit consent or silence on the part of the consumer does not suffice. If the GTC handed over or sent together with the original information already deviate from or contradict the original information, the entrepreneur behaves inconsistently, meaning that they cannot rely on the deviating GTC.[8]

### c) *Duties of Information as a Prerequisite for the Conclusion of a Contract?*

**485.** Due to Article 4 no. 5 of the Directive on Better Enforcement and Modernisation of Union Consumer Protection Rules,[9] a new Article 6a was inserted into the CRD. This creates additional specific information requirements for contracts concluded on online marketplaces. According to its first section, 'on an online marketplace, the provider of the online marketplace shall, without prejudice to Directive 2005/29/EC, provide the consumer with the following information in a clear and comprehensible manner and in a way appropriate to the means of distance communication', for example, about the parameters based on which the ranking of offers on the online marketplace is generated. This information must be given '[b]efore a consumer is bound by a distance contract, or any corresponding offer, on an online marketplace'.

---

7 CJEU, 10 July 2019, Case C-649/17, *Amazon*, ECLI:EU:C:2019:576. On the issue of the 'availability' of the telephone number within the meaning of Article 6(1)(c), (h) and (4) in conjunction with Annex I Part A CRD. Annex I Part A CRD see CJEU, 14 May 2020, Case C-266/19, *EIS*, ECLI:EU:C:2020:384, paras. 37 ff.

8 BT-Drucks. 17/12637, p. 54. The above does not apply to contracts for financial services, as sec. 312d(2) of the German Civil Code does not contain a provision corresponding to sec. 312d(1) of the German Civil Code. The legislator was not bound by Article 6(5) CRD in this respect, as it does not extend to financial services.

9 Directive (EU) 2019/2161, OJ 2019 L 328/7.

**486.** This wording seems misleading in that it could be understood to mean that the provision of the information must have caused the consumer's consent to the contract. However, this reading would neither make sense nor be intended: In practice, it would create great legal uncertainty, as it would be unclear in many contracts whether the information was provided correctly. Moreover, Recital 57 to Directive 2019/2161 clarifies that national contract law remains unaffected, 'regulating for instance, the conclusion or the validity of a contract in cases such as lack of consent or unauthorised commercial activity'. In this respect, the general principles of the respective Member State's law on the conclusion of contracts also apply, i.e. in Germany, sec. 145 et seq. of the German Civil Code.

### 2. IN PARTICULAR: DUTIES OF INFORMATION ABOUT COSTS

**487.** Pursuant to Article 6(5) CRD, the trader has to provide cost-related duties of information before distance contracts and contracts concluded away from business premises are concluded.

**488.** In particular, the trader has to inform the consumer about the total price of goods or services (including all taxes and duties) as well as the way the price is calculated in cases where, due to the nature of the goods or services, it cannot reasonably be calculated in advance. If the business and the consumer have not agreed to pay additional costs, there is no contractual right to compensation. However, even if it can be inferred from the interpretation of the contract that the consumer is to bear the costs in the usual amount, the obligation to pay only exists if the consumer has been informed accordingly. This information duty covers the delivery, freight and shipping costs expressly listed in Article 6(5) CRD.

## III. TRANSCRIPTS AND CONFIRMATIONS

**489.** According to Articles 7(2) and 8(7) CRD, businesses must provide the consumer with a copy or confirmation of the contract after it has been concluded. The provision thus serves to protect the consumer by providing comprehensive documentation;[10] it extends to contracts concluded away from business premises, distance contracts and contracts for the supply of digital content that is not on a physical medium. If the content of the contract confirmation differs from the concluded contract, this must not be detrimental to the consumer.

---

10 Cf. BT-Drucks. 17/12637, p. 55. The regulation does not apply to contracts for financial services due to sec. 312f(4) of the German Civil Code. However, there are special regulations for these contracts in sec. 312d(2), 491 ff. of the German Civil Code.

## IV. SPECIAL OBLIGATIONS IN E-COMMERCE

**490.** E-commerce contracts only partially overlap with distance selling contracts. There are special specific information duties that the entrepreneur must fulfil whenever they engage in e-commerce, which lie irrespective of the existence of a consumer contract. These duties can be traced back to Articles 10, 11 and 18 of the E-Commerce Directive.[11]

**491.** Electronic devices are indeed often used in B2C relations. However, even today, consumers are often less experienced in dealing with electronics and are, therefore, particularly vulnerable to the resulting dangers. Other purposes include consumer confidence in e-commerce (Recital 7 E-Commerce Directive) and the promotion of economic growth (Recital 2 E-Commerce Directive).

**492.** Electronic commerce is defined as an entrepreneur using a telecommunication service or other electronic media to conclude a contract to deliver goods or provide services. This term is considerably narrower than the means of distance communication, which also includes, for example, letters and telephone calls. As to tele- or media services, Recital 17 of the E-Commerce Directive refers to 'electronic equipment for the processing (including digital compression) and storage of data', which provides services at the individual request of a recipient. According to Recital 18 of the E-Commerce Directive, the business activities covered take place online; offline services are outside of its scope of application. Essentially, the E-Commerce Directive probably only covers offers and orders by email or Internet, not by telephone.

**493.** According to Annex I no 2, indents 1 and 2 of Directive (EU) 2015/1535,[12] services provided with electronic devices but in a tangible form, e.g. cash dispensers or ticket machines, are also not covered. It is unavoidable that this will lead to demarcation difficulties.[13]

**494.** In e-commerce, the business must provide the customer with appropriate, effective and accessible technical means to enable the customer to recognise and correct input errors before placing their order.

---

11 Directive 2000/31/EC, OJ 2000 L 178/1.

12 Directive (EU) 2015/1535, OJ 2015 L 241/1.

13 Cf. C. Wendehorst, in *Münchener Kommentar zum BGB*, 9th ed. (Munich: C.H. Beck, 2022), §312i para. 19.

## V. LEGAL CONSEQUENCES IN CASE OF VIOLATIONS

**495.** As shown above, the duties of information that apply to businesses are extremely extensive and complex. Therefore, frequent noncompliance is to be expected. The legal consequences of violations are, therefore, all the more important. In some cases, there are special legal consequences; in all other cases, general principles can be applied. Article 6(9) CRD assigns the burden of proof regarding the fulfilment of the statutory duty to inform to the entrepreneur. This rules also applies to claims for damages by the consumer due to breaches of the information duty.

**496.** The most important sanction results from Article 10 CRD: If the trader has not provided the consumer with the information on the right of withdrawal as required by Article 6(1)(h) CRD, the withdrawal period shall expire 12 months from the end of the initial withdrawal period.

**497.** Besides, pursuant to Article 6(6) CRD, if the trader has not complied with the information requirements on additional charges or other costs as referred to in Article 6(1)(e) CRD, or on the costs of returning the goods as referred to in Article 6(1)(i) CRD, the consumer shall not bear those charges or costs. If, however, the trader has not complied with the information duties set up in Article 8(2) CRD, the consumer shall not be bound by the contract or order.

**498.** Clearly, as EU law does not prescribe a fully-fledged legal framework on damages for non-compliance, domestic law must react to breaches of information duties.

# §12. OFFER AND ACCEPTANCE

## CONTENTS

References: H. Kötz, *European Contract Law*, 2nd ed. (Oxford: Oxford University Press, 2017), §2; J. Schmidt, *Der Vertragsschluss – ein Vergleich zwischen dem deutschen, französischen, englischen Recht und dem CESL* (Tübingen: Mohr Siebeck, 2013); R. Schulze, 'Grundsätze des Vertragsschlusses im Acquis communautaire', *GPR* 2005, 56; R. Schulze/F. Zoll, *European Contract Law*, 3rd ed. (Munich: C.H. Beck, 2021), pp. 126 ff.

# I. PRINCIPLE OF CONSENSUS

## 1. BASICS: THE WILL PARADIGM

**499.** A contract is the binding regulation of legal relations between two legal entities. Its binding effect derives its legitimacy from the parties' consensus concerning the contractual regulation of essential points (the *essentialia negotii*) that have been freely and without relevant coercion agreed upon. If this consensus does not exist, a contract is not concluded due to the presence of a dissent (e.g. sec. 154(1) of the German Civil Code). If the consensus is formally present, but the underlying agreement of wills was reached incorrectly, the legal transaction is valid but may be voidable, depending on the system. In the current *acquis communautaire*, there are no explicit regulations spelling out the legal consequences for different defects of volition.[1]

## 2. THE CONCLUSION OF CONTRACTS IN THE *ACQUIS COMMUNAUTAIRE*

### *a) Agreement*

**500.** Contract law is based – arguably worldwide – on the consent principle.[2] The situation is similar in European contract law, despite the fragmentary nature

1 On the treatment of the defects of will see para. 555 below.

2 Cf. e.g. Article 1128 n° 1 of the French Code civil (as stipulated by Article 2 of the Ordonnance n° 2016-131 du 10 février 2016): 'Sont nécessaires à la validité d'un contrat: 1° Le consentement des parties; [...].'

of the system.[3] There is no EU regulation on the conclusion of contracts,[4] but European contract law implicitly presupposes the consent principle. Notably, Article 27 CRD provides that the delivery of unsolicited goods or digital content or the provision of unsolicited services exempts the consumer from the obligation to provide the consideration; the absence of a response from the consumer is not deemed to constitute consent.[5] Furthermore, Article 7(1) CSD allows for an 'agreement' between the seller and consumer on the shortening of the warranty period up to one year in accordance with Member State law.[6]

**501.** The fact that the principle of consensus is part of the unspoken *acquis communautaire* can also be inferred from Article 30 of the proposal for a Common European Sales Law, which regulates the requirements for the conclusion of a contract. According to para. 1 of the provision, a contract is 'concluded if (a) the parties reach an agreement; (b) they intend the agreement to have legal effect; and (c) the agreement, supplemented if necessary by rules of the Common European Sales Law, has sufficient content and certainty to be given legal effect'. According to para. 2 of the provision, '[an] agreement is reached by acceptance of an offer. Acceptance may be made explicitly or by other statements or conduct.'

**502.** These formulations can be traced back to the Draft Common Frame of Reference, which is, in turn, based on the CISG.[7] Article II.-4:101 DCFR reads as follows: 'A contract is concluded, without any further requirement, if the parties: (a) intend to enter into a binding legal relationship or bring about some other legal effect; and (b) reach a sufficient agreement.' Offer and acceptance are governed by Article II.-4:201, 4:204 DCFR; but here, the principle of consensus dominates, so that in the case of contract conclusions where the parties are located in different places, it is no longer relevant what constitutes an offer and what constitutes acceptance. In this respect, Article II.-4:211 DCFR makes it clear that the relevant provisions of the DCFR apply accordingly.

---

3 See para. 403 above.

4 For example, Recital 57 of Directive 2019/2161 on better enforcement and modernisation of Union consumer protection rules clearly states: 'This Directive should not affect aspects of national contract law that are not regulated by it. Therefore, this Directive should be without prejudice to national contract law regulating for instance the conclusion or the validity of a contract in cases such as lack of consent or unauthorised commercial activity.' More on this Directive at para. 993 below.

5 Likewise already Article 9 Distance Selling Directive.

6 Cf. Riesenhuber, *Europäisches Vertragsrecht*, 2nd ed. 2006, paras. 327 ff.

7 Cf. B. *Lurger*, in C. Wendehorst/B. Zöchling-Jud (eds.), *Am Vorabend eines Gemeinsamen Europäischen Kaufrechts. Zum Verordnungsentwurf der Europäischen Kommission vom 11.10.2011* (Vienna: Manz 2012), pp. 63, 73 ff.; *Looschelders*, *AcP* 212 (2012), 581, 605 ff.

**503.** The consent principle should also apply if non-monetary remuneration is owed. This could be considered doubtful, for example, if digital content is not provided in exchange for money but in exchange for the provision of other digital content (for example, in the form of personal data). The Digital Content Directive, which governs such constellations, does not regulate the conclusion of the contract itself. If the question of the parties' intention to be legally bound was to be left to the regulation by the legal systems of the Member States, this could lead to massive inequalities in the application of the law so that the *effet utile* of the Directive would be called into question. In any case, it is clear from the Directive that the conclusion of a contract does not require monetary consideration (Article 3(1) subpara. 2 Digital Content Directive).[8]

*b) Revocability of Contractual Offers*

**504.** It is interesting to analyse the external effects of a declaration of intent; in other words: How long is an offer freely revocable? According to German law, a declaration of intent becomes effective upon receipt by the recipient of the declaration (sec. 130(1) of the German Civil Code). This is not the case if it is preceded or accompanied by a revocation (sec. 130(1) of the German Civil Code). If the binding force has not been excluded (sec. 145 of the German Civil Code), an offer is irrevocable once it has been received by the recipient of the declaration.

**505.** English law adopts a rather extreme position in this respect. According to the so-called Mailbox Theory, an offer to conclude a contract becomes effective not only when the recipient receives it but already when the will is expressed, e.g. when it is posted. However, an offer is, in principle, freely revocable as long as it has not yet been accepted. The reason for this is the requirement of *consideration*, without which a contract cannot be concluded. The recipient of the declaration can, therefore, only create a contractual obligation by performing a contractual duty in *consideration of the offer* or by confirming the obligation by *deed*.[9]

**506.** French law takes an intermediate position. In principle, it is also assumed that a declaration of intent can be freely revoked even after it has been expressed since the binding effect is only brought about with the offer's acceptance.[10]

---

8 See para. 937 below.

9 The classic formulation is in *Currie* v. *Misa* (1875) L.R. 10 Ex. 153, 162 (Lush J.): 'A valuable consideration, in the sense of the law, may consist in some right, interest, profit, or benefit accruing to the one party, or some forbearance, detriment, loss, or responsibility given, suffered, or undertaken by the other.' The consideration can thus also consist of a counter-promise.

10 H.J. Sonnenberger/C. Autexier, *Einführung in das französische Recht*, 3rd ed. (Fachmedien Recht und Wirtschaft in Deutscher Fachverlag GmbH, 2000), p. 123.

However, as a rule, the addressee of the declaration of intent is granted a reasonable period to consider the matter (*délai raisonnable*) – the offering party may owe damages based on the general tort clause of Article 1240 of the Civil Code,[11] namely, if the legitimate expectations of the offeree regarding the continuation of the offer have been disappointed.[12]

**507.** Again, the *acquis communautaire* does not yet exhibit any illustrative examples. The DCFR instead follows the model of English law: According to Article II.-4:202 DCFR, an offer can be revoked if the revocation reaches the addressee before they have sent the declaration of acceptance. Exceptions exist if the offering party has excluded revocation or promised a fixed offer period or if the offeree was entitled to trust that the offer was irrevocable and acted accordingly. Following this model, Article 32(1) CESL also follows the 'mailbox rule', according to which a declaration of intent can be withdrawn at any time before the recipient has declared its acceptance. Only in exceptional cases, in particular, if the recipient could reasonably rely on the irrevocability of the offer and acted in reliance on the offer, is the withdrawal of the offer invalid (Article 32(3)(c) CESL).

## II. SPECIAL CONDITIONS FOR EFFECTIVENESS

### 1. OBSERVANCE OF THE LEGAL AND MORAL ORDER

**508.** Every legal system regulates some external limits to contractual freedom. In German law, these are, in particular, violations of a statutory prohibition (sec. 134 of the German Civil Code), cases of immorality (sec. 138 of the German Civil Code) and non-compliance with any prescribed form of the legal transaction (sec. 125 of the German Civil Code). Immorality is used to incorporate ethical and fundamental considerations into the legal system.

**509.** English law also refuses to recognise a contract that violates public policy. In this respect, instruments such as (economic) duress, undue influence and unconscionability are also comparable since they also represent reactions of the legal system to such contracts that were concluded under completely unfair conditions.[13]

---

11 In the version of Article 2 of Ordonnance n° 2016-131 du 10 février 2016.

12 Some commentators instead assume the existence of an implied pre-contract to maintain the offer for a certain period of time.

13 Cf. Stürner, *Der Grundsatz der Verhältnismäßigkeit im Schuldvertragsrecht*, 2010, pp. 79 ff.

**510.** According to traditional French law, the contract must pursue a permissible purpose (*cause licite*), Article 1131 Code civil (old version). The cause is to be understood in an extensive manner; the term includes not only the reason for the contract but, in a broader fashion, the objectives pursued with the conclusion of the contract (e.g. the purchase of a house to establish a brothel). Also, a certain object of the contract (*objet*) must be established, Article 1128 Code civil (old version). Thus, only such objects are considered negotiable that are '*dans le commerce*'. A contract for carrying a child to term, for example, is not based on a permitted *objet*.[14] *Objet* and *cause* cannot always be separated clearly. Following the reform of the French Code of Obligations in 2016, Article 1128 no. 3 Code civil now requires '*un contenu licite et certain*'; the traditional categories of *objet* and *cause* are, thus, completely dissolved. The old concept of cause is effectively abandoned.[15]

**511.** Again, EU law does not relate to the described outer limits of contractual freedom. This can be explained, on the one hand, by the fact that questions of morality and moral laws are deeply rooted in a country's respective legal culture, which suggests a certain legislative restraint. On the other hand, however, there is no regulatory desideratum from an EU point of view: The internal market is primarily promoted by the fact that contracts are concluded because this promotes the exchange of goods and services. Therefore, the aim of most regulatory measures is to increase the attractiveness of a (cross-border) contract for the consumer. The DCFR also does not contain a distinct European definition of the limits of the freedom to contract; rather, Article II.-7:301 and 7:302 DCFR refer to the law of the Member States ('Contracts infringing a principle recognised as fundamental in the laws of the Member States' or 'contracts infringing mandatory rules are void').

**512.** The proposal for a Common European Sales Law also lacks a provision on unconscionability or other instances in which contracts are void; only usury is standardised in Article 51 CESL. The proposal leaves open whether this is conclusive or whether the Member States would be free to apply their own standards of nullity. In principle, the CESL itself should determine the conditions under which a legal transaction is null and void. Article 1(1) of the CESL states that '[the] parties are free to conclude a contract and to determine its contents, *subject to any applicable mandatory rules*'.[16] It is not immediately clear whether only those mandatory provisions are included that can be found in the Uniform Law on the Sale of Goods itself or whether this also refers to other mandatory laws outside of it.

---

14 The establishment of a filiation relationship between sperm donor and child is excluded under Article 311-19 Code civil.

15 Cf. Weller, in *Festschrift für Müller-Graff*, 2015, p. 109; Babusiaux/Witz, *JZ* 2017, 496, 501 f.

16 Emphasis added.

**513.** If one ought to understand the latter as a general opening clause along the DCFR lines, the question arises as to which mandatory standards are thus applicable. In this regard, a working group of the Max Planck Institute in Hamburg has suggested using a European standard.[17] This solution would be consistent and in favour of uniformity. In practice, however, it is likely to cause legal uncertainty because the grounds due to which legal transactions can be objected sometimes diverge extensively between individual Member States. It must be admitted that there is perhaps little need for such considerations in the area of sales law. Usury, which, from a German point of view, is the most important case in practice that is typically considered immoral, is contained in the uniform law on the International Sale of Goods in Article 51 CESL under the designation 'unfair exploitation' (in the form of a contestation element).[18]

**514.** In this respect, it seems more plausible to assume that an opening clause in favour of mandatory rules of subsidiary applicable national law was intended. This would undoubtedly be detrimental to further unification, but given the rare cases where this is applicable, this appears tolerable.

**515.** The Commission's accompanying Communication on the proposed CESL Regulation states succinctly: 'If [the entrepreneur] concludes a contract with a consumer from another Member State, he would no longer need to take into account the mandatory law of that Member State'.[19] If the CESL wanted to exclude all mandatory laws, this should be clearly stated in its codification.

## 2. RECONFIRMATION AS A CONDITION OF VALIDITY

**516.** Whether specific contracts should only be valid if they have been reconfirmed is a somewhat different issue, but it also falls under the framework of effectiveness requirements. The draft of the E-Commerce Directive contained such a requirement.[20] Accordingly, an electronic contract could only be considered concluded when, after a concurring offer and acceptance, both parties

---

17 Max Planck Institute, *RabelsZ* 75 (2011), 371, 406 f.

18 This is to be seen critically because the usurious legal transaction is seen here as an expression of the lack of will. In this respect, the consequence of voidability is consistent. However, the reason for the objectionability of the usurious legal transaction actually lies in the exploitation of the weaker contractual partner. Here, nullity would be the more appropriate legal consequence. For more details, cf. Stürner, *Der Grundsatz der Verhältnismäßigkeit im Schuldvertragsrecht*, 2010, pp. 88 ff.

19 COM(2011) 636 final, p. 11.

20 Proposal for a Directive of the European Parliament and of the Council on certain legal aspects of electronic commerce in the Internal Market, COM(98) 586 final.

had also reconfirmed the contract electronically.[21] Eventually, this proposal was not implemented. Article 11(1) E-Commerce Directive only codified the provider's obligation to send the contractual partner a confirmation of the order. Anyhow, the wording of this draft provision would not have constituted a constitutive regulation of the conclusion of the contract. Its purpose is limited to informing the customer about the acceptance of the order.[22]

**517.** The proposal for a Common European Sales Law also contained a comparable provision: Article 8(2) CESL-Regulation provides that a contract between a trader and a consumer shall only be valid 'if the consumer's consent is given by an explicit statement which is separate from the statement indicating the agreement to conclude a contract'. In the case of online contracts, this requirement is fulfilled simply by the consumer ticking another mandatory opt-in checkbox in addition to agreeing to the entrepreneur's GTC and further declarations, such as on the use of data.[23]

**518.** The provision exhibits parallels to Article 1341(2) of the Italian Codice civile, which tightens the inclusion requirements for specific clauses that are typically particularly dangerous to the other party in that they can only be validly agreed upon if the other party has expressly consented to them by signing them (so-called '*doppia firma*'). It is not without a certain irony that consumers must be warned about this, of all things, given that the entrepreneur chooses a uniform European sales law that explicitly refers to its high level of consumer protection in Article 1(3) CESL.

## III. SPECIAL FORMS OF DISTRIBUTION

### 1. CONSUMER CONTRACTS CONCLUDED AWAY FROM BUSINESS PREMISES

#### *a) 'Doorstep Selling' as a Regulatory Problem*

**519.** The conclusion of a contract is based on a free consensus of the parties. In some situations, however, this freedom is restricted. This may be the case for what is called doorstep selling, where the trader visits the consumer at their

21 Article 11(1)(a) of the draft reads: 'the contract is concluded when the recipient of the service: – has received from the service provider, electronically, an acknowledgement of receipt of the recipient's acceptance, and – has confirmed receipt of the acknowledgement of receipt.'

22 Riesenhuber, *Europäisches Vertragsrecht*, 2nd ed. 2006, para. 335.

23 Wendehorst, in Schulze, *Common European Sales Law – Commentary*, 2012, Art. 8 VO paras. 5 f.

home or workplace, where the contract is then initiated or concluded. Here, it is typically more difficult to rationally weigh up the pros and cons of the offer due to the familiar surroundings. In many cases, therefore, entrepreneurs have taken advantage of this sales model, often resulting in undesirable contractual obligations from the consumer's point of view. The legislator reacted to this problem with the implementation of a right of withdrawal.

### b) *Genesis and Function*

#### aa) The Regulation of 'Doorstep Selling' by the Doorstep Selling Directive

**520.** In 1985, Directive 85/577/EEC to protect the consumer in respect of contracts negotiated away from business premises (hereinafter the Doorstep Selling Directive) was adopted. According to the directive's Recitals, it responds to the observation that the conclusion of contracts away from the entrepreneur's business premises is a form of commercial practice frequently encountered in the Member States.

**521.** Essentially, the protection afforded by the Doorstep Selling Directive comprised three situations (Article 1(1) Doorstep Selling Directive):[24] (1) On the occasion of a visit of the entrepreneur to the consumer in their home or in the home of another consumer, (2) on the occasion of a visit of the entrepreneur to the consumer at their place of work, or (3) during a trip organised by the entrepreneur outside their business premises. A doorstep situation in the literal sense only exists in the first group of cases. However, in those other cases, the consumer often also cannot compare the quality and price of the offer with other offers; here, too, the element of surprise due to the unique situation often contributes to the conclusion of the contract. As a reaction, the Doorstep Selling Directive gave the consumer the opportunity to reconsider the obligation resulting from the contract and granted them a withdrawal period of seven days. This unilateral right to dissolve the contract protects consumers from abusive commercial practices; the Doorstep Selling Directive thus also pursues fair trading objectives.[25]

#### bb) The Recast in the CRD

**522.** A significant change was brought about by the CRD, which, among other things, repealed the Doorstep Selling Directive. The CRD significantly expanded the situations worthy of protection by no longer positively defining

---

[24] For development also P. Bülow/M. Artz, *Verbraucherprivatrecht*, 6th ed. (Heidelberg: C.F. Müller, 2018), paras. 216 ff.

[25] See again the Recitals to the Doorstep Selling Directive.

individual doorstep situations but instead covering all contracts concluded away from business premises (Article 2 nos. 8, 9 CRD). In contrast to the Doorstep Selling Directive, which only prescribed a minimum level of protection, i.e. left it up to the Member States to increase the level of protection, the CRD is fully harmonising (Article 4 CRD),[26] i.e. it does not allow any deviation in favour of the consumer. In this way, uniform conditions for contracts concluded away from business premises are created within the internal market.

**523.** While the term 'off-premises contract' seems to be more suitable to cover the broader range of protection, the CRD does not aim to achieve harmonisation at the linguistic level (Recital 15 CRD), so that the term doorstep selling may still be used. Moreover, the concept of contracts concluded away from business premises was no new creation of the CRD. Instead, it was already the basis of the Doorstep Selling Directive. Recital 21 of the CRD states that the consumer may be subject to psychological pressure or surprises away from business premises.

**524.** Compared to the legal situation with the former doorstep selling (Article 1(1) Doorstep Selling Directive), the consumer is also protected if they have brought about the contact with the entrepreneur themselves (cf. Recital 21 of the CRD). Only Article 16(h) CRD takes up the idea behind the old provision that a consumer cannot be taken by surprise if they have brought about the 'doorstep situation' themselves and excludes a consumer's right of withdrawal if they have expressly requested the entrepreneur to call on them. However, this exception only applies in the case of urgent repair and maintenance measures and only in relation to the work for which the entrepreneur was requested. If the entrepreneur provides further services in this context or supplies goods that are not necessarily needed as spare parts for the requested repair or maintenance, this exception does not apply.

### c) *The Scope of Protection*

#### aa) Contract Concluded Away from Business Premises

**525.** Article 2 no. 8 CRD conclusively determines when a contract concluded away from business premises exists.

##### (1) Business Premises

**526.** Because of the extensive scope of application of the term 'doorstep selling', the definition of business premises is crucial. According to Article 2 no. 9 CRD,

[26] See para. 78 above.

this includes immovable commercial premises in which the entrepreneur carries out their activity permanently, as well as movable commercial premises in which the entrepreneur habitually carries out their activity. With a view to Recital 22 CRD, this includes shops, stalls, sales carts, sales premises where the entrepreneur carries out their business on a seasonal basis (e.g. during the high season in a ski resort), and, in principle, also fair and exhibition stalls if the entrepreneur usually carries out their business there.

**527.** In the latter case, however, keeping the protective purpose of the provision in mind is essential. The consumer should not be exposed to any psychological pressure or element of surprise when concluding the contract. This can only be assumed if the consumer is confronted at the market, trade fair or exhibition with products unrelated to the subject of the market, trade fair or exhibition. What matters in this respect is whether the average consumer, who is reasonably well informed and reasonably observant and circumspect, could rationally expect, in the light of the appearance of the entrepreneur's stall and the information disseminated on the spot at the fair itself, that the entrepreneur would carry on their activities there and approach them to conclude a contract; overall, this has to be determined by national courts.[27] For example, a consumer contract concluded at a sales stall operated by an entrepreneur on the occasion of a trade fair immediately after the consumer, who was strolling through an aisle between several various sales stands in the trade fair's exhibition hall, was approached by that entrepreneur, is considered to fall under Article 2 nos. 8 and 9 CRD.[28]

**528.** Business premises do not include places accessible to the public, such as streets, shopping centres, beaches, sports facilities as well as public transport, which the entrepreneur exceptionally uses for their business activities, as well as retail shops of other businesses where the entrepreneur sets up a stall once or sporadically and addresses customers.[29] The same applies to private flats or workplaces.[30]

**529.** The classification of commercial premises that do not belong to the entrepreneur appears problematic: Here, the situation of being taken by surprise, which is typical for doorstep transactions, is not likely to exist since the consumer is already located in a business-related environment. However,

---

27 CJEU, 7 August 2018, Case C-485/17, *Verbraucherzentrale Berlin/Unimatic*, ECLI:EU:C:2018:642, para. 43.

28 CJEU, 17 December 2019, Case C-465/19, *B & L Elektrogeräte*, ECLI:EU:C:2019:1091, paras. 27 ff.

29 Recital 22 CRD.

30 CJEU, 7 August 2018, Case C-485/17, *Verbraucherzentrale Berlin/Unimatic*, ECLI:EU:C:2018:642, para. 42.

the definition crucially depends on the fact that the business premises of the entrepreneur in question are concerned.

### (2) Off-Premises Conclusion of Contracts

**530.** First of all, an off-premises contract in the above-mentioned sense is defined as a contract concluded with the simultaneous physical presence of the consumer and the entrepreneur at a location that is not the entrepreneur's business premises. Recital 5 CRD refers to 'direct selling' in this respect. This includes, in particular, the consumer's private home and workplace, but also, for example, the conclusion of the contract in a restaurant that is not the business premises of the contracting entrepreneur, in a department store or in other areas accessible to the public.

### (3) Leisure Events

**531.** The definition in Article 2(8)(d) CRD covers contracts concluded on trips or excursions organised by or with the help of the entrepreneur in order to advertise the sale of goods or the provision of services to the consumer. The case in which an entrepreneur other than the business offering the goods or services organises the excursion is also covered. This applies, for example, to wine-tasting trips organised by a bus tour operator if another entrepreneur is allowed to sell their wines. Here, the contract must be concluded on the occasion of the trip, i.e. a causal connection needs to exist, which is further indicated by a close temporal and spatial relationship.[31]

### (4) Binding Offer of the Entrepreneur is Sufficient

**532.** Consumer protection also extends to situations where the consumer has already made a binding offer to enter into a contract in the circumstances mentioned (Article 2(8)(b) CRD). An offer by the entrepreneur is not mentioned in the CRD. The decisive factor here is that it makes no difference to the consumer's need for protection whether the entrepreneur has also made their contractual declaration of intent outside business premises.

### (5) Contract Initiation is Sufficient

**533.** Furthermore, contracts are covered which are concluded on the business premises of the entrepreneur using distance communication, but where the consumer has previously been addressed personally outside of the

31 Cf. German case law. e.g. BGH NJW 2009, 431, 432.

entrepreneur's business premises (with both the consumer and the entrepreneur being physically present, see Article 2(8)(c) CRD). In particular, the provision covers cases where the entrepreneur addressed the consumer in front of the entrepreneur's shop on public streets, for example, by handing out a leaflet, because in these situations, too, the consumer can feel surprised or coerced to conclude a contract. The provision does not include cases where the entrepreneur first comes to the consumer's home to take measurements or give an estimate without any obligation on the consumer's part, and the contract is only concluded at a later stage at the entrepreneur's premises or using means of distance communication. In these cases, it is assumed that the consumer had sufficient time to consider the contract's conclusion.[32]

bb) Participants

**534.** The CRD regime applies to the conclusion of contracts where the supplier is an entrepreneur and the customer is a consumer (cf. Article 1 and 2(5) and (6) CRD)). A simultaneous physical presence within the meaning of Article 2(8)(a) CRD can thus also be assumed if, for example, a representative or agent of the entrepreneur concludes a contract with a consumer.[33] In other words, it was deemed irrelevant whether the entrepreneur or one of their agents acted. This is in line with the wording of Article 2(2) CRD.

**535.** By contrast, the CRD does not address the consumer's right of representation. Considering the protective effect of the Directive, one may assume that the agent must have been in a situation for the consumer at the time of the conclusion of the contract in which it was not possible for them to consider the matter carefully and to compare prices.

cc) Personal Guarantee

**536.** There has been some discussion about whether or not the conclusion of a personal guarantee falls under the material scope of the CRD. Given the open wording of Article 3(1) CRD, which applies to 'any contract concluded between a trader and a consumer', there seems to be no major problem.

**537.** However, another issue arises: In the *Dietzinger* decision on the Doorstep Selling Directive, the CJEU opined that the guarantor and debtor must be a consumer and that the principal debt must originate from a doorstep selling situation in order for the right to withdrawal to be exercised.[34] The court's

---

[32] Cf. Recital 21 CRD.

[33] CJEU, 25 October 2005, Case C-229/04, *Crailsheimer Volksbank*, ECLI:EU:C:2005:640.

[34] CJEU, 17 March 1998, Case C-45/96, *Dietzinger*, ECLI:EU:C:1998:111, para. 22.

solution, which was based on the ancillary nature of guarantees, was quite rightly disapproved by many legal scholars: The protection of the guarantor who has been taken by surprise must not depend on the principal debtor being taken by surprise. Accordingly, only the existence of a doorstep situation on the part of the guarantor is relevant. From an EU perspective, such a deviation from the CJEU's case law was previously not objectable, as the Member States were free to establish more favourable regulations for consumers within the framework of the Doorstep Selling Directive, which brought about a minimum harmonisation only.

**538.** However, given the fully harmonising nature of the CRD, it could be concluded that the Member States were no longer free to do so. This is, of course, only provided that the *Dietzinger* decision was still good law under the CRD. However, since the CRD brought about numerous substantive changes compared to the Doorstep Selling Directive, this might now be understood to represent a relevant discontinuity in opposition to the continued validity of the *Dietzinger* case law. It can, therefore, be assumed that the German Federal Court of Justice's case law is in conformity with the CRD.[35] However, this does seem to be an *acte clair*, so that a Member State's court in a given case might be under an obligation to submit the question to the CJEU again.[36]

#### dd) Burden of Proof

**539.** The CRD does not state who has to prove the conditions of a contract concluded away from business premises. According to general principles, therefore, the consumer has to present and, if necessary, prove these prerequisites.

## 2. DISTANCE SELLING CONTRACTS

### *a) The Regulatory Purpose of Distance Selling Law*

**540.** Increasing distance selling is of great importance to the internal market; enormous growth potential can be assumed in this respect. Since, according to the EU Commission, the inconsistency of legal regulations in the Member States undermined confidence in the internal market and thus constituted a barrier to trade, the Distance Selling Directive brought about an approximation of laws for distance selling transactions (Recital 4 Distance Selling Directive). Today, the CRD has replaced the Distance Selling Directive and now regulates

35 Cf. e.g. Janal, *WM* 2012, 2314, 2315; Schürnbrand, *WM* 2014, 1157, 1160.

36 Cf. Grüneberg, in Grüneberg, *BGB Kommentar*, 84th ed. 2025, §312 para. 5; against this, however, Schürnbrand, *WM* 2014, 1157, 1161.

distance selling law in a fully harmonised manner. In contrast to the minimum harmonisation approach of the Distance Selling Directive, the Member States are, therefore, not permitted to establish a higher level of protection in the area of distance contracts than that prescribed by the Directive.

**541.** In contrast to the regulation on off-premises contracts, the protective regime for distance selling contracts does not react to a risk to the consumer created by the entrepreneur. Rather, the behaviour of the entrepreneur in distance selling may be irreproachable and this may have been chosen by the consumer themselves. The fact that the consumer should nevertheless have the right to special information and to withdrawal is based on the assumption that distance selling is particularly prone to irregularities: the supplier and the consumer do not physically meet, and the consumer cannot inspect the goods or services before the contract is concluded.[37] Moreover, the consumer often did not receive information in a reliable and permanent manner. It was, therefore, an aim of the Distance Selling Directive and equally of the CRD to give the consumer the possibility to look at or try out the goods or to take note of the characteristics of the service in detail. In particular, this was made possible by introducing the consumer's right of withdrawal.[38] The German Federal Court of Justice referred to this as a 'compensation of dangers due to the invisibility of the contracting party and the product'.[39] As with off-premises contracts, the law thus reacts to a situational deficit of the consumer. In light of this comparability, the German Civil Code refers to both types of contracts as special forms of distribution and regulates them in an interconnected manner.

### *b) Scope of Application and Requirements*

**542.** According to Article 2(7) CRD, distance contracts are contract concluded between the trader and the consumer under an organised distance sales or service-provision scheme without the simultaneous physical presence of the trader and the consumer, with the exclusive use of one or more means of distance communication up to and including the time at which the contract is concluded.

### *c) Third Parties*

**543.** The CRD is concerned with B2C situations only. In the case of agency, a personal contact of the represented consumer with the entrepreneur excludes an application of the CRD regime if the representative acts according to specific

[37] Recital 14 Distance Selling Directive and Recital 37 CRD.

[38] Recital 14 Distance Selling Directive.

[39] Cf. the decision of the German Federal Court of Justice in BGHZ 187, 268 para.23 (withdrawal of a distance selling contract for a waterbed).

instructions: It would be unviable, for example, for the consumer to examine the goods in the shop and then to instruct a representative to place an order by telephone with the intent to contract into a right of withdrawal. Thus, Member States are free to exclude such a constellation from the material scope of the protection, as according to Recital 14 of the CRD, the CRD does not affect national contract law. Moreover, the examples cited in Recital 20 of the CRD also support this perspective.[40]

*d) Particularities of the Contract's Conclusion*

**544.** The characteristic feature of the distance contract is not its subject matter but how it is concluded: According to Article 2(7) CRD, there must be an organised distance sales or service-provision scheme without the simultaneous physical presence of the trader and the consumer, with the exclusive use of one or more means of distance communication. This results in three constituent elements:

aa) Means of Distance Communication

**545.** The means of distance communication that characterise distance selling are mentioned in Recital 20 CRD as including mail order, Internet, telephone or fax. It follows from those examples that means of distance communication are not only electronic means of communication but include letters, catalogues (mail orders) and phone calls. They all have in common that they can be used without the simultaneous physical presence of the trader and the consumer (Article 2(7) CRD). Whether or not a contract concluded with the intervention of a messenger depends on whether the messenger is aware of the entrepreneur's contractual performance.[41]

bb) Exclusive Use of Means of Distance Communication

**546.** A distance contract only exists if both the contract negotiations and the conclusion of the contract take place exclusively using means of distance communication. Thus, the scope of application of the CRD is not limited to request and acceptance; instead, personal contacts of the parties also play a role in the mere initiation of the contract. Recital 20 of the CRD suggests the following distinction: If the consumer visits the business premises merely to

---

40 C. Wendehorst, in *Münchener Kommentar zum BGB*, 9th ed. (Munich: C.H. Beck, 2022), §312c paras. 20 f.

41 Cf. BGHZ 160, 393; against the qualification of messengers as means of distance communication C. Wendehorst, in *Münchener Kommentar zum BGB*, 9th ed. (Munich: C.H. Beck, 2022), §312c para. 14.

obtain information in order to negotiate and conclude the contract at a distance subsequently, the protective regime applies. If, in contrast, the contract is already negotiated on the business premises and ultimately concluded using means of distance communication, this does not amount to a distance contract in the legal sense. The consumer's need for protection is reduced in this case because they still had time to consider, and a protection would be pointless. The situation might be different if there is a relevant time gap between the personal contact and the contract's conclusion through means of distance communication. In German case law, this has been ruled to be about one and a half months.[42]

**547.** A related question arises in the case of personal contacts of the parties after the contract's preliminary conclusion. An example is the case where a repair contract is concluded by phone, and it is to be clarified in person whether, how and at what cost repairs can be carried out. Recital 20 CRD suggests that, in such cases of successive contract specification, the applicability of the protective regime will also have to be denied if the personal contact has taken place before the contractual duty's final determination. Furthermore, this is also significant for contracts with a doctor or lawyer, for example, if the service to be provided can only be specified after personal contact. Similarly, reservations made by a consumer via distance communication means to perform a service, such as a consumer's telephone call to make an appointment with a hairdresser, are not to be regarded as distance contracts.

cc) Organised Distance Sales or Service-Provision Scheme

**548.** Finally, the contract must have been concluded using a distribution or service system organised for distance selling. The entrepreneur must have created all prerequisites (regarding their employees, tools and business organisation) in order to conclude distance contracts regularly. Only sporadic distance selling is, therefore, insufficient, as this cannot be called an 'organised distance sales or service-provision scheme'. It is not intended that entrepreneurs who regularly conclude contracts locally are prevented by the obligations incumbent on the entrepreneur from shipping goods based on an exceptional use of distance communication means.

**549.** Sales or service systems offered by third parties and used by the entrepreneur also fall under Article 2(7) CRD. This includes online platforms in particular. On the other hand, the protective regime does not apply in cases where websites only offer information about the entrepreneur, their goods and/or

---

[42] Cf. e.g. AG Frankfurt a.M. MMR 2011, 804.

services and their contact details.[43] This is of particular importance for contracts with lawyers, for example. A simple law firm website with information about involved lawyers and fields of practice does not yet constitute a service system organised for distance selling. This should undoubtedly be judged differently when 'online legal advice' is offered.

**550.** The definition contained in Article 2(7) CRD does not refer to the allocation of the burden of proof. Consequently, Member States' law may prescribe that the entrepreneur bears the burden of proof that the contract was not concluded within the framework of their distribution or service system organised for distance selling. This is appropriate because those facts relate to the entrepreneur's sphere.[44]

## IV. FORMAL PROVISIONS

References: H. Kötz, *European Contract Law*, 2nd ed. (Oxford: Oxford University Press, 2017), §5.

**551.** The principle of party autonomy includes the freedom to choose a contract's form. Where the law prescribes a certain form, such requirements are mostly sanctioned by nullity of the contract (e.g. sec. 125 of the German Civil Code). Formal requirements pursue several purposes; in particular, they amount to a warning function: The addressees of the formal requirements are to be protected from hasty and ill-considered decisions in comparably risky transactions. In addition, formal requirements usually serve to provide evidence of the contractual agreement since the existence and content of a written or even notarised legal transaction can be proven more easily in the event of a dispute.

**552.** One may safely say that EU private law has a different view on formal requirements. At the outset, it focuses on promoting the conclusion of contracts. Hence, no excessive formal requirements are to be expected. The notarial form is nowhere to be found, as the Member States' legal systems vary greatly in this respect. Formal requirements are primarily used for the effective communication of information. According to Article 6(1)(h) CRD, the consumer must be informed of the existence and modalities of the right of withdrawal's exercise using a standardised template. The sanction for non-compliance, however, is not the invalidity of the contract, but that the limitation in time for exercising the right of withdrawal does not start to lapse (Article 10 CRD). The same applies to

43 Cf. Recital 20 CRD.
44 Cf. BT-Drucks. 17/12637, p. 50.

the information to be given before the conclusion of a consumer loan contract (Article 5(1) Consumer Credit Directive).

**553.** However, the idea that a certain formal requirement facilitates proof can also be found in EU directives. For example, consumer loan contracts must be drawn up on paper or another durable medium; furthermore, all contracting parties must receive a copy (Article 10(1) Consumer Credit Directive). The same applies to timeshare agreements (Article 5(1), (5) Timeshare Directive) and commercial guarantees (Article 17(2) Sale of Goods Directive). However, the legal consequences of infringement are not explicitly prescribed by the EU directives. Instead, they are left to the law of the Member States, who must ensure that the requirements of EU law are complied with (see, for example, Article 23(1) CRD). However, the rule of Article 17(3) of the Sale of Goods Directive must also be considered: According to this provision, the commercial guarantee binds the guarantor even if the formal requirements for the guarantee declaration set out in para. 2 of the provision are not complied with.

**554.** Besides, there is EU legislation that aims to simplify formal requirements. For example, by establishing common standards for electronic signatures, the Signatures Directive[45] pursued the goal of promoting the internal market by strengthening trust in electronic communication (Recital 4 Signatures Directive). The Signatures Directive has since been superseded by the eIDAS Regulation,[46] but the latter, too, pursues the same purpose (cf. Recital 2 eIDAS Regulation). The E-Commerce Directive also aims to strengthen the (electronic) internal market (Article 1(1) as well as Recitals 3-5, 7 E-Commerce Directive) by equating in its Article 9(1) the electronic form with standard written form requirements. The reason is that cross-border contracts are more easily concluded electronically than in written form; the E-Commerce Directive, therefore, aims to promote electronic form. Some exceptions exist, particularly for real estate transactions, sureties and family and inheritance law contracts (Article 9(2) E-Commerce Directive).

## V. DEFECTS OF WILL

References: H. Kötz, *European Contract Law*, 2nd ed. (Oxford: Oxford University Press, 2017), §§9–10; S.A.E. Martens, 'Die Regelung der Willensmängel im Vorschlag für eine Verordnung über ein Gemeinsames Europäisches Kaufrecht', *AcP* 211 (2011), 845.

[45] Directive 1999/93/EC.
[46] Regulation (EU) No 910/2014, OJ 2014 L 257/73.

**555.** A legal system based on the principle of mutual consent needs protective mechanisms concerning the freedom of will. Union law does not contain any such provisions. Only in the proposal for a Common European Sales Law did provisions on defects of agreement and their consequences exist (Articles 48–57 CESL).[47] They refer to the legal consequences of error, fraudulent misrepresentation and threat. In addition, unfair exploitation (Article 51 CESL) may also be seen as reacting to a defect in the agreement.[48]

## VI. STANDARD TERMS

**556.** In principle, the inclusion of standard terms into a contract also belongs in this section. However, due to the close regulatory context, they are considered within the context of the Unfair Terms Directive and thus in the section on the contract's content.[49]

47 Cf. Jansen, in Schulte-Nölke/Zoll/Jansen/Schulze, *Der Entwurf für ein optionales europäisches Kaufrecht*, 2012, p. 169; Looschelders, *AcP* 212 (2012), 581, 618 ff.; Martens, *AcP* 211 (2011), 845.

48 On the corresponding rules in the PECL and DCFR Stürner, *Der Grundsatz der Verhältnismäßigkeit im Schuldvertragsrecht*, 2010, pp. 88 ff.

49 See para. 633 below.

# §13. RIGHTS OF WITHDRAWAL AND CONSEQUENCES OF WITHDRAWAL

## CONTENTS

References: T. Finkenauer, 'Vertragstreue und Vertragsreue', in *Festschrift für Müller-Graff* (Baden-Baden: Nomos, 2015), p. 146; F. Schurr, *Geschäftsimmanente Abstandnahme* (Tübingen: Mohr Siebeck, 2006); H. Kötz, *European Contract Law*, 2nd ed. (Oxford: Oxford University Press, 2017), §11; J. Watson, 'Withdrawal Rights', in C. Twigg-Flesner (ed.), *Research Handbook on EU Consumer and Contract Law* (Cheltenham: Edward Elgar Publishing, 2016), p. 241.

# I. THE RIGHT OF WITHDRAWAL FROM CONSUMER CONTRACTS

## 1. BASICS

**557.** The right of withdrawal is one of the most important instruments of consumer protection under EU private law. It gives the consumer the right to withdraw from the contract concluded with the entrepreneur within a certain period of time; any services or goods that have already been exchanged are to be reversed. In contrast to other ways to get rid of the obligation, however, withdrawal does not require a legal reason to cancel the contract: The consumer status as such is sufficient. However, there is no general consumer right of revocation, but rather does the law prescribe its existence and conditions separately for each type of contract. For this purpose, as for the distance and off-premises contracts regulated in the CRD, the right of withdrawal can be linked to the form of distribution. It can also be linked to the content of the contract, as is the case with the Consumer Credit Directive or the Timeshare Directive.

## 2. RATIONALE AND LEGAL NATURE

### a) *Justification*

**558.** The main rationale for the right of withdrawal is consumer protection. As has been explained earlier, one pillar of consumer protection is the obligation for the trader to inform the consumer about the goods or services on offer and the modalities of the prospective contract.[1] However, this concept has its weaknesses. It fails, for example, in the case of the conclusion or initiation of a contract outside business premises, where the consumer is typically taken by surprise.[2] Furthermore, the situation is different in the case of distance contracts, where consumers cannot inspect the goods or services themselves.[3]

1 See para. 477 above.
2 See para. 519 above.
3 In this sense, for example, Recital 37 of the CRD, see also para. 545.

Finally, things also differ with regard to contracts on financial and insurance products, distance learning, timeshare or instalment delivery. Due to the usually long duration and complexity of such contracts, the financial consequences of the concluded obligations can usually only be realistically assessed after a certain period of reflection. In all these cases, according to the relevant EU law provisions, it does not matter whether the information model has actually failed or if an information asymmetry really existed in the individual case. In other words, the consumer who is not taken by surprise at the doorstep but thoughtfully concludes the magazine subscription is also entitled to a right of withdrawal. The same applies to the consumer who orders a product they already know well online. Furthermore, a distance learning, insurance, or financial services contract may also be withdrawn from by someone who does not use the reflection period at all in the described sense. The right of withdrawal is mandatory. The consumer may not even contract out of the right to withdrawal to get a better price for the good or service.

**559.** From an economic point of view, the right of withdrawal has been criticised as it is likely to make consumer contracts more expensive overall; the majority of consumers who do not make use of the option to withdraw from the contract thus subsidise those who exercise their right of withdrawal.[4] The mandatory character of the right of withdrawal can lead to this inefficiency in particular. *De lege ferenda*, optional withdrawal rights might seem reasonable;[5] however, the European legislator adheres to the non-dispositive form.

*b)* Pacta (Non) Sunt Servanda?

**560.** As Article 12 CRD states, the exercise of the right of withdrawal terminates the obligations of the parties. One can infer that, initially, the contract had been validly concluded. Before the withdrawal, both parties can therefore demand performance. The withdrawal is irrevocable and unconditional, just like the corresponding declaration itself.

**561.** Whether the right of withdrawal is a dilution or a confirmation of the principle of contractual obligation (*pacta sunt servanda*) is judged differently. Especially in the wake of the implementation of the early consumer protection directives, there was a strong view in German scholarship that the right of withdrawal introduced the principle of '*pacta non sunt servanda*' for consumer

4 Cf. Eidenmüller, *AcP* 210 (2010), 67, 71 ff.

5 On the different models in relation to distance contracts Eidenmüller, *AcP* 210 (2010), 67, 77 ff. Generally on the legitimacy of mandatory consumer law in the European acquis G. Wagner, in Eidenmüller/Faust/Grigoleit/Jansen/Wagner/Zimmermann, *Revision des Verbraucher-acquis*, 2011, pp. 1, 21 ff.; *Lurger*, ZEuP 2018, 788.

contracts.[6] On the other hand, it must be kept in mind that the right of withdrawal is not at the consumer's discretion but is limited to specific contract categories or conclusion situations. Even if the ensuing rationales appear to be quite heterogeneous and even contestable, it can nevertheless be seen as an inherent restriction to the principle of contractual obligations, which does not fundamentally call into question the principle *pacta sunt servanda*.[7]

### c) *Contractual Freedom*

**562.** Outside the statutory rights of withdrawal, the principle of party autonomy prevails so that the parties can freely agree on a contractual right of withdrawal. There must be enough evidence to assume that the period for exercising such a contractually agreed right of withdrawal is only to begin if the entrepreneur has additionally provided the consumer with instructions that meet the requirements for a statutory right of withdrawal. The 'right to return or exchange', which is often granted to customers in non-distance selling, e.g. in a shopping centre, thus is based on party autonomy only. Its content may be defined in greater detail in the general terms and conditions. Conversely, the clause 'products cannot be returned or exchanged' has mainly a declarative meaning in contracts with no statutory right of withdrawal.

## 3. EXISTENCE OF A RIGHT OF WITHDRAWAL

**563.** For distance contracts and off-premises contracts, Article 9(1) CRD establishes a right of withdrawal for the consumer. However, in numerous cases there are exceptions to this rule. These cases are listed in Article 16 CRD. It goes without saying that the parties can agree on an exclusion of the exclusion.[8] If one tries to establish commonalities, the following groups may be identified.

### a) *Impracticability of the Return*

**564.** The reversal and thus also the withdrawal in the case of contracts for the delivery of goods appears to be simply impracticable if these are mixed with other goods after delivery due to their nature, for example, in the case of the

6 Term coined by F.A. Schurr, *Geschäftsimmanente Abstandnahme* (Tübingen: Mohr Siebeck, 2006), p. 213.

7 Cf. M.-P. Weller, *Die Vertragstreue* (Tübingen: Mohr Siebeck, 2009), pp. 294 ff. See para. 416 above.

8 Cf. e.g. sec. 312g(2) of the German Civil Code, according to which the parties may not have 'otherwise agreed'.

delivery of heating oil due to the mixing with residual quantities in the tank (Article 16(f) CRD).

### b) *Significant Loss of Value or Unusability of the Service in the Event of Withdrawal*

**565.** The right of withdrawal is also excluded if the entrepreneur's interest in continuing the contract far outweighs the consumer's interest in withdrawing. This may be the case if the goods would be almost unusable for the entrepreneur in the event of a withdrawal. This is true for goods that are not prefabricated and are made based on an individual choice by the consumer, as well as goods that are tailored to the personal needs of the consumer (Article 16(c) CRD). These cannot be sold elsewhere or only with considerable discounts.

**566.** Similar considerations apply to goods that perish quickly (e.g. certain foodstuffs) or whose expiry date has passed already (Article 16(d) CRD) and to sealed goods that are not suitable for return for reasons of health protection or hygiene, provided the seal has been removed after delivery (Article 16(e) CRD). There is also no right of withdrawal for contracts for the delivery of newspapers, periodicals or magazines (Article 16(j) CRD), as these products lose their value through obsolescence. Calendars are not mentioned, although the idea of obsolescence also applies to them. The exception does not cover subscriptions, so a right of withdrawal exists in this case.

**567.** A disputed question was whether mattresses were hygiene articles in the sense of Article 16(e) CRD, meaning that withdrawal would be excluded after removing the protective foil. The wording ('hygiene reasons') is ambivalent in this respect. According to the meaning and purpose of the right of withdrawal existing in distance contracts, the consumer is to be protected in the unique situation of concluding a contract in distance e-commerce because here, an opportunity to review the product before concluding the contract or to take note of the characteristics of the service does not exist. This disadvantage is to be compensated by the right of withdrawal, which grants the consumer a reasonable reflection period to examine and try out the purchased goods. In this respect, Article 16(e) CRD is to be interpreted narrowly and as an exception.[9]

**568.** In light of these considerations, this exception only intervenes if, after the sealing of the packaging has been removed, the goods contained therein are no longer marketable for health protection or hygiene reasons. This may be the case if the nature of the goods makes it impossible or excessively difficult

[9] CJEU, 27 March 2019, Case C-681/17, *slewo*, ECLI:EU:C:2019:255, paras. 33 f.

for the entrepreneur to make them saleable again without failing to meet the requirements of health protection or hygiene reasons.[10] It must be noted that one and the same mattress serves a great many successive hotel guests; there is also a market for clean, used mattresses.[11] Moreover, concerning the right of withdrawal, a mattress can be equated with a piece of clothing, which can also come into direct contact with the human body. Concerning both goods, the trader can make them suitable for reuse by a third party and, thus, for placing them on the market again through a treatment such as cleaning or disinfection, which satisfies the requirements of health protection or hygiene.[12] A mattress whose protective film has been removed by the consumer is thus not covered by the exception.

**569.** Furthermore, there is an exception in Article 16(l) CRD for the provision of accommodation other than for residential purpose, transport of goods, car rental services, catering or services related to leisure activities if the contract provides for a specific date or period of performance. The entrepreneur's salient capacity to provide services at a 'specific date or period' may no longer be meaningful if a right of withdrawal was accepted. Examples include renting a car,[13] booking hotel rooms or holiday flats, and ordering tickets for opera, theatre, cinema or catering. A common prerequisite is always the provision of a service, which must be understood broadly under EU law. Regarding the transport of goods, it is not necessary that the respective item is tradable. This also includes, for example, items that are transported for disposal.[14]

### c) *Disloyal Behaviour*

**570.** In several cases, dissolving the contract by means of a right of withdrawal would run contrary to good faith. This concerns, for example, speculative transactions such as contracts for the delivery of alcoholic beverages to be delivered at the earliest 30 days after the conclusion of the contract, if the price was agreed upon at the time of the conclusion of the contract and the current value depends on market fluctuations over which the entrepreneur has no influence (Article 16(g) CRD). This includes, for example, contracts for the delivery of wine where the delivery is to take place long after the conclusion of a sales contract of a speculative nature ('*vin en primeur*').[15]

---

10 CJEU, 27 March 2019, Case C-681/17, *slewo*, ECLI:EU:C:2019:255, para. 40.

11 CJEU, 27 March 2019, Case C-681/17, *slewo*, ECLI:EU:C:2019:255, para. 42.

12 CJEU, 27 March 2019, Case C-681/17, *slewo*, ECLI:EU:C:2019:255, paras. 43 ff.

13 Recital 27 CRD. See CJEU, 10 March 2005, Case C-336/03, *easyCar*, ECLI:EU:C:2005:150 (referring to the slightly different setting under the Distance Selling Directive).

14 Cf. BT-Drucks. 17/12637, p. 57.

15 Cf. BT-Drucks. 17/12637, p. 56 with reference to Recital 49 of the CRD.

**571.** Contracts for goods (e.g. precious metals and raw materials) and financial services whose price is subject to fluctuations in the financial market over which the entrepreneur has no influence and which may occur within the withdrawal period are also not revocable (Article 16(b) CRD). The law also mentions shares, certain share certificates, other tradable securities, foreign exchange, derivatives and money market instruments as examples.[16] The consumer should not be able to speculate to the detriment of the entrepreneur, i.e. to pass on an unfavourable course of events to the entrepreneur by withdrawing the contract. The controversial question of whether the exception also covers the supply of heating oil that was not ordered at a fixed price should be decided in the negative, as there is no inherent speculative character.[17]

**572.** The same applies to contracts for the provision of betting and lottery services. Here, withdrawal must be ruled out after the decision or draw because the object of the transaction is the probability of an event (Article 3(3)(c) CRD).

**573.** In the case of contracts on the supply of sealed audio or sealed video recordings or sealed computer software, it would be virtually an invitation to cancel the contract if the seal was removed after delivery. Here, there is a risk that the consumer has produced a copy; therefore, a right of withdrawal does not exist (Article 16(i) CRD). However, data carriers that are not sealed in the first place should not fall under this exclusion.

**574.** This rationale for exceptions includes cases in which the contract came into existence due to a prior order by the consumer. However, according to Article 16(h) CRD, this only applies if the contract relates to urgent repair and maintenance measures. In practice, contracts concluded away from business premises are likely to be affected by the exception. The reason is that contracts for repair and maintenance works are generally not concluded at a distance but only when the entrepreneur gained an impression of the services to be provided on the spot. The exclusion of the right of withdrawal only covers urgent works for which the consumer called the entrepreneur. However, if the entrepreneur provides further services in this context or supplies goods that are not necessarily needed as spare parts for the requested repair or maintenance, there is a right of withdrawal.[18]

---

16 For certificates cf. the German decisions in BGHZ 195, 375; BGH NJW 2013, 1223.

17 Cf. the decision of the German Federal Court of Justice, BGH NJW 2015, 2959, para. 20 and the critique by Henning-Bodewig, *EuCML* 2016, 87.

18 Cf. BT-Drucks. 17/12637, p. 57.

*d) Auctions*

**575.** For obvious reasons, pursuant to Article 16(k) CRD, the right of withdrawal is excluded in the case of auctions open to the public.

*e) Contracts Certified by Deed*

**576.** Finally, a last group of cases concerns notarised contracts, which are excluded altogether from the material scope of application of the CRD (Article 3(3)(i) CRD).

## II. EXERCISING THE RIGHT OF WITHDRAWAL

**577.** Articles 11 to 14 CRD contain the basic requirements for exercising the right of withdrawal as well as general statements on the legal consequences of withdrawal, each of which relate to all rights of withdrawal stipulated in Article 9 CRD.

### 1. ELIGIBILITY

**578.** The consumer is primarily entitled to withdraw from the contract (cf. Article 9(1) CRD), even if they were represented at the conclusion of the contract. If several consumers conclude a consumer loan contract with an entrepreneur as a lender, each may independently withdraw their declaration of intent.[19] If spouses are involved in the conclusion of a consumer contract, they should, however, in principle, only be able to exercise the right of withdrawal jointly. If the performance is divisible (e.g. in the case of collective orders), a partial withdrawal of the consumer should be permissible, but not if it relates to a uniform subject matter.

### 2. DECLARATION OF WITHDRAWAL

**579.** Withdrawal is exercised through a declaration of withdrawal (Article 11(1) CRD); a statement of reasons for the withdrawal is not required. The word 'withdrawal' does not have to be mentioned explicitly. As with other rights, the declaration's content must be determined by interpretation. It must follow from

[19] BGHZ 212, 207 para. 15.

such declaration with sufficient clarity that the consumer wishes to withdraw from the contract (Article 11(1)(b) CRD).[20]

**580.** The trader may give the consumer the option of completing the model withdrawal form as set out in Annex I(B) to the CRD (Article 11(1)(a) CRD). If the consumer makes use of this, the entrepreneur must immediately confirm receipt of the declaration of withdrawal to the consumer on a durable medium (Article 11(3) CRD). This procedure has advantages for both the entrepreneur and the consumer: The entrepreneur can carry out the reversal automatically and assign it directly to the customer account; the consumer, who bears the burden of proof for the timely declaration of the right's exercise, immediately receives a confirmation of the receipt of their declaration of withdrawal.[21]

## 3. FORM

**581.** The declaration of withdrawal does not require a specific form. However, it is still advisable for the consumer to withdraw in text form[22] since they bear the burden of proof for exercising the right of withdrawal according to Article 11(4) CRD. Based on its wording, the exercise of the right of withdrawal could also be read as to relate only to the declaration of withdrawal by the consumer. However, systematic reasons suggest that the phrase 'exercising the right of withdrawal' is to be understood comprehensively and includes the beginning of the withdrawal period. Thus, Article 11(4) CRD refers to the entire content of Article 11 CRD. Article 11(2) CRD refers to Articles 9(2) and 10 CRD. Both provisions also deal with the withdrawal period, compliance with which is a prerequisite for exercising the right of withdrawal. It cannot, therefore, be assumed that Article 11(4) CRD does not cover the beginning of the withdrawal period. Returning the goods without comment is insufficient for exercising the right of withdrawal unless there is a corresponding contractual agreement (Article 11(3) CRD).

## 4. WITHDRAWAL PERIOD

**582.** The withdrawal period for all rights of withdrawal is 14 days (Article 9(1) CRD). It usually begins with the conclusion of the contract (Article 9(2) CRD). To comply with this limitation in time, it is sufficient to send the notice of withdrawal in due time (Article 11(2) CRD).

20 See also Recital 44 CRD.
21 BT-Drucks. 17/12637, p. 60.
22 Cf. explicitly Recital 44 CRD.

**583.** In the case of contracts for the supply of digital content (Article 2 no. 11 CRD), the right of withdrawal expires when the entrepreneur has begun with the performance of the contract after the consumer has expressly consented to the entrepreneur doing so before the expiry of the withdrawal period. Clearly, it is not sufficient if the consumer merely accepts the commencement of the performance of the contract by the entrepreneur. The consumer must be aware that they lose their right of withdrawal upon the complete performance of the contract by the entrepreneur and confirm this to the entrepreneur. If the consumer can withdraw from the contract due to the lack of the aforementioned prerequisites, the entrepreneur has no claim for compensation against the consumer.

**584.** In extreme situations, the consumer's exercise of the right of withdrawal may be considered an abuse.[23] This may be the case, for example, if the lack of information obviously played no role regarding the consumer's intention to conclude the contract or if the withdrawal would be legally abusive due to superior special knowledge[24] or equivalent to a self-contradiction.[25] It is always insufficient if the protective purpose intended by the legislator in granting the right of withdrawal was not the guiding principle for the exercise of the right of withdrawal.[26]

**585.** Forfeiture of the right of withdrawal is also possible.[27] In this respect, it is always necessary to consider the individual case; there are no general presumptions.[28] In any case, forfeiture cannot be considered if a longer period of time has passed since the conclusion of the contract. Furthermore, the statutory maximum periods of limitation cannot be used to infer a 'minimum period of time'.[29] In addition to temporal concerns, the element of circumstance is particularly problematic. In some cases, it has been assumed that the other party's reliance on the absence of the declaration of withdrawal already results from the complete fulfilment of the contract by both parties.[30] Other court decisions are clearly more restrictive.[31] As a general rule, however, the creation of legitimate expectations on the part of the entrepreneur will already be prevented by any

23 See in general Mankowski, *JZ* 2016, 787; Rieländer, *AcP* 216 (2016), 763.

24 OLG Stuttgart VersR 2015, 878 paras. 38 ff.

25 OLG Frankfurt, 7 August 15, Az 19 U 5/15, juris paras. 52 ff.; p.a. OLG Stuttgart, 6 December 16, Az 6 U 95/16, juris paras. 22 ff.: unconditional continuation of payment.

26 BGHZ 211, 105 para. 23.

27 Leading cases are BGHZ 211, 105 para. 39; BGHZ 211, 123 paras. 31 ff.

28 BGH WM 2018, 2274 para. 14; BGH WM 2018, 2275 para. 12 on the consumer loan contract.

29 BGH WM 2017, 2247 para. 9.

30 In this sense OLG Köln WM 2012, 1532; KG GuT 2013, 213; OLG Düsseldorf NJW 2014, 1599 and OLG Frankfurt BKR 15, 245; for limitation also Scholz/Schmidt/Ditté, *ZIP* 2015, 605 (due to 'institutional abuse of rights' by exercising the right of withdrawal).

31 OLG Karlsruhe ZIP 2015, 1011; OLG Hamm ZIP 2015, 1113 para. 16.

incorrect information on the right of withdrawal.[32] The German Federal Court of Justice seems to permit the plea of forfeiture, especially for a withdrawal after the termination of the contract at the consumer's request,[33] as the subsequent instruction is then no longer reasonably possible.

**586.** It may be questioned whether or not this is a violation of secondary law as there might be possible frictions with Article 14(1) CRD.[34] The German Federal Court of Justice considers this question to be an *acte clair*, i.e., an issue that does not need further clarification.[35] For this purpose, the court can rely on a decision of the CJEU on insurance contract law, in which the court stated the following:[36] '[...] [W]here information, including incorrect information, does not essentially limit the circumstances in which the policyholder can exercise their right of cancellation as compared with the circumstances in which they could have done so if the information had been correct, it would be disproportionate to allow the latter to be released from obligations arising from a contract concluded in good faith.' Moreover, the CJEU considers the prohibition of abuse of rights a general principle of EU law,[37] so the forfeiture objection is only problematic if it affects the *effet utile* of the CRD.[38] Given the strict conditions that exist for such objection, this should usually not be the case.

## III. REVERSAL OF THE CONTRACTUAL PERFORMANCES AFTER WITHDRAWAL

### 1. BASIC ASSUMPTIONS

**587.** According to Article 12 CRD, the contractual parties are no longer bound by their declarations of intent to conclude the contract in the event of the consumer's withdrawal. This means there is no (longer) a legal justification to keep any obtained benefits. Consequently, a legal mechanism is needed to control the contractual performance's reversal. As there are no detailed prerequisites in the CRD, the Member States are fairly free to use existing mechanisms. In the German Civil Code, for example, the law on enrichment (sec. 812 et seq. of the

32 BGHZ 201, 101 para. 39; BGH WM 2015, 2311 para. 27.
33 BGHZ 211, 105 para. 41; BGHZ 212, 207 para. 30; BGH NJW-RR 2017, 812 para. 28; BGH WM 2017, 2248 para. 26.
34 LG Ravensburg BeckRS 2020, 3265 paras. 82 ff.
35 Cf. BGH WM 2020, 371.
36 CJEU, 19 December 2019, Cases C-355/18 *e.a.*, *Rust-Hackner*, ECLI:EU:C:2019:1123, para. 79.
37 Cf. CJEU, 6 February 2018, Case C-359/16, *Altun*, ECLI:EU:C:2018:63, para. 49 with references.
38 On the prohibition of abuse of rights cf. also at para. 456 above.

German Civil Code) or the law on the consequences of withdrawal (sec. 346 et seq. of the German Civil Code) would be available for this purpose. For some time now, however, an independent regime on the consequences of withdrawal was included in sec. 357–357c of the German Civil Code.

## 2. REVERSAL OF CONTRACTUAL PERFORMANCE

**588.** Articles 13 and 14 CRD neatly distinguish between the legal position of the trader and the consumer.

### *a) Repayment Duty of the Trader*

**589.** The immediate restitution must be made without undue delay and within the maximum period of 14 days.[39] The costs of delivery must be borne by the trader, as Article 13(1) CRD explicitly states following the CJEU's case law on the old Distance Selling Directive.[40] An exception exists in Article 13(2) CRD only insofar as the goods were dispatched at the consumer's request by a method of delivery other than the standard delivery offered by the entrepreneur. This restriction means that the consumer is not entitled to the difference between the standard delivery offered and the actual delivery method.

**590.** The trader must use the same means of payment for the refund as the consumer used for the payment (Article 13(1) CRD). Hence, if the consumer paid in cash, the entrepreneur must also reimburse them in cash; if the payment was made by bank transfer or direct debit, the entrepreneur must reimburse the amount to the consumer's account. A voucher can only be issued to the consumer in cases where the consumer has also used a voucher for the payment.

**591.** When it comes to sales contracts, Article 13(3) CRD stipulates that, unless the trader has offered to collect the goods himself, he may withhold the reimbursement until he has received the goods back, or until the consumer has supplied evidence of having sent back the goods, whichever is the earliest.

### *b) Obligation of the Consumer to Return the Goods*

**592.** The consumer's obligations arising from the declaration of withdrawal are regulated by Article 14 CRD. The 14-day period begins to run when the consumer submits the declaration of withdrawal. The time limit is met by the

39 Cf. Articles 13(1), 14(1) CRD.
40 CJEU, 15 April 2010, Case C-511/08, *Heinrich Heine*, ECLI:EU:C:2010:189.

timely dispatch of the goods (Article 14(1) CRD). However, this does not apply if the entrepreneur has offered to collect the goods. Some courts have even held a clause in traders' standard terms to be effective which makes it compulsory for the consumer to collect the goods, as the law considers the collection of the goods by the entrepreneur to be a favourable arrangement for the consumer compared to the return of the goods.[41] If the consumer nevertheless returns the goods in this case, they may be in breach of this contractual duty.

**593.** The entrepreneur bears the risk of loss of the goods when returning them, sec. 355(3) of the German Civil Code. However, the consumer is obliged to pack the goods appropriately, whereby the original packaging does not necessarily have to be used.[42] The consumer is therefore liable for damage caused by inadequate packaging of the goods.

**594.** If the consumer exceeds the 14-day deadline, default occurs immediately.[43] In this case, obligations to pay damages may arise. This does not run counter to the ban on additional claims against the consumer as stipulated by Article 14(5) CRD, as this provision only concerns the regulatory area of the withdrawal itself, but not such obligations that are not direct consequences of it. Article 3(5) CRD, in conjunction with Recital 48 of the CRD explicitly allows the application of general contract law in this respect.[44] This does not affect the consumer's liability under the general provisions for damages unrelated to withdrawal and its consequences, such as liability for a breach of protective duties.

**595.** Otherwise, according to Article 14(1), subpara. (2) CRD, the consumer only has to bear the direct costs of returning the goods. However, this is subject to the twofold condition that (1) the trader has agreed (e.g. in their standard terms) to bear these costs or (2) the trader has failed to inform the consumer that they have to bear these costs. This is an essential change compared to the previous legal situation. Under the old regime, in principle, the entrepreneur had to bear the costs of the return, but these could be imposed on the consumer under certain conditions, in particular, if the price of the goods was less than 40 euros. In the case of distance contracts, the consumer must also be informed of the costs of returning the goods if they cannot be returned by post.

---

41 OLG Düsseldorf NJW-RR 2015, 877.

42 Cf. BT-Drucks. 17/12637, p. 60.

43 J. Fritsche, in *Münchener Kommentar zum BGB*, 9th ed. (Munich: C.H. Beck, 2022), §357 para. 5; Mörsdorf, in *BeckOGK-BGB* (1 August 2024), §355 paras. 110 ff.; against this cf. Schärtl, *JuS* 2014, 577, 581.

44 Wendelstein/Zander, *JURA* 2014, 1191, 1206.

**596.** Article 14(1), subpara. 3 CRD contains a special provision for contracts concluded away from business premises. In the case of off-premises contracts where the goods have been delivered to the consumer's home at the time of the conclusion of the contract, the trader shall at his own expense collect the goods if, by their nature, those goods cannot normally be returned by post. With the expiry of the deadline set in Article 14(1) CRD, default of acceptance occurs. The consumer may then also be entitled to compensation for any storage costs.

**597.** If the trader provides digital services or delivers digital contents, these cannot in fact be returned after the consumer has withdrawn from the contract. If the withdrawal was not excluded anyway in the case of the delivery of digital content, the trader is then entitled to claim compensation from the consumer within the limits set by Article 14(4)(b) CRD.

*c) The Consumer's Obligation of Compensation for Loss of Value*

**598.** The case may arise that, for example, a purchased good is damaged before the withdrawal is declared. As this does not in itself exclude the withdrawal, it must be determined under which conditions and to what extent the consumer has to compensate the trader. In this respect, Article 14(2) CRD sets up a fairly clear rule. Its aim is to balance the interests of the consumer and the trader. In particular, this concerns the reduction in the item's value (which is usually free of defects) because it may no longer be returned to the trader 'as new'. In the case of e.g. motor vehicles, furniture and clothing, this can amount to a considerable loss. The objective value of the goods is to be taken as the basis for calculating the compensation claim. The trader may thus not claim compensation for the profit associated with the contract. However, the amount of the compensation claim is limited to the contractual remuneration if the good's objective value exceeds it.[45] However, the consumer can avoid the obligation to pay compensation if they return the goods to their original condition at their own expense.[46]

**599.** According to Article 14(2) CRD, there is no obligation to compensate for such degradations exclusively due to the inspection of the goods' quality, characteristics and functioning. The consumer is, therefore, only liable if the goods are used for their intended purpose, but this goes beyond what would be necessary to test the goods. Furthermore, the consumer is liable for all

---

45 In that sense for the withdrawal from doorstep contracts BGHZ 185, 192 para. 31; likewise Grüneberg, in Grüneberg, *BGB Kommentar*, 84th ed. 2025, §357 para. 11. Differently with reference to Article 14(2) CRD Mörsdorf, in *BeckOGK-BGB* (1 August 2024), §357 para. 75. However, the effet utile of the CRD speaks against such a narrow interpretation.

46 Schwab, *JZ* 2015, 644, 650.

deteriorations resulting from the goods not being used for their intended purpose. In principle, the aim is to create a standard comparable to a situation where the consumer would try out and test the goods in a store. For example, the consumer should be able to try on an item of clothing but not wear it.[47] In many cases, however, the inspection granted to the consumer will not be possible without at least opening the original packaging and partially destroying it in the process or even changing the item itself.[48] Certain items, such as medicine and hygiene products, can usually be tested without opening the packaging. It is further required for the obligation to pay compensation in Article 14(2) CRD that the consumer has been informed about the conditions, the time limits and the procedure for exercising the right of withdrawal.

## IV. WITHDRAWAL IN THE CASE OF LINKED AND INTERRELATED CONSUMER CONTRACTS

References: M. Stürner, 'Verbundene und zusammenhängende Verbraucherverträge', *JURA* 2016, 739.

### 1. BASIC POINTS

**600.** Consumer transactions are often financed by third parties. This usually requires the conclusion of two contracts: One for the actual performance that is ultimately sought (e.g. a contract for the sale of goods or a contract for work and services) and a second contract to finance the remuneration owed under the first contract. This second contract is usually a consumer loan and is concluded with another contractual partner, usually a bank. From an economic point of view, financing may be advantageous, but from a legal point of view, the existence of two distinct contracts entails risks for the consumer: For example, a withdrawal from the loan (Article 14(1) Consumer Credit Directive II) is of little use to a consumer if they cannot also withdraw from the contract for the sale of goods. Conversely, withdrawal from the latter (e.g. according to Article 9 CRD) is useless if the consumer remains bound to the loan. Furthermore, splitting a transaction into a loan and a procurement contract can also entail other risks: Objections arising from the purchase contract do not automatically affect the lender's claim.

---

47 Example from Recital 47 CRD. Further examples in Schwab, *JZ* 2015, 644, 647 ff.

48 Cf. BGHZ 187, 268: withdrawal possible even if the consumer has been filling a waterbed. Things are different, however, when a catalytic converter is installed and then used in the context of a short test drive, cf. BGHZ 212, 248, paras. 24 ff.

**601.** These considerations are addressed by Articles 14(4) and 15 Consumer Credit Directive II, which contain provisions on the fate of the linked contract in the event of withdrawal from the other contract.[49] By the same token, Article 11(1) of the Timeshare Directive obliges the Member States to ensure that, in the event of withdrawal from the timeshare contract, 'any exchange contract ancillary to it or any other ancillary contract is automatically terminated, at no cost to the consumer'.[50] The same applies according to Article 11(2) of the Timeshare Directive to all financing agreements concluded to finance the timeshare contract: These must be terminated without compensation. Comparable provisions are contained in Article 6(7) of the Distance Marketing of Consumer Financial Services Directive. In addition, Article 15 CRD contains another provision on 'ancillary contracts'. However, this provision only deals with the effects of exercising the right of withdrawal and leaves details to the law of the Member States. The Mortgage Credit Directive, on the other hand, does not contain any specific provisions on linked contracts.

**602.** In principle, the aforementioned directives are all fully harmonising.[51] However, their regulatory claim does not always extend to all aspects of linked contracts; also, within the framework of 'targeted full harmonisation', there are sometimes opening clauses for Member State law.

## 2. THE WITHDRAWAL'S EFFECT ON LINKED CONTRACTS

### a) *Linked Contracts*

**603.** The definition of a linked contract goes back to Article 3(n) Consumer Credit Directive 2008. According to this definition, a linked credit agreement exists if the credit in question serves exclusively to finance an agreement for the supply of specific goods or the provision of a specific service, and if those two agreements form, from an objective point of view, a commercial unit. Still according this definition, the latter is the case where the supplier or service provider himself finances the credit for the consumer or, if it is financed by a third party, where the creditor uses the services of the supplier or service provider in connection with the conclusion or preparation of the credit agreement, or where the specific goods or the provision of a specific service are explicitly specified in the credit agreement.

---

49 On the Consumer Credit Directive see para. 1004 below.

50 On the Timeshare Directive see para. 1041 below.

51 On this harmonisation approach see para. 73 above.

### b) *Consequences*

**604.** According to Article 15(1) Consumer Credit Directive 2008, where the consumer has exercised a right of withdrawal, based on Community law, e.g. under Article 9 CRD, concerning a contract for the supply of goods or services, they shall no longer be bound by a linked credit agreement. The loan is therefore, as it were, accessory to the procurement contract. The new Consumer Credit Directive 2023 does not change this approach as can be seen in its Article 26(6).

**605.** By the same token, Article 15(1) CRD provides that if the consumer exercises his right of withdrawal from a distance or an off-premises contract in accordance with Articles 9 to 14 of this Directive, any ancillary contracts shall be automatically terminated, without any costs for the consumer, except as provided for in Article 13(2) and in Article 14 of this Directive. It follows from this, that claims against the consumer for interest and costs arising from the reversal of the loan are excluded. The lender is therefore not only worse off compared to the general rules in that a revocation does not have to be declared to them. Rather, they are additionally disadvantaged in the reversal of the loan. If the loan only partially serves to finance a related contract, the said rule is only applicable to this part, but not to the remaining amount of the loan paid out to the borrower themselves, according to the case law of the Federal Court of Justice.[52]

**606.** Article 14(4) Consumer Credit Directive 2008 deals with the opposite constellation: The consumer does not withdraw from the procurement contract but from the consumer credit agreement. In such cases, the consumer shall no longer be bound by the ancillary service contract.

**607.** According to CJEU case law,[53] there is no violation of Article 3(2)(a) of the Doorstep Selling Directive to exclude contracts for the sale of immovable property even where they are merely a component of an investment scheme financed by a loan for which the negotiations prior to the conclusion of the contract were held in a doorstep-selling situation, both as regards the contract for the purchase of the immovable property and the loan agreement serving solely to finance that purchase. Therefore, the legal consequences of withdrawal could be limited to the loan contract. In particular, it was usually not objectionable that the consumer's withdrawal from the loan contract had unfavourable legal consequences for them. However, this did not apply if the credit institution did not inform the consumer about the right of withdrawal, and if the consumer who had been informed could have avoided the risks arising from the transaction.[54]

---

52 BGH NJW 2011, 1063.

53 CJEU, 25 October 2005, Case C-350/03, *Schulte/Badenia*, ECLI:EU:C:2005:637.

54 CJEU, 25 October 2005, Case C-350/03, *Schulte/Badenia*, ECLI:EU:C:2005:637, paras. 99 ff.

Since Article 3(2)(e) CRD contains a provision corresponding to Article 3(2)(a) of the Doorstep Selling Directive, one must assume that this question is answered along these lines on the basis of the CRD.

## 3. THE WITHDRAWAL'S EFFECT ON RELATED CONTRACTS

**608.** The extension of the right of withdrawal to related contracts serves the right of withdrawal's practical effectiveness: A consumer should not be prevented from a possible withdrawal because they remain bound to another contract related to the withdrawn contract (Recital 47 CRD). Article 15(1) CRD refers to 'ancillary contracts'. According to the definition in Article 2 no. 15 CRD, this is a contract by which the consumer acquires goods or services related to a distance contract or an off-premises contract and where these goods or services are supplied by the entrepreneur or a third party based on an agreement between that third party and the trader. Article 6(7) Distance Marketing of Consumer Financial Services Directive and Article 11(1) of the Timeshare Directive contain similar provisions in their respective field of application.

## 4. CONTRACTUAL OBJECTIONS AND DEFENCES WITHIN LINKED CONTRACTS

**609.** According to Article 15(2) Consumer Credit Directive 2008, where the goods or services covered by a linked credit agreement are not supplied, or are supplied only in part, or are not in conformity with the contract for the supply thereof, the consumer shall have the right to pursue remedies against the creditor if the consumer has pursued his remedies against the supplier but has failed to obtain the satisfaction to which he is entitled according to the law or the contract for the supply of goods or services. In such cases, the consumer may refuse performance vis-à-vis the lender.

# CHAPTER 3
# CONTENT OF THE CONTRACT

## §14. CONTENT AND INTERPRETATION OF CONTRACTS

CONTENTS



References: J. Barrij/L. Macgregor/D. Cabrelli (eds.), *Interpretation of Commercial Contracts in European Private Law* (Cambridge: Intersentia, 2020); L. Hübner, 'State of play der englischen Vertragsauslegung', *ZEuP* 2018, 684; P. Jung (ed.), *Europäisches Privatrecht in Vielfalt geeint. Richterliche Eingriffe in den Vertrag* (Munich: Sellier, 2013); H. Kötz, *European Contract Law*, 2nd ed. (Oxford: Oxford University Press, 2017), §6; E.A. Kramer, 'Konzeptionsfragen zur Vertragsinhaltskontrolle', *ZSR* 2018, 295; K. Riesenhuber, 'Kein Zweifel für den Verbraucher', *JZ* 2005, 829; C. Wendehorst, 'Methodennormen in kontinentaleuropäischen Kodifikationen', *RabelsZ* 75 (2011), 730.

## I. CONTRACTUAL FREEDOM

### 1. BASICS

**610.** With the contract, the parties determine which legal relationship ought to apply between them. French law is particularly clear on this point: '*Les conventions légalement formées tiennent lieu de loi à ceux qui les ont faites.*' (Article 1103 Code civil). In this respect, private autonomy grants both parties freedom of conclusion and content. Regarding their personal needs, the contracting parties are the most knowledgeable; they can best decide which content is most favourable to them. In this respect, it is possible to speak cautiously of a certain probability of correctness of private legal relationships.[1] This is also accompanied by the freedom to conclude disadvantageous contracts. The legal system merely sets outer limits, for example, through statutory prohibitions (sec. 134 of the German Civil Code) or good morals (sec. 138 of the German Civil Code).[2] The principle of good faith (sec. 242 of the German Civil Code) may also prevent the exercise of a legal position in individual cases.[3]

## 2. SCRUTINY OF THE CONTRACT'S CONTENT

**611.** The control of the content of private autonomous agreements thus initially appears as a foreign body in a system based on such a liberal basic conception.[4] An example of this is the case law of the German Imperial Court, which, in a decision issued before the entry into force of the Civil Code, rejected any review of the content[5] and later also allowed a review of standard terms only in the case of a monopoly position of the user.[6]

**612.** Reflecting the increasingly complex economic conditions and an increasingly frequent disparity in the bargaining power of market participants, judicial review of contracts increased dramatically in the second half of the last century. Since a landmark decision in 1956, the German Federal Court of Justice has subjected contractual clauses to a substantive review based on the standard of good faith (sec. 242 of the German Civil Code).[7] The legislator later reacted by enacting the German Act on standard terms which entered into force in 1977. Even outside its scope of application, case law had, in the meantime, subjected wide areas of contractual agreements in the field of, for example, labour law,[8] residential tenancy law[9] and company law[10] to content-related judicial review;

1 See para. 419 above.
2 See para. 422 above.
3 See para. 448 above.
4 Cf. W. Flume, Allgemeiner Teil des Bürgerlichen Rechts, Volume II: Das Rechtsgeschäft, 4th ed. (Berlin: Springer, 1992), p. 8; for a comparative perspective, cf. Kramer, *ZSR* 2018, 295.
5 RGZ 11, 100, 110: admissibility of a liability waiver despite it being 'not very fair and equitable' with reference to contractual freedom.
6 RGZ 62, 264, 266; RGZ 79, 224, 229; RGZ 143, 24, 28 f.; RGZ 161, 76, 80: unconscionability if the monopoly holder exploits his position of power by inserting disproportionate clauses into the contract.
7 BGHZ 22, 90, 97 ff.
8 BVerfGE 33, 125, 158 f.
9 BVerfGE 89, 1, 6.
10 Cf. Coester-Waltjen, *AcP* 190 (1990), 1, 5 ff.

even surety agreements, commercial agency agreements and legal transactions under family law are nowadays not exempt from review.[11]

**613.** However, any kind of control presupposes that the content of the contractual agreement is fixed. This is determined by interpretation. Each legal system has its own methods of interpreting contracts for this purpose.[12] A content review can only take place once the process of interpretation has been undertaken.

## 3. CONTRACT INTERPRETATION

**614.** Many legal systems allow judicial intervention in the contractual structure that has been established autonomously by the parties. In German law, this is referred to as supplementary contract interpretation. This means that 'the contract is interpreted in such a way that the parties would have agreed upon in good faith, had they been aware of the invalidity of the clause'.[13] Ultimately, however, the case law aims to undertake this kind of interpretation from a somewhat objective perspective since it is usually not based on the interests of the parties involved, as provided for in sec. 157 of the German Civil Code, but more generally on the interests of the public typically involved in legal transactions of this kind.[14]

**615.** English law also recognises the method of supplementary interpretation of the contract in the case of gaps within the contractual regulations. The question guiding the interpretation of the implication of a term is 'whether such provision would spell out in express words what the instrument, read against the relevant background, would reasonably be understood to mean'.[15] In other words, the court must determine the contract's wording that corresponds to the hypothetical intention of the parties from the perspective of an objective third party. A gap cannot be filled if it improves the text of the contract or facilitates the execution of the contract.[16]

**616.** Under the guise of contract interpretation, the court may in fact change the content of a contract, too. However, this is not a content review in the

---

11 BVerfGE 89, 214 ('guarantee'); BVerfGE 81, 242 ('commercial agent'); BVerfGE 103, 89 ('marriage contract').

12 See para. 618 below.

13 This is an often used formulation, cf. for instance BGHZ 90, 69, 75; BGHZ 137, 153, 158.

14 BGHZ 164, 297, 317; BGH NJW-RR 2005, 1040, 1041; BGHZ 107, 273, 276 f.

15 *Attorney-General of Belize* v. *Belize Telecom Ltd.* [2009] UKPC 10, 21 (PC).

16 *Liverpool City Council* v. *Irwin* [1977] AC 239, 266: 'The touchstone is always *necessity* and not merely *reasonableness*.'

sense described above. This is because supplementary contract interpretation is usually only applied if the contract is incomplete, for example, because the parties forgot to agree on a problem that is now virulent. In principle, dispositive statutory law is available to fill the gap. However, supplementary interpretation of the contract goes beyond this if the law does not provide a rule. In these cases, the decisive factor is the question of what the parties would have agreed upon in good faith and according to custom if they had known about the loophole when concluding the contract.[17] There are certainly points of contact here with the scrutiny of the contract's content.[18] Furthermore, the situation is similar in the case of disruptions or frustration of contract. Here, too, the legal consequence is usually a judicial adjustment of the contract (cf. sec. 313(1) of the German Civil Code).

**617.** However, there is an essential difference insofar as, in these cases, where a fundamental change of circumstances occurred, it is the parties who have not recognised or regulated a point that needs to be regulated. Contrary to this, reviewing the contract's content is about scrutinising provisions that are part of the contract according to the parties' intention.

## II. THE INTERPRETATION OF CONTRACTS

References: J. Baaij/L. Macgregor/D. Cabrelli (eds.), *Interpretation of Commercial Contracts in European Private Law* (Cambridge: Intersentia, 2020); J.H. Herbots, 'Interpretation of Contracts', in J.M. Smits/J. Husa/C. Valcke/M. Narciso (eds.), *Elgar Encyclopedia of Comparative Law* (Cheltenham: Edward Elgar Publishing, 2023), p. 273.

### 1. REGULATORY ABSTINENCE OF EU LAW

**618.** European contract law does not deal with the question of how the content of a contract is to be determined. Only the proposal for a Common European Sales Law is an exception.[19] A contract is interpreted according to the applicable non-uniform national law. In German law, sec. 133, 157 of the German Civil Code provide a rather vague framework; more precise standards have emerged under judicial law. The German Civil Code does not have any special methodological provisions.[20]

17 BGHZ 16, 71, 76.
18 Kötz, *European Contract Law*, 2nd ed. 2017, p. 153.
19 See para. 623 below.
20 Cf. amply on the meaning of such methodological norms Wendehorst, *RabelsZ* 75 (2011), 730.

**619.** The purpose of contract interpretation under English law (construction or interpretation of terms of contract) is to determine a contract's meaning and legal effects. The aim is to determine the common intention of the parties.[21] The basis is an objectified standard: the question is what meaning the contractual provisions have from the point of view of an objective third party with the necessary background knowledge that the parties had or reasonably ought to have had when they concluded the contract.[22] The starting point is always the wording of the contract.[23] There is a presumption that the parties' intention is reflected in the wording chosen in the contract[24] and that the parties have used a term in its natural and ordinary meaning.[25]

**620.** A contractual provision must not be considered in isolation; instead, the context of the entire contract remains vital.[26] In addition, the actual circumstances of the conclusion of the contract are also used to determine the intention of the parties in order to determine how the contract's wording would be understood from the perspective of an objective third party in the position of the contractual parties.[27] The more precise and unambiguous the literal meaning is, the less willing the English courts will be to give a different meaning to the contractual provision.[28] This applies to legal terms in particular: Here, too, there is a presumption that the parties intended to ascribe the 'usual' meaning to them.[29] The conduct of the parties after the conclusion of the contract, on the other hand, may not be taken into account when interpreting the contract.[30] The

---

[21] *Marquis of Cholmondeley* v. *Clinton* (1820) 2 Jacob & Walker, 1, 91 (English Reports, Volume 37).

[22] *Investors Compensation Scheme Ltd.* v. *West Bromwich Building Society* [1998] 1 WLR 896, 912 (HL).

[23] Cf. *Total Gas Marketing Ltd.* v. *Arco British Ltd. and others* [1998] 2 Lloyd's Rep. 209, 215 (HL); *Albion Sugar Co. Ltd.* v. *William Tankers Ltd. and Davies (the 'John S. Darbyshire')* [1977] 2 Lloyd's Rep. 457, 466.

[24] *British Movietonews Ltd.* v. *London and District Cinemas Ltd.* [1952] AC 166 (HL).

[25] *Investors Compensation Scheme Ltd.* v. *West Bromwich Building Society* [1998] 1 WLR 896, 912 (HL).

[26] *North Eastern Railway* v. *Hastings* [1900] A.C. 260, 267 (HL).

[27] *Investors Compensation Scheme Ltd.* v. *West Bromwich Building Society* [1998] 1 WLR 896, 913 (HL); *Bayerische Vereinsbank Aktiengesellschaft* v. *National Bank of Pakistan* [1997] 1 Lloyd's Rep. 59, 63; *Harvey Shopfitters Ltd.* v. *ADI Ltd.* [2004] 91 Con LR 71 (CA); *Lymington Marina Ltd.* v. *Macmanara and others* [2006] EWHC 704 (ChD); *Vaverakis* v. *Compagnia de Navegacion Artico S.A.* [1976] 2 Lloyd's Rep. 250, 255; see also S.A. Smith, *Atiyah's Introduction to the Law of Contract*, 6th ed. (Oxford: Clarendon Press, 2006), p. 149.

[28] *Melanesian Mission Trust Board* v. *Australian Mutual Provident Society* [1997] 1 N.Z.L.R. 391, 394 (PC).

[29] Cf. A.G. Guest, in *Chitty on Contracts*, Volume I: General Principles, 31st ed. (London: Sweet & Maxwell, 2012), para. 12-053.

[30] *L. Schuler AG* v. *Wickman Machine Tools Sales Ltd.* [1974] AC 235, 261, 263 (HL). For a critical account of this cf. J. Beatson/A.S. Burrows/J. Cartwright, *Anson's Law of Contract*, 29th ed. (Oxford: Oxford University Press, 2010), p. 168.

same applies to the pre-contractual negotiations between the parties: According to English case law, it is usually not permissible to take them into account, as they are more capable of supporting the subjective intentions of the parties than the actual contractual content, which must be determined from the perspective of an objective third party.[31]

**621.** If an interpretation based on the wording leads to absurd or contradictory results, or if a contractual obligation follows from this which the parties could not reasonably have intended, a deviation from such an interpretation is necessary.[32] The same applies to evident linguistic confusion (*falsa demonstratio non nocet*).[33] If there are several possible interpretations, the one that leads to the contract's validity must be chosen,[34] and otherwise, the one that most closely corresponds to the intention of the parties or the business common sense of the respective industry.[35]

**622.** As in German law, the interpretation of contracts in English law generally follows the maxim that the parties' intentions, as reflected in the contract's text, shall be determined.[36] English case law is even more oriented towards the contract's wording, whereas German law focuses on the economic purpose of the agreement. Exceptionally, a supplementary filling of gaps can also be considered.

## 2. THE REGULATIONS ON CONTRACT INTERPRETATION IN THE CESL

**623.** Just like the DCFR,[37] the CESL contains rules on the interpretation of contracts (Articles 58–65 CESL).[38] According to those provisions, what matters

---

31 *Prenn* v. *Simmonds* [1971] 1 WLR 1381, 1384 (HL); *Chartbrook Ltd.* v. *Persimmon Homes Ltd.* [2009] 1 AC 1101 (HL), paras. 28 ff. (toon the rule), paras. 35 ff. (on the exceptions). Critically for instance *Lord Nicholls* (2005) 121 LQR 577.

32 *L. Schuler AG* v. *Wickman Machine Tools Sales Ltd.* [1974] AC 235, 251 (HL).

33 See the references on the pertinent case law in A.G. Guest, in *Chitty on Contracts*, Volume I: General Principles, 31st ed. (London: Sweet & Maxwell, 2012), para. 12-075.

34 See for example *Pioneer Freight Futures Co. Ltd.* v. *TMT Asia Ltd. (No 2)* [2011] 2 Lloyd's Rep. 565, 574; J. Beatson/A.S. Burrows/J. Cartwright, *Anson's Law of Contract*, 29th ed. (Oxford: Oxford University Press, 2010), p. 169.

35 *Antaios Compania Naviera SA* v. *Salen Rederierna A.B.* (The Antaios) [1984] A.C. 191, 201 (HL); *Chartbrook Ltd.* v. *Persimmon Homes Ltd.* [2009] 1 AC 1101 (HL), para. 16.

36 Cf. Kötz, in *Festschrift für Zeuner* (Tübingen: Mohr Siebeck, 1994), pp. 219 ff.; see further K. Zweigert/H. Kötz, *Introduction to Comparative Law*, 3rd ed. (Oxford: Clarendon Press, 1996), §30.

37 Cf. Maultzsch, GPR 2011, 114.

38 Cf. Hardy, *ERPL* 2011, 817 (on the Feasibility Study); C. Wendehorst, in C. Wendehorst/B. Zöchling-Jud (eds.), *Am Vorabend eines Gemeinsamen Europäischen Kaufrechts. Zum Verordnungsentwurf der Europäischen Kommission vom 11.10.2011* (Vienna:

in the first place is the parties' shared intentions, even if these do not coincide with the ordinary meaning of the expressions used in the contract (Article 58(1) CESL). Article 59 CESL contains a detailed and non-exhaustive list of circumstances that may be taken into account during the interpretation of the contract. Finally, Article 64 CESL establishes the principle of consumer-friendly interpretation.

**624.** The content of the contract shall be determined following Articles 66–78 CESL.[39] According to Article 66 CESL, the contractual provisions are derived from (a) the parties' agreements; (b) usages and customs insofar as a binding obligation exists according to Article 67 CESL; (c) non-waived dispositive provisions of the CESL, and (d) so-called additional contractual provisions according to Article 68 CESL: In essence, this is an adoption of the doctrine of implied terms from common law or the continental doctrine of supplementary contract interpretation. Article 70 CESL contains an obligation to refer to contractual provisions that have not been individually negotiated.[40]

---

Manz 2012), pp. 87–88 ff.; E. Clive, in L. Moccia (ed.), *The Making of European Private Law* (Munich: Sellier, 2013), p. 181; Rott-Pietrzyk, *ZEuP* 2014, 371.

39 Cf. C. Wendehorst, in C. Wendehorst/B. Zöchling-Jud (eds.), *Am Vorabend eines Gemeinsamen Europäischen Kaufrechts. Zum Verordnungsentwurf der Europäischen Kommission vom 11.10.2011* (Vienna: Manz 2012), pp. 87, 91 ff.; Looschelders, *AcP* 212 (2012), 581, 635 ff.

40 For a critical discussion see Mansel, *WM* 2012, 1309, 1317.

# §15. STANDARD TERMS

## CONTENTS

References: F. Bonke, *Europäische Klauselkontrolle im unternehmerischen Geschäftsverkehr* (Berlin: Duncker & Humblot, 2020); D. Coester-Waltjen/M. Coester, 'Deutsches AGB-Recht unter dem Einfluss europäischen Gemeinschaftsrechts', in *Festschrift für Köhler* (Munich: C.H. Beck, 2014), p. 63; M. Fornasier, 'A Short Biography of the Unfair Contract Terms Directive on the Occasion of Its 30th Anniversary', (2023) *European Review of Private Law*, 1143; C. Gardiner, *Unfair Contract Terms in the Digital Age. The Challenge of Protecting European Consumers in the Online Marketplace* (Cheltenham: Edward Elgar Publishing, 2022); B. Gsell/M. Fervers, 'Control of Price Related Terms in Standard Form Contracts', in M. Schmidt-Kessel (ed.), *German National Reports on the 20th International Congress of Comparative Law* (Tübingen: Mohr Siebeck, 2018), p. 283; B. Heiderhoff, *Europäisches Privatrecht*, 6th ed. (Heidelberg: C.F. Müller, 2023), paras. 399 ff.; P. Hellwege, 'It is necessary to strictly distinguish two forms of fairness control!', *EuCML* 2015, 129; C. Herresthal, 'Vertragsrecht', in K. Langenbucher, *Europäisches Privat- und Wirtschaftsrecht*, 5th ed. (Baden-Baden: Nomos, 2022), §2 paras. 118 ff.; H. Kötz, *European Contract Law*, 2nd ed. (Oxford: Oxford University Press, 2017), §8; E. Mišćenić/P. Tereszkiewicz/M. Infantino, 'The Interplay Between the CJEU and National Courts in the Case Law on Unfair Contract Terms in Foreign Currency Loans: A Comparative Overview', *ERCL* 2023, 346; C. Poncibò, 'The UCTD 30 Years Later: Identifying and Blacklisting Unfair Terms in Digital Markets', *ERCL* 2023, 321; P. Rott, 'Unfair contract terms', in C. Twigg-Flesner (ed.), *Research Handbook on EU Consumer and Contract Law* (Cheltenham: Edward Elgar Publishing, 2016), p. 287; M. Stürner, 'Amtsprüfung im Mahnverfahren und Unzulässigkeit der Vertragsanpassung bei missbräuchlicher Verzugszinsklausel', *ZEuP* 2013, 671; M. Stürner, 'Die Rolle des EuGH bei der Kontrolle missbräuchlicher Klauseln in Verbraucherverträgen', in C. von

Bar/A. Wudarski (eds.), *Deutschland und Polen in der europäischen Rechtsgemeinschaft* (Munich: Sellier, 2012), p. 65; M. Wendland, *Vertragsfreiheit und Vertragsgerechtigkeit. Subjektive und objektive Gestaltungskräfte im Privatrecht am Beispiel der Inhaltskontrolle Allgemeiner Geschäftsbedingungen im unternehmerischen Geschäftsverkehr* (Tübingen: Mohr Siebeck, 2019); A. Zaccaria, 'Anmerkungen zur Umsetzung der Richtlinie 93/13/EWG über missbräuchliche Klauseln in Verbraucherverträgen in Europa', *ZEuP* 2016, 159

# I. FUNDAMENTALS AND LEGAL FRAMEWORK

## 1. THE USE OF STANDARD TERMS

**625.** The use of standard terms streamlines legal transactions. It simplifies concluding a contract insofar as the parameters do not have to be specifically negotiated. However, this is precisely what threatens to present disadvantages for a contracting party: By introducing standard terms into the negotiations, by making them a condition of the conclusion of the contract, as it were, it is usually only a choice of between accepting the contract with these clauses or not at all. Typically, the user of the standard terms will exploit the leeway left to them by the dispositive law to introduce regulations into the contract that are advantageous for them. In order to avoid completely one-sided contractual conditions and, thus, an imbalance in the contract, legal regulation and scrutiny of standard terms is necessary. This relates to three main options: The inclusion of the clauses (inclusion control),[1] their regulatory content (content control)[2] and their comprehensibility (transparency control).[3]

## 2. THE UNFAIR TERMS DIRECTIVE

### a) Purpose

**626.** The Council Directive 93/13/EEC of 5 April 1993 on unfair terms in consumer contracts (in short: Unfair Terms Directive) serves to approximate the laws, regulations and administrative provisions of the Member States on unfair terms in contracts between traders and consumers (Article 1(1) Unfair Terms Directive). As usual, the applicability of the Directive depends on the contracting parties, i.e. whether or not they are acting in the course of their trade, business or profession.[4] Consumers are considered worthy of protection,

[1] See para. 633 below.
[2] See para. 641 as well as para. 654.
[3] See para. 669.
[4] CJEU, 17 May 2018, Case C-147/16, *de Grote*, ECLI:EU:C:2018:320, para. 53.

as they are in a weaker position than the trader and possess less information; furthermore, consumers usually cannot influence the content of the standard terms.[5] As in other contexts as well, therefore, even a lawyer, who certainly has a far above-average level of professional knowledge, is regarded as a consumer within the meaning of Article 2(b) Unfair Terms Directive if they conclude a contract unrelated to their professional activity.[6] An employee who concludes a contract with their employer other than an employment contract can thus also be classified as a consumer.[7] On the other hand, persons other than natural persons do not fall within the scope of protection of the Unfair Terms Directive.[8]

**627.** The Unfair Terms Directive is based on the EU's general legislative competence regarding the establishment of the internal market.[9] Consequently, the recitals emphasise the importance of eliminating unfair terms from consumer contracts to establish the internal market. Since consumers are generally unaware of the legislation applicable to the purchase of goods and the offer of services in other Member States, they are reluctant to order goods and services directly in other Member States (Recital 5 of the Unfair Terms Directive). It is, therefore, essential to remove unfair terms from these contracts (Recital 6 of the Unfair Terms Directive). This would also make it easier for sellers of goods and providers of services to sell both in their own country and throughout the internal market, thereby promoting competition and providing consumers with more choices (Recital 7 of the Unfair Terms Directive).

### *b) No General Fairness Control*

**628.** The 'Proposal for a Council Directive on unfair terms in consumer contracts'[10] submitted by the Commission in 1990 had stipulated that individual contracts should also fall within the scope of the Directive. Moreover, the proposal allowed for the interpretation that the price-performance ratio and the service description could also be subject to a fairness control.[11] Such a power of review would be difficult to reconcile with basic assumptions of contractual freedom.[12] Hence, the version of the Unfair Terms Directive adopted by the Council no

---

5 CJEU, 3 September 2015, Case C-110/14, *Costea*, ECLI:EU:C:2015:538, para. 18; CJEU, 21 March 2019, Case C-590/17, *Pouvin*, ECLI:EU:C:2019:232, para. 25. On this line of reasoning in more detail para. 643 below.

6 CJEU, 3 September 2015, Case C-110/14, *Costea*, ECLI:EU:C:2015:538, paras. 26 f.

7 CJEU, 21 March 2019, Case C-590/17, *Pouvin*, ECLI:EU:C:2019:232, para. 29.

8 CJEU, 22 November 2001, Joined Cases C-541/99 and C-542/99, *Cape and Idealservice MN RE*, ECLI:EU:C:2001:625, para. 16; CJEU, 2 April 2020, Case C-329/19, *Condominio di Milano*, ECLI:EU:C:2020:263, paras. 24 ff.

9 At that time Article 100a TEC, today Article 114 TFEU, see para. 220 above.

10 Of 3 September 1990, COM(90) 322 final.

11 See the broad formulation in Articles 2(1) and 3 of the draft, COM(90) 322 final.

12 Cf. only Canaris, in *Festschrift für Lerche* (Munich: C.H. Beck, 1993), p. 873.

longer contained such a broad scope of contractual scrutiny. Article 4(2) of the Unfair Terms Directive explicitly excludes the main contractual obligations from fairness control – as long as the relevant clauses are drafted 'in plain intelligible language'.

**629.** Article 3(1) Unfair Terms Directive restricts the scope of control of the directive to terms that have not been negotiated individually. In this context, the primary obligations are only indirectly important for scrutinizing the contractual content. Recital 19 of the Unfair Terms Directive contains, in addition to this general statement, the indication that the unfairness of clauses in insurance contracts that define the primary obligations in more detail can be assessed concerning the question of whether limitations of the scope of benefits are reflected in the premiums to be paid.

**630.** The Unfair Terms Directive only contains a standard for the control's density in the form of a general clause in Article 3(1) Unfair Terms Directive. Only in the form of an annex does the Unfair Terms Directive contain an 'indicative and non-exhaustive list of the terms which may be regarded as unfair' (Article 3(3) Unfair Terms Directive). There is some confusion about the meaning of this 'grey list', as will be explained later on. The Unfair Terms Directive is of a minimum harmonizing nature (Article 8 Unfair Terms Directive) so that the Member States can enact stricter – i.e. more consumer-friendly – provisions. The Member States had to implement the Unfair Terms Directive by 31 December 1994.[13]

### c) *Excluded Areas*

**631.** The control of the contractual content does not extend to clauses based on mandatory law, nor does it apply if clauses merely repeat dispositive norms. The first follows from Article 1(2) of the Unfair Terms Directive, which provides an exception for contractual clauses based on mandatory law. That is to be understood as referring to contractual terms which reflect mandatory statutory or regulatory provisions and the provisions or principles of international conventions to which the Member States or indeed the EU are party. According to the CJEU's case law, this exception is justified because the balanced regulation of all rights and obligations of the parties in specific contracts intended by the national legislators should be respected.[14] However, the exception should not apply in a purely national consumer contract clause according to which the place

---

[13] See para. 682 below.

[14] CJEU, 7 August 2018, Case C-96/16, *Banco Santander and Escobedo Cortés*, ECLI:EU:C:2018:643, para. 43; CJEU, 3 April 2019, Case C-266/18, *Aqua Med/Skóra*, ECLI:EU:C:2019:282, para. 33; CJEU, 3 March 2020, Case C-125/18, *Gómez*, ECLI:EU:C:2020:138, paras. 29 ff.

of jurisdiction for disputes between the parties should be determined following the relevant provisions. The CJEU held that this clause was, in principle, open to review since it was not a binding provision within the meaning of the narrowly interpreted exception of Article 1(2) of the Unfair Terms Directive.[15] However, the question of abusiveness was nevertheless to be assessed by the national court – since the term did not merely repeat a specific provision but referred to a particular set of rules, it was not clear how the wording of the contractual term and its impact on the consumer's expectations had to be assessed.[16] If, however, the clause only reflects mandatory statutory law, a violation of the law cannot be grounded on the contractual agreement but, at most, on higher-ranking law.

**632.** The latter is because clause control can only react to the degree of deviation of the contractual agreement from the normative area marked by dispositive rules. The normative scope itself, in turn, cannot be evaluated by the law of general terms and conditions without a suitable (external) standard of application.[17]

## II. PREREQUISITES FOR THE INCLUSION OF STANDARD TERMS

### 1. THE DEFINITION OF STANDARD TERMS AND THE POSSIBILITY OF TAKING NOTICE

**633.** The Unfair Terms Directive defines the term standard terms as a clause that 'has been drafted in advance and the consumer has therefore not been able to influence the substance of the term, particularly in the context of a pre-formulated standard contract' (Article 3(2) subpara. 1 Unfair Terms Directive). The Directive is essentially based on the fact that the clause is not negotiable, i.e. the consumer could not influence the content of the clause. It is irrelevant that parts of a clause were negotiated after all; this applies in any event if, according to the overall situation, it must nevertheless be classified as a pre-formulated standard contract (Article 3(2) subpara. 2 Unfair Terms Directive). Since the entrepreneur bears the burden of proof that a standard contract term has been negotiated in detail (Article 3(2) subpara. 3 Unfair Terms Directive), in the case of pre-formulated contract terms, there is a presumption that they are standard terms within the Directive's meaning. In order to avoid

---

15 CJEU, 3 April 2019, Case C-266/18, *Aqua Med/Skóra*, ECLI:EU:C:2019:282, paras. 33 ff.

16 See Piekenbrock/Rodi, *GPR* 2019, 233.

17 The deviation from the standard of dispositive law is also used in various cases as a justification of the clause control itself, see para. 649 below.

a content review, the consumer must therefore have been offered a negotiation for each clause.

**634.** In some systems, like the German, surprising clauses do not become part of the contract. They are contractual provisions 'which in the circumstances, in particular with regard to the outward appearance of the contract, are so unusual that the party contracting with the user need not expect to encounter them' (sec. 305c(1) German Civil Code). The provision thus protects the trust in the GTC's functional design.[18] Here, too, it is irrelevant whether they have actually been noticed. Hence, the law prevents the user of the GTC from 'sneaking' into the contract terms that have nothing to do with the actual subject matter of the contract. The aim is to protect the opposing party's trust that the general terms and conditions do not deviate too far from those customary and conceivable in comparable legal transactions.[19] The Unfair Terms Directive does not contain any such provisions, but it does not prohibit this mode of consumer protection (Article 8 Unfair Terms Directive).

## 2. INCLUSION AND CONTROL OF THIRD-PARTY STANDARD TERMS

**635.** Difficulties arise in constellations where the requirement of including GTC is not easily fulfilled. This can be the case if the GTC originate from a third party who does not become a contracting party themselves. Such triangular relationships are frequent in sales via online platforms. Here, the question arises whether the platform's GTC also affect the relationship between seller and buyer and how this can be justified doctrinally. The following case, which has been decided by the German Federal Court of Justice, can illustrate this.[20]

**636.** V offers his car for auction on the platform www.ricardo.de for 10 euros. However, he actually wanted to enter 10,000 euros as the minimum bid. The car is auctioned off by K for 15,000 euros. V expected at least 20,000 euros and refused to deliver the car. He claims he had no intention of being legally bound. The general terms and conditions of www.ricardo.de explicitly state that the contract is concluded with the bidder who has made the highest bid at the end of the auction period. Can K demand the car from V?

**637.** For a contract to be concluded, there must be two concurrent declarations of intent. Can V's intention to be legally bound arise from the platform's general

---

18 BGH WM 1992, 1895.
19 In that sense BT-Drucks. 7/3919, p. 19.
20 BGHZ 149, 129.

terms and conditions? Here it is problematic to what extent the general terms and conditions of the auction platform are to apply in the relationship between V and K. The purchase contract is not concluded with the auction platform: The purchase contract is not concluded with the platform, but between the two auction participants. The starting point is therefore that the GTC of the auction platform, which both parties acknowledged vis-à-vis the platform when registering on it, were not 'provided' by either party in the relationship between V and K, so that neither party to the contract is a 'user' within the meaning of sec. 305(1) of the German Civil Code.[21] However, the bidder, in this case V, may, from an objective recipient's point of view (sec. 157 German Civil Code), understand the posting of the item for sale as meaning that the auction is carried out according to the conditions stated in the platform's GTC.[22]

**638.** But suppose the seller uses GTC as well. How do they relate to the contradictory GTC of the platform and whether a review of the clause's content appears possible in a situation where the platform's GTC appear to be abusive? First of all, the declarations of intent of the contracting parties have to be interpreted according to a reasonable third party's understanding (see above). If, based on this, a clause of the seller was not included, a content review does not apply anyway.[23] According to the Unfair Terms Directive, the only decisive factor for the existence of GTC is that the consumer did not influence the clause's content (Article 3(2) Unfair Terms Directive).[24] Therefore, from this perspective, it appears like the general terms and conditions of third parties might also be subject to scrutiny.[25] This applies at least as long as they are 'terms used in a contract concluded with a consumer by a seller or supplier' (Article 6(1) Unfair Terms Directive). If, for example, the platform GTC contained a clause that the consumer must always pay all fees or a clause that always prescribes a general exclusion of liability in favour of the seller, these could certainly be subject to scrutiny from the point of view of the Unfair Terms Directive. After all, the general aim is to eliminate unfair terms from consumer contracts (Recital 4 Unfair Terms Directive).

**639.** However, the Directive does not regulate how these terms become part of the contract between the business and the consumer. According to the case law developed by the German Federal Court of Justice, no content review would be carried out due to the lacking inclusion of such general terms and conditions by the user, but the principle of good faith would be called upon. This would also

21 BGHZ 149, 129, para. 40.

22 BGHZ 149, 129, paras. 26 ff.

23 Heiderhoff, *Europäisches Privatrecht*, para. 402, advocates a content review also for GTC of the provider, as this is necessary for consumer protection reasons.

24 On this already para. 634 above.

25 Heiderhoff, *Europäisches Privatrecht*, para. 402. A plea for reform can be found in Möslein, *ERCL* 2023, 300.

be acceptable from the point of view of the Unfair Terms Directive: Article 7(1) Unfair Terms Directive leaves it up to the Member States to decide how to prevent the abuse of clauses. However, these must be 'adequate and effective means' to 'prevent the continued use of unfair terms in contracts concluded with consumers by sellers or suppliers'. Within the *effet utile* of the Directive, as defined in this way, there is thus freedom for the Member States regarding the manner of implementation.

**640.** Since the approach of the Member States was somewhat inconsistent in this and other areas of consumer law, the Directive on Better Enforcement and Modernisation of the Union Consumer Protection Rules[26] introduced a series of measures to facilitate a more uniform imposition of sanctions. To achieve this, a new Article 8b was inserted into the Unfair Terms Directive, which now lists exemplary and non-exhaustive criteria, such as the nature, gravity, extent and duration of the infringement, as well as any compensation received by the consumer from the business for the damage caused.

## III. THE LEGITIMACY OF FAIRNESS CONTROL OF GENERAL TERMS AND CONDITIONS

References: P. McColgan, *Abschied vom Informationsmodell im Recht allgemeiner Geschäftsbedingungen* (Tübingen: Mohr Siebeck, 2020).

**641.** There is quite some disagreement about the rationale of standard terms control: Why is it justified to control a private law agreement beyond the threshold of public policy? Why does it make sense to allow any content-related scrutiny of general terms and conditions and basically not of individual agreements?[27]

### 1. STARTING POINT: DISTURBANCE OF THE CONTRACTUAL PRESUMPTION OF CORRECTNESS

**642.** The presumption of 'correctness' of the contract's content is inherent in every formally valid contract.[28] The idea of the parties' autonomy as legal

---

26 Directive (EU) 2019/2161 of the European Parliament and of the Council of 27 November 2019 amending Council Directive 93/13/EEC and Directives 98/6/EC, 2005/29/EC and 2011/83/EU of the European Parliament and of the Council with regard to better enforcement and modernisation of Union consumer protection laws, OJ L 328/7.

27 L. Fastrich, *Richterliche Inhaltskontrolle im Privatrecht* (Munich: C.H. Beck, 1992), pp. 29 ff.; Leuschner, *AcP* 207 (2007), 491, 493 ff. For the following, see already Stürner, *Der Grundsatz der Verhältnismäßigkeit im Schuldvertragsrecht*, 2010, pp. 100 ff.

28 On this and on the relativisation of the concept of 'correctness' already para. 419 above.

subjects allows the legal system to refrain from checking the contract's content in order to validate whether a party has acted in accordance with their autonomy: this inherent freedom goes so far as individuals may conclude disadvantageous or even frivolous contracts. This suggests that reviewing individual contractual terms is legitimate when this presumption appears false.[29] The difficulty, however, lies in defining criteria for such a disturbance of the correctness of the contract. For the use of GTC, such a disturbance was typically defined on a case-by-case basis in court decisions and later by the legislator.[30] However, there is still disagreement about the legitimacy of this approach.

## 2. JUSTIFICATION OF THE CONTROL OF GTC

**643.** The reasons for the intervention in the contractual structure within the framework of the control of GTC are ever-changing. In the 1950s and later on, the focus was primarily on the exploitation of the trader's superior bargaining power; today, the idea of a market failure is increasingly used to justify the control of GTC.[31]

### *a) 'Imbalance' between the User and the Contracting Party?*

**644.** In the past, a justification for the control of GTC was often seen in an economic, social, intellectual or other imbalance between the trader and the contracting party, which the latter exploited to enforce their contractual terms.[32] According to this conception, the review of the GTC's content serves to protect the weaker contractual partner and, as such, is ultimately only an instrument of consumer protection.[33]

**645.** However, at least today, this justification is contradicted by the fact that, at least in some systems like Germany, standard terms in B2B contracts are, in principle, also subject to review. Typically, there will undoubtedly be a certain

---

29 Coester-Waltjen, *AcP* 190 (1990), 1, 14 ff.; L. Fastrich, *Richterliche Inhaltskontrolle im Privatrecht* (Munich: C.H. Beck, 1992), pp. 55 ff. Some even argue for a constitutional imperative of clause control, e.g. H. Hanau, *Der Grundsatz der Verhältnismäßigkeit als Schranke privater Gestaltungsmacht* (Tübingen: Mohr Siebeck, 2004), p. 124 as well as Leuschner, *AcP* 207 (2007), 491, 509 ff. (with reference to BVerfG NJW 2005, 2376 and BVerfG NJW 2006, 1783).

30 Cf. BGHZ 101, 350, 354 (in connection with the control of the content of notarial contracts). See in general on the control of content already para. 612 above.

31 On the European discussion Jansen, *ZEuP* 2010, 69, 83 ff.

32 Cf. for example Reich, *ZRP* 1974, 187, 192; Damm, *JZ* 1978, 173, 178.

33 In that sense, before the AGBG came into force, BGHZ 60, 243, 245 ('considerable economic and intellectual preponderance'); cf. also the government's explanatory memorandum to the draft AGBG, BT-Drucks. 7/3919, p. 43.

'imbalance of bargaining power' between the user and the other contracting party; this applies above all to consumer contracts. However, the control of general terms and conditions is not exclusively linked to this but merely intervenes situationally if pre-formulated clauses are used.[34] A lack of experience or any other inferior position of the other contracting party is irrelevant, so a lawyer who concludes a contract outside their professional activity can also benefit from the control of GTC.

**646.** The principle of protection has greater weight in the domain of the Unfair Terms Directive, which only covers consumer contracts. According to the concept of the Directive, unfair terms are to be fought against in order to protect the consumer.[35] According to the case law of the CJEU, the consumer is in a weaker negotiating position vis-à-vis the trader and generally has less information and knowledge than the latter.[36] This leads to the consumer agreeing to terms drawn up in advance by the seller without being able to influence the content of the terms.[37]

### b) *Unilateral Use of the Freedom of Contract*

**647.** A more modern approach to this argument refers to the unilateral use of contractual freedom by the user of GTC, who, by establishing rules in their favour, prevents the other party from legally shaping their own interests. This, so it is argued, would then be an abuse of contractual freedom. This theory of institutional abuse of rights goes back to Ludwig Raiser;[38] it is also used in the case law of the German Federal Court of Justice.[39] A similar rationale can be found in the Unfair Terms Directive, where Recital 9 speaks of 'abuse of power by the seller or supplier', against which the consumer must be protected. Article 3(2) of the Unfair Terms Directive also refers to the consumer's lack of

---

34 Critical of the 'inferiority thesis' Lieb, *AcP* 178 (1978), 196, 200; B. Dauner-Lieb, *Verbraucherschutz durch Ausbildung eines Sonderprivatrechts für Verbraucher: Systemkonforme Weiterentwicklung oder Schrittmacher der Systemveränderung?* (Berlin: Duncker & Humblot, 1983), pp. 141 ff.; Coester-Waltjen, *AcP* 190 (1990), 1, 19 ff.; L. Fastrich, *Richterliche Inhaltskontrolle im Privatrecht* (Munich: C.H. Beck, 1992), p. 91; Wackerbarth, *AcP* 200 (2000), 45, 51 ff.; in this sense also BGH NJW 1976, 2345, 2346.

35 Cf. Recitals 4 and 6 Unfair Terms Directive.

36 CJEU, 30 April 2014, Case C-26/13, *Kásler*, ECLI:EU:C:2014:282, paras. 39 f.

37 CJEU, 27 June 2000, Joined Cases C-240/98 to C-244/98, *Océano*, ECLI:EU:C:2000:346, para. 25; CJEU, 26 October 2006, Case C-168/05, *Centro Móvil*, ECLI:EU:C:2006:675, para. 25.

38 L. Raiser, *Das Recht der allgemeinen Geschäftsbedingungen* (Hamburg: Hanseatische Verlags-Anstalt, 1935), pp. 277 ff.; *id.*, in summum ius, summa iniuria, 1963, p. 145, 152. Likewise Grüneberg, in Grüneberg, *BGB Kommentar*, 84th ed. 2025, before §305 para. 8.

39 BGHZ 51, 55, 59; BGH NJW 1976, 2345, 2346; BGHZ 70, 304, 310; BGHZ 126, 326, 332 f.; BGH NJW 2004, 1454, 1455; on this L. Fastrich, *Richterliche Inhaltskontrolle im Privatrecht* (Munich: C.H. Beck, 1992), pp. 47 ff.

influence on the contract's content and thus suggests that the content review is some sort of compensation for the unequal negotiating power.[40]

**648.** This approach has a reasonable core; it draws the legitimacy of the content review from the fact that the user of GTC does not usually aim to create a balanced compromise between the parties' interests but focuses primarily on their own interests. Nevertheless, this justification is insufficient since the freedom of *both* contracting parties is not one of the indispensable prerequisites for the conclusion of a contract. By contrast, it is not one of the essentialia of the conclusion of a contract that both contracting parties are able to shape the content of the contract. On the contrary, an offer can be accepted with a simple 'yes'. The customer always has the option to refrain from concluding the contract altogether if they disagree with the GTC.[41] The prevention of a real possibility for the contracting party to influence the formulation of contractual terms and conditions by the user's provision of GTC is, therefore, no criterion for the effective conclusion of a contract and cannot serve as a justification for controlling GTC.[42]

### c) *Unilateral Displacement of Dispositive Statutory Law*

**649.** Another approach for justifying the scrutiny of GTC is to regard the user 'quasi as a substitute legislator in his own cause'.[43] Accordingly, the mass use of unilateral clauses displaces the legislator, which makes the contract's content objectionable. It is in the nature of dispositive law that the parties waive it by drafting their own contracts. Instead, the real problem is that the balance of interests created by dispositive law[44] is replaced en masse by clauses that primarily serve the user's interests.[45] This gives the contractual partner 'the impression of legality, completeness and balance' of the provision.[46] Consequently, the degree

---

40 In that sense CJEU, 27 June 2000, Joined Cases C-240/98 to C-244/98, *Océano*, ECLI:EU:C:2000:346, para. 27.

41 Zöllner, *AcP* 196 (1996), 1, 31; *id.*, AcP 176 (1976), 221, 235 f.; Coester-Waltjen, *AcP* 190 (1990), 1, 20 f.; Wackerbarth, *AcP* 200 (2000), 45, 63 ff.

42 However, the case law of the Federal Court of Justice goes partly in this direction, cf. e.g. BGHZ 74, 204, 209 ff.

43 G. Nobbe, in B. Dauner-Lieb/M. Henssler/U. Preis (eds.), *Inhaltskontrolle im Arbeitsrecht. Zwischen Zivilrecht und arbeitsrechtlichen Besonderheiten* (Baden-Baden: Nomos, 2006), pp. 38, 41.

44 On the justice value of dispositive statutory law also Hesselink, *ERCL* 2005, 44, 51 ff.; on the criteria for the dispositivity of statutory law L. Kähler, *Begriff und Rechtfertigung abdingbaren Rechts* (Tübingen: Mohr Siebeck, 2012); J. Cziupka, *Dispositives Vertragsrecht. Funktionsweise und Qualitätsmerkmale gesetzlicher Regelungsmuster* (Tübingen: Mohr Siebeck, 2010); F. Möslein, *Dispositives Recht - Zwecke, Strukturen und Methoden* (Tübingen: Mohr Siebeck, 2011).

45 Zöllner, *JuS* 1988, 329, 333; *id.*, RdA 1989, 152, 157.

46 In that sense BGHZ 101, 350, 354 for a notarial contract.

of deviation of the GTC from the dispositive statutory law may be used as a yardstick for the unreasonable disadvantage caused by the term.

**650.** This approach does not attribute a normative quality to GTC, as the so-called norm theories have sometimes done explicitly or implicitly.[47] However, due to the focus on the mass displacement of dispositive statutory law, this approach is unable to explain why a general terms and conditions control de *lege lata* already intervenes in the case of pre-formulated terms and conditions for a large number of contracts and is by no means based on the mass dissemination.[48] In addition, it presupposes the dissemination of unfair general terms and conditions, i.e. it looks at the situation retrospectively, whereas the general terms and conditions control considers the dispositive statutory law as the standard for the unreasonableness of a clause, but does not presuppose the large-scale suppression of dispositive norms by GTC.[49]

### *d) Partial Market Failure*

**651.** In more recent academic literature, partial market failure is predominantly used as a justification for the control of GTC.[50] The reason for this is not the unilateral power of the user to shape the contract but the insight that a functioning market does not exist among the GTC of different providers, as the customer does not and cannot regularly control their content: The effort to determine any disadvantages in the clauses and to identify alternatives would not be worthwhile for them because of prohibitively high transaction costs.[51] They usually have neither the time nor the expertise to compare the clauses

47 In this regard, L. Fastrich, *Richterliche Inhaltskontrolle im Privatrecht* (Munich: C.H. Beck, 1992), pp. 29 ff.; M. Habersack, in P. Ulmer/H.D. Brandner/H.E. Hensen, *AGB-Recht*, 13th ed. (Cologne: Otto Schmidt, 2022), Einl. paras. 39 ff.

48 According to German case law, it is sufficient if a form contract is used three times, see BGH NJW 1998, 2286, 2287; BGH NJW 2002, 138, 139.

49 Critically also Coester-Waltjen, *AcP* 190 (1990), 1, 24.

50 H. Kötz, Gutachten A zum 50. Deutschen Juristentag (Munich: Beck, 1974), pp. 29 ff.; H. Kötz, in C. Ott/H.-B. Schäfer (eds.), Allokationseffizienz in der Rechtsordnung. Beiträge zur ökonomischen Analyse des Zivilrechts (Berlin: Springer, 1989), pp. 189, 190 ff.; H.-B. Schäfer/C. Ott, Lehrbuch der ökonomischen Analyse des Zivilrechts, 5th ed. (Berlin/Heidelberg: Springer, 2013), pp. 552 ff.; B. Dauner-Lieb, *Verbraucherschutz durch Ausbildung eines Sonderprivatrechts für Verbraucher* (Berlin: Duncker & Humblot, 1983).
pp. 72 ff.; A. Fuchs, in PP. Ulmer/H.D. Brandner/H.E. Hensen, *AGB-Recht*, 13th ed. (Cologne: Otto Schmidt, 2022), introduction to §307 paras. 32 ff.; Leuschner, AcP 207 (2007), 491, 502 ff.

51 On this point Koller, in *Festschrift für Steindorff* (Berlin: De Gruyter, 1990), pp. 667, 669 f.; Coester-Waltjen, *AcP* 190 (1990), 1, 24 ff.; H.-B. Schäfer/C. Ott, ibid., pp. 553 f. Competition in the area of GTC thus risks to become a 'market for lemons' (fundamentally Akerlof, 84 *Quarterly Journal of Economics*, 488 [1970]), since the user can enforce the terms most favourable to them without risk due to the lack of control by the customer. As a result, balanced GTC tend to be driven out of the market, leaving behind Akerlof's 'lemons', i.e. GTC that are disadvantageous for the customer.

of different providers.[52] Competition is usually limited to the quality of the offer and the price. For this reason, there is no incentive for a rational user to formulate balanced GTC, as this would not be advantageous for them in terms of their greater attractiveness on the market. GTC control compensates for this functional deficit by declaring certain clauses invalid and replacing them with the rules of otherwise applicable dispositive law.[53]

**652.** Nevertheless, even this justification remains incomplete. If one assumes a market failure, then, from an economic point of view, a control is not justified for those areas where a market for GTC exists, i.e. if a rational customer can determine and compare the clauses of different providers with reasonable effort. In this respect, the control of GTC therefore reaches too far. On the other hand, from an economic point of view, it does not necessarily seem compelling that any control may only take place if it concerns clauses which are pre-formulated for a large number of contracts and which the user includes themselves; a market failure can also exist in the case of individual contractual agreements: If one assumes that parties tend to be over-optimistic concerning their performance,[54] then a content review would also make sense outside these specifications, for example, in the case of contractually and individually agreed lump-sum damages or contractual penalties.[55]

### *e) Proportionality Principle and GTC Control*

**653.** The central importance of the principle of proportionality within European contract law has already been emphasised.[56] It also contributes to the implementation of contractual equivalence in the area of GTC, which not only extends to the primary obligations but to the entire contract.[57] Nevertheless, the control of secondary obligations is structured differently than the scrutiny

---

52 T. Miethaner, *AGB-Kontrolle versus Individualvereinbarung. Zweck und Grenzen der Inhaltskontrolle vorformulierter Klauseln* (Tübingen: Mohr Siebeck, 2010), pp. 63 ff., speaks of the 'legitimate ignorance of the opponent of use towards pre-formulated provisions'.

53 In contrast, clause control does not lead to a restoration of competition on terms, cf. A. Fuchs, in P. Ulmer/H.D. Brandner/H.E. Hensen, *AGB-Recht*, 13th ed. (Cologne: Otto Schmidt, 2022), vor §307 para. 37.

54 Eidenmüller, *JZ* 2005, 216, 218 ff. on a corresponding correction of the model of homo oeconomicus by behavioural psychological findings.

55 On this point Rachlinski, 85 *Cornell L. Rev.* 739, 747 ff., 758, 760 ff. (2000).

56 See para. 460 above.

57 Equivalence is also understood in this sense, for example, by Bartholomeyczik, *AcP* 166 (1966), 30, 31; M. Wolf, *Rechtsgeschäftliche Entscheidungsfreiheit und vertraglicher Interessenausgleich* (Tübingen: Mohr Siebeck, 1970), p. 35; F. Bydlinski, *System und Prinzipien des Privatrechts* (Vienna: Springer, 1996), p. 156 with note 165, 756 ff. (according to whom the concept of equivalence has acquired its greatest significance precisely in the case of blatantly unequal distribution of risk through GTC); Canaris, *AcP* 200 (2000), 271, 285, 325 ff.

of primary obligations.[58] The prerequisite for controlling GTC is not an existing restriction of the freedom of decision. Instead, content control applies irrespective of whether the customer decides to conclude the contract in full knowledge of the GTC or if they do not pay any attention to them. The unique situation of a market failure in the area of GTC, which can be used to justify the content review, is not a constituent element, but, as shown, a justification of the review of clauses. Because of the diversity of the secondary contractual obligations, a comparison of different secondary obligations would not make sense. Thus, the individual clause to be assessed within the scope of the GTC review must be considered in light of the dispositive statutory law's standards or, in the case of non-regulated contract types, the purpose of the contract. Since many aspects can speak for an unreasonable disadvantage towards the customer, the user's interests in the validity of the clause and the interest in customer protection have to be considered. The material fairness standard for the proportionality test in GTC thus ultimately results from the legal transaction itself: The dispositive statutory law, which is the primary point of reference, also represents (albeit from the perspective of the legislator) what contracting parties would agree upon as an appropriate balance of interests. If there is no rule in this respect, the nature of the contract must be taken into account.

## IV. CONTENT REVIEW ACCORDING TO THE UNFAIR TERMS DIRECTIVE

### 1. CONTROL MECHANISMS

**654.** At the core of the Unfair Terms Directive lies the control of a clause's unfairness in Article 3(1) of the Directive, which concerns such provisions that 'contrary to the requirement of good faith, it causes a significant imbalance in the parties' rights and obligations arising under the contract, to the detriment of the consumer'; such clauses are non-binding for the consumer according to Article 6(1) of the Directive. This general provision is accompanied by an 'indicative and non-exhaustive list' of terms which, according to Article 3(3) of the Unfair Terms Directive, serve as a model of unfairness. The question here is whether the principle of autonomous interpretation of EU law also applies to

[58] In contrast, Canaris (*AcP* 200 [2000], 271, 326) sees a connection between the basic structures of the control of GTC and the elements required in sec. 138(2) German Civil Code. The parallel appears doubtful: in order to achieve a parallelism with the inferiority situation required by sec. 138(2) German Civil Code, this assumption would presuppose that the valid reason for the GTC control is an impairment of the customer's actual freedom of choice. Canaris himself justifies this, however, among others as here with the aspect of market failure (loc. cit., pp. 321 ff.).

the general clause of Article 3(1) of the Unfair Terms Directive and what role the 'grey list' in the Annex to the Directive plays.

**655.** This aspect became relevant in the *Freiburger Kommunalbauten* case, in which the German Federal Court of Justice had to review the validity of a property developer's contract clause according to which the purchase price was due irrespective of the progress of construction if only the property developer provides a guarantee for any claim the consumer might have against the developer out of the contract. The decisive question was whether this constituted an unfair disadvantage. This could be argued by the fact that the purchaser is deprived of the right of retention and has to prove the existence of a defect in order to obtain liability under the guarantee.[59] However, the court did not see any unfair disadvantage since the developer's liquidity is increased by advance performance; furthermore, the construction becomes cheaper, and the guarantee insofar secures any claims. Still, the court had doubts as to the compatibility with the Unfair Terms Directive and referred the question to the CJEU.[60]

## 2. CRITERIA OF ABUSE CONTROL

### *a) Requirements of the Directive*

**656.** The concept of unfairness, which requires a comprehensive assessment of both the subject matter of the contract and the circumstances of the conclusion of the contract, is central to the review of GTC. A clause may never be considered in an isolated perspective: according to Article 4(1) of the Unfair Terms Directive, the content of other contractual terms and even of terms of other contracts must always be considered whenever they appear to be connected with the clause in question. The Directive thus seems to prescribe the necessity of an overall assessment which must ponder the advantages and disadvantages of the individual provisions carefully. A seemingly unfair clause may be compensated elsewhere by the user's generosity. In addition, an examination of the circumstances of the conclusion of the contract is necessary: Here, too, the European legislator pursues a specific protective direction in favour of the 'inferior' consumer. Recital 16 of the Unfair Terms Directive specifies that the requirement of good faith includes 'the overall evaluation of the different interests involved'. Hence, it depends on the balance of power between the parties in the individual case; in particular, it might be important whether the user pushed the consumer in any way to conclude the contract or whether the conclusion of

59 In that sense OLG Karlsruhe BB 2001, 1325 as lower court.

60 BGH NZM 2002, 754; see subsequently CJEU, 1 April 2004, Case C-237/02, *Freiburger Kommunalbauten*, ECLI:EU:C:2004:209; see also para. 663 below.

the contract came about at the consumer's instigation, for example in the context of a custom-made product.[61]

*b) Autonomous Interpretation of the Directive's Requirements?*

**657.** Since these requirements are formulated in a general clause-like breadth despite the aforementioned guiding principles, the question arises as to how they can be fulfilled: Autonomously with the help of EU law standards or based on the respective applicable national law? A distinction must be made between the abstract interpretation of Article 3(1) of the Unfair Terms Directive and the concrete assessment of the unfairness of a term in an individual case. The latter is carried out according to the standard of the dispositive law otherwise applicable to the contract. The unfairness of the term is thus first determined by comparing it with those rules of the law applicable to the contract which the legislator considered to be a fair and balanced balance of interests, or, in the absence of such rules, by taking an evaluative stance regarding the regulatory purpose of the contract.[62]

**658.** Nevertheless, the concept of unfairness in Article 3(1) of the Unfair Terms Directive must be interpreted autonomously[63] and concretised with the help of the existing rules of EU law.[64] First, the legal principles in the Directives on private law can be used for further concretisation.[65] Since the European Court of Justice is increasingly developing a body of common European legal principles, the possibility of an autonomous European concretisation of the Unfair Terms Directive does not seem impossible in the medium or long term.[66]

---

61 Therefore, the term 'circumstancial inappropriateness' is sometimes used, cf. Heinrichs, *NJW* 1993, 1817, 1820.

62 So also CJEU, 1 April 2004, Case C-237/02, *Freiburger Kommunalbauten*, ECLI:EU:C:2004:209, paras. 21, 23.

63 For a case study highlighting the practical shortcomings concerning uniform interpretation, cf. Mišćenić/Tereszkiewicz/Infantino, *ERCL* 2023, 346.

64 On the concretisation of general clauses in European private law W.-.H. Roth, in *Festschrift für Drobnig*, (Tübingen: Mohr Siebeck, 1998), pp. 135, 145 ff.; Franzen, *Privatrechtsangleichung durch die Europäische Gemeinschaft*, 1999, p. 536 ff.; A. Röthel, *Normkonkretisierung im Privatrecht* (Tübingen: Mohr Siebeck, 2004), pp. 316 ff.; I. Wolff, *Die Verteilung der Konkretisierungskompetenz für Generalklauseln in privatrechtsgestaltenden Richtlinien* (Baden-Baden: Nomos, 2002), pp. 67 ff.; C. Schmid, *RabelsZ* 71 (2007), 147, 152 ff. See also the various contributions in C. Baldus/P.C. Müller-Graff (eds.), *Die Generalklausel im Europäischen Privatrecht. Zur Leistungsfähigkeit der deutschen Wissenschaft aus romanischer Perspektive* (Munich: Sellier, 2006).

65 Franzen, *Privatrechtsangleichung durch die Europäische Gemeinschaft*, 1999, pp. 564 ff.

66 In favour: Riesenhuber, *Europäisches Vertragsrecht*, 2nd ed. 2006, paras. 627 ff. Sceptical views in this respect prevail: Herresthal, in Langenbucher, *Europäisches Privat- und Wirtschaftsrecht*, §2 para. 122; Franzen, *Privatrechtsangleichung durch die Europäische Gemeinschaft*, 1999, pp. 571 ff.; M. Stoffels, *Gesetzlich nicht geregelte Schuldverträge. Rechtsfindung und Inhaltskontrolle* (Tübingen: Mohr Siebeck, 2002), pp. 507 ff.

This would be vital, for example, in the – currently – unlikely case that the DCFR is upgraded in some way so that an instrument would be available that contains rule-based expressions of common European legal principles.[67] The adoption of the proposal for a Common European Sales Law (currently equally unlikely) could have a similar effect: Both instruments would add to a body of dispositive law on an EU level which would have to be taken into account in the control of standard terms.

### c) *The Significance of the 'Grey List'*

**659.** In addition to the general provision of Article 3(1), the Unfair Terms Directive contains non-binding proposals in its annex regarding terms that can be regarded as unfair.[68] The Commission's draft of the Unfair Terms Directive still prescribed their binding nature; however, this version was not implemented, in particular at the instigation of the German government.[69] In this sense, the CJEU has also ruled that the transposition of the Unfair Terms Directive into Swedish national law without the 'grey list' does not constitute a violation of Article 249(3) TEC (now Article 288(3) TFEU).[70] Nevertheless, the role of the list of clauses is quite significant. It certainly has authority for the national legislator that goes beyond the character of a mere 'food for thought' kind of list. It should serve as a source of information for all individuals concerned; to this end, the list must be known to the general public.[71] Moreover, from the CJEU's point of view, the list can serve to specify the general clause of unfairness contained in Article 3(1) of the Unfair Terms Directive; according to the CJEU, the list has an 'indicative *and illustrative value*'.[72] The court considers it to be an 'essential element on which the competent court may base its assessment as to the unfair nature of that term'.[73]

---

67 On Article 3(1) of the Unfair Terms Directive as a lever for the advancement of legal harmonisation already Leible, *RIW* 2001, 422, 425 ff.

68 Making the case for a 'black list': Poncibò, *ERCL* 2023, 321.

69 Cf. the Green Paper on consumer goods guarantees and after-sales services, COM(1993) 509 final, pp. 70 ff.

70 CJEU, 7 May 2002, Case C-478/99, *Commission/Sweden*, ECLI:EU:C:2002:281. In doing so, the CJEU opposed the position of the Commission, which had considered a full transposition of the list to be necessary, cf. the 'Report from the Commission on the implementation of Council Directive 93/13/EEC of 5 April 1993 on unfair terms in consumer contracts', COM(2000) 248 final, p. 18.

71 This can be done, for example, as in Sweden, by publication in the legislative materials, cf. CJEU, 7 May 2002, Case C-478/99, *Commission/Sweden*, ECLI:EU:C:2002:281, para. 23. In this respect, the CJEU emphasised the Nordic legal tradition, according to which the legislative materials constitute an important aid to statutory interpretation.

72 CJEU, 7 May 2002, Case C-478/99, *Commission/Sweden*, ECLI:EU:C:2002:281, para. 22 (emphasis added).

73 CJEU, 3 April 2014, Case C-342/13, *Sebestyén*, EU:C:2014:1857, para. 32; CJEU, 19 September 2019, Case C-34/18, *Tóth*, ECLI:EU:C:2019:764, para. 45.

**660.** Hence, an indirect binding effect of the grey list does exist. Such a view also appears to be in line with the purpose of the Unfair Terms Directive as set out in Recital 15, which is to give the consumer a certain degree of certainty about the protection against unfair terms.[74] Even if the national legislator is free to deviate from this catalogue of clauses,[75] the terms on the grey list may nevertheless serve to interpret Article 3(1) of the Unfair Terms Directive.[76]

**661.** However, if the disproportional nature of a clause is beyond question, then the unfairness follows directly from the Directive itself; the CJEU found this to be the case in particular for a form-based choice of court agreement in a consumer contract.[77] In the decision in question, the CJEU had to decide on the validity of a jurisdiction clause which assigned jurisdiction for all disputes arising from the contract to the court in whose district the trader had their place of business. Here, in particular, the clause's unfairness was established by reference to the group of terms listed in point 1 q) of the Annex to the Unfair Terms Directive.[78] Such a term forces the consumer to accept the exclusive jurisdiction of a court that may be far from their domicile, which may make it difficult for them to appear in court. For small claims disputes, the consumer's costs of appearing in court could be a deterrent and discourage them from taking legal action or even defending themselves. On the other hand, this clause allows the entrepreneur to concentrate all litigation relating to their business in front of the court in whose district they are established, which both facilitates their appearance in terms of organisation and reduces the costs involved.[79] This leads to a significant and unjustified imbalance in the contractual rights and obligations of the contracting parties pursuant to Article 3(1) of the Unfair Terms Directive, so that such a clause must be considered unfair.[80]

---

74 Also Riesenhuber, *Europäisches Vertragsrecht*, 2nd ed. 2006, paras. 640 ff. For an opposing view, cf. Franzen, *Privatrechtsangleichung durch die Europäische Gemeinschaft*, 1999, pp. 558 ff., who argues that the grey list should only serve to concretise the corresponding national transposition provision.

75 Cf. explicitly CJEU, 7 May 2002, Case C-478/99, *Commission/Sweden*, ECLI:EU:C:2002:281, para. 20; likewise CJEU, 1 April 2004, Case C-237/02, *Freiburger Kommunalbauten*, ECLI:EU:C:2004:209, para. 20.

76 Riesenhuber, *Europäisches Vertragsrecht*, 2nd ed. 2006, para. 643, 648 ff.

77 CJEU, 27 June 2000, Joined Cases C-240/98 to C-244/98, *Océano*, ECLI:EU:C:2000:346, paras. 21 ff.

78 CJEU, 27 June 2000, Joined Cases C-240/98 to C-244/98, *Océano*, ECLI:EU:C:2000:346; CJEU, 4 June 2009, Case C-243/08, *Pannon GSM*, ECLI:EU:C:2009:350.

79 CJEU, 27 June 2000, Joined Cases C-240/98 to C-244/98, *Océano*, ECLI:EU:C:2000:346.

80 A particular setting was to be found in CJEU, 3 April 2019, Case C-266/18, *Aqua Med/Skóra*, ECLI:EU:C:2019:282: Here, a purely national consumer contract contained the following clause: '[t]he court which has jurisdiction to hear disputes between the parties shall be the court which has the jurisdiction under the relevant provisions.' The CJEU held that this clause was in principle capable of being reviewed, as the clause was not based on a binding provision within the meaning of Article 1(2) of the Unfair Terms Directive (paras. 33 ff.). See para. 631 above.

**662.** Apart from such evident exceptions, however, the control of the clause is left to national law.[81] Thus, in the view of the CJEU, a contract term which has not been negotiated in detail and which aims to shift the burden of proof to the detriment of the consumer or has the effect of doing so cannot be qualified as unfair in general, despite the wording in Annex no. 1(q) of the Unfair Terms Directive.[82]

**663.** In the *Freiburger Kommunalbauten* case, the core issue to be examined is whether the pertinent provision of the German Civil Code,[83] according to which the remuneration is only due upon acceptance of the work, was effectively waived by the contractual clause. In principle, this provision was dispositive.[84] However, it is possible that the contractual clause leads to an unreasonable disadvantage for the purchaser and is thus invalid. This is supported by the fact that the advance payment agreed in the form of a contract deprives the orderer of the right to refuse performance. The legal concept, according to which the contractor is in principle obliged to perform in advance, is reversed. In addition, the burden of proof that a defect in the work exists now rests with the buyer.[85] In this respect, the agreement deviates from the essential basic ideas of the contractor's advance performance obligation thus and disadvantages the consumer in an unfear manner.[86]

**664.** On the other hand, such a contractual clause has the effect of increasing the developer's liquidity with the possible consequence that the construction becomes cheaper. The contractual partner is sufficiently secured by the guarantee in case the work has defects.[87] This legitimate interest is reflected in a provision according to which the contractor can demand partial payments depending on the progress of the construction. Furthermore, the guarantee minimises the risk of insolvency, since in the event of the developer's insolvency a third party is liable in the form of the bank. If this view is taken under domestic law, there is no unreasonable disadvantage.

---

81 CJEU, 1 April 2004, Case C-237/02, *Freiburger Kommunalbauten*, ECLI:EU:C:2004:209, para. 22.

82 CJEU, 19 September 2019, Case C-34/18, *Tóth*, ECLI:EU:C:2019:764, paras. 45 ff.

83 Today, there is a special provision for construction contracts in sec. 650g(4) German Civil Code, which also applies to consumer construction contracts in accordance with sec. 650i German Civil Code.

84 J. Busche, in *Münchener Kommentar zum BGB*, 9th ed. (Munich: C.H. Beck, 2023), §641 paras. 12, 16.

85 The situation may be different if a guarantee is provided on first demand. In this case, there is no need to prove a defect.

86 Therefore making the case for an invalidity of the clause: OLG Karlsruhe BB 2001, 1325 (as appellate court).

87 Cf. BGH NZM 2002, 754 (order referring requesting a preliminary ruling).

**665.** However, this result might contradict the requirements of the Unfair Terms Directive. The question is whether the agreement must be considered unfair within the meaning of Article 3(1) of the Unfair Terms Directive. First of all, there could be a violation of the clauses listed in the Annex to the Unfair Terms Directive under point 1 lit. b and o. This, in itself, is problematic, as it is not possible to determine whether the agreement is unfair. The problem here, however, is that the clauses listed in the Annex are not binding and merely serve as examples. The question, therefore, arises as to how the unfairness in Article 3(1) Unfair Terms Directive is to be understood. In principle, an autonomous interpretation of the directive provision is necessary. However, this is difficult in the case of a general clause such as this. According to Article 4 of the Unfair Terms Directive, the nature of the goods and services that are the subject of the contract as well as all circumstances surrounding the conclusion of the contract must be taken into account. This also requires an assessment of the consequences that the clause may have in the context of the law applicable to the contract. Thus, a complete assessment can only be made by considering the rules of the respective national legal system as well.[88] However, since the CJEU is not called upon to assess national law, a complete concretisation of the concept of unfairness remains impossible.

**666.** At most, it could be argued that a clause is unfair if it violates fundamental legal principles recognised in all private law systems. In the present case, it could be argued that the contractual clause violated the principle that performances are to be fulfilled step by step in a reciprocal relationship, and, thus, procedural equality of the contracting parties is waived to the consumer's detriment, especially if there is a dispute about defects of the construction work.[89] However, this does not seem compelling, given the guarantee provided. The CJEU stated that the specification of the concept of unfairness is left to the courts of the Member States, at least to the extent that 'without having to consider all the circumstances in which the contract was concluded and without having to assess the advantages and disadvantages that that term would have under the national law applicable to the contract'.[90] According to Article 4(1) of the Unfair Terms Directive, this must be done by taking into account the nature of the goods or services which are the subject of the contract and all the circumstances surrounding the conclusion of the contract. Here, according to the CJEU, the consequences that the clause may have in the context of the law applicable to

---

[88] CJEU, 1 April 2004, Case C-237/02, *Freiburger Kommunalbauten*, ECLI:EU:C:2004:209, para. 21.

[89] See the party submission to this effect: CJEU, 1 April 2004, Case C-237/02, *Freiburger Kommunalbauten*, ECLI:EU:C:2004:209, para. 17.

[90] CJEU, 1 April 2004, Case C-237/02, *Freiburger Kommunalbauten*, ECLI:EU:C:2004:209, para. 23. For further details, see Stürner, in von Bar/Wudarski (eds.), *Deutschland und Polen in der Europäischen Rechtsgemeinschaft*, 2012, pp. 65 ff.

the contract must also be assessed, which implies an examination of the national legal system.[91] However, it does not follow from this that an exceptionally knowledgeable consumer is less worthy of protection.[92] The standard remains a general one; exceptions seem to be appropriate at most if the GTC were only made for a few contracts.

### d) *Proportionality as a Guiding Principle of Abuse Control*

**667.** The wording of Article 3(1) of the Unfair Terms Directive already indicates that a term appears to be unfair whenever it deprives the consumer of rights to which they would otherwise be entitled or imposes obligations on them that do not exist and, in return, relieves the user of the GTC, so that a significant and unjustified imbalance of the respective rights and obligations of the contracting parties arises. This touches on the principle of proportionality: A relationship is established between the purpose pursued by the user with the clause and the intensity of the curtailment of consumer rights: The lower the user's creditable interest in a clause, the more likely it is that an 'unjustified' imbalance will exist and vice versa. This is confirmed by clause no 1 lit. e of the 'Grey List': According to this clause, a consumer who does not fulfil their contractual obligations may not be charged a disproportionately high amount of compensation. What is disproportionately high in this context depends, among other things, on the purpose of the provision, the type of breach of contractual duty and the amount of damage incurred.

**668.** In addition, granting a unilateral power to change prices by the user is in principle only permissible if the consumer is granted a right to dissolve the contract if the final price is 'too high' compared to the agreed price. This results from clause no 1 lit. l in the Annex to the Unfair Terms Directive, which covers price adjustment clauses.[93] This is also an instance of an application of the principle of proportionality: It cannot be determined abstractly when the final price is 'too high'. Instead, this again requires consideration of the interest that the user has in such a unilateral price change clause. In any case, cost increases over which the user has no influence are acceptable.[94]

---

91 CJEU, 1 April 2004, Case C-237/02, *Freiburger Kommunalbauten*, ECLI:EU:C:2004:209, para. 21.

92 Cf., however, Remien, *ZEuP* 1994, 34, 53; cf. also S. Grundmann, *Europäisches Schuldvertragsrecht* (Berlin: De Gruyter, 1999), p. 264.

93 See also para. 682 below.

94 Another provision on the right to change prices can be found in Article 4(4) of the Package Travel Directive; however, unlike the price adjustment clause, this stipulates exclusive criteria according to which a change may be made.

## 3. TRANSPARENCY CONTROL

References: F. Esposito/M. Grochowski, 'The Consumer Benchmark, Vulnerability, and the Contract Terms Transparency: A Plea for Reconsideration', *ERCL* 2022, 1; M.B.M. Loos, 'Crystal Clear? The Transparency Requirement in Unfair Terms Legislation', *ERCL* 2023, 281.

**669.** According to Article 5 of the Unfair Terms Directive, clauses 'must always be drafted in plain, intelligible language'.[95] Even if the Directive does not link any direct sanction to this postulate – except in connection with primary obligations (Article 4(2) Unfair Terms Directive) – the lack of transparency is nevertheless a factor to be taken into account in the context of abuse control according to Article 3(1) Unfair Terms Directive.[96]

**670.** According to the interpretation of the CJEU, the term 'main subject-matter of the contract', which must be understood identically in both Article 4(2) and Article 5 of the Unfair Terms Directive,[97] includes those clauses which determine the primary performance of the contract and characterise it as such, i.e., provisions which define the essence of the contractual relationship itself. This is determined by considering the nature, the system and the provisions of the contract as well as the legal and factual context in which it is embedded. Note that clauses of a merely ancillary nature, do not fall under this concept.[98]

**671.** In the case of clauses relating to the primary performance obligations, transparency requires not only that they are grammatically comprehensible for the consumer;[99] rather, they must also enable the consumer to assess the resulting economic consequences for them on the basis of precise and comprehensible criteria.[100] This can be problematic in the case of clauses that regulate processing fees in the context of consumer loans. Here, the consumer must be able to check based on the clauses that the various fees or services do not overlap. However,

---

95 For a detailed account of the requirements of this provision and consequences of violations, cf. Loos, *ERCL* 2023, 281.

96 CJEU, 3 October 2019, Case C-621/17, *Kiss*, ECLI:EU:C:2019:820, para. 49.

97 CJEU, 30 April 2014, Case C-26/13, *Kásler*, ECLI:EU:C:2014:282, paras. 67 ff.; CJEU, 3 October 2019, Case C-621/17, *Kiss*, ECLI:EU:C:2019:820, para. 36.C.

98 CJEU, 20 September 2017, Case C-186/16, *Andriciuc*, ECLI:EU:C:2017:703, paras. 35 f.; CJEU, 3 October 2019, Case C-621/17, *Kiss*, ECLI:EU:C:2019:820, paras. 32 f.

99 The CJEU commonly refers to the 'average consumer', as mentioned in Recital 18 of the Unfair Terms Directive, cf., e.g. CJEU, 30 April 2014, Case C-26/13, *Kásler*, ECLI:EU:C:2014:282, para. 74; CJEU, 3 October 2019, Case C-621/17, *Kiss*, ECLI:EU:C:2019:820, para. 27. For a critical account of the approach the CJEU takes, cf. Esposito/Grochowski, *ERCL* 2022, 1.

100 CJEU, 9 July 2015, Case C-348/14, *Bucura*, ECLI:EU:C:2015:447, para. 55; CJEU, 3 October 2019, Case C-621/17, *Kiss*, ECLI:EU:C:2019:820, para. 37; CJEU, 3 March 2020, Case C-125/18, *Gómez*; ECLI:EU:C:2020:138, paras. 46, 50.

this does not mean that a clause specifying the amounts of the handling fee and the commitment fee to be paid by the consumer, the method of calculating them, and the date on which they are due must also specify in detail all the services provided in return for the amounts in question.[101]

## 4. EX OFFICIO JUDICIAL REVIEW?

References: A. Beka, *The Active Role of Courts in Consumer Litigation. Applying EU Law of the Nationale Courts' Own Motion* (Cambridge: Intersentia, 2018).

**672.** Since the civil procedural systems are still largely in the realm of domestic law, procedural contexts can arise in which a claim is successfully granted by a court even though it is based on an unfair clause. This may be the case, for example, in order for payment proceedings, where, at most, a conclusiveness check of the asserted claim is carried out. This undoubtedly affects the practical effectiveness of the Unfair Terms Directive. In this respect, the CJEU has assumed that the content review should be carried out ex officio, if necessary.[102] This should at least apply if the court has the necessary legal and factual competence to do so.[103]

**673.** This issue can be particularly problematic for the European order for payment procedure under Regulation (EC) 1896/2006. This is based precisely on a reduced standard of review. Otherwise, it could not fulfil its function of offering a simple and quick way to acquire an enforceable title throughout the EU (Article 1 with Recitals 9 and 29 European Order for Payment Procedure Regulation). For the debtor, there is certainly the risk of surrendering to the order for payment without objection, even if it was issued based on an unreasonable contractual clause. In order to prevent this, the court hearing the application for an order for payment may have to request further information from the creditor ex officio in order to assess the possible unfairness of a contractual term.[104]

101 CJEU, 3 October 2019, Case C-621/17, *Kiss*, ECLI:EU:C:2019:820, paras. 42 ff.

102 CJEU, 14 June 2012, Case C-618/10, *Banco Español de Crédito*, ECLI:EU:C:2012:349; also CJEU, 19 December 2019, Joined Cases C-453/18 and C-494/18, *Bondora*, ECLI:EU:C:2019:1118. However, this ex officio review only extends to the clauses directly at issue, CJEU, 11 March 2020, Case C-511/17, *Lintner*, ECLI:EU:C:2020:188, paras. 30 ff. See already para. 1374 above.

103 CJEU, 4 June 2009, Case C-243/08, *Pannon GSM*, ECLI:EU:C:2009:350, para. 32; CJEU, 7 November 2019, Joined Cases C-419/18 and C-483/18, *Profi Credit Polska*, ECLI:EU:C:2019:930, para. 42; CJEU, 19 December 2019, Joined Cases C-453/18 and C-494/18, *Bondora*, ECLI:EU:C:2019:1118, para. 42.

104 CJEU, 19 December 2019, Joined Cases C-453/18 and C-494/18, *Bondora*, ECLI:EU:C:2019:1118, paras. 47 ff. referring to the principle of fair trial in Article 38 of the Charter of Fundamental Rights.

**674.** If this is established, the court is generally obliged to inform the parties of this and hear the case in the form provided for this by the respective procedural rules.[105] However, the decision to seek the appropriate remedy rests with the consumer: The Unfair Terms Directive does not oblige the court to leave unfair contract terms unenforced if the consumer does not wish to claim unfairness and non-bindingness after notice from this court.[106] Consequently, this does not mean that the legal examination must always be carried out before the defence has been filed.[107] Such a compulsory ex officio examination would nevertheless be permissible under European Union law.[108]

## 5. LEGAL CONSEQUENCES IN THE EVENT OF UNFAIRNESS

References: C. Bresci, 'Transparency Claims, Intellectual Services and Consumer Contracts: A Case of Consumer Over-Protection and Under-Protection?', *ERCL* 2023, 394; M. Ginestri, 'Equality or Superiority of the Weak Party? Consumer Protection and the Issues at Stake', *ERCL* 2023, 375; B. Gsell, 'Lückenfüllung insbesondere durch ergänzende Vertragsauslegung und Schicksal des Gesamtvertrages bei missbräuchlichen Klauseln in Verbraucherverträgen – Einfluss des EuGH auf die Rechtsprechung des BGH', in J. Kindl/T. Arroyo Vendrell (eds.), *Die Rechtsprechung des EuGH und ihr Einfluss auf die nationalen Privatrechtsordnungen* (Baden-Baden: Nomos, 2019), p. 63; B. Gsell/M. Fervers, 'Ergänzende Vertragsauslegung bei der AGB-Kontrolle im unionsrechtlichen Kontext', *NJW* 2019, 2569; A.D. Tassikas, 'The Court and the Sleeping Beauty 2.0: Filling the Contractual Gap, or Making Valid Consumer Contracts to the Detriment of the Non-consumer?', *ERCL* 2023, 422.

### a) *Unfair Clause Not Binding*

**675.** The Unfair Terms Directive only stipulates in Article 6(1) that unfair terms shall not bind the consumer; more detailed requirements are found in the laws of the Member States. The latter should also provide that the contract remains binding for both parties on the same basis if it can exist without the unfair terms in question.

[105] CJEU, 21 February 2013, Case C-472/11, *Banif Plus Bank*, ECLI:EU:C:2013:88, paras. 31 f.; CJEU, 7 November 2019, Joined Cases C-419/18 and C-483/18, *Profi Credit Polska*, ECLI:EU:C:2019:930, para. 70; CJEU, 11 March 2020, Case C-511/17, *Lintner*, ECLI:EU:C:2020:188, para. 42.

[106] CJEU, 4 June 2009, Case C-243/08, *Pannon GSM*, ECLI:EU:C:2009:350, para. 33; CJEU, 11 March 2020, Case C-511/17, *Lintner*, ECLI:EU:C:2020:188, para. 43.

[107] In that sense, however, Rieländer, *GPR* 2020, 55, 62 ff.

[108] This follows from the principle of minimum harmonisation, Article 8 Unfair Terms Directive: CJEU, 11 March 2020, Case C-511/17, *Lintner*, ECLI:EU:C:2020:188, para. 41.

### b) *No Reduction of Unfair Terms in Order to Preserve their Validity*

**676.** Reducing an invalid clause to preserve its validity is generally understood to mean a reduction to a level that no longer brings about the legal consequence disapproved of by the law.[109] This can be achieved by bringing the clause to what maybe seen to be fair and balanced.[110] But one could also think of reducing the unfairness to a level just below what is deemed to be unfair.[111] Such reduction of objectionable GTC to preserve their validity seems to run counter the idea to remove unfair terms from B2C contracts, as stipulated in Recital 6 of the Directive and repeated in its Article 7(1) and Recital 24. It is the clear intention of Article 6(1) Unfair Terms Directive, which stresses that unfair clauses must not be binding on the consumer, to prevent the user from using objectionable clauses without risk.[112] In addition, a cleansing function of the control of GTC may be called upon, which is intended to ensure that, because of the sanction of nullity, only fair standard terms are used from the outset, and in this way, the customer is provided with clear information on the scope of their rights and obligations (transparency principle).[113] Finally, it is argued that it is not the judge's but the trader's task to intervene in the structure of the contract and to determine the permissible content of the contract.[114]

**677.** The fact that the total nullity of objectionable clauses resulting from the prohibition of a reduction that preserves the validity of the contract can, in turn, lead to inappropriate results by disadvantaging the user unilaterally is also brought forward by opponents of such a reduction. In order to avoid these contradictions, various solutions have been suggested, above all the supplementary interpretation of the contract.[115] This solution is particularly important in cases where the filling of contractual gaps by dispositive statutory law because there is no suitable provision, for example, because the respective clause is contained in a type of contract that is not regulated by law. In the case

---

109 H. Schmidt, in P. Ulmer/H.D. Brandner/H.E. Hensen, *AGB-Recht*, 13th ed. (Cologne: Otto Schmidt, 2022), §306 para. 14.

110 Canaris, in *Festschrift für Steindorff* (Berlin: De Gruyter, 1990), pp. 519, 529 f., 549 f.; also J. Hager, *JZ* 1996, 175, 176; H. Roth, *JZ* 1989, 411, 414 f., 417 f.

111 In that sense BGHZ 90, 69, 81 f.

112 See, for example, BGHZ 84, 109, 116; BGH NJW 2006, 1059, 1060; H. Schmidt, in P. Ulmer/H.D. Brandner/H.E. Hensen, *AGB-Recht*, 13th ed. (Cologne: Otto Schmidt, 2022), § 306 para. 14; Grüneberg, in Grüneberg, *BGB Kommentar*, 84th ed. 2025, §306 para. 6. Critically, J. Hager, *JZ* 1996, 175, 176 ff.

113 BGHZ 96, 18, 25 f.; BGH NJW 2006, 1059, 1060; H. Schmidt, in P. Ulmer/H.D. Brandner/H.E. Hensen, *AGB-Recht*, 13th ed. (Cologne: Otto Schmidt, 2022), §306 para. 14.

114 BGH NJW 1984, 48, 49.

115 Detailed account given in *Uffmann, Das Verbot der geltungserhaltenden Reduktion*, 2010, pp. 120 ff., 149 ff., 175 ff.

law of the German Federal Supreme Court,[116] it is recognised that in the absence of dispositive statutory rules in individual proceedings,[117] a supplementary interpretation of the contract is to be made, which creates a regulation in line with the interests of the parties instead of the invalid clause.[118] In this way, a completely one-sided preferential treatment of the customer is prevented.[119]

**678.** According to the case law of the CJEU, filling gaps by means of dispositive statutory law is only in line with the Unfair Terms Directive as long as it prevents the total nullity of the contract, which is detrimental to the consumer.[120] However, a judicial contract adjustment does not occur if an unfair term is invalid.[121] According to the wording of Article 6(1) Unfair Terms Directive, the unfair term cannot be amended by the national court. This follows from the fact that the contract must, in principle, continue to exist unchanged but without the respective clause – in so far as, in the words of the CJEU, in accordance with the rules of domestic law, such continuity of the contract is legally possible.[122] The Unfair Terms Directive aims to achieve a balance between the parties.[123] Hence, whether the contract could continue without the unfair term is not to be assessed solely based on whether an overall nullity of the contract proves

---

116 BGH NJW 2008, 2172, 2175 as well as previously BGHZ 90, 69, 75; BGH NJW 1984, 1180, 1181; BGH NJW 1985, 621, 622 with further references (price adjustment clauses).

117 In collective proceedings, the question of gap filling of the individual contract does not arise, cf. H. Schmidt, in P. Ulmer/H.D. Brandner/H.E. Hensen, *AGB-Recht*, 13th ed. (Cologne: Otto Schmidt, 2022), § 306 para. 36.

118 The German legal literature predominantly agrees with the established case law of the BGH, cf. Grüneberg, in Grüneberg, *BGB Kommentar*, 84th ed. 2025, § 306 para. 13; H. Schmidt, in P. Ulmer/H.D. Brandner/H.E. Hensen, *AGB-Recht*, 13th ed. (Cologne: Otto Schmidt, 2022), § 306 para. 34 ff. with further references; H. Roth, *AcP* 190 (1990), 292, 312 ff.; M. Stoffels, *Gesetzlich nicht geregelte Schuldverträge. Rechtsfindung und Inhaltskontrolle* (Tübingen: Mohr Siebeck, 2002), pp. 536 ff. Against this approach e.g. Steindorff, *ZHR* 148 (1984), 271, 276 f.; Häsemeyer, in *Festschrift für Ulmer* (Berlin: De Gruyter, 2003), pp. 1097, 1106 f. (the supplementary interpretation leads to a 'judicial petrification' of the party-autonomous options for drafting).

119 BGHZ 137, 153, 157.

120 CJEU, 30 April 2014, Case C-26/13, *Kásler*, ECLI:EU:C:2014:282, paras. 82 ff.; CJEU, 7 August 2018, Case C-96/16, *Banco Santander and Escobedo Cortés*, ECLI:EU:C:2018:643, para. 74; CJEU, 20 September 2018, Case C-51/17, *OTP Bank and OTP Faktoring*, ECLI:EU:C:2018:750, para. 61; CJEU, 14 March 2019, Case C-118/17, *Dunai/ERSTE Bank Hungary*, ECLI:EU:C:2019:207, para. 54; CJEU, 26 March 2019, Joined Cases C-70/17 and C-179/17, *Abanca*, ECLI:EU:C:2019:250, paras. 56 ff.; CJEU, 3 October 2019, C-260/18, *Dziubak*, ECLI:EU:C:2019:819, para. 48; CJEU, 3 March 2020, Case C-125/18, *Gómez*; ECLI:EU:C:2020:138, paras. 61 ff.

121 CJEU, 14 June 2012, Case C-618/10, *Banco Español de Crédito*, ECLI:EU:C:2012:349. See Stürner, *ZEuP* 2013, 671.

122 CJEU, 14 June 2012, Case C-618/10, *Banco Español de Crédito*, ECLI:EU:C:2012:349, para. 65.

123 As previously CJEU, 15 March 2012, Case C-453/10, *Pereničová*, ECLI:EU:C:2012:144, para. 31.

to be advantageous for the consumer in the specific individual case.[124] The CJEU based this finding essentially on the deterrent effect that Article 6(1) of the Unfair Terms Directive was intended to have: If the entrepreneur could rely on the fact that an unfair term was not ineffective but would be amended by way of adaptation to a level that was no longer unfair, this could actually create an incentive to include unfair terms in the contract. This would jeopardise the objective pursued by Article 7(1) as well as Recital 24 of the Unfair Terms Directive to 'prevent the continued use of unfair terms in consumer contracts'.[125]

**679.** These statements of the CJEU are, in themselves and especially from a German perspective, not particularly spectacular at first. It has long been recognised in the case law of the Federal Court of Justice that a so-called reduction of unfair terms in order to preserve their validity would be incompatible with the protective purpose of standard terms control.[126] The preventive idea behind this, among other things, coincides with the argumentation used by the CJEU. The rest of the contract remains valid; the gap created by the nullity of the unfair term is filled by dispositive statutory law. In the absence of corresponding provisions, the principles of supplementary contractual interpretation apply.[127] This is based on the consideration that, for example, the omission without replacement of a price adjustment clause that unreasonably disadvantages the customer would shift the contractual structure unilaterally in the customer's favour.[128] Only then, if no balanced solution can be found that considers both parties' interests, is the contract as a whole to be denied validity. This step-by-step examination considers the principle expressed in Article 6(1) Unfair Terms Directive of the maintenance of the contract.[129] Usually, it also protects the customer since a total nullity of the contract would deprive them of the benefits of the legal transaction; services already exchanged would have to be reversed.

---

124 CJEU, 15 March 2012, Case C-453/10, *Pereničová*, ECLI:EU:C:2012:144, para. 32. Nevertheless, the law of that Member State law may provide for this legal consequence in view of the minimum harmonising character of the Clauses Directive (loc. cit., para. 34).

125 CJEU, 14 June 2012, Case C-618/10, *Banco Español de Crédito*, ECLI:EU:C:2012:349, para. 68.

126 Cf. BGHZ 84, 109, 114 ff.; BGHZ 143, 103, 119; BGH NJW 2011, 139 para. 27 with further references. Other legal systems also limit themselves in principle to the total nullity of objectionable clauses without considering a reduction that preserves the validity, see the references in von Bar/Clive (eds.), *Principles, Definitions and Model Rules of European Private Law, Full Edition*, Volume I, 2009, Note 9 on Article II.-9:408 DCFR (where again essentially the content of the Unfair Terms Directive is repeated without taking a position on the problem).

127 See only BGHZ 137, 153, 157.

128 BGHZ 90, 78.

129 On this point, Stürner, *Der Grundsatz der Verhältnismäßigkeit im Schuldvertragsrecht*, 2010, pp. 131 f.

**680.** However, it is questionable whether the filling of gaps by supplementary contractual interpretation undertaken by case law can be upheld in view of the requirements of the *Banesto* decision.[130] This is because the CJEU's argumentation is essentially based on the fact that the review of terms should be dissuasive; only in this way, the court argues, could the long-term goal of the Unfair Terms Directive – the elimination of all unfair terms from consumer contracts – be achieved. Hence, one might object to the supplementary interpretation of contracts. From a functional point of view, it could be considered an inadmissible change in the content of the unfair term. Such a view, however, would fail to take into account the fact that the Unfair Terms Directive does indeed have a market-regulating function; in principle, the Directive aims to leave the contractual equivalence relationship untouched.[131] The question of gap-filling was only indirectly addressed by the CJEU in the *Banesto* case; it is governed by Member State law in any case. A unilateral shift of the contractual balance in favour of the customer does not create the 'effective balance' that the CJEU calls for.[132] Supplementary contract interpretation should therefore continue to be permissible as long as it does not counteract the deterrent effect intended by the Unfair Terms Directive.[133] This initially concerns contracts in which the loophole would result in disadvantages for the consumer. In practice, however, this case is hardly conceivable since the omission of an unfair term puts the consumer in a better position per se. However, constellations are possible in which the contract as a whole would be invalid according to Article 6(1) Unfair Terms Directive.[134] This could be the case with the notoriously controversial ancillary price agreements. If, for example, in the case of ineffective price adjustment clauses in natural gas supply contracts, one party claims a substantial disruption of the equivalence relationship because of the clause being null and void, nullification of the contract would lead to a substantial disadvantage for the customer. What remains here is the option to fill the gap through a supplementary contract interpretation, which, however, can only be considered if leaving the gap in the contract 'leads to a result that no longer takes account

[130] Stürner, *ZEuP* 2013, 671.

[131] Rott, *ERCL* 2012, 470, 476 f., focusing unilaterally on the former point of view and without discussing the admissibility of supplementary contract interpretation. The consequences of this approach remain largely blurred.

[132] CJEU, 14 June 2012, Case C-618/10, *Banco Español de Crédito*, ECLI:EU:C:2012:349, para. 63. For a critical account of the approach taken by the CJEU, cf. Tassikas, *ERCL* 2023, 422.

[133] In this sense also *Grüneberg*, in Grüneberg, BGB Kommentar, 84th ed. 2025, §306 para. 13; Schlosser, *IPRax* 2012, 507, 514 f.; see already Stürner, *Der Grundsatz der Verhältnismäßigkeit im Schuldvertragsrecht*, 2010, pp. 131 f. However, Uffmann, *NJW* 2012, 2225, 2229 f. probably differs, who apparently assumes that supplementary contract interpretation is inadmissible within the scope of the Clause Directive.

[134] See also Schlosser, *IPRax* 2012, 507, 515.

of the mutual interests in a justifiable manner, but rather shifts the contractual structure unilaterally in favour of the customer'.[135]

**681.** The German Federal Court of Justice ruled in this sense in two judgments of 23 January 2013, again on gas supply contracts.[136] The supplementary interpretation of the contract had not been addressed by the CJEU in the *Banesto* case; the Court had only rejected the reduction that preserved the validity of the contract. The possibility of a referral to the CJEU was not even addressed by the court. Nevertheless, doubts remain whether the legal consequences found within case law for ineffective clauses are sufficient in all facets to fulfil the CJEU's categorical prohibition of a contract adjustment. Commentators have indeed criticised such supplementary contract interpretation, claiming that it is a reduction that preserves the contract's validity in disguise. Since the interests of the public involved in legal transactions of this kind are essentially used to determine the hypothetical will of the parties, and thus an objective standard is applied, this type of gap-filling does not differ fundamentally from a judicial supplementation of the contract in the form of a reduction that preserves the validity of the contract, at least if one assumes that this does not necessarily mean a reduction to the content that is still legally permissible, but rather the achievement of an appropriate solution.[137]

### c) *In Particular: Legal Consequences in Case of Transparency Control*

**682.** Under German law, the intransparency of a clause may entail the invalidity of the standard term.[138] With regard to the legal consequences, this leads to the problem that an unclearly formulated promise of performance by the user would be void; however, this would not serve the consumer. Some cases can be solved on the factual level since the lack of transparency does not necessarily lead to invalidity. The reverse case of a hidden price increase in an unclearly formulated clause is also discussed controversially. One consequence of the invalidity of the clause is plain: There would be no price agreement at all. The ramifications of this case can be illustrated by cases regarding price adjustment clauses:[139]

---

135 BGH NJW 2008, 2172, 2175; BGH NJW 2010, 993, 997, in each case with references.

136 BGH NJW 2013, 991 and BGH EnWZ 2013, 225.

137 Canaris, in *Festschrift für Steindorff* (Berlin: De Gruyter, 1990), pp. 519, 552 ff.; K. Uffmann, *Das Verbot der geltungserhaltenden Reduktion* (Tübingen: Mohr Siebeck, 2010), pp. 57 ff, 149 ff., 175 ff.; Ginestri, *ERCL* 2023, 375; see also Stürner, *Der Grundsatz der Verhältnismäßigkeit im Schuldvertragsrecht*, 2010, pp. 129 ff., 432 ff. A reduction that preserves validity is advocated in particular if the provision intended by the clause was based on a justifiable legal opinion, i.e. the user was in good faith with regard to its effectiveness, see Kötz, *NJW* 1979, 785, 789; H. Roth, *JZ* 1989, 411, 418.

138 See para. 669 above.

139 For other examples, cf. Bresci, *ERCL* 2023, 394.

**683.** A Consumer orders a new car from an authorised car dealer; the delivery time is six months. The purchase contract contains the following clause: 'The current list price on the day of delivery applies.' At the time of delivery, the list price is 10% higher than the price at the time of the conclusion of the contract. The consumer wants to know whether he has to pay the increase.[140]

**684.** The German Federal Court of Justice found this term to be invalid. For the Court, an unfair disadvantage lies in the fact that it is not comprehensible for consumers how the final price is being determined. Moreover, not only does the term enable the dealer to pass on direct price increases (e.g. due to increased energy costs). Rather, the trader can exploit a changed market situation in general, which allows for larger profit margins, to increase prices almost at will. Such a unilateral right to determine performance violates the principle of equivalence. This assessment is in line with the Unfair Terms Directive. Here, the clause in Annex no. 1(l) Unfair Terms Directive can be used to interpret Article 3(1) Unfair Terms Directive,[141] so that the interpretation of the German Federal Court of Justice, in any case, meets the requirements of the Directive. The CJEU also requires price adjustment clauses to be transparent.[142]

**685.** The question arises, then, how to fill this gap. First, dispositive statutory law may be referred to. However, since the price adjustment clause concerns a primary obligation, there are no such provisions.[143] Therefore, by way of a supplementary interpretation of the contract, the Federal Court of Justice filled the gap to the effect that, although the price at the time of delivery applies, the buyer has a right of withdrawal if this price deviates too much from the original list price. At least from a formal point of view, this does not appear to be an inadmissible reduction that preserves the contract's validity, but a fair balance of the parties' interests.

**686.** This can be extended to all price adjustment clauses: They must be formulated in such a way that the customer can check the relevant cost elements; furthermore, the weight of these elements for the price must be indicated, and finally, it must be possible to compensate for the increase of one cost factor by the

140 BGHZ 90, 69.

141 On the significance of the 'grey list', see para. 659.

142 CJEU, 26 April 2012, Case C-472/10, *Invitel*, ECLI:EU:C:2012:242, paras. 27 ff.; CJEU, 30 April 2014, Case C-26/13, *Kásler*, ECLI:EU:C:2014:282, paras. 60 ff.

143 BGHZ 90, 69, 80 ff. Price adjustment clauses with unilateral price determination are unreasonably disadvantageous to the consumer, if they allow the seller to unilaterally increase the purchase price without any limitation beyond passing on cost increases, cf. BGHZ 82, 21, 25 ff.

reduction of other costs.[144] The courts have often had to review the admissibility of such clauses in the energy sector. For special customers, the CJEU has ruled that price change clauses can be void if they do not present the reason and the implementation of the change in a sufficiently transparent manner at the time of the conclusion of the contract.[145] In addition, the possibility of termination granted to the customer must not be merely formal.[146] For private households, the CJEU has ruled that a Member State's regulation is not in conformity with EU law if it provides for the possibility to change the rate of supplies but does not ensure that consumers are informed of the reason, conditions and scope of this change in due time before it enters into force.[147]

## 6. DELIMITATION TO OTHER EU ACTS

### a) *Choice of Court Agreements, Article 25 Brussels Ibis Regulation*

**687.** Jurisdiction agreements are also often made based on pre-formulated clauses. The CJEU has deemed such a clause without cross-border reference to be unfair.[148] The requirements set out in Article 25 of the Brussels Ibis Regulation[149] are, in principle, conclusive with regard to the formal validity of the choice-of-court agreement. Thus, the CJEU had previously rejected any supplementary abuse control, at least in the case of cases relating to the internal market.[150] However, the situation should be different in the case of third-country cases.[151] Nevertheless, the opening clause of Article 67 of the Brussels Ibis Regulation gives priority to the Unfair Terms Directive, with the result that, in consumer contracts, jurisdiction clauses in GTC must be subject to an ex officio abuse control based on the respective applicable national provision, which implements Article 3(1) of the Unfair Terms Directive.[152] Of course, this is usually only relevant where Article 25(4), 19 Brussels Ibis Regulation does not apply in favour of the consumer anyway.

---

144 See, e.g. BGH DB 2005, 2813; BGH ZIP 2007, 914, there also on the question of compensation through a right of the customer to terminate the contract; BGHZ 180, 257; BGHZ 182, 59; BGH NJW 2017, 325; Thomas, *AcP* 209 (2009), 84.

145 CJEU, 21 March 13, Case C-92/11, *RWE Vertrieb*, ECLI:EU:C:2013:180, paras. 49 ff.

146 CJEU, 21 March 13, Case C-92/11, *RWE Vertrieb*, ECLI:EU:C:2013:180, para. 54.

147 CJEU, 23 October 14, Joined Cases C-359/11 and C-400/11, *Schulz and Egbringhoff*, ECLI:EU:C:2014:2317, para. 53.

148 CJEU, 27 June 2000, Joined Cases C-240/98 to C-244/98, *Océano*, ECLI:EU:C:2000:346; see para. 661above.

149 See para. 1453.

150 CJEU, 16 March 1999, Case C-159/97, *Trasporti Castelletti*, ECLI:EU:C:1999:142, para. 49.

151 See the references in B. Hess, *Europäisches Zivilprozessrecht*, 2nd ed. (Berlin: De Gruyter, 2020), para. 147.

152 CJEU, 9 November 2010, Case C-137/08, *VB Pénzügyi Lízing Zrt.*, ECLI:EU:C:2010:659.

### b) *Choice of Law Agreements, Article 3(5) Rome I Regulation*

**688.** Choice of law agreements according to Article 3 Rome I Regulation[153] are often made in GTC. Their effectiveness is determined by the law that is presumably applicable to the contract (Articles 3(5), 10 Rome I Regulation). In this context, a conflict of the chosen law with the Unfair Terms Directive may arise.[154] The CJEU ultimately measures the choice of law agreement directly against the standard of Article 3(1) of the Unfair Terms Directive. According to the Court's view, the choice of law and its consequences must be made sufficiently transparent to the other party.[155]

### c) *Consent Based on the GDPR*

References: P. Hacker, 'Daten als Gegenleistung: Rechtsgeschäfte im Spannungsfeld von DS-GVO und allgemeinem Vertragsrecht', *ZfPW* 2019, 148; C. Wendehorst/F. Graf von Westphalen, 'Das Verhältnis zwischen Datenschutz-Grundverordnung und AGB-Recht', *NJW* 2016, 3745.

**689.** Consent under data protection law is often given in a pre-formulated manner. Therefore, the question arises as to what extent these might be scrutinised as GTC. If the data protection declaration merely serves to provide the information on data protection required by Articles 13 and 14 GDPR without particular regulations on the rights and obligations of the parties, there is no room for a review under GTC law.[156] However, if the data protection statement forms the basis for a pre-formulated declaration of consent to data processing or if it is a pre-formulated description of services which makes data collection 'necessary' for the fulfilment of the contract, it is subject to control given that it is a pre-formulated contractual term.[157] Recital 42 of the GDPR explicitly emphasises through reference to the Unfair Terms Directive that a declaration of consent should not 'contain unfair terms', which is why it must be assumed that a review of the GTC must be possible in addition to the GDPR's own control mechanisms.[158] Furthermore, the GDPR does not contain any provisions dealing with the mutual rights and obligations arising from contractual relationships,

---

153 See para. 1156.

154 Some commentators deny their applicability to choice-of-law clauses, see W.-H. Roth, *IPRax* 2017, 449, 455 ff.

155 CJEU, 28 July 2016, Case C-191/15, *Amazon*, ECLI:EU:C:2016:612. More details on this issue below at paras. 1197 ff.

156 OLG Hamburg GRUR-RR 2015, 361, paras. 48 ff.

157 Wendehorst/Graf von Westphalen, *NJW* 2016, 3745, 3748.

158 Similarly Hacker, *ZfPW* 2019, 148, 184 (the reference to Recital 32 GDPR is probably due to inadvertence).

so a blocking effect of the GDPR vis-à-vis the general GTC control cannot be assumed either.[159]

### d) *Content Control in Other Directives*

**690.** Several directives contain provisions which may overlap with the requirements of the Unfair Terms Directive. This applies in particular to Article 7(1) of the CSD. According to this provision, contractual clauses or other agreements that directly or indirectly waive or restrict the rights granted under the CSD shall not be binding for the consumer under the respective national law. A similar provision regarding the mandatory nature of the protection granted is also found in Article 25(2) of the CRD; according to this provision, contractual clauses that directly or indirectly waive or restrict the rights arising from this Directive are not binding for the consumer.[160] Both provisions are more recent and more specific than the Unfair Terms Directive and, therefore, take precedence.

**691.** A remarkably detailed provision on contract terms is contained in Article 7 of the Late Payment Directive. Here, however, there is no overlap with the Unfair Terms Directive since the Late Payments Directive concerns business transactions, i.e. transactions between businesses or between businesses and public bodies (Articles 1(1) and 2 no. 1 Late Payments Directive).[161]

### e) *Control of Standard Terms within the Platform Regulation*

References: F. Möslein, 'Digitized Terms: The Regulation of Standard Contract Terms in the Digital Age', *ERCL* 2023, 300; H. Wais, 'B2B-Klauselkontrolle in der Plattform-Ökonomie: Der Kommissionsvorschlag für eine Verordnung über Online-Vermittlungsdienste', *EuZW* 2019, 221.

**692.** Similarly, the Platform Regulation only applies to business transactions;[162] it does not affect EU law that protects consumers (Article 1(5) Platform Regulation). It only applies to commercial users, i.e. any private person acting in the course of a trade, business or profession or any legal person offering goods or services to consumers through online intermediary services and for

159 Likewise Wendehorst/Graf von Westphalen, *NJW* 2016, 3745, 3748.

160 See further Article 12(1) Timeshare Directive.

161 On that Directive see para. 762 below.

162 Regulation (EU) 2019/1150 of the European Parliament and of the Council of 20 June 2019 on promoting fairness and transparency for business users of online intermediary services. See on this para. 989 below.

purposes related to their trade, business, craft or profession (Article 2 no. 1 Platform Regulation). However, the Regulation nevertheless also aims to protect consumers, as Recital 3 of the Platform Regulation explains: By creating transparency and trust in the relationships between companies, it should indirectly contribute to increasing consumer confidence in the economy of online platforms as well.

**693.** The Platform Regulation contains in its Article 3(1) – including the sanction of invalidity of the GTC (Article 3(3) Platform Regulation) – among other things, the requirement that the GTC of the providers of online intermediary services must be clearly and understandably formulated and readily available. The provider must always inform customers about proposed changes to the GTC; in such cases, the contractual partner has a right to terminate the contract according to Article 3(2) of the Platform Regulation.

**694.** Following Article 8 of the Platform Regulation, providers may not make retroactive changes to their GTC unless this is done in order to fulfil a regulatory obligation or for the benefit of the commercial users (lit. a). In addition, the platform's GTC must provide information on the conditions under which the commercial users can terminate the contractual relationship with the provider of online intermediary services (lit. b). Finally, the platform GTC must describe the existing or non-existing technical and contractual means of access to the information provided or generated by the commercial user that the platform retains after the contract between the provider of online intermediary services and the commercial user has expired (lit. c). This ensures that contractual relations between online intermediary service providers and commercial users are conducted in good faith and based on fair dealing, as the provision states in very general terms. The Platform Regulation does not contain a specific rule relating to any sanctions following a violation of these requirements. Therefore, Member State law applies in this matter, which must, however, be both effective and dissuasive (Article 15 of the Platform Regulation).

## V. CLAUSE CONTROL IN THE PECL, DCFR AND CESL

References: F. Bonke, *Europäische Klauselkontrolle im unternehmerischen Geschäftsverkehr. Grundsätze und Lehren aus dem gescheiterten GEKR* (Berlin: Duncker & Humblot, 2020); T. Pfeiffer, 'Die Wahrnehmung grenzüberschreitender Privatautonomie in der EU: Zur AGB-Kontrolle im Bereich externer Lücken des Gemeinsamen Europäischen Kaufrechts', in *Festschrift für Müller-Graff* (Baden-Baden: Nomos, 2015), p. 129.

**695.** The PECL regulate the law of unfair terms and conditions in their Article 4:110.[163] This provision is very closely related to Article 3(1) and (4) of the Unfair Terms Directive, but in contrast to that, does not only apply to consumer contracts but to all.[164] Likewise, the DCFR does not only relate to consumer contracts; in contrast to the PECL, it even contains three different standards for an 'unfair term', depending on whether it is made by a trader vis-à-vis a consumer or whether it is contained in a contract between two non-traders or two traders, cf. Article II.-9:404 ff. DCFR.[165] In contrast, the proposal for a Common European Sales Law contains only two different standards of control.

## 1. SIGNIFICANT IMBALANCE OF CONTRACTUAL RIGHTS AND OBLIGATIONS

**696.** Clauses dealing with primary contractual obligations are not subject to review unless they violate the principle of transparency, Article 4:110(2)(a) PECL. The adequacy of performance and counter-performance is also not scrutinised, cf. Article 4:110(2)(b) PECL. For the PECL, the central criterion for the unfairness of a term that has not been individually negotiated is the substantial imbalance of contractual rights and obligations, which is to be interpreted in the same way as Article 3(1) of the Unfair Terms Directive because of the directive's above-mentioned relationship to the PECL.[166] On the one hand, this can be an unjustified economic burden on the other party, or on the other hand, it can also be any other legal disadvantage.[167] According to the so-called 'mirror rule' in the PECL commentary, this is supposed to be the case if the clause confers rights on one party but not on the other.[168]

**697.** How a clause is supposed to stand up to scrutiny according to this rule remains unclear, as it is in the nature of GTC that the user restricts the rights of

163 Article 4:110 PECL reads: 'Unfair Terms not Individually Negotiated. (1) A party may avoid a term which has not been individually negotiated if, contrary to the requirements of good faith and fair dealing, it causes a significant imbalance in the parties' rights and obligations arising under the contract to the detriment of that party, taking into account the nature of the performance to be rendered under the contract, all the other terms of the contract and the circumstances at the time the contract was concluded. (2) This Article does not apply to: (a) a term which defines the main subject matter of the contract, provided the term is in plain and intelligible language; or to (b) the adequacy in value of one party's obligations compared to the value of the obligations of the other party.'

164 Cf. Comment A to Article 4:110 PECL.

165 See Pfeiffer, in Schulze, Common Frame of Reference and Existing EC Contract Law, 2009, p. 177.

166 Cf. explicitly note 3 to Article 4:110 PECL.

167 Cf. comment G on Article 4:110 PECL.

168 Cf. again comment G on Article 4:110 PECL.

the other party or imposes obligations on them. The 'mirror rule' can, therefore, only deliver meaningful results if not only a single clause is considered but the entire contract. The admissibility of such an approach indirectly originates in Article 4:110(1) PECL, according to which all other contract terms must also be included during the examination. The PECL contains only vague indications of how the concept of material imbalance must be specified. A 'grey list' along the lines of the Unfair Terms Directive was discarded, as it seemed impossible to compile such a list due to the multitude of potential scenarios.[169] Instead, the commentary on Article 4:110 PECL refers to the 'grey list' of the Unfair Terms Directive, from which the legal practitioner can 'draw inspiration'.[170]

**698.** The DCFR also follows the model of the Unfair Terms Directive. A significant difference, however, is that its scope of application is not limited to contracts between entrepreneurs and consumers. In order to do justice to the differences in interests between the diverse areas of application of the clause control, there are three distinctions regarding the standard of unfairness: While Article 3(1) of the Unfair Terms Directive is linked to a 'significant imbalance in the parties' rights and obligations arising under the contract, to the detriment of the consumer', Article II.-9:404 DCFR requires that the clause 'significantly disadvantages the consumer'. This is probably not intended to change the standard of control. In addition, the DCFR distinguishes contracts between traders from other contracts. If it is a contract between parties who are not traders ('non-business parties'), then a term is ('only') unfair if it 'significantly disadvantages the other party', Article II.-9:405 DCFR. The standard is thus no different from a contract between a trader and a consumer.

**699.** In contrast, a term in a contract between traders is only unfair if 'its use grossly deviates from good commercial practice, contrary to good faith and fair dealing', Article II.-9:406 DCFR. Accordingly, an unfair disadvantage of the contracting party does not seem necessary as long as there is no extreme deviation from the relevant commercial practice. Compared to the two preceding provisions, this was probably intended to reduce the intensity of the examination of clauses. However, this does not appear to be compelling. It is more likely that even in contracts between traders, there must be a disadvantage to the other party through the clause; this is usually the case if there is a significant deviation from commercial practice, which is the standard

169 Cf. comment B on Article 4:110 PECL.

170 Cf. again comment B on Article 4:110 PECL. The fact that the 'grey list' only looks at consumer contracts and can therefore hardly serve as a model for commercial transactions is not given any consideration.

for a balanced consideration of the interests of both parties.[171] In contrast to the PECL, Article II.-9:411 DCFR contains a binding 'black list' of objectionable terms for contracts between traders and consumers, which is very closely based on the 'grey list' contained in the Annex to the Unfair Terms Directive and is a specification of Article II.-9:404 DCFR. Article II.-9:410 DCFR regulates the special case of a jurisdiction agreement in GTC in favour of the trader's domicile to the consumer's detriment. Such clauses are always unfair if the prorogated jurisdiction coincides with the consumer's domicile jurisdiction. This rule has no equivalent in the Unfair Terms Directive; it builds on the CJEU's *Océano* ruling.[172]

**700.** Articles 79to 86 CESL contain provisions on unfair contract terms.[173] The central rule of Article 83 of the CESL is based on Article 3(1) of the Unfair Terms Directive; there are no relevant differences with regard to the content of the term 'unfair'. In contrast to the EU Directive on Unfair Terms, which only contains a catalogue of unfair terms as a non-binding annex ('grey list'), unfair or presumably unfair terms are listed per se in Articles 84 and 85 of the CESL. The problem is that the catalogues also cover matters that do not fall under the scope of the CESL, such as provisions on tortious liability, set-off, assignment or procedural assertion of claims, and are, thus, strictly speaking, ultra vires.[174] Article 86 CESL contains a separate provision on unfair contract terms in contracts between entrepreneurs.[175]

## 2. LEGAL CONSEQUENCES

**701.** It must be noted that, according to the PECL, an unfair term is not invalid or non-binding, but the disadvantaged party may avoid it (Article 4:110(1) PECL). This unusual model is justified by the fact that, without a list of standard examples and precedents, a concretisation of the provision 'will usually ... not be possible'.[176] This means that the legal consequence is the same as that

---

171 Cf. in this context the concretisation of sec. 307(1) German Civil Code by sec. 307(2) no. 1 German Civil Code, in which the otherwise applicable dispositive law is defined as the standard of review for the unfairness of the clause.

172 CJEU, 27 June 2000, Joined Cases C-240/98 to C-244/98, *Océano*, ECLI:EU:C:2000:346.

173 On this, cf. Ernst, in O. Remien/S. Herrler/P. Limmer, *Common European Sales Law for the EU?* (Munich: Beck, 2012), p. 93; C. Wendehorst, in C. Wendehorst/B. Zöchling-Jud (eds.), *Am Vorabend eines Gemeinsamen Europäischen Kaufrechts. Zum Verordnungsentwurf der Europäischen Kommission vom 11.10.2011* (Vienna, Manz 2012), pp. 87, 95 ff.; Loos, in L. Moccia (ed.), *The Making of European Private Law* (Munich: Sellier, 2013), p. 191; Graf von Westphalen, *ZIP* 2011, 1985; Pfeiffer, in *Festschrift für Müller-Graff*, 2015, p. 129.

174 Cf. C. Wendehorst, in C. Wendehorst/B. Zöchling-Jud, ibid. , pp. 87, 103 ff.

175 See Gramlich, *GPR* 2014, 62.

176 See comment C on Article 4:110 PECL.

of unreasonable exploitation regulated in Article 4:109 PECL: Here, too, the protection of the disadvantaged party is not achieved through nullification of the contract but through a right of avoidance. The grounds for this defence in Chapter 4 of the PECL are all subject to a time limit: Article 4:113(1) PECL prescribes a 'reasonable time, with due regard to the circumstances' for the right's exercise, which begins with the knowledge of the grounds for avoidance. However, this provision would not serve the avoidance of unfair terms directly, so Article 4:113(2) PECL links this to the use of an unfair term; the disadvantaged party must then again challenge this within a reasonable period of time. The result seems to be the same as in those models that declare the unfair term per se invalid.[177] Nevertheless, the latter is preferable since it is not discernible what advantage an unfair term should have for the contracting party that could induce them to waive the declaration of avoidance: The rest of the contract remains in force. However, if the exercise of the right of avoidance is a mere formality, the outright invalidity of the clause appears to be a better solution because it avoids the risk of the contracting party to not recognise the disadvantage as such and let the avoidance period expire.

**702.** In contrast, the unfair term under Article II.-9:409(1) DCFR does not bind the party who did not make it ('not binding on the party who did not support it'). The DCFR thus again follows the conventional solution suggested by the consumer acquis in the form of the Unfair Terms Directive. The solution is the same in the CESL (Article 79(1) CESL: an unfair term is 'not binding').

## VI. PLANNED REFORM STEPS AND THEIR FAILURE

### 1. NO FULL HARMONISATION OF CLAUSE CONTROL

**703.** In the proposal for a Consumer Rights Directive,[178] the Commission aimed at a full harmonisation of consumer law. The concept of minimum harmonisation pursued in the previous directives on consumer law was found to be incompatible with the internal market: It led to companies still having to comply with different legal provisions when offering goods and services in the internal market, a circumstance which made cross-border trade more expensive and – most likely – an obstacle. Full harmonisation, which sets a fixed level of consumer protection and is binding for all Member States, and thus does not allow for more consumer-friendly rules, as has been the case up until now, should provide a remedy here. This would result in a uniform level

[177] Comment C on Article 4:110 PECL apparently assumes this.
[178] COM(2008) 614 final, on this see para. 127 as well as para. 1300 above.

of protection throughout the EU, removing any uncertainty for consumers regarding their cross-border demand for goods and services. This seems questionable because even a full harmonisation of the control of preformulated clauses does not set any standard for the decisive unfairness criterion. Furthermore, it does not seem at all certain that consumers will engage in cross-border trade more easily in a 'fully harmonised' internal market, in particular, given that linguistic and cultural differences between the Member States still pose considerable barriers.

**704.** In the area of laws on GTC, the draft provided for two major innovations:[179] First, the draft contained an annex with a list of terms that should be considered unfair in any case, a so-called black list.[180] Another annex contained a list of terms whose unfairness was only to be assumed (by means of a rebuttable presumption) and which was therefore widely referred to as 'the grey list'.[181] Moreover, in order to adapt these lists of clauses to the changing case law, it was planned to use a procedure that was highly problematic from the point of view of democratic legitimacy and transparency, the so-called comitology procedure.[182] According to this procedure, the Member States were to notify the Commission of clauses considered unfair by the national courts. On this basis, it was planned to give the Commission the power to amend the annexes with the prohibited clauses (outside of the normal legislative procedure, supported by an appropriate committee of experts).[183]

**705.** In the Consumer Rights Directive, which has entered into force, the scope of clause control has been almost eliminated; As a reminiscence of the original concept, Article 32 CRD contains a reporting obligation of the Member States concerning the adoption of such provisions of national law that provide for a higher level of protection than the Unfair Terms Directive envisages. This obligation refers in particular to provisions which (1) extend the unfairness assessment to individually negotiated contractual terms or to the adequacy of the price or remuneration, or (2) contain lists of contractual terms which shall be considered as unfair. Hence, there are still no binding unfair terms catalogues at the European level.

---

179 On clause control in the proposal, cf. Kieninger, *RabelsZ* 73 (2009), 792; Jansen, *ZEuP* 2010, 73.

180 Article 34 of the Proposal in conjunction with Annex II.

181 Article 35 of the Proposal in conjunction with Annex III.

182 Article 40(2) of the Proposal refers in this respect to Articles 5a(1) to (4), 7 and 8 of Decision 1999/468/EC, OJ 1999 L 184/23, as amended by Decision 2006/512/EC, OJ 2006 L/11.

183 Articles 39 and 40 of the Proposal.

## 2. THE SIGNIFICANCE OF THE PROPOSAL FOR A COMMON EUROPEAN SALES LAW

**706.** According to the proposal for a Common European Sales Law,[184] which is not being pursued any further, the parties to a cross-border sales contract should have been able to opt for the validity of the European uniform sales law. This uniform sales law would have served as a standard for the specification of the abuse of contractual terms in Article 3(1) of the Directive. This would initially apply in the event that the parties choose it because then, there would be a series of dispositive rules at the EU level against whose standard it could be judged whether a contractual agreement caused a substantial imbalance.

**707.** However, it is questionable whether the dispositive statutory law of a Common Sales Law could also be used as such a standard to specify the unfairness if the parties had not or not successfully opted into the CESL. Consequently, another legal system could apply to the case. The character of the CESL as a component of positive EU law could speak in favour of this. So far, however, it is not self-evident that another secondary legal act can be used to define a legal concept contained in a directive (in this case: abusiveness). According to the case law of the CJEU, 'every provision of Community law must be placed in its context and interpreted in the light of the provisions of Community law as a whole [...]'.[185] The intensity of this systematic interpretation depends, of course, to a large extent on the degree of harmonisation in the relevant area of law. So far, harmonisation in private law has been sector-specific; the EU legislator has often pursued different regulatory objectives in the various legal acts or has not always sufficiently harmonised the individual legal acts. With the CESL, in contrast, this sector-specific approach would be abandoned (for the first time) and a 'horizontal' set of rules created, representing a further development of the consumer acquis. Hence, even if the parties had not chosen the uniform sales law, and, consequently, the respective applicable national law would govern their contractual relationship, nevertheless, a CESL, once adopted, would embody common legal principles of EU law, which would have a guiding character even if its rules are not directly applicable to the contract. In contrast to dispositive national law, the CESL would have to be chosen by the parties in order to apply; rules of dispositive national law, on the other hand, would have to be waived by an agreement of the contractual parties. However, the significance of both sets of rules for the specification of the offence of abuse is comparable insofar as these provide information on how a balanced distribution of contractual rights and obligations should look according to the ideas of the respective legislator.

---

[184] See para. 130 above.

[185] CJEU, 6 October 1982, Case 283/81, *CILFIT*, ECLI:EU:C:1982:335, para. 20.

## 3. CLAUSE CONTROL ACCORDING TO DCFR STANDARDS?

**708.** In contrast, the use of the DCFR as a reference instrument appears to be far more problematic. Despite its funding by the Commission under the 6th Research Framework Programme and its design as a model code, the DCFR is a purely academic work without any claim to normative validity. As such, it is fundamentally unsuitable to concretise the applicable EU law due to its lack of legislative legitimacy. This would not change even if the DCFR were formally elevated to the rank of EU law – following the original plan – since it was only planned to serve as an internal reference instrument for the EU legislative bodies, from which they can draw inspiration. In this case, too, no sufficient will on the part of the EU legislator would be discernible to regard the model rules of the (then political) DCFR as an expression of the private law acquis. It would then be precisely the provisional character of a 'toolbox' that would speak against such an assumption.

# CHAPTER 4
# EXECUTION OF THE CONTRACT

## §16. OBLIGATIONS ARISING FROM THE CONTRACT

CONTENTS



References: M.-P. Weller, Die Vertragstreue (Tübingen: Mohr Siebeck, 2009).

## I. THE CONTRACTUAL OBLIGATIONS

**709.** The contract forms the basis for the exchange of performances between the parties. Given its importance for the private law system, the domestic law of the Member States has developed more or less sophisticated approaches to systematise the obligations following from the contract. On way to see things is to distinguish between primary and secondary obligations.[1] In the case of mutual contracts, the former concern those contractual obligations that characterise the contractual relationship and are connected in such a way that the performance of one obligation stands or falls with the other. In this respect, one may speak of synallagmatic performance obligations. The primary claim, which is at least in most continental European systems directed towards specific performance, enforces primary obligations.[2]

[1] Cf. Olzen, in Staudinger, *BGB Kommentar* (2024), §241 paras. 144 ff. with references.
[2] On the enforcement of primary claims see §17 below.

**710.** In addition to these primary (performance) obligations, there are numerous secondary (performance) obligations, e.g. duties to protect the other party's valid interests.[3] Furthermore, there may be duties of loyalty, care, information, cooperation and consideration. Their violation triggers a different sanction regime than in relation to primary obligations: Here, secondary claims take effect, in particular damages, but also rescission. According to the prevailing view, ancillary duties are not enforceable independently.[4]

**711.** There is no such elaborated doctrine in European contract law. Here, too, the piecemeal approach to regulation is clearly evident.

## II. PRIMARY OBLIGATIONS

**712.** Regulations concerning primary obligations can be found where directives standardise certain contracts, such as in sales contracts, loan contracts or time-share contracts. In some cases, there are also provisions regarding breaches of primary contractual obligations and the resulting legal consequences. These will be explained individually in connection with the respective legal act.[5]

**713.** Only in rare cases are there isolated provisions on the obligations relating to the primary performance. Particularly noteworthy is the Late Payments Directive, which deals with the consequences for business transactions of late payment of sums of money owed as remuneration for services in business-to-business transactions or business-to-public transactions (Article 1(2) Late Payments Directive). This will also be considered in detail later.[6]

## III. ANCILLARY PERFORMANCE OBLIGATIONS

### 1. GENERAL INFORMATION

**714.** All contractual obligations that are not primary ones can be described as secondary or ancillary obligations. The contract as such does not depend on them: If there is agreement on the essentials of the contract, the contract is concluded even if the parties have not reached a consensus otherwise, for example, regarding the delivery date. The dispositive statutory law then takes the

---

3 For details, see Olzen, in Staudinger, *BGB Kommentar* (2024), §241 paras. 163 ff.

4 Differently, however, C. Wendelstein, *Pflicht und Anspruch* (Tübingen: Mohr Siebeck, 2020), passim.

5 See para. 839, para. 1009 as well as para. 1027 below.

6 See para. 762.

place of the party's agreement. Because of the selective harmonisation, it is not surprising that European contract law knows only comparatively few regulations on ancillary obligations. Of great importance are information duties, which are typically imposed on the trader in consumer contracts. In addition, there are duties to cooperate in certain contexts.

## 2. IN PARTICULAR: DUTIES TO PROVIDE INFORMATION

**715.** European contract law provides various information duties that regularly apply to the trader vis-à-vis the consumer. One of the basic principles of European consumer law is to enable an informed consent. This intends to compensate for the consumer's inferior position vis-à-vis the trader. In this regard, consumer law often aims to compensate for this information deficit. The general purpose is to ensure that a well-considered decision regarding the conclusion of the contract is made by correcting the existing information asymmetry.[7] Consequently, these information duties can already be found in the pre-contractual stage.[8]

**716.** Information duties also exist when the contract is executed. For example, in the case of a contract for the sale of goods with digital elements, the seller must ensure that the consumer is informed of available updates (Article 7(3) of the Sale of Goods Directive); the same applies to contracts for the provision of digital content (Article 8(2) of the Digital Content Directive).

## 3. IN PARTICULAR: DUTIES OF COOPERATION

**717.** A special form of secondary obligations are the so-called duties of cooperation. They are vital in the case of continuing obligations. In the area of European contract law, it is above all the Commercial Agents Directive, which, in Article 3(1) and 4(1), regulates the obligation of the parties to the commercial agency contract to act in good faith. The commercial agent must endeavour to arrange and conclude the transactions entrusted to them (Article 3(2) Commercial Agents Directive). This will be discussed in a separate chapter.[9]

**718.** However, more and more frequently, exchange contracts, such as the sales contract or the contract for the provision of digital content or digital services, incorporate continuing obligations.[10] For example, in a contract for

---

7 See para. 477 above.

8 See para. 480 above.

9 See §27.

10 On the regulation of long-term contracts in the DCFR, H. Unberath, in G. Wagner (ed.), *The Common Frame of Reference: A View from Law & Economics* (Munich: Sellier, 2009), p. 87.

the sale of goods with digital elements, the seller owes certain updates on an ongoing basis;[11] the same is true concerning contracts for the provision of digital content.[12] In this respect, the consumer must cooperate by installing these updates. The sanction for non-performance does not consist of in obligation to pay damages but rather only limits the liability of the trader under certain conditions (Article 7(4) Sale of Goods Directive; Article 8(3) Digital Content Directive). Article 12(5) Digital Content Directive also standardises such a duty to cooperate. According to this provision, the consumer shall cooperate with the trader to the extent reasonably necessary and possible to establish whether the cause of the lack of conformity of the digital content or service lies in the consumer's sphere. The sanction for failure to cooperate does again not give rise to any liability for damages; it is merely the burden of proof for the existence of the lack of conformity that is shifted to the consumer – but only if the trader has informed the consumer of this obligation in a clear and comprehensible manner before the conclusion of the contract.

---

11 See para. 851.

12 See para. 962.

# §17. BREACH OF CONTRACT

## CONTENTS

References: R. Feltkamp/F. Vanbossele, 'The Optional Common European Sales Law: Better Buyer's Remedies for Seller's Non-performance in Sales of Goods?', *ERPL* 2011, 873; B. Gsell, 'Non-performance and Remedies in General', in S. Leible/M. Lehmann (eds.), *European Contract Law and German Law* (Alphen aan den Rijn: Kluwer, 2014), p. 375; H. Kötz, *European Contract Law*, 2nd ed. (Oxford: Oxford University Press, 2017), §12; L. Leuschner, 'Grenzen der Vertragsfreiheit im Rechtsvergleich', *ZEuP* 2017, 335; T. Riehm, *Der Grundsatz der Naturalerfüllung* (Tübingen: Mohr Siebeck, 2015); M. Schmidt-Kessel, 'Supervening Events and Force Majeure', in J.M. Smits/J. Husa/C. Valcke/M. Narciso (eds.), *Elgar Encyclopedia of Comparative Law* (Cheltenham: Edward Elgar Publishing, 2023), p. 457; M. Stürner, 'Die Grenzen der Primärleistungspflicht im Europäischen Vertragsrecht', *ERPL* 2011, 167; M. Torsello, 'Remedies for Breach of Contract', in J.M. Smits/J. Husa/C. Valcke/M. Narciso (eds.), *Elgar Encyclopedia of Comparative Law* (Cheltenham: Edward Elgar Publishing, 2023), p. 325; M.-P. Weller, 'Die Struktur des Erfüllungsanspruchs im BGB, common law und DCFR – ein kritischer Vergleich', *JZ* 2008, 764; M.-P. Weller, *Die Vertragstreue* (Tübingen: Mohr Siebeck, 2009); M.-P. Weller, 'Der Vertrag: Haftungs- oder Erfüllungsversprechen? – von *Holmes* über *Rabel* und *Rheinstein* zu *Unberath*', in *Gedächtnisschrift für Hannes Unberath* (Munich: C.H. Beck, 2015), p. 443; H. Unberath, *Die Vertragsverletzung* (Tübingen: Mohr Siebeck, 2007).

## I. NORMATIVE STARTING POINT: THE DIFFERENT APPROACHES OF CIVIL LAW AND COMMON LAW

**719.** A central category within contract law doctrine is the breach of contract and, here in particular, its consequences.[1] Non-compliance with the contractual obligations entails sanctions in all legal systems. However, there are differences in how they are applied, especially regarding the enforcement of the primary obligation. In this respect, the basic positions will be discussed first. Continental civil law regards performance in kind as a rule,[2] whereas, in common law, it is only granted as an exception.[3] Any European harmonisation approach has to position itself in this respect.[4] Depending on the general approach, the scope of the existing exceptions is particularly important.

---

1 On the following subject see previously Stürner, *ERPL* 2011, 167.
2 See para. 720 below.
3 See para. 735 below.
4 See para. 744 below.

## 1. CHARACTERISTICS OF THE CONTINENTAL SYSTEM: THE GERMAN EXAMPLE

### a) *The Primary Claim as an Actionable Right*

**720.** When a contract is concluded, mutual rights and obligations arise. 'By virtue of an obligation', according to sec. 241(1) of the German Civil Code, 'an obligee is entitled to claim performance from the obligor'. According to the German Civil Code, the establishment of an obligation thus entails two things: First, it already gives rise to an enforceable right to demand that another person must do or refrain from doing something. The enforceability of the claim is inherent to it and is a material part. Consequently, in sec. 656 of the German Civil Code for the marriage brokerage contract or in sec. 762 of the German Civil Code for gambling and betting, the legislator had to expressly stipulate that an obligation is not be created by such legal transactions. Only in these explicit cases, commonly referred to as imperfect obligations, does the claim lack enforceability.[5] Moreover, no other circumstances – beyond the conclusion of the contract – are required for a claim to a performance in kind to be enforceable. The assertion of the primary claim is not a legal remedy linked to separate preconditions but a self-evident rule. It does not only arise in the case of non-performance but already with the obligation itself.[6]

### b) *The Limits of the Primary Duty to Perform*

**721.** The described structure of the primary claim as a right that can be enforced without further preconditions has consequences for determining the limits of the debtor's performance obligation. The formulation of these limits is of considerable importance. Since the modernisation of the law of obligations, the German Civil Code provides for a double possibility of relief for the debtor: The exclusion of the obligation to perform according to sec. 275 German Civil Code on the one hand and the adjustment of the contract due to disturbance of the basis of the contract according to sec. 313 German Civil Code on the other hand.

---

5 In-depth analysis in G. Schulze, *Die Naturalobligation* (Tübingen: Mohr Siebeck, 2008), pp. 262 ff.

6 On this subject, see comprehensively M.-P. Weller, *Die Vertragstreue* (Tübingen: Mohr Siebeck, 2009), pp. 316 ff., 371 ff., 464 ff.; cf. further H. Unberath, *Die Vertragsverletzung* (Tübingen: Mohr Siebeck, 2007), pp. 210 ff.; K. Zweigert/H. Kötz, *Introduction to Comparative Law*, 3rd ed. (Oxford: Clarendon Press, 1996), §35.

### aa) Development

**722.** According to the original concept of the German Civil Code, the category of impossibility was the central concept for regulating the limits of performance obligations. The claim to performance lapsed if, and only if, performance was impossible for the debtor or for anyone else. Particularly in the wake of the upheavals caused by the war and later by inflation, the German Imperial Court initially used the legal institution of impossibility to dissolve contractual obligations that were considered unreasonable and coined the concept of economic impossibility for this purpose.[7] The legal instrument of impossibility was thus understood, beyond the actual cases of physical impossibility, as any circumstance that unreasonably impeded the performance of the service.[8] However, the German Imperial Court then quickly used sec. 242 of the German Civil Code to apply the instrument of frustration of contract developed by Oertmann, which was itself based on Windscheid's 'doctrine of the prerequisite'.[9]

**723.** Windscheid considered the 'prerequisite' to be an implicit restriction of the intention of the legal transaction, meaning that this intention should only be valid in case of the existence or continuance of particular circumstances. Windscheid regarded as prerequisites such circumstances that come close to a requirement in the technical sense but are taken for granted by at least one party so that they are not explicitly formulated.[10] The prerequisite thus stands between the legally irrelevant motive and the genuine condition. However, Windscheid's doctrine did not achieve widespread acceptance. Above all, *Lenel* criticised the doctrine of the prerequisite, arguing that it was too broad and could not be distinguished from a general motive. An intermediate phenomenon between motive and condition, he claimed, could not exist.[11] The drafters of the German Civil Code, therefore, refrained from including a general provision on the fate of contracts in the event of changed circumstances, because 'this doctrine endangers the safety of legal transactions and is, therefore, not suitable as a basis for the Code'. Windscheid was right after all when he said: 'It is my firm conviction that

---

7 Cf. for example the decision of the German Imperial Court in RGZ 102, 272, 273 (exceeding the 'sacrifice limit'); on this in more detail G. Kegel/H. Rupp/K. Zweigert, *Die Einwirkung des Krieges auf Verträge* (Berlin: De Gruyter, 1941), pp. 51 f., 71 ff.; summarising G. Kegel, 'Gutachten für den 40. Deutschen Juristentag', 1953, pp. 150 ff.

8 Critically, H.H. Jakobs, *Unmöglichkeit und Nichterfüllung* (Bonn: Röhrscheid, 1969), pp. 67 ff.

9 P. Oertmann, *Die Geschäftsgrundlage. Ein neuer Rechtsbegriff* (Leipzig: A. Deichert, 1921). On this, see for example K. Larenz, *Geschäftsgrundlage und Vertragserfüllung*, 3rd ed. (Munich: Beck, 1963), pp. 5 ff.

10 B. Windscheid, *Die Lehre des römischen Rechts von der Voraussetzung* (Düsseldorf: Buddeus, 1850), pp. 80 ff.

11 Lenel, *AcP* 74 (1889), 213; Lenel, *AcP* 79 (1892), 49.

the tacitly declared premise [...] will always reassert itself. Thrown out of the door, it comes in again through the window.'[12]

**724.** The modernisation of the law of obligations then standardised a triad of notable impediments to performance in sec. 275 German Civil Code: Impossibility, a disproportionate effort to perform and unreasonableness of personal performance. The consequences of supervening events were codified in sec. 313 of the German Civil Code.

bb) Impossibility and Difficulties of Performance

**725.** While the revised rule on impossibility in sec. 275(1) of the German Civil Code is now intended to cover only actual physical impossibility,[13] the legislator has entered uncharted territory with the defence of a disproportionate effort to perform in sec. 275(2) of the German Civil Code: The provision does not merely form a sub-category of impossibility, but it opens up an independent right to refuse performance, which is ultimately based on the prohibition of abuse of rights and may thus be categorised as a special variant of the principle of good faith as enshrined in sec. 242 German Civil Code.[14]

**726.** In order to determine the limits of the debtor's obligation to perform, sec. 275(2) German Civil Code requires a process of balancing the effort to be made by the debtor to perform on the one hand and the creditor's interest in receiving performance on the other. The specific content of the obligation, the principle of good faith and a possible obligation of the debtor to act in relation to the performance impediment must be taken into account. If there is a gross disproportion between these reference points within the framework of this balancing exercise, the debtor may refuse performance.

**727.** While the courts now seem more and more open to the application of sec. 275(2) German Civil Code,[15] the provision has been heavily criticised. The essence of the criticism is that it shifts the limits of contractual obligations to the debtor's detriment by imposing on them a further obligation to perform beyond what is contractually owed. To illustrate the problem, *Picker* put forward the fictitious case of a convertible car sold to a buyer in Germany that was however

---

12 Windscheid, *AcP* 78 (1892), 161, 197.

13 Government draft BT-Drucks. 14/6040, p. 128.

14 For a detailed discussion, cf. Stürner, *Der Grundsatz der Verhältnismäßigkeit im Schuldvertragsrecht*, 2010, pp. 185 ff.

15 BGHZ 163, 234; on this C. Hirsch, *JURA* 2006, 120; Keilmann, *NJW* 2006, 2526; Gutzeit, *NJW* 2007, 956; see further BGH NJW 2005, 3284; BAGE 111, 191; BGH NJW 2008, 3122, 3123; also BGH NJW 2008, 3123, 3125. On the last two judgments in more detail Stürner, in *Festschrift für von Brünneck* (Baden-Baden: Nomos, 2011), p. 360.

stolen the night before it was due to be handed over to the buyer and turned up again later in Murmansk, Russia.[16] The seller can retrieve the car there but would have to make a substantial financial effort for this which equals the purchase price agreed for the car. The question is whether the buyer can still demand performance, i.e. delivery and transfer of ownership of the car, or whether the seller can refuse performance.[17]

**728.** Critics see the balancing process required by sec. 275(2) German Civil Code as disregarding the parties' own choices made within private autonomy.[18] In fact, the rule only considers the contract in the context of weighing the creditor's interest and the debtor's effort. However, it should go without saying that an interpretation of the contract is already necessary to determine the performance's content in the first place.[19] Only on this foundation is it possible to determine the extent to which the creditor's insistence on their claim for performance would be regarded as an abuse of rights. Sec. 275(2) of the German Civil Code is intended to set a limit within an inherently existing claim to performance; hence, the rule precisely only limits the debtor's obligation to perform, and does not extend it. On the other hand, this must not undermine the principle *pacta sunt servanda*: The legislator seeks to achieve this by applying the threshold of intervention only in the case of gross disproportion. Consequently, the rule does not already apply if the debtor might prospectively conclude a better deal with someone else or if the creditor could procure the object of the contractual obligation in some other way.[20]

**729.** Even if, against the backdrop of the requirements set out in sec. 275(2) German Civil Code, one might call the proportionality test to be carried out within the rule's framework a cost-benefit analysis,[21] this should not give way to a purely efficiency-oriented analysis. A demand for performance contrary to good faith may be regarded as inefficient, whereas the reverse implication is not

16 Picker, *JZ* 2003, 1035.

17 Cf. the controversy between Picker and Canaris: Picker, *JZ* 2003, 1035, reply by Canaris, *JZ* 2004, 214; on this again Picker, in *Festschrift für Konzen* (Tübingen: Mohr Siebeck, 2006), pp. 687, 696 f., 700 ff.

18 Cf. in particular Wilhelm, *JZ* 2001, 861, 866 f. (sec. 275(2) German Civil Code as a 'freak'); *Picker, JZ* 2003, 1035; Picker, in *Festschrift für Konzen*, ibid., p. 687; in detail T. Lobinger, *Die Grenzen rechtsgeschäftlicher Leistungspflichten* (Tübingen: Mohr Siebeck, 2004), pp. 238 ff. who even considers sec. 275(2) German Civil Code to be unconstitutional.

19 BT-Drucks. 14/6040, p. 127.

20 On the notion of efficient breach of contract cf. below at paras. 757–758.

21 For example Ernst, in *Münchener Kommentar zum BGB*, 9th ed. (Munich: C.H. Beck, 2023), §275 paras. 83 f., who nevertheless classifies the provision as an example of the prohibition of abuse of rights.

necessarily true.[22] If one considers the enforceability of the primary claim to be efficient because it gives the market actors certainty as well as confidence in the market and, in this way, reduces transaction costs,[23] then this also bears consequences for the definition of the limits of the obligation to perform. Sec. 275(2) German Civil Code is also important from an efficiency point of view, as it defines the presumed will of the parties in a way that minimises transaction costs.[24] If rationally acting parties had expected the increase in production costs before the conclusion of the contract, they would have agreed on a specific limit of the obligation to perform by agreeing on an obligation to compensate that amounts to the respective party's interest in performance. The fact that sec. 275(2) German Civil Code does not apply this limit until there is a gross disproportion correctly emphasises the relevance of the primary claim.

**730.** In contrast to sec. 275(2) German Civil Code, which explicitly requires a disproportion between the debtor's effort and the creditor's interest, para. 3 of this rule is linked to the unreasonableness of the performance. The right to refuse performance only applies to those cases in which the performance is both possible and the debtor has to perform personally, but in the case of an impediment that is so serious that the debtor can no longer be expected to perform the contract. This may be the case, for example, if an opera singer's child falls seriously ill on the day of the performance.[25] The existence of unreasonableness must be determined in a balancing process, just as in sec. 275(2) German Civil Code, as para. 3 expressly says. As in para. 2, the reference point is the creditor's interest in the performance. However, this is contrasted by different aspects on the debtor's side:[26] Whereas para. 2 focuses on the economic effort necessary to overcome the obstacle to performance, para. 3 exclusively covers non-material obstacles to perform that relate only to the debtor. These are not to be taken into account in the context of para. 2. Finally, while it is true that both elements of the defence

22 A question to be distinguished from this is whether a party acting rationally in a situation in which the breach of contract would be efficient but the disproportion between the debtor's effort and the creditor's interest has not reached the threshold of sec. 275(2) German Civil Code would not try by way of a negotiated solution with the creditor to cancel the obligation to perform in exchange for the sharing of the (potential) additional profit between the parties resulting from the breach of contract. Such a cancellation solution would be efficient – if one did not take into account the transaction costs incurred. See Eidenmüller, *JZ* 2005, 216, 222; Maultzsch, *AcP* 207 (2007), 530, 539 ff.

23 H.-B. Schäfer/C. Ott, *Lehrbuch der ökonomischen Analyse des Zivilrechts*, 5th ed. (Berlin/ Heidelberg: Springer, 2013), pp. 427 ff.; Unberath, *Die Vertragsverletzung*, 2007, pp. 232 ff.; M.-P. Weller, *Die Vertragstreue* (Tübingen: Mohr Siebeck, 2009), pp. 366 ff.

24 Unberath, ibid., pp. 237 ff., 277 ff.; *Köndgen*, in *Festschrift für Hans-Bernd Schäfer* (Wiesbaden: Gabler, 2008), pp. 275, 280 ff.

25 According to the government's explanatory statement, BT-Drucks. 14/6040, p. 130.

26 C.-W. Canaris, in *Studi in onore di Giorgio Cian* (Padua: CEDAM, 2010), pp. 383, 385 ff., essentially points out that in sec. 275(3) of the German Civil Code, the debtor's interest is in the foreground, whereas in sec. 275(2) it is primarily the creditor's interest that is important.

ultimately concretise the prohibition of abuse of rights[27] (for that reason, there is no *lex specialis* relationship between the two paragraphs[28]), they ultimately relate to different conflicts of interest.[29]

cc) Frustration of Contract, Sec. 313 German Civil Code

**731.** The German Civil Code provides yet another way for the debtor to get rid of their originally stipulated obligation, namely if circumstances essential to the contract have fundamentally changed so that it appears unreasonable to adhere to the contract.[30] The institution of frustration of contract, as enshrined in sec. 313 of the German Civil Code since 2002, protects the parties from the realisation of such risks that were not foreseeable at the time of the conclusion of the contract unless they are attributed to them according to the structure of the contract. In this way, a balance is created between the legitimate interests of one party in the existence of the contract and its performance and those of the other party in reducing or lifting the burden which has become unreasonable for them.

dd) The Demarcation between Sec. 275(2) and Sec. 313 German Civil Code

**732.** While the modernised German Civil Code provides different rules that limit the primary obligation to perform, the question of the respective scope of application arises. Because of the different legal consequences – the right to refuse performance on the one hand, contract adjustment on the other – the demarcation is certainly of practical importance.[31]

**733.** Although both sec. 275(2) German Civil Code and the institution of frustration of contract have their roots in sec. 242 German Civil Code and

27 Cf. Canaris, ibid., pp. 383, 386 f.

28 For a diverging approach cf. Ernst, in *Münchener Kommentar zum BGB*, 9th ed. (Munich: C.H. Beck, 2022), §275 para. 125.

29 Similarly S. Greiner, *Ideelle Unzumutbarkeit* (Berlin: Duncker & Humblot, 2004), pp. 371 ff., 383. Likewise, in conclusion, Canaris, in *Studi in onore di Giorgio Cian* (Padua: CEDAM, 2010), pp. 383, 386, who for this reason even assumes that sec. 275(3) German Civil Code, compared to para. 2, has 'a considerably larger and more varied practical field of application'.

30 P. Oertmann, *Die Geschäftsgrundlage. Ein neuer Rechtsbegriff* (Leipzig: A. Deichert, 1921), p. 37: 'The basis of the transaction is the idea of a party to the transaction, which comes to light at the time of the conclusion of the transaction and whose significance is recognised and not objected to by the possible opponent, or the common idea of the several parties to the transaction of the existence or occurrence of certain circumstances, on the basis of which the intention of the transaction is built.' Likewise BGH NJW-RR 2006, 1037, 1038. For a comparative perspective cf. Kramer, *SJZ* 2014, 273.

31 For further details cf. Stürner, *JURA* 2010, 761; Schmidt-Recla, in *Festschrift für Laufs* (Berlin/Heidelberg: Springer, 2005), pp. 641, 659 ff.

thus in the legal idea of equity,[32] both are linked to different disturbances of the contractual relationship. The systematic vicinity to sec. 275(1) German Civil Code shows that sec. 275(2) German Civil Code contains a rule on the transfer of risk, which regulates the risk of the realisation of contract-related disturbances. The area of regulation of frustration of contract must be distinguished from this: It is already clear from the wording of sec. 313 German Civil Code that, here, a regulation is being made for the distribution of other risks, namely those that have not expressly or implicitly found their way into the contract itself.[33] This results from the concept of the basis of the contract ('*Geschäftsgrundlage*'): Those circumstances described as the basis of the contract have not become part of it.[34] They do not designate the contractually agreed modalities of the exchange of performances, but merely its external framework conditions, on whose existence a party relied and was entitled to rely.

**734.** Consequently, the law regulates the consequences of the two disturbances in different ways: While only the primary claim may be objected against according to sec. 275(2) German Civil Code, the debtor may also be liable for damages under sec. 275(4), 280 ff. German Civil Code. Furthermore, the original obligation to perform ceases to operate altogether in the case of considerable disturbances to the basis of the contract. As a legal consequence, the contract is usually adapted; if even the modified performance obligation would be unreasonable, a rescission right arises. Obligations to pay damages do not follow from the discontinuation of the basis of the contract.

## 2. THE REMEDY CONCEPT IN THE COMMON LAW

### a) *The Unenforceability of the Primary Claim*

**735.** While the German Civil Code at the outset assumes the enforceability of each and every claim, the obligation to perform in kind, at least outside of monetary payment obligations, is not, according to the understanding of common law, a component of a contractual obligation that would be enforceable per se:

---

32 On the development in detail Schermeier, in *Historisch-Kritischer Kommentar zum BGB* (Tübingen: Mohr Siebeck, 2007), §275 paras. 42, 62 ff.

33 Similarly, for a justification of the institute of the basis of the contract with risk considerations, W. Fikentscher, *Die Geschäftsgrundlage als Frage des Vertragsrisikos* (Munich: C.H. Beck, 1971), pp. 31 ff.; Medicus, in *Festschrift für Flume I* (Cologne: Otto Schmidt, 1978), pp. 629, 630 ff.; W. Flume, *Allgemeiner Teil des Bürgerlichen Rechts*, vol. II: Das Rechtsgeschäft, 2nd ed. (Berlin/Heidelberg: Springer 1975), §26, 3 (p. 501); M. Köhler, in *Festgabe 50 Jahre Bundesgerichtshof*, vol. I, (Munich: C.H. Beck, 2000), pp. 295, 300 ff.

34 K. Larenz, *Geschäftsgrundlage und Vertragserfüllung*, 3rd ed. (Munich: Beck, 1963), passim; H. Köhler, *Unmöglichkeit und Geschäftsgrundlage bei Zweckstörungen im Schuldverhältnis* (Munich: Beck, 1971), pp. 132 ff.

The enforceability of a claim is not considered to be an exclusively substantive question but also carries elements of procedural law. Only the combination of substantive claim requirements and their procedural assertion decides whether performance in kind is granted.

**736.** The obligation to perform in kind also does not result directly from the contractual obligation but is regarded as a remedy that only arises based on the fulfilment of certain conditions, which include the breach of the contractual promise. Above all, however, the conditions of this remedy are not standardised abstractly, but it is at the discretion of the court whether or not it is granted. Thus, according to the understanding of common law, specific performance is the exception, not the rule.[35]

### *b) The Requirements for a Specific Performance*

#### aa) Specific Performance as a Legal Institution of Equity

**737.** From a historical point of view, one reason for the need to justify performance in kind can be found in the traditional division of English jurisdiction into Courts of Common Law and Courts of Equity. The action system developed by the Courts of Common Law were originally unfamiliar with any action for claims in kind that were not directed to a monetary compensation. It was only with the emergence of equity as a subsidiary system of fairness and the corresponding procedural institutions that the possibility arose to enforce other claims compulsorily.

**738.** The original form of remedy in equity still shapes the remedy of specific performance today, well over a century and a half after the formal abolition of the forms of action and the merger of common law and equity by the Judicature Acts 1873/75.[36] However, the concept of equity has become largely 'juridified'; in today's law, it is absorbed e.g. into the instrument of judicial discretion.[37] Due to its origins as an instrument of equity, the court's discretion concerning orders for performance in kind is still guided primarily by the overarching goal to reach a fair solution.[38] However, the reasons for the English courts' reluctance to order specific performance also lie in the law of enforcement: If the debtor does not comply with the court-sanctioned obligation to perform, this constitutes

---

35 Cf. *Sky Petroleum Ltd.* v. *V.I.P. Petroleum Ltd* [1974] 1 *WLR* 576, 578 (ChD); K. Zweigert/ H. Kötz, *Introduction to Comparative Law*, 3rd ed. (Oxford: Clarendon Press, 1996), §35; S.A. Smith, *Contract Theory* (Oxford: Oxford University Press, 2004), pp. 398 ff.

36 On the development Stürner, *ZVglRWiss* 99 (2000), 310, 313 ff.

37 On the exercise of discretion by English civil courts and their reviewability on appeal M. Stürner, *Die Anfechtung von Zivilurteilen* (Munich: Beck, 2002), pp. 199 ff.

38 *Shell U.K. Ltd.* v. *Lostock Garages Ltd.* [1976] 1 WLR 1187.

contempt of court, which can be punished with up to two years' imprisonment of the debtor.[39] Under this 'sword of Damocles', the performance of the contract might appear untenable for the debtor.[40] In contrast, concerning obligations towards a specific result, such as work contract, uncertainties regularly exist to a lesser extent due to the usually shorter duration of the contractual relationship.[41]

### bb) Discretionary Aspects

**739.** The court hearing the creditor's action for performance in kind exercises its discretion according to several considerations. English law contains only partial express statutory provisions on specific performance. For example, sec. 52(1) Sale of Goods Act 1979 made provision for specific performance a remedy for breach of contract.[42] However, the court only granted this claim 'if it thinks fit', i.e. if it considers it appropriate.[43] The decisive factor here is the extent to which a replacement for the purchased item can be procured. For easily available goods, a claim for specific performance is ruled out from the outset.[44] If, on the other hand, the goods are difficult to procure or even unique, such as real estate property, the debtor is usually ordered to perform in kind.[45]

---

39 Regulated inter alia by sec. 14 ff. Contempt of Court Act 1981; on this Unberath, *Die Vertragsverletzung*, 2007, p. 178.

40 Lord Hoffmann's expression in *Co-operative Insurance Society Ltd.* v. *Argyll Stores* (Holdings) Ltd [1998] AC 1, 13.

41 See, for example, *Jeune* v. *Queens Cross Properties Ltd* [1974] Ch. 97, 99 ff., ChD (Pennycuick VC).

42 'Sec. 52 Specific performance: (1) If any action for breach of contract to deliver specific or ascertained goods the court may, if it thinks fit, on the plaintiff's application, by its judgment or decree direct that the contract shall be performed specifically, without giving the defendant the option of retaining the goods on payment of damages.' The Sale of Goods Act 1979 ceased to have effect on 1 October 2015. Since then, the Consumer Rights Act 2015 has applied. See on the reform Twigg-Flesner, *ZEuP* 2019, 170.

43 For consumer sales contracts, pursuant to sec. 48E(2) Sale of Goods Act 1979 specific performance was the rule. The Consumer Rights Act 2015 has changed this considerably, as sec. 54(7)(c) mentions specific performance as a possible remedy of the consumer, but not as a standard case. Comment no 273 to the explanations states: '"Specific performance" is a direction a court can make, to compel a party to perform their obligations under a contract. It is an equitable remedy, meaning it is not available to consumers as a right, but at the court's discretion. It will not be ordered if damages are adequate to compensate the consumer – generally, damages will be adequate unless the subject matter of the contract is unique as the consumer can use damages to buy a replacement.'

44 Cf. the references in G.H. Treitel/E. Peel, *The Law of Contract* 12th ed. (London: Sweet & Maxwell, 2007), para. 21-019. This corresponds to the solution in Article 9:201(2)(d) PECL – a restriction that the DCFR has not adopted. For more details, see para. 751 below.

45 Cf. the references in G.H. Treitel, in *Chitty on Contracts*, 30th ed. (London: Sweet & Maxwell, 2008), para. 27-014. Particularly in the case of 'commercially unique goods', an order for performance in kind can also be considered, cf. *Behnke* v. *Bede Shipping Co. Ltd* [1927] 1 KB 649, 660 ff., KBD (Wright J.) (in relation to a ship). See, on the other hand, *Société des Industries Metallurgiques p.A.* v. *The Bronx Engineering Co. Ltd* [1975] 1 Lloyd's Rep. 465, 468 f., CA (Lord Edmund Davies), where specific performance was not granted in a contract

**740.** The court also considers the economic effects of an order for specific performance. In particular, it takes into account the possibility of satisfying the creditor by ordering them to pay damages. The discretionary decision also openly includes considerations that appear foreign to classical private law, namely the extent to which an order for specific performance would be a waste of public resources. Where an order for specific performance would lead to an artificial prolongation of a failed contractual relationship that would provoke new litigation, granting the remedy of specific performance is opposed by the overriding public interests of saving court resources and the idea of legal certainty.

### cc) Limits to the Primary Duty to Perform

**741.** In a system such as the common law, which regards the specific performance of the contractual obligation as a mere remedy, the limits of the performance obligations naturally have a different meaning than in continental civil law. If performance in kind is impossible, a corresponding conviction is ruled out from the outset.[46] If performance is not impossible, but would be excessively burdensome for the debtor, a court order for specific performance will usually not be issued since it would not bring about a fair solution for the disturbed contract.[47] Here, too, the creditor must settle with a claim for damages.

**742.** In the common law, there is also an equivalent to sec. 313 of the German Civil Code: The doctrine of frustration of contract. It only applies if an unforeseeable event[48] beyond the control of the parties has so fundamentally changed the circumstances of the performance of the contract that it would amount to an entirely different performance than the contractually agreed one,[49]

---

for the supply of a machine, although the (nevertheless possible) covering purchase was connected with a waiting period of almost one year.

46 Cf. *Forrer* v. *Nash*, 35 Beav. 167 = 55 Eng. Rep. 858 (1865); *Elliott & Elliott (Builders) Ltd.* v. *Pierson* [1948] Ch. 453; *Watts* v. *Spence* [1976] Ch. 165. On the historical development R. Zimmermann, *The Law of Obligations – Roman Foundations of the Civilian Tradition* (Oxford: Oxford University Press, 1990), pp. 776 ff.

47 *Tito* v. *Waddell (no 2)* [1977] Ch. 106, 326; *Handley Page Ltd.* v. *Commissioners of Customs and Excise* [1970] 2 Lloyd's Rep. 459, but see *Mountford* v. *Scott* [1975] Ch. 258; *Howard E. Perry & Co.* v. *British Railways Board* [1980] 1 WLR 1375.

48 In some cases this requirement is not considered essential, as by Lord Denning in *Ocean Tramp Tankers Corp. v. V/O Sovfracht (The Eugenia)* [1964] 2 QB 226, 238. See G.H. Treitel, *Frustration and Force Majeure*, 2nd ed. (London: Sweet & Maxwell, 2004), para. 13-011.

49 *Davis Contractors Ltd.* v. *Fareham Urban District Council* [1956] A.C. 696 (HL); *National Carriers Ltd.* v. *Panalpina (Northern) Ltd* [1981] AC 675 (HL), 700 (Lord Simon); G.H. Treitel, ibid., para. 2-044 ff. In summary, cf. K. Zweigert/H. Kötz, *Introduction to Comparative Law*, 3rd ed. (Oxford: Clarendon Press, 1996), §37 IV; see also S.A. Smith, *Contract Theory* (Oxford: Oxford University Press, 2004), pp. 371 ff.

i.e. if the debtor can say: 'It was not this that I promised to do.'[50] The contract's frustration leads to the contract's annulment; an adjustment is not at the discretion of the court. This makes sense: Because of the lack of an obligation to perform in kind, it would not be reasonable to adjust the contractual obligation to perform in the first place. The frustration of contract thus does not have its essential function in the area of the primary obligation to perform but instead serves to limit the debtor's obligation to pay damages.

#### dd) Comparison with German Law

**743.** Both German and English law thus set a limit to the debtor's claim for performance in kind whenever this would lead to an excessive burden for the debtor. However, there is a fundamental difference in the doctrinal foundations of this limitation of the claim: English law, which only grants the claim for payment in kind as a remedy, already carries out a balancing act at this point. The court must consider not only the interests of the parties but also considerations of procedural economy. The burden that would arise for the debtor through performance in kind is only one factor to be considered, which, however, will regularly lead to the remedy of specific performance being ruled out. In German law, on the other hand, the balancing in sec. 275(2) German Civil Code is only to be carried out in exceptional cases. The requirements are strict; the defence will only prevail in cases of obvious disproportion. The regulation is thus rather creditor-friendly, whereas English law tends to relieve the debtor.

## II. THE LINK BETWEEN THE DUTY TO PERFORM IN KIND AND THE REMEDY CONCEPT IN PECL AND DCFR

References: F. Hofmann/F. Kurz (eds.), *Law of Remedies. A European Perspective* (Cambridge: Intersentia, 2019); M. Schmidt-Kessel, 'The Right to Specific Performance under the DCFR', in G. Wagner (ed.), *The Common Frame of Reference: A View from Law & Economics* (Munich: Sellier, 2009), p. 69.

### 1. THE CLAIM FOR SPECIFIC PERFORMANCE AS A RULE

**744.** Following the PECL, the DCFR explicitly endorses the principle of performance in kind, i.e. it follows the civil law solution:[51] Article III.-3:302(1)

[50] Such is the formulation of Lord Radcliffe in *Davis Contractors Ltd.* v. *Fareham Urban District Council* [1956] A.C. 696, 729; similarly *Ocean Tramp Tankers Corp.* v. *V/O Sovfracht (The Eugenia)* [1964] 2 QB 226, 238 (Lord Denning).

[51] On this point also de Vries, *ERPL* 2009, 581.

DCFR[52] grants the creditor a right to enforce an obligation with consists in something other than the payment of money. Pursuant to Article III.-1:110(1) DCFR, this explicitly includes cases where performance has become more onerous for the debtor because the costs of performance have increased since the conclusion of the contract or due to the fact that the value of the remuneration has decreased.[53] The proposal for a Common European Sales Law (CESL) also follows this concept.

## 2. THE DESIGN OF THE CLAIM FOR SPECIFIC PERFORMANCE AS A MERE REMEDY

**745.** Nevertheless, the DCFR – again following the PECL – follows the remedy concept insofar as the actionable claim for specific performance does not follow precisely from the conclusion of the contract and, thus, from the nature of the obligation itself. Instead, it is linked to the conditions in Article III.-3:101(1) DCFR[54] relating to the non-fulfilment of the obligation and the lack of exemption from liability.[55] In addition, there are special provisions in Article III.-3:301 or III.-302 DCFR depending on whether the claims are monetary or not.

**746.** An exemption is provided if the non-performance is due to an obstacle beyond the debtor's control (Article III.-3:104(1) DCFR). The DCFR thus adopts, *mutatis mutandis*, the force majeure rule known from Article 79(1) CISG. Accordingly, the debtor is released from claims for damages to which the creditor is entitled in the event of non-performance if they could not perform due to force majeure.[56]

**747.** Structurally, the DCFR has thus adopted the common law approach. This solution generally favours the debtor: The creditor who wants to enforce performance in kind must, in addition to the conclusion of the contract, also set out and prove the facts giving rise to the claim, namely the non-performance of the obligation and the lack of exemption. The fact that these are adverse facts only exonerates the creditor (and plaintiff) to a limited extent.

---

52 Likewise Article 9:102(1) PECL.

53 Cf. comment A on Article III.-1:110 DCFR.

54 Likewise Article 8:101(1) PECL.

55 Similar in substance are Article 9:101 and 9:102 PECL; here too the claim for performance is referred to as a remedy. For a critical discussion of the concept, cf. Weller, *JZ* 2008, 764.

56 Cf. note I. 1. to Article III.-3:104 DCFR; on this also Unberath, *Die Vertragsverletzung*, 2007, pp. 336 ff. The relationship between the provision on excused non-performance and the exemptions from performance, e.g. on the grounds of impossibility, is unclear. According to Comment A on Article III.-1:110 DCFR, the task of demarcation between cessation of the basis of the contract and impossibility is left to legal practice.

## 3. LIMITS OF THE DUTY TO PERFORM

**748.** The limits of the obligation to perform in kind are also standardised as negative elements of the rule (Article III.-3:302(3) DCFR). They concern the legal or physical impossibility,[57] the impediment to performance and the unreasonableness of personal performance. The factual requirements are standardised in abstract and general terms. In contrast to the common law approach, the judge does not have discretion in this regard.

### *a) Refusal of Specific Performance Due to Undue Burden*

**749.** According to Article III.-3:302(3)(b) DCFR, specific performance is excluded if it would cause too much effort or cost. However, in contrast to German law, the DCFR does not give any precise indications as to when specific performance is 'unreasonably burdensome or expensive'. In particular, this standard does not prescribe a comparison of the debtor's effort and the creditor's interest in the performance.[58] What is to be understood by 'reasonableness' therefore depends on the respective context of the rule and the possibly conflicting values behind them, which are to be balanced in each specific case.[59] This only makes sense because a uniform concept of 'reasonableness' throughout Europe does not exist. It is related, if not identical, to the terms appropriate, proportionate, or unreasonable.[60] In this context, the term reasonableness serves to assess issues of contractual balance from the perspective of a neutral third party.[61]

**750.** The explanatory notes to Article III.-3:302 DCFR expressly exclude the consideration of whether performance and consideration were adequate or

---

57 On the corresponding provisions in the PECL, cf. C. Düchs, *Die Behandlung von Leistungsstörungen im Europäischen Vertragsrecht* (Berlin: Duncker & Humblot, 2006), pp. 158 ff.

58 Article III.-3:303 DCFR stipulates that even if performance cannot be demanded due to disproportionate effort, the creditor's claims for damages remain unaffected. Cf. in this respect sec. 275(4) German Civil Code. While according to sec. 280 ff. German Civil Code it is decisive for the existence of the claim for damages whether the debtor is responsible for the breach of duty, relief under Article III.-3:104(1) DCFR only occurs if the non-performance is due to force majeure, cf. on the parallel predecessor regulation of the PECL Lando, *RabelsZ* 67 (2003), 231, 239.

59 The authors of the DCFR explicitly point this out in the introduction: DCFR Full Edition, 2009, Introduction no. 22.

60 Cf. J. Schmidt, in *Festschrift für Großfeld* (Heidelberg: Recht und Wirtschaft, 1999), pp. 1017, 1027. Critically, Troiano, in Schulze (ed.), *New Features in Contract Law*, 2007, pp. 375, 377.

61 On these cases also Troiano, in Schulze (ed.), *New Features in Contract Law*, 2007, pp. 375, 398 f., 410 ff. According to Troiano, reasonableness is a 'balance component' within the concepts of good faith and diligence, namely as an 'intersection between colliding interests'. Reasonableness, however, almost completely coincides with the concept of *equità* (equity).

whether the parties made a good or a bad bargain.[62] The example given in the commentary to the Article of a yacht that sank on the way to being handed over to the buyer shows that the additional costs incurred by the debtor due to the impediment to performance and other expenses necessary for the fulfilment of the contract are to be taken into account. In the given case, these exceed the yacht's value by a factor of forty; the performance of the contract can thus be refused. It is already apparent at this point that the creditor's interest in performance is not the decisive factor but rather the effort to be made by the debtor. However, the complete absence of a creditor's interest in specific performance is of decisive importance if insisting on it would amount to vexatious behaviour.[63]

**751.** The PECL had excluded the claim for specific performance if 'the aggrieved party may reasonably obtain performance from another source'.[64] Meanwhile, the DCFR has adopted this restriction of the claim for performance, which is unknown from a continental perspective, only in a weakened form (Article III.-3:302(5) DCFR): If a creditor unreasonably insists on the claim for performance, although she could make a reasonable substitute transaction ('without significant effort or expense'), she cannot claim damages in this respect. Therefore, in the event of non-performance of the contract, the creditor will have a strong interest, if a substitute transaction seems possible, to abandon the demand for performance at an early stage and to switch to a claim for damages.[65] As a result, this again can be understood as an approximation to the common law solution.

### b) *Change in Material Circumstances*

**752.** In addition to the aforementioned exception to the claim for performance in kind, the DCFR also includes a provision in Article III.-1:110 DCFR on the adjustment of the contract if, due to subsequent changes in circumstances, the performance of the contractual obligation has become so onerous for the debtor that it would be manifestly unjust to enforce performance.[66] The relatedness to undue performance, as discussed above, is striking: In both cases, it depends on

---

62 Cf. note F to Article III.-3:302 DCFR.

63 Article III.-1:103 DCFR obliges the parties to observe the principle of good faith. Cf. further note F to Article III.-3:302 DCFR, which is similar to the case of *Tito* v. *Waddell* (no 2) [1977] Ch. 106.

64 Article 9:102(2)(d) PECL. In justification of this, the materials state that in this case it is in the presumed interest of the parties to procure a replacement themselves on the market and to liquidate any additional costs as damages from the debtor. Cf. note H to Article 9:102 PECL.

65 According to U. Huber, *ZEuP* 2008, 708, 722 the intended acceleration effect could also be achieved more simply, namely through a 'more expedient regulation of the abstract calculation of damages'. Critical of the concept also van Kogelenberg, *ERPL* 2009, 599, 616 ff.

66 On this point Lilleholt/Mikelsen, *ERPL* 2009, 573.

whether the performance has become excessively burdensome for the debtor. Thus, in light of the different legal consequences – exclusion of the obligation to perform on the one hand, adjustment of the contract on the other – the necessity to delimitate these two defences also arises here.

753. In this respect, one might be tempted to conclude that the element of adjustment of the contract in the case of frustration of contract would be meaningless since every change of circumstance covered by this would simultaneously lead to the excuse of an impediment to performance, which in turn excludes the primary obligation to perform and the claim for damages according to Article III.-3:104 DCFR.[67] The fact that this cannot be the case follows from the materials on the corresponding predecessor provision of the PECL:[68] It expressly postulates the priority of the provisions on the frustration of contract over undue performance. Thus, the debtor is not *eo ipso* released from his obligation to perform and pay damages in the event of a subsequent change in the circumstances essential to the contract. Only if the prerequisites of the contract's frustration are not met can the debtor be released from the obligation to perform due to an obstacle to performance outside of his influence.[69]

## 4. A MEANINGFUL COMPROMISE?

754. Overall, there seems to be a consensus that the debtor cannot be forced to perform in kind if it is impossible or would require excessive efforts. However, the starting points are very different: The continental legal systems are based on the assumption that the debtor's obligation to perform results from the obligation itself. This is different in common law: Here, specific performance is the exception that requires justification; it is not part of the obligation but a remedy. This is a significant structural difference.[70]

755. The drafters of the DCFR, like the creators of the PECL, have tried to find a compromise between the two approaches by treating performance in kind as a rule rather than an exception, unlike in English law.[71] Nevertheless, both

67 In this direction Weller, *JZ* 2008, 764, 772.

68 Cf. comment F on Article 9:102 PECL. Likewise U. Huber, *ZEuP* 2008, 708, 736.

69 Cf. Lilleholt/Mikelsen, *ERPL* 2009, 573, 577, who assume (without justification) that this precedence no longer applies under the DCFR.

70 For a critical perspective, cf. Weller, *JZ* 2008, 764.

71 The UN Convention on Contracts for the International Sale of Goods is different, as Articl 28 CISG subjects the consequences of the obligation to perform in kind to the law of the respective state of the court: The CISG grants the primary claim comprehensively on the substantive level, but subjects its enforcement to the same restrictions that would exist for corresponding actions for performance under the law of the respective state of jurisdiction. For more details on the implications of this concession to the common law

sets of rules structurally implement the remedy concept, which does not link the claim for performance in kind to the creation of the obligation, but to the non-performance for which the debtor is responsible. The remedy approach separates the creation of the obligation from the rights that follow from it. The breach of contract, which may consist of non-performance, triggers the claim for specific performance as one of the possible remedies. This approach favours the debtor, as it does not suffice for the creditor merely to prove the conclusion of the contract in order to assert a claim for performance in kind.[72]

**756.** The approach chosen by the authors of the DCFR to list the creditor's rights with maximum transparency are to be commended. The notion of non-performance remains central (Article III.-3:101(1) DCFR). If the non-performance is not excused, the creditor has several remedies at their disposal. However, demanding the contractually promised performance is only one of these remedies, albeit the most important one.

## III. ECONOMIC PERSPECTIVE: THE THEORY OF EFFICIENT BREACH OF CONTRACT

**757.** The theory of efficient breach of contract states that a contractual obligation should not be fulfilled from an economic point of view if it leads to a waste of resources, and, consequently, to inefficiency.[73] On the one hand, this is the case if the costs of fulfilling the contract incurred by the debtor exceed its benefits for the creditor, for example, due to increased procurement costs.[74] In this case, the breach of contract helps the debtor minimise losses. On the other hand, a breach of contract is already considered efficient if the debtor receives a higher offer for the subject matter of the contract after its conclusion, provided that this allows them to satisfy the creditor's interest in performance. In this case, the item goes where it provides the greatest economic benefits – namely,

---

states, see Müller-Chen, in P. Schlechtriem/I. Schwenzer/U.G. Schroeter, *Kommentar zum UN-Kaufrecht (CISG)*, 7th ed. (Basel/Munich: C.H. Beck/Helbing & Lichtenhahn, 2019), Art. 28 paras. 1 ff.

72 However, according to U. Huber, *AcP* 210 (2010), 319, 321 note 2, these differences must not be overemphasized.

73 Representative for many R. Posner, *Economic Analysis of Law*, 7th ed. (New York: Aspen, 2007), p. 56. The problem of efficient breach only arises in the case of an imperfect contract, i.e. when the negative cost-benefit balance is not known to the parties at the time of the conclusion of the contract; a party acting rationally would not conclude such a contract in the first place, knowing the circumstances. In general on the economic analysis of continental contract law, Hatzis, in Grundmann/Schauer (eds.), The Architecture of European Codes and Contract Law, 2006, p. 159.

74 Cf. H.-B. Schäfer/C. Ott, *Lehrbuch der ökonomischen Analyse des Zivilrechts*, 5th ed. (Berlin/Heidelberg: Springer, 2013), pp. 495 ff.

to the person who is willing to pay the most for it.[75] In this constellation, the breach of contract thus serves to maximise profit. Even if exactly the same result could be achieved by the third party buying the good from the creditor at a higher price,[76] this would entail the execution of two contractual relationships and, thus, higher transaction costs.[77]

**758.** In practice, the theory of efficient breach of contract leads to the abandonment of the principle of specific performance since the debtor is granted the right to choose between performance in kind and compensation for the monetary interest in the performance. This would amount to a proportionality test in such a way that the costs incurred by the debtor through the performance of the contract would be weighed against the benefit accruing to the creditor. There would be no need to weigh the costs against the benefits, as the cost-benefit comparison would only include quantifiable values that could be expressed in monetary terms. A mere preponderance of the debtor's costs over the creditor's benefit (i.e. the interest in performance) would be sufficient to render the obligation to perform in kind invalid. As outlined above, this is not in line with the civil law approach to grant the creditor a right to specific performance. It does, however, reflect a pragmatic viewpoint underlying many business transactions.

## IV. BREACH OF CONTRACT IN EU PRIVATE LAW

References: S. Engelmann, *Die Fristsetzung als Voraussetzung für Leistungsstörungsrechte* (Baden-Baden: Nomos, 2019); M.W. Hesselink, *Justifying Contract in Europe. Political Philosophies of European Contract in Europe* (Oxford: Oxford University Press, 2021), p. 196.

**759.** In EU private law as it currently stands, outside the realm of sales law, the non-fulfilment of performance obligations has only been subject to regulatory interventions in the context of certain types of contracts. A general regime for rights in the event of a breach of contract, as regulated in Article 45(1) CISG, for example, does not exist in European contract law. An exception exists for the default of payment, on which a directive was adopted.

---

[75] According to the so-called Coase theorem, this is in the nature of the market: In a perfect market, according to *Coase*, the goods (property rights) tend to go to the market participant who benefits most from them, regardless of their initial distribution: This is the one who pays the highest price for them; in this way, the Pareto optimum is necessarily achieved in the final allocation. Cf. Coase, *Journal of Law and Economics*, 3 (1960), 1.

[76] This is the solution according to Coase's view, see previous note.

[77] R. Posner, *Economic Analysis of Law*, 7th ed. (New York: Aspen, 2007), p. 61.

## 1. NON-COMPLIANCE

**760.** The Consumer Sales Directive and its successor, the Sale of Goods Directive, contain provisions on the requirements that must be met by the purchased goods in order for them to be considered in conformity with the contract (Article 2(2) Consumer Sales Directive and Articles 5–9 Sale of Goods Directive).[78] There is only an indirect reference to the primary performance obligations in the definition standard of Article 2 no. 1 Sale of Goods Directive. This states that a sales contract is any contract 'under which the seller transfers or undertakes to transfer ownership of goods to a consumer, and the consumer pays or undertakes to pay the price thereof'. Nevertheless, this does not impose any requirements on the Member States concerning the primary obligations of the parties The core of the directive are secondary claims. These include, in particular, the right to have the goods brought into conformity as a kind of 'secondary primary claim'.

**761.** According to the Payment Services Directive, which deals with the rights and obligations of payment service users and payment service providers in the professional or commercial provision of payment services, there is an obligation on the payment service provider to credit the amount of the payment transaction to the payee's payment service provider's account by the end of the following business day (Article 83(1) Payment Services Directive). If this limitation is time is exceeded, 'the payer's payment service provider shall, [...] be liable to the payer for correct execution of the payment transaction' (Article 89(1) subpara. 1 Payment Services Directive). For direct debit (Article 89(2) Payment Services Directive), in the case of non-performance, the payee may demand from the payment service provider, that this payment order be transferred without undue delay, where necessary once again, to the payer's payment service provider. These claims are only excluded in cases of unusual and unforeseeable events (Article 93 Payment Services Directive).

## 2. LATE PERFORMANCE

References: M.-P. Weller/C. Harms, 'Die Kultur der Zahlungstreue im BGB – Zur Umsetzung der neuen EU-Zahlungsverzugs-RL ins deutsche Recht', *WM* 2012, 2305.

### a) *The Late Payment Directive*

**762.** The Late Payments Directive responds to the sometimes poor payment behaviour in business transactions. Recital 3 of the Late Payments Directive

[78] See para. 839 below.

states this clearly: 'Although the goods are delivered or the services performed, many corresponding invoices are paid well after the deadline. Such late payment negatively affects liquidity and complicates the financial management of undertakings. It also affects their competitiveness and profitability when the creditor needs to obtain external financing because of late payment. The risk of such negative effects strongly increases in periods of economic downturn when access to financing is more difficult.' In response to that, the Directive postulates that in business-to-business transactions, the creditor is entitled to interest for late payment, without the need for a reminder, if they have fulfilled their contractual and legal obligations and have nevertheless not received the amount due on time, unless the debtor is not responsible for the delay in payment; this applies from the agreed due date, but no later than 30 days after the due date and receipt of an invoice (Article 3(1) and (3) Late Payment Directive).

**763.** Moreover, Article 6(1) of the Late Payment Directive stipulates that in these cases, the creditor has a claim against the debtor for payment of a lump sum of at least 40 euros. The German legislator has implemented this so-called lump sum for recovery in sec. 288(5) of the German Civil Code; according to this, the creditor of a claim for payment can demand a lump sum of 40 euros in addition to the other items if the debtor is in default. This is independent of any proven damage; also, an additional reminder is not necessary. The EU legislator considered the provision to be appropriate in order to deter the debtor from exceeding the payment deadlines (Recitals 19, 33 Late Payment Directive); the standard thereby becomes an incentive for good payment practices.[79]

### *b) Lump-Sum Recovery Fees in the Case of Periodically Recurring Performance Obligations*

**764.** Even if the sum of 40 euros mentioned in sec. 288(5) German Civil Code might be bearable in an individual case, things will certainly look different in the case of repetition. The problem arises above all in the case of periodically recurring services: The question here is whether sec. 288(5) German Civil Code or, indeed, comparable provisions of national law, apply to each individual claim for payment or only once in total.[80]

**765.** First of all, it should be clear that in the case of a plurality of remuneration claims from similar contractual relationships, there is a claim to payment of several lump sums: Each individual contract gives rise to remuneration claims with which the debtor can be in default. This is not so clear, however,

[79] Cf. BAG NZA 2019, 121 para. 51.
[80] Cf. BGH WM 2020, 192 (however leaving the issue unsolved).

if default occurs in the case of periodically arising remuneration claims from a single contractual relationship: Does a claim to payment of only one lump sum or several lump sums arise here? For instalment and progressive payments, sec. 288(5) German Civil Code expressly stipulates the latter. For all other cases, it depends on an interpretation of the norm. Looking at the wording of sec. 288(5) German Civil Code, it is obvious to generally follow the second view: Remuneration claims arise monthly in the present contractual relationship. This so-called receipt-based accrual can become a considerable burden for the debtor, especially if they consider themselves no longer bound by the contract because of a declared termination. It is therefore sometimes suggested to refer to balances that are to be assessed over a period of time or are otherwise related; one can speak of a process-oriented accrual of remuneration claims. However, it would be difficult to develop easily manageable criteria according to which claims could be summarised. If one considers that the lump sum comes into being without a reminder and without causing damages, this argues against any kind of cumulation. Also, excessively large units would, under certain circumstances, drastically limit the deterrent effect of sec. 288(5) German Civil Code.[81] The better reasons thus speak for a receipt-oriented view.

**766.** This result is in line with the Late Payment Directive. According to Article 3(1), Article 6(1) Late Payment Directive, the Member States can freely increase the lump sum of 40 euros. In this respect, it must be noted that the directive follows the principle of minimum harmonisation insofar as the Member States are allowed to enact more creditor-friendly provisions than those provided for in the Directive (Article 12(3) Late Payments Directive). However, it also follows from the objective of the Directive: Consequences of late payments must be dissuasive (Recitals 19 and 33 Late Payment Directive). Any kind of aggregation of individual claims, as explained above, would be detrimental to this objective. According to Article 6(2) of the Late Payments Directive, Member States shall ensure that the lump sum is payable without any reminder and as compensation for the creditor's recovery costs. Another advantage is the fact that this kind of obligation can be determined easily.

### *c) Compensation for Recovery Costs*

**767.** Article 6(3) Late Payments Directive allows for a combination of the lump sum (Article 6(1) Late Payments Directive) and the appropriate compensation provided in Article 6(3) Late Payments Directive.[82]

---

[81] Cf. Dornis, in *BeckOGK-BGB* (1 June 2024), §288 paras. 68 ff.

[82] CJEU, 19 April 2019, Case C-131/18, *Gambietz/Ziegler*, ECLI:EU:C:2019:306.

## 3. NON-CONTRACTUAL PERFORMANCE

### a) *Reduction*

**768.** Price reduction as a reaction to a breach of contract by the seller is found, in particular, in the law of sales of goods. Article 3(3) and (5) of the Consumer Sales Directive give the consumer a right 'to an appropriate reduction of the price'; however, the calculation method is left to the respective Member State's law. With a similar starting point, the Sale of Goods Directive now contains in its Article 15a definition of what constitutes a 'proportionate reduction in the price' within the meaning of Article 13(1) and (4) of the Sale of Goods Directive: A reduction according to the ratio of the reduced value of the goods to the value the goods would have had if they had conformed with the contract. The provision in Article 14(5) Digital Content Directive is similar.

### b) *Rescission and Adjustment of the Contract*

References: J.C. Dastis, *Das Rücktrittsrecht des Käufers im Europäischen Privatrecht* (Baden-Baden: Nomos, 2017); H. Kötz, *European Contract Law*, 2nd ed. (Oxford: Oxford University Press, 2017), §13; M. Sonnentag, *Das Rückgewährschuldverhältnis* (Tübingen: Mohr Siebeck, 2016).

**769.** In a legal system which values the binding effect of contractual commitments,[83] it seems logical that an adjustment or termination of a contract may only be granted in exceptional cases. Therefore, rescission is only possible if an adjustment of the contract is impossible or unreasonable for one party. This is based on the fact that the termination of the contract, as opposed to its adjustment, interferes more profoundly with private autonomy.

**770.** According to Article 3(6) of the Consumer Sales Directive, the consumer does not have the right to dissolve the contract in the case of only minor non-conformities. Thus, the right to terminate the contract (as a right based on defects liability) is subject to the proviso that a certain triviality threshold is exceeded. This illustrates both the favour contractus underlying the Consumer Sales Directive[84] and the principle of proportionality, as the Council explicitly stated in its Common Position on the Directive as justification for the exclusion of contract termination for minor breaches of contract.[85]

---

83 On the principle of *pacta sunt servanda*, see para. 412 above.

84 Cf. C. M. Bianca, in S Grundmann/C.M. Bianca (eds.), *EU Sales Directive* (Antwerp/New York: Intersentia, 2002), Art. 3 para. 36.

85 Cf. the explanations on Article 3 in Council Common Position no 51/98, OJ 1998 C 333/46, p. 53.

771. In the past, European contract law did not regulate the consequences of the rescission of a contract.[86] Now, a regulatory framework of sorts exists in Article 16(3) of the Sale of Goods Directive and Article 16, 17 of the Digital Content Directive.[87] They are structurally similar to the consequences of consumer withdrawal, for which quite detailed regulations exist in Articles 12–15 Consumer Rights Directive.[88] However, the rationale for the right of withdrawal is not a breach of contract but a statutory right.

### c) *Damages*

References: C. Heinze, *Schadensersatz im Unionsprivatrecht* (Tübingen: Mohr Siebeck, 2017); H. Kötz, *European Contract Law*, 2nd ed. (Oxford: Oxford University Press, 2017), §14.

772. In business transactions, even in civil law systems, the claim for damages is often of more central importance than the (primary) claim for performance. It is, therefore, no coincidence that common law considers the primacy of the damages claim to be the general rule: This reflects the interests of the parties in normal cases; claims for specific performance must be the exception.[89] In consumer contracts, however, different interests are at play. Here, the proper fulfilment of the contractual obligations is what counts. European sales law primarily contains claims regarding the restoration of consumer goods to their contractual condition through repair or replacement (Article 3(2) Consumer Sales Directive or Article 13(1) and (2) Sale of Goods Directive). Subsequent claims facilitate a reasonable reduction of the purchase price or a termination of the contract (Article 3(5) Consumer Sales Directive or Article 14(4) and (5) Sale of Goods Directive). Neither the Consumer Sales Directive nor the Directive replacing it regulate claims for damages; their regulation is rather left to the law of the Member States. As their traditions are too different, a standardisation has, hence, not been undertaken.[90]

773. In contrast, the Commission's proposal for a Digital Content Directive contained a claim for damages in Article 14. This claim should arise in the case of non-compliance with the contract or non-performance (probably in the sense of Article 11 draft Digital Content Directive); liability extends to any economic damage to the consumer's digital environment and, in principle, includes a restoration of the status quo ante. However, the relationship to the respective

86 See on this from the perspective of a future common European private law *Dastis*, *Das Rücktrittsrecht des Käufers im Europäischen Privatrecht*, 2017, pp. 283 ff.
87 See paras. 890 and 981 below.
88 See para. 587 above.
89 See para. 735 above.
90 See para. 870 below.

liability laws of the Member States was unclear.[91] In the adopted version, Article 3(10) Digital Content Directive, therefore, 'shall not affect the freedom of Member States to regulate [...] the right to damages'. Recital 73 of the Digital Content Directive explains this by stating that such a right to damages already exists in all Member States and that it is, therefore, unnecessary to regulate it in the Directive.

**774.** Although Article 7 of Regulation (EC) no 261/2004 also provides for a lump-sum compensation claim in the event of flight delays, it does not provide an independent claim for damages. Rather, according to Article 12 of Regulation 261/2004, further claims for damages by the passenger under applicable national law remain unaffected.[92]

**775.** In contrast to this, the Package Travel Directive in Article 14(2) Directive 2015/2302 regulates a claim against the tour operator for reasonable compensation for the damage suffered by the traveller as a result of the lack of conformity, irrespective of fault and to be paid without delay.[93]

**776.** Another independent claim for damages[94] is contained in Article 35a of the Credit Rating Agencies Regulation,[95] which investors and issuers can assert against a rating agency if it has committed one of the infringements listed in Annex III to the Credit Rating Agencies Regulation intentionally or with gross negligence and this has had an effect on a rating. Claims for damages existing under national law are not excluded (Article 35a(5) Credit Rating Agencies Regulation). From a European point of view, these are non-contractual claims as long as the ratings were not specifically prepared for certain investors or issuers. From an objective point of view, the claim requires one of the almost 100 infringements listed in Annex III to the Credit Rating Agencies Regulation. This infringement must have affected the rating.[96] An investor is entitled to a claim 'where it establishes that it has reasonably relied, in accordance with Article 5a(1) or otherwise with due care, on a credit rating for a decision to invest into, hold onto or divest from a financial instrument covered by that credit rating' (Article 35a(1) of the Credit Rating Agencies Regulation). In

---

91 See para. 985 below.

92 However, compensation granted under the Air Passenger Rights Regulation may be offset against such a claim for damages, see para. 1073 below.

93 See para. 1037 below.

94 For an overview of liability provisions in EU private law, see Heinze, *Schadensersatz im Unionsprivatrecht*, 2017, pp. 120 ff.

95 As amended by Regulation (EU) No 462/2013 of the European Parliament and of the Council of 21 May 2013 amending Regulation (EC) No 1060/2009 on credit rating agencies, OJ 2013 L 146/1.

96 For more details see Wojcik, *NJW* 2013, 2385, 2387.

this respect, the substantiation of the claim is alleviated to a certain degree (Article 35a(2) Credit Rating Agencies Regulation). In any case, liability requires gross negligence on the part of the agency (Article 35a(1) of the Credit Rating Agencies Regulation);[97] Article 35a(4) of the Credit Rating Agencies Regulation subjects legal questions not regulated in the ordinance to the applicable national law. Limitations of liability are possible under the conditions of Article 35a(3) Credit Rating Agencies Regulation.

97 Critical of this limitation is G. Wagner, in *Festschrift für Blaurock* (Tübingen: Mohr Siebeck, 2013), pp. 467, 491 ff., who advocates liability for slight negligence in combination with a maximum liability amount.

# CHAPTER 5
# NON-DISCRIMINATION

## §18. EQUAL TREATMENT AND PRIVATE LAW

CONTENTS



References: G. Bachmann, 'Der Gleichbehandlungsgrundsatz im Zivilrecht', *ZHR* 170 (2006), 144; M. Grünberger, *Personale Gleichheit. Der Grundsatz der Gleichbehandlung im Zivilrecht* (Baden-Baden: Nomos, 2013); C. Herresthal, 'Vertragsrecht', in K. Langenbucher, *Europäisches Privat- und Wirtschaftsrecht*, 5th ed. (Baden-Baden: Nomos, 2022), §2 paras. 112 ff.; M. Lehmann, 'Diskriminierungsschutz und Vertragsrecht – Entwicklungstendenzen im Rechtsvergleich', in R. Schulze (ed.), *New Features in Contract Law* (Munich: Sellier, 2007), p. 67; S. Leible/M. Schlachter (eds.), *Diskriminierungsschutz durch Privatrecht* (Munich: Sellier, 2006); D. Looschelders, 'Diskriminierung und Schutz vor Diskriminierung im Privatrecht', *JZ* 2012, 105; A. Metzger, 'Allgemeine Rechtsgrundsätze in Europa – dargestellt am Beispiel des Gleichbehandlungsgrundsatzes', *RabelsZ* 75 (2011), 845; O. Mörsdorf, *Ungleichbehandlung als Norm – eine dogmatische Analyse des unional determinierten Antidiskriminierungsrechts in Deutschland* (Tübingen: Mohr Siebeck, 2018); J. Neuner, 'Protection against Discrimination in European Contract Law', (2006) *European Review of Contract Law* 2, 35; K. Riesenhuber, *EU-Vertragsrecht* (Tübingen: Mohr Siebeck, 2013), §6; B. Schöbener/F. Stork, 'Anti-Diskriminierungsregelungen der Europäischen Union im Zivilrecht – zur Bedeutung der Vertragsfreiheit und des Rechts auf Privatleben', *ZEuS* 2004, 43; F. Stork, 'Das Gesetz zum Schutz vor Diskriminierungen im Zivilrecht. Umsetzung der Richtlinien 2000/43/EG und 2004/113/EG in das deutsche Privatrecht', *ZEuS* 2005, 1; A.-S. Vandenberghe, 'Non-discrimination on the grounds of age and disability in private contracting for goods and services: Economic analysis of the European 2008 Proposal for a new Directive', *ZEuP* 2011, 235; M. Zoppel, *Europäische Diskriminierungsverbote und Privatrecht* (Tübingen: Mohr Siebeck, 2015).

# I. NON-DISCRIMINATION AS A RATIONALE IN PRIVATE LAW?

777. Since the Age of Enlightenment, one of the pillars of private law, especially contract law, has been the right to freely choose one's contractual partner and determine the content of contractual agreements on one's own accord. No justification – positive or negative – is required; arbitrariness and discrimination are, hence, actually permitted in private law. According to this traditional view, exceptions, such as compulsory contracting, only exist in the area of services of general interest or if the provider has a factual monopoly on the respective good or service.

778. However, this formal interpretation of private law as a mere external regulatory framework in the context of private equality has fundamentally changed in recent years. These tendencies towards so-called materialisation have already been described;[1] they primarily concern the sphere of commutative justice. The concept of non-discrimination practically does not occur here. In public law categories, contract law is the domain of liberty; equality plays a very subordinate role – distributive justice is organised by the state and is not the responsibility of private legal subjects.[2] Thus, according to the traditional view, the principle of equal treatment is not a component of general private law.[3] Here it was primarily the impulses of Community law that forced many Member State legal systems to reconsider this orthodox viewpoint.

# II. PRECONDITIONS OF EU LAW

## 1. NON-DISCRIMINATION AS A CROSS-CUTTING ISSUE

779. Whereas in national legal systems, an often quite sharp separation of public and private law prevents or at least complicates direct horizontal protection against discrimination, the EU legislator is less bound by such distinctions. As has already been discussed, directives in the context of private law, in particular, could also be implemented in the guise of public law, such

1 See para. 419 above.

2 For the distinction between iustitia commutativa and iustitia distributva, which goes back to Aristotle, see para. 425above.

3 However, the discussion here is rather dynamic, at least in Germany, see for example G. Hueck, *Der Grundsatz der gleichmäßigen Behandlung im Privatrecht* (Munich: Beck, 1958), p. 61; Bachmann, *ZHR* 170 (2006), 144; Grünberger, *Personale Gleichheit. Der Grundsatz der Gleichbehandlung im Zivilrecht*, 2013; O. Mörsdorf, *Ungleichbehandlung als Norm – eine dogmatische Analyse des unional determinierten Antidiskriminierungsrechts in Deutschland* (Tübingen: Mohr Siebeck, 2018).

as prohibitions and restrictions subject to fines, within the framework of the Member States' freedom of implementation under Article 288(3) TFEU.[4] This explains why non-discrimination is not seen exclusively as a state duty to protect but as an issue that relates to both private and public law.

**780.** For example, the Equal Treatment Directive 2004/113/EC stipulates in its Recital 2 that 'the right to equality before the law and protection against discrimination for all persons constitutes a universal right [...]'. However, Recital 3 goes on to say that, 'while prohibiting discrimination, it is important to respect other fundamental rights and freedoms [...]'. Article 3(2) Directive 2004/113/EC then reads: 'This Directive does not prejudice the individual's freedom to choose a contractual partner as long as an individual's choice of contractual partner is not based on that person's sex.' This is to be understood as an attempt to bring the rights of freedom and equality of those involved in legal transactions into a meaningful balance. It must be absolutely clear that a stronger emphasis on equality rights can only be achieved at the expense of freedom rights – what matters in this respect is the practical harmony between the two spheres, which can be achieved with the help of the proportionality principle.[5]

## 2. LEGISLATIVE COMPETENCE

**781.** The legal basis for directives in the field of anti-discrimination derives primarily from Article 19 TFEU (ex-Article 13 EC; introduced by the Treaty of Amsterdam). According to this, the Council 'may take appropriate action to combat discrimination based on sex, racial or ethnic origin, religion or belief, disability, age or sexual orientation'. The principle of unanimity applies. The provision deliberately describes the form of regulation openly, meaning that all forms of action listed in Article 288 TFEU are to be considered. In addition, Article 157(3) TFEU (ex-Article 141(3) EC) allows for regulation regarding equal pay. The pertinent legislation is adopted in the ordinary legislative procedure, i.e. with the double consent of Parliament and Council (Article 294 TFEU).

## 3. EXISTING DIRECTIVES

**782.** Based on the EU's legislative powers regarding the protection against such forms of discrimination, a whole series of directives have been issued in this area, all of which serve to implement the principle of equal treatment in the Member States:

---

4 See para. 311 above.
5 As discussed in para. 460 above.

**783.** (1) The Racial Equality Directive 2000/43/EC of 29 June 2000: Its purpose is to establish a framework for combating discrimination based on race or ethnicity (Article 1 Directive 2000/43/EC). According to its Article 3(1), it applies equally to public and private relationships, including public bodies, and covers the areas of employment and occupation (above all labour law), education, health and social benefits, as well as access to publicly offered goods and services, including housing; the latter area concerns general private law, above all.

**784.** (2) The Framework Directive Employment 2000/78/EC of 27 November 2000: Its purpose is to establish a general framework to combat discrimination on the grounds of religion or belief, disability, age or sexual orientation in employment and occupation (Article 1 Directive 2000/78/EC). The latter, at the same time, outlines the scope of application defined in greater detail in Article 3(1) of Directive 2000/78/EC, which primarily concerns access to education and employment, employment and working conditions as well as membership in workers' and employers' organisations and, thus, lies in the realm of labour law.

**785.** (3) Directive 2004/113/EC on gender equality outside the workplace of 13 December 2004 (the so-called Unisex Directive): Its purpose is to establish a framework for combating gender discrimination regarding the access to and supply of goods and services (Article 1 Directive 2004/113/EC). According to its Article 3, it applies to all persons providing goods and services which are available to the public in both public and private sectors, including public bodies, and are offered outside the sphere of private and family life. It does not apply to employment and occupation, including self-employment, or education. It is intended as a complementary instrument to the Employment Equality Directives; it covers, in particular, access to publicly provided goods and services in bulk transactions and insurance under private law (Recital 15 of Directive 2004/113/EC).

**786.** (4) The Equal Treatment Directive 2006/54/EC of 5 July 2006: This directive aims to ensure the implementation of the principle of equal opportunities and equal treatment of men and women in matters of employment and occupation. It consolidates the legal situation and repeals the directives in force in this field until then.[6] It concerns access to employment, including promotion and vocational training, working conditions, including pay, and occupational social security schemes (Article 1 Directive 2006/54/EC).

---

6 The following Directives were repealed with effect of 15 August 2009 (Article 34(1) Directive 2006/54/EC): 75/117/EEC, 76/207/EEC, 86/378/EEC and 97/80/EC; for a full list see Annex I Part A of Directive 2006/54/EC.

## 4. REFORM

**787.** Already in July 2008, the Commission had presented the proposal for a Council Directive on implementing the principle of equal treatment between persons irrespective of religion or belief, disability, age or sexual orientation.[7] This proposal was intended to complement the existing legal framework as established by the Directives 2000/43/EC, 2000/78/EC and 2004/113/EC,[8] in which the prohibition of discrimination on the grounds of religion or belief, disability, age or sexual orientation applies only in employment, occupation and vocational training. The proposal was intensively discussed in the Council until 2011.[9] However, no agreement could be reached. Later, in 2014, the Council was unable to reach the required unanimity.[10] Since 2016, the proposal has been back on the agenda. The status since then is summarised in a Council document of 26 June 2019;[11] a conclusion of the legislative process is currently not expected. As there was no foreseeable agreement, the Commission has eventually withdrawn the proposal in its Work Programme 2025.[12]

## 5. DISCRIMINATION THROUGH NON-DISCRIMINATION DIRECTIVES?

References: C. Armbrüster, *Das Unisex-Urteil des EuGH (Test-Achats) und seine Auswirkungen* (Bonn: Zentrum für Europäisches Wirtschaftsrecht, 2012); J.D. Lüttringhaus, 'Europaweit Unisex-Tarife für Versicherungen!', *EuZW* 2011, 296; K. Purnhagen, 'Zum Verbot der Risikodifferenzierung aufgrund des Geschlechts – Eine Lehre des EuGH zur Konstitutionalisierung des Privatrechts am Beispiel des Versicherungsvertragsrechts?', *EuR* 2011, 690.

**788.** In order to achieve a gradual transition to full gender equality,[13] the Unisex Directive 2004/113/EC contained an opening clause in Article 5(2) for insurance contracts, allowing Member States to allow proportional differences in premiums and benefits before the entry into force of the Directive on 21 December 2007 'where the use of sex is a determining factor in the assessment of risk based on relevant and accurate actuarial and statistical data'. This was to take account of the fact that certain categories of risk may be different for men and women and that gender may be a determining factor in

[7] COM(2008) 426 final.
[8] See para. 782 above.
[9] Summary of the state of affairs in Council document 16525/11 of 15 November 2011.
[10] Minutes of the Council meeting of 11 December 2014, Council document 16887/14, pp. 7 f.
[11] Consolidated version of the Directive, Council document 10740/19.
[12] Cf. Commission Work Programme 2025, COM(2025) 45 final, Annex IV no. 26.
[13] See Recital 18 of Directive 2004/113/EC.

the assessment of the risks insured. In the case of such contracts, Member States should initially be allowed to derogate from the principle of gender-neutral premiums and benefits, provided that the difference in treatment was based on transparent actuarial and statistical data (Recital 19 of Directive 2004/113/EC). After five years, a review was to be carried out by the Member States, the results of which were to be forwarded to the Commission, which was then to submit proposals for amendments to the Council on this basis (Article 16 Directive 2004/113/EC).

**789.** The CJEU, however, considered this opening clause a violation of primary law.[14] As a standard of review, the court referred, in particular, to Articles 21 and 23 of the Charter of Fundamental Rights, which prohibits discrimination on the grounds of gender and demands equality between women and men in all areas. Although the Charter only came into force on 1 December 2009, and thus after the Unisex Directive 2004/113/EC, the CJEU used it as a basis for the review. This is justified by the fact that the Directive explicitly refers to these Charter provisions in its Recital 4.[15] However, one should not be inclined to deduce from this that the EU legislator may use provisions that are not in force (e.g. soft law[16]) to give them authority that they have not acquired through democratic legitimacy.[17] Rather, this is a case of application of the hierarchy of norms, albeit *pro futuro*.

**790.** According to the case law of the CJEU, like situations must not be treated differently, and different situations may not be treated equally unless such treatment is objectively justified.[18] However, since the Directive itself obviously assumes, at least from the CJEU's perspective, that the situation of women and men is comparable concerning the premiums and benefits of the insurance policies they take out, a theoretically unlimited validity of the opening clause according to the Directive is not compatible with the principle of equal treatment; the CJEU, therefore, deemed it invalid as of 21 December 2012.[19] Other Charter rights, such as the freedom to conduct a business, or indeed the requirement of an objective rationale for the unequal treatment, were not discussed.[20] The decision has led to a recalculation of all tariffs for contracts concluded after that date in the insurance industry.

---

14 CJEU, 1 March 2011, Case C-236/09, *Test-Achats*, ECLI:EU:C:2011:100.
15 CJEU, 1 March 2011, Case C-236/09, *Test-Achats*, ECLI:EU:C:2011:100, para. 17.
16 On the DCFR see para. 122 above.
17 In this direction, see Purnhagen, *EuR* 2011, 690, 698.
18 CJEU, 16 December 2008, Case C-127/07, *Arcelor Atlantique et Lorraine*, ECLI:EU:C:2008:728, para. 23; CJEU, 1 March 2011, Case C-236/09, *Test-Achats*, ECLI:EU:C:2011:100, para. 28.
19 CJEU, 1 March 2011, Case C-236/09, *Test-Achats*, ECLI:EU:C:2011:100, paras. 31 ff.
20 Critically, hence, Lüttringhaus, *EuZW* 2011, 296.

# §19. PRIVATE LAW PROVISIONS AIMING AT NON-DISCRIMINATION

## CONTENTS



References: C. Armbrüster, 'Kontrahierungszwang im Allgemeinen Gleichbehandlungsgesetz?', *NJW* 2007, 1494; M. Benecke/G. Kern, 'Sanktionen im Antidiskriminierungsrecht: Möglichkeiten und Grenzen der Umsetzung der Europäischen Richtlinien im deutschen Recht', *EuZW* 2005, 360; M. Heese, 'Offene Preisdiskriminierung und zivilrechtliches Benachteiligungsverbot', *NJW* 2012, 572; K. Sponholz, *Die unionsrechtlichen Vorgaben zu den Rechtsfolgen von Diskriminierungen im Privatrechtsverkehr* (Baden-Baden: Nomos, 2017); F. Stork, *Das Anti-Diskriminierungsrecht der Europäischen Union und seine Umsetzung in das deutsche Zivilrecht* (Frankfurt am Main, Lang, 2006); G. Thüsing/K. von Hoff, 'Vertragsschluss als Folgenbeseitigung: Kontrahierungszwang im zivilrechtlichen Teil des Allgemeinen Gleichbehandlungsgesetzes', *NJW* 2007, 21; G. Wagner/N. Potsch, 'Haftung für Diskriminierungsschäden nach dem Allgemeinen Gleichbehandlungsgesetz', *JZ* 2006, 1085.

## I. CONTENT

### 1. MATERIAL SCOPE

**791.** The requirements of the EU directives can essentially be categorised using two criteria: The first relates to the material scope of application; this concerns occupation, education and employment on the one hand, i.e. to labour law, and access to publicly offered goods and services, including housing, on the other, and thus general private law. The second criterion of classification concerns the grounds of discrimination: The Directives differentiate between discrimination based on racial or ethnic origin, sex, religion or belief, disability, age or sexual orientation. This corresponds to the list in Article 19(1) TFEU.

## 2. REGULATORY DESIGN IN THE PROCESS OF TRANSPOSITION

**792.** In transposing the directives, the Member States had to decide whether each directive should be transposed separately in the regulatory context that suited them or whether an overarching form of regulation would be more suitable. In Germany, for instance, the second approach was preferred. The German General Equal Treatment Act, entered into force in 2006, goes beyond the requirements of the aforementioned directives in that it does not retain the combination of classification criteria used there in each case, but significantly expands them. According to sec. 1 German General Equal Treatment Act, the aim of the law is to prevent or eliminate discrimination on grounds of racial or ethnic origin, gender, religion or belief, disability, age or sexual identity. Thus, all the grounds of discrimination listed in Article 19(1) TFEU are mentioned. However, in the area of civil law as well as in the area of labour law, the provisions of the Directive only require the implementation of the characteristics of race, ethnic origin and gender; the other characteristics are only relevant for the area of labour law. In the area of civil law, which is of interest here, there is thus an overextended transposition[1] – only discrimination on the grounds of ideology was not adopted here.[2]

**793.** The same can be said for the intensity of discrimination: According to the standards of the Directives, one-off acts are regularly not sufficient; this results, for example, from Article 2(3) of Directive 2000/43/EC (Racial Equality Directive). According to this, the harassment must create a 'hostile environment', which requires continuous action.[3] In contrast, sec. 3(3) of the German General Equal Treatment Act allows only one instance of harassment to be sufficient.[4] The German Federal Labour Court requires the cumulative existence of a violation of a person's dignity and a 'hostile environment', which will regularly require conduct of a certain duration. However, in individual cases, particularly serious one-off conduct may also be sufficient.[5]

---

1 In general see para. 366 above.

2 Instructive on this, is for example BGH WM 2020, 1387: Justification of age discrimination via freedom of entrepreneurial activity ('Adults-Only-Hotel'); no reference for a preliminary ruling.

3 Bauer/Thüsing/Schunder, *NZA* 2005, 32, 33.

4 Baumgärtner, in *BeckOGK-BGB* (1 November 2024), §3 AGG para. 110 with further references.

5 BAG NZA 2010, 387 para. 32.

# II. PERTINENT ISSUES

## 1. PRECLUSION PERIOD FOR THE ASSERTION OF CLAIMS

**794.** Under German law, in the field of labour law, claims for compensation due to violation of the prohibition of discrimination must be filed within two months after receipt of the rejection (sec. 15(4) German General Equal Treatment Act). A similar provision is found for claims under general private law in sec. 21(5) German General Equal Treatment Act. In both cases, this is a preclusive deadline, the exceeding of which leads to material preclusion.[6] If one considers that one of the main objectives of the non-discrimination directives is to provide effective protection against discrimination, these preclusion periods could appear problematic insofar as they could actually curtail the remedies available.[7]

**795.** The question of the compatibility of national law rules that preclude claims for damages within a certain period of time arises. A preliminary ruling pertaining to sec. 15(4) German General Equal Treatment Act against the backdrop of the Employment Framework Directive 2000/78/EC was therefore sought from the CJEU. The facts of the case were as follows:[8] Ms Bulicke, aged 41, applied for a job on 16 November 2007 in response to a job advertisement placed by Deutsche Büro Service in a newspaper. The job advertisement read as follows: 'We are looking for motivated members of staff (male/female) for our young team in the City. Do you like talking on the phone? Then you are exactly the right person for us. We'll give you the opportunity to earn money doing it. You are between 18–35 years of age, with a good knowledge of German and looking for a full-time job? …' On 19 November 2007, Ms Bulicke was informed by telephone that her application had not been considered. This rejection was confirmed in a letter dated 21 November 2007, according to which all positions had been filled. However, it turned out that two persons aged 20 and 22 had been recruited on 19 November 2007. Similar job advertisements were subsequently published several times. On 29 January 2008, Ms Bulicke brought an action before the Hamburg Labour Court for compensation for the age-related disadvantage she claimed to have suffered. At that time, the preclusive period under sec. 15(4) German General Equal Treatment Act had already expired, given that Ms Bulicke became aware of the discrimination on 21 November 2007 at the latest.[9]

---

6 See OLG Hamm NJW-RR 2011, 762, 764; G. Thüsing, in *Münchener Kommentar zum BGB*, 10th ed. (Munich: C.H. Beck, 2025), §21 AGG para. 60 with further references.

7 See also *Grünberger, Personale Gleichheit*, 2013, pp. 306 ff., 311 ff.

8 CJEU, 8 July 2010, Case C-246/09, *Bulicke*, ECLI:EU:C:2010:418.

9 LAG Hamburg LAGE §15 AGG no. 9, para. 65.

**796.** The CJEU first discussed the requirements of the EU law's equivalence principle, according to which the provision of sec. 15(4) German General Equal Treatment Act must apply in the same way to actions based on the violation of EU law as to those based on the violation of domestic law, provided that these actions have a similar subject matter and legal basis.[10] However, this does not mean that the most favourable national law must be applied to enforce the legal positions determined by the EU, as long as there is no disadvantage.

**797.** Consequently, a violation of the EU law's requirement of *effet utile* was considered by the court. In principle, preclusion periods are unproblematic in terms of legal clarity.[11] Problems concerning the effectiveness can, therefore, only arise if the time limit is so short or its commencement is so late that the actual assertion of the claim is made excessively difficult. The CJEU did not have any issues regarding the time limit's duration; in particular, the court considered the beginning of the time limit valid if, following a teleological interpretation of sec. 15(4) German General Equal Treatment Act, it does not necessarily begin with the receipt of the rejection but with the point in time at which the person concerned becomes aware of the alleged age-related discrimination.[12]

## 2. OTHER LAWS VIOLATING THE DIRECTIVES

**798.** As is otherwise the case in non-discrimination law, the preconditions of the relevant directives must be observed within all areas of law. It is, therefore, not sufficient if the specific act adopted in transposition of the Directive meets all the necessary requirements.[13] Rather, the entire legal order must be in conformity with EU law, as shows an example taken from German labour law. The question of a possible violation of EU law arose in the context of sec. 622(2) of the German Civil Code (old version). According to that provision, periods of employment before the employee reached the age of 25 were not to be taken into account when calculating the relevant period of employment for the notice period for termination of contract.[14] The CJEU considered this provision to be a violation of the Framework Employment Directive, which applies to

---

10 See e.g. CJEU, 1 December 1998, Case C-326/96, *Levez*, ECLI:EU:C:1998:577, para. 41; CJEU, 16 May 2000, C-78/98, *Preston*, ECLI:EU:C:2000:247, para. 55; CJEU, 29 October 2009, Case C-63/08, *Pontin*, ECLI:EU:C:2009:666, para. 45; CJEU, 8 July 2010, Case C-246/09, *Bulicke*, ECLI:EU:C:2010:418, para. 26.

11 See, for example, CJEU, 10 July 1997, Case C-261/95, *Palmisani*, ECLI:EU:C:1997:351, para. 28.

12 CJEU, 8 July 2010, Case C-246/09, *Bulicke*, ECLI:EU:C:2010:418, paras. 35 ff.

13 Cf. above at paras. 346 ff.

14 The provision was repealed with effect from 1 January 2019 by Article 4d of the Act to Strengthen Opportunities for Qualification and for More Protection in Unemployment Insurance (Qualification Opportunities Act) of 18 December 2018, Federal Law Gazette I, p. 2651.

dismissals under Article 3(1)(c) of Directive 2000/78/EC, as there was no viable objective rationale for not taking into account the period of employment prior to the employee's 25th birthday, which could have served as justification under Article 6(1) of Directive 2000/78/EC.[15]

## 3. OBLIGATION TO CONCLUDE A CONTRACT?

**799.** The question of whether a duty to conclude a contract can follow from a relevant discrimination has been and still is highly controversial in Germany. As a legal consequence of discrimination under sec. 19 German General Equal Treatment Act, claims for removal and damages arise under sec. 21(1) and (2) German General Equal Treatment Act. However, the law does not explicitly provide for a claim that leads to the conclusion of a contract. However, can such a claim possibly arise from general principles? The following fictitious example will illustrate the problem: A is of non-German descent. He wants to rent a flat in a small German town. At the viewing appointment, the landlord V informs him that he only intends to rent his total of 100 flats to Germans. A is outraged and wants to know if he can force V to rent out the flat to him.

**800.** Under German law as it stands, sec. 19(3) German General Equal Treatment Act allows for grounds for justification with regard to the allocation of the flat with a view to creating and maintaining socially stable resident structures and balanced settlement structures as well as balanced economic, social and cultural conditions. The landlord would have to make a corresponding commitment here, so that the discrimination would eventually be justified.

**801.** If, based on the interpretation of German law, one were to conclude that A does not have a claim to the elimination of discrimination, this result would have to conform with the European requirements. In this respect, the requirements of Article 2(1) and (2)(a), Article 3(1)(h) of Directive 2000/43/EC must be taken into account. The purpose of this Directive is to achieve equal treatment irrespective of racial or ethnic origin. Exceptions for apartment rental contracts are not provided. Sec. 19(3) of the German General Equal Treatment Act thus violates the provisions of the Racial Equality Directive.[16]

---

15 CJEU, 19 January 2010, Case C-555/07, *Kücükdeveci*, ECLI:EU:C:2010:21; also in the follow-up decision in BAG NJW 2011, 1626, 1627. For details on the decision see para. 265 above.

16 Stork, *Das Anti-Diskriminierungsrecht der Europäischen Union und seine Umsetzung in das deutsche Zivilrecht*, 2006, pp. 294 ff.; Mörsdorf, in *BeckOGK-BGB* (1 July 2024), §19 AGG para. 70; G. Thüsing, in *Münchener Kommentar zum BGB*, 10th ed. (Munich: C.H. Beck, 2025), §19 AGG paras. 77, 87.

**802.** Since a horizontal direct effect of the Directive is ruled out,[17] A cannot rely on the fact that the Racial Equality Directive prohibits discrimination like the one at issue here. However, Member State law must exhaust all methodologically possible ways to meet the requirements of the Directive.[18] An interpretation of sec. 19(3) German General Equal Treatment Act in conformity with the Directive may be considered. The effect of such an approach would be to disapply this provision in the case of discrimination on grounds of racial or ethnic origin.[19] Consequently, there is a claim for removal and also a claim for damages.

**803.** It is disputed whether this results in a veritable duty to conclude a contract. There is no explicit rule in the German General Equal Treatment Act. For labour contracts, sec. 15(6) German General Equal Treatment Act provides that no claim to the establishment of an employment relationship follows from a relevant discrimination. This is sometimes referred to as a systematic argument in favour of the obligation to conclude a contract in general private law.[20] Other approaches depart from the claim for removal under sec. 21(1) German General Equal Treatment Act; the *actus contrarius* for the discriminatory refusal to conclude a contract lies precisely in the conclusion of the very contract.[21] Alternatively, one may refer to the claim for damages under sec. 21(2) German General Equal Treatment Act: its content is measured according to sec. 249(1) German Civil Code; a restitutio in integrum is therefore owed, which may imply the conclusion of a contract.[22]

**804.** The opposing view refers to the massive encroachment on contractual freedom that such a contractual obligation undoubtedly causes.[23] Especially in the case of continuing obligations, this leads to potentially conflict-ridden party relationships. Irrespective of this, it will often be difficult to prove that the contract would have been concluded with the discriminated party without the disadvantage, especially in the case of mass transactions. If one did not want to

---

17 See para. 392 above.

18 See para. 348 above.

19 In favour of this also e.g. G. Thüsing, in *Münchener Kommentar zum BGB*, 10th ed. (Munich: C.H. Beck, 2025), §19 AGG para. 87; Mörsdorf, in *BeckOGK-BGB* (1 July 2024), §19 AGG para. 70. Different methodological approach in Singer, in *Festschrift für Adomeit* (Cologne: Luchterhand, 2008), pp. 703, 710, who assumes that sec. 19(2) AGG takes precedence by way of interpretation of the law in line with the Directive.

20 G. Thüsing, in Münchener Kommentar zum BGB, ibid., §21 AGG para. 18; Sponholz, Die unionsrechtlichen Vorgaben zu den Rechtsfolgen von Diskriminierungen im Privatrechtsverkehr, 2017, pp. 235 ff.

21 For example G. Thüsing, in *Münchener Kommentar zum BGB*, ibid., §21 AGG para. 17 with further references.

22 In this sense Rolfs, *NJW* 2007, 1489, 1493.

23 For references cf. K. Riesenhuber, in W. Erman, *BGB Kommentar*, 17th ed. (Cologne: Otto Schmidt, 2023), §21 AGG para. 19.

require this proof, this would possibly lead to multiple contracts that would not make much sense, especially in the case of tenancies, for example if in the above case V had rejected further interested parties because of their ethnic origin.[24] In this case, it would amount to a plea of impossibility under sec. 275(1) of the German Civil Code, so that the disadvantaged party who demanded the conclusion of the contract first would ultimately be the one to benefit.

**805.** In this respect, the question of whether European Directive law requires compulsory contracting is particularly important. An argument in favour of this could be that, in some cases, only the fulfilment in kind would constitute an effective sanction in the sense of, for example, Article 15 of the Racial Equality Directive. The Unisex Directive also clearly states in its Article 3(2) Directive 2004/113/EC that a person's free choice of contractual partner is not affected as long as their choice does not depend on the person's gender. However, a similar formulation is not found in other directives. Since the EU directives generally do not intend to interfere with the general principles of contract law of the Member States,[25] it seems more reasonable to assume that compulsory contracting is not required under EU law as a matter of principle.[26] Only if all relevant sanctions under Member State law are ineffective, granting a right to contract might be necessary.[27]

**806.** Irrespective of this, it is, of course, possible under the principle of minimum harmonisation (e.g. Article 7(1) Directive 2004/113/EC or Article 6(1) Directive 2000/43/EC) to provide for stricter sanctions for relevant disadvantages.

## 4. THE AMOUNT OF COMPENSATION

**807.** An important aspect of the effectiveness of non-discrimination law from the perspective of EU law concerns the sanctions for violations.[28] For example, according to Article 15 of the Racial Equality Directive 2000/43/EC, Member States shall determine the sanctions to be imposed in case of a breach of the relevant transposition law and shall take all appropriate measures to ensure that they are enforced. The Racial Equality Directive explicitly mentions compensation to victims as an appropriate sanction. As elsewhere, all sanctions

24 Likewise sec. 22(2) Draft ADG, BT-Drucks. 15/4538, p. 44.

25 See also para. 407 above.

26 Likewise Bruns, *JZ* 2007, 385, 389; cf. also the approach in Zoppel, *Europäische Diskriminierungsverbote und Privatrecht*, 2015, pp. 166 ff.

27 Similarly Heese, *NJW* 2012, 572, 575 f.

28 See also Sponholz, Die unionsrechtlichen Vorgaben zu den Rechtsfolgen von Diskriminierungen im Privatrechtsverkehr, 2017, pp. 186 ff.

must be effective, proportionate and dissuasive. Here, on the one hand, there is a wide margin of implementation of the Member States. On the other hand, purely symbolic amounts of damages do not meet the requirements of the Directive. The following case may serve as an example:[29]

**808.** G, a German-born son of a Togolese woman, brought an action against D, who runs a nightclub in an industrial area, because on 5 November 2010 he was allegedly refused entry with the remark that there were 'already enough black people in there'. G demands injunctive relief and payment of damages for pain and suffering of at least 5,000 euros.

**809.** Since nightclubbing is a mass business in the sense of sec. 19(1) no. 1 German General Equal Treatment Act, the claim for injunctive relief arises relatively unproblematically from sec. 21(1) German General Equal Treatment Act, so that in the future, D must not refuse entry because of G's ethnic origin. However, it is questionable whether a claim for compensation for immaterial damages also arises.[30] According to sec. 21(2) German General Equal Treatment Act, the disadvantaged person can demand appropriate compensation in money. However, what amount is appropriate in the sense of the provision? All the circumstances of the individual case must be taken into account.[31] The Stuttgart Higher Regional Court considered the amount of 5,000 euros to be excessive given the weight of the incident and taking into account general preventive considerations, and also disproportionate in view of the damages for pain and suffering awarded in other cases for the disregard of a person's general right of personality. In the court's view, compensation of 900 euros was appropriate instead.[32] The court calculated this amount from the turnover that D made that evening in his nightclub with 150 guests.[33] This reasoning appears convincing overall in light of the Directive's requirements. The Directive indeed requires that sanctions have a deterrent effect. However, this is only one consideration among others; the principle of proportionality requires that the disadvantage's nature and extent must also be considered.

---

29 OLG Stuttgart NJW 2012, 1085.

30 Other claims in tort are not excluded under sec. 21(3) AGG (see OLG Köln NJW 2010, 1676: §§831, 823 BGB). However, with regard to the amount of the claim for compensation, the same considerations apply as for sec. 21(2) AGG.

31 On the concretisation of open legal concepts by way of balancing, see Stürner, *Der Grundsatz der Verhältnismäßigkeit im Schuldvertragsrecht*, 2010, pp. 347 ff.

32 This was not the case with the lower court, which was of the opinion that the humiliating treatment did not exceed the level of injustice and offence that ultimately happens to every person on a daily basis: LG Tübingen BeckRS 2012, 01258.

33 Critically Liebscher, *NJW* 2012, 1087, who considers an orientation on the total turnover of D on that evening (i.e. including drinks) to be preferable.

# CHAPTER 6
# SPECIFIC TYPES OF CONTRACTS

## §20. SPECIFIC TYPES OF CONTRACT AND EU LAW: GENERAL REMARKS

CONTENTS



References: C. Baldus *e.a.*, 'Forum: Neue Richtlinien, neue Vertragstypensystematik?', *GPR* 2019, 258; L. Specht, 'Daten als Gegenleistung – Verlangt die Digitalisierung nach einem neuen Vertragstypus?', *JZ* 2017, 763; M. Wendland, 'Digitale Inhalte und Vertragstypenlehre: Dogmatische Grundfragen des Digitalen Vertragsrechts', in M. Weller/M. Wendland (eds.), *Digital Single Market – Bausteine eines Rechts in der Digitalen Welt* (Tübingen: Mohr Siebeck, 2019), p. 71; F. Zoll, 'Die Vertragstypen im Vorschlag für das Gemeinsame Europäische Kaufrecht', in *Festschrift für Müller-Graff* (Baden-Baden: Nomos, 2015), p. 118.

## I. A DOCTRINE OF SPECIFIC TYPES OF CONTRACT?

**810.** The German Civil Code is sometimes considered a prime example of an inaccessible body of law. Its abstract style can be seen in many formulations, but also in the technique of 'bracketing out' ('*vor die Klammer ziehen*', a term coined by Gustav Boehmer[1]), which was implemented with the German Civil Code's General Part. This refers to the effort to consolidating the common elements of a set of rules in abstract and general rules rather than spelling out every detail over and over again in each and every section of the code. In doing so, the creators of the German Civil Code pursued a rationalisation approach intended to prevent the duplication of similar rules in different sub-areas of the law, which was

[1] G. Boehmer, *Einführung in das Bürgerliche Recht*, 2nd ed. (Tübingen: Mohr Siebeck, 1965), p. 74.

perceived as less than elegant.[2] The Second Book of the German Civil Code, the Law of Obligations, for its part – unlike the other books – also was given its own General Part, contained in sec. 1 to 7. The subsequent part on specific obligations contains regulations for types of obligations that occur particularly frequently in practice, which include contractual and non-contractual obligations.

**811.** The types of contracts regulated there – such as purchase, lease, contract for work and services or service contract – are therefore not comprehensively regulated. Rather, it is the interplay of general and special norms that provides the normative framework. The parties are by no means bound to the types of contracts as standardised in the German Civil Code: Unlike in property law, for example, there is no fixation of legal institutions. Rather, the existing contract types can be modified or combined with each other (mixed contract); the parties are even free to conclude contracts completely outside such types (atypical contract). However, the vast majority of contractual obligations are likely to be within the legally standardised contract types. In this respect, the doctrine of specific types of contracts primarily has a rationalisation function: It is not necessary, for example, to make special provisions on liability for defects in the contract of sale, since a regime is prescribed by law that provides a legally secure and, at least for typical constellations, fair and balanced regulation.[3]

**812.** Many legal systems are similarly based on a more or less differentiated doctrine of specific types of contracts. The DCFR has also adopted that approach: Book IV (Specific Contracts) regulates several important contracts, similar to many continental codifications; however, this is not understood to represent a conclusive regulation.[4] Even systems without comprehensive codifications are familiar with individual regulations for contract types that occur frequently in practice, such as the Sale of Goods Act 1979 in England.[5]

## II. EUROPEAN CONTRACT TYPES

**813.** These considerations cannot be transferred indiscriminately to European private law since it represents a regulatory system without codification and any

---

2 See Petersen, *JURA* 2011, 759.

3 In general, on the function of dispositive law, see law L. Kähler, Begriff und Rechtfertigung abdingbaren Rechts (Tübingen: Mohr Siebeck, 2012); J. Cziupka, Dispositives Vertragsrecht. Funktionsweise und Qualitätsmerkmale gesetzlicher Regelungsmuster (Tübingen: Mohr Siebeck, 2010); F. Möslein, Dispositives Recht – Zwecke, Strukturen und Methoden (Tübingen: Mohr Siebeck, 2011).

4 Zoll, in Festschrift für Müller-Graff, 2015, p. 118.

5 The Sale of Goods Act 1979 expired on 1 October 2015. Since then, the Consumer Rights Act 2015 has applied.

overarching legislative power. However, it can be stated that the doctrine of contract types has also found its way into EU law. Private law directives and regulations refer back to, and sometimes adopt, the terminology used in the law of the Member States. The 1968 Brussels Convention[6] already contained rules on jurisdiction that referred to certain contract types, such as sale (Article 13–15 Brussels Convention) and rent (Article 16 no. 1 Brussels Convention). With increasing regulatory density, other types of contracts were added. As a general rule, the terms used in EU legal instruments are to be interpreted autonomously and can thus have a different meaning than those in the Member States' legal systems. This is clearly shown, for example, by the service contract, which is understood much more narrowly in German law (sec. 611 German Civil Code) than in EU law (e.g. in Article 4(1)(b) Rome I Regulation).[7]

**814.** Occasionally, EU law has introduced entirely new types of contracts, such as the time-share contract,[8] the package travel contract[9] or the contract for the supply of digital content and digital services.[10] In some cases, recognised contract types have been modified: The Sale of Goods Directive contains rules on the law of sales only concerning a contract of sale concluded between a trader and a consumer.[11] The same applies to consumer credit agreements.[12]

**815.** The Directive's regulatory technique and the obligation to transpose it into the law of the Member States make it possible to integrate these new or modified contract types into the national legal systems. This does not fundamentally call into question the doctrine of types of contracts, but rather confirms it.

## III. DIGITALISATION AS A CROSS-SECTIONAL TASK

**816.** The process of integrating contract types found in EU law into the national regulatory system now faces a particular challenge with regard to contracts for the provision of digital content, which the Digital Content Directive has introduced.[13] This Directive deals primarily with the content and enforcement of such contracts. It does not specify which type of contract should be concerned. The Digital Content Directive is at odds with the traditional doctrine of contract

6 See para. 1413 below.
7 More at para. 1173 below.
8 See §26 below.
9 See §25 below.
10 See §23 below.
11 See para. 836 below.
12 See §24 below.
13 See the contributions in Baldus *e.a.*, *GPR* 2019, 258.

types because it does not focus on the mutual performance obligations to characterise the contract but on the subject matter of the performance (the digital content) instead.[14] Therefore, it seems possible to create special regulations for the types of contracts under consideration if digital content is the subject matter of the contract.[15]

**817.** As will be explained in more detail later on, the contracts concluded on online platforms also transcend, to some extent, the classical doctrine of contract types. However, this is not so much about the legal nature of the contracts concluded within the framework of the platform economy but rather the fact that a third party has a decisive influence on the parameters of the contract's conclusion. From the perspective of EU law, this is arguably a regulatory problem rather than one of contract law.[16]

---

14 See Specht, *JZ* 2017, 763; Wendland, in Weller/Wendland, *Digital Single Market – Bausteine eines Rechts in der Digitalen Welt*, 2019, p. 71.

15 More on this at para. 944 below.

16 See Regulation (EU) 2019/1150 of the European Parliament and of the Council of 20 June 2019 on promoting fairness and transparency for business users of online intermediary services, OJ 2019 L 186/57. More on this 'Platform Regulation' below at para. 989 below.

# §21. THE SALES CONTRACT

## CONTENTS

References: F. Bien, 'Vermögensschäden in der Absatzkette', *ZEuP* 2012, 644; S. Bucher, *Gewährleistungsrecht im Gemeinsamen Europäischen Kaufrecht* (Baden-Baden: Nomos, 2016); R. Canavan, 'Contracts of sale', in C. Twigg-Flesner (ed.), *Research Handbook on EU Consumer and Contract Law* (Cheltenham: Edward Elgar Publishing, 2016), p. 266; C. Goanţă, *Convergence in European Consumer Sales Law. A Comparative and Numerical Approach* (Cambridge: Intersentia, 2016); S. Grundmann, 'Verbraucherrecht, Unternehmensrecht, Privatrecht – warum sind sich UN-Kaufrecht und EU-Kaufrechts-Richtlinie so ähnlich?', *AcP* 202 (2002), 40; M. Heese, 'Europäische Kaufrechtsharmonisierung: Stand, Grundfragen, Perspektiven', in *Festschrift für Bamberger* (Munich: C.H. Beck, 2017), p. 109; B. Heiderhoff, *Europäisches Privatrecht*, 6th ed. (Heidelberg: C.F. Müller, 2023), paras. 478 ff.; C. Herresthal, in K. Langenbucher, *Europäisches Privat- und Wirtschaftsrecht*, 5th ed. (Baden-Baden: Nomos, 2022), §2 paras. 171 ff.; V. Heutger, *Ein gemeineuropäisches Kaufrecht?* (Frankfurt am Main: Lang, 2007); H.-P. Mansel, 'Kaufrechtsreform in Europa und die Dogmatik des deutschen Leistungsstörungsrechts: Kaufrecht in Europa nach der Umsetzung der Verbrauchsgüterkauf-Richtlinie', *AcP* 204 (2004), 396; K. Riesenhuber, *EU-Vertragsrecht* (Tübingen: Mohr Siebeck, 2013), §§11–13; G. Wagner, 'Der Blue Button klemmt', *ZEuP* 2012, 455; G. Wagner, 'Der Verbrauchsgüterkauf in den Händen des EuGH: Überzogener Verbraucherschutz oder ökonomische Realität?', *ZEuP* 2016, 87.

## I. THE SIGNIFICANCE OF THE SALE OF GOODS

**818.** The contract for the sale of goods usually serves as a prototype of the contract of obligation in legal education. The transaction brought about by the sales contract occurs extremely frequently in everyday life so that economic backgrounds – unlike, for example, leasing, time-sharing or factoring – do not need to be explained to students. In quantitative terms, the contract of sale is probably one of the most important contract types in Europe.[1]

**819.** This empirical assessment is also confirmed by a look at the legal framework of the contract of sale: In the Law of Obligations of the German Civil Code (section 8 of book 2), the law on sales contracts is found at the very beginning (title 1). Such is the case also e.g. in the Swiss Code of Obligations,[2] in the French Code civil[3] and in the Italian Codice civile.[4] Likewise, the DCFR begins Book IV on the individual contract types with the sales contract.[5] It is no coincidence that efforts to standardise contract law, especially in the area of sales law, have been successful at the international level: The Vienna Sales Convention (CISG) is one of the most prominent examples of international legal unification.[6]

**820.** In general, the structure of sales law also has a significant effect as a blueprint for the general doctrine of contract law. This can be seen, for example, in the German Civil Code, where the law on contracts for work and services was restructured according to the sales law model as part of the modernisation of the law of obligations in 2001. In some legal systems, the rules pertaining to sales contracts are extended to contracts not explicitly regulated by the law. Hence, they serve as a substitute of sorts of a general part of the law of obligations.[7]

**821.** The sales contract also plays an extremely important role in EU law. With the Consumer Sales Directive, a core area of contract law was partially regulated in 1999. This legal act was rightly described as a crystallisation point for European contract law.[8] The proposal for a Common European Sales Law of 2011 also shows the central importance of the matter for the internal market. Even though this initiative ultimately failed, it has left its mark on the Sale of Goods Directive of 2019. Similar initiatives in other areas of the law of obligations, such as in the law on contracts for services or contracts for work and services, are not to be found. Especially in the law of service contracts, which is highly relevant to the internal market, has not been regulated, with the Services Directive[9] explicitly

---

1 Cf. Mansel, *AcP* 204 (2004), 396, 399. Likewise the assessment in the Comments on Article IV.A.-1:101 DCFR.

2 Articles 184 ff. OR.

3 Articles 1582 ff. Code civil.

4 Articles 1470 ff. Codice civile.

5 Articles IV.A.-1:101 ff. DCFR.

6 See para. 92 above.

7 See the examples given in the notes to Article IV.A.-1:101 DCFR.

8 Cf. Mansel, *AcP* 204 (2004), 396, 397.

9 Directive 2006/123/EC of the European Parliament and of the Council of 12 December 2006 on services in the internal market, OJ 2006 L 376/36.

excluding contractual relations between the service provider and the customer from its scope of application.[10]

## II. THE DEVELOPMENT OF SALES LAW IN THE EU

### 1. THE CONSUMER SALE OF GOODS DIRECTIVE

**822.** The legislative process regarding the Consumer Sales Directive (CSD) was initiated with a proposal submitted by the Commission on 23 August 1996.[11] It was based on the EU's general internal market competence (ex-Article 100a EC, today Article 114 TFEU). Consequently, the explanatory memorandum emphasises the importance of a uniform minimum standard for the confidence of consumers and entrepreneurs in the internal market: According to the memorandum, the legal fragmentation leads to distortions of competition. Following a series of amendments proposed by the European Parliament, the Commission submitted an amended proposal on 31 March 1998.[12] After further amendments, Parliament and Council then approved the Directive in May 1999. It entered into force in July 1999 and was to be implemented by 1 January 2002 (Article 11(1) CSD).

**823.** Only Austria, Finland, and Germany transposed the law on time. Infringement proceedings were initiated against France, Belgium and Luxembourg[13] with respective affirmative judgements of the CJEU in 2004.[14] Most Member States pursued a minimal solution, which regularly consisted of transposition into national consumer protection laws. A far-reaching change to the general law on sales or even the general law on performance deficits was only made in Germany.

**824.** The Directive follows the principle of minimum harmonisation (Article 8(2) CSD). The Member States can, therefore, adopt or maintain more consumer-friendly regulations.[15] In order to achieve the goal of establishing

10 Recital 90 Directive 2006/123/EC.

11 Proposal for a Directive of the European Parliament and of the Council on the sale of consumer goods and associated guarantees, COM (95) 520 final. This was preceded by the Green Paper on consumer goods guarantees and after-sales services, COM (93) 509 final.

12 Amended proposal for a Directive of the European Parliament and of the Council on the sale of consumer goods and associated guarantees, COM(1998) 217 final.

13 For more details on the implementation process, see Mansel, *AcP* 204 (2004), 396, 402 ff.

14 CJEU, 19 February 2004, Case C-310/03, *Commission/Luxembourg*, ECLI:EU:C:2004:115; CJEU, 19 February 2004, Case C-311/03, *Commission/France*, ECLI:EU:C:2004:405; CJEU, 19 February 2004, Case C-312/03, *Commission/Belgium*, ECLI:EU:C:2004:116.

15 On the principle of minimum harmonisation see para. 75 above.

a uniform minimum protection for consumers in the internal market (cf. Recitals 2, 5 CSD), the Directive creates a mandatory minimum standard: Hence, the rights granted to the consumer cannot be derogated from (Article 7(1) CSD). This means that even informed consumers (who are therefore no longer worthy of protection) cannot waive their rights out of their own interest. Thus, for example, a technically skilled amateur mechanic cannot waive his warranty rights when buying a used car that he wants to use for stripping even if the commercial seller grants a substantial price reduction in return.

## 2. THE SALES LAW IN THE DCFR

References: U. Huber, 'Modellregeln für ein Europäisches Kaufrecht', *ZEuP* 2008, 709; M. Loos, 'Sales Law in the DCFR', in V. Sagaert/M.E. Storme/E. Terryn (eds.), *The Draft Common Frame of Reference: national and comparative perspectives* (Cambridge: Intersentia, 2012), p. 453.

**825.** The PECL[16] establish rules on general contract law; they do not contain provisions on the law of sales or other types of contracts. In contrast, the DCFR[17] contains a separate book on sales law (Book IV, Part A. Sales). Since this is a purely academic model code, its content cannot be presented in depth here.[18]

## 3. THE GENESIS OF THE CONSUMER RIGHTS DIRECTIVE AND THE LAW OF SALES

References: G. De Cristofaro/A. de Franceschi (eds.), *Consumer Sales Law in Europe – After the Implementation of the Consumer Sales Directive* (Cambridge: Intersentia, 2016); M. Loos, 'Consumer Sales Law in the Proposal for a Consumer Rights Directive', *ERPL* 2010, 15.

**826.** In moving away from the approach of a (political) frame of reference, the Commission had argued for a fully harmonising horizontal directive. In the proposal for a Directive on Consumer Rights,[19] an overarching approach could be established, which also covered the CSD, among other things.[20] Article 21 to 29 of the proposal regulated the consumer sales contract.[21] What

16 See para. 161 above.
17 See para. 120 above.
18 For more details see U. Huber, *ZEuP* 2008, 709; Loos, in Sagaert/Storme/Terryn, *The Draft Common Frame of Reference: national and comparative perspectives*, 2012, p. 453.
19 Of 8 October 2008, COM(2008) 614 final.
20 On this already para. 127 above and para. 1150 below.
21 See for example Jud, in Jud/Wendehorst (ed.), *Neuordnung des Verbraucherprivatrechts in Europa?*, 2009, p. 119; C. Twigg-Flesner, in G.G. Howells/R. Schulze (ed.), *Modernising*

was remarkable about this was not so much the regulatory content but rather the fact that the proposal moved from the minimum harmonization approach pursued by the CSD to full harmonisation. The accompanying restriction of the Member States' regulatory autonomy, which has already been criticised,[22] has particularly pronounced consequences in the law of sales since a central area of any code of obligations is concerned here. This already affects the general regulatory technique in the Member States' civil codes, at least for those Member States, such as Germany, which pursue a far-reaching transposition of the Directive's requirements into their national codification, as the separation between consumer law and the general law of obligations will certainly be very visible.[23]

**827.** It may have been the sometimes strongly defensive attitude of several Member States towards the draft that led the Commission to pursue a double strategy by introducing an optional European Contract Law in parallel with the work on the Directive. The Commissioner for Justice, Fundamental Rights and Citizenship at the time, Viviane Reding, had announced further steps towards a European Contract Law in early 2010.[24] The Common Frame of Reference was to be completed and enter into force in the form of a legal act.[25] This project was supposed to be at least as important as the adoption of the planned Consumer Rights Directive. In the Communication 'EUROPE 2020: A strategy for smart, sustainable and inclusive growth',[26] the Commission also announced that, in parallel to the harmonisation of consumer protection rules, it was also striving for 'making progress towards an European Contract Law'.[27]

---

*and Harmonising Consumer Contract Law* (Munich: Sellier, 2009), p. 147; Gsell, in Gsell/Herresthal (ed.), *Vollharmonisierung im Privatrecht*, 2009, p. 219; Loos, *ERPL* 2010, 15.

22 See the statement of the German Bundesrat of 6 March 2009, BR-Drucks. 765/08(B), p. 4; also Reich, *ZEuP* 2010, 7, 37 as well as Riehm, in Gsell/Herresthal (eds.), *Vollharmonisierung im Privatrecht*, 2009, pp. 83, 111, who assume a disproportionate restriction of Member State autonomy through the approach of the draft directive.

23 More in detail Loos, in Stürner (ed.), *Vollharmonisierung im Europäischen Verbraucherrecht?*, 2010, pp. 47, 65 ff.

24 Speech of 15 March 2010 at the Consumer Days in Madrid, see V. Reding, SPEECH/10/91; likewise already the Commissioner's position at a hearing before the European Parliament on 7 January 2010, CM\800797EN.doc, PE431.139v02-00.

25 V. Reding, CM\800797EN.doc, PE431.139v02-00, p. 7: 'I want to make substantial progress in the work towards a European contract law [...]. I therefore intend to complete – with the help of academic expertise from across Europe – the work on the common frame of reference in the course of 2010, and to include it thereafter into a well-publicised legal instrument.'

26 COM(2010) 2020 final.

27 COM(2010) 2020 final, p. 21: 'The Commission will propose action to tackle bottlenecks in the single market by: [...] Making it easier and less costly for businesses and consumers to conclude contracts with partners in other EU countries, notably by offering harmonised solutions for consumer contracts, EU model contract clauses and by making progress towards an optional European Contract Law.' The Action Plan prepared by the Commission to implement the Council's Stockholm Programme, Delivering an area of freedom, security

## 4. THE PROPOSAL FOR A COMMON EUROPEAN SALES LAW

**828.** The implementation of the proposal for a Common European Sales Law would have brought about a significant step towards further harmonisation. The circumstances and implications of its emergence and failure have already been discussed.[28] Even though, according to the Commission's communication, the proposal has not been pursued in this form since the end of 2014 at the latest,[29] the main provisions of sales law will be introduced below. This appears justified given that the proposal represents a consolidated version of the PECL, DCFR and Feasibility Study.

## 5. THE GENESIS OF THE DIRECTIVE ON CONTRACTUAL ASPECTS OF THE SALE OF GOODS

References: I. Bach, 'Neue Richtlinien zum Verbrauchsgüterkauf und zu Verbraucherverträgen über digitale Inhalte', *NJW* 2019, 1705; E. Helmig, 'Die neuen Richtlinien zum europäischen Verbraucherkaufrecht. Überlegungen zum Kauf eines Fahrzeugs als Ware mit digitalem Inhalt', *IWRZ* 2019, 200; D. Staudenmayer, 'Kauf von Waren mit digitalen Elementen – Die Richtlinie zum Warenkauf', *NJW* 2019, 2889.

### a) *The Commission's Proposal*

References: N. Härting/P. Gössling, 'Online-Kauf in der EU – Harmonisierung des Kaufgewährleistungsrechts. Was würde sich durch den Vorschlag der EU-Kommission v. 9.12.2015 wie verändern?', *CR* 2016, 165; M. Lehmann, 'A Question of Coherence: The Proposals on EU Contract Rules on Digital Content and Online Sales', (2016) *Maastricht Journal of European and Comparative Law*, 752; F. Maultzsch, 'Der Entwurf für eine EU-Richtlinie über den Online-Warenhandel und andere Formen des Fernabsatzes von Waren', *JZ* 2016, 236; P. Ostendorf, 'Geplanter neuer Rechtsrahmen für Online-Warenhandel und Bereitstellung digitaler Inhalte im Europäischen Binnenmarkt', *ZRP* 2016, 69; M. Schmidt-Kessel/K. Erler/A. Grimm/M. Kramme, 'Die Richtlinienvorschläge der Kommission zu Digitalen Inhalten und Online-Handel', *GPR* 2016, 2 and 54; S. Stiegler/D. Wawryka, 'Umbruch der Gewährleistungsrechte beim Fernabsatzverkehr? Der Richtlinienvorschlag über vertragliche Aspekte des Online-Warenhandels', *BB* 2016, 903; M. Stürner, 'Zur Fortentwicklung des EU-Vertragsrechts: Der Richtlinienvorschlag zum Online-Warenhandel', *JURA* 2016, 884; M. Wendland, 'Ein

and justice for Europe's citizens – Action Plan Implementing the Stockholm Programme, COM(2010) 171 final, formulates this less clearly but is comparable in content.

28 See para. 130 above.

29 In the 'Work Programme 2015 – A New Start' of 16 December 2014, COM(2014) 910 final, the Commission announced that it no longer intended to maintain the proposal in this form, see on the CESL in Annex II at no. 60: 'Modified proposal in order to fully unleash the potential of e-commerce in the Digital Single Market.'

neues europäisches Vertragsrecht für den Online-Handel? Die Richtlinienvorschläge der Kommission zu vertragsrechtlichen Aspekten der Bereitstellung digitaler Inhalte und des Online-Warenhandels', *EuZW* 2016, 126.

**829.** After the failure of the proposal for a Common European Sales Law, the Commission presented its 'A Digital Single Market Strategy for Europe' on 6 May 2015.[30] Here, the Commission announced an extension of fully harmonising rules for online transactions. On 9 December 2015, the Commission then published two proposals for fully harmonising Directives: the proposal concerning the provision of digital content,[31] and the proposal concerning certain aspects of contract law applicable to online sales of goods and services and other forms of distance sales of goods (hereinafter: Distance Selling Directive Proposal).[32]

**830.** Regarding its content, the proposal for a Distance Selling Directive was largely built on familiar grounds; it can be seen as a rather conventional evolution of the CSD that mainly considered the relevant case law of the CJEU.[33] The proposal took a very selective approach, which – above all due to the fully harmonising approach – entailed the danger of fragmentation of the Member States' legal systems and, thus, contrary to the aim of harmonisation, would not have created uniform market conditions. Distance selling, particularly online purchases, was to receive privileged treatment and would have been uncoupled from stationary trade.[34] This was primarily based on economic considerations: The Commission wanted to create a digital single market because it still sees great growth potential here – apparently in contrast to offline trade.[35] In this respect, the Commission considers the differences in the legal rules of the Member States as the main obstacles.[36] This obscures the fact that there is no solid empirical foundation to prove that consumers would be deterred from buying goods across borders precisely because of legal differences within the Single Market. Language barriers, a lack of confidence in the smooth handling

---

30 COM(2015) 192 final.

31 Proposal for a Directive of the European Parliament and of the Council on certain aspects of contract law relating to the provision of digital content, COM(2015) 634 final; see para. 942 below.

32 Proposal for a Directive of the European Parliament and of the Council on certain aspects of contract law applicable to online and other distance marketing of goods, COM(2015) 635 final.

33 On this already Stürner, *JURA* 2016, 884.

34 Critically also Maultzsch, *JZ* 2016, 236, 238.

35 Recital 3 Draft Distance Selling Directive: 'E-commerce is the main driver for growth within the Digital Single Market. However its growth potential is far from being fully exploited. In order to strengthen Union competitiveness and to boost growth, the Union needs to act swiftly and encourage economic actors to unleash the full potential offered by the Digital Single Market.'

36 Recitals 6 and 7 Draft Distance Selling Directive.

of the purchase as well as concerns about problems in enforcing warranty rights are more likely to be the decisive factors.

**831.** Inevitably, this approach would have created demarcation difficulties, on the one hand, concerning the parallel proposal of the Digital Content Directive,[37] and on the other hand, regarding general private law, which is only partly harmonised.[38] The latter applies to general contract law, which the Directive proposal – like the CSD – deliberately excluded (Article 1(4) draft Distance Selling Directive), and above all, to claims for damages for breach of contract.[39] In this context, it would also have been necessary to clarify to what extent the respective autonomous tort law of the Member States could have been applied, for example, in the case of the so-called 'ancillary damages'.[40] In terms of its content, there was a large overlap with the CSD; Article 19(1) of the draft Distance Selling Directive, therefore, only provided for an amendment of the CSD to the extent that it was intended to exclude distance contracts from its scope of application.

### *b) Amendments by Parliament and Council*

**832.** During the legislative procedure, one of the main criticisms of the Commission's proposal concerned the restriction to long-distance and other online contracts.[41] Both Parliament and Council called for coherence between distance contracts and those concluded in the traditional retail sector. An impact assessment carried out on behalf of the European Parliament[42] found that abandoning the limitation of the scope to distance and other online contracts was preferable.[43] As a result, the Commission submitted a recast of the proposal on 31 October 2017,[44] which now covered the entire material scope of the CSD. After further deliberations in the trilogue, Directive (EU)

37 On this point, Schmidt-Kessel/Erler/Grimm/Kramme, *GPR* 2016, 2, 4 f.

38 More in detail Schmidt-Kessel/Erler/Grimm/Kramme, *GPR* 2016, 2, 5 f.

39 These are reserved for national law, cf. the reference in the Commission proposal, COM(2015) 635 final, p. 4.

40 On this, Ostendorf, *ZRP* 2016, 69, 71. On the comparable problem in the context of the CESL already Wendelstein, *GPR* 2013, 70.

41 See for example Lehmann, Maastricht Journal of European and Comparative Law 2016, 752.

42 European Parliamentary Research Service (EPRS), 'Online and other distance sales of goods. Impact assessment of substantial amendments', July 2017, PE 603.258, available at https://www.europarl.europa.eu/RegData/etudes/STUD/2017/603258/EPRS_STU(2017)603258_EN.pdf.

43 EPRS, ibid., pp. 32 ff., 105 ff.

44 Amended proposal for a Directive of the European Parliament and of the Council on certain aspects of contract law relating to trade in goods, amending Regulation (EC) No 2006/2004 of the European Parliament and of the Council and Directive 2009/22/EC of the European Parliament and of the Council and repealing Directive 1999/44/EC of the European Parliament and of the Council, COM(2017) 637 final.

2019/771 of the European Parliament and of the Council of 20 May 2019 on certain aspects of the law applicable to contracts concerning the sale of goods, amending Regulation (EU) 2017/2394 and Directive 2009/22/EC and repealing Directive 1999/44/EC was adopted.[45] The Sale of Goods Directive was to be implemented by the Member States by 1 July 2021; the corresponding provisions apply from 1 January 2022 (Article 24 Sale of Goods Directive). The CSD has become obsolete and ceased to apply on that date (Article 23 Sale of Goods Directive). The Sale of Goods Directive is fully harmonising (Article 4 Sale of Goods Directive), but in several aspects it gives the Member States the freedom to exceed the specified level of protection or to extend the material or personal scope of application of the Directive.[46]

## III. SCOPE AND STRUCTURE OF THE SALE OF GOODS DIRECTIVE

References: I. Bach, 'Neue Richtlinien zum Verbrauchsgüterkauf und zu Verbraucherverträgen über digitale Inhalte', *NJW* 2019, 1705; E. Helmig, 'Die neuen Richtlinien zum europäischen Verbraucherkaufrecht. Überlegungen zum Kauf eines Fahrzeugs als Ware mit digitalem Inhalt', *IWRZ* 2019, 200; D. Staudenmayer, 'Kauf von Waren mit digitalen Elementen – Die Richtlinie zum Warenkauf', *NJW* 2019, 2889; B. Zöchling-Jud, 'Das neue Europäische Gewährleistungsrecht für den Warenhandel', *GPR* 2019, 115.

### 1. MATERIAL SCOPE OF APPLICATION

**833.** The Sale of Goods Directive (SGD) regulates individual aspects of sales contracts. In particular, it contains provisions on the conformity of the goods with the contract, remedies in the event of a lack of conformity, the modalities for claiming these remedies, and commercial guarantees (Article 1 SGD). Furthermore, contracts for the provision of goods which have yet to be manufactured or produced are also covered (Article 3(2) SGD). Contracts for the provision of digital content or digital services are not subject to the Sale of Goods Directive but to the Digital Content Directive[47] unless they are to be regarded as part of the goods (so-called goods with digital elements, Article 2 no. 5 lit. b SGD) – the latter is presumed according to the rule of Article 3(3) SGD.

---

45 OJ 2019 L 136/28.

46 Regarding this 'targeted full harmonisation' see para. 84 above. On both aspects of gold-plating see para. 366 above.

47 See para. 944 below.

**834.** The sales contract is defined in Article 2 no. 1 SGD as a 'contract under which the seller transfers or undertakes to transfer ownership of goods to a consumer, and the consumer pays or undertakes to pay the price thereof'. The CSD did not contain a corresponding definition. Nevertheless, the CJEU had already ruled that the concept of a sales contract was to be interpreted autonomously and, as such, uniformly throughout the EU.[48] Since the CSD heavily draws on the UN Sales Convention, in principle, the CISG's concept of a contract can be used so that the transfer of a good against payment is constitutive.[49] Hence, this includes contracts for the provision of goods that still have to be manufactured or produced, Article 1(4) CSD or Article 3(2) SGD, but not contracts in which an element of service dominates.[50]

**835.** Where the CSD still spoke of consumer goods, the Sale of Goods Directive now refers to goods as 'tangible movable items' (Article 2 no. 5 lit. a SGD) without any change in substance. Water, electricity and gas are excluded unless they are offered for sale in a limited volume or quantity.[51]

## 2. PERSONAL SCOPE OF APPLICATION

**836.** The Sale of Goods Directive applies to sales contracts for goods concluded between a seller and a consumer (so-called B2C contract, Article 3(1) SGD). The term 'consumer' used in Article 2 no. 2 SGD does not introduce any innovations compared to other directives. In contrast, the concept of entrepreneur used in the Consumer Rights Directive is not taken over, but the concept of seller defined in Article 2 no. 3 SGD is functionally equivalent.

**837.** With regard to the term 'consumer', the Directive leaves it up to the Member States to include, for example, start-ups or even small and medium-sized enterprises (SMEs) in the scope of protection of the transposed Directive (Recital 21 SGD). They may also widen the material scope of the term 'consumer' to the extent that so-called dual use contracts are included (Recital 22 SGD).[52] As opposed to Recital 17 CRD, the Sale of Goods Directive is based on a narrower understanding of the term 'consumer'.[53]

---

48 CJEU, 7 September 2017, Case C-247/16, *Schottelius*, ECLI:EU:C:2017:638, para. 32 referring to CJEU, 18 October 2011, Case C-34/10, *Brüstle*, ECLI:EU:C:2011:669, para. 26 (this decision referred to the interpretation of the term 'human embryo' in Directive 98/44/EC on the legal protection of biotechnological inventions).

49 See in this respect also Article IV A.-1:202 DCFR.

50 CJEU, 7 September 2017, Case C-247/16, *Schottelius*, ECLI:EU:C:2017:638, paras. 44 ff.

51 Same content as Article 1(2)(b) CRD and Article 2 no. 3 IRD.

52 On this already para. 36 above.

53 Likewise the Digital Content Directive, see para. 951 below.

### 3. STRUCTURE

**838.** The structure of the Sale of Goods Directive largely corresponds to that of the CISG.[54] First and foremost, it regulates the conformity of the goods with the contract and the remedies in the event of non-conformity, namely, first and foremost, repair or replacement, and secondarily reduction and rescission. Here, in particular, the relevant provisions have been expanded and specified, in many cases incorporating the relevant case law of the CJEU. The provisions on digital content, which was not yet recognised as a regulatory problem when the CSD was introduced and which is now often a component of goods, are particularly new.

## IV. THE CONFORMITY OF THE GOODS WITH THE CONTRACT

References: I. Bach, 'Neue Richtlinien zum Verbrauchsgüterkauf und zu Verbraucherverträgen über digitale Inhalte', *NJW* 2019, 1705; A.M. Geiger-Wieske, 'Das "Bastlerfahrzeug" und die Richtlinien über digitale Verträge – Anforderungen an eine ausdrückliche Erklärung', *GPR* 2020, 76; E. Helmig, 'Die neuen Richtlinien zum europäischen Verbraucherkaufrecht. Überlegungen zum Kauf eines Fahrzeugs als Ware mit digitalem Inhalt', *IWRZ* 2019, 200; D. Staudenmayer, 'Kauf von Waren mit digitalen Elementen – Die Richtlinie zum Warenkauf', *NJW* 2019, 2889; B. Zöchling-Jud, 'Das neue Europäische Gewährleistungsrecht für den Warenhandel', *GPR* 2019, 115.

### 1. THE APPROACH OF THE CONSUMER SALES DIRECTIVE

**839.** Following the CSD's focus on the internal market, consumers in all Member States should encounter uniform legal standards when buying consumer goods (Recitals 7–9 CSD). Accordingly, the seller should always be liable if the goods do not meet these requirements. For this purpose, Article 3 CSD introduces a respective liability regardless of negligence or fault.

**840.** Article 2 CSD positively defines the contractual nature of the goods by introducing a gradual specification (from specific to general aspects). In this respect, the legislator of the Directive was guided by Article 35 CISG.[55] Individual agreements by the parties on quality are possible and thus individually determine the standard of conformity with the contract. In the absence of such

54 A very helpful concordance table can be found in Annex I to the Sale of Goods Directive.

55 COM(95) 520, pp. 6, 13; Grundmann, *AcP* 202 (2002), 40, 45 ff.; Staudenmayer, *ERPL* 2001, 547, 553 at note 9.

an agreement, the usual quality is deemed to be agreed (Article 2(2)(d) CSD). In view of the consumer-protecting purpose of the Directive, it sometimes appears problematic to what extent the seller can exclude or reduce their liability by a restrictive description of the good's quality. Therefore, any defects must be described in sufficiently concrete terms. 'Purchased as seen' is probably not sufficient.[56] Article 2(3) CSD allows the exclusion of liability for defects the buyer knows or should reasonably have known about. Accordingly, the warranty is excluded if the buyer is aware of the defect. If the lack of knowledge is due to gross negligence, warranty rights can only be asserted if the seller has fraudulently concealed the defect or in the case of the assumption of a guarantee.

**841.** The guideline for the good's conformity with the contract is the buyer's reasonable expectation (Article 2(2)(d) CSD).[57] This constitutes an objective standard: Above all, public statements of the seller, the manufacturer or their representative, such as advertising, are included. Thus, circumstances outside the actual conclusion of the contract also play a role. However, this does not automatically lead to the inclusion of the entire value chain because the Directive expressly refers only to statements by such actors where attribution to the seller's sphere of influence seems, due to the authority of their authors, plausible from the consumer's point of view.[58] Also, the seller is not bound by such public statements under Article 2(4) CSD if they prove that they were not aware or should not have been aware of the statement in question, that the statement in question had already been corrected at the time of the conclusion of the contract or that the decision to buy could not have been influenced by the statement in question.

## 2. THE CRITERIA OF THE SALE OF GOODS DIRECTIVE

**842.** Similarly to the Consumer Sales Directive, the regulation of the conformity of the goods with the contract also occupies a central position in the Sale of Goods Directive. However, unlike the Consumer Sales Directive, there

56 Staudenmayer, *NJW* 1999, 2393.

57 In the Green Paper on consumer goods guarantees and after-sales service, the Commission had still proposed to take the 'legitimate expectations' of the consumer as a yardstick, COM(93) 509 final, pp. 86 ff. This objective concept of contractual conformity would have entailed a clear restriction of contractual freedom. In the Commission proposal, this was then no longer included, COM(95) 520, p. 12. In general, the 'legitimate expectations' of a party are also not to be regarded as an independent legal figure in EU private law, see para. 446 above.

58 S. Grundmann, in S Grundmann/C.M. Bianca (eds.), *EU Sales Directive* (Antwerp/New York: Intersentia, 2002), Art. 2 para. 29.

is no longer a presumption of conformity. Instead, the Sale of Goods Directive describes standards the seller must comply with.

### a) *The Conformity of the Goods*

**843.** Just as the Consumer Sales Directive, the Sale of Goods Directive also uses a combination of objective and subjective criteria for the conformity of the goods with the contract (Article 5–9 SGD).

#### aa) Subjective Elements

**844.** The decisive and primary factor for conformity with the contract is an agreement of whatever kind between the seller and the consumer (Article 6 SGD). The original proposal still contained a provision to the effect that a connection to pre-contractual declarations of the seller could also be made, provided that these have become part of the contract.[59] However, the version of the Sale of Goods Directive that has entered into force has not adopted a corresponding provision. Recital 32 SGD should also be mentioned. According to this, a pre-contractual declaration which is part of the sales contract and contains specific information on the good's durability is to be regarded as part of the subjective requirements of conformity with the contract.

**845.** In particular, conformity with the contract according to Article 6(d) SGD requires that the goods receive the contractually owed updates. This concerns goods with digital elements (cf. Article 2 no. 5 lit. b SGD). These may be security-relevant updates or technical innovations; thus, the provision of the contractually owed updates during the entire term is owed. If the updates are deficient, incomplete or not provided at all, the goods as a whole are to be regarded as not in conformity with the contract (Recital 28 SGD). It can be inferred from this that the updates do not represent a mere secondary obligation but a primary contractual obligation.

**846.** The non-conformity cannot be excluded simply if the consumer was aware of the non-conformity or could not reasonably have been unaware of it, as provided for in Article 2(3) CSD. Rather, according to Article 7(5) SGD, the consumer must now be specifically informed that a certain characteristic of the goods deviates from the objectively required standard; in addition, they must have expressly and separately consented to said deviation at the time of conclusion of the contract. Only if these conditions are met does the Directive

---

59 Article 4(1)(c) Draft Distance Selling Directive.

permit a detrimental deviation from the objective standard (Article 21(1) SGD).[60]

bb) Objective Elements

**847.** In addition to the subjective criteria, the objective requirements mentioned in Article 7 SGD must also be met. The latter thus functions as a minimum standard that every good – subject to the express waiver of the consumer just mentioned – must comply with.[61] In particular, the goods must be suitable for the purposes for which goods of the same kind are normally used (Article 7(1)(a) SGD). This is to be determined, where appropriate, by taking into account existing EU and national law, technical standards or – in the absence of such technical standards – applicable sector-specific codes of conduct, as the provision explicitly states.

**848.** Moreover, in terms of quantity, quality and other characteristics (such as durability,[62] functionality, compatibility and safety), the goods must correspond to what is usual for goods of the same kind and what the consumer can reasonably expect in light of the nature of the goods (Article 7(1)(d) SGD). In determining this standard, account must also be taken of public statements made by or on behalf of the seller or any other person in preceding links of the value chain, including the producer, in particular in advertising or on the product's packaging and labelling. The legislator thus makes it clear that statements along the entire value chain are now covered. However, according to Article 8(2) SGD, the seller can exonerate himself by proving that he could not reasonably have been aware of such a statement. This possibility was essentially taken over from the Consumer Sales Directive. However, it could now be of greater importance.

**849.** The conformity of the goods with the contract also includes appropriate accessories such as packaging or assembly instructions (Article 7(1)(c) SGD). If the seller has provided the consumer with a sample or specimen before the conclusion of the contract, the goods must correspond to this in terms of quality and description (Article 7(1)(b) SGD).[63]

**850.** Whether the far-reaching objective requirements for the conformity of the goods, especially in Article 7 SGD, still leave substantial room for deviating

---

60 More in detail Geiger-Wieske, *GPR* 2020, 76.

61 Wendland, *EuZW* 2016, 126, 129 f.

62 The term 'durability' of a product is not to be confused with its 'reparability' – when adopted, the Sale of Goods Directive did not contain this requirement, see critically Kieninger, ZEuP 2020, 264, 274 ff. For a recent change see para. 42 above.

63 It is debatable whether this is not rather a subjective criterion – this was still the view of Article 4(1)(a) Draft Distance Selling Directive.

contractual agreements is certainly open to doubt. If, for example, the parties agree that the car sold does not have to be roadworthy because the buyer wants to strip it for spare parts, it seems questionable whether this does not conflict with Article 7(1)(a) SGD because goods of the same kind (i.e. cars) are usually used in road traffic. The rule would have to be interpreted to mean that in this case it concerns the good 'scrap cars'. Here, in order to avoid legal uncertainty, the parties would have to reach an agreement in the sense of Article 7(5) SGD.[64]

cc) In Particular: The Supply of Updates

**851.** The Sale of Goods Directive contains a real innovation in Article 7(3) and (4) SGD concerning goods with digital elements (definition: Article 2 no. 5 lit. b SGD). In this respect, even in the absence of a corresponding agreement (in which case Article 6(d) SGD applies), the seller must inform the consumer of any updates that are necessary to maintain the goods' conformity with the contract and to provide them during the period that the consumer can reasonably expect, given the nature and purpose of the goods and the digital elements and taking into account the circumstances and the nature of the contract, if the sales contract provides for the digital content or service to be provided once (Article 7(3)(a) SGD). If, on the other hand, the contract of sale provides for the continuous provision of the digital content or service over a period of time, the obligation to provide updates extends over the entire period during which the seller is liable for the conformity of the goods with the contract (Article 7(3)(b) SGD), which is two years according to Article 10(2) SGD.[65]

**852.** While the latter is simply a consequence of the corresponding agreement and can thus be justified by private autonomy, the seller's obligation under lit. a to continuously provide updates extends the contractual programme of obligations beyond what traditionally followed from a purchase contract, i.e. the obligation to deliver a purchased good in conformity with the contract or free of defects at the time of the risk transfer. In contrast, the obligation to provide updates gives the sales contract a continuing obligation. The pre-existing obligation to remedy a lack of conformity has already led to a departure from the idea of the purchase contract as a simple exchange contract.[66] However, the connecting factor for this obligation of the seller could always be found in the lack of conformity of the

64 It would have been preferable to include a clarifying wording in Article 7(1) of the CESL, based on the wording in Article 99(2) of the CESL, to the effect that the objective standards set out in Article 7 of the CESL only apply unless the parties have agreed otherwise. On the comparable problem in the Distance Selling Directive, see Stürner, *JURA* 2016, 884, 887. On the other hand, Maultzsch, *JZ* 2016, 236, 239, assumes a subsidiary application of Articles 5 to 7 of the Distance Selling Directive.

65 In addition see para. 891 below.

66 For example, V. Kitz, *Die Dauerschuld im Kauf* (Baden-Baden: Nomos, 2004).

goods with the contract at the time of the risk transfer. In the case of goods with digital elements, this is missing: The obligation to provide updates finally exists even if the object of sale was completely in conformity with the contract at the time of the risk transfer.

**853.** The Directive offers a twofold justification for this: On the one hand, the digital environment of the corresponding goods is subject to permanent change, which could impair their functionality. On the other hand, however, goods with digital elements never completely leave the seller's sphere, since the seller, possibly via third parties, can regularly update the digital elements of the goods even from a distance (Recital 31 SGD). This is linked to the time of risk transfer, which is normally decisive for allocating responsibility and liability in the sales contract. However, this does not necessarily hold completely, as the consumer determines whether the seller has access to the goods, even in the case of goods with digital elements. The fact that updates can also be provided remotely does not change this; it could also be argued that in the case of goods without digital elements, such access by the seller is possible by the consumer handing over the goods to the seller, for example, for repair or replacement.

**854.** While, in the case of a contractual agreement on updates (Article 6(d) SGD), the seller may also have to provide updates that extend or improve the product's functionality, the seller's objective obligation under Article 7(3) SGD only exists concerning those updates necessary for the goods to continue to meet the requirements of conformity with the contract under Articles 6 and 7 SGD. The seller is, therefore, usually not obliged to provide improved versions of the digital content or services of the goods or to improve or extend the functions of the goods (Recital 30 SGD).

**855.** Since the seller cannot impose updates on the consumer, the Sale of Goods Directive only obliges them to provide information and to make the updates available, for example, by sending a corresponding hyperlink. The consumer now has an obligation to install the update within a reasonable time. If they fail to do so, the seller's liability for a possible lack of conformity resulting solely from the lack of the corresponding update may lapse. However, this is subject to a twofold restriction according to Article 7(4) SGD: First, the seller must have informed the consumer about the availability of the update and about the consequences if the consumer does not install it (lit. a). The former follows from Article 7(3) SGD. The latter extends the existing Duties of information even further. This is comparable to the information duties on the liability for any loss of value of the goods after withdrawal in distance and off-premises contracts (Article 14(2) in conjunction with Article 6(1)(h) CRD). Second, the fact that the consumer has not installed the update or has installed it improperly must not be due to defective installation instructions provided to the consumer (Article 7(4)(b) SGD).

This also extends the seller's duties of information once again: The information about the existence of the update and the possible exclusion of liability in case of a failure to install it is not sufficient; in addition, installation instructions must be provided, which in turn must not be defective as such.

dd) Improper Assembly or Installation

**856.** Article 8 SGD describes the lack of conformity caused by improper assembly or installation and is thus linked to Article 2(5) CSD. According to the clear wording of Article 8 SGD, it does not matter whether the assembly was contractually agreed upon or based on a subsequent agreement between the parties; this also includes assembly carried out purely for convenience.

ee) Third-Party Rights

**857.** Finally, the goods must be free from third-party rights if, otherwise, the use of the goods was prevented or restricted within the meaning of the conformity requirement (Article 9 SGD).[67]

*b) Relevant Time for Determining Conformity with the Contract*

**858.** The regulation of risk transfer is of central importance for sales law. In particular, it determines who bears the risk of losing or damaging the good. In principle, it will, therefore, regularly depend on the possibility of influencing the object. Thus, the risk should pass to the buyer when the good is handed over. The Consumer Sales Directive stipulates the delivery of the good as the relevant point in time for determining lack of conformity (Article 3(1), Article 5(1), (3) CSD). In contrast to this, the proposal of the Distance Selling Directive contained a much more detailed regulation in Article 8. According to its wording, it only concerned the point in time that is decisive for determining the lack of conformity: As a general rule, this was the physical taking of possession of the goods by the consumer or a third party commissioned by them. However, the rule also combined elements from Article 105 CESL (decisive point in time) and Article 142(1) CESL (transfer of risk). This was to be understood to also regulate the passing of risk, as follows from Recital 24 of the draft Distance Selling Directive: In order to ensure coherence between the Distance Selling Directive and the Consumer Rights Directive, the time of the transfer of risk should be specified as the time for determining the conformity of the goods with the contract.[68]

67 Critical of the less precisely formulated provision in Article 7 Draft Distance Selling Directive Maultzsch, *JZ* 2016, 236, 240.

68 This is also the case in the explanations to Article 8 of the Distance Selling Directive, see COM(2015) 635 final, p. 17. Cf., however, Schmidt-Kessel/Erler/Grimm/Kramme, *GPR* 2016, 54, 66 with reference to Article 20 of the Directive.

**859.** In the version of the Sale of Goods Directive that has entered into force, a corresponding provision is now found in Article 10 SGD: This provision also regulates the period during which the seller is liable for lack of conformity. However, according to Article 10(1) SGD, the decisive factor is now the delivery of the goods. However, the Directive does not contain a corresponding definition of this term. Recital 38 SGD shows that this is a deliberate omission so that Member State law applies in this respect. In particular, the aforementioned recital clarifies that the reference to the delivery time does not affect the provisions on the risk transfer in Article 20 CRD. According to this provision, the risk of loss or damage passes to the consumer when they or a third party designated by them have taken possession of the goods. This separates the transfer of risk from the time of delivery. However, it would hardly be possible to design Member State law concerning the time of delivery in such a way that the two are separated. This is because Article 18(1) CRD defines the delivery of goods as the transfer of physical possession of or control over the goods to the consumer. Although the main purpose of this provision is to determine the time of delivery (immediately, but not later than thirty days after the conclusion of the contract), the rules on the place and modalities of delivery and for determining the conditions and time of transfer of ownership of the goods remain reserved for Member State law (Recital 51 CRD).

**860.** If the goods are assembled or installed by or under the seller's responsibility, Article 8(2) of the draft Distance Selling Directive stated that the physical acquisition of ownership happens when the assembly or installation is completed. While this fiction could still be justified by the seller's remaining possibility to influence the good's condition, sentence 2 shifted the contractual balance strongly to the seller's disadvantage. It moved the relevant point in time further back in time, despite the handover of the goods, even if the goods were intended for assembly or installation by the consumer. By means of a rebuttable[69] presumption, the relevant point in time was placed on the completion of assembly or installation. However, this should only apply if this has been done within a reasonable time. Physical acquisition of ownership should also be assumed here at the latest 30 days after the regular point in time (Article 8(1) draft Distance Selling Directive). It hardly appears possible for the seller to provide evidence to the contrary.[70]

**861.** The version of the Sale of Goods Directive that has entered into force has not adopted this provision. This makes sense because it does not refer to the

[69] Cf. also Recital 26 Draft Distance Selling Directive.

[70] Critical of this regulation are Stiegler/Wawryka, *BB* 2016, 903, 907, who see a high potential for abuse for the consumer.

physical acquisition of ownership of the goods but to their delivery. Recital 40 SGD at least contains the indication that in cases where the contract of sale provides that the goods are to be assembled or installed by the seller or under the seller's responsibility, the goods are deemed to have been delivered to the consumer when the assembly or installation has been completed. As said Recital states clearly, this should apply when the consumer cannot use the goods or detect defects before the assembly or installation is completed.

### c) *Burden of Proof*

**862.** If, from the point of view of the Sale of Goods Directive, the question of the good's conformity with the contract depends on the time of delivery, the problem of the respective burden of proof might arise: As a general rule, it will be the consumer who invokes a lack of the good's conformity with the contract and demands redress. According to general principles, it is then up to the consumer to prove that the goods do not meet the contractual or legal requirements and that this was already the case at the time of delivery. Only in the rarest of cases will this not be problematic. Since the effectiveness of the Directive depends on the effectiveness of the remedies it grants, it postulates a reversal of the burden of proof: According to Article 11(1) SGD, in the case of lack of conformity that becomes apparent within one year after delivery of the goods, it is presumed that the lack of conformity already existed at that time. In this respect, the seller must prove the contrary. Only when it is incompatible with the nature of the goods or the nature of the lack of conformity this presumption does not apply.

**863.** This provision is closely connected to Article 5(3) CSD, according to which there is a presumption that the lack of conformity already existed at the time of delivery if it becomes apparent within six months after the risk transfer. In German law, sec. 477 German Civil Code (previously sec. 476 German Civil Code (old version)) implements these requirements. According to the German Federal Court of Justice,[71] this presumption did not concern the question of the existence of the defect itself but only the question of the time of its existence; any further shift of the burden of proof after the transfer of risk was, according to this understanding, not intended.[72] The buyer must prove that a defect exists. This means that a material defect that occurs within the six months after the transfer of risk does not trigger the presumption that it is based on an already existing defect at the time of the risk transfer.[73]

71 BGHZ 159, 215; see also BGHZ 200, 1.

72 Hondius, in Bianca/Grundmann, Directive on the International Sale of Goods, 2002, Art. 5 paras. 20 f.

73 For a different view, cf. Lorenz, *NJW* 2004, 3020.

**864.** However, in the *Faber* case[74] the CJEU favoured a different interpretation: The consumer must prove that the goods sold are not in conformity with the contract and that the lack of conformity in question became apparent within six months of the delivery of the goods. The consumer does not have to prove the cause of the lack of conformity or that its origin is attributable to the seller. The presumption can only be invalidated if the seller proves that the cause or origin of the lack of conformity lies in conditions occurring after the delivery of the goods.[75] The restrictive case law of the German Federal Court of Justice was hence not in line with this and was abandoned in a subsequent decision.[76]

**865.** Consequently, sec. 477 German Civil Code was henceforth to be understood to cover cases where the defective condition that became apparent within six months after the transfer of risk already existed, at least in principle, at the time of the risk transfer. This relieves the buyer of the burden of proving that an apparent defect that has been proven to have occurred only after the transfer of risk has its cause in a previously existing, 'latent' defect. The distinction between apparent and latent defects previously made by the German Federal Supreme Court case law thus becomes obsolete. The question of whether the presumption of conformity only applies to the initial stage of a later defect or also to a basic defect preceding it is also of no practical significance because the general terminology ('at the outset') chosen by the CJEU in the *Faber* case covers both types of case due to its broad meaning.[77] This basically engenders a de facto durability guarantee for the first six months after the risk transfer.[78]

**866.** The Commission's proposal of Article 8(3) of the draft Distance Selling Directive had even extended the presumption to be interpreted in this sense within two years after the point in time in Article 8(1) and (2) of the draft Distance Selling Directive. In principle, this was also supposed to apply to used goods[79] – for these, it would have depended on a corresponding interpretation of the exception in Article 8(3) of the Distance Selling Directive, which should apply if the presumption is incompatible with the type of goods or lack of conformity. As a result, the Directive proposal would have brought with it a two-year guarantee of durability in many cases. Such a consumer privilege in

---

74 CJEU, 4 June 2015, Case C-497/13, *Faber*, ECLI:EU:C:2015:357.

75 CJEU, 4 June 2015, Case C-497/13, *Faber*, ECLI:EU:C:2015:357, paras. 69 ff.

76 BGHZ 212, 224 paras. 36 ff.

77 For references see BGHZ 212, 224 paras. 49 ff.

78 In that sense S. Lorenz, in *Münchener Kommentar zum BGB*, 9th ed. (Munich: C.H. Beck, 2024), §477 para. 31; Hübner, *NJW* 2015, 2241; Ruckteschler, *ZEuP* 2016, 538, 541.

79 The proposal for the Distance Selling Directive – unlike Article 7(1)(2) of the Directive – did not provide for the possibility of agreeing on time limits of liability of up to one year for second-hand goods.

distance sales, in contrast to other forms of sale, hardly seemed justified since the quality of the goods in no way depends on the type of distribution.[80]

**867.** Criticism also arose from the Member States concerning the temporal scope of the reversal of the burden of proof, i.e. the fact that the presumption only applies for one year after delivery (Article 11(1) SGD). However, since some Member States had already provided for longer periods, Article 11(2) SGD allowed to maintain or introduce a period of two years starting from the delivery of the goods.

**868.** The above-mentioned rules apply to goods with digital elements as well (Article 11(1) SGD). However, since such contracts include a continuing obligation,[81] a simple reference to the delivery time would not have made sense. If the sales contract provides for the continuous provision of the digital content or service over a period of time, the seller bears the burden of proving that the digital content or service conformed with the contract within the period referred to in the cited Article (Article 11(3) SGD) in the event of a lack of conformity which becomes apparent within two years after delivery or, if contractually agreed, beyond that period (Article 10(2) SGD).

## V. CONSEQUENCES ARISING FROM THE LACK OF CONFORMITY

### 1. THE BUYER'S REMEDIES UNDER THE SALE OF GOODS DIRECTIVE

#### a) *Overview*

**869.** Like the Consumer Sales Directive, the Sale of Goods Directive provides various remedies if the goods do not conform with the contract. These continue to be, as mentioned in Article 13(1) SGD, (1) the restoration of the goods to their contractual condition (Article 13(2) and (3), Article 14 SGD), (2) the reduction of the price (Article 13(4), Article 15 SGD), and (3) the rescission of contract (Article 13(4) and (5), Article 16 SGD); in addition, the consumer has a right of retention, the modalities of which are determined by Member State law, regulated in Article 13(6) SGD.

---

80 On the criticism of the Commission proposal Stiegler/Wawryka, *BB* 2016, 903, 907; Stürner, *JURA* 2016, 884, 889.

81 See para. 851 above.

**870.** The Sale of Goods Directive does not regulate claims for damages either. In this respect, the law of the Member States also applies (Article 3(6) SGD). However, the legislator does not fail to point out in Recital 61 SGD that, from the perspective of EU law, the seller's liability for damages is also an essential element of sales contracts, and consumers should therefore have a right to compensation for all damages caused by a breach of this Directive by the seller, including damages caused as a result of a lack of conformity. However, a uniform regulation was unnecessary, as such a claim for damages already existed in all Member States. It appears unclear what requirements for Member State law could be derived from this with regard to the *effet utile* of the Directive. Since it only contains a general exclusion, the regulatory autonomy of the Member States concerning the claim for damages should be unfettered and allow for regulations that place the burden of proof on the consumer.

**871.** The proposal for a Distance Selling Directive contained a provision on contributory negligence on the part of the consumer: Insofar as the consumer themselves had contributed to the lack of conformity of the goods, they should not be entitled to redress (Article 9(5) draft Distance Selling Directive). This would have created considerable uncertainty, as the rule's wording would have allowed any causal contribution to suffice.[82] It is possible that improper assembly would have been sufficient, partly due to faulty assembly instructions but also due to the consumer's negligence. According to the wording of the proposed provision, the fact that the consumer was aware of the lack of conformity of the goods at the time of the passing of the risk would not have been relevant. In the version of the Sale of Goods Directive that came into force, this provision was not adopted; it was replaced by an opening clause according to which the Member States can regulate whether and to what extent a consumer's contribution to the lack of conformity affects the consumer's right to redress (Article 13(7) SGD). Here, too, the *effet utile* of the Directive should ultimately prevent too much consideration of contributory negligence on the part of the consumer.

*b) Hierarchy of Remedies*

**872.** The Consumer Sales Directive prescribes a hierarchy of remedies to the extent that reduction and termination of the contract can only be claimed in the event of failure to repair or subsequent delivery (Article 3(3) and (5) CSD); termination of the contract is in turn excluded in the event of a minor lack of conformity (Article 3(6) CSD). Most Member States have adopted this hierarchy; in some cases, however, consumers are free to choose between individual

---

[82] So also Stiegler/Wawryka, *BB* 2016, 903, 908.

remedies.[83] This privileged consumer position, which is possible under the minimum harmonising Consumer Sales Directive, is excluded under the fully harmonising Sale of Goods Directive. In this case, the seller's restoration of the contractual condition has priority over the other remedies; only in the event of their failure do the other remedies come into play (Article 13(4) SGD).

**873.** Termination by rescission is also impossible in the case of minor breaches of contract (Article 13(5) SGD).[84] The Commission's proposal still provided for the discontinuation of this threshold.[85] The justification given for this was that it should create an incentive for the seller to remedy the situation at an early stage.[86] However, this seemed hardly convincing. Especially in the case of minor defects, repair or replacement will not make economic sense from the seller's point of view, so the contract's possible termination could hardly provide an incentive. Rather, the provision would have unnecessarily undermined the principle of contractual compliance. Moreover, the parallelism of the Consumer Sales Directive with the CISG would have been abandoned.[87]

### c) *Repair and Replacement*

**874.** Like the Consumer Sales Directive, with respect to the right to have the goods brought into conformity, the Sale of Goods Directive distinguishes between repair and replacement. The consumer still has the right to choose between these two remedies (Article 13(2) SGD).[88]

#### aa) Overview

**875.** As before, the seller can object that – in addition to impossibility[89] – either remedy would cause disproportionately high costs compared to the other. The guiding parameters for this weighing of all relevant circumstances remain essentially unchanged; during the consideration of what could be dubbed test of relative disproportionality, the following aspects are to be taken into account in particular: (1) The value of the goods in contractual condition; (2) the significance of the lack of conformity, and (3) the question of whether

---

83 COM(2015) 635 final, pp. 6 f.

84 The same applies to the provision in Article 114(2) CESL.

85 This has been assessed differently, positively by Wendland, *EuZW* 2016, 126, 131; critically by Ostendorf, *ZRP* 2016, 69, 70.

86 Recital 29 Draft Distance Selling Directive.

87 See e.g. Stürner, *Der Grundsatz der Verhältnismäßigkeit im Schuldvertragsrecht*, 2010, pp. 238 ff.

88 But see at paras. 897 ff. below for recent changes.

89 The unlawfulness of the chosen type of subsequent performance, as it had been mentioned in Article 11 Draft Distance Selling Directive, is not mentioned.

the alternative remedy can be provided without considerable inconvenience for the consumer.

**876.** Repair or replacement is, as before, also free of charge for the consumer (Article 14(1)(a) SGD). The seller must provide repair or replacement within a reasonable period of time, which is determined from the time the consumer has informed the seller of the lack of conformity (Article 14(1)(b) SGD). Thus, the Directive does not introduce any indirect obligation to notify the consumer of a lack of conformity (cf. Article 12 SGD). This remains within the legislative power of the Member States. Where no such obligation exists, this leads to a higher level of consumer protection, which must be tolerated (Recital 46 SGD). Obviously, at least in the case of repair, it is not enough for the consumer to inform the entrepreneur of the lack of conformity, as Recital 50 SGD states. In many cases, the seller must take physical possession of the goods.[90] According to Recital 55 SGD, in determining the reasonableness of the time limit, the nature and complexity of the goods, the nature and seriousness of the lack of conformity and the effort required to repair or replace the goods must also be considered. The Directive leaves it up to the Member States to determine fixed time limits which might be generally considered reasonable for certain categories of products. At the same time, it cannot be at the consumer's discretion to override the seller's right of a second tender by delaying the return of the good in order to be then able to invoke a period that is no longer reasonable within the meaning of Article 13(4)(d) SGD.

**877.** Finally, the repair or replacement must not cause significant inconvenience to the consumer. Here too, the nature of the goods and the purpose for which the consumer needs the goods must be taken into account (Article 14(1)(c) SGD). This provision is essentially akin to the preceding standard (Article 3 subpara. 3 CSD). The Directive contains sanctions for a breach of these provisions only to the extent that the consumer can then, under certain circumstances, resort to a reduction or termination of the contract (Article 13(4)(d) SGD). However, claims for compensation for successful but considerably inconvenient instances of repair or replacement are left to the law of the Member States (Recital 61 SGD). The same applies to the case that the repair or replacement was too late.

bb) Absolute Disproportionality

**878.** So far, no European regulation has been agreed upon for instances of so-called absolute disproportionality.[91] This is meant to describe cases where

90 On the question of the place of performance for repair see para. 885 below.

91 See, however, Article 110(3)(b) CESL proposal.

both repair and replacement would create disproportionate costs. Neither the proposal of the Distance Selling Directive nor the Consumer Sales Directive contains any provision in this respect. However, under German law, the seller could refuse both repair and replacement under the conditions set out in sec. 439(4) German Civil Code. Now if the purpose of the Consumer Sales Directive was to exempt the seller with regard to the remaining type of supplementary performance only when impossibility occurred, then the German transposition, which already allows the limit of disproportionality to suffice for this, would in any case mean a restriction of the consumer's rights. At least if one assumes that subsequent performance in one of the variants is more favourable for the consumer than price reduction or termination of the contract. The German Federal Court of Justice did not seem to rule out from the outset that the concept of impossibility used in the Directive was not defined in it and that its fulfilment was therefore left to national law.[92] For the Court it was implausible that the Directive only assumed an exclusion of the obligation of subsequent performance in cases of physical impossibility; this could lead to economically unreasonable burdens being imposed on the seller.[93]

**879.** However, in response to a request for referral by the German Federal Court of Justice, the CJEU ruled in joined cases *Weber and Putz*,[94] that the Consumer Sales Directive precludes absolute disproportionality. The German legislator subsequently reacted by inserting sec. 475(4) German Civil Code as of 1 January 2018: According to this provision, the objection of absolute disproportionality is cut off for consumer sales contracts.[95] By contrast, the Sale of Goods Directive now contains an explicit rule on absolute disproportionality in Article 13(3) SGD.

cc) Duty to Take the Sold Goods Back in Case of Replacement

**880.** If the seller remedies the lack of conformity by replacement, he must take back the non-conforming goods at his own expense; the consumer makes the goods available to the seller for this purpose (Article 14(2) SGD). The Directive Proposal had provided for the possibility of a deviating agreement after the consumer had informed the seller of the lack of conformity of the goods (Article 10(1) draft Distance Selling Directive). However, this is not

92 BGH NJW 2009, 1660, 1662 (referring to CJEU, 16 June 2011, Joined Cases C-65/09 and C-87/09, *Weber* and *Putz*, ECLI:EU:C:2011:396).

93 BGH NJW 2009, 1660, 1662.

94 CJEU, 16 June 2011, Joined Cases C-65/09 and C-87/09, *Weber* and *Putz*, ECLI:EU:C:2011:396.

95 It has been argued on various occasions, that this infringes the Directive, see for example *Georg*, NJW 2018, 199.

part of the Directive that has entered into force. If the seller and the consumer agree that the goods, which are worthless for the seller, are to remain with the consumer, this will be regarded as the conclusion of a gift contract. Passing on the costs of returning the goods is therefore ruled out, as are agreements that were made after notification of the lack of conformity that indirectly restrict the consumer's legal position, for example, by connecting the delivery of a replacement to the consumer's assumption of an obligation to carry the costs of returning the goods.

dd) No Compensation for Use in Case of Replacement

**881.** The consumer does not owe compensation for the normal use of the replaced goods before the replacement (Article 14(4) SGD). This implements the *Quelle* ruling of the CJEU.[96] Assigning the costs of use to the seller seems generally justified because the responsibility for the lack of conformity stems from their sphere.

ee) Dismantling and Re-Installation Costs

**882.** In contrast, the duty to bear the costs of removal and installation regulated in Article 14(3) SGD is much less clear-cut. The Directive adopts the basic statement of the above-mentioned *Weber and Putz* ruling of the CJEU. According to this, the seller not only has to take back the goods that are not in conformity with the contract but is also obliged to remove the goods if they have been assembled or installed by the consumer in accordance with their nature and purpose. Moreover, they owe the assembly and installation of the replacement goods or at least the payment of the costs for both. As a result, in the context of supplementary performance, the seller's obligations thus extend beyond the primary performance obligations agreed in the sales contract: As the seller has a duty to have the defective good removed and the replacement good installed, the performance of a service is also owed. The justification for this again lies in the lack of conformity with the contract, which is not necessarily the seller's fault, but in any case, originates in his scope of responsibility.

**883.** According to the wording of Article 14(3) SGD, the relationship between the obligation to remove and install the goods on the one hand and the seller's assumption of costs on the other remains unclear. The wording ('or') suggests the consumer has a right to choose. But how can the seller fulfil the obligation

[96] CJEU, 17 April 2008, Case C-404/06, *Quelle*, ECLI:EU:C:2008:231. See para. 349 above.

to remove and install the product? Is it sufficient to object that he does not have the necessary skills himself, or does the law require him to assign the task to a professional? The wording of the explanation of the Directive proposal, however, rather speaks in favour of the seller's right to choose.[97]

**884.** The part of the *Weber and Putz* decision of the CJEU dealing with a cap on the costs caused by removal and installation is not reflected in the text of the Directive. In *Weber and Putz*, the CJEU had decided that Article 3(3) CSD does not preclude the consumer's claim for reimbursement of the costs of removing the defective consumer goods and installing the consumer goods supplied as replacement in such a case from being limited to the assumption of a reasonable amount by the seller.[98] The Commission's proposal also did not address this issue. This was worthy of criticism, as the seller would not have been able to invoke the objection of absolute disproportionality, i.e. installation and removal costs would also have to be reimbursed, which might reach a multiple of the good's value.[99] However, the fact that the Sale of Goods Directive, which has entered into force, still does not regulate a cap on the costs of removal or installation is negligible because Article 13(3) SGD now allows raising the objection of absolute disproportionality, so that there is an upper limit for the expenses to be paid by the seller.

ff) Place of Performance for the Supplementary Performance

**885.** The Sale of Goods Directive does not regulate the place of performance for supplementary performance (Recital 56 SGD). Concerning the Consumer Sales Directive, the CJEU had ruled that, in principle, it was the Member State's up to the Member States to determine this – with due regard to the requirements of the Directive, which did not aim to impose any significant inconvenience on the consumer.[100] These requirements will likely continue to apply under the law as it now stands, as it must be possible to exercise the remedy without significant inconvenience to the consumer under Article 14(1)(c) SGD.

---

97 COM(2015) 635 final, p. 18. Cf. also Maultzsch, *JZ* 2016, 236, 243 with further references.

98 CJEU, 16 June 2011, Joined Cases C-65/09 and C-87/09, *Weber* and *Putz*, ECLI:EU:C:2011:396, para. 78.

99 Critically Maultzsch, *JZ* 2016, 236, 243. From the seller's point of view, one solution could have been to refuse to restore the contractual condition altogether, so that the subsidiary remedies in Article 9(3)(d) Draft Distance Selling Directive would apply. In particular, the termination of the contract by the consumer only leads to a reversal of the services received (Article 13(3)(a) Draft Distance Selling Directive), but does not include a claim for compensation by the consumer. This view would have hardly been in line with the intention underlying Article 10(2) of the Distance Selling Directive.

100 CJEU, 23 May 2019, Case C-52/18, *Fülla*, ECLI:EU:C:2019:447.

*d) Price Reduction*

**886.** Article 15 SGD contains specifications for calculating the price reduction in case of a defect. The provision is concise but more detailed than Article 3(5) CSD, which only regulated the prerequisites for the reduction, but not its implementation.[101]

*e) Termination by Rescission*

**887.** On par with the reduction is the consumer's right to terminate the contract in Article 16 SGD.[102] As already mentioned, this is subject to the condition that the lack of conformity is not insignificant (Article 13(5) SGD). It is exercised by a declaration addressed towards the seller, indicating the consumer's decision to terminate the contract (Article 16(1) SGD). Article 13(1) draft Distance Selling Directive was formulated in a much more extensive manner: A 'notice to the seller given by any means' was considered to be sufficient. This would also have included the return of the goods to the seller, as long as it was clearly recognisable that it was not the repair or replacement that was desired, but rather repayment of the purchase price. It seems that, in the light of this, Article 16(1) SGD may be interpreted accordingly.

**888.** The provision on the partial termination of the contract in Article 16(2) SGD is not formulated very precisely. It obviously reflects the principle of preserving the contract, but it can also be justified under the general objective of sustainability: Termination of the contract can only be sought for that part of the delivered goods, including accessories, to which the lack of conformity relates. A prerequisite for the applicability of this standard is probably the divisibility of the delivery of goods. Cases of quantitative divisibility (e.g. five identical jumpers, one of which has a hole) or the purchase of different types of goods (e.g. order of three different books, one of which is defectively bound) prove comparatively unproblematic.

**889.** It remains unclear, however, whether a termination of the contract should also be possible if the lack of conformity of a part of the goods leads to the consumer no longer having any interest in the contract as a whole. Article 13(4)(d) SGD does not provide a solution in this respect: Termination could be based on the fact that supplementary performance would mean considerable

[101] In terms of content, it is based on Article 120(1) CESL proposal.

[102] The use of the term 'right to terminate' (*Recht auf Beendigung*) in Article 16(1) Sale of Goods Directive on the one hand and the term 'shall (not) be entitled to the termination' (*Anspruch auf Beendigung*) in Article 13(4) and (5) Sale of Goods Directive on the other hand seems to be rather unfortunate.

inconvenience for the consumer. However, this only opens up the possibility to terminate the contract according to Article 16 SGD, which includes the application of paragraph 2 on partial withdrawal. There, the restriction on partial withdrawal has been relaxed to the effect that it does not apply unless the consumer can reasonably be expected to accept to keep only the goods that conform with the contract. This can be used to illustrate many of the cases in which the consumer's interests in keeping the good have ceased to exist.

**890.** Finally, Article 16(3) SGD contains a partial regulation of the legal consequences of the termination of the contract. There are similarities to the provisions of the Consumer Rights Directive on the contract's reversal after consumer withdrawal (Articles 13 and 14 CRD), but without the same level of detail. Both parties must return the performance received: First, the consumer must return the goods to the seller at the seller's expense. As soon as the seller receives the goods or the consumer provides proof that they have returned the goods, the seller must refund the purchase price. Thus, the seller has a right of retention concerning the purchase price refund.[103] The Member States may determine the modalities of return and refund. The question of refund claims in case of damage to the goods can also be regulated autonomously in national law.

*f) Temporal Limitation of Consumer Rights*

**891.** According to Article 10(1) SGD, all claims for redress by the consumer can only be asserted insofar as the lack of conformity becomes apparent within two years after the delivery date. Member States can introduce or maintain longer periods (Article 10(3) SGD). Conversely, for used goods, Article 10(6) SGD allows the Member States to agree on a contractual reduction of the liability period or the limitation period of up to one year. This corresponds to the previous legal situation in Article 7(1) subpara. 2 CSD.

**892.** Article 10(2) SGD contains a special rule for goods with digital elements: If the continuous provision of the digital content or service is agreed upon in the purchase contract, the seller is liable for any lack of conformity during a period of two years. The liability period is extended for contracts the duration of which exceeds this period. Thus, if the seller promises to provide software updates for a mobile navigation system or a smartwatch for three years and delivers a defective software patch after two years and eight months, this constitutes a lack of conformity (Article 7(3)(c) SGD) that will give rise to the remedies set out in Article 13 SGD.

---

[103] Cf. the corresponding provision for reversal after withdrawal in Article 13(3) Consumer Rights Directive. The Commission proposal remained silent on this point.

**893.** Concerning the remedies mentioned in Article 13 SGD, the Member States are free to introduce a limitation in time as an alternative to a provision on the maximum liability period, or even both (Article 10(4) and (5) SGD). This must not restrict the scope of the consumer's rights.[104]

## 2. COMMERCIAL GUARANTEES

**894.** In practice, commercial guarantees are of enormous importance. They provide the consumer with an additional debtor, such as the product manufacturer or a third-party supplier. This way, on the one hand, the insolvency risk of the seller can be absorbed, and on the other hand, the guarantee often offers better conditions than the statutory warranty, for example, concerning the distribution of the burden of proof. Article 6 CSD already provided some minimum standards. The Consumer Rights Directive built on this: Article 2 no. 14 CRD defines the commercial guarantee as 'any undertaking by the trader or a producer (the guarantor) to the consumer, in addition to his legal obligation relating to the guarantee of conformity, to reimburse the price paid or to replace, repair or service goods in any way if they do not meet the specifications or any other requirements not related to conformity set out in the guarantee statement or in the relevant advertising available at the time of, or before the conclusion of the contract'. The Consumer Rights Directive contains pre-contractual duties of information regarding such guarantees (Article 5(1)(e); Article 6(1)(m) CRD. Furthermore, the Sale of Goods Directive contains several more substantive rules in this respect: For example, in cases where the commercial guarantee contains less favourable conditions for the consumer than the relevant advertising, the more favourable conditions should usually apply (Article 17(1) subpara. 2 SGD).

**895.** Furthermore, the Directive clarifies that pre-contractual information provided by the seller and relevant advertising available before the conclusion of the contract also bind the guarantor (Article 17(1) SGD). Several formal requirements are set out in Article 17(2) SGD, but the guarantee statement is binding on the guarantor even if they do not comply with them (para. 3). Finally, Article 17(4) SGD contains an exception to the principle of full harmonisation: Concerning commercial guarantees, the Member States are allowed to introduce special provisions for aspects not regulated in the Directive, which may concern, for example, the language in which the guarantee statement must be provided to the consumer.

---

104 On the ambivalence of the two parts of the proposed Directive in Article 14 Draft Distance Selling Directive, see Maultzsch, *JZ* 2016, 236, 245.

### 3. RIGHT OF REDRESS

**896.** Concerning the seller's right of redress against intermediaries or manufacturers (Article18 SGD), the Sale of Goods Directive is also connected closely to the predecessor regulation in Article 4 CSD. This is not consumer law in the narrower sense, as the recourse will be between two entrepreneurs. Article 18 SGD closely follows Article 4 CSD in its content and structure. In addition to clarifying that the right of recourse also applies to the failure to provide updates for goods with digital elements according to Article 7(3) SGD, Article 18 SGD only states in more general terms, but probably without any difference in substance, that this can be any person in preceding links of the contractual value chain. In this respect, Article 4 CSD still referred to the manufacturer, a previous seller within the same contractual chain or another intermediate person.[105] Therefore, the right of redress should continue to exist vis-à-vis the person or persons liable within the contractual chain. Further details are left to the legal systems of the Member States (Article 18 SGD). There, it can be regulated, for example, that debtors other than the guarantor are included in the commercial guarantee insofar as these provisions do not impair the protection otherwise granted by the Sale of Goods Directive (Recital 62 SGD).

## VI. INCENTIVES FOR A SUSTAINABLE EXERCISE OF CONSUMER RIGHTS

**897.** It has already been mentioned that the EU is more and more concerned about sustainability issues in consumer law.[106] The Right to Repair Directive, adopted in 2024, confers a right to repair on the consumer. However, it operates outside the sales contract and addresses only the manufacturer of a product.[107] Still, one may ask whether the right to repair may have repercussions on the contractual relationship between seller and buyer. Indeed, the Right to Repair Directive itself brings about changes to the Sale of Goods Directive.[108] These are meant to incentivise consumers to choose repair to bring goods into conformity within the liability of the seller, and therefore to promote repair (Recitals 40 to 42 Right to Repair Directive).

---

[105] In Article 16 Draft Distance Selling Directive, the formulation was used that the action or omission of a person before the conclusion of the contract must lead to the seller's liability towards the consumer. Despite this more open formulation, no deviation from the previous law was intended here either.

[106] See at paras. 42 ff. above.

[107] On the right to repair cf. §22.

[108] Cf. Hanecker/Schmidt-Kessel, *GPR* 2024, 236.

**898.** This concerns, firstly, an extension of the objective requirements for conformity as provided in Article 7(1) Sale of Goods Directive. Here, repairability is added to the list. There is no corresponding definition for this characteristic in the Right to Repair Directive. The list in Article 2(11) of the Directive does not provide a satisfactory answer for the context of sales law.

**899.** Clearly, the notion of repairability has to be read in the light of the Sale of Goods Directive and the legal framework it provides. A good may not be construed in a way that repair is impossible from the outset, or indeed possible only at disproportionate costs. This new item on the list of objective requirements for conformity thus may be seen to serve to combat what is called planned obsolescence. By the same token, repairability of a good – which means any tangible good within the meaning of Article 2(5) Sale of Goods Directive, not the much narrower scope of application in Article 5(1) Right to Repair Directive – may only be seen as an objective requirement for conformity within the liability period of the seller, which runs two years from the point in time when the good was delivered (Article 10(1) Sale of Goods Directive). As will be explained later, the right to repair under Directive 2024/1799 has a totally different temporal scope.[109]

**900.** The second incentive for consumers to have a defective good repaired rather than replaced, is provided by a new Article 10(2a) Sale of Goods Directive. This provision provides that, where repair takes place as the remedy to bring the goods into conformity, the liability period shall be extended once by 12 months, or, if Member States think fit, even longer, as the amended Article 10(3) Sale of Goods Directive provides. In any case, Member States must ensure that the liability of the seller or the limitation period for remedies in the event of repair is at least equivalent to three years (Article 10(5) Sale of Goods Directive).

**901.** Thirdly, pursuant to the new Article 13(2a) Sale of Goods Directive, before the seller provides the remedy to bring the goods into conformity, the seller shall inform the consumer about the consumer's right to choose between repair and replacement, as well as about the possible extension of the liability period, provided for in Article 10(2a). Again, as Recital 41 states, this is meant to raise awareness about both alternatives and the advantage of choosing repair. That information requirement would encourage sustainable consumption and contribute to a circular economy.[110]

---

109 See the similar approach taken by Hanecker/Schmidt-Kessel, *GPR* 2024, 236, 239.

110 For possible consequences of non-compliance with this duty of information cf. Hanecker/Schmidt-Kessel, *GPR* 2024, 236, 240 ff.

**902.** Lastly, Article 14(1) Sale of Goods Directive is amended by what can be seen to be a mirror image of Article 5(2)(c) and (d) Right to Repair Directive: Pursuant to this amendment, during repair, depending on the specificities of the relevant category of goods, in particular of the need of the consumer to have such goods permanently available, the seller may provide the consumer free of charge with a replacement good, including a refurbished good, on loan. As explained above, just as the manufacturer, the seller is of course free to offer whatever he wishes to the consumer. As Recital 42 Right of Repair Directive makes clear, this provision serves as a further incentive for repair, and also as a boost for the emerging market of refurbished goods.

**903.** This does not give repair priority over replacement in legal terms. Clearly, Article 13(2) Sale of Goods Directive, which gives the consumer the free choice between repair and replacement (outside impossibility or disproportionality), remains unchanged. From the nature of the changes to other provisions (only) of the Sale of Goods Directive, one must draw the counter-inference that replacement may still be chosen by the consumer without any further justification. It remains to be seen whether or not the massive incentives given by the Right to Repair Directive towards repair will nudge the consumer towards this presumably more sustainable way to bring goods in conformity with the contract.

# §22. THE RIGHT TO REPAIR

CONTENTS



References: S. Jung/M. Back, 'Das neue EU-Recht auf Reparatur', *JZ* 2025, 21; E. M. Kieninger, 'Recht auf Reparatur ("Right to Repair") und Europäisches Vertragsrecht', *ZEuP* 2020, 264; F. Zoll, 'From a Product-Based Economy to Services? Legal Aspects of an Economy in Transition', in Keirsbilck/Terryn, *Consumer Protection in a Circular Economy* (Cambridge: Intersentia 2019), p. 149.

**904.** In its Action Plan for the Circular Economy of 11 March 2020,[1] the EU Commission had proposed to establish a 'right to repair'.[2] After political and parliamentary debates, on 13 June 2024, the European Parliament and the Council have adopted Directive (EU) 2024/1799 on common rules promoting the repair of goods.[3]

## I. SUSTAINABLE CONSUMPTION AND CIRCULAR ECONOMY

**905.** In its first Recital, the legislative act reminds us that the 2019 Sale of Goods Directive pursued the double objective of 'improving the functioning

[1] A new action plan for the circular economy. Towards a cleaner and more competitive Europe, COM(2020) 98 final.

[2] COM(2020) 98 final, p. 6. See e.g. E. Terryn, in Keirsbilck/Terryn, *Consumer Protection in a Circular Economy*, 2019, p. 127; Kieninger, *ZEuP* 2020, 264, 274 ff.

[3] Directive (EU) 2024/1799 of the European Parliament and of the Council of 13 June 2024 on common rules promoting the repair of goods and amending Regulation (EU) 2017/2394 and Directives (EU) 2019/771 and (EU) 2020/1828, OJ 2024 L 2024/1799.

of the internal market, while achieving a high level of consumer protection as well as increased circularity within the economy'. While it is not easy to find evidence to support this last statement, the Recital goes on to state that '[i]n the context of the green transition, this Directive pursues the objective of improving the functioning of the internal market, while promoting more sustainable consumption, and thereby complements the objective pursued by Directive (EU) 2019/771'. To this end, in the words of Recital 3, '[i]n order to reduce premature disposal of viable goods purchased by consumers and to encourage consumers to use their goods longer, it is necessary to strengthen the provisions related to the repair of goods, allowing consumers to seek affordable repair from the repair service provider of their choice. Repair should result in sustainable consumption, since it is likely to generate less waste caused by discarded goods, less demand for resources, including energy, caused by the process of manufacturing and sale of new goods replacing defective goods, as well as less greenhouse gas emissions. This Directive promotes sustainable consumption with a view to achieving benefits for the environment, by promoting a life cycle of goods which includes re-use, repair and refurbishment, while also producing benefits for consumers by avoiding costs associated with new purchases in the short term'.

## II. FULL HARMONISATION

**906.** It is no surprise that the Right to Repair Directive, like most, if not all, pertinent Directives in the area of consumer law since at least 2011, aims at full harmonisation. This means, as Article 3 Right to Repair Directive spells out, that Member States shall not maintain or introduce in their national law provisions diverging from those laid down in this Directive. Full harmonisation has become the standard model for directives in the field of consumer law. Member States may not go beyond the protective standards set by the Directive, even though this would give the consumer more rights. The so-called gold-plating, i.e. a transposition implementing the requirements of the Directive in an 'excessive' manner, runs counter to the intention of the fully harmonising Directive, to set a level-playing field for companies in the internal market (cf. Article 19(5) as well as Recital 2 of the Right to Repair Directive). Member States must transpose the Directive into national law by 31 July 2026 and apply those measures from this date at the latest (Article 22 Right to Repair Directive).

## III. THE OBLIGATION OF THE MANUFACTURER TO REPAIR CERTAIN GOODS

**907.** As one of the central provisions of the legal act, Article 5(1) Right to Repair Directive introduces an obligation of the manufacturer to repair goods for which, and to the extent that, repairability requirements are provided for by Union legal acts listed in Annex II, unless repair of such goods is impossible. By contrast, a manufacturer may not refuse to repair goods for the sole reason that a previous repair has been performed by other repairers or by other persons (Article 5(7) Right to Repair Directive).

**908.** As can be inferred from this, the Right to Repair Directive distinguishes between the repairer and the manufacturer. The former is defined by Article 2(2) Right to Repair Directive as 'any natural or legal person who, related to that person's trade, business, craft or profession, provides a repair service, including manufacturers and sellers that provide repair services and repair service providers whether independent or affiliated with such manufacturers or sellers'. The definition of manufacturer as the obligee of the duty to repair, however, is contained in Article 2, point (42), of the Ecodesign Regulation (EU) 2024/1781, to which Article 2(5) Right to Repair Directive merely makes reference. There, 'manufacturer' is defined as 'any natural or legal person that manufactures a product or that has a product designed or manufactured, and markets that product under their name or trademark'.

**909.** The manufacturer is not obliged to carry out the repair in person. Rather, he may subcontract repair in order to fulfil its obligation to repair (Article 5(1) Right to Repair Directive). Where the manufacturer is established outside the Union, Article 5(3) Right to Repair Directive imposes a duty to designate an authorised representative in the Union who shall perform the obligation of the manufacturer. Where the manufacturer fails to designate an authorised representative in the Union, the importer of the good concerned shall perform the obligation of the manufacturer. Lastly, where there is no such importer, the distributor of the good concerned shall perform the obligation of the manufacturer. Like the manufacturer himself, the authorised representative, importer and distributor may sub-contract repair in order to fulfil their obligation to repair. To keep the consumer informed about the repair services offered by the manufacturer or, as the case may be, the authorised representative, importer or distributor, these entities shall provide relevant information on that (Article 6 Right to Repair Directive). This will be explained in more detail below.

**910.** Repair shall be carried out either free of charge or for a reasonable price and within a reasonable period of time. Moreover, as Article 5 of the Directive goes on to say in an attempt to implement further consumer rights in a soft, nudging way, the manufacturer may provide the consumer with the loan of a replacement good free of charge or for a reasonable fee for the duration of the repair; and offer the consumer a refurbished good where repair is impossible. Both is of course perfectly possible under the principle of contractual freedom under the law as it stands.

**911.** As transpires from Article 4(3) Right to Repair Directive, where a diagnostic service, including a physical or remote examination, is needed to identify the nature of the defect, the type of repair and to estimate the price of repair, the repairer may request the consumer to pay the necessary costs of this service. The repairer shall inform the consumer about the costs of the diagnostic service.

**912.** It cannot be emphasised enough that, as a matter of principle, the obligation to repair operates outside the existing contract between consumer and trader. The seller of the good is not under any obligation to repair the good sold unless there is a non-conformity of the good with the requirements following either from the contract or from the objective standards set by the applicable law: in that case, as explained above, the consumer has the right to choose between repair and replacement (Article 13(2) Sale of Goods Directive) within the relevant period of time as defined pursuant to Article 10 Sale of Goods Directive. This legal setting remains largely unaffected by the Right to Repair Directive.[4] Rather, the right of repair as stipulated by the new Directive concerns the manufacturer of the good, and it does not presuppose any non-conformity of the good with the contractual obligation.

**913.** The obligation of the manufacturer of the good to carry out repair of the good does not correspond with a duty of the consumer to have it repaired in the first place. As before, the consumer may choose to buy a new good instead. Besides, consumers are by no means bound to have the good repaired by the manufacturer as defined in the Directive. They are entirely free to seek repair from any repairer of their choice, as Article 5(8) Right to Repair Directive makes clear.

## IV. MATERIAL SCOPE OF APPLICATION

**914.** As already mentioned, the obligation to repair of the manufacturer does not extend to each and every good. Instead, Annex II refers to legal acts in force in the EU laying down repairability requirements for, e.g., household appliances such as washing machines, washer-dryers, tumble dryers, dishwashers, refrigerating appliances, and vacuum cleaners. Furthermore, it extends to goods incorporating light means of transport batteries, to welding equipment, electronic displays, servers, data storage products, mobile phones, cordless phones, and slate tablets. This list provided in Annex II is conclusive. Under the

---

4 Note that Article 16 Right to Repair Directive brings about a number of changes to the Sale of Goods Directive. This will be explained in more detail below.

principle of full harmonisation, a Member State is not in a position to extend this list of goods to e.g. cars or bicycles. Such an obligation would constitute actual or potential obstacles to the functioning of the internal market, adversely affecting cross-border transactions of economic operators acting on that market, as Recital 2 of the Right to Repair Directive underlines.

**915.** The Directive does not explicitly state for which period of time the manufacturer is obliged to repair a given good. Consequently, it is open to discussion whether this obligation extends to a good fabricated, say, 5, 10, or even 15 years ago. Clearly, there must be a temporal limitation to the right of repair under Article 5 of the Directive. This understanding seems to underlie the information duty following from Article 6 Right to Repair Directive, which refers to 'the entire duration of their obligation to repair pursuant to Article 5'. Recital 21 states as one of the goals of the Directive to avoid overburdening manufacturers and to ensure they are able to perform their obligation to repair. Consequently, pursuant to Article 5(1) of the Directive, the right to repair exists only to the extent that repairability requirements are provided for by Union legal acts listed in Annex II to the Directive.

**916.** The obligation to provide spare parts is key to the understanding of this provision. Recital 18 of the Directive reiterates that spare parts should be made available at least for the time period set out in Union legal acts. To give an example, Commission Regulation (EU) 2019/2023 on ecodesign requirements for household washing machines and household washer-dryers[5] lays down the obligation of manufacturers, importers or authorised representatives of household washing machines and household washer-dryers to make available to professional repairers certain spare parts for a minimum period of 10 years after placing the last unit of the model on the market (Annex II, Ecodesign Requirements, No. 8). For mobile phones and smartphones, Commission Regulation (EU) 2023/1670 on ecodesign requirements for smartphones, mobile phones other than smartphones, cordless phones and slate tablets[6] provides that manufacturers, importers or authorised representatives shall make available to professional repairers certain spare parts until at least 7 years after the date of end

5 Commission Regulation (EU) 2019/2023 of 1 October 2019 laying down ecodesign requirements for household washing machines and household washer-dryers pursuant to Directive 2009/125/EC of the European Parliament and of the Council, amending Commission Regulation (EC) No 1275/2008 and repealing Commission Regulation (EU) No 1015/2010, OJ 2019 L 315/285.

6 Commission Regulation (EU) 2023/1670 of 16 June 2023 laying down ecodesign requirements for smartphones, mobile phones other than smartphones, cordless phones and slate tablets pursuant to Directive 2009/125/EC of the European Parliament and of the Council and amending Commission Regulation (EU) 2023/826, OJ 2023 L 214/47.

of placement on the market, when present (Annex II, Ecodesign Requirements, A 1.1.(1) and B 1.1.(1)).

**917.** According to Recital 21 of the Right to Repair Directive, the obligation to repair should correspond to the scope of the repairability requirements, for instance, ecodesign requirements might apply only to certain components of the goods or a specific period of time might be set to make spare parts available. Consequently, the right to repair exists at least during the period of time during which spare parts for the specific good must be made available according to the relevant Regulation.[7]

## V. INFORMATION ABOUT THE RIGHT TO REPAIR

**918.** Pursuant to Article 6 Right to Repair Directive, the manufacturer (or his authorised representative, importer or distributor) is under an obligation to make available free of charge, at least for the entire duration of their obligation to repair pursuant to Article 5, information on their repair services in an easily accessible, clear and comprehensible manner. To help spread information on any available repair service, a European online platform for repair shall be established to allow consumers to find repairers, to be set up by 31 July 2027 (Article 7 Right to Repair Directive). Moreover, the Member States shall take appropriate measures to ensure that information on the rights of consumers under the Right to Repair Directive are available to consumers (Article 12 Right to Repair Directive).

## VI. (INFORMATION ABOUT THE) CONTENT OF THE REPAIR CONTRACT

**919.** Pursuant to Article 4 Right to Repair Directive, repairers may provide the consumer with the European Repair Information Form set out in Annex I. While the information duties in Articles 6 and 7 Right to Repair Directive explained above aim at bringing consumers in a position to decide where a certain good may be repaired, the European Repair Information Form is designed to streamline the individual contract between a repairer and the consumer. To this end, the form shall be provided within a reasonable period of time after the request and before the consumer is bound by a contract for the provision of repair services. In this form, certain conditions of repair shall be specified, and they shall be binding for at least 30 days running from the

[7] Cf. Jung/Back, *JZ* 2025, 21, 27 f.

date on which that form was provided to the consumer (Article 4(4) and (5) Right to Repair Directive). From the perspective of contract law, this provision defines the content of the offer of the repairer. Pursuant to Article 4(5) Right to Repair Directive, where the consumer accepts, within the period of validity, the conditions set out in the European Repair Information Form, the repairer shall be obliged to perform the repair service under those conditions.

**920.** It should go without saying that an offer and a matching acceptance result in a binding contract, and that the extent of the contractual obligation is defined by the content of the parties' mutual intent. Insofar, the mechanism described is purely descriptive. Moreover, the title of the relevant Article 4 – European Repair Information Form – is slightly misleading, as the real intention of the provision is the regulation of the conclusion of the contract between consumer and repairer. It should be stressed in that context, that the use of the form is not mandatory, as is made clear by Article 4(1) Right to Repair Directive. However, two points must be mentioned: first, where the repairer has supplied a complete and accurate European Repair Information Form to the consumer, it shall be deemed to have complied with the numerous information requirements as set up in the Consumer Rights Directive 2011/83/EU (Article 4(6) Right to Repair Directive). And second, the conditions of the offer as specified in the form must not be changed for at least 30 calendar days from the date on which that form was provided to the consumer. Insofar, the Directive sets up a binding requirement for the repairer which diverts from the usual standard e.g. in German law, where the offeror is free to determine the period of time for the acceptance of an offer (sec. 148 German Civil Code).

## VII. A NEW PARADIGM?

**921.** It must be reiterated that the Right to Repair Directive does not bring about any changes to the obligations arising from the sales contract. The right to repair arises outside the sales contract. It does not relate to any defect of the good sold, and, hence, is not a remedy of the consumer against the seller. It gives rise to an obligation of the manufacturer to conclude, under certain conditions, a repair contract with the consumer. This contract is not a sales contract, but rather a contract for services – more specifically, a contract for work.

**922.** An exception may be said to exist in the case of direct sales, i.e. if the seller is also the manufacturer. In this case, the obligation to repair comes into existence in addition to the obligations arising from the sales contract. But even in that case the legal basis of the obligation to repair is separate and distinct from the sales contract.

**923.** In principle, therefore, the sales contract remains an exchange contract and does not become a continuing obligation. The right to repair remotely resembles the obligation to provide updates in contracts for the supply of digital content and digital services under Directive (EU) 2019/770. However, the obligation to provide updates is directed against the trader as transpires from the objective requirements for conformity laid down in Article 8 Directive (EU) 2019/770.

**924.** The Right to Repair Directive introduces under certain circumstances an obligation of the manufacturer to conclude a contract. The manufacturer may fulfil this obligation by subcontracting repair, but there is no way simply to reject justified requests of consumers for repair of a good falling within the scope of Article 5 of the Directive. Such an obligation to enter into a contract is something unusual under private autonomy, which ordinarily allows for a free choice of contracting partners – at least outside monopolies. What is more, this obligation to enter into a contract extends to an economic activity in which the manufacturer may not be interested in, let alone have the necessary equipment and expertise. Clearly, in many cases subcontracting will be the only option for a manufacturer to dispose of the obligation to repair.

**925.** Moreover, every buyer of a good within the meaning of Article 5 of the Directive has a right to repair. Therefore, one may say that the sales contract gains an additional legal dimension, some sort of a contractual triangle between seller, manufacturer/repairer and consumer. But there is not much that can be inferred from this: the right to repair exists vis-à-vis a certain good, irrespective of the legal title the consumer has with respect to that good. The consumer need not be the owner of the good, he may have leased, lent or even stolen it.

**926.** However, the Right to Repair Directive has also brought about significant changes to the Sale of Goods Directive. It has upgraded the remedy of repair in cases of non-conformity of the good with the contract. Formally, repair and replacement are still on equal footing. Yet the new provisions confer very considerable advantages on the consumer if he chooses to have the good repaired rather than replaced. Without openly introducing a new hierarchy of remedies, the Directive nudges the consumer softly into repairing goods that are indeed repairable.[8] In more general terms, with the increasing availability of sharing or leasing offers, some commentators assume that the legal significance of the sales contract could diminish anyway.[9]

---

8 Some commentators infer from this the end of the sales contract as a mere exchange contract, cf. *Hanecker/Schmidt-Kessel*, GPR 2024, 236, 247.

9 In that sense *Zoll*, in Keirsbilck/Terryn, Consumer Protection in a Circular Economy, 2019, p. 149.

**927.** Whether the Right to Repair Directive will lead to more sustainability in the sale of goods remains to be seen. Anyway, it is difficult, if not impossible, to assess the sustainability gain in the first place. It is completely unclear how many consumers will exercise their right to repair. After all, although the directive introduces a new right, it does not necessarily create a completely new market: many manufacturers already offer repair options for their products. Likewise, numerous non-branded repair shops offer repair as well. The question is whether the repair obligation introduced by the Directive will lower the price level here or even lead to smaller businesses being pushed out of the market. This is clearly not the intention of the Directive. The decisive factor will be what price level is to be regarded as 'reasonable' within the meaning of the Directive. This can hardly be reviewed in court – after all, the question of a fair price is as old as contract law itself. If the market price is considered reasonable, the price level will hardly change as a result of the repair obligation. At most, individual products could become more expensive if manufacturers pass on the additional costs of setting up an infrastructure for repairs to customers in their calculations.

**928.** It should also be borne in mind that a repair seems not necessarily always to be preferable to a new purchase in terms of sustainability. After all, more modern appliances are generally more energy-efficient and therefore more environmentally friendly. In any case, the obligation to repair could tend to slow down the replacement of old appliances with new ones. Overall, the approach of the Directive is novel in that it is less about consumer protection and more about a form of consumer empowerment to achieve sustainability goals, the latter being at least doubtful for the time being.

# §23. CONTRACT LAW IN THE DIGITAL AGE

## CONTENTS

References: M. Auer, 'Digitale Leistungen', *ZfPW* 2019, 130; A. *De Franceschi/R. Schulze, Harmonizing Digital Contract Law: The Impact of EU Directives 2019/770 and 2019/771 and the Regulation of Online Platforms* (Baden-Baden/Munich/Oxford: Nomos/C.H. Beck/Hart Publishing, 2023); S. Grundmann (ed.), *European Contract Law in the Digital Age* (Cambridge: Intersentia, 2018); S. Grundmann/F. Möslein (eds.), *Vertragsrecht und Innovation* (Tübingen: Mohr Siebeck, 2019); J.D. Lüttringhaus, 'Das internationale Datenprivatrecht: Baustein des Wirtschaftskollisionsrechts des 21. Jahrhunderts – Ein Beitrag zum IPR der Haftung für Verstöße gegen die EU-Datenschutzgrundverordnung', *ZVglRWiss* 117 (2018), 50; G. Resta, 'Personal Identity and European Contract Law', *ERCL* 2022, 205; R. Schulze, 'European Private Law in the Digital Age – Developments, Challenges and Prospects', in A. Janssen/M. Lehmann/R. Schulze (eds.), *The Future of European Private Law* (Baden-Baden: Nomos, 2023), p. 141; R. Schulze/D. Staudenmayer (eds.), *Digital Revolution: Challenges for Contract Law in Practice* (Baden-Baden: Nomos, 2016).

## I. DIGITAL CONTENT AS THE SUBJECT OF CONTRACTUAL RIGHTS AND OBLIGATIONS

**929.** After the failure of the proposal to introduce a Common European Sales Law,[1] the Commission focused on improving the Digital Single Market, which was expected to have considerable growth potential.[2] A whole set of measures was initiated. In the context of contract law, Directive (EU) 2019/770 on certain aspects of contract law relating to the provision of digital content and digital services (Digital Content Directive) is of particular importance.[3]

### 1. DIGITAL CONTENTS

**930.** The growing importance of the internet at the end of the 1990s had already triggered an initial regulatory push at the EC level. In this respect,

[1] On this see para. 130 above.
[2] See the Digital Single Market Strategy of 5 May 2015, COM(2015) 192 final.
[3] See para. 943 below.

the Distance Selling Directive,[4] the E-Commerce Directive or the Signatures Directive are particularly noteworthy.[5] While this was primarily intended to be a legal framework for digital communication as a means of concluding contracts, more recent legislative activities have concentrated on digital content as the contractual subject. This, in itself, is not new: The legal classification of contracts for the provision of standard software, for example, was already discussed earlier;[6] however, the plea for legislative action was not yet heard. However, this has changed for some time now, as the mass distribution of smartphones and the ubiquitous and often free availability of apps has given rise to a whole series of legal questions for which a reference to case law no longer seemed sufficient.

**931.** Article 2 no. 11 CRD defines digital content as 'data which are produced and supplied in digital form'. The proposal for a Common European Sales Law contains a corresponding provision.[7] After its failure, the Commission transferred essential contents into an independent legal act: The Digital Content Directive (DCD), which contains provisions on certain requirements for contracts for the provision of digital content or digital services between entrepreneurs and consumers (Article 1 DCD).[8]

## 2. DATA AS A COUNTER-PERFORMANCE

References: P. Hacker, 'Daten als Gegenleistung: Rechtsgeschäfte im Spannungsfeld von DS-GVO und allgemeinem Vertragsrecht', *ZfPW* 2019, 148; C. Langhanke, *Daten als Leistung. Eine rechtsvergleichende Untersuchung zu Deutschland, Österreich und der Schweiz* (Tübingen: Mohr Siebeck, 2018); C. Langhanke/M. Schmidt-Kessel, 'Consumer Data as Consideration', *EuCML* 2015, 218; D. Linardatos, 'Daten als Gegenleistung im Vertrag: Modell der Richtlinie über digitale Inhalte', in L. Specht-Riemenschneider/N. Werry/S. Werry (eds.), *Datenrecht in der Digitalisierung* (Berlin: Eric Schmidt, 2020), p. 506; S. Lohsse/R. Schulze/D. Staudenmayer (eds.), *Data as Counterperformance – Contract Law 2.0?* (Baden-Baden/Oxford: Nomos/Hart Publishing, 2020); L. Mischau, 'Daten als 'Gegenleistung' im neuen Verbrauchervertragsrecht', *ZEuP* 2020, 335; T. Pertot, 'Die Auslegung des datenschutzrechtlichen Koppelungsverbots – Lockerung durch den Corte di Cassazione', *GPR* 2019, 54; T. Riehm, 'Freie Widerruflichkeit der Einwilligung und Struktur der Obligation – Daten als Gegenleistung?', in T. Pertot (ed.), *Rechte an Daten* (Tübingen: Mohr Siebeck, 2020), p. 175 (im Erscheinen); A. Scheuch, 'Daten als Gegenstand von Leistung und Gegenleistung im UN-Kaufrecht', *ZVglRWiss* 118 (2019), 375; M. Schmidt-Kessel/A. Grimm, 'Unentgeltlich oder entgeltlich? – Der vertragliche

[4] In addition see para. 546 above.
[5] On both points see para. 554 above.
[6] The leading case is BGHZ 102, 135, 145: in any case application of sales law by analogy.
[7] Cf. para. 948 below.
[8] For their histories of origin see para. 148 and 942, for their contents see para. 944 below.

Austausch von digitalen Inhalten gegen personenbezogene Daten', *ZfPW* 2016, 84; S. Schwamberger, 'Reichweite des datenschutzrechtlichen Koppelungsverbots nach alter und neuer Rechtslage', *GPR* 2019, 57.

### *a) Personal Data*

**932.** At the European level, the General Data Protection Regulation (GDPR) provides a framework that is also relevant to private law. In particular, according to Article 82 GDPR, any person who has suffered material or non-material damage due to a breach of this regulation has a claim for damages against the controller or the processor. Given its nature as a tort claim,[9] it is not considered in detail in this volume.

**933.** Data protection law may be seen as a specific variant of the right to informational self-determination, which originates in a person's personality rights. In the words of the German Federal Constitutional Court, it prescribes 'under the modern conditions of data processing, the protection of the individual against unlimited collection, storage, use and disclosure of his or her personal data'.[10] From this is derived the right of the individual to determine for themselves the disclosure and use of their personal data. In precise terms, Article 16(1) TFEU and, with identical wording, Article 8(1) CFR state: 'Everyone has the right to the protection of personal data concerning them.' These provisions regulate the relationship of the individual to the state, but they are of indirect importance in horizontal relationships.[11]

**934.** However, it cannot be inferred from this that data is a commodity that cannot be commercialised. A statement made by the (then) European Data Protection Supervisor (EDPS) Buttarelli in March 2017, for example, could be understood in this direction, as he stated the following concerning the Commission's proposal for the Digital Content Directive:[12]

**935.** 'The EDPS supports the aim of the Commission's initiative, which is to enhance consumer rights. I consider this an opportunity to harness synergies

9 Cf. Frenzel, in B.P. Paal/D. Pauly, *DS-GVO/BDSG*, 3nd ed. (Munich: C.H. Beck, 2021), Art. 82 DSGVO para. 1; B. Kreße, in G. Sydow, *Europäische Datenschutzgrundverordnung*, 3nd ed. (Baden-Baden/Vienna/Zurich: Nomos/Manz/Dike, 2022), Art. 82 para. 4. On the qualification of data protection claims under the Brussels Ibis Regulation Stürner/ Wendelstein, *JZ* 2018, 1083.

10 The leading case is BVerfGE 65, 1, 41 ff.

11 See, for example, on the 'right to be forgotten' CJEU, 13 May 2014, Case C-131/12, *Google Spain*, ECLI:EU:C:2014:317, paras. 69, 74. More generally on the horizontal effect of fundamental freedoms, see para. 263 above.

12 See the press release of 15 March 2017, available at https://edps.europa.eu/press-publications/ press-news/press-releases/2017/edps-sees-opportunities-stronger-consumer-and-data_en.

between consumer and data protection law in the interests of the individual. The proposed directive should avoid unintentional interference with the data protection rights and obligations set down by the EU last year in the General Data Protection Regulation. *Individuals should not be required to disclose personal data in "payment" for an online service. Rather, their rights and interests should be safeguarded by coherent application of up-to-date rules in the consumer and data protection area.*'[13]

**936.** Consequently, the business model 'app for data' would be obsolete. The fact that this corresponds neither to the requirements of primary law nor to the systematics of the legal acts of European secondary law is explained below.[14]

*b) Data as Consideration*

**937.** The Digital Content Directive deals with contracts for the provision of digital content.[15] It starts with the ordinary constellation that the digital content is provided against payment (Article 3(1) subpara. 1 DCD), which is understood as 'money or a digital representation of value that is due in exchange for the supply of digital content or a digital service' (Article 2 no. 7 DCD). However, since the business model of many providers of digital content provides the respective service 'for free' or 'free of charge', the legislator had to choose whether to include this type of contract in the regulatory concept, leave the regulation to the law of the Member States or prohibit it completely.

**938.** The Directive proposal[16] defined the scope of application in Article 3(1) in such a way that it should also cover contracts for the provision of digital content where the consumer 'actively provides counter-performance other than money in the form of personal data or any other data'.[17] Further differentiation according to the type of consideration would, in the Commission's view, 'Introducing a differentiation depending on the nature of the counter-performance would discriminate between different business models; it would provide an unjustified incentive for businesses to move towards offering digital content against data.' (Recital 13 draft Digital Content Directive). The resulting equation of data as payment was met with criticism and opposition, especially with regard to personal data, or even complete rejection of such commercialisation by the European Data Protection Supervisor just quoted.

---

13 Emphasis added.

14 On the transformation of the traditional idea of 'inalienability' of personality rights, cf. Resta, *ERCL* 2022, 205.

15 For more on this see para. 944 below.

16 COM(2015) 634 final.

17 Additionally see para. 946 below.

**939.** The wording found in the adopted version of the Digital Content Directive weakens the connection between data and the contractual performance obligation but remains in line with the content of the draft: According to its Article 3(1) subpara. 2, the Digital Content Directive also applies 'where the trader supplies or undertakes to supply digital content or a digital service to the consumer, and the consumer provides or undertakes to provide personal data to the trader [...]'. Although a reciprocal connection between performance (the provision of digital content by the entrepreneur) and consideration (the provision of data by the consumer) cannot be directly established from these rules, this is, of course, precisely what is meant.[18] Recital 24 DCD takes up the widespread use of such business models and formulates a clear desideratum: The 'Directive should ensure that consumers are, in the context of such business models, entitled to contractual remedies'.[19] At the same time, the Directive's aim to establish a safeguard against excessive commercialisation by referring to the protection of personal data under fundamental rights in the same Recital, which could, therefore, not be regarded as a commodity.

**940.** This obscures the actual problems for several reasons: For one, the wording's clarity – data are not goods – is achieved, at least in the German language version, through a terminological choice that leads away from the actual problem: According to the definition in Article 2 no. 5 SGD, goods are movable objects, so that data cannot be regarded as goods for this reason alone already. The distinction between the singular (goods as an object capable of being commercialised) and the plural (goods as objects of sale) does not seem very distinctive here. The English language version is clearer ('personal data cannot be considered as a commodity').[20] Furthermore, the aforementioned Recital 24 DCD may give rise to an internal contradiction: If data is something other than money (or its digital representation) and, moreover, is not to be considered a commodity, it should also not be able to be provided as contractual consideration. However, since the Digital Content Directive legitimises precisely this,[21] it is very much a question of the content of the legal framework within which the data-related performance takes place.

---

18 Cf. Metzger, *JZ* 2019, 577, 579; Staudenmayer, *ZEuP* 2019, 663, 669.

19 Staudenmayer, *ZEuP* 2019, 663, 669, speaks of a 'groundbreaking innovation' that opens up a 'new dimension of the adaptation of private law to the transition to the digital economy'. In view of the freedom of contract generally accepted in all Member State legal systems, this is at most true to the extent that there is now a positive-law regulation (also) at EU level.

20 The French version ('*les données à caractère personnel ne peuvent être considérées comme des marchandises*') also makes a clearer linguistic distinction (definition of goods in Article 2 no. 5 SGD: '*bien*') than the German version.

21 It is also recognised in the context of sec. 312(1) of the German Civil Code that the 'performance for consideration' required there for the applicability of the consumer protection provisions does not have to consist of money, so that personal data in particular can also constitute consideration, see BT-Drucks. 17/13951, p. 72.

**941.** The protection of fundamental rights, which is, first and foremost, to be granted concerning data in the form of data protection by the GDPR or Member State data protection law, partly contradicts this view since it assumes, in principle, the person's right to free disposition of data. Hence, Article 7(4) GDPR stresses that the voluntary nature of the granting of consent under data protection law may be lacking if 'the performance of a contract, including the provision of a service, is conditional on consent to the processing of personal data that is not necessary for the performance of that contract'. Furthermore, consent should not provide a valid legal ground for the processing of personal data in a specific case, where there is a 'clear imbalance' between the controller and the data subject (Recital 43 GDPR).[22] The problems associated with this will be discussed later.[23]

## II. THE DIGITAL CONTENT DIRECTIVE

### 1. ORIGINS AND BACKGROUND

References: I. Bach, 'Neue Richtlinien zum Verbrauchsgüterkauf und zu Verbraucherverträgen über digitale Inhalte', *NJW* 2019, 1705; B. Gsell, 'Der europäische Richtlinienvorschlag zu bestimmten vertragsrechtlichen Aspekten der Bereitstellung digitaler Inhalte', *ZUM* 2018, 75; E. Helmig, 'Die neuen Richtlinien zum europäischen Verbraucherkaufrecht. Überlegungen zum Kauf eines Fahrzeugs als Ware mit digitalem Inhalt', *IWRZ* 2019, 200; A. Metzger, 'Verträge über digitale Inhalte und digitale Dienstleistungen: Neuer BGB-Vertragstypus oder punktuelle Reform?', *JZ* 2019, 577; R. Schulze, 'Die Digitale-Inhalte-Richtlinie – Innovation und Kontinuität im europäischen Vertragsrecht', *ZEuP* 2019, 695; R. Schulze/D. Staudenmayer (eds.), *Digital Revolution: Challenges for Contract Law in Practice* (Baden-Baden: Nomos, 2016); G. Spindler/K. Sein, 'Die endgültige Richtlinie über Verträge über digitale Inhalte und Dienstleistungen', *MMR* 2019, 415; G. Spindler/K. Sein, 'Die Richtlinie über Verträge über digitale Inhalte – Gewährleistung, Haftung und Änderungen', *MMR* 2019, 488; D. Staudenmayer, 'Die Richtlinien zu den digitalen Verträgen', *ZEuP* 2019, 663; M. Wendland, 'Sonderprivatrecht für Digitale Güter: Die neue Europäische Digitale Inhalte-Richtlinie als Baustein eines Digitalen Vertragsrechts für Europa', *ZVglRWiss* 118 (2019), 191.

**942.** Directive (EU) 2019/770 of 20 May 2019 on certain aspects concerning contracts for the supply of digital content and digital services (Digital Content Directive, DCD) is of key importance for the Digital Single Market. It was preceded by the proposal for a Directive on certain contract law aspects of the supply of digital content.[24] This proposal also invokes the improvement of the

---

22 Pertot, *GPR* 2019, 54; Schwamberger, *GPR* 2019, 57.

23 See para. 965 below.

24 COM(2015) 634 final.

internal market as legitimisation. It seems a little alarmistic, when reference was made to relevant legislation in Great Britain and the Netherlands, which is why, according to the Commission, haste was called for to prevent further fragmentation of the law due to new different national provisions.[25] The lengthy legislative process has already been discussed.[26] Besides the treatment of data as consideration, central points of contention were, for example, the obligation to provide updates or the question of the regulation of a claim for damages; the coordination with the Sale of Goods Directive, which was discussed in parallel, was also important.[27] Like the Sale of Goods Directive, the Digital Content Directive is fully harmonising (Article 4 DCD). However, it also grants the Member States the freedom to exceed the specified level of protection or to extend the material or personal scope of application of the Directive in a number of points.[28]

**943.** For the first time, EU law regulates exchange contracts in which the consideration does not consist of the payment of a sum of money but the handing over of data; it takes up a phenomenon that is now very common in practice.[29] The importance of user data for entrepreneurs lies in the fact that it can be used to better understand the consumer's demands, which are of enormous economic importance, for example, for the creation of individualised advertising. From the user's point of view, the threshold to disclose such data is very low, so it is often transmitted rather thoughtlessly.

## 2. THE SCOPE OF THE DIGITAL CONTENT DIRECTIVE

### *a) Subject Matter*

**944.** The Directive regulates contracts for the supply of digital content and digital services to consumers; in particular, it prescribes the requirements for the conformity of digital content and digital services with the contract, remedies for lack of conformity or non-delivery and the use thereof, as well as provisions on the modification of digital content and services (Article 1 DCD).

---

25 Explanation on the Commission proposal COM(2015) 634 final, p. 3.

26 See para. 148 above.

27 This mainly concerned the regulation of goods with digital elements, which were finally added to the Sale of Goods Directive, see also Staudenmayer, *ZEuP* 2019, 663, 666 f.

28 On this 'targeted full harmonisation', see para. 84 above; on both aspects of the gold-plating see para. 366 above.

29 On this point cf. already Langhanke/Schmidt-Kessel, *EuCML* 2015, 218.

### aa) Performance and Counter-Performance

**945.** The material scope of application is positively described in Article 3(1) DCD as covering all contracts where an entrepreneur supplies or agrees to supply digital content or services to a consumer, and the consumer pays or agrees to pay a price.[30]

**946.** The Directive also applies when the consumer does not pay a price in return but provides or agrees to provide personal data.[31] The restriction to the 'active' provision of non-monetary consideration, which was still contained in the proposal for a Directive, was not very convincing[32] and is not reflected in the adopted text of the directive. On the other hand, it is not a relevant consideration in the sense of the Directive if the data transmitted by the consumer are necessary for the performance of legal provisions (Article 3(1) subpara. 2 DCD). This applies, in any case, insofar as the supplier uses the data transmitted to them only for that very purpose.

**947.** It can, therefore, be concluded that commercial use of this data contrary to the agreement – as a sanction, so to speak – opens up the material scope of application of the Directive. However, this raises several issues. First of all, the consumer is not likely to be aware of this fact, so they are typically not fully aware of their rights. Apart from that, the Directive would only apply at the moment of the improper use of the data. It would then be unclear, for example, whether the supply of digital content owed by the supplier under Article 5 DCD is deemed to have taken place at the actual time (which might have happened long ago) or whether one must assume that the supply can only be considered to have taken place when the Directive becomes applicable (i.e. at the time of the improper use). This can have serious consequences because the liability of the supplier (Article 11(1) DCD) and the consumer's remedy in the event of failure to supply (Article 13(1) DCD) primarily depend on the lack of conformity at the time of the supply.

### bb) Digital Content

**948.** The term digital content is defined in Article 2 no. 1 DCD. It corresponds to the definition contained in Article 2 no. 11 CRD and includes data created or

---

30 Contracts developed according to consumer specifications are also covered (Article 3(2) Digital Content Directive).

31 On data as counterperformance see para. 932 above.

32 It would hardly be plausible if the simple toleration of data collection by the provider (e.g. collection of geodata) did not fall within the material scope of the Directive. According to Recital 14 DCD, it should be sufficient if the consumer actively provides the provider with access to the corresponding data, for example by registering individually.

made available in digital form. The term is extensive and technology-neutral in order to take into account future technical developments. Recital 19 DCD lists a whole range of examples (including software, applications or video, audio and music files.[33] The type of access to this digital content is irrelevant.[34] For the national transposition laws, this would mean that the Member State legislators could also assume a uniform term.

cc) Exceptions

**949.** Several exceptions, such as financial and gambling services, can be found in Article 3(5) DCD. In the case of mixed contracts, the Directive is to apply to that part of the contract which concerns the supply of digital content (Article 3(6) DCD).[35] Like the Sale of Goods Directive, the Digital Content Directive excludes general questions of the formation and validity of contracts and – in contrast to the Directive proposal[36] – the question of damages (Article 3(10) DCD).

dd) A New Type of Contract?

**950.** With the digital content and the digital services, the Directive places the object of the agreement at the centre of the regulatory concept and not, as is otherwise the case, the rights and obligations of the parties relating to it.[37] The Directive is, therefore, not limited to a specific type of contract, such as a sales contract. Yet it also does not necessarily introduce a new contract type but leaves it up to the Member States to determine the 'legal form' of such contracts (Recital 12 DCD). Thus, the supply of digital content can take place within the framework of various types of contracts already existing under national law, such as sales, rental, lease, service or work contracts.[38] It is obvious that this approach, especially in connection with full harmonisation, leads to problems in transposing it into national law and even has the potential to disrupt the national systems: If a new type of contract were standardised, such as a 'contract for the supply of digital content', which only applies to digital content, then there would be a variety of problems in delimiting it from the existing types of contract. If one were to leave it at that, however, the Directive would require modifications

---

33 The list of examples still contained in Article 3(1) of the Commission proposal has thus been moved to the Recitals.

34 Staudenmayer, *ZEuP* 2019, 663, 671, sees this as a change towards the 'access economy'.

35 The relationship to the Sale of Goods Directive and other legal acts will be dealt with later, see para. 954below; on the relationship to the Sale of Goods Directive see para. 833 above.

36 See para. 985 below.

37 Critical of this regulatory approach F. Faust, *Digitale Wirtschaft – Analoges Recht: Braucht das BGB ein Update?, Gutachten A für den Deutschen Juristentag* (Munich: C.H. Beck, 2016), pp. 5 f.

38 Staudenmayer, *ZEuP* 2019, 663, 668.

for every single obligatory relationship in the respective contexts in which the supply of digital content can occur. This, in turn, leads to a multiplication of very similar rules.

*b) Personal Scope of Application*

**951.** The Digital Content Directive only covers contracts between entrepreneurs and consumers.[39] The definition of entrepreneur[40] in Article 2 no. 5 DCD is identical to that of the seller in Article 2(3) SGD.[41] The term 'consumer' defined in Article 2 no. 4 DCD is almost[42] identical in wording to Article 2 no. 1 CRD. The definition of consumer in Article 2 no. 6 DCD also follows established conventions. According to Recital 16 DCD, the Member States can define national transposition law more broadly and extend it, for example, to start-ups, SMEs or contracts between entrepreneurs.

**952.** No special mention is made of contracts with dual purposes, which are certainly not uncommon, especially in the case of digital content.[43] For such dual-use contracts, Recital 17 CRD states that the consumer status does not cease to exist if the commercial purpose does not predominate in the overall context of the contract. Because of the comparable regulatory context, a systematic interpretation could easily conclude that this assessment could also apply to the Digital Content Directive. Recital 17 DCD, however, instructs the legal practitioner otherwise: According to this, dual-use contracts are not covered by the Directive; however, the Member States are free to extend the national transpositions to such contracts. This dichotomy of the term 'consumer' within substantive EU law does not appear to be a good solution, especially since a differentiation in content is not obvious.[44] It is unclear whether the consumer status under the Directive also ceases to apply if the professional or commercial element is only very minor, as the CJEU ruled in the *Gruber* case on consumer

---

39 Critically, F. Faust, *Digitale Wirtschaft – Analoges Recht: Braucht das BGB ein Update?, Gutachten A für den Deutschen Juristentag* (Munich: C.H. Beck, 2016), p. 6.

40 The Directive Proposal used the term 'supplier' instead of entrepreneur, although the content was the same.

41 The clarification in Article 2(c) Distance Selling Directive that the definition of seller only applies to contracts covered by the Directive seems superfluous. This passage is also missing in Article 2 no. 3 DCD.

42 Why a different wording was chosen here is not apparent.

43 Spindler, *MMR* 2016, 147, 149. The same applies to the Sale of Goods Directive, see para. 837 above. For general information on the definition of the term consumer, see para. 31 above.

44 See, however, Staudenmayer, *ZEuP* 2019, 663, 674 ff. with reference to the significantly higher cost burden that the extended term 'consumer' entails for the entrepreneur, whereas the duties of information to be fulfilled under the Consumer Rights Directive are generic and thus comparatively cheap to fulfil. This is not convincing, because the right of withdrawal under the Consumer Rights Directive also entails costs that are quite comparable to the remedies available under the Digital Content Directive.

jurisdiction in the framework of the Brussels regime.[45] For reasons of coherence, this should be answered in the affirmative; it would also hardly be acceptable to have otherwise not two but even three different notions of consumer in EU private law.

### c) *Spatial Scope of Application*

**953.** The Digital Content Directive also applies not only to cross-border but also to purely national contracts. This again contrasts to a certain extent with the Directive's underlying goal to promote cross-border digital content offerings.[46] Nevertheless, here too, it seems reasonable to advocate for an application to all contracts since otherwise, suppliers might have to have different contractual clauses depending on whether they conclude cross-border or purely national contracts. Particularly in the online sector, this is often not apparent when contracts are concluded.

### d) *The Directive's Relationship to Other Legal Acts*

**954.** The Digital Content Directive has many points of contact with other legal areas. First and foremost, data protection law must be mentioned. Since the Digital Content Directive accepts personal data as consideration for supplying digital content and services, such cases regularly constitute instances of data processing (Article 4 no. 2 GDPR). The resulting data protection issue is excluded from the Digital Content Directive; its regulation is left to the GDPR in particular, as Article 3(8) DCD explicitly clarifies.[47] This provision further clarifies that, in the event of contradictions, the GDPR shall take precedence. Delimitation problems arise in particular concerning the question of how the subject matter of 'performance data' must be considered under contract law, as well as in connection with the contractual consequences of a possible withdrawal of the declaration of consent under data protection law.[48]

**955.** There is no regulation in the Directive regarding so-called End-User Licence Agreements (EULA), which the holder of the rights to the digital content regularly concludes with the consumer. According to Article 3(9) DCD, the provisions on copyright and related rights also remain unaffected.[49] Finally, Article 3(7) DCD stipulates that in all other cases of conflict with other sectoral

[45] CJEU, 20 January 2005, Case C-464/01, *Gruber*, ECLI:EU:C:2005:32, paras. 32 f. See para. 36 above.

[46] Commission proposal COM(2015) 634 final, pp. 5 ff.; Recitals 1 and 4 to 7 DCD also focus very significantly on cross-border contracts.

[47] Schantz, *NJW* 2016, 1841; Spindler, *MMR* 2016, 147.

[48] On both points see para. 964 below.

[49] On this point, Spindler, *MMR* 2016, 147, 149.

or subject-matter-specific acts of EU law, such provisions take precedence. This applies, in particular, to the Sale of Goods Directive; for cases of doubt, this is stipulated explicitly by Article 3(4) DCD (for example, if the goods sold also include digital content, such as the software in a washing machine).

## 3. DUTIES OF THE ENTREPRENEUR

### *a) Supply of the Digital Content*

**956.** The entrepreneur's primary performance obligation is to supply digital content without delay (Article 5(1) DCD). This requires the entrepreneur to supply or make available the digital content or to deliver it to a physical or virtual facility designated by the consumer for this purpose or to use any other means suitable for accessing or downloading the digital content. If the supply of a digital service is owed, it must be made available to the consumer or a physical or virtual facility designated by them for this purpose (Article 5(2) DCD).

### *b) Conformity of the Digital Content with the Contract*

**957.** The contractual obligation is only performed if the content supplied conforms with the contract. Articles 6 to 9 DCD and Articles 5 et seq. SGD distinguish between subjective and objective criteria. First, the contractual agreements determine what is owed (Article 7(a) DCD). This rule corresponds to Article 6 SGD.[50] In the Commission proposal, there was an addendum to the effect that conformity with the contract must also be measured against pre-contractual information duties.[51] This systematically inadequate provision was rightly not included in the adopted text of the Directive: If the entrepreneur performs the obligations of information incumbent on them, they regularly become part of the contract even without a legislative order, at least by implied consent of the consumer. If, however, they do not perform them, they could, at best, find their way into the contract through an appropriately formulated objective concept of conformity.

**958.** Furthermore, the digital content must be suitable for the purpose intended by the consumer, which the consumer also has brought to the supplier's attention at the time of the contract's conclusion and to which the supplier has agreed (Article 7(b) DCD). This is also a simple contractual agreement. According to

---

50 See para. 844 above.

51 Article 6(1)(a) Draft Digital Content Directive. Such obligations were not standardised in the proposal for a Directive, but may result from national standards that implement Article 5 CRD.

general principles of contract law, it can be assumed that the supplier's consent can also be implied, for example, by supplying the digital content without comment. In addition, the provision of 'instructions and customer assistance' is owed, provided this meets the requirements of the contract (lit. c); the same applies to updates (lit. d). If the latter has not been contractually agreed, Article 8(2) and (3) DCD apply.

**959.** Also, as a minimum standard and parallel to Article 7 SGD, Article 8(1) DCD prescribes objective criteria that the digital content supplied must meet in any case. First, such digital content must be suitable for the purposes for which digital content of the same type is usually used (lit. a). Furthermore, it must meet the usual standards regarding quantity, characteristics and performance features such as functionality, compatibility, accessibility, continuity and security (lit. b). In addition, this provision considers the consumer's 'reasonable expectations' of such characteristics based on public declarations by the entrepreneur or persons attributable to them, provided that the entrepreneur cannot exonerate themselves in this respect. The latter is the case, for example, in the event of evidence that the entrepreneur did not know and could not reasonably have known the relevant public statement, typically in the form of an advertisement (lit. b sublit. i).[52]

**960.** The Directive proposal differentiated between cases where the supply was made against payment of a price or consideration other than money (Article 6(2)(a) draft Digital Content Directive). In this respect, it was unclear whether, in the case of monetary consideration, there should be higher requirements than otherwise. This interpretation would have been intuitively conceivable since legal transactions generally regard the supply of digital content in exchange for personal data as 'free of charge', but this would hardly have corresponded to the difference between monetary and non-monetary consideration underlying the proposal. The final version of the Directive consequently no longer contained a distinction in this regard.

**961.** Unless otherwise agreed, digital content and services must be provided in the latest version available at the time of the contract's conclusion (Article 8(6) DCD); they must also be free of third-party rights (Article 10 DCD). By way of a declarative clarification, Article 8(4) DCD states that, if continuous supply is agreed upon, the obligation to supply digital content in accordance with the contract applies to each delivery.

---

52 Article 7(1)(d) and (2) SGD (see para. 848 above) are almost identical in content.

**962.** Because of the rapid technical development, the question of digital content and services updates is crucial. In terms of contract law, the case is clear where there is an explicit agreement to that extent: Here, the provision of updates is part of the existing contractual obligations (Article 7(d) DCD). Without such a subjective requirement of conformity with the contract, the entrepreneur's obligation would, by way of a converse argument, only apply to the one-time supply of digital content. However, in the case of software or apps, for example, legal transactions have adjusted to permanent updating without additional costs or a separate agreement. This applies, in any case, to so-called security updates. This is mirrored by Article 8(2) and (3) DCD, which corresponds *cum grano salis* to Article 7(3) and (4) SGD.[53] If it is a one-off supply of digital content, it all boils down to the question of what the consumer's 'reasonable expectations' are concerning the provision of updates. The entrepreneur will ultimately only be able to avoid a continuous update obligation through clear contractual agreements or by launching a completely new version of the software or app on the market: By definition, it is then no longer possible to speak of updating.

**963.** If the digital content or services provided are integrated into the consumer's digital environment, any lack of conformity caused thereby is also to be regarded as a lack of conformity of the digital content if the integration was carried out by or under the responsibility of the entrepreneur or, in any event, if it is due to defective instructions given by the entrepreneur (Article 9 DCD). Here, therefore, it is not the lack of conformity at the time of the supply of the digital content that is to be considered, but the completion of the integration. The digital environment is defined by Article 2 no. 9 DCD as hardware, software and network connections of all kinds used by the consumer to access or use digital content or services.

## 4. THE CONSUMER'S COUNTER-PERFORMANCE

**964.** The Directive assumes that a reciprocal contract is concluded between the entrepreneur and the consumer, which obliges the entrepreneur to supply digital content or services, and the consumer to pay a price (Article 2 no. 7 DCD) or to provide other consideration in the form of personal data.[54] It is thus clarified that the contract is already concluded when the consumer provides the entrepreneur with corresponding data, i.e., not only with the supply of the digital content by the entrepreneur itself.

---

[53] On this also see para. 851 above.

[54] Cf. on the problem area of 'data as consideration' see para. 937 above.

**965.** Still unresolved is the issue of the contractual consequences of a withdrawal of consent to the transfer of personal data, which is possible at any time under Article 7(3) GDPR.[55] The regulation of possible consequences, notwithstanding other EU regulations, such as in the GDPR, is thus within the competence of the respective autonomous Member State law.[56] If, for example, the applicable data protection law allows for a free withdrawal of consent to the transfer of personal data, the supplier is regularly obliged to delete this data. Under private law, however, the consumer's conduct constitutes a breach of contract; the supplier's claim to the transfer of the data continues to exist. In any case, the withdrawal of the consumer's consent under data protection law cannot be regarded as a termination of the contract since the digital content or services were provided properly (Article 13 DCD), and there is also no lack of conformity (Article 14 DCD). The Directive does not contain any provisions on the legal position of the entrepreneur if the consumer acts in breach of contract; in this respect, the provisions of the respective applicable national law apply. It was debated whether this could also grant the entrepreneur a right of withdrawal.[57] Irrespective of this, the consumer's withdrawal under data protection law could be classified as an offer to terminate the contract. The legal consequences in the case of an acceptance of such an offer by the supplier would then follow from Article 17 DCD.

## 5. LEGAL CONSEQUENCES OF BREACHES OF CONTRACT

**966.** The entrepreneur is liable for any failure to supply digital content and services in accordance with Article 5 DCD (Article 11 DCD). The Directive distinguishes between two different remedies: On the one hand, remedies for non-delivery (Article 13 DCD) and, on the other hand, remedies for lack of conformity (Article 14 DCD). This includes the remedies already contained in Article 5 DCD (obligation to make the digital content available) and Article 6 DCD (obligation to perform the subjective and objective requirements of conformity with the contract).

### *a) Liability of the Entrepreneur*

**967.** Article 11(1) DCD first clarifies the entrepreneur's liability (Article 12(1) DCD) for any failure to supply digital content and services in accordance with

[55] On the specific problem of the ordinance of minors over their personal data, which is not permissible under data protection law, Spindler, *MMR* 2016, 147, 148 (surrender of transmitted data via the law of enrichment). See also F. Faust, *Digitale Wirtschaft – Analoges Recht: Braucht das BGB ein Update?, Gutachten A für den Deutschen Juristentag* (Munich: C.H. Beck, 2016), pp. 8–12; Langhanke/Schmidt-Kessel, *EuCML* 2015, 218, 222.

[56] Cf. the wording in Recital 40 DCD, see Staudenmayer, *ZEuP* 2019, 663, 670.

[57] In that sense Staudenmayer, *ZEuP* 2019, 663, 670.

Article 5 DCD. This includes cases of failure to supply as well as late supply. The legal consequence results from Article 13 DCD.

**968.** The entrepreneur's liability for a lack of conformity according to Articles 7 to 9 DCD, i.e. for qualitative negative deviations, is regulated by Article 11(2) and (3) DCD; both provisions differentiate between contracts that mandate a one-time supply only and those that contain a duty for a continuous supply. Culpability is not required in any case, meaning the entrepreneur is liable regardless of negligence or fault. Corresponding rules on the burden of proof can be found in Article 12(2–5) DCD; the legal consequences of breaches of contract follow from Article 14 DCD.

**969.** The liability period is generally determined by Member State law. In the case of a one-time supply of digital content and services, it may not be shorter than two years from the time of supply (Article 11(2) subpara. 2 DCD). Here, too, Directive law takes into account the fact that some Member States do not regulate the duration of liability by means of such maximum periods but through the legal institution of limitation instead:[58] Any limitation period must, therefore, not be detrimental to the consumer (Article 11(2) subpara. 3 DCD).

**970.** In the case of a continuous supply due under the contract, the entrepreneur is liable for any lack of conformity occurring or becoming apparent during this period (Article 11(3) subpara. 1 DCD). Again, any limitation period under national law must not negatively affect the consumer's legal position (Article 11(3) subpara. 2 DCD).

*b) Burden of Proof*

**971.** According to Article 12(1) DCD, the entrepreneur bears the burden of proof for properly supplying digital content or services. Mutatis mutandis, this also applies to breaches of contract: In case of a contract for the one-off supply of digital content or services, the entrepreneur must prove that these conform with the contract at the time of supply. This applies to any lack of conformity that becomes apparent within one year of the content's supply (Article 12(2) DCD).[59] If the continuous supply of digital content or services is agreed on, the entrepreneur has to prove conformity with the contract for each instance of lacking conformity that becomes apparent within the relevant period (Article 12(3) DCD).[60]

---

58 Cf. para. 891 above.

59 On the comparable provision in Article 11(1) Sale of Goods Directive see para. 862 above.

60 The Sale of Goods Directive also contains a parallel standard in Article 11(3), see para. 868 above.

**972.** The only exception relates to the case of incompatibility between digital content and the consumer's digital environment, provided that the supplier has informed the consumer of these requirements before the conclusion of the contract (Article 12(4) DCD). This will give rise to corresponding pre-contractual duties of information.[61]

**973.** Finally, the consumer's duty to cooperate with the supplier to determine the cause of the lack of conformity of the digital content or service, as standardised in Article 12(5) DCD, must be mentioned. The scope of this duty appears unclear. Violations are sanctioned by the exclusion of the reversal of the burden of proof concerning the cases mentioned in Article 11(2) and (3) DCD – but only if the consumer was informed of this in a clear and comprehensible manner before the conclusion of the contract.

### c) *Remedies for the Consumer*

**974.** The entrepreneur's liability under Article 11 DCD triggers remedies for the consumer, which are regulated in Articles 13 and 14 DCD. In accordance with the Directive's system, here, too, a distinction is made between cases of non-performance (Article 13 DCD) and lacking conformity (Article 14 DCD). In both cases, as in the Consumer Sales Directive, a variety of sanctions exist, with the termination of the consumer's contract by rescission as a final consequence.[62]

#### aa) Remedies in the Event of Failure to Supply

**975.** If the entrepreneur fails to fulfil his contractual obligation to supply digital content or services, the consumer will initially demand performance; if the entrepreneur continues to be in default, the consumer may terminate the contract (Article 13(1) DCD). The right thus granted to the entrepreneur for a second tender must be exercised 'without undue delay' or 'within an additional period of time, as expressly agreed to by the parties'. This can only be understood insofar as any performance not made immediately only does not entitle the consumer to terminate the contract if they have previously expressly agreed to a different period.

**976.** In contrast to this, the consumer is entitled to terminate the contract immediately according to Article 13(2) DCD if the entrepreneur is obviously not prepared to provide the service and has also declared this (lit. a), or if the

61 Cf. Spindler, *MMR* 2016, 147, 153 (on the Directive Proposal).

62 In general see para. 872 above; on the concurrent approach of the Sale of Goods Directive see para. 869 above.

contract stands or falls with the provision of the service at a certain point in time and this was also agreed upon or is clearly evident from the circumstances surrounding the conclusion of the contract (lit. b). In both cases, a right for the entrepreneur to a second tender would obviously be pointless.

#### bb) Remedies for Lack of Conformity

**977.** Article 14 DCD regulates in great detail the consumer's remedies in the event of a lack of conformity. Here, according to para. 1, a distinction is made between the restoration of the contractual condition (paras. 2 and 3), as well as the reduction (paras. 4 and 5) and the termination of the contract (paras. 4 and 6 in conjunction with Articles 15 to 17 DCD). The Digital Content Directive does not contain a claim for damages either.

##### (1) Free Restoration of the Contractual Condition

**978.** Under EU law, the free-of-charge creation of the contractual condition is the prioritised remedy. The Digital Content Directive does not differentiate between repair or replacement. The claim is excluded in cases of impossibility or disproportionality (Article 14(2) DCD). Only disproportionality is defined in greater detail, which is not designed as an objection by the entrepreneur but apparently as a negative element of the remedy. The legal situation seems unclear, for example, if the entrepreneur supplies 'contractual' digital content despite objective disproportionality – could this be seen an offer to conclude a new contract? The balancing to be carried out here clearly borrows from the relative disproportionality criterion known from Article 13(2) SGD;[63] however, it is (necessarily) designed as absolute disproportionality. The entrepreneur has a reasonable period starting from the moment the consumer notifies him of the lack of conformity to restore the contractual condition. The remedy must be provided without significant inconvenience to the consumer (Article 14(3) DCD).

##### (2) Reduction of Price

**979.** The remedy of reduction of the prise according to Article 14(4) DCD applies in particular in the event of a failure to produce a condition in conformity with the contract within a reasonable period or without significant inconvenience. This remedy is only available to the consumer if the consumer's consideration consists of paying a price. The modalities of calculation is laid down in Article 14(5) DCD and largely corresponds to Article 15 SGD.

---

[63] See para. 875 above.

**980.** The Directive explicitly does not regulate the question of how the price reduction becomes effective, nor its legal consequences. One viable approach would be to apply the law of the Member States, as may be inferred from Article 3(10) DCD. However, this would contradict the fully harmonising approach of the Directive, which also concerns remedies. Given the parallel design of reduction and termination by rescission expressed in Article 14(4) DCD, it seems logical to require a declaration of reduction in the sense of Article 15 DCD. It can also be concluded from Article 18(1) DCD that a declaration by the consumer is necessary for a price reduction. This also implies that the entrepreneur must refund the amount overpaid.

### (3) Termination of Contract

**981.** The remedy of termination by rescission in case of a lack of conformity is carried out by a corresponding declaration of the consumer (Article 15 DCD). As with reduction, it presupposes the entrepreneur's failure to realise the contractual condition owed or comparable circumstances (Article 14(4) DCD). The consumer, therefore, has the choice of either sticking to the contract, with an adjusted price, or terminating it. However, the termination of the contract is subject to the condition that the lack of conformity is not minor, which is generally presumed (Article 14(6) DCD).[64] However, this only applies to those contracts where the consumer's consideration consists of a price payment. Conversely, for all other contracts within the meaning of Article 3(1) subpara. 2 DCD, termination is possible even for minor breaches of contract.

**982.** The legal consequences of terminating the contract are regulated by Articles 16 and 17 DCD. These two provisions differentiate between the obligations of the entrepreneur and those of the consumer. First, the entrepreneur has to reimburse the consumer for all amounts paid under the contract. This includes, first and foremost, the price the consumer paid for the digital content and services. In the case of contracts that provide for continuous performance, a refund may only be made on a pro rata basis (Article 16(1) DCD). The refund must be made without delay and in any case within 14 days of the day on which the entrepreneur was informed of the consumer's decision to terminate the contract (Article 18(1) DCD). A fee for the refund may not be charged (Article 18(3) DCD).

[64] This did not implement the approach contained in the Directive Proposal, according to which a termination of the contract would only be possible if the lack of conformity affected the functional scope, interoperability and other essential performance features of the digital content (accessibility, continuity and, if applicable, security). This was a kind of material threshold that functionally corresponded to the de minimis clause already contained in the Consumer Sales Directive.

**983.** If the consideration did not consist in the payment of a price, the Directive endeavours to adequately circumscribe the reimbursement owed by obliging the entrepreneur to restore the status quo ante: In principle, the entrepreneur may no longer use the content provided by the consumer in the context of the use that is not personal data (Article 16(3) DCD); exceptions exist, for example, if this content is only related to the use of the digital content or services provided by the entrepreneur (lit. b) or if it can be aggregated with other data and disaggregated only with disproportionate effort (lit. c). Beyond these exceptional cases, the entrepreneur must make such content available to the consumer 'at the request of the consumer'; the consumer can demand that it must be made available 'free of charge, without hindrance from the trader, within a reasonable time and in a commonly used and machine-readable format' (Article 16(4) DCD). Although not quite correct from a systemic point of view, Article 16(5) DCD also contains a right of the entrepreneur: After the contract's termination, the entrepreneur may block any existing user account of the consumer and prevent the consumer's access to the digital content and services provided.

**984.** The consumer also has obligations in connection with the termination of the contract (Article 17 DCD). They may not continue to use the digital content or services provided to them (para. 1). If the supply was made on a physical data carrier, it must be returned at the entrepreneur's request and the entrepreneur's expense (para. 2).[65] The consumer does not owe a fee for the use of the digital content before termination of the contract insofar as the lack of conformity existed (para. 3).

cc) No Regulation of the Claim for Damages

**985.** In contrast to the proposal for a Distance Selling Directive, the proposal for the Digital Content Directive contained in its Article 14a claim for damages irrespective of fault. This was supposed to arise in the case of non-compliance with the contractual obligation[66] or non-performance (probably in the sense of Article 11 draft Digital Content Directive). The liability should extend to any economic damage to the consumer's digital environment and, in principle, include restoration of the status quo ante. Further details regarding the exercise of this right were supposed to be regulated by the Member States' legal systems. Functionally, such a claim for damages found a normative model in the provision

65 The issue of the fate of any copies made is not regulated. Article 13(2)(e)(ii) of the Draft Directive on Digital Content had postulated an obligation on the part of the consumer to delete or render illegible such copies. The version that has entered into force does not contain such a provision. In this respect, the consumer's obligation to refrain from using this content, as regulated in Article 17(1) DCD, remains in force.

66 Objectively, there should be no difference here to the lack of conformity.

of Article 35a of the Rating Regulation,[67] where further claims for compensation under national law are expressly permitted. It appeared to require clarification what regulatory leeway should exist, in particular, whether further-reaching claims relating to any damage outside the consumer's digital environment should be possible under national law and whether these could be linked to fault on the part of the entrepreneur. Given the problems involved, the adopted version of the Digital Content Directive now abstains from regulating such a claim for damages. According to Article 3(10) DCD, Member State law applies in this respect.

## 6. CHANGE OF THE DIGITAL CONTENT

**986.** Article 19 DCD contains a special provision for contracts that have as their object the supply of digital content or services during a period of time. This standard regulates the entrepreneur's possibility to make changes to the digital content or services to be provided. A unilateral change would be in breach of contract. If the change goes beyond what is necessary to establish conformity with the contract within the meaning of Articles 7 and 8 DCD, it must be covered by the party's consent; moreover, it requires a viable reason (Article 19(1)(a) DCD). It must not result in additional costs for the consumer (lit. b), and the entrepreneur must provide clear and comprehensible information (lit. c). If the change affects the consumer's access to or use of the digital content or services, the consumer has the right to terminate the contract within 30 days, except for minor changes (Article 19(2) DCD). The entrepreneur must inform the consumer of both the change and the resulting right to terminate the contract within a reasonable period of time in advance (Article 19(1)(d) DCD). If the change does not lead to disadvantages for the consumer because the contractual condition is maintained without further costs, the right to terminate the contract does not apply (Article 19(4) DCD). The entrepreneur must also inform the consumer of this consequence in advance (Article 19(1)(d) DCD).

## 7. THE RIGHT TO TERMINATE LONG-TERM CONTRACTS

**987.** The right to terminate long-term contracts, which was still contained in the proposal of the Directive (Article 16 draft Digital Content Directive), according to which the consumer could terminate contracts of more than twelve months or unlimited duration at any time within a termination period of 14 days calculated from the date of notification, was not implemented.

---

67 See para. 776 above.

## 8. REDRESS

**988.** Finally, Article 20 DCD contains the right of redress along the contractual value chain known from Article 18 SGD so that the entrepreneur who is liable regardless of fault can pass on the damage caused by the consumer's remedy. Further details are determined by Member State law.

# III. REGULATING THE PLATFORM ECONOMY

References: M.-E. Ancel, 'Regulating digital platforms' autonomy', in M.M. Fogt (ed.), *Private International Law in an Era of Change* (Cheltenham: Edward Edgar Publishing, 2024), p. 69; C. Busch, 'Fairness und Transparenz in der Plattformökonomie. Der Vorschlag für eine EU-Verordnung über Online-Plattformen', *IWRZ* 2018, 147; C. Busch/G. Dannemann/H. Schulte-Nölke/A. Wiewiórowska-Domagalska/F. Zoll, 'The ELI Model Rules on Online Platforms', *EuCML* 2020, 61; C. Busch/H. Schulte-Nölke/A. Wiewiórowksa-Domagalski/F. Zoll, 'The Rise of the Platform Economy: A New Challenge for EU Consumer Law?', *EuCML* 2016, 3; B. Devolder (ed.), *The Platform Economy. Unravelling the Legal Status of Online Intermediaries* (Cambridge: Intersentia, 2019); T. Lutzi, *Private International Law Online. Internet Regulation and Civil Liability in the EU* (Oxford: Oxford University Press, 2020); H. Schweitzer, 'Digitale Plattformen als private Gesetzgeber. Ein Perspektivwechsel für die europäische "Plattform-Regulierung"', *ZEuP* 2019, 1.

## 1. THE ENTREPRENEURIAL SPHERE

**989.** The so-called Platform Regulation[68] regulates legal relationships between providers of online intermediary services and online search services and professional users, the latter understood as any private person acting in the course of a business or professional activity or any legal person offering goods or services to consumers through online intermediary services and for purposes related to their trade, business, craft or profession (Article 2 no. 1 Platform Regulation). Indirectly, the Regulation also protects consumers, as Recital 3 Platform Regulation explains: 'Ensuring the transparency of, and trust in, the online platform economy in business-to-business relations could also indirectly help to improve consumer trust in the online platform economy'. It has been applicable since 12 July 2020 (Article 19(2) Platform Regulation).

---

[68] Regulation (EU) 2019/1150 of the European Parliament and of the Council of 20 June 2019 on promoting fairness and transparency for business users of online intermediary services, OJ 2019 L 186/57, preceded by a Commission proposal of 26 April 2018, COM(2018) 238 final.

**990.** For contract law, the regulation is only indirectly significant, above all in that it makes specifications for the design of the GTC of providers of online intermediary services (Articles 3, 7 to 9 Platform Regulation).[69] It must be noted how strongly the legislator refers to the principle of good faith, in particular, to legitimise the interference with the entrepreneur's freedom to contract (Article 8 of the Platform Regulation).[70] From the perspective of German law, this is trite law, which already follows from the central role of sec. 242 German Civil Code. Also, GTC control in business transactions, albeit somewhat restricted (sec. 310(1) German Civil Code), is nevertheless possible to a considerable extent. Other Member States, on the other hand, have implemented the Unfair Terms Directive purely as an instrument of consumer protection; for such legal systems, a provision such as Article 8 of the Platform Regulation certainly requires justification.

**991.** In addition to these provisions relevant to the providers of online intermediary services, the Platform Regulation also contains some rules for the providers of online search engines. These provisions, which are closer to competition law, concern the transparency of rankings, which is, according to the definition in Article 2 no. 8 of the Platform Regulation, 'the relative prominence given to the goods or services offered through online intermediation services, or the relevance given to search results by online search engines, as presented, organised or communicated by the providers of online intermediation services or by providers of online search engines, respectively, irrespective of the technological means used for such presentation, organisation or communication' (Article 5 of the Platform Regulation).

**992.** Furthermore, according to Article 7(2) of the Platform Regulation, providers of online search engines shall explain any differentiated treatment of goods and services offered to consumers via these online search engines either by that provider itself or by users with a corporate website controlled by that provider on the one hand and by other users with a corporate website on the other hand.

## 2. TRANSPARENCY

**993.** Article 4 no. 5 of the Directive on Better Enforcement and Modernisation of Union Consumer Protection Rules[71] introduced a new Article 6a into

---

69 See para. 962 above.
70 On this also see para. 452 above.
71 Directive (EU) 2019/2161 of the European Parliament and of the Council of 27 November 2019 amending Council Directive 93/13/EEC and Directives 98/6/EC, 2005/29/EC and

the Consumer Rights Directive. This creates additional special duties of information for contracts concluded on online marketplaces. According to its first paragraph, the provider of an online marketplace shall inform the consumer 'in a clear and comprehensible manner and in a way appropriate to the means of distance communication' about the parameters based on which the ranking of the offers on the online marketplace are generated, whether the third party provider is an entrepreneur or not, if applicable, that EU consumer rights do not apply to the contract and, if applicable, how the contractual obligations are shared between the third-party provider and the provider of the online marketplace.

**994.** These requirements are only baseline standards; according to Article 6a(2) Directive 2019/2161, Member States may provide additional information duties for online marketplaces providers, provided that they are proportionate, non-discriminatory and justified for consumer protection reasons.

## 3. LEGISLATIVE PROJECTS

**995.** The regulation of service providers such as Airbnb or Uber poses increasing challenges for the courts. Several times, the CJEU had to deal with the question of whether such companies are to be classified as an 'information society service' within the meaning of the E-Commerce Directive.[72] If the answer is to the affirmative, the country-of-origin principle (Article 3(1) of the E-Commerce Directive) applies, according to which regulation of such services is reserved for their country of domicile.

**996.** The E-Commerce Directive is currently being revised; it is to be transformed into the Digital Services Act. The first consultations took place in the European Parliament on 18 February 2020. This Digital Services Act is one of the core elements of the European Commission's digital agenda. At its core, it deals with the responsibility and liability of platforms.[73]

2011/83/EU of the European Parliament and of the Council on better enforcement and modernisation of Union consumer protection laws, OJ 2019 L 328/7.

[72] In an affirmative sense CJEU, 19 December 2019, Case C-390/18, *Airbnb Ireland*, ECLI:EU:C:2019:1112; in a negative sense, however, CJEU, 20 December 2017, Case C-434/15, *Uber Spain*, ECLI:EU:C:2017:981; CJEU, 10 April 2018, Case C-320/16, *Uber France*, ECLI:EU:C:2018:221.

[73] On the legislative process https://ec.europa.eu/digital-single-market/en/digital-services-act-package; on the liability of platforms G. Wagner, GRUR 2020, 329 and 447; on the ELI project concerning platforms Busch/Dannemann/Schulte-Nölke/Wiewiórowska-Domagalska/Zoll, *EuCML* 2020, 61.

# IV. ALGORITHMS AS A SUBSTITUTE FOR A CONTRACT?

References: A. Bonomi/M. Lehmann/S. Lalani (eds.), *Blockchain and Private International Law* (Leiden: Brill, 2023); L.A. DiMatteo/C. Poncibó/G. Howells (eds.), *The Cambridge Handbook of AI and Consumer Law – Comparative Perspectives* (Cambridge: Cambridge University Press, 2024); M. Ebers/C. Poncibò/M. Zou (eds.), *Contracting and Contract Law in the Age of Artificial Intelligence* (Oxford: Bloomsbury Publishing, 2022); Expert Group on Liability and New Technologies, 'New Technologies Formation, Liability for Artificial Intelligence and other Emerging Digital Technologies', 2019; F. Graf von Westphalen, 'Datenvertragsrecht – disruptive Technik – disruptives Recht. Kollisionsrecht und Haftungsrecht', *IWRZ* 2018, 9; M. Hennemann, 'Die personalisierte Vertragsanbahnung. Regulierungsbedarf für den digitalen Massenverkehr', *AcP* 219 (2019), 818; T. Rademacher, 'Wenn neue Technologien altes Recht durchsetzen: Dürfen wir es unmöglich machen, rechtswidrig zu handeln?', *JZ* 2019, 702; G. Wagner/H. Eidenmüller, 'In der Falle der Algorithmen? Abschöpfen von Konsumentenrente, Ausnutzen von Verhaltensanomalien und Manipulation von Präferenzen: Die Regulierung der dunklen Seite personalisierter Transaktionen', *ZfPW* 2019, 220.

## 1. SMART CONTRACTS

References: J.G. Allen, 'Wrapped and Stacked: 'Smart Contracts' and the Interaction of Natural and Formal Language', *ERCL* 2018, 307; M. Corrales Compagnucci/M. Fenwick/S. Wrbka (eds.), *Smart Contracts. Technological, Business and Legal Perspectives* (London: Hart Publishing, 2021); M. El Harrak, 'Do Smart Contracts Need New Conflict-of-Laws Rules?', in A. Bonomi/M. Lehmann/S. Lalani (eds.), *Blockchain and Private International Law* (Leiden: Brill, 2023), p. 479; T. Kuntz, 'Konsens statt Recht? Überlegungen zu Chancen und Herausforderungen der Blockchain-Technologie aus juristischer Sicht', *AcP* 220 (2020), 51; D. Linardatos, 'Smart Contracts – einige klarstellende Bemerkungen', *K&R* 2018, 85; O. Meyer, 'Stopping the Unstoppable: Termination and Unwinding of Smart Contracts', *EuCML* 2020, 17; B.P. Paal/M. Fries (eds.), *Smart Contracts* (Tübingen: Mohr Siebeck, 2019); A. Savelyev, 'Contract law 2.0: "Smart" contracts as the beginning of the end of classic contract law, (2017) 26(2) *Information and Communications Technology Law* 116.

### *a) Forms of Appearance and Technical Background*

**997.** Since computers have existed, people have been looking for ways to automate the application of the law. Today, Legal Tech (short for Legal Services Technology) is mainly about processing large amounts of data in legal processes. Legal jobs are supported or even replaced by algorithms, and law is thus supposed to be created ex machina.[74] Global law firms see great potential in

[74] See O. Raabe/R. Wacker/D. Oberle/C. Baumann/C. Funk, *Recht ex machina: Formalisierung des Rechts im Internet der Dienste* (Berlin: Springer, 2012), using the example of data

using legal tech to optimise knowledge management and, above all, simplify contract drafting.[75] In the context of this volume, so-called smart contracts are of particular interest.[76] According to a widespread definition, a smart contract is a programme that is stored in a tamper-proof manner and is guaranteed to execute predefined actions when certain conditions occur.[77] For this purpose, certain contractual obligations and presuppositions are fed into the software, which in turn uses other data sources to recognise events that are supposed to trigger the specified legal consequences. Smart contracts are intended to make going to court or other dispute resolution bodies largely superfluous, as they have already integrated the application and enforcement of the law into the contract structure, making the contract 'self-executing'.

**998.** Firstly, this may solve the problem of advance performance: The contracting party obliged to perform in advance must trust in the other party's faithfulness to the contract, provide collateral, or insist on the involvement of a third party, such as a notary,[78] as a trustee.[79] The smart contract can replace such constructions. Secondly, smart contracts promise efficient control of the parties' compliance with the contract for continuing obligations that have been put into effect: For example, if contractually agreed instalment payments are not made, sanctions automatically take effect without any further party intervention. Such sanctions can range from an automated penalty payment to the suspension of counter-performance and the termination of the contract. Eventually, enforcement could also become superfluous.

**999.** In this respect, the distributed ledger technology, e.g. on a blockchain, promises objectivity and protection against forgery. The blockchain is a decentralised database in a global network that mirrors the information it contains on all participating servers. The large number of computers involved and how the information to be stored is generated and validated ensures the information's authenticity, completeness and immutability. The contractual agreement is appended to the blockchain by adding a key provided with the personal signature. It is validated by duplicating the information on other computers and adding a timestamp. This is done by so-called mining, i.e. the

protection law. For a critique of this, see Kotsoglou, *JZ* 2014, 451; Engel, *JZ* 2014, 1096; Kotsoglou, *JZ* 2014, 1100.

75 M. Hartung/M.-M. Bues/G. Halbleib, *Legal Tech – Die Digitalisierung des Rechtsmarkts* (Munich: C.H.Beck, 2018).

76 The term probably goes back to Nick Szabo, Smart Contracts, 1994.

77 Heckelmann, *NJW* 2018, 504; Allen, *ERCL* 2018, 307, 313, each with further references.

78 This ultimately also includes financial service providers in the area of e-commerce such as PayPal; in this regard BGHZ 217, 33 as well as BGH ZIP 2018, 226; likewise for the 'a-to-z guarantee' on the Amazon Marketplace BGH MDR 2020, 717.

79 C. Moes, Vertragsgestaltung (Munich: C.H. Beck, 2020), §14.

calculation of a matching hash value and thus the generation and attachment of a block to the blockchain, which is carried out by individual network members. For this, the network rewards the miners, who usually have powerful computer farms, e.g. with a certain amount in the cryptocurrency of the blockchain. Since the blockchain cannot be subsequently changed, the information it contains is – at least in theory – highly trustworthy.[80] Forgeries are conspicuous because they are only accepted if more than half of the participants in the network trace them.[81]

**1000.** Ethereum, for instance, a system that has already established itself as the architecture for executing smart contracts in blockchain technology, has been available since 2013.[82] Ethereum offers the cryptocurrency Ether as a means of payment, one of the most widespread of its kind alongside Bitcoin.[83] However, the scope of application of such smart contracts has so far been limited to a few areas, such as trading in virtual currencies and securities.[84] Initial Coin Offerings (ICOs), a kind of digital crowdfunding, have also gained prominence.[85] Nevertheless, it is to be expected that the availability of the new technology will sooner or later also cover areas of everyday legal transactions.

### *b) Preconditions in EU Law for Smart Contracts*

**1001.** As a form of contracting permissible under contractual freedom, smart contracts are, in principle, also permissible under EU law.[86] In practice, they come into consideration when precisely definable actual events are to trigger clear legal consequences that can already be determined ex-ante. For example, the lump-sum compensation claims under the EU Air Passenger Rights Regulation[87] could certainly be processed automatically. If digital content or services are the subject of a smart contract, the provisions of the Digital Content Directive apply. This does not generally cover financial services (Article 3(5)(e) DCD). However, it also includes transactions in which cryptocurrencies such as bitcoins play a role; nevertheless, the latter are not digital content or services within the meaning of the said Directive.[88] If smart contracts have a cross-border dimension, the Rome I Regulation applies in this respect.[89]

---

80 But see the incident 'the DAO'; on this Heckelmann, *NJW* 2018, 504, 509 as well as para. 1210 below.
81 More in detail Schrey/Thalhofer, *NJW* 2017, 1431.
82 Behind this is a foundation under Swiss law, see Martiny, *IPRax* 2018, 553 at note 2.
83 See https://coinmarketcap.com/.
84 Kaulartz/Heckmann, *CR* 2016, 618, 620 (derivatives trading).
85 Glatz, in Blocher/Heckmann/Zech, DGRI Jahrbuch 2016, 2017, p. 81.
86 On the recognition of private autonomy in EU law, supra para. 409 above.
87 See §28 below.
88 Cf. Recital 30 Digital Content Directive.
89 See para. 1206 below.

## 2. DYNAMIC PRICING

**1002.** Another phenomenon of digitalisation is so-called dynamic pricing. Here, the price is constantly adjusted to the market situation with the help of algorithms.[90] In itself, this is nothing unusual; in essence, it simply reflects the interplay of supply and demand.[91] What is new is that the use of algorithms allows prices to be changed as quickly and frequently as desired. Dynamic pricing must be distinguished from personalised contract initiation, where a different price is charged for the same product depending on the individual.[92] Nevertheless, dynamic and personalised pricing are often combined.[93] From the point of view of market participants, this leads to a reduction in market and price transparency.[94]

**1003.** A seller is indeed, in principle, free to determine prices,[95] provided that there are no violations prohibited of competition by the Unfair Commercial Practices Directive.[96] Dynamic pricing could be seen as 'unfair' in the sense of this Directive if the price change takes place after a product has already been placed in the digital shopping basket.[97] Measures to promote transparency could possibly also be taken with the help of antitrust law.

---

90 Cf. amply Hofmann, *WRP* 2016, 1074; Hennemann, *AcP* 219 (2019), 818, 822 ff.

91 Tietjen/Flöter, *GRUR-Prax* 2017, 546.

92 Cf. the Opinion by the German Advisory Council for Consumer Affairs: Zander-Hayat/Domurath/Groß, 'Personalisierte Preise', SVRV Working Paper No 2, 2016, p. 2.

93 Cf. Hennemann, *AcP* 219 (2019), 818, 822. On personalized prices, cf. Akon, *ERCL* 2024, 77.

94 Cf. from the perspective of the German Price Indication Ordinance Wenglorz, in K.-H. Fezer/W. Büscher/E.I. Obergfell, *Lauterkeitsrecht*, 3rd ed. (Munich: C.H. Beck, 2016), §14 PAngV para. 81e.

95 Cf. BGH NJW 2003, 2096, according to which a seller may increase or decrease the price at any time he deems reasonable, unless there is a conflict with price regulations or unfair circumstances prevail.

96 Directive 2005/29/EC of the European Parliament and of the Council of 11 May 2005, *OJ 2005 L 149/22*.

97 Guidelines on the transposition/application of Directive 2005/29/EC on Unfair Commercial Practices of 25 May 2016, SWD (2016) 163 final, pp. 166 ff.

# §24. CONSUMER CREDIT CONTRACTS

CONTENTS



References: E. Arroyo Amayuelas, 'A Third Directive on Consumer Credit', *ERCL* 2024, 1; B. Gsell/H.M. Schellhase, 'Vollharmonisiertes Verbraucherkreditrecht – Ein Vorbild für die weitere europäische Angleichung des Verbrauchervertragsrechts?', *JZ* 2009, 20; R. Harnos, 'Schadensersatz wegen fehlerhafter Kreditwürdigkeitsprüfung', *JZ* 2017, 552; C. Herresthal, 'Unionsrechtliche Vorgaben zur Sanktionierung des Verstoßes gegen die Kreditwürdigkeitsprüfung', *EuZW* 2014, 497; A. Piekenbrock, 'Die geplante Umsetzung der Wohnimmobilienkreditvertragsrichtlinie', *GPR* 2015, 26; F.L. Schäfer, 'Wohnimmobilienkreditrichtlinie. Geschichte und Umsetzung im Verbraucherdarlehensrecht', *VuR* 2014, 207; T. Riehm/B. Schreindorfer, 'Das Harmonisierungskonzept der neuen Verbraucherkreditrichtlinie', *GPR* 2008, 244; C. Wendehorst, 'Das deutsche Umsetzungskonzept für die Verbraucherkreditrichtlinie', *ZEuP* 2011, 263; P. Wösthoff, *Die Verbraucherkreditrichtlinie 2008/48/EG und deren Umsetzung ins deutsche Recht* (Frankfurt am Main: Lang, 2011); B. Zapf, 'Die Wohnimmobilienkreditrichtlinie 2014/17/EU – Am Ziel einer langen Reise?', *ZEuP* 2016, 656.

## I. OVERVIEW

**1004.** The consultation process for harmonising consumer credit law began as early as 1975. The (first) Consumer Credit Directive was adopted in 1986.[1] In an integrated market, consumer credits are fundamentally desirable from an economic point of view. Hence, the harmonisation of the law was intended to increase supply and demand in the loan market.[2] In practice, the matter is of great importance: 50–65% of all consumers have consumer credits at their disposal; in 2001, the volume of credit in the then 15 Member States amounted

[1] Council Directive 87/102/EEC of 22 December 1986 for the approximation of the laws, regulations and administrative provisions of the Member States concerning consumer credit, OJ 1987 L 42/48.

[2] Scholz, *MDR* 1988, 730 f.

to more than 500 billion euros, i.e. more than 7% of GDP.[3] In 2008, it was over 800 billion euros.[4]

**1005.** In September 2002, the Commission presented a proposal to revise the Directive,[5] as the level of protection of the Directive was not considered sufficient and, in addition, the credit market developed very differently in the Member States. Here, too, the Commission argued that the concept of minimum harmonisation pursued by the Directive had led to a higher, but again unequal, level of protection in the individual Member States. A major point of criticism concerned the prohibition of negotiating credit agreements away from business premises contained in Article 5 of the proposal.[6] In October 2004, the Commission presented an amended proposal for the revision of the Consumer Credit Directive,[7] in which this prohibition was no longer included – the Doorstep Selling Directive now covered this constellation. A further amendment proposal by the Commission followed in October 2005.[8] In addition to strengthening the duties of information through a Europe-wide uniform 'European Credit Information Form', this also provided for a standardised calculation of the annual percentage rate of charge (APR), a right of withdrawal, and binding rules on advertising and loan-related information. After approval by the Council and Parliament, the new Consumer Credit Directive[9] entered into force on 12 May 2010.[10] Unlike its predecessor, it is now, following a general trend, fully harmonising (Article 22(1) Directive 2008/48/EC). This approach appears problematic, especially with regard to the high level of consumer protection to be achieved, as it may prevent or freeze competition between different providers.[11]

**1006.** Mortgage loans are excluded from the scope of the Consumer Credit Directive (Article 2(2)(a–c) Directive 2008/48/EC); early attempts to bring about legal harmonisation in this respect[12] had failed due to the resistance

---

3 Cf. COM(2002), 443 final, p. 2.
4 EC Commission press release of 16 January 2008 on the new Consumer Credit Directive.
5 Proposal of 11 September 2002 for a Directive on the harmonisation of the laws, regulations and administrative provisions of the Member States concerning consumer credit, COM(2002), 443 final.
6 COM(2002), 443 final, pp. 13 f.
7 COM(2004), 747 final.
8 COM(2005) 483 final.
9 Directive 2008/48/EC of the European Parliament and of the Council of 23 April 2008 on credit agreements for consumers and repealing Council Directive 87/102/EEC, OJ 2008 L 133/66.
10 Gsell/Schellhase, *JZ* 2009, 20.
11 On the concept of full harmonisation see para. 78 above.
12 Proposal for a Council Directive on freedom of establishment and freedom to provide services in the field of mortgage credit, 4 February 1985, COM(84) 730 final.

of the Member States.[13] In the meantime, the Commission tried to proceed with a recommendation and, thus, not with binding legislation,[14] but this was unsuccessful in practice. It was not until 2011 that the Commission made a new attempt and presented a proposal for a directive[15] that also regulated aspects of mortgage lending under supervisory and professional law and represented an attempt to learn lessons from the financial and banking crisis of 2008. This is remarkable insofar as the Commission had previously very clearly endeavoured to make subprime loans, which were widespread in the British real estate market and ultimately triggered the crisis, acceptable throughout Europe.

**1007.** After numerous amendments, the Directive was finally adopted at the beginning of 2014[16] and had to be transposed into Member State law by 21 March 2016 (Article 42(1) Directive 2014/17/EU). It is noteworthy that, unlike other consumer protection legislation, the Directive follows the principle of minimum harmonisation (Article 2(1) Directive 2014/17/EU). Only in some cases, it prohibits stricter, i.e. more consumer-protective regulations: On the one hand, concerning the provision of pre-contractual information through a 'European Standardised Information Sheet' (so-called ESIS leaflet), on the other hand, with regard to the calculation of the APR (Article 2(2) Directive 2014/17/EU). This was to prevent individual Member States from having to lower the level of consumer protection again (Recital 7 Directive 2014/17/EU).

**1008.** A Proposal for a recast Commercial Credit Directive was presented by the EU Commission on 20 June 2021.[17] After debates in Council and Parliament, the new Directive (EU) 2023/2225 on credit agreements for consumers was adopted on 18 October 2023.[18] Member States shall implement the Directive by 20 November 2025. The new regime applies from 20 November 2026 (Article 48 Directive). The scope of application of new Directive was slightly expanded, and it seeks to take into account recent developments regarding digitalisation.[19]

---

13 On the development Schäfer, *VuR* 2014, 207.

14 Commission Recommendation of 1 March 2001 on pre-contractual information to be provided to consumers by lenders offering home loans, COM(2001) 477 final.

15 Proposal of 31 March 2011 for a Directive on credit agreements relating to residential immovable property, COM(2011) 142 final.

16 Directive 2014/17/EU of the European Parliament and of the Council of 4 February 2014 on credit agreements relating to residential immovable property for consumers and amending Directives 2008/48/EC and 2013/36/EU and Regulation (EU) No 1093/2010, OJ 2014 L 60/34.

17 COM(2021) 347 final.

18 Directive (EU) 2023/2225 of the European Parliament and of the Council of 18 October 2023 on credit agreements for consumers and repealing Directive 2008/48/EC, OJ 2023 L 2023/2225.

19 See the overview given by Arroyo Amayuelas, *ERCL* 2024, 1.

# II. ESSENTIAL AREAS OF REGULATION

## 1. OBJECT

**1009.** The Consumer Credit Directive covers credit agreements (Article 2(1) Directive 2008/48/EC); these are agreements whereby a creditor grants or promises to grant credit to a consumer in the form of a deferred payment, a loan or other similar financial assistance (Article 3(c) Directive 2008/48/EC). Like other consumer protection directives, the it relies heavily on the creditor's duties of information to enable the consumer to decide full knowledge of the essential parameters of the obligations arising from the conclusion of the contract (Articles 4 et seq. Directive 2008/48/EC).[20] The credit agreement itself must also contain a large number of compulsory details, which are listed in Article 10(2) Directive 2008/48/EC, such as the annual percentage rate of charge.[21]

**1010.** In addition, Article 8(1) Directive 2008/48/EC obliges the creditor to assess the consumer's creditworthiness. The legal consequences of violations of this are not regulated. Article 23 Directive 2008/48/EC requires effective sanctions. For German law, sec. 505d(1) German Civil Code provides for the reduction of the contractually agreed debit interest rate to the market interest rate. By contrast, a Member State regulation whereby an infringement at the consumer's request leads to the invalidity of the credit agreement and an obligation on the consumer to repay the principal is not in conformity with the Directive.[22]

**1011.** The Directive of 1986 had left it up to the Member States to provide for a right of withdrawal in their legal systems. For credit agreements concluded in particularly dangerous doorstep situations, the protection of the (then) Doorstep Selling Directive also applied.[23] Furthermore, Article 14(1) of Directive 2008/48/EC provides for a general consumer-friendly right of withdrawal and justifies this quite sweepingly with the need to harmonise the different legal situations in the Member States (Recitals 9 and 34 of Directive 2008/48/EC). Its ratio is clearly different from that used to justify a right of withdrawal for contracts concluded away from business premises and

20 On the duties of information see §11 above.

21 The indication of a margin between a minimum and a maximum interest rate does not comply with this requirement, see CJEU, 19 December 2019, Case C-290/19, *Home Credit Slovakia*, ECLI:EU:C:2019:1130, para. 36.

22 CJEU, 5 March 2020, Case C-679/18, *OPR-Finance*, ECLI:EU:C:2020:167, paras. 29 ff. referring to a corresponding provision of Czech law.

23 The Doorstep Selling Directive was not designed to be subsidiary to the Consumer Credit Directive, see CJEU, 13 December 2001, Case C-481/99, *Heininger*, ECLI:EU:C:2001:684, paras. 38 ff.

distance contracts: The consumer need not have been surprised by the consumer credit contract, nor is a distance selling transaction necessary. Rather, the right of withdrawal ensures a period of reflection to allow for reconsideration of the decision to conclude and the resulting long-term commitment, the financial magnitude of which may, due to the complexity of some contracts, not have been properly assessed before the conclusion of the contract.

**1012.** The Mortgage Credit Directive applies to credit agreements secured either by a mortgage or functionally comparable security or by a right in residential immovable property, as well as to credit agreements intended for the acquisition or maintenance of property rights in land or an existing or planned building (Article 3(1) Directive 2014/17/EU). For these, it contains a colourful bouquet of various regulations that can be assigned to different areas of law, in particular, extensive pre-contractual duties of information of the creditor (Articles 10 et seq. Directive 2014/17/EU), specifications for calculating the APR (Article 17 Directive 2014/17/EU), an obligation to check the creditworthiness of the consumer (Articles 18 et seq. Directive 2014/17/EU), standards for advisory services (Article 22 Directive 2014/17/EU) and on early repayment of the credit amount by the consumer (Article 25 Directive 2014/17/EU) as well as on requirements for credit intermediaries and their representatives and other supervisory provisions (Articles 29 et seq. Directive 2014/17/EU).

**1013.** Like the Consumer Credit Directive, the Mortgage Credit Directive also grants the consumer a period of reflection within which they can withdraw from the contractual obligation without negative consequences. This is intended to give the consumer sufficient time, as Article 14(6) subpara. 1 Directive 2014/17/EU carefully formulates, to compare the offers, assess their effects and make an informed decision. However, there are clear differences here in two respects: On the one hand, the relevant period in the case of real estate credit is at least seven days; on the other hand, Member States are free to decide whether this period is a reflection period before the conclusion of the credit agreement or a period during which there is a right of withdrawal after the conclusion of the credit agreement, or both.

## 2. SELECTED PROBLEM AREAS

### a) *Information about the Withdrawal Period*

**1014.** The information to be provided by the creditor includes, in particular, information on the right of withdrawal, which, according to Article 10(2)(p) Directive 2008/48/EC, must be given 'in a clear and concise manner' in the credit contract on paper or on another durable medium. This information is necessary to make the consumer aware of their rights and obligations.[24] In the light of Recital 31 of Directive 2008/48/EC and the principle of *effet utile*, this includes not only 'the existence or absence of a right of withdrawal' and 'the period during which that right may be exercised' but also 'conditions governing the exercise thereof', which, according to the interpretation of the CJEU, also includes the parameters for calculating the withdrawal period provided for in Article 14(1) subpara. 2 of Directive 2008/48/EC.[25]

**1015.** According to the CJEU's assessment, the standard clause used by many German banks and savings banks since June 2010, according to which the revocation period only starts to run after the borrower has received all the mandatory information according to sec. 492(2) German Civil Code,[26] does not meet this requirement. At first, it could be argued that the mere reference to statutory law as such should always be in conformity with the law. However, the issue here is not the clause control itself, but the information contained therein: In order to determine the revocation period, a chain of references through the German Civil Code or Introductory Act to the German Civil Code must be followed, which is way too complex for ordinary people. The information given in the contract should render a look into the law superfluous; the content of the legal rules must be explained in an understandable form.[27] For the 'tiered reference' contained in the above-mentioned clause, this means that it does not meet the requirements of Article 10(2) Directive 2008/48/EC, so that the withdrawal period contained in Article 14(1) subpara. 2 lit. b Directive 2008/48/EC should not start to run.[28]

**1016.** It is interesting to note that in a decision from 2016, the German Federal Supreme Court had declared a corresponding contractual arrangement in real estate loan agreements to be lawful.[29] A referral to the CJEU was not considered there and also not later,[30] as the Consumer Credit Directive does not apply

24 CJEU, 9 November 2016, Case C-42/15, *Home Credit Slovakia*, ECLI:EU:C:2016:842, para. 31.

25 CJEU, 26 March 2020, Case C-66/19, *JC*, ECLI:EU:C:2020:242, paras. 34 ff.

26 See the standard term quoted in CJEU, 26 March 2020, C-66/19, *JC*, ECLI:EU:C:2020:242, para. 14: 'Right of withdrawal. The borrower may withdraw from the contractual obligation, without having to provide any reasons, within 14 days and in writing (for example, by letter, fax or email). The period begins after conclusion of the agreement, but not before the borrower has received all mandatory information referred to in sec. 492(2) of the [German Civil Code] (for example, information concerning the type of loan, information relating to the net loan amount, information concerning the contractual term).'

27 CJEU, 26 April 2012, Case C-472/10, *Invitel*, ECLI:EU:C:2012:242, para. 29; CJEU, 21 March 13, Case C-92/11, *RWE Vertrieb*, ECLI:EU:C:2013:180, para. 50.

28 CJEU, 26 March 2020, Case C-66/19, *JC*, ECLI:EU:C:2020:242, paras. 43 ff.

29 BGHZ 213, 52 paras. 18 ff.

30 BGH WM 2019, 864 para. 17; in detail already OLG Stuttgart ECLI:DE:OLGSTUT:2019:0204.6U88.18.00 para. 15 ff.

to real estate loan agreements. Moreover, it was sufficiently clear that not all information within the meaning of Article 14(1) Directive 2008/48/EC had to be listed in the cancellation information when describing the conditions for the start of the cancellation period.[31] Finally, German law could not be interpreted in conformity with the Directive anyway, so that the question referred for a preliminary ruling ultimately remained hypothetical, as it could not be relevant to the decision in relation to the current proceedings.[32] The wording of the clause is identical to the corresponding passage of the model for a revocation information for consumer loan agreements created by the legislator itself in Annex 6 to Article 247 sec. 6(2) of the Introductory Act to the German Civil Code (old version).[33] A referral to the CJEU was then made by the Saarbrücken Regional Court.[34] The decision made in Luxembourg in the *JC* case[35] could trigger a wave of withdrawals in Germany, as a result of which the BGH did have to rule again on the legality of the clause.[36] It will then depend on the question whether the requirements of the Consumer Credit Directive are to be followed for German law even where there is no formal binding effect.[37] However, a legislative reform finally closed the curtain (for the time being).[38]

**1017.** The CJEU (Grand Chamber) has also decided in this context, that, 'where information provided by the creditor to the consumer under Article 10(2) of Directive 2008/48 proves to be incomplete or incorrect, the withdrawal period starts to run only if the incomplete or incorrect nature of that information is not capable of affecting the consumer's ability to assess the extent of his or her rights and obligations under that directive or his or her decision to conclude the contract and, where relevant, is not capable of depriving him or her of the possibility of exercising his or her rights, in essence, under the same conditions as would have prevailed if that information had been provided in a complete and correct manner'.[39]

---

31 Cf. ECLI:DE:OLGSTUT:2019:0204.6U88.18.00, para. 23; likewise BGH WM 2019, 864 para. 17.

32 Cf. ECLI:DE:OLGSTUT:2019:0204.6U88.18.00, paras. 18 ff.; likewise BGH WM 2019, 864 para. 17.

33 Today: Annex 7.

34 LG Saarbrücken WM 2019, 1444.

35 CJEU, 26 March 2020, Case C-66/19, *JC*, ECLI:EU:C:2020:242.

36 Cf. BGHZ 227, 253 para. 16; BGH ZIP 2021, 26 para. 17; BGH BKR 2021, 371.

37 In general see para. 374 above.

38 Gesetz zur Anpassung des Finanzdienstleistungsrechts an die Rechtsprechung des Gerichtshofs der Europäischen Union vom 11. September 2019 in der Rechtssache C-383/18 und vom 26. März 2020 in der Rechtssache C-66/19 vom 9. Juni 2021, BGBl. I, p. 1666.

39 CJEU, 21 December 23, Joined Cases C-38/21, C-47/21, C-232/21, *BMW Bank*, ECLI:EU:C:2023:1014, para. 265 citing CJEU, 9 November 2016, Case C-42/15, *Home Credit Slovakia*, ECLI:EU:C:2016:842, para. 72, CJEU, 19 December 2019, Joined Cases C-355/18 to C-357/18 and C-479/18, *Rust-Hackner and Others*, ECLI:EU:C:2019:1123, para. 81.

### b) *Leasing*

**1018.** Leasing, which can be described roughly as an atypical rental contract with elements of a sales contract, is particularly popular in practice. The original Consumer Credit Directive applied to leasing cases in which ownership was eventually transferred to the lessee; the situation was different only if the use of the goods was the primary purpose (Article 2(1)(b) Directive 87/102/EEC). The application of the Directive was disputed if the purchase was only structured as an option.[40] In this case, the applicability of the Consumer Credit Directive was supported by the fact that the consumer also needed the information from Article 4 of Directive 87/102/EEC in order to be able to think about exercising the option to purchase. In addition, in some cases, the regulation on overdraft facilities from Article 6(3) of Directive 87/102/EEC was applicable, as here too there is a need for information, although, at the time of conclusion of the contract, it is not yet clear whether the overdraft facility will be needed.[41]

**1019.** The recast Consumer Credit Directive now contains an exception for rental or leasing contracts in which neither the agreement itself nor a separate agreement provides for an obligation to purchase the rental or leasing object; such an obligation is to be assumed if the creditor decides on it unilaterally (Article 2(2)(d) Directive 2008/48/EC).

### c) *Personal Guarantee*

**1020.** According to the German Federal Court of Justice, the personal guarantee, as a form of credit security, is not a consumer credit as it lacks the characteristic feature of counter-performance.[42] Criticism was voiced in the legal literature in this regard: The comparability with the contract of adhesion to a debt, for which the existence of a right of revocation is affirmed by the German Federal Court of Justice,[43] argues for an analogous applicability of the consumer protection provisions to the guarantee; a right of revocation should exist if the protected contract is a credit agreement.[44]

**1021.** Under the First Consumer Credit Directive, the CJEU was asked whether this result conformed with European law. In the *Berliner Kindl* decision,

---

[40] In favour of the applicability of Directive 87/102/EEC: BGH NJW 1985, 1539.

[41] S. Grundmann, *Europäisches Schuldvertragsrecht* (Berlin: De Gruyter, 1999), p. 668.

[42] BGHZ 138, 321, 326.

[43] BGHZ 129, 371, 380; BGHZ 134, 94; BGH ZIP 2000, 1523.

[44] For example P. Bülow/M. Artz, *Verbraucherprivatrecht*, 6th ed. (Heidelberg, C.F. Müller, 2018), paras. 325 ff.; Holznagel, *JURA* 2000, 582; Tiedtke, *NJW* 2001, 1027; Zahn, *ZIP* 2006, 1069.

the Court held that the Directive did not apply to guarantees.[45] It referred to the systematic structure of the Directive: According to Annex I no. 1 lit. vi Directive 87/102/EEC, securities must also be stated. This was an indication that the Directive made a distinction between credit and credit security. On the other hand, the guarantee was not explicitly mentioned. However, the purpose of the Directive, i.e., the protection of the consumer, did not indicate any other result since the content of the Directive did not bring any advantages to the guarantor: Essentially, it was about informing the principal debtor about the extent of their obligation. The guarantor's interest, however, was primarily to be informed about the main debtor's ability to pay. In particular, the fact that such agreements are ancillary to the principal agreement whose performance they underwrite does not change anything here.[46] This is remarkable because in the *Dietzinger* case,[47] which had been decided shortly before, the CJEU had (incorrectly) based the applicability of the Doorstep Selling Directive on guarantees on this very argument.[48]

**1022.** The new Consumer Credit Directive does not explicitly cover guarantees either. It is questionable, however, whether the national legislator might now be prevented from including the guarantee in the regulatory scope of the respective national consumer credit law due to the full harmonisation postulated in Article 22(1) of Directive 2008/48/EC. This depends on whether the full harmonisation also has a negative blocking effect or simply does not want to apply to this area. According to Recital 10 of Directive 2008/48/EC, the obligation of the Member States to transpose the provisions of this Directive is to extend only to the areas defined by these definitions. However, it is not intended to prevent the Member States from applying, in accordance with EU law, the provisions of this Directive to areas which do not fall within its scope. Since the definitions in Article 3 of Directive 2008/48/EC do not cover guarantees, neither directly nor indirectly, a blocking effect cannot be assumed.[49]

---

45 CJEU, 23 March 2000, Case C-208/98, *Berliner Kindl*, ECLI:EU:C:2000:152, paras. 25 ff.

46 CJEU, 23 March 2000, Case C-208/98, *Berliner Kindl*, ECLI:EU:C:2000:152, para. 26.

47 CJEU, 17 March 1998, Case C-45/96, *Dietzinger*, ECLI:EU:C:1998:111, para. 22.

48 See para. 537 above.

49 See Möller, in *BeckOK-BGB* (1 May 2024), §491 para. 53.

# §25. PACKAGE TRAVEL CONTRACTS

## CONTENTS



References: S. Bergmann, *Das neue Reiserecht. Die Umsetzung der EU-Pauschalreiserichtlinie* (Munich: C.H. Beck, 2018); A. Chambellan, *Europäisierung des Reisevertragsrechts. Die Mängelrechte des Reisenden im deutsch-polnischen Rechtsvergleich* (Tübingen: Mohr Siebeck, 2016); E. Führich, 'Das neue Pauschalreiserecht – Umsetzung der Pauschalreiserichtlinie (EU) 2015/2302 in deutsches Recht', *NJW* 2017, 2945; M.B.M. Loos, 'Precontractual information obligations for package travel contracts', *EuCML* 2016, 125; M. Sonnentag, 'Das neue Reisevertragsrecht', *VersR* 2018, 967.

## I. REGULATORY OBJECTIVE

**1023.** The tourism sector is of great economic importance in the EU.[1] Since mostly service contracts play a role here, there is a direct relevance to the internal market: the Treaty of Lisbon even created a separate title for tourism within the framework of the internal policies and measures of the Union with Article 195 TFEU. With the increase in package travel offers, the Commission noted major differences in the legal systems of the Member States, which hindered the free movement of services in the field of package travel contracts and led to distortions of competition between entrepreneurs in the travel industry established in various Member States (Recital 3 Directive 90/314/EEC). It also discouraged consumers from booking packages with suppliers in other Member States (Recital 8 Directive 90/314/EEC).

**1024.** The justification for this legislative intervention follows usual patterns: Harmonisation of package travel law in the Community would stimulate

1 In 2018, for example, the direct share of the travel and tourism sector in the gross domestic product of the EU Member States was 3.9% according to the Fact Sheet of the EU Parliament, and even 10.3% when tourism-related economic sectors are added, see https://www.europarl.europa.eu/factsheets/de/sheet/126/tourism.

stronger growth and increased productivity, which would not only be to the benefit of consumers but would also attract travellers from third states who would benefit from the guaranteed minimum services in package travel (Recital 7 Directive 90/314/EEC). The legal basis for the Package Travel Directive of 13 June 1990 was the then-applicable Article 100a EC, i.e. the general internal market competence.[2]

**1025.** More than 20 years later, the legal framework created by this was considered inadequate. The classic package travel regulated by it, which consisted of both transport services and accommodation and possibly also other tourist services put together by the supplier (Article 2 no. 1 Directive 90/314/EEC), is increasingly being replaced by other supply forms.[3] The Commission also stated that legal fragmentation still existed, which led to distortions in the market and discouraged consumers from requesting package tours from providers in other Member States (Recitals 4 and 6 Directive 2015/2302). Consequently, the revision of the Package Travel Directive comes with a fully harmonizing approach (Article 4 Directive 2015/2302), again in the weakened form of 'targeted' full harmonisation, which opens up regulatory leeway for the Member States at appropriate points.[4] The general contract law of the Member States, which concerns, for example, the validity, formation or effects of a contract, remains unaffected by the Directive; the same applies to all aspects of general contract law that are not regulated in the Directive (Article 1(3) Directive 2015/2302).

**1026.** The revised Package Travel Directive had to be transposed by 31 December 2017; the transposition standards apply since 1 July 2018 (Article 28 Directive 2015/2302).

## II. THE PACKAGE TRAVEL CONTRACT

**1027.** The definition of the regulation's subject matter, the package travel contract, is of central importance. The first Package Travel Directive defined the package in its Article 2 no. 1 as a 'pre-arranged combination of not fewer than two of the following when sold or offered for sale at an inclusive price and when the service covers a period of more than twenty-four hours or includes overnight accommodation: (a) transport; (b) accommodation; (c) other tourist services not ancillary to transport or accommodation and accounting for a significant proportion of the package'. Thus, a package of travel services must always be booked. In this respect, it is irrelevant if the consumer puts the services together

2 Today Article 114 TFEU, on this generally para. 220.
3 In more detail Führich, *NJW* 2016, 1204.
4 On this already above para. 84.

themselves.[5] The actual travel service does not necessarily have to be provided by the contracting party itself; its role can be limited to that of an intermediary (definitions in Article 2 nos. 2 and 3 Directive 90/314/EEC).

**1028.** The revised Package Travel Directive essentially retains this basic framework but expands and specifies the definition of a package (Article 2(1) and (2); Article 3 nos. 1 to 3 Directive 2015/2302).[6] A notable novelty is the category of 'linked travel arrangements', i.e. those travel services where entrepreneurs assist the traveller in acquiring the travel service and where the traveller concludes contracts with various service providers via linked booking procedures, which do not have the characteristics of a package (Article 19 with Recital 9 Directive 2015/2302).

**1029.** With regard to the personal scope of application, the revision no longer covers consumer contracts exclusively; the Directive now protects 'travellers', as it is not always easy to distinguish whether the journey is booked for private or (also) business purposes. Article 3 no. 6 Directive 2015/2302 defines the traveller as any person who wishes to conclude a package travel contract or is entitled to any travel that is subject to the Directive. This, therefore, covers business travellers who book package travel for business purposes, but not if there is a framework contract for the provision of business travel that is used to book the travel (so-called business travel, see Article 2(2)(c) Directive 2015/2302).

**1030.** The pre-contractual duties of information, which were extended in the revised Package Travel Directive[7] and now also require, for example, information on the approximate time of departure and return (Article 5(1)(a)(ii) Directive 2015/2302), continue to be of major importance. This information becomes an integral part of the package travel contract and can only be changed by explicit agreement between the contracting parties; costs not communicated before the conclusion of the contract are not borne by the traveller (Article 6 Directive 2015/2302). The legislative intention – the informed conclusion of the contract – and the regulatory system are similar to those of the Consumer Rights Directive.[8]

**1031.** The Directive does not contain any other sanctions for breaches of the duties of information.[9] In particular, there is no connection to the period

---

5 CJEU, 30 April 2002, Case C-400/00, *Club-Tour*, ECLI:EU:C:2002:272.

6 For details see Führich, *NJW* 2016, 1204, 1206.

7 Loos, *EuCML* 2016, 125.

8 On this already above paras. 477 ff.

9 The remedies for breaches of duties of information in consumer contracts were already discussed, cf. above at paras. 495 ff.

of a right of withdrawal. The Directive does not contain such a right either; it merely allows Member States to introduce a right of withdrawal in their law for package travel contracts concluded away from business premises (Article 12(5) Directive 2015/2302). The right of withdrawal thus given is only excluded if the oral negotiations preceding the conclusion of the contract were conducted on the initiative of the consumer.

## III. CONSEQUENCES OF NON-PERFORMANCE

### 1. WITHDRAWAL BEFORE THE START OF THE JOURNEY

**1032.** According to Article 12(1) of Directive 2015/2302, the traveller may withdraw from the package travel contract at any time before the obligations have been performed but may then owe the payment of a reasonable and justifiable withdrawal fee if this has been contractually agreed.

**1033.** Such a fee does not apply if rescission before departure is due to unavoidable, extraordinary circumstances at or near the destination, which substantially affect the performance of the package travel contract or the carriage of persons to the destination. The term 'unavoidable and extraordinary circumstances' replaces the term '*force majeure*' still used in the predecessor Directive. Article 3 no. 12 Directive 2015/2302 defines this in line with, for example, the Air Passenger Rights Regulation[10] as 'a situation beyond the control of the party who invokes such a situation and the consequences of which could not have been avoided even if all reasonable measures had been taken'. The traveller is then entitled to a full refund of all payments made for the package; however, they cannot claim additional compensation (Article 12(2) Directive 2015/2302).

### 2. BREACHES OF CONTRACT DURING THE TRIP

**1034.** Once the journey has begun, the organiser is liable for the provision of the travel services included in the package travel contract; this applies to their own services as well as to those provided by third parties on their behalf; Member State law may also extend this liability to travel agents (Article 13(1) Directive2015/2302). The traveller has an Obligation to inform the organiser immediately of any lack of conformity. The tour operator is thus allowed to remedy the situation unless this is impossible or involves disproportionately high

10 See paras. 1064 ff. below.

costs (Article 13(3) Directive 2015/2302). In this case, the traveller is entitled to a price reduction or damages (Article 14 Directive 2015/2302).

**1035.** The traveller may set a deadline for the tour operator to remedy the lack of conformity and, if the deadline expires without remedy, remedy the lack of conformity themselves. If setting a deadline is pointless because the tour operator refuses to remedy the situation or the lack of conformity must be remedied immediately, the deadline does not apply (Article 13(4) Directive 2015/2302). This regulation, which deviates from sales law, where subsequent performance by the buyer is generally not permitted,[11] is explained by the limited duration of the trip, due to which the remedy makes less sense over time. This also explains the obligation of the tour operator to offer the traveller reasonable other arrangements for the continuation of the trip if the remedy becomes pointless because a significant part of the travel services can no longer be provided; corresponding losses in terms of the owed quality are to be compensated with a price reduction (Article 13(4) Directive 2015/2302).

**1036.** Rescission is only possible if the lack of conformity significantly impacts the travel services and the tour operator has failed to remedy the situation within the deadline. A cancellation fee is not due; also, claims for reduction and damages may arise (Article 13(6) and Article 14 Directive 2015/2302).

## 3. DAMAGES

**1037.** While the Sale of Goods Directive or the Digital Content Directive do not provide for a claim for damages and leave this legal consequence of a breach of contract to the law of the Member States, Article 14(2) Directive 2015/2302 gives rise to a claim against the tour operator for reasonable compensation for the damage suffered by the traveller as a result of the lack of conformity. This claim is independent of fault. However, tour operators may exonerate themselves by proving that the lack of conformity is attributable to the travellers themselves or a third party if the lack of conformity was neither foreseeable nor avoidable. The claim is also excluded if unavoidable, extraordinary circumstances caused the lack of conformity (Article 14(3) Directive 2015/2302).

**1038.** The first Package Travel Directive already had a similarly structured claim for damages in Article 5(2) of Directive 90/314/EEC. In this respect, it was unclear whether immaterial damages should also be included, especially a loss of holiday enjoyment. The CJEU had to decide on this question in the

---

[11] See para. 972 above.

*Leitner* case.[12] The Austrian plaintiff had been served salmonella-contaminated food in a Turkish hotel during a package tour organised by the defendant's travel company. She suffered salmonella poisoning and demanded compensation for a loss of holiday enjoyment. The Austrian law in force at the time recognised 'the feelings of dissatisfaction and negative impressions caused by disappointment' as immaterial damages but did not contain any grounds for a claim for the constellation in question.[13]

**1039.** The CJEU considered a loss of holiday enjoyment to be compensable. The court argued that the obligation to pay damages also includes non-material damages; the transposition of the Directive into national law can, therefore, not be restricted to quantifiable damages only.[14] The court further argued that non-material damages can be compensated under the law of many Member States so that the absence of such an obligation in other states would lead to noticeable distortions of competition. However, this argument hardly leads anywhere as long as this requirement does not follow from the Directive itself; it is rather circular in character. The CJEU then cited the rationale of the directive, in particular its Article 5, which lies in the protection of consumers; in the case of holiday travel, damages for loss of holiday enjoyment are of particular importance. Hence, the Court found that the directive implicitly recognises a fundamental right to compensation for non-bodily harm, including non-material harm, in that Article 5(2) subpara. 4 allows Member States to permit compensation for non-bodily harm to be limited by contract, provided that this limitation is not unreasonable.[15] It follows from this that the concept of damage in Article 5(2) of Directive 90/314/EEC includes both material and immaterial damages.

**1040.** The revised Package Travel Directive leaves the legal situation unchanged: Recital 34 Directive 2015/2302 now succinctly clarifies that damages should also include non-material damage, such as a loss of holiday enjoyment as a result of significant problems in the provision of the travel services in question. The text of Article 14 of Directive 2015/2302 itself does not contain a corresponding provision, but the legal situation is thus sufficiently clear, also in light of the established *Leitner* case law.

---

12 CJEU, 12 March 2002, Case C-168/00, *Leitner*, ECLI:EU:C:2002:163.

13 CJEU, 12 March 2002, Case C-168/00, *Leitner*, ECLI:EU:C:2002:163, para. 10.

14 CJEU, 12 March 2002, Case C-168/00, *Leitner*, ECLI:EU:C:2002:163, paras. 20 ff.

15 CJEU, 12 March 2002, Case C-168/00, *Leitner*, ECLI:EU:C:2002:163, para. 23.

# §26. TIMESHARE CONTRACTS

CONTENTS



References: C. Busch, 'Der Vorschlag der EU-Kommission für eine Reform der Timeshare-Richtlinie – ein richtiger Schritt auf dem Weg zur Überarbeitung des Verbraucheracquis?', *GPR* 2008, 13; M.C. Dias Urbano de Sousa, *Das Timesharing an Ferienimmobilien in der EU* (Baden-Baden: Nomos, 1998); M. Franzen, 'Neue Regeln zum Time-Sharing. Das 'Gesetz zur Modernisierung der Regelungen über Teilzeit-Wohnrechteverträge, Verträge über langfristige Urlaubsprodukte sowie Vermittlungsverträge und Tauschsystemverträge"', *NZM* 2011, 217; S. Friesen, *Auswirkungen der Richtlinie 2008/122/EG auf das Internationale Timesharingrecht in der EU* (Jena: JWV, 2017); C. Jehle, *Die Timesharing-Richtlinie der EU vom 26. Oktober 1994 und deren Umsetzung in den deutschsprachigen Ländern* (Basel: Helbing & Lichtenhahn, 2001); G. Mäsch, 'Licht und Schatten im Europäischen Verbraucherschutzrecht', *EuZW* 1995, 8; G. Mäsch, 'Das deutsche Time-Sharing-Recht nach dem neuen Teilzeit- Wohnrechte-Gesetz', *DNotZ* 1997, 180; K. Schubert, 'Neues bei den Teilzeit-Wohnrechten (Timesharing). Der Vorschlag der EU-Kommission für eine Reform der Richtlinie 94/47/EG', *NZM* 2007, 665; K. Tonner, *Das Recht des Time-sharing an Ferienimmobilien* (Munich: Beck, 1997).

## I. HISTORY AND BACKGROUND

**1041.** The legal basis for the Timeshare Directive of 1994[1] was the then-applicable Article 100a TEC, i.e. the general internal market competence.[2] Its objective was the approximation of the laws, regulations and administrative provisions of the Member States relating to contracts which directly or indirectly concern the acquisition of the right to use one or more immovable properties on a timeshare basis ('time-sharing') (Article 1 Directive 94/47/EC).[3] In this respect, the Commission argued that the differences between national laws on

1 Directive 94/47/EC of the European Parliament and of the Council of 26 October 1994 on the protection of purchasers in respect of certain aspects of contracts relating to the purchase of the right to use immovable properties on a timeshare basis, OJ 1994 L 280/83. On this point Mäsch, *EuZW* 1995, 8.

2 See Dias Urbano de Sousa, *Das Timesharing an Ferienimmobilien in der EU*, 1998, p. 270.

3 Jehle, *Die Timesharing-Richtlinie der EU vom 26. Oktober 1994 und deren Umsetzung in den deutsprachigen Ländern*, 2001, p. 56; Dias Urbano de Sousa, *Das Timesharing an Ferienimmobilien in der EU*, 1998, p. 265.

timeshare contracts were likely to hinder the proper functioning of the internal market and to create distortions of competition and partitioning of national markets (Recital 1 Directive 94/47/EC).

**1042.** However, the Directive only covered certain aspects of the conclusion of the contract, namely the information on the contents of the contract and the details of the respective transmission as well as the procedures and details of the right of withdrawal (Recital 2 Directive 94/47/EC).[4] It does not regulate questions regarding the admissibility of timeshare contracts or concerning their content or legal nature (Recital 4 Directive 94/47/EC).[5] In essence, these are rules on consumer protection.[6]

**1043.** As the timeshare market continued to evolve and new, similar holiday products were introduced to the market (which were not covered by Directive 94/47/EC), the need to revise the act arose (Recital 1 Directive 2008/122/EC).[7] This occurred with the adoption of the Timeshare Directive of 14 January 2009 on the protection of consumers in respect of certain aspects of timeshare contracts, long-term holiday product contracts and resale and exchange contracts.[8] In terms of content, the recast led, among others, to an extension of the scope of application, a standardisation and extension of the withdrawal period, an extension of the prohibition of advance payment, and the introduction of general rules on terminating ancillary contracts.[9]

**1044.** While the Directive of 1994 still pursued the approach of minimum harmonisation, the new version now establishes fully harmonising rules for consumer protection in timeshare contracts.[10] However, according to Article 1(2) Directive 2008/122/EC, Member States may continue to apply certain national provisions, such as rules on general contract law remedies (lit. a). This is based on the legislative approach of 'targeted full harmonisation'.[11]

---

4 Jehle, *Die Timesharing-Richtlinie der EU vom 26. Oktober 1994 und deren Umsetzung in den deutsprachigen Ländern*, 2001, p. 54; Dias Urbano de Sousa, *Das Timesharing an Ferienimmobilien in der EU*, 1998, p. 265.

5 Jehle, *Die Timesharing-Richtlinie der EU vom 26. Oktober 1994 und deren Umsetzung in den deutsprachigen Ländern*, 2001, p. 56.

6 Dias Urbano de Sousa, *Das Timesharing an Ferienimmobilien in der EU*, 1998, p. 265.

7 On this point Schubert, *NZM* 2007, 665, 665 f.

8 Directive 2008/122/EC of the European Parliament and of the Council of 14 January 2009 on the protection of consumers in respect of certain aspects of timeshare, long-term holiday product, resale and exchange contracts, OJ 2009 L 33/10. See Busch, *GPR* 2008, 13.

9 Schubert, *NZM* 2007, 665, 666 ff.; Busch, *GPR* 2008, 13 ff.

10 Schubert, *NZM* 2007, 665, 670; Busch, *GPR* 2008, 13, 16.

11 See the explanatory memorandum of the Commission proposal, COM(2007) 303 final, p. 9; on this, Schubert, *NZM* 2007, 665, 670. On a reading that places Article 1(2) of the draft Directive in the context of the horizontal instrument planned at about the same time (on this,

## II. SPECIFIC ASPECTS OF THE TIMESHARE CONTRACT

**1045.** According to the definition in Article 2(a) Directive 2008/122/EC, a timeshare contract is a contract of a duration of more than one year under which a consumer, for consideration, acquires the right to use one or more overnight accommodation for more than one period of occupation. Further definitions can be found for contracts for a long-term holiday product (Article 2(1)(b) Directive 2008/122/EC or 481a German Civil Code) as well as resale and exchange contracts (Article 2(1)(c) and (d) Directive 2008/122/EC).

**1046.** According to Article 5(1) of Directive 2008/122/EC, these contracts must be in writing; electronic form is generally considered equivalent. They must be drawn up in the language of the Member State in which the consumer is domiciled or of which the consumer is a national; otherwise, the contract is void; if there are several official languages, the consumer has a right to choose between them.

**1047.** Prior to the conclusion of the contract, the entrepreneur must provide the consumer with correct and sufficient information on the contract's content in due time before the performance of a contractual obligation (Article 4(1) of Directive 2008/122/EC) by sending the forms referred to therein.

## III. CONSUMER RIGHTS

**1048.** In addition to the duties of information following the principle of 'informed consent',[12] the revised Timeshare Directive in Article 6(1) gives the consumer the right to withdraw from the timeshare contract, the long-term holiday product contract, the resale contract or the exchange contract within 14 days without giving reasons. After withdrawal, the consumer's obligations are terminated without any costs incurred by the consumer (Article 8 Directive 2008/122/EC). The same applies to all exchange contracts or other accessory contracts subordinate to these contracts: These are also automatically terminated without any costs for the consumer (Article 11(1) Directive 2008/122/EC).

**1049.** All consumer protection laws of the Directive cannot be derogated from (Article 12(1) Directive 2008/122/EC). This applies at least to the extent that the

---

cf. paras. 127 ff. above), so that ultimately there would be no exceptions to full harmonisation, see Busch, *GPR* 2008, 13, 16.

[12] Cf. para. 477 above.

law of a Member State applies to the timeshare contract. If, on the other hand, such a contract is governed by the law of a third country, consumers may not be deprived of the protection granted to them by this Directive as implemented by the Member State of the court before which the case is brought (Article 12(2) Directive 2008/122/EC).[13] This applies in any case if one of the immovable properties concerned is situated in the territory of a Member State or, in the case of a contract which does not directly relate to immovable property, the entrepreneur pursues a commercial or professional activity in a Member State or directs that activity in any way to a Member State and the contract falls within the scope of that activity.[14]

13 Leible/Leitner, *IPRax* 2013, 37, 39 ff.

14 Staudinger, *NZM* 2011, 601; Leible/Leitner, *IPRax* 2013, 37, 40 (also on questions of jurisdiction).

# §27. THE COMMERCIAL AGENCY CONTRACT

CONTENTS



References: R. Emde, 'Die Handelsvertreter-Richtlinie 1986 und ihre Folgen', *ZVertriebsR* 2014, 218; R. Emde/D. Valdini, 'Die Handelsvertreter-Richtlinie', *ZVertriebsR* 2016, 353 and 2017, 3; H. Fischer, 'Der Handelsvertreter im deutschen und europäischen Recht', *ZVglRWiss* 101 (2002), 143; R. Guski, 'Der Ausgleichsanspruch des Handelsvertreters und seine Verwirkung: zur prinzipienorientierten Teleologie des Gemeinschaftsprivatrechts', *GPR* 2009, 286; G. Heinicke, 'Stolpersteine im grenzüberschreitenden Handelsvertreterrecht', *ZVertriebsR* 2013, 275; S. Huber, 'Distributionsgeschäfte', in H. Kronke/W. Melis/H. Kuhn (eds.), *Handbuch Internationales Wirtschaftsrecht*, 2nd ed. (Cologne: Otto Schmidt, 2017), Teil G; M.F. Müller, 'Internationale Anwendbarkeit des handelsvertreterrechtlichen Ausgleichsanspruchs – Vom Intervall Ingmar und Unamar zum Dreiklang mit Agro', *GPR* 2017, 203; B. Rohrßen, 'Handelsvertreter als Ein- und Mehrfirmenvertreter sowie im Nebenberuf: Die Irrelevanz von Tätigkeitsort und -art (stationär, ambulant oder online)', *ZVertriebsR* 2019, 153; U. Sellhorst, 'Die Umsetzung der Handelsvertreterrichtlinie', *EWS* 2001, 481; C. Stempel, *Treu und Glauben im Unionsprivatrecht* (Tübingen: Mohr Siebeck, 2016), pp. 237–244, 279–280, 290–295; J. Teichmann/U. Wauschkuhn, 'Die Anwendung der zwingenden Vorschriften der §§ 84 ff. HGB auf Handelsvertreter und Vertragshändler im internationalen Kontext', *ZVertriebsR* 2012, 274; K.-H. Thume, 'Der Provisionsanspruch des Handelsvertreters: Grenzen der Vertragsgestaltung', *BB* 2012, 975.

## I. HISTORY AND BACKGROUND

**1050.** The Commercial Agents Directive of 1986,[1] based on Article 57(2) and the internal market clause of Article 100 EEC Treaty, is clearly modelled after German law, which has a long-standing history in the field.[2] Harmonisation is justified because the differences between national laws in the field of commercial agency contracts affect the conditions of competition and the cross-border exercise of the profession. This affects the scope of protection of commercial agents and the security in commercial transactions and makes it more difficult

[1] Council Directive 86/653/EEC of 18 December 1986 on the co-ordination of the laws of the Member States relating to self-employed commercial agents, OJ 1986 L 382/17.

[2] Kindler, *RIW* 1990, 358; in-depth on the genesis Emde/Valdini, *ZVertriebsR* 2016, 353.

to conclude and perform agency contracts between an entrepreneur and a commercial agent established in different Member States (Recitals 2 and 3 Directive 86/653/EEC).

**1051.** The directive aims at reaching three goals: to protect the interests of commercial agents vis-à-vis entrepreneurs, to promote the security of commercial transactions and to facilitate the exchange of goods between Member States by approximating the legal systems of the Member States.[3] A commercial agent is a person who, as an independent[4] trader, is permanently entrusted with arranging the sale or purchase of goods for an entrepreneur[5] or with concluding such transactions in the name and on behalf of the entrepreneur (Article 1(2) Directive 86/653/EEC). The Directive regulates the rights and obligations of the parties to the agency contract, remuneration and commission claims, the conclusion and termination of the agency contract and, in particular, post-contractual compensation claims and non-competition clauses. It is a minimum harmonising directive in so far as Member States may introduce or maintain stricter provisions for the protection of commercial agents.[6]

**1052.** The Commission's evaluation report published on 16 July 2015[7] assesses the directive positively and recommends keeping it unchanged.

## II. CONTRACTUAL RIGHTS AND OBLIGATIONS

**1053.** In Article 3(1) and 4(1), the Commercial Agents Directive standardises the mutual obligation for the parties to the agency contract to act in good faith.[8] These are mandatory duties, as follows from Article 5 Directive 86/653/EEC. For both parties, there are more detailed specifications in this respect, which are, however, by no means conclusive. The commercial agent must make reasonable efforts to arrange and, if necessary, conclude the transactions entrusted to them; they are accountable to the entrepreneur and are bound by their instructions (Article 3(2) Directive 86/653/EEC). The entrepreneur, in turn, must provide the

3 See CJEU, 3 December 2015, Case C-338/14, *Quenon*, ECLI:EU:C:2015:795, para. 23 with references.

4 On the question of the independence of the commercial agent CJEU, 21 November 2018, Case C-452/17, *Zako*, ECLI:EU:C:2018:935. On this issue CJEU, 16 March 2006, Case C-3/04, *Poseidon Chartering*, ECLI:EU:C:2006:176.

5 It is not sufficient that the trader acts on account of an entrepreneur but in their own name, CJEU, 10 February 2004, Case C-85/03, *Mavrona*, ECLI:EU:C:2004:83.

6 Emde/Valdini, *ZVertriebsR* 2016, 353, 354.

7 Commission Staff Working Document: Evaluation of the Council Directive on the Coordination of the Laws of the Member States Relating to Self-Employed Commercial Agents (Directive 86/653/EEC) / Refit Evaluation, SWD(2015) 146 final, p. 4.

8 For details Emde/Valdini, *ZVertriebsR* 2017, 3.

commercial agent with the necessary documents relating to the goods concerned, give them the information necessary for the performance of the agency contract and, in particular, inform them within a reasonable period of time as soon as they foresee that the volume of business will be considerably less than the commercial agent could normally have expected and, finally, inform them within a reasonable period of the acceptance or refusal and the non-performance of the transactions arranged by the commercial agent (Article 4(2) Directive 86/653/EEC).

**1054.** Should the parties have not agreed on a monetary compensation, a commercial agent shall be entitled to the remuneration that commercial agents appointed for the goods forming the subject of his agency contract are customarily allowed in the place where he carries on his activities and, if no such customs exist, to a reasonable remuneration (Article 6(1) Directive 86/653/EEC). The latter should occur only rarely.[9] A sub-category of remuneration is commission. Under the conditions of Article 7 to 11 of Directive 86/653/EEC, the commercial agent is entitled to such commission, which arises when the transaction is due to their activity. The Directive does not specify which requirements must be met regarding the causal link between the activity of the commercial agent and the right to commission. In this respect, there is a certain margin of implementation in Member State law. However, the requirements are not too strict, as can be seen on the one hand from the general idea of protection in favour of the commercial agent, and on the other hand from the fact that the Directive, as may be derived from Article 8(1)(a), also provides for stricter standards.[10]

## III. CONCLUSION, TERMINATION AND POST-CONTRACTUAL OBLIGATIONS

**1055.** Articles 13 to 20 of Directive 86/653/EEC regulate the conclusion, duration and termination of the commercial agency contract as well as the post-contractual obligations of the parties. In order to protect the commercial agent, a contract concluded for a definite period of time which is continued by both parties after the end of the respective term must be converted into a contract concluded for an indefinite period of time (Article 14 of Directive 86/653/EEC). Contracts concluded indefinitely may be terminated by either party subject to a notice period. This mandatory period of notice is extended with each year of the contract's duration (Article 15 Directive 86/653/EEC). Here, the protection of the economically weaker commercial agent is also pursued.

---

9 Emde/Valdini, *ZVertriebsR* 2017, 3, 4.

10 Emde/Valdini, *ZVertriebsR* 2017, 3, 5.

**1056.** In addition, the commercial agent's post-contractual claims for compensation or damages (Articles 17 to 19 Directive 86/653/EEC) are of great practical importance. The Directive leaves it to the Member States to decide what kind of claims they want to regulate (Article 17(1) Directive 86/653/EEC).[11] In most cases, the compensation model already in force in Germany (Article 17(2) Directive 86/653/EEC) is adopted.[12] According to the CJEU, such post-contractual compensation claims are considered to be overriding mandatory provisions in the sense that they also prevail over laws of a third state chosen by the parties.[13]

**1057.** Finally, the Directive contains a provision on post-contractual competition agreements (Article 20 Directive 86/653/EEC). This provision makes such agreements, which are extremely restrictive for the commercial agent, subject to the threefold proviso that they must be in writing, that they cover the territory or client base allocated to the commercial agent and give details on the categories of goods which, according to the contract, are the subject of their representation, and that they must be valid for a maximum of two years after the termination of the contractual relationship.

---

11 Cumulation is also possible in principle, as long as such a provision does not lead to a double compensation of the commercial agent for the loss of commissions as a result of the termination of the agency contract, cf. CJEU, 3 December 2015, Case C-338/14, *Quenon*, ECLI:EU:C:2015:795.

12 More in detail Emde/Valdini, *ZVertriebsR* 2017, 3, 9. These claims also exist if the contract is terminated during a contractually agreed probationary period, CJEU, 19 April 2018, Case C-645/16, *Conseils et mise en relations (CMR) SARL/Demeures terre et tradition SARL*, ECLI:EU:C:2018:262.

13 CJEU, 9 November 2000, Case C-381/98, *Ingmar*, ECLI:EU:C:2000:605. For more details see para. 1271 below.

# §28. TRANSPORT CONTRACTS

## CONTENTS



References: J. Karsten/A. Seidenspinner, '"Zum Vorteile des Verkehrsnutzers" - Zwanzig Jahre EU-Passagierrecht im Spannungsfeld zwischen international governance und europäischen Nutzerrechten', *ZEuP* 2010, 830; S. Keiler, 'Der Vorschlag für eine Änderung der Fluggastrechte-VO – Eine Analyse aus wissenschaftlicher Sicht', *RRa* 2013, 163; U. Lienhard, 'Europäisches Schuldrecht im Flugverkehr', *GPR* 2004, 259; T. Richter/ M.F. Monteiro, 'Passagierrechte bei Flugverspätungen', *GPR* 2012, 199; H. Rösler, 'Billigfluglinien im EU-Wirtschaftsrecht - Marktordnungs-, Beihilfe- und Fluggastrecht', *ZHR* 170 (2006), 336; J. Schindler/M.-M. Bues, 'Die Reform der FluggastrechteVO – Was lange währt, wird endlich gut?', *ZLW* 2014, 188-223; R. Schmid/H. Hopperdietzel, 'Die Fluggastrechte - eine Momentaufnahme', *NJW* 2010, 1905; R. Schmid, 'Die "Unvollendete": Zehn Jahre Fluggastrechte-Verordnung. Ausgewählte noch offene oder nicht befriedigend gelöste Rechtsfragen der VO (EG) Nr. 261/2004', *NJW* 2015, 513; A. Staudinger/R. Schmidt-Bendun, 'Neuregelung über Ausgleichs- und Unterstützungsleistungen für Fluggäste', *NJW* 2004, 1897; K. Tonner, 'Die EG-Verordnung über Ausgleichsleistungen bei Nichtbeförderung, Annullierung und großer Verspätung – ein wichtiger Beitrag des Rechts zur Qualitätssicherung im Luftverkehr', *RRa* 2004, 59; B. Wagner, 'Verbesserung der Fluggastrechte durch die Verordnung (EG) Nr 261/2004? Praktische Probleme aus Verbrauchersicht', *VuR* 2006, 337.

# I. AIR TRAFFIC

## 1. GENESIS AND BACKGROUND

**1058.** A regulation with great practical importance in practice exists in the area of air transport, where the Air Passenger Rights Regulation[1] regulates, among other things, compensation claims against airlines in the cases of overbooking and delay of a flight. It replaces the predecessor regulation,[2] which has been in force since 1991, and which laid down common minimum standards for compensation in the event of denied boarding following the liberalisation of air transport in the Common Market. The regulatory aim was to maintain the quality of the airline services in the context of increasing competition in air transport (Recital 4 of Regulation 295/91). The revision became necessary because it became apparent that the measures taken did not have the desired effect: Despite the obligation to pay compensation, the number of passengers denied boarding against their will was still too high; the same applied to unannounced cancellations and long delays (Recital 3 of Regulation 261/2004).

**1059.** The new regulation was based on the then-applicable Article 80(2) TEC (now Article 100(2) TFEU), i.e., it was issued within the framework of the common transport policy. It entered into force on 17 February 2005. Compared to the previous regulation, its scope of application was extended: charter flights are now also covered in addition to scheduled flights. The regulation also applies to certain third-country constellations (Article 3 of Regulation 261/2004). The existing air passenger rights based on the Package Travel Directive[3] remain unaffected; the Air Passenger Rights Regulation does not apply to cases in which a package tour is cancelled for reasons other than the cancellation of the flight (Article 3(6) of Regulation 261/2004). However, a proposal submitted by the Commission in 2013 to revise the Air Passenger Rights Regulation[4] has not progressed significantly so far. After several years of standstill, a

1 Regulation (EC) No 261/2004 of the European Parliament and of the Council of 11 February 2004 establishing common rules on compensation and assistance to passengers in the event of denied boarding and of cancellation or long delay of flights, and repealing Regulation (EEC) No. 295/91, OJ 2004 L 46/1.

2 Council Regulation (EEC) No 295/91 of 4 February 1991 establishing common rules for a denied boarding compensation system in scheduled air transport, OJ 1991 L 36/5.

3 For this purpose para. 1032 above.

4 Proposal of 13 March 2013 for a Regulation of the European Parliament and of the Council amending Regulation (EC) No 261/2004 establishing common rules on compensation and assistance to passengers in the event of denied boarding and of cancellation or long delay of flights, and Regulation (EC) No 2027/97 on air carrier liability in respect of the carriage of passengers and their baggage by air, COM(2013) 130 final. See Keiler, *RRa* 2013, 163.

comprehensive study on the status of passenger rights has been published.[5] On 23 November 2023, the Proposal for a Regulation regarding enforcement of passenger rights in the Union has been published.[6] It does not aim at a complete overhaul of the Air Passenger Rights Regulation, but proposes a series of minor amendments.

## 2. AIR TRAVEL CONTRACTS

**1060.** The Air Passenger Rights Regulation regulates the rights of air passengers in the event of denied boarding against their will, cancellation or delay of the flight (Article 1(1) Regulation 261/2004). It primarily applies to passengers who board their flight from a Member State or EEA state.[7] Flights from third countries to the EU are also covered if the flight is operated by an air carrier established in the EU unless passengers have received compensation or assistance in that third country (Article 3(1) of Regulation 261/2004). Flights from third countries operated by third-country airlines are not covered by the scope of application of the regulation.

**1061.** Unlike other regulations, the Air Passenger Rights Regulation does not define the air travel contract. Nevertheless, it implicitly assumes that the flight is based on a contractual relationship. This results, for example, from the definition of the 'operating air carrier' in Article 2(b) of Regulation 261/2004, which is described as an air carrier that 'performs or intends to perform a flight under a contract with a passenger or on behalf of another person, legal or natural, having a contract with that passenger'.[8] Moreover, according to Article 3(5) of Regulation 261/2004, the Air Passenger Rights Regulation assumes that an operating air carrier that does not have a contractual relationship with the passenger fulfils obligations under this Regulation if it acts on behalf of the person having a contractual relationship with the passenger concerned.[9]

---

5 Study on the current level of protection of air passenger rights in the EU. Final report (Study contract no MOVE/B5/2018 – 541), as of January 2020. It can be accessed here: https://ec.europa.eu/transport/sites/transport/files/studies/isbn-978-92-76-14244-7-study-on-the-current-level-of-protection-of-air-passenger-rights-in-the-eu.pdf.

6 Proposal for a Regulation of the European Parliament and of the Council amending Regulations (EC) No 261/2004, (EC) No 1107/2006, (EU) No 1177/2010, (EU) No 181/2011 and (EU) 2021/782 as regards enforcement of passenger rights in the Union, COM/2023/753 final.

7 On the interpretation of the relevant Article 3(1)(a) of Regulation 261/2004, cf. CJEU, 10 July 2008, Case C-173/07, *Emirates/Schenkel*, ECLI:EU:C:2008:400; CJEU, 31 May 2018, Case C-537/17, *Wegener/Royal Air Maroc*, ECLI:EU:C:2018:361.

8 On the concretisation of this term in the case of the use of a subcontractor by hiring out an aircraft with crew ('wet lease') CJEU, 4 July 2018, Case C-532/17, *Wirth*, ECLI:EU:C:2018:527; see also BGH NJW 2018, 1251.

9 CJEU, 13 February 2020, Case C-606/19, *flightright*, ECLI:EU:C:2020:101, para. 34.

The formation and validity of the contract of carriage shall be governed by the law applicable to the contract (Article 5 Rome I Regulation).[10] Claims arising from the contract may be asserted in the special jurisdiction of the place of performance, even if no contract was concluded between the passenger and the operating air carrier and the flight performed by the air carrier was provided for in a package travel contract which also included accommodation and was concluded with a third party).[11]

## 3. ISSUES OF PERFORMANCE

**1062.** The relevant categories are denied boarding (Article 4 of Regulation 261/2004), cancellation (Article 5 of Regulation 261/2004) or delay of the flight (Article 6 of Regulation 261/2004).

### *a) Denied Boarding*

**1063.** Since flights are often deliberately overbooked in order to be able to cushion foreseeable cancellations at short notice, it can happen that not all passengers can be transported as booked. Article 4 of Regulation 261/2004 provides for a proportionate reaction of the carrier in this case: The air carrier must first try to persuade individual passengers to voluntarily give up their seat, combined with an offer for subsequent carriage, reimbursement of expenses and a monetary incentive; Article 8 of Regulation 261/2004 regulates this in more detail. If insufficient volunteers are found, individual passengers may be refused boarding; in this case, they are entitled to compensation according to Articles 7 to 9 of Regulation 261/2004.

### *b) Cancellation*

**1064.** If the entire flight is cancelled,[12] the mechanism of Article 5 of Regulation 261/2004 applies. The operating air carrier has to inform passengers about a possible alternative transport and additionally provide support services according to Article 7 of Regulation 261/2004, possibly also compensation and assistance services according to Articles 8 and 9 of Regulation 261/2004. The

---

10 More on this below at para. 1201.

11 CJEU, 26 March 2020, Case C-215/18, *Primera Air Scandinavia*, ECLI: ECLI:EU:C:2020:235, paras. 39 ff.; more on this case below at paras. 1432 ff.

12 Cancellation means non-operation of a planned flight for which at least one seat was reserved, Article 2(l) of Regulation 261/2004. This includes the case that the aircraft took off but subsequently had to return to the airport of departure, for whatever reason, and the passengers were rebooked on other flights, see CJEU, 13 October 2011, Case C-83/10, *Sousa*, ECLI:EU:C:2011:652, para. 35.

possibility of relief according to Article 5(3) of Regulation 261/2004 is of great practical importance: If the operating air carrier can prove that the cancellation is due to extraordinary circumstances which could not have been avoided even if all reasonable measures had been taken, the carrier is not obliged to pay compensation according to Article 7 of Regulation 261/2004.

**1065.** In principle, the concept of extraordinary circumstances covers all circumstances the air carrier cannot control, regardless of their nature and severity.[13] Recital 14 of Regulation 261/2004 provides further clarification. Such circumstances can be assumed, in particular, in the case of political instability, weather conditions incompatible with the operation of the flight in question, safety risks, unexpected flight safety defects and strikes affecting the operation of an operating air carrier. According to the case law of the CJEU, such circumstances must arise from an event which is not part of the normal activities of the air carrier concerned and which, by its nature or cause, is effectively beyond the carrier's control.[14]

**1066.** In this regard, extensive case law exists, for example, on the relevance of technical problems,[15] the effect of strikes,[16] the failure of computer systems in the check-in area,[17] the closure of airspace[18] or bird collisions.[19] It is also necessary to clarify which measures appear reasonable for the air carrier; the

---

13 CJEU, 31 January 2013, Case C-12/11, *McDonagh*, ECLI:EU:C:2013:43, para. 29.

14 See, for example, CJEU, 22 December 2008, Case C-549/07, *Wallentin-Herman*, ECLI:EU:C:2008:771, para. 23; CJEU, 19 November 2009, Joined Cases C-402/07, C-432/07, *Sturgeon and Böck*, ECLI:EU:C:2009:716, para. 70.

15 These can be included among the unexpected aviation safety deficiencies if they concern an occurrence which is not part of the normal exercise of the activity of the air carrier concerned and which, by its nature or cause, is effectively beyond its control, see CJEU, 22 December 2008, Case C-549/07, *Wallentin-Herman*, ECLI:EU:C:2008:771, paras. 23, 34; CJEU, 19 November 2009, Joined Cases C-402/07, C-432/07, *Sturgeon and Böck*, ECLI:EU:C:2009:716, para. 70; CJEU, 17 September 2015, Case C-257/14, *van der Lans*, ECLI:EU:C:2015:618, para. 36; CJEU, 4 April 2019, Case C-501/17, *Germanwings*, EU:C:2019:288, para. 20; CJEU 26 June 2019, Case C-159/18, *Moens*, EU:C:2019:535, para. 16; CJEU, 12 March 2020, Case C-832/18, *Finnair*, ECLI:EU:C:2020:204, para. 38.

16 The spontaneous absence of a significant part of the flight staff ('wildcat strike') does not fall within the notion of 'extraordinary circumstances' if it results from the surprise announcement of restructuring plans by an operating air carrier and follows a call not disseminated by the company's workers' representatives but spontaneously by the workers themselves who called in sick, cf. CJEU, 17 April 2018, Case C-195/17, *Krüsemann*, ECLI:EU:C:2018:258. Things are possibly different in the case of an external strike at the service provider of the handling systems, cf. BGH NJW 2014, 3304, paras. 10 ff. on the air traffic controllers' strike or BGH NJW 2019, 300, para. 10 on the strike of employees of control centres.

17 BGH NJW 2019, 1369, paras. 14 ff.

18 Thus after the eruption of the Icelandic volcano Eyjafjallajökull, see CJEU, 31 January 2013, Case C-12/11, *McDonagh*, ECLI:EU:C:2013:43, paras. 27 ff.

19 CJEU, 4 May 2017, Case C-315/15, *Pešková*, ECLI:EU:C:2017:342, paras. 24 f., considering as irrelevant whether this collision actually caused damage to the aircraft concerned.

circumstances of the individual case are always decisive in this regard.[20] In any case, it is not sufficient that an air carrier has carried out the legally prescribed minimum maintenance work on an aircraft.[21]

### c) Delay

**1067.** In practice, flight delays are arguably the most important issue. They seem almost unavoidable due to the density of today's air traffic. Article 6 of Regulation 261/2004 provides for some generalised rules, which, depending on the route to be flown, prescribe a temporal threshold, the exceeding of which gives rise to compensation claims according to Article 9 of Regulation 261/2004, and in the case of long delays of more than five hours, also to claims for assistance according to Article 8 of Regulation 261/2004.

**1068.** There is no definition of the term 'delay' in the regulation. According to the case law of the CJEU, a flight is delayed if the actual departure time is later than the scheduled departure time.[22] From a practical point of view, because of the often long taxiing times, it is important that the term 'arrival time', on which the extent of the delay incurred by passengers depends, stands for the time at which at least one of the aircraft doors is opened, provided that the passengers are allowed to leave the aircraft at that moment.[23]

**1069.** Even if the delay is significant, a delayed flight cannot be considered cancelled if it is operated in accordance with the air carrier's original flight schedule.[24] Since Article 6 of Regulation 261/2004 does not refer to Article 7 of Regulation 261/2004, which regulates compensation claims, the reverse conclusion could be that only assistance and support services are owed. However, the CJEU, referring to Recital 15 of Regulation 261/2004, where the concept of long delay is mentioned in the context of extraordinary circumstances, concluded that the legislator also linked it to the compensation claim.[25] Regarding its impact on the affected passengers, no distinction can be made

---

20 CJEU, 4 May 2017, Case C-315/15, *Pešková*, ECLI:EU:C:2017:342, para. 30. Note the comments at para. 38 ff. as to what precautionary measures the air carrier must take to avoid bird strike.

21 CJEU, 22 December 2008, Case C-549/07, *Wallentin-Herman*, ECLI:EU:C:2008:771, paras. 38 ff.

22 CJEU, 19 November 2009, Joined Cases C-402/07, C-432/07, *Sturgeon and Böck*, ECLI:EU:C:2009:716, para. 32.

23 CJEU, 4 September 2014, Case C-452/13, *Germanwings/Henning*, ECLI:EU:C:2014:2141, para. 25.

24 CJEU, 19 November 2009, Joined Cases C-402/07, C-432/07, *Sturgeon and Böck*, ECLI:EU:C:2009:716, para. 34.

25 CJEU, 19 November 2009, Joined Cases C-402/07, C-432/07, *Sturgeon and Böck*, ECLI:EU:C:2009:716, paras. 43, 62 ff.

in any case as to whether the loss of time incurred was due to cancellation or delay; any different treatment would, therefore, not be justifiable.[26] Due to the *effet utile* of the regulation, this means that passengers of delayed flights can be treated in the same way as passengers of cancelled flights concerning the application of the compensation claim. Thus, they can claim the compensation provided for in Article 7 of Regulation 261/2004; the restrictions of Article 5(3) of Regulation 261/2004 continue to apply.[27]

**1070.** If the destination is not reached on a direct route but only via connecting flights (Article 2(h) Regulation 261/2004), the obligation of the operating air carrier to compensate for a long delay does not require a departure delay of the magnitude provided for in Article 6 of Regulation 261/2004; rather, the sole criterion is whether the destination of the last flight was reached with a delay of three hours or more compared to the scheduled arrival time.[28]

## 4. LEGAL CONSEQUENCES

**1071.** The Air Passenger Rights Regulation essentially provides three different categories of legal consequences in the event of service disruptions: A claim for compensation under Article 7 of Regulation 261/2004, a claim for reimbursement or re-routing under Article 8 of Regulation 261/2004, and a claim for assistance under Article 9 of Regulation 261/2004. Claims for damages existing under national law, which give passengers further claims, remain unaffected in principle, Article 12 of Regulation 261/2004.

### *a) Compensatory Claims*

**1072.** According to Article 7 of Regulation 261/2004, passengers receive compensation payments under the conditions of Articles 4 to 6 of Regulation 261/2004 in the event of denied boarding and cancellation of the flight (and also in the event of long delays) according to a system of tiered lump-sums, the amount of which depends on the distance of the flight in question. The grounds of this assessment in the case of flight connections is only the distance between the place of the first

---

26 CJEU, 19 November 2009, Joined Cases C-402/07, C-432/07, *Sturgeon and Böck*, ECLI:EU:C:2009:716, paras. 55 ff.

27 CJEU, 19 November 2009, Joined Cases C-402/07, C-432/07, *Sturgeon and Böck*, ECLI:EU:C:2009:716, para. 69.

28 CJEU, 26 February 2013, Case C-11/11, *Folkerts*, ECLI:EU:C:2013:106, para. 35. This may also apply if, according to the underlying uniform booking, the final destination is to be reached from an airport in the territory of the EU with a direct connecting flight via a third country and the customer arrives there with a long delay as a result of a delay of the first flight, see BGH MDR 2019, 982.

departure and the final destination, which is to be determined according to the 'Great Circle' method, irrespective of the distance actually travelled.[29] If an operating air carrier transfers a passenger to a lower class than that for which the ticket was purchased, a claim for reimbursement also arises, which is, however, only granted on a pro rata basis and is again granted depending on the distance (Article 10(2) of Regulation 261/2004).[30] A passenger who has received a compensation payment due to the cancellation of a flight and accepted an alternative flight offer and now has another relevant delay on the latter flight is also entitled to compensation if the air carrier operating the alternative flight is the same as the one operating the cancelled flight.[31] No compensation payment is owed if the connecting flight reaches the final destination without a relevant delay, even if a rebooking was made for parts of the journey.[32]

### b) *Entitlement to Reimbursement or Re-Routing*

**1073.** In the event of denied boarding or cancellation, passengers are entitled to reimbursement or re-routing under Article 8 of Regulation 261/2004; passengers may choose between the modalities specified therein (reimbursement, possibly combined with a return flight, re-routing, as soon as possible or later). In the event of a delay of more than five hours, a right to reimbursement is also provided for (Article 6(1)(c)(iii), Article 8(1)(a) of Regulation 261/2004).

**1074.** Passengers whose flights are part of a package travel contract may also assert rights under Article 8(1)(a) of Regulation 261/2004. However, an exception applies concerning the right to reimbursement standardised therein insofar as this arises from Directive 90/314/EEC on Package Travel: According to Article 8(2) of Regulation 261/2004, the existence of a claim for reimbursement under Directive 90/314/EEC is sufficient to preclude a passenger whose flight is part of a package from claiming reimbursement of their ticket costs under the Air Passenger Rights Regulation from the operating air carrier.[33] Since the Air Passenger Rights Regulation does not contain any of the exceptions regulated in Article 8(2) concerning the compensation payments regulated in Article 6 and 7, these claims can also exist if the purchased flight is part of a package travel contract, without this having any effect on any claims resulting from Directive 90/314/EEC.[34]

---

29 CJEU, 7 September 2017, Case C-559/16, *Bossen*, ECLI:EU:C:2017:644, paras. 25 ff.

30 On the modalities in more detail CJEU, 22 June 2016, Case C-255/15, *Mennens*, ECLI:EU:C:2016:472.

31 CJEU, 12 March 2020, Case C-832/18, *Finnair*, ECLI:EU:C:2020:204, paras. 28 ff.

32 CJEU, 30 April 2020, Case C-191/19, *Air Nostrum*, ECLI:EU:C:2020:339, paras. 30 ff.

33 See CJEU, 10 July 2019, Case C-163/18, *Aegean Airlines*, ECLI:EU:C:2019:585, para. 31.

34 CJEU, 26 March 2020, Case C-215/18, *Primera Air Scandinavia*, ECLI: ECLI:EU:C:2020:235, paras. 34 ff.

### c) *Right to Care*

**1075.** In the event of denied boarding or cancellation as well as long flight delays, passengers have a right to care according to Article 9 of Regulation 261/2004. In detail, these are meals and refreshments (in a reasonable proportion to the waiting time), depending on the length of stay also hotel accommodation as well as transport services between the airport and the place of accommodation; in addition, 'passengers shall be offered free of charge two telephone calls, telex or fax messages, or e-mails' – an option that is unlikely to be of any significance today in times of ubiquitously available communication possibilities.

### d) *Further Damages*

**1076.** According to Article 12 of Regulation 261/2004, further claims for damages of the passenger remain unaffected. However, the compensation granted according to the Air Passenger Rights Regulation can be offset against such a claim for damages. Essentially, this concerns claims for damages existing under the respective applicable national law.[35] In this context, not only material but also immaterial damages are covered, as the Air Passenger Rights Regulation does not provide for a corresponding differentiation.[36] On the other hand, national law may not provide that passengers whose flight was delayed or cancelled are to be reimbursed for the costs they incurred due to the violation of the support and assistance obligations incumbent on that carrier under Articles 8 and 9 of Regulation 261/2004. This already follows from the wording of Article 12 of Regulation 261/2004, which only covers further-reaching claims for damages, meaning that the Air Passenger Rights Regulation conclusively regulates the categories mentioned.[37]

**1077.** However, the significance of these further claims for damages is reduced due to the deduction option under Article 12(1) of Regulation 261/2004.[38] Therefore, according to the Air Passenger Rights Regulation, compensation claims granted due to long delays are to be set off against claims for damages for breach of the contract of carriage due to the same long delay. In this regard, the

---

35 Under German law, these can follow from sec. 280(1) German Civil Code, cf. BGH NJW-RR 2010, 1641. The claim for repayment of part of the travel price due to a reduction on account of a long delay in the return flight pursuant to sec. 651d German Civil Code also falls under Article 12(1) of Regulation 261/2004, see BGH NJW 2015, 553, 554; on this, Kotzur/Krauß, *GPR* 2015, 72.

36 CJEU, 13 October 2011, Case C-83/10, *Sousa*, ECLI:EU:C:2011:652, paras. 36 ff. For the corresponding discussion on the Package Travel Directive, see paras. 1038 ff. above.

37 CJEU, 13 October 2011, Case C-83/10, *Sousa*, ECLI:EU:C:2011:652, paras. 42 f.

38 BGH NJW 2015, 553; BGH MDR 2019, 1437.

regulation runs parallel to the Package Travel Directive.[39] While Article 12(1) of Regulation 261/2004 allows the national court having jurisdiction to deduct the compensation granted under that regulation from further compensation, it does not require it to do so.[40]

#### e) *The Obligation to Inform Passengers of their Rights*

**1078.** Finally, Article 14 of Regulation 261/2004 regulates the obligation to inform passengers about their rights, which is probably known to every air passenger. An operating air carrier that has complied with its obligation to inform passengers under Article 14(2) of Regulation 261/2004 is, in principle, not liable on the basis of the applicable national law for the costs of the initial assertion of the claim by a lawyer instructed by the passenger. However, this might not be the case if the instructions given are incomplete, incomprehensible or otherwise so unclear that the passenger cannot be sure what they must do.[41]

## II. RAIL TRANSPORT

**1079.** A similar protection desideratum as in air travel also exists concerning rail passengers. In this respect, the Rail Passenger Rights Regulation applies.[42] In particular, this standardises liability for delays, missed connections and train cancellations.

---

[39] See Article 14(5) and Recital 36 of Directive (EU) 2015/2302; reference to this is made in BGH MDR 2019, 1437.

[40] See CJEU, 29 July 2019, Case C-354/18, *Rusu*, ECLI:EU:C:2019:637, para. 47.

[41] BGH NJW 2016, 2883.

[42] Regulation (EC) No 1371/2007 of the European Parliament and of the Council of 23 October 2007 on rail passengers' rights and obligations, OJ 2007 L 315/14.

# PART THREE
# CONFLICT OF LAWS ISSUES

References: S. Arnold (ed.), *Grundfragen des Europäischen Kollisionsrechts* (Tübingen: Mohr Siebeck, 2016); J.F. Baur/H.-P. Mansel (eds.), *Systemwechsel im Europäischen Kollisionsrecht* (Munich: C.H. Beck, 2002); S. Bruinier, *Der Einfluss der Grundfreiheiten auf das Internationale Privatrecht* (Frankfurt am Main: Lang, 2003); M. Fallon/P. Lagarde/S. Poillot-Peruzzetto, *Quelle architecture pour un code européen de droit international privé?* (Brussels: Lang, 2011); M.M. Fogt (ed.), *Private International Law in an Era of Change* (Cheltenham: Edward Elgar Publishing, 2024); K. Funken, *Das Anerkennungsprinzip im internationalen Privatrecht* (Tübingen: Mohr Siebeck, 2009); J. von Hein/G. Rühl (eds.), *Kohärenz im Internationalen Privat- und Verfahrensrecht der Europäischen Union* (Tübingen: Mohr Siebeck, 2016); K.F. Kreuzer, 'Zu Stand und Perspektiven des Europäischen Internationalen Privatrechts', *RabelsZ* 70 (2006), 1; K. Kroll-Ludwigs, *Die Rolle der Parteiautonomie im europäischen Kollisionsrecht* (Tübingen: Mohr Siebeck, 2013); S. Leible/H. Unberath (eds.), *Brauchen wir eine Rom 0-Verordnung?* (Jena: JWV, 2013); J. Leifeld, *Das Anerkennungsprinzip im Kollisionsrechtssystem des internationalen Privatrechts* (Tübingen: Mohr Siebeck, 2010); J.D. Lüttringhaus, 'Übergreifende Begrifflichkeiten im europäischen Zivilverfahrens- und Kollisionsrecht', *RabelsZ* 77 (2013), 31; H.-P. Mansel, 'Anerkennung als Grundprinzip des Europäischen Rechtsraums', *RabelsZ* 70 (2006), 651; T. Nehne, *Methodik und allgemeine Lehren des europäischen Internationalen Privatrechts* (Tübingen: Mohr Siebeck, 2012); S. Nietner, *Internationaler Entscheidungseinklang im europäischen Kollisionsrecht* (Tübingen: Mohr Siebeck, 2016); C.F. Nordmeier, 'Stand, Perspektiven und Grenzen der Rechtslagenanerkennung im europäischen Rechtsraum anhand Entscheidungen mitgliedstaatlicher Gerichte', *IPRax* 2012, 31; G. Rühl, 'Die rechtsaktübergreifende Auslegung im europäischen Internationalen Privatrecht: Art. 6 der Rom I-VO und die Rechtsprechung des EuGH zu Art. 15 Brüssel I-VO', *GPR* 2013, 122; R. Schaub, 'Grundlagen und Entwicklungen des europäischen Kollisionsrechts', *JZ* 2005, 328; K. Schilling, *Binnenmarktkollisionsrecht* (Berlin:De Gruyter, 2006); H.J. Sonnenberger, 'Randbemerkungen zum Allgemeinen Teil eines europäisierten IPR', in *Festschrift für Kropholler* (Tübingen: Mohr Siebeck, 2008), p. 227; H.J. Sonnenberger, 'Anerkennung statt Verweisung?', in *Festschrift für Spellenberg* (Munich: Sellier, 2010), p. 371; M. Stürner, 'Europäisierung des (Kollisions-)Rechts und nationaler ordre public', in *Festschrift für von Hoffmann* (Bielefeld: Gieseking, 2011), p. 463; D. Trüten, *Die Entwicklungen des Internationalen Privatrechts in der Europäischen Union. Auf dem Weg zu einem europäischen IPR-Gesetz* (Bern: Stämpfli, 2015); M.-P. Weller, 'Anknüpfungsprinzipien im Europäischen Kollisionsrecht: Abschied von der '"klassischen" IPR-Dogmatik?', *IPRax* 2011, 429; F.M .Wilke, *A Conceptual Analysis of European Private International*

*Law. The General Issues in the EU and its Member States* (Cambridge: Intersentia, 2019); M. Würdinger, 'Das Prinzip der Einheit der Schuldrechtsverordnungen im Europäischen Internationalen Privat- und Verfahrensrecht: eine methodologische Untersuchung über die praktische Konkordanz zwischen Brüssel I-VO, Rom I-VO und Rom II-VO', *RabelsZ* 75 (2011), 102; C.S. Rupp *e.a.* (eds.), *IPR zwischen Tradition und Innovation* (Tübingen: Mohr Siebeck, 2019).

# §29. THE ROLE OF PRIVATE INTERNATIONAL LAW

## CONTENTS



References: M. Stürner, 'Vom Nutzen des Internationalen Privatrechts in der juristischen Ausbildung', *JURA* 2018, 349.

## I. TASK AND FUNCTION OF PRIVATE INTERNATIONAL LAW

**1080.** Private international law (PIL) or conflict of laws determines which legal system is applicable in private law relationships with a cross-border element. This establishes the applicable law that is then responsible for the substantive assessment of the relevant legal questions. The application of the conflict-of-laws rules thus necessarily precedes any application of substantive laws. In this context, the term substantive law is used to distinguish those from conflict-of-laws rules. Contrary to what typical issues in legal education might suggest, in practice, it may well happen that a foreign legal system decides on the existence and scope of a claim. Thus, courts are confronted with the necessity to determine and apply the relevant norms of English, French, or German law, or, indeed, any other state's law.

**1081.** Two points follow from this: First, PIL rules are necessary if there are different states to which a legal relationship has a connection. Second, however, this only applies if and to the extent that these states have different private law systems. In other words: Within the scope of international uniform law, such as the UN Sales Convention, which currently applies to 97 states,[1] PIL provisions are superfluous and do not apply.[2] Conversely, this also means that states without a uniform private law system need internal conflict-of-laws rules for their part. In the US, for example, each state has its own private law. In the case of so-called interstate conflicts, interlocal conflict-of-laws rules must be referred to in order to decide which legal system is applicable.

## II. THE DISTINCT METHODOLOGY OF PRIVATE INTERNATIONAL LAW

References: R.J. Bader, *Koordinationsmethoden im Internationalen Privat- und Verfahrensrecht* (Tübingen: Mohr Siebeck, 2019); F. Berner, *Kollisionsrecht im Spannungsfeld von Kollisionsnormen, Hoheitsinteressen und wohlerworbenen Rechte* (Tübingen: Mohr Siebeck, 2017), pp. 131 ff.; G. Cuniberti, 'Should European Teachers Focus on European Private International Law?', in J. von Hein/E.-M. Kieninger/G. Rühl (eds.), *How European is European Private International Law? Sources, Court Practice, Academic Discourse* (Cambridge: Intersentia, 2019), p. 355; C. Harms, *Neuauflage der Datumtheorie im Internationalen Privatrecht* (Tübingen: Mohr Siebeck, 2019); T. Kadner Graziano, 'Private International Law in Legal Education in Europe and Selected Other Countries', in von J. Hein/E.-M. Kieninger/G. Rühl (eds.), *How European is European Private International Law? Sources, Court Practice, Academic Discourse* (Cambridge: Intersentia, 2019), p. 333; X. Kramer/L. Carballo Piñeiro (eds.), *Research Methods in Private International Law. A Handbook on Regulation, Research and Teaching* (Cheltenham: Edward Elgar Publishing, 2024); M. Lehmann, 'Auf der Suche nach dem Sitz des Rechtsverhältnisses: Savigny und die Rom I-Verordnung', in *Festschrift für Spellenberg* (Munich: Sellier, 2010), p. 245; H.P. Mansel, 'Privatrechtsdogmatik und Internationales Privatrecht', in *Festschrift für Canaris* (Berlin: De Gruyter, 2017), p. 739; C.F. Nordmeier, 'Stand, Perspektiven und Grenzen der Rechtslagenanerkennung im europäischen Rechtsraum anhand Entscheidungen mitgliedstaatlicher Gerichte', *IPRax* 2012, 31; K. Schurig, 'Das Fundament trägt noch', in H.J. Mansel (ed.), *Internationales Privatrecht im 20. Jahrhundert* (Tübingen: Mohr Siebeck, 2014), p. 5: A.S. Schwemmer, *Anknüpfungsprinzipien im europäischen Kollisionsrecht. Integrationspolitische Zielsetzungen und das Prinzip der engsten Verbindung* (Tübingen: Mohr Siebeck, 2018); H.J. Sonnenberger, 'Anerkennung statt Verweisung?', in *Festschrift für Spellenberg* (Munich: Sellier, 2010), p. 371; M.-P. Weller, 'Vom Staat zum Menschen: Die Methodentrias des Internationalen Privatrechts unserer Zeit', *RabelsZ* 81 (2017), 747; F.M. Wilke, *A Conceptual Analysis of European Private International Law. The General Issues in the EU and its Member States* (Cambridge: Intersentia, 2019).

1 See https://uncitral.un.org/en/texts/salegoods/conventions/sale_of_goods/cisg/status.

2 BGHZ 134, 201, 206 on the old law. As a result, this also applies to the relationship with the Rome I Regulation; cf. OLG Köln IHR 2018, 71, 74. See also paras. 1151 ff. below.

## 1. THE RELATIONSHIP BETWEEN PIL AND SUBSTANTIVE LAW

**1082.** Since PIL pursues fundamentally different goals as compared to substantive law, it has also developed its own methodology. This, in turn, results in legal techniques unknown to substantive law and also produces new terminology. While substantive rules basically serve to create, delimit or terminate rights and obligations in private legal transactions, PIL rules primarily resolve conflicts of applicability as between different legal systems by allocating the facts in question to one or more of these legal systems.

**1083.** Contrary to what the name might suggest, private international law is, at least originally, national law: Each legal system has its own conflict-of-laws rules. These can differ quite considerably from each other. This is particularly evident in the area of international procedural law: if, in a particular cross-border legal dispute, international jurisdiction exists for the courts of several states, the plaintiff can choose between these different jurisdictions: There is no superior authority in the inter-state sphere that could assign the dispute to a particular court. When deciding on a particular jurisdiction – this is referred to as a forum – it will certainly play a role to which substantive law the respective applicable PIL leads to and which consequences this might have for the outcome of the case.

**1084.** Choosing a forum in this sense is generally referred to as forum shopping. Various means are available to prevent it: in Anglo-American legal systems, the defendant may raise the objection of *forum non conveniens*, which is used to argue that another forum has far closer links to the subject matter of the dispute. The continental European tradition, on the other hand, tends to narrow the choice of the forum from the outset in order to reduce the options available. Within the EU, the Brussels Ibis Regulation establishes a uniform system of jurisdiction for all Member States.[3] One of the objectives of this regulation is to prevent forum shopping, even if this is not entirely successful.

## 2. SPECIAL FEATURES OF THE PIL METHODOLOGY

### *a) Savigny and the Principle of the Closest Connection*

**1085.** Given the different tasks of conflict of laws and substantive law, it is not surprising that PIL has developed its own methodology and terminology. Many terms and doctrinal concepts were developed in the 19th century. The works of Friedrich Carl von Savigny (1779–1861) proved to be particularly influential. In

[3] More on this below paras. 1413 ff.

Volume VIII of the monumental work *System des heutigen Römischen Rechts*, published in 1849, he laid the foundation for modern conflict of laws. In this work, Savigny turned away from the hitherto prevailing law-based approach (so-called statute theory), which focused on the domestic law's intent to apply to cross-border situations.[4] Instead, he considered the respective legal relationship to be the central point of reference in conflict of laws. Accordingly, the object of conflict-of-laws analysis was not a law (statute) but a legal relationship, for example, a contract, a marriage relationship or a will. This development was rightly described as the 'Copernican turn' in the conflict of laws (Paul Heinrich Neuhaus).[5]

**1086.** According to Savigny, the task of conflict of laws should be 'to select for each legal relationship that area of law to which this legal relationship belongs or is subject according to its peculiar nature (in which it has its seat)'.[6] This leads to the fact that 'the judge must apply the local law to which the legal relationship in dispute belongs, irrespective of whether this local law is the judge's domestic law or the law of a foreign state'.[7] This is based on the postulate of the equivalence of all legal systems: For Savigny, the legal relationship's seat is determined objectively-territorially and initially without regard to the outcome. The guiding principle for this spatial allocation is to be the principle of the closest connection, not a substantive criterion of any kind. This fact-oriented approach is intended to guarantee that 'in cases of a conflict of laws, the legal relationships can expect the same assessment, without distinction as to whether the judgment is pronounced in this or that state'.[8]

**1087.** This concept is based on the ideal of international unity of decision-making: Everywhere, a legal case ought to be decided in the same way, irrespective of the court or state in which the dispute arises. Even if this often remains a mere theoretical postulate, especially since PIL today is much less 'neutral' than it might have been in the past,[9] it is emblematic of the discipline's universality.

---

4 This is not to conceal the fact that criticism of the statute doctrine had already been voiced before. In this context, von Wächter, *AcP* 24 (1841), 230 and AcP 25 (1842), 1, 161 and 361 should be mentioned in particular.

5 Neuhaus, *RabelsZ* 15 (1949/50), 364, 366.

6 System des heutigen römischen Rechts, Vol. VIII, 1849, pp. 108, 118.

7 System des heutigen römischen Rechts, Vol. VIII, 1849, p. 32.

8 System des heutigen römischen Rechts, Vol. VIII, 1849, p. 27, also p. 129 (emphasis in original).

9 On Savigny's legacy in the Rome I Regulation Lehmann, in *Festschrift für Spellenberg*, 2010, p. 245.

**1088.** In fact, the academic discipline of conflict of laws – quite in line with the subject matter – has developed a far more transnational thinking than private law in particular, where the major codifications had an inhibiting effect to a certain extent, as they directed the doctrinal perspective 'inwards'. In PIL, there were only rudimentary black letter rules in many systems until well into the second half of the 20th century. Throughout Europe, French doctrine was influential for a long time, which is why concepts and legal figures such as *renvoi* (referral and re-referral), *dépeçage* (different connection of related factual questions, for example, through a partial choice of law), *ordre public* (public policy) or others, which give the subject its exotic appearance, have survived until today. In terms of their content, these terms and others reflect the special features of PIL: The coexistence of two or more legal systems (the 'conflict') entails the use of special legal instruments that the substantive law does not need.

**1089.** If a fictitious legislator were entrusted with the task of regulating such 'conflicts', a system would at least theoretically be conceivable that would manage to get by with a single collision rule formulated in the manner of a general clause: The legal relationship is to be subordinated to the legal system with which – in Savigny's sense – it has the closest spatial connection. However, further individual taxonomy of individual cases would lead to considerable legal uncertainty. Thus, it is not surprising that the concept of the closest connection in force today has experienced a great degree of differentiation in legislation and jurisprudence and was concretised for individual legal relationships. The conflict-of-laws rules contained in the EU regulations on PIL[10] distinguish between main categories, such as contracts, non-contractual obligatory relationships, property law legal relationships, etc., and subcategories, such as contracts of carriage, consumer contracts and insurance contracts; for each category, different criteria for the so-called 'connection' are decisive. The connection is understood to be the link between the connecting factor as standardised in an abstract-general conflicts rule (such as the domicile or habitual residence of a person or the location of a thing) with a specific applicable legal system (such as the law of the seller's domicile).

**1090.** In addition, there are ancillary conflicts rules and principles which regulate issues arising for all forms of connection, such as the scope of the reference to a foreign system,[11] the subordinate connection in the case of reference in states without a uniform legal system[12] or the so-called public policy

---

10 On the Europeanization of conflict of laws Stürner, in Langenbucher, *Europäisches Privat- und Wirtschaftsrecht*, §8.
11 See paras. 1236 ff. below.
12 See paras. 1262 ff. below.

exception.[13] A factual situation with a foreign connection must now be located in this web of rules; this process is called qualification (or characterisation).[14] Due to this analytical approach,[15] a single set of facts may be subject to different conflict-of-laws rules, and even different substantive laws might need to be applied to partial aspects of the case. In extreme cases, this can lead to contradictions because the legal systems called upon to apply are not coordinated in terms of their content. Because such a legal situation cannot be tolerated, PIL provides various instruments that can be used to bring about a synthesis, such as adaptation, transposition or substitution.[16]

### b) *Referral, Recognition and the Relevance of Local Data*

**1091.** Even today, the rules of PIL aim to determine the applicable substantive law in an abstract-general manner for those subject matters falling under their scope of application to which the respective case has the closest connection.[17] This is done primarily through a reference to a particular legal order: The pertinent conflict-of-laws rule determines the relevant (partial) legal system which then determines the merit of the claims and defences. A somewhat opposing model seems to be that of recognition, according to which the 'legal situations' existing under foreign law are accepted ('recognised') as such, i.e. without substantive application of the *lex causae* (the law applicable to the concrete legal question). Furthermore, the possibility of 'taking into account' foreign norms or circumstances ('local data') is found in various conflict-of-laws rules. This has been dubbed the 'methodological triad of PIL',[18] even if this may be an overemphasis of the differences: The reference method remains the principal method; recognition and the process o taking into account local data merely accompany it.

#### aa) Referral to a (Substantive) Legal System

**1092.** The conflict-of-laws rules are usually designed as references;[19] they use certain systematic concepts, the so-called connecting factors, which determine in an abstract-general manner for specific areas of private law which substantive rules are to be applied. For example, in the case of a cross-border sales contract,

---

13 See paras. 1283 ff. below.

14 See paras. 1102 ff. below.

15 The term was coined by Goldschmidt, in *Festschrift für M. Wolff*, 1952, pp. 203, 208 ff.

16 On these terms von Hein, in *Münchener Kommentar zum BGB*, 9th ed. (Munich: C.H. Beck, 2024), Einl. IPR paras. 247 ff.

17 On the principle of the closest connection, see below para. 1114.

18 Weller, *RabelsZ* 81 (2017), 747.

19 On the principle of closest connection in European PIL Weller, *IPRax* 2011, 429; *id.*, in Arnold, *Grundfragen des Europäischen Kollisionsrechts*, 2016, p. 133.

the law of the country in which the seller has his habitual residence is generally applicable, unless the parties agree otherwise, Article 4(1)(a) Rome I Regulation. Accordingly, where the contractual performance was or would have been performed is irrelevant. In contrast, the applicable law is determined differently in tort law: in the case of a cross-border tort, according to Article 4(1) Rome II Regulation, the law of the place where the damage occurred, which is to be understood as the place of the legal infringement, is decisive.

bb) Recognition (Of Legal Situations)

**1093.** In addition to such referral rules, PIL also knows rules that result in the recognition of legal situations.[20] These must not be confused with recognition in the procedural sense, as set out in Article 36(1) Brussels I-bis Regulation: in the case of the latter, the effects of a judgment rendered in one Member State, are extended to the state of recognition.[21]

**1094.** An example of a 'recognition of a legal situation' can be found in property law where in most systems the *lex rei sitae* principle applies, according to which property rights that have been validly established under foreign law are, in principle, accepted, where chattel has been transferred from one state to the other.[22] The new rules do not interfere with the pre-existing legal situation (unless public policy concerns are raised), so that, for example, the acquisition of a right in rem affirmed by the law of the state of origin is always accepted by the new statute if the legal transaction in question was already completed validly under the previous law.

**1095.** Similarly, based on the CJEU's case law,[23] there is also a 'recognition principle' in cross-border transfer of seat of companies.[24] However, this only means that the legal personality founded under foreign law abroad and the ensuing legal capacity are respected when operating (from abroad) in the country to which the company is being transferred. In fact, the need for a recognition of European companies, which results from the freedom of establishment (Articles 49 and 54 TFEU), has lead to the replacement of the

---

20 Cf. Mansel, RabelsZ 70 (2006), 651; Coester-Waltjen, IPRax 2006, 392; Funken, *Das Anerkennungsprinzip im internationalen Privatrecht*, 2009; Leifeld, *Das Anerkennungsprinzip im Kollisionsrechtssystem des internationalen Privatrechts*, 2010; Sonnenberger, in *Festschrift für Spellenberg*, 2010, p. 371; Nordmeier, *IPRax* 2012, 31.

21 On this already above paras. 1425 ff.

22 Mansel, in Staudinger, *BGB Kommentar* (2015), Art. 43 EGBGB para. 1264 ('*Hinnahmetheorie*').

23 The leading case is CJEU, 9 March 1999, Case C-212/97, *Centros*, ECLI:EU:C:1999:126; cf. Stürner, in Erman, *BGB Kommentar*, 17th ed. 2023, Annex Art. 12 EGBGB paras. 6 ff.

24 More a detailed discussion, cf. Kindler, in *Münchener Kommentar zum BGB*, 9th ed. 2025, Internationales Wirtschaftsrecht Teil 8, paras. 317 ff.

seat principle by the incorporation principle, which prescribes the application of the state where the corporation was first incorporated, and thus does not lead to a change of the applicable law even in the case of a cross-border transfer of the administrative seat of the corporation. This also reveals a fundamental connection: Under conflict of laws, the incorporation principle refers to the law of the company's incorporating state. Thus, the recognition principle becomes practical on a meta-level: It influences the reference but does not function as a conflict-of-laws principle itself.

cc) Taking into Account Local Data

**1096.** In addition, some PIL rules call for the taking into account of local data. Thus, Article 17 Rome II Regulation requires 'as a matter of fact and in so far as is appropriate' the taking into account of rules of safety and conduct in force at the place and time of the event giving rise to liability when the conduct of a person giving rise to liability is assessed. In the field of contract law, Article 9(3) Rome I Regulation allows foreign overriding mandatory provisions to be 'taken into account'.[25] By the same token, Article 12(2) Rome I Regulation concedes, in the interest of the compatibility of the contract statute as a comprehensive (Article 12(1) Rome I Regulation) *lex causae*, that the legal situation at the place of performance cannot be ignored and, therefore, shall be had regard to.[26]

**1097.** This goes back to the so-called local data approach, which was originally developed by Ehrenzweig[27] and which has recently been the subject of renewed academic interest.[28] Note that Ehrenzweig initially pursued a purely descriptive approach concerning US conflict of laws: he aimed to show the extent to which courts resort to legal rules that do not belong to the substantive law referred to by the pertinent PIL rule, but continue to have real significance for the case (the 'local data') and must, therefore, be taken into account similarly to facts. Hence, there was no normative concern behind this.[29] In essence, the local data approach has a more factual nature; it always presupposes a 'regular' conflict-of-laws reference within the framework of which local data may be included in a corrective or supplementary manner.[30]

---

25 See paras. 1274 ff.

26 See para. 1237 below.

27 E. Jayme, in *Gedächtnisschrift für Ehrenzweig* (Karlsruhe: C.F. Müller, 1976), p. 37.

28 M. Weller, in M. *Gebauer/H.-P. Mansel/G. Schulze* (eds.), *Die Person im IPR* (Tübingen: Mohr Siebeck, 2019), p. 53; Harms, *Neuauflage der Datumtheorie im Internationalen Privatrecht*, 2019.

29 Cf. M. Reimann, in *Der Einfluß deutscher Emigranten auf die Rechtsentwicklung in den USA und in Deutschland* (Tübingen: Mohr Siebeck, 1993), pp. 397, 414 f.

30 See for example on Article 9(3) Rome I Regulation below paras. 1274 ff.

### c) *Adjustment*

References: S.L. Gössl, 'Anpassung im EU-Kollisionsrecht', *RabelsZ* 82 (2018), 619.

**1098.** Due to the analytical method of PIL, references may, due to the design of different connecting factors, lead to the application of different legal systems to one set of facts. In individual cases, this may lead to results that do not harmonise with each other or even lead to some kind of deprivation of rights. On the one hand, such disharmony occurs because of a lack of rules: In this case, the relevant provisions of all legal systems in question are inapplicable; this would lead to a result that is not desired by any of the legal systems involved. On the other hand, an unwanted cumulation of rules is conceivable: The applicable substantive provisions contradict each other, meaning that the result is incompatible with either of the two legal systems.

**1099.** In such cases, the contradiction must be resolved either by substantive law (by adaptation of the substantive rules or by modification or creation of ad-hoc legal solutions) or by conflict-of-laws methods (harmonisation by restriction or extension of the reference's scope).[31] The conflict-of-laws approach is generally preferable, as it is normally less intrusive; however, the decision can only be made in light of the specific case.

**1100.** European PIL does not contain any explicit rules on adjustment. However, there are indications that a 'legal transport' of a certain rule into a new legal environment may make modifications to the content necessary. This applies, in particular, to cross-border enforcement: In this respect, Article 54 Brussels I-bis Regulation regulates the case where a judgment contains a measure or order that is not known in state where enforcement is sought. Since the free movement of judgments requires enforcement for such verdicts as well, the respective measure or order must be adapted as far as possible to a measure or order that is known in the law of the respective Member State and which is associated with comparable effects and pursues similar aims and interests; however, this must not lead to any effects that go beyond those provided for in the law of the Member State where the verdict originated.

**1101.** From this, one can at least deduce for conflict of laws that an adjustment in the described sense is not generally excluded. Again, such an adaptation is generally preferable.[32] General solutions do not exist; however, the adaptation must not affect the *effet utile* of the relevant regulations.

---

[31] Cf. in general Kropholler, in *Festschrift für Ferid* (Munich: Beck, 1978), p. 279.

[32] For more details cf. Gössl, *RabelsZ* 82 (2018), 619, 626 ff.

## III. THE LEGISLATIVE TECHNIQUE OF PIL: CLASSIFICATION

**1102.** In general, each substantive rule might be accompanied by a conflict-of-laws rule in order to clarify its applicability in cross-border situations. However, this would hardly make sense, as it would result in a very confusing legal situation. The PIL, therefore, pursues efficiency by subjecting entire groups of legal relationships to a uniform connection. For example, the Rome I Regulation – including technical provisions on its entry into force, etc. – contains just 29 articles but covers the entire law of contractual obligations.

**1103.** However, since every legal relationship is to be covered by the connecting factor of a certain conflict-of-laws rule – for example, as a matter of contract or tort law – an allocation must be made in each case: This means that a decision must be made as to how a certain legal term is to be classified, i.e., whether it fits under into a given rule. This classification process, therefore, decides which conflict-of-laws rule applies. The conflict-of-laws rules must be interpreted for this purpose. Since they are to be applied in light of a certain substantive law, it is primarily the latter to determine the scope of the respective conflict-of-laws provision. In this context, one can speak of classification according to the *lex fori* (the law of the court's state).

**1104.** However, one must not stop here: As a hinge between the domestic and the immense variety of legal systems existing worldwide, conflict-of-laws rules must also be flexible enough to be able to classify foreign legal institutions unknown to the domestic system. The classification of such legal institutions is done from a functional perspective so that the legal system in question can provide the necessary context of such legal institution of the foreign law. Their substantive content must be assessed to establish the relationship to functionally corresponding provisions of domestic substantive law to be able to classify within the conflict of laws.[33] If the scope of a particular conflict-of-laws rule is clear, the legal question arising from the facts of the case can be subsumed under it.[34]

---

33 The leading case is BGHZ 29, 137, 139: 'The task incumbent on the German judge in this respect is to grasp the provisions of the foreign law, in particular if it contains a legal figure unknown to German law, according to their meaning and purpose, to assess their meaning from the point of view of the foreign law and to compare them with institutions of the German legal order. On the basis thus obtained, it is to be assigned to the features of the German conflict-of-laws rules [...] built up from the concepts and delimitations of the German legal system.'

34 On the qualification in more detail Stürner, in Erman, *BGB Kommentar*, 17th ed. 2023, Einl. Art. 3 EGBGB paras. 58 ff.

**1105.** In principle, this approach also works for EU conflict of laws and, in particular, to contract law issues as covered by the Rome I Regulation. However, since the latter takes precedence over national PIL, its applicability must first be determined. Here, too, classification is required: The various regulations contain a multitude of connecting factors. The interpretation of uniform conflict-of-laws rules is not carried out according to the standard of the *lex fori* but uniformly according to the meaning and purpose of the regulations, considering their international character. In this respect, classification is, therefore, autonomous, i.e. detached from a specific national legal system. Note that this process is at the outset identical to the interpretation of other EU secondary law.[35]

[35] Cf. paras. 326 ff. above.

# §30. CONFLICT OF LAWS IN THE FIELD OF CONTRACT LAW: GENERAL PRINCIPLES

CONTENTS



References: S. Arnold, 'Gründe und Grenzen der Parteiautonomie im Europäischen Kollisionsrecht', in S. Arnold (ed.), *Grundfragen des Europäischen Kollisionsrechts* (Tübingen: Mohr Siebeck, 2016), p. 23; J. Basedow, 'Theorie der Rechtswahl oder Parteiautonomie als Grundlage des Internationalen Privatrechts', *RabelsZ* 75 (2011), 32; K. Kroll-Ludwigs, *Die Rolle der Parteiautonomie im europäischen Kollisionsrecht* (Tübingen: Mohr Siebeck, 2013); P. Lagarde, 'Le principe de proximité dans le droit international privé contemporain, Recueil des Cours', in Recueil des Cours, Vol. 196 (Leiden: Martinus Nijhoff, 1986), p. 9; H.P. Mansel, 'Parteiautonomie, Rechtsgeschäftslehre der Rechtswahl und Allgemeiner Teil des europäischen Kollisionsrechts', in S. Leible/ H. Unberath (eds.), *Brauchen wir eine Rom 0-Verordnung?* (Jena: JWV, 2013), p. 243; H.P. Mansel, 'Privatrechtsdogmatik und Internationales Privatrecht', in *Festschrift für Canaris II* (Munich: Beck, 2017), p. 739; A. Mills, *Party Autonomy in Private International Law* (Cambridge: Cambridge University Press, 2018); G. Rühl, *Statut und Effizienz* (Tübingen: Mohr Siebeck, 2011); H.M. Watt, 'A Private International Law Perspective on the Creation of Norms and Transnational Governance', in S. Grundmann/M. Grochowski (eds.), *European Contract Law and the Creation of Norms* (Cambridge: Intersentia, 2021), p. 149.

## I. PARTY AUTONOMY AND ITS LIMITS

### 1. CHOICE OF LAW

**1106.** The question of whether party autonomy represents a fundamental connecting principle within the conflict of laws has been debated since the beginning of modern PIL. The general freedom to act (enshrined e.g. in Article 2(1) German Basic Law), and likewise in internal market cases the fundamental freedoms of the TFEU, also encompass conflict of laws-related party autonomy. The fact that this goes further than the freedom to contract because it opens up the possibility for the parties to change the entire legal system, including its mandatory rules, and not only to waive the dispositive provisions, does not lead to a different conclusion.[1]

**1107.** Besides, some scholars refer to the parties' common intention as a justification,[2] while others see it as the most efficient connecting factor[3] or simply the 'reality of the interests at play'.[4] The opposite stance is taken by those authors who see freedom of a choice of law as a mere 'secondary solution': for them, party autonomy can only come into play if no clear objective connecting factor is provided for.[5] Today, this can probably be considered outdated; in view of an ever stronger focus on the individual in many areas of the law, party autonomy in conflict of laws can be considered a 'tool for a self-assignment of the individual to a legal order'.[6] Whether this may even be rooted in natural law principles,[7] however, does not seem compelling. This discussion cannot be traced any further here. In any case, it should be noted that the freedom of choice of law has come to play a vital role in EU conflict of laws and virtually dominates international contract law.[8]

**1108.** A compilation of choice of law-related best practices can be found in the Hague Principles on Choice of Law in International Commercial Contracts (2015). This soft law instrument is, first of all, addressed towards states and, in this respect, has the character of a model code (despite the statement to the contrary in Introduction I.8, I.5 and I.9 as well as Preamble no. 2). At the same time, it is also addressed to private parties who, by referring to the Principles, are allowed to make them the basis of their choice of law agreement, provided that the respective *lex fori* permits this.[9]

---

1 Kroll-Ludwigs, *Die Rolle der Parteiautonomie im europäischen Kollisionsrecht*, 2013, pp. 223 f.

2 Leible, in *Festschrift für Jayme*, Vol. I, (Munich: Sellier, 2004), 2004, p. 485; Basedow, *RabelsZ* 75 (2011), 32, 50 ff.

3 Rühl, *Statut und Effizienz*, 2011, p. 347 ff.; from the perspective of the internal market also Weller, *IPRax* 2011, 429, 433.

4 A. Flessner, *Interessenjurisprudenz im internationalen Privatrecht* (Tübingen: Mohr Siebeck, 1990), pp. 98 ff.

5 G. Kegel/K. Schurig, *Internationales Privatrecht*, 9th ed. (Munich: Beck, 2004), §18 I 1 c (p. 653) for the law of obligations.

6 In that sense Mansel, in Leible/Unberath (eds.), *Brauchen wir eine Rom 0-Verordnung?*, 2013, pp. 241, 262; cf. Looschelders, in Staudinger, *BGB Kommentar* (2024), Einl. IPR para. 159.

7 In that sense Basedow, *RabelsZ* 75 (2011), 32, 50 ff., 57 (the legal-theoretical justification of party autonomy in international treaty law lies 'in a pre-state subjective right of the individual to subject himself to a certain positive legal order by private expression of will').

8 See paras. 1156 ff. below.

9 Martiny, *RabelsZ* 79 (2015), 624, 632; Basedow, in *Festschrift für Schnyder* (Zürich: Schulthess Verlag, 2018), p. 3; Rühl, in *Festschrift für Kronke* (Bielefeld: Gieseking, 2020), p. 485.

## 2. INDIRECT PARTY AUTONOMY

**1109.** The increase in the number of connecting factors in EU conflict-of-laws rules that give the parties a 'de facto choice of law' (such as the increased use of the habitual residence as a connecting factor, for example, in family and succession law, or in the law of persons), has been pointed out on various occasions. This is referred to as 'indirect party autonomy'.[10] This intends to express that such connecting factors are relatively easy to influence, so certain parallels arise with the choice of law. However, both categories should be kept neatly apart. Ultimately, almost every connecting factor can be influenced without bringing about a change of the legal system that is comparable to a choice of law. A prime example is the alternative application of local laws regarding the formal validity of legal transactions (Article 11(1) Rome I Regulation).[11] In this respect, calls for limiting the 'abusive' exercise of such 'indirect party autonomy'[12] must be met with caution. If the legislator chooses to insert such connecting factors in conflict-of-laws rules, this is generally acceptable: The use of an existing leeway within PIL norms is, as such, legitimate and, therefore, does not violate public policy.[13] The latter is not already affected in cases where the habitual residence was merely fabricated.[14] Things can be seen differently in the case of a true evasion of the law.[15] Here, general restrictions apply, so that, in the end, there is no difference compared to choice of law cases.[16]

## 3. OVERRIDING MANDATORY PROVISIONS

**1110.** The freedom to choose the applicable law under Article 3(1) Rome I Regulation extends, in principle, to all legal systems of states; the rule does not prescribe any specific proximity to the chosen legal system.[17] However, it does not follow from this that the chosen law cannot be escaped without any restriction. Generally, the so-called overriding mandatory provisions of a legal

10 In that sense Coester-Waltjen, *JZ* 2017, 1073, 1074 f., who sees indirect party autonomy and choice of law as being equal.

11 Cf. below at paras. 1244 ff.

12 Cf. Grünberger, *IPRax* 2017, 147.

13 Cf. also Weller/Benz/Thomale, *ZEuP* 2017, 250, 269 ff. On the public policy exception cf. below at paras. 1283 ff.

14 On the so-called insolvency tourism Stürner, *KTS* 2017, 291, 293 ff.

15 See G. Kegel/K. Schurig, *Internationales Privatrecht*, 9th ed. (Munich: Beck, 2004), §14 VII 1 (pp. 491 f.).

16 Further examples are given in Weller/Benz/Thomale, *ZEuP* 2017, 250, 272 ff.

17 This is different, for example, in international family or inheritance law: in these fields of law, only the choice of certain legal systems is permitted, such as the law of the habitual residence of the spouses (Article 22(1)(b) European Matrimonial Property Regime Regulation) or of the testator (Article 22(1) European Succession Regulation).

system (*lois de police*, *Eingriffsnormen*) prevail over the law designated by the parties' choice of law.[18]

**1111.** According to the definition provided in Article 9(1) Rome I Regulation, overriding mandatory provisions are 'provisions the respect for which is regarded as crucial by a country for safeguarding its public interests, such as its political, social or economic organisation, to such an extent that they are applicable to any situation falling within their scope, irrespective of the law otherwise applicable to the contract under this Regulation'.[19] These provisions of the *lex fori* are governed by a special conflict-of-laws rule; in this way, certain areas which are perceived by the respective national legal system as being particularly important for the protection of its public interests are excluded from the codified system of conflict-of-laws rules. Hence, overriding mandatory provisions already serve as an exception to the conflict-of-laws provisions, which do not apply from the outset. With the recognition of overriding mandatory rules, certain groups of cases were decoupled from the system of conflict-of-laws rules and, as it were, made independent under private international law.

**1112.** The increased reference to the *lex fori* enhances the value of a state's own law vis-à-vis foreign law. The axiomatic presumption of the equivalence of all legal systems, which is the basis of classical PIL, is thus abandoned to a certain extent. The same applies to the increasing recourse to unilateral conflict-of-laws rules, i.e. conflict-of-laws rules that primarily refer to the *lex fori*.[20]

## II. THE PRINCIPLE OF THE CLOSEST CONNECTION

References: S. Reuter, 'Das Rechtsverhältnis im Internationalen Privatrecht bei Savigny', *RabelsZ* 81 (2017), 661.

**1113.** As explained above, the system of conflict-of-laws rules classically follows the criterion of proximity. The statutes in the field of PIL aim to determine in an abstract-general manner for the facts falling within their scope of application that substantive law (or those substantive laws) to which such facts have the closest connection.[21] It is, therefore, a matter of a spatial allocation of a set of facts or the legal question connected with it to a legal system. The principle of

---

18 For further limits to the choice of law, see para. 1164 below.

19 The other EU PIL regulations (mostly) contain similar rules on overriding mandatory rules, cf. e.g. Article 16 Rome II Regulation.

20 For example, Stürner, in *Festschrift für Kronke*, 2020, p. 545.

21 Cf. B. von Hoffmann/K. Thorn, Internationales *Privatrecht*, 9th ed. (Munich: C.H. Beck, 2007), §1 paras. 3 ff.

the closest connection postulated by Savigny functions as a *leitmotif* here. The European regulations on conflict of laws take as their starting point – in the spirit of Savigny – a division of legal relationships into groups or classes. For each of those, the appropriate connecting factors are determined according to the principle of the closest connection. This explains, for example, the reference to the law of the place of location for contracts that have as their object a right in rem in immovable property (Article 4(1)(c) Rome I Regulation). Without such further specification, the criterion of the closest connection is reflected in exception clauses, such as Articles 4(3), 5(3), and 8(4) Rome I Regulation or Article 4(3) Rome II Regulation. The catch-all clauses, which aim to encompass legal relationships for which more typical conflict-of-laws rules do not fit, are also regularly based on the principle of the closest connection (e.g. Article 4(4) Rome I Regulation).[22]

## III. POLITICISED OR NEUTRAL-TECHNICAL PIL?

References: V. van den Eeckhout, 'The instrumentalisation of private international law; quo vadis? Rethinking the neutrality of private international law in an era of globalisation and Europeanisation of private international law', in J.-S. Bergé/S. Francq/M. Gardenes Santiago (eds.), *Boundaries of European private international law/Les frontières de droit international privé européen/Las fronteras del derecho internacional privado europea* (Brussels: Bruylant, 2015), p. 387; X. Kramer/L. Carballo Piñeiro (eds.), *Research Methods in Private International Law. A Handbook on Regulation, Research and Teaching* (Cheltenham: Edward Elgar Publishing, 2024); S.L. Gössl *e.a.* (eds.), *Politik und Internationales Privatrecht* (Tübingen: Mohr Siebeck, 2017); P. Mankowski, Interessenpolitik und europäisches Kollisionsrecht (Baden-Baden: Nomos, 2011); H. Muir Watt/D.P. Fernández Arroyo (eds.), *Private International Law and Global Governance* (Cheltenham: Edward Elgar Publishing, 2015); M. Stürner, 'Politische Interessen und Internationales Privatrecht', in *Festschrift für Kronke* (Bielefeld: Gieseking, 2020), p. 545.

**1114.** Recently, some developments can be observed that can be described as a certain politicisation of private international law.[23] The more technical

22 See para. 1178 below. Especially in the area of family law, there are catch-all clauses that refer to the lex fori, e.g. for the divorce statute in Article 8(d) Rome III Regulation or the law applicable to maintenance obligations in Article 15 European Maintenance Regulation in conjunction with Article 4(2) of the Hague Protocol of 23 November 2007 on the Law Applicable to Maintenance Obligations.

23 For example, Mankowski, *Interessenpolitik und europäisches Kollisionsrecht*, 2011; Muir Watt/Fernández Arroyo (eds.), *Private International Law and Global Governance*, 2015; Gössl e.a. (eds.), *Politik und Internationales Privatrecht*, 2017. Cf. also the contibutions by Whytock, Kinsch and Ruiz Abou-Nigm/Michaels, in Kramer/Carballo Piñeiro (eds.), *Research Methods in Private International Law. A Handbook on Regulation, Research and Teaching*, 2024.

description of PIL rules as the realisation of a 'closest connection' of a spatial-horizontal nature may, however, obscure that tangible legal-political interests lie behind numerous conflict-of-laws rules. The postulates of neutrality and result-blindness of PIL can be upheld especially when the choice of the connecting factor already ensures that the applicable substantive law system leads to an acceptable result. Thus, the Rome I and II Regulations (which apply to contractual and non-contractual relationships), in particular, were 'objects of hard-hitting legal policies'.[24] The central question of the proper seat of the legal relationship can be answered in very different ways depending on the interests involved. Hence, the answer to the question, to which legal system there is the closest connection lies in the eye of the beholder. Because of the considerable differences in the respective substantive laws, even within the EU, the conflict-of-laws rules are of decisive importance. It is thus obvious that policy must already start at the level of PIL. The fact that certain lobby groups have discovered conflict of laws as a field of legal policy may be due to the increasing internationalisation of trade or simply to the fact that many areas of conflict of laws were mere case law not so long ago and thus were less prone to lobbying activities than today.

**1115.** The global enforcement of human rights due diligence has become particularly important today. Beyond the WTO rules, global trade in goods and services is comparatively weakly regulated. As a general rule, local rules apply, for example, concerning labour protection, safety and wages. Globally active entrepreneurs exploit the resulting legal discrepancies by relocating their production. If accidents occur at the production site, EU conflict of laws regularly refers to the liability standard operating at the place of the offence (*lex loci delicti commissi*, Article 4(1) Rome II Regulation).[25] In this sense, a factual determination of the applicable law can ultimately result in misconduct remaining without sanction. In this context, PIL is sometimes accused of wrongly insisting on its traditional neutrality; instead, the argument goes, it must actively contribute to ensuring that abuse of 'private sovereignty' can be prosecuted under civil law.[26] Consequently, it is submitted that the law of the company's domicile, which is supposedly better suited to enforce human rights-related duties of conduct, should be applied rather than the law at the place where the damage occurred.[27]

---

[24] Mankowski, *Interessenpolitik und europäisches Kollisionsrecht*, 2011, p. 17 with numerous examples.

[25] On this already Stürner, in *Festschrift für Coester-Waltjen* (Bielefeld: Gieseking, 2015), pp. 843, 848 ff.

[26] H. Muir Watt, *Transnational Legal Theory* 2011, 2(3), 347.

[27] See for example Weller/Thomale, *ZGR* 2017, 509, 523 ff.; Thomale/Hübner, *JZ* 2017, 385, 391 ff.

**1116.** International standards on human rights due diligence already exist, such as the UN Guiding Principles on Business and Human Rights (2011) or the OECD Guidelines for Multinational Enterprises (2011). However, in terms of conflict of laws, these have, at best, an indirect effect, as these instruments are ultimately soft laws without any direct binding force. Therefore, if one wanted to establish due diligence obligations for domestic entrepreneurs with global effect, the only way to do so would be through substantive law. The corporate due diligence obligations to be standardised there would have to be applicable extraterritorially, meaning that they would have to be regarded as overriding mandatory rules within the meaning of Article 16 Rome II. This is indeed the approach taken by the Directive No 2024/1760 of 13 June 2024 of the European Parliament and of the Council on Corporate Sustainability Due Diligence.[28] The corporate obligations standardised in this Directive, which must be transposed into national law by 26 July 2026, are intended to regulate the due diligence requirements to be observed in a mandatory manner and without regard to the law governing the non-contractual obligatory relationship under private international law. This includes civil liability of a company for damage caused to a natural or legal person because the company failed to comply with the obligations laid down in the Directive (Article 29 Directive 2024/1760). While the effective implementation of CSR may call for such a broad approach, this entails to a certain extent a departure from multilateralism in that the enforcement of human rights-related standards of conduct is not left with the law where the damage occurred, as it is characterised as deficient in this respect.

**1117.** Private international law is thus certainly suitable to transmit political interests and is increasingly being used for this purpose. For this end, the universality of conflict-of-laws rules is being abandoned in favour of an increasing primacy of domestic law. The multilateralist approach of classical private international law, at least at the outset, seems to be on the retreat. This may be based on pragmatism in legal policy, which can certainly justify a synchronisation of international jurisdiction and applicable law. However, this should always be based on factual arguments and interests specific to the conflict of laws and not on the conviction, perhaps only motivated by day-to-day politics, that one's own law is the better one as compared to the laws of other countries.

---

28 OJ 2024 L 2024/1760.

# §31. EUROPEAN CONFLICT OF LAWS IN THE FIELD OF CONTRACT LAW: FUNDAMENTAL ISSUES

CONTENTS



References: J. von Hein/E.-M. Kieninger/G. Rühl (eds.), *How European is European Private International Law? Sources, Court Practice, Academic Discourse* (Cambridge: Intersentia, 2019); D. Martiny, 'Europäisches Internationales Schuldrecht – Feinarbeit an Rom I- und Rom II-Verordnungen', *ZEuP* 2018, 218; T. Pfeiffer, 'Rechtsvergleichung und Internationales Privatrecht in der Berliner Republik – national, europäisch, global', in T. Duve/S. Rupper (eds.), *Rechtswissenschaft in der Berliner Republik* (Berlin: Suhrkamp, 2018), p. 147; R. Schaub, 'Gemeinsame Strukturelemente der europäischen Verordnungen zum Internationalen Privatrecht – Zugleich ein Beitrag zur Diskussion über IPR als Pflichtfach', *JURA* 2017, 611; M. Stürner, 'Internationales Privatrecht', in K. Langenbucher, *Europäisches Privat- und Wirtschaftsrecht*, 5th ed. (Baden-Baden: Nomos, 2022), §8 paras. 29–56

## I. PIL IN THE INTERNAL MARKET

**1118.** In the area of judicial cooperation, the EEC Treaty of 1957 did not yet contain any legislative powers for legal harmonisation. Rather, it was up to the Member States, based on the then-applicable Article 220 of the EEC Treaty, to pursue the reduction of formalities for the mutual recognition and enforcement of judicial decisions and arbitral awards by means of intergovernmental cooperation. After the Brussels Convention on Jurisdiction and the

Enforcement of Judgments (Brussels Convention) entered into force in 1973,[1] the Rome Convention on the law applicable to contractual obligations (Rome Convention) was enacted in 1980,[2] which contained conflict-of-laws rules for cross-border contractual relationships. In the process of the Europeanisation of legislative powers in the field of judicial cooperation, the Treaty of Amsterdam of 2 October 1997, which entered into force on 1 May 1999, also established a respective competence title in Article 81(2)(c) TFEU. The TFEU also introduced an EC competence for PIL.[3] On these grounds, several regulations were adopted in the field of International Civil Procedure and PIL, including the Rome I Regulation on the law applicable to contractual obligations.

**1119.** This multitude of legal acts of European conflict of laws should not obscure the fact that EU law is not the only source of conflict-of-laws provisions. In principle, PIL is – contrary to what the term 'international might' suggest – national law: each state determines autonomously – by virtue of its state sovereignty – how to deal with cross-border cases. Some systems have adopted specific legislation in the field of PIL, which more or less strives at a coherent and comprehensive set of conflict-of-laws rules, while others still heavily rely on judge-made law.

## II. EU REGULATIONS IN THE FIELD OF CONFLICT OF LAWS

**1120.** The following EU regulations contain conflict-of-laws rules (in chronological order):

- Non-contractual obligations: Rome II Regulation;[4]
- Contractual obligations: Rome I Regulation;[5]
- Divorce and legal separation: Rome III Regulation;[6]

---

1 The Convention contains rules on international jurisdiction, recognition and enforcement as well as on the settlement of positive conflicts of jurisdiction in civil and commercial matters. It was 'communitarised' in 2001 by the Brussels I Regulation.

2 Rome Convention on the Law Applicable to Contractual Obligations of 19 June 1980, consolidated version, OJ 1998 C 27/34.

3 On this Wilke, *A Conceptual Analysis of European Private International Law*, 2019, pp. 303 ff. Cf. in general on judicial cooperation Stürner, *JURA* 2015, 813 as well as below at paras. 1415 ff.

4 Regulation (EC) No 864/2007 of the European Parliament and of the Council of 11 July 2007 on the law applicable to non-contractual obligations (Rome II), OJ 2007 L 199/40.

5 Regulation (EC) No 593/2008 of the European Parliament and of the Council of 17 June 2008 on the law applicable to contractual obligations (Rome I), OJ 2008 L 177/6.

6 Council Regulation (EU) No 1259/2010 of 20 December 2010 implementing enhanced cooperation in the area of the law applicable to divorce and legal separation, OJ 2010 L 343/10.

- Maintenance claims: European Maintenance Regulation[7] (in conjunction with the Hague Protocol on the law applicable to maintenance obligations of 2007);
- Succession and testamentary matters: the European Succession Regulation;[8]
- Matrimonial property law: Regulations on matrimonial property law in marital unions[9] and in registered civil partnerships;[10]
- Insolvency law: the European Insolvency Regulation 2000[11] and European Insolvency (Recast) Regulation[12] contain some special provisions, for example for insolvency set-off.

## III. INTERPRETATION OF EU CONFLICT-OF-LAWS RULES

**1121.** There are no special features regarding the interpretation of the EU conflict-of-laws rules. As a general rule, the principle of autonomous interpretation applies.[13] This ensures the uniformity of the application of the law in all Member States; it also serves the goal of uniform legal consequences regarding the applicable law, regardless of the competent court, and thus, legal certainty. Even the more general concept of a contract is determined autonomously; the CJEU defines it as any obligation entered into voluntarily.[14]

---

7 Council Regulation (EC) No 4/2009 of 18 December 2008 on jurisdiction, applicable law, recognition and enforcement of decisions and cooperation in matters relating to maintenance obligations, OJ 2009 L 7/1.

8 Regulation (EU) No 650/2012 of the European Parliament and of the Council of 4 July 2012 on jurisdiction, applicable law, recognition and enforcement of decisions and acceptance and enforcement of authentic instruments in matters of succession and on the creation of a European Certificate of Succession, OJ 2012 L 201/107.

9 Council Regulation (EU) 2016/1103 of 24 June 2016 implementing enhanced cooperation in the area of jurisdiction, applicable law and the recognition and enforcement of decisions in matters of matrimonial property regimes, OJ 2016 L 183/1.

10 Council Regulation (EU) 2016/1104 of 24 June 2016 implementing enhanced cooperation in the area of jurisdiction, applicable law and the recognition and enforcement of decisions in matters of the property consequences of registered partnerships, OJ 2016 L 183/30.

11 Council Regulation (EC) No 1346/2000 of 29 May 2000 on insolvency proceedings, OJ 2000 L 160/1.

12 Regulation (EU) 2015/848 of the European Parliament and of the Council of 20 May 2015 on insolvency proceedings (recast), OJ 2015 L 141/19.

13 For more details see Langenbucher/Donath, in Langenbucher, *Europäisches Privat- und Wirtschaftsrecht*, §1 paras. 5 ff.; Nehne, *Methodik und allgemeine Lehren des europäischen Internationalen Privatrechts*, 2012, pp. 40 ff.

14 The starting point is again the law of international jurisdiction, cf. the references in Martiny, in *Münchener Kommentar zum BGB*, 9th ed. 2025, Art. 1 Rom I-VO paras. 8 ff. On the notion of contract cf. above at paras. 19 ff, 1144 ff.

**1122.** Case law of the CJEU on the European PIL regulations is currently still relatively rare. In many cases, it is possible to refer to case law on procedural law, in particular, on the Brussels I and I-bis Regulations, or even the Brussels Convention. However, this presupposes that respective terminology is used uniformly.[15] This is not always the case, so it must be examined for each legal term whether relevant case law can be transferred. The legislator itself regularly assumes that there is a certain degree of uniformity between procedural and conflict-of-laws regulations.[16]

**1123.** In case of doubt regarding the interpretation, the preliminary ruling procedure according to Article 267 TFEU is – as usual – available, sometimes even mandatory, to the courts of the Member States.[17]

## IV. GAPS

**1124.** EU conflict of laws now covers many areas of the law. However, there are still non-harmonised areas. In these residual fields, the respective autonomous PIL of the Member States remains applicable.[18] This concerns, in particular, the following areas:

- The status or legal capacity of natural persons (cf. Article 1(2)(a) Rome I Regulation): in addition to Article 13 Rome I Regulation, the relevant domestic PIL applies here.
- The law applicable to arbitration agreements and choice of court agreements (Article 1(2)(e) Rome I Regulation): While there is a rule for the latter in Article 25(1) Brussels Ibis Regulation,[19] the conflict of laws in the field of arbitration is unregulated and disputed.[20]
- The law applicable to the name of a natural person: In this respect, EU laws do not (yet) exist.
- The law on agency (cf. Article 1(2)(g) Rome I Regulation).
- Non-contractual liability arising from damage caused by nuclear energy and non-contractual liability for personal injury (cf. Article 1(2)(f) and (g) Rome II Regulation).
- Property law has also not been regulated by EU law.

---

15 Cf. below at paras. 1174 ff.

16 Cf. Recitals No 7, 17 and 24 Rome I Regulation, Recital No 7 Rome II Regulation, and Recital No 10 Rome III Regulation.

17 Cf. above at paras. 1415 ff.

18 On the future significance of national codifications in the field of PIL Jayme, *IPRax* 2017, 179.

19 Cf. below at paras. 1453 ff.

20 On the law applicable to arbitration agreements, cf. e.g. Stürner/Wendelstein, *IPRax* 2014, 473.

- Parts of international family law, in particular the PIL of marriage, parentage, adoption, guardianship, care and custody.
- Company law (cf. Article 1(2)(f) Rome I Regulation; Article 1(2)(d) Rome II Regulation).[21]

**1125.** However, European influences still might play a role in these areas; this concerns, in particular, the fundamental freedoms of the TFEU.[22]

## V. FURTHER DEVELOPMENTS: DO WE NEED A 'ROME 0 REGULATION'?

References: M. Czepelak, 'Would we like to have a European Code of Private International Law?', *ERPL* 2010, 705; C. Heinze, Bausteine eines Allgemeinen Teils des europäischen Internationalen Privatrechts, in *Festschrift für Kropholler* (Tübingen: Mohr Siebeck, 2008), p. 105; M. Kieninger, 'Das Europäische IPR vor der Kodifikation?', in *Festschrift für von Hoffmann* (Bielefeld: Gieseking, 2011), p. 184; S. Leible/M. Müller, 'The Idea of a Rome 0 Regulation', in *Yearbook of Private International Law Vol. XIV, 2012/2013* (Munich: Sellier, 2013), 137; S. Leible/H. Unberath (eds.), *Brauchen wir eine Rom 0-Verordnung?* (Jena, JWV, 2013-; R. Michaels, 'A Global Restatement of Private International Law?', in *Festschrift für Kronke* (Bielefeld: Gieseking, 2020), p. 387.

**1126.** For some time now, there has been a discussion, especially among academics, about the need for a European Code on Private International Law[23] or a 'Rome 0 Regulation'.[24] This includes the plea for a consolidation of the rules common to all EU regulations on PIL in a single legal act. Beyond that, some authors even argue for a comprehensive codification of PIL.[25] This discussion has also found its way into legal policy: The Legal Affairs Committee of the EU Parliament commissioned an in-depth analysis, which was published at the end of 2012 under the title 'Current gaps and future perspectives in European private international law: towards a code on private international law?'.[26] The author of

21 Cf. Stürner, in Langenbucher, *Europäisches Privat- und Wirtschaftsrecht*, §8 paras. 103 ff.

22 Cf. Stürner, in Langenbucher, *Europäisches Privat- und Wirtschaftsrecht*, §8 paras. 98 ff.; Repasi, *Wirkungsweise des unionsrechtlichen Anwendungsvorrangs im autonomen IPR* (Tübingen: Mohr Siebeck, 2018), pp. 294 ff.

23 Cf. X.E. Kramer, 'European Private International Law: The way forward', Study PE 509.987, pp. 77, 93 f., 101 f.; see further the 'Embryon de Règlement portant Code europeén de droit international privé' authored by Lagarde, published in *RabelsZ* 75 (2011), 673; Fallon/Lagarde/Poillot-Peruzzetto, *Quelle architecture pour un code européen de droit international privé?*, 2011.

24 Leible/Unberath (eds.), *Brauchen wir eine Rom 0-Verordnung?*, 2013; Wilke, *GPR* 2012, 334.

25 For further references, cf. von Hein, in *Münchener Kommentar zum BGB*, 9th ed. (Munich: C.H. Beck, 2024), Art. 3 EGBGB para. 69.

26 Study PE 462.476 from 14 December 2012 (Author: Xandra Kramer).

the study, professor Xandra Kramer, recommends a tiered approach, despite all sympathy for an overall codification.[27] The Commission, in its Communication on the EU Justice Agenda 2020, has nevertheless stated that 'The EU should examine whether codification of the existing instruments could be useful, notably in the area of conflict of laws'.[28]

**1127.** The calls for creating a Rome 0 Regulation do not necessarily seem compelling. The desired increase in coherence through such a consolidation of the instruments of what may be called a 'General Part of the PIL' is more likely to entail other problems, which would lie in particular in the demarcation of the Rome 0 Regulation from the specific regulations that would then have to be modified.[29] A political will to this effect does currently not exist anyway.[30]

## VI. PRACTICAL EFFECTIVENESS OF EU CONFLICT-OF-LAWS RULES

References: P. Beaumont, 'When Should EU Private International Law Require that Foreign Law be Applied?', in J. von Hein/E.-M. Kieninger/G. Rühl (eds.), *How European is European Private International Law? Sources, Court Practice, Academic Discourse* (Cambridge: Intersentia, 2019), p. 177; M. Hellner, 'The Application of European Private International Law by National Judges: Making the Job Easier', in J. von Hein/ E.-M. Kieninger/G. Rühl (eds.), *How European is European Private International Law? Sources, Court Practice, Academic Discourse* (Cambridge: Intersentia, 2019), p. 205; M. Requejo Isidro, 'The Application of European Private International Law and the Ascertainment of Foreign Law', J. in von Hein/E.-M. Kieninger/G. Rühl (eds.), *How European is European Private International Law? Sources, Court Practice, Academic Discourse* (Cambridge: Intersentia, 2019), p. 139; M. Stürner, 'Effektivität des europäischen Kollisionsrechts und nationales Verfahrensrecht', in *Festschrift für Rolf Stürner, Volume II* (Tübingen: Mohr Siebeck, 2013), p. 1071; M. Stürner/F. Krauß, *Ausländisches Recht in deutschen Zivilverfahren. Eine rechtstatsächliche Untersuchung* (Baden-Baden: Nomos, 2018); M. Stürner, 'Wie kann der Zugang zu ausländischem Recht in Zivilverfahren verbessert werden?', *ZVglRWiss* 117 (2018), 1; C. Trautmann, *Europäisches Kollisionsrecht und ausländisches Recht im nationalen Zivilverfahren* (Tübingen: Mohr Siebeck, 2011).

---

27 Study PE 462.476, p. 18.

28 Communication 'The EU Justice Agenda for 2020 – Strengthening Trust, Mobility and Growth in the Union', 1 March2014, COM (2014) 144 final, p. 9.

29 Weighing up advantages and disadvantages von Hein, in *Münchener Kommentar zum BGB*, 9th ed. (Munich: C.H. Beck, 2024), Art. 3 EGBGB paras. 70 ff. On the question of competence Wilke, *A Conceptual Analysis of European Private International Law*, 2019, pp. 303 ff.

30 On the parallel discussion about a 'Brussels 0 Regulation' Stürner, *ZVglRWiss* 219 (2020), 143, 164 ff.

## 1. *EFFET UTILE*

**1128.** EU conflict-of-laws rules are guided, among other things, by the purpose of giving legal practice the greatest possible certainty regarding the applicable law and thus making the outcome of legal disputes predictable. They aim to invoke the same law at all times, regardless of the forum, for a given set of facts.[31] Whether or not this works out depends very much on how such harmonising conflict-of-laws rules are applied by the courts.

**1129.** However, the procedural framework for the application of conflict-of-laws rules has so far not been harmonised.[32] Each Member State applies its autonomous procedural law when it comes to ascertaining and applying the foreign law as designated by EU conflict-of-laws rules.[33] Hence, divergences concerning the application of the law may arise.[34] But how does this get along with the *effet utile* of the choice-of-law rules, the postulate of the practical effectiveness of EU law, which permeates all directives and regulations?[35] The ascertaining and application of foreign law are thus caught between the postulate of the effectiveness of EU conflict-of-laws rules and national procedural autonomy.[36]

**1130.** An important aspect in this respect is the courts' practical approach to conflict of laws. It has always been argued that the courts have a 'homeward bias' in applying PIL rules, i.e. they tend to favour the application of domestic law whenever possible.[37] This is not necessarily because chauvinistic tendencies are pursued. Rather, the additional loop required by conflict of laws consumes time and effort. If the conflict-of-laws rules lead to the designation of a foreign legal system, considerable further efforts arise from the identification of the relevant

---

31 Recital No 6 Rome I Regulation puts it very succinctly.

32 The European Commission has not taken up proposals of the European Parliament to standardise the ascertaining of foreign law in the context of the discussion on the Rome II Regulation. In this respect, only the review clause of Article 30(1) Rom II Regulation can be found in the adopted text. On the evolution cf. Dickinson, *The Rome II Regulation* (Oxford: Oxford University Press, 2008), paras. 14.67 ff.

33 Cf. especially Articles 1(3) Rome I Regulation and 1(3) Rome II Regulation. There is a vast amount of literature on the different approaches. Cf. e.g. Nishitani (ed.), *Treatment of Foreign Law – Dynamics towards Convergence?* (Cham: Springer, 2017); Verhellen, *Journal of Private International Law* 12 (2016), 281; Þorláksson, *Journal of Private International Law* 12 (2016), 301; Wilke, *A Conceptual Analysis of European Private International Law*, 2019, pp. 236 ff.

34 Cf. Kreuzer, in Jud/Rechberger/Reichelt, 'Kollisionsrecht in der Europäischen Union', pp. 1, 9 ('birth defect'); similar von Hein, *RabelsZ* 73 (2009), 461, 506 f. ('blind spot').

35 Cf. above at paras. 309, 347.

36 Cf. Trautmann, *Europäisches Kollisionsrecht und ausländisches Recht im nationalen Zivilverfahren*, 2011, pp. 265 ff.; M. Stürner, in *Festschrift für Rolf Stürner*, 2013, p. 1071.

37 The term was already used by A. Nussbaum, *Deutsches Internationales Privatrecht* (Tübingen: Mohr, 1932), p. 43; cf. also R. Fentiman, *Foreign Law in English Courts* (Oxford: Oxford University Press, 1998), pp. 29 ff.

legal provisions; their application ultimately represents considerable potential for error due to the courts' lack of experience and familiarity with that specific foreign system.[38]

**1131.** All European civil procedural systems must be interpreted in light of the principle of effectiveness.[39] In principle, this also applies to EU conflict of laws: Practical effectiveness must also be ensured for these secondary law provisions.[40] This postulate is not only a guiding principle in interpreting secondary law but also concerns the relationship of European law to national law in general. Since European legislation is, in almost all cases, not accompanied by procedural rules,[41] the question of their practical effectiveness hinges on the corresponding provisions of the Member States' legal systems. According to the established case law of the CJEU, these 'must not be framed in such a way as to render impossible in practice the exercise of rights conferred by the Community law (principle of effectiveness)'.[42]

## 2. PROCEDURAL AUTONOMY OF THE MEMBER STATES?

**1132.** One might wonder to what extent the applicability of EU conflict-of-laws rules is also capable of influencing national procedural law through the postulate of *effet utile*, with the consequence that the regulatory autonomy of the Member States would be subject to restrictions. The 'secret king' of PIL, to use Gerhard Kegel's words,[43] would then no longer be procedural law for cross-border proceedings, but the principle of effectiveness.

**1133.** The effectiveness of the conflict-of-laws rules and the goal of uniformity in application that they pursue depend decisively on the approach that the domestic procedural law chooses concerning the way how foreign law is

[38] In-depth on the options available under sec. 293 ZPO for ascertaining foreign law M. Stürner/F. Krauß, *Ausländisches Recht in Zivilverfahren* (Baden-Baden: Nomos, 2018), paras. 32 ff.; Hellner, in von Hein/Kieninger/Rühl, *How European is European Private International Law?*, 2019, p. 205.

[39] Cf. CJEU, 8 November 2005, Case C-443/03, *Leffler*, ECLI:EU:C:2005:665, para. 51; B. Hess, *Europäisches Zivilprozessrecht*, 2nd ed. (Berlin: De Gruyter, 2020), §4 paras. 69 ff.

[40] Cf. e.g. J. von Hein, in T. Rauscher (ed.), *Europäisches Zivilprozess- und Kollisionsrecht*, 5th ed. (Cologne: Otto Schmidt, 2023), Einl. Rom I-VO para. 62.

[41] Exceptions concern in particular the European Small Claims Regulation and the European Order for Payment Regulation.

[42] Cf. e.g. CJEU, 16 March 2006, Case C-234/04, *Kapferer/Schlank & Schick*, ECLI:EU:C:2006:178, para. 22; CJEU, 13 July 2006, Joined Cases C-205/04 to C-298/04, *Manfredi*, ECLI:EU:C:2006:137, para. 62, with further references.

[43] Kegel, in *Festschrift für Nipperdey* (Munich: Beck, 1965), pp. 453, 462.

introduced into domestic proceedings and whether it actually can facilitate the ascertaining and the application of the designated law.

**1134.** First, it could be argued that the Member States have complete regulatory autonomy as to procedural rules which concern the ascertaining and application of the law designated pursuant to conflict-of-laws provisions. Such an interpretation could, at least superficially, be based on the regulatory abstinence of the European legislator. All secondary laws, including those in the field of conflict of laws, determine their own material scope of application. For example, the Rome II Regulation, according to its Article 1(1), applies to non-contractual obligations in civil and commercial matters. There are numerous exceptions in this respect within Article 1(1) and (2). The most important exception in the present context, however, is found in Article 1(3) of the Rome II Regulation: According to this rule, the Regulation 'shall not apply to evidence and procedure'. The same exception applies to contractual matters pursuant to Article 1(3) Rome I Regulation. It reflects the general *lex fori* principle. However, for the ascertaining and application of the designated law, this may lead to a limitation of the practical effectiveness of the regulation.

**1135.** In the context of the creation of the Rome II Regulation, it was precisely this point that the European Parliament raised in its resolution of 6 July 2005. It was proposed that the parties should be obliged to give notice of the law they consider applicable if the claim or counterclaim asserted falls within the scope of application of the Rome II Regulation (Article 12 of the Parliament's draft). In addition, an obligation to ascertain foreign law was included (Article 13(1) of the Parliament's draft). However, both points were not pursued further in the subsequent legislative process in order to avoid jeopardising the success of the proposed regulation as a whole.[44] The only thing that remained was the review clause of Article 30(1)(i) Rome II Regulation, according to which the European Commission had to report by 20 August 2011 on the 'effects of the way in which foreign law is treated in the different jurisdictions and on the extent which courts in the Member States apply foreign law in practice pursuant to this Regulation'. This deadline was not met. However, the Commission has initiated a study on the reality of the application of foreign law and is also cooperating with the Hague Conference on Private International Law under the general theme

---

44 On the course of the legislative procedure in this respect R. Wagner, in *Festschrift für Kropholler*, 2008, pp. 715, 728; A. Dickinson, *The Rome II Regulation* (Oxford: Oxford University Press, 2008), paras. 14.67 ff.; J. Müller, *Die Behandlung ausländischen Rechts im Zivilverfahren* (Berlin: Lang, 2011), pp. 18 ff.

'Access to Foreign Law in Civil and Commercial Matters'. This joint venture has discussed ways to improve access to foreign law for legal practice.[45]

**1136.** However, it would be unviable to infer from the European legislator's regulatory abstinence that the Member States have complete freedom in implementing the conflict-of-laws reference to foreign law. If this were the case, Member States could allow the application of the foreign law to be de facto rendered null and void by designing procedural provisions which would effectively allow for an application of forum law. It is well-established in the case law of the CJEU that national procedural principles may remain operative even if they lead to a certain restriction of Union law rules. This has been decided, for example, for the principle of res judicata[46] or the abuse of rights.[47] The limit, however, remains always the *effet utile*.[48] Thus, in each case, it must be determined by a balancing exercise how far the regulatory claim of the domestic legal act in question extends.

**1137.** Against this backdrop, it must be noted that the Member States cannot have complete regulatory autonomy in the area of procedural law.[49] This also follows from the exceptions contained in Article 1(3) of the Rome I and Rome II Regulations for procedural law.[50] From these Regulations, it can only be deduced that both do not claim to regulate the procedural rights of the Member States. However, the general claim of EU law to be effectively applied must be distinguished from this. If and to the extent that the objectives of a certain predictability of conflict-of-laws rules[51] and international unity of decisions can be jeopardised by procedural rights of the Member States, a complete 'immunisation' through these exceptions is out of question. Rather, these are to be interpreted in the light of *effet utile*.[52]

---

45 Cf. M. Stürner/F. Krauß, *Ausländisches Recht in Zivilverfahren* (Baden-Baden: Nomos, 2018), paras. 69 ff.

46 Cf. for the principle of res iudicata CJEU, 16 March 2006, Case C-234/04, *Kapferer/Schlank & Schick*, ECLI:EU:C:2006:178, paras. 20 f.; CJEU, 1 June 1999, Case C-126/97, *Eco Swiss*, ECLI:EU:C:1999:269, paras. 43 ff.

47 CJEU, 12 May 1998, Case C-367/96, *Kefalas*, ECLI:EU:C:1998:222, para. 20 f.; CJEU, 23 March 2000, Case C-373/97, *Diamantis*, ECLI:EU:C:2000:150, paras. 33 ff.

48 As to the abuse of rights, cf. CJEU, 23 March 2000, Case C-373/97, *Diamantis*, ECLI:EU:C:2000:150, para. 34.

49 A noteworthy plea for a party-autonomous view of the determination of foreign law, however, was made for example by Beaumont, in von Hein/Kieninger/Rühl, *How European is European Private International Law?*, 2019, p. 177.

50 But see G. Wagner, *ZEuP* 1999, 6, 39 f.

51 Recitals No 6 and 12 Rome I Regulation; cf. CJEU, 6 October 2009, Case C-133/08, *Intercontainer Interfrigo*, ECLI:EU:C:2009:617, paras. 23, 44, 62 (on the Brussels Convention).

52 Cf. amply Trautmann, *Europäisches Kollisionsrecht und ausländisches Recht im nationalen Zivilverfahren*, 2011, pp. 285 ff.

## 3. PROBLEMATIC ISSUES

**1138.** Since the exceptions relating to procedural law contained in Articles 1(3) Rome I and Rome II Regulations cannot keep that area of domestic law completely unaffected by the influences of EU law, it is necessary to identify possible areas of conflict.[53] Probably the most important one concerns introducing foreign law into the proceedings and thus the question of the optional character of the conflict of laws. If, as is the practice in some legal systems, the reference to foreign law by at least one of the parties is considered a prerequisite for the judicial consideration of conflict-of-laws rules, this seems to negate the conflict-of-laws rules in many cases. The case law of the CJEU on the admissibility of the defence of *forum non conveniens* under European law could also be used for this purpose.[54] Here, the CJEU ruled that the national procedural law of a Member State could not establish exceptions to the jurisdictional system of the Brussels Convention. The introduction of foreign law seems comparable, as a conflict-of-laws system that would (hypothetically) be entirely at the parties' disposal would lead to such exceptions as well.[55] However, such a parallel assessment would only be valid if the application of the European conflict-of-laws rules – just like the dismissal of a claim on the grounds of *forum non conveniens* – were left to the court's discretion. However, such a discretionary conflict-of-laws system[56] would violate European prerequisites.[57] By contrast, it is much more difficult to argue for a violation of the *effet utile* with a view to a conflict-of-laws system at the disposition of the parties. If one considers the history of the Rome II Regulation, there is much to suggest that the European legislator deliberately accepted restrictions regarding the effectiveness of the conflict-of-laws rules.[58] As a side note, whether in a given procedural context, foreign law is to be regarded as a question of law or a question of fact is irrelevant from a European perspective.

---

53 Comprehensive analysis in Trautmann, *Europäisches Kollisionsrecht und ausländisches Recht im nationalen Zivilverfahren*, 2011, pp. 289–401.

54 CJEU, 1 March 2005, Case C-281/02, *Owusu/Jackson*, ECLI:EU:C:2005:120.

55 With this consequence J. Müller, *Die Behandlung ausländischen Rechts im Zivilverfahren* (Berlin: Lang, 2011), pp. 156 ff.

56 A discretion of the court to this effect is (arguably) only to be found in French law, cf. Trautmann, *Europäisches Kollisionsrecht und ausländisches Recht im nationalen Zivilverfahren*, 2011, pp. 86 ff., 331.

57 Trautmann, *Europäisches Kollisionsrecht und ausländisches Recht im nationalen Zivilverfahren*, 2011, p. 335; G. Wagner, *ZEuP* 1999, 6, 42 ff. (breach of iura novit curia); from an economic perspective also Rühl, *Statut und Effizienz*, 2011, pp. 390 f.

58 In this sense Trautmann, *Europäisches Kollisionsrecht und ausländisches Recht im nationalen Zivilverfahren*, 2011, pp. 319 ff.; A. Dickinson, *The Rome II Regulation* (Oxford: Oxford University Press, 2008), paras. 14.70 ff.; A. Briggs, *The conflict of laws*, 5th ed. (Oxford: Oxford University Press, 2024), pp. 34 f.; Rühl, *Statut und Effizienz*, 2011, pp. 380 ff.

**1139.** Nevertheless, one restriction is necessary. EU law that is at the parties' disposition cannot exist if the relevant provisions of secondary law aim to protect weaker parties. The CJEU has decided accordingly several times, especially as to the Unfair Terms Directive.[59] With regard to European conflict of laws, this means that, for example, the specific conflict-of-laws rules for consumers, employees and policy holders must be taken into account ex officio.[60] In procedural terms, this usually means that the court must give the parties an indication of the cross-border dimension of the case.[61] However, a procedural rule of a Member State which allows a party to waive the protection granted to it under conflict of laws does not restrict the *effet utile*.[62]

**1140.** In practice, this restriction should not result in any major changes to the procedural systems of the Member States. It should be borne in mind that international jurisdiction and applicable law often run parallel, so that the question of foreign law does not arise in the first place.[63] This also results from EU conflict-of-laws rules insofar as a choice of law in favour of the forum is usually possible, for example, according to Article 5(1)(d) Rome III Regulation or Article 15 of the EU Maintenance Regulation in conjunction with Article 7 of the Hague Protocol on the law applicable to maintenance obligations of 2007. In consumer and labour matters, the objective connecting factor regularly leads to a concurrence of forum and ius. In many cases, the choice of law and the forum will run parallel, as Recital 12 to the Rome I Regulation favours an implied choice of law in favour of the *forum prorogatum*.[64]

**1141.** Still, from the perspective of EU law, it is problematic to resort to the lex fori too quickly, if the ascertainment of foreign law appears to be costly and cumbersome, or altogether impossible. It appears necessary under EU law to refer to a substitute legal system that is most closely related to the *lex causae*, or

---

59 Cf. already above at paras. 672 ff. and 1374 ff.

60 Trautmann, *Europäisches Kollisionsrecht und ausländisches Recht im nationalen Zivilverfahren*, 2011, pp. 303 ff.

61 This is also the recommendation of the report of the Institut suisse de droit comparé, The Application of Foreign Law in Civil Matters in the EU Member States and its Perspectives for the Future – JLS/2009/JCIV/PR/0005/E4, 2011, Part III, at para. 7.1.

62 Cf. CJEU, 4 June 2009, Case C-243/08, *Pannon GSM*, ECLI:EU:C:2009:350, paras. 32–35: The obligation to review a term ex officio does not exist if the consumer does not wish to assert the unfairness and non-binding nature of the term after a court notice.

63 Cf. J. Müller, *Die Behandlung ausländischen Rechts im Zivilverfahren* (Berlin: Lang, 2011), pp. 63 ff.

64 Cf. J. von Hein, in T. Rauscher (ed.), *Europäisches Zivilprozess- und Kollisionsrecht*, 5th ed. (Cologne: Otto Schmidt, 2023), Art. 3 Rom I-VO paras. 20 ff.

to refer to alternative conflict-of-laws rules; only in this way will the reference be given the greatest possible effect.[65]

**1142.** Hence, upon closer examination, the statement made at the beginning, i.e., that the procedural law of the Member States is not immune to the influence of European conflict of laws, has hardly led to any noteworthy frictions. Only in some rare instances is the practical effectiveness of European conflict of laws restricted to the extent that makes it necessary to apply the national procedural rules in conformity with Union law.

[65] Trautmann, *Europäisches Kollisionsrecht und ausländisches Recht im nationalen Zivilverfahren*, 2011, pp. 386 ff.

# §32. THE ROME I REGULATION

## CONTENTS

References: E. Guinchard (ed.), *Rome I and Rome II in Practice* (Cambridge: Intersentia, 2020); S. Leible/M. Lehmann, 'Die Verordnung über das auf vertragliche Schuldverhältnisse anzuwendende Recht ("Rom I")', *RIW* 2008, 528; U. Magnus, 'Die Rom I-Verordnung', *IPRax* 2010, 27; P. Mankowski, 'Die Rom I-Verordnung: Änderungen im europäischen IPR für Schuldverträge', *IHR* 2008, 133; D. *Martiny*, 'Neues deutsches internationales Vertragsrecht', *RIW* 2009, 737; D. Solomon, 'Die Rom I-Verordnung in der deutschen ordentlichen Gerichtsbarkeit', *ZVglRWiss* 115 (2016), 586.

## I. HISTORY OF ORIGINS AND OBJECTIVE

**1143.** The Rome I Regulation superseded the Rome Convention on the law applicable to contractual obligations of 19 June 1980 (Rome Convention) and transformed it into an EU Regulation. The aim of the Regulation is 'to improve the predictability of the outcome of litigation, certainty as to the law applicable and the free movement of judgments'. Thus, it draws its legitimacy from the goal of the 'proper functioning of the internal market' (Recital 6 Rome I Regulation).[1] The Rome I Regulation only applies to contracts concluded after its entry into force on 17 December 2009, Article 28 Rome I Regulation.[2]

1 Cf. C.F. Nordmeier, in M. Weller (ed.), *Europäisches Kollisionsrecht* (Baden-Baden: Nomos, 2016), pp. 127 ff.; Riesenhuber, *EU-Vertragsrecht*, 2013, §4.

2 Originally, the Rome I Regulation contained diverging wordings in Article 28 (to be applied 'after 17 December 2009') and Article 29(2) ('shall apply from 17 December 2009'). This obvious contradiction made it necessary to amend Article 28 Rome I Regulation accordingly.

# II. MAIN CONTENTS

## 1. MATERIAL SCOPE

### a) *Contractual Obligations*

**1144.** The Rome I Regulation applies to contractual obligations in civil and commercial matters with a cross-border dimension (Article 1(1) Rome I Regulation). The Regulation is designed parallel to the Rome II Regulation and the Brussels Ibis Regulation, which is emphasised in Recital 7 of the Rome I Regulation. Excluded are, in particular,[3] family and matrimonial obligations (Article 1(2)(b), (c) Rome I Regulation), company law (Article 1(2)(f) Rome I Regulation), agency (Article 1(2)(g) Rome I Regulation) and, in principle, issues of evidence and procedure (Article 1(3) Rome I Regulation, but note Article 18 Rome I Regulation).

**1145.** The concept of contractual obligations is to be interpreted autonomously, so that the understanding in the Member States' legal systems is not important, at least at the outset. According to the case law of the CJEU, the characteristic of the voluntariness of entering into an obligation is of paramount importance.[4] In this respect, the creation of a legal 'special relationship' vis-à-vis the other party by voluntarily entering into an obligation is required.[5]

### b) *In Particular: The Delimitation of Contract and Tort*

**1146.** The relationship between the Rome I Regulation and the Rome II Regulation is of particular importance. Both regulations taken together are intended to span the entire law of obligations: the Rome I Regulation applies to contractual and the Rome II Regulation to non-contractual obligations. While the Rome II Regulation contains a definition in Article 2(1), according to which the Regulation covers all consequences arising out of tort, unjust enrichment, *negotiorum gestio* and *culpa in contrahendo*, the Rome I Regulation does not define contractual obligations. The already mentioned Recital 7 establishes a reference to the Brussels Ibis Regulation and emphasises the substantive coherence of both legal acts. This shows that the concept of contract should

[3] Cf. Stürner, in Erman, *BGB Kommentar*, 17th ed. 2023, Art. 1 Rom I-VO paras. 5 ff.

[4] Cf. CJEU, 17 June 1992, Case C-26/91, *Handte*, ECLI:EU:C:1992:268, para. 15; CJEU, 14 March 2013, Case C-419/11, *Česká spořitelna*, ECLI:EU:C:2013:165, para. 47; CJEU, 18 July 2013, Case C-147/12, *ÖFAB*, ECLI:EU:C:2013:490, para. 33; CJEU, 21 April 2016, Case C-572/14, *Austro-Mechan*, ECLI:EU:C:2016:286, para. 36; CJEU, 8 May 2019, Case C-25/18, *Kerr/Postnov*, ECLI:EU:C:2019:376, para. 25.

[5] Martiny, in *Münchener Kommentar zum BGB*, 9th ed. 2025, Art. 1 Rom I-VO para. 8; Magnus, in Staudinger, *BGB Kommentar* (2021), Art. 1 Rom I-VO para. 29.

also be identical. It has already been mentioned that, according to the definition of the CJEU, the concept of a contractual obligation presupposes a special relationship that has been entered into voluntarily.[6] This also includes unilateral legal obligations, such as those arising from promises of prizes,[7] competitions and prize competitions or letters of comfort and other reinforcing promises of performance. By contrast, claims arising from pre-contractual negligence (*culpa in contrahendo*, Article 1(2)(i) Rome I Regulation), for which Article 12 Rome II Regulation provides a specific provision, do not qualify as contractual claims.[8]

**1147.** With regard to non-contractual obligations, the CJEU engages in a negative delimitation: A 'tort, delict and quasi-delict' in Article 7 no. 2 Brussels Ibis Regulation refers to all actions 'which seek to establish liability of a defendant and which are not related to a 'contract' within the meaning of [Article 7 no. 1 lit. a Brussels Ibis Regulation]'.[9] A classification of a claim for damages as both contractual and tortious is therefore ruled out.[10] Accordingly, it is not sufficient for the classification of a claim for damages as contractual that a contract exists between the parties. Rather, an action for damages only concerns a 'contract or claims arising out of a contract' within the meaning of Article 7 no. 1 Brussels Ibis Regulation if the alleged conduct can be regarded as a breach of the obligations established by the contract, as they can be determined based on the subject matter of the contract.[11] In other words, it must be assessed whether no liability for damages would follow from the event without a contractual agreement[12] or whether an interpretation of the contract appears indispensable to clarify whether the claimant's conduct is lawful or unlawful.[13]

**1148.** In the light of Recital 7 of the Rome I Regulation, these principles may also be applied to conflict-of-laws issues. Difficult cases may be dealt with via exception clauses, especially Article 4(3) Rome I Regulation. In the area of international jurisdiction, the conflict becomes more obvious, as the recent case law of the CJEU on ancillary tort claims shows.[14]

---

6 Cf. above at para. 1145.

7 CJEU, 20 January 2005, Case C-27/02, *Engler*, ECLI:EU:C:2005:33.

8 Cf. below at paras. 1231 ff.

9 CJEU, 27 September 1988, Case 189/87, *Kalfelis*, ECLI:EU:C:1988:459, para. 17; CJEU, 13 March 2014, C-548/12, *Brogsitter*, ECLI:EU:C:2014:148, para. 20.

10 CJEU, 13 March 2014, Case C-548/12, *Brogsitter*, ECLI:EU:C:2014:148, para. 27; cf. Dornis, *GPR* 2014, 352, 353; Wendelstein, *ZEuP* 2015, 624, 626; Klöpfer/Wendelstein, *JZ* 2017, 99.

11 CJEU, 13 March 2014, Case C-548/12, *Brogsitter*, ECLI:EU:C:2014:148, para. 24; CJEU, 14 July 2016, Case C-196/15, *Granarolo*, ECLI:EU:C:2016:559, para. 21.

12 Cf. Wendelstein, *ZEuP* 2015, 624 ff.

13 CJEU, 13 March 2014, Case C-548/12, *Brogsitter*, ECLI:EU:C:2014:148, para. 26.

14 CJEU, 2 April 2020, Case C-500/18, *Reliantco*, ECLI:EU:C:2020:264, paras. 67 ff.; cf. below at paras. 1447 ff.

### c) The Application of the Rome I Regulation in Arbitration

References: S. Gößling, *Europäisches Kollisionsrecht und internationale Schiedsgerichtsbarkeit. Die Bedeutung der Rom I-Verordnung bei der Bestimmung des anwendbaren materiellen Rechts durch internationale Handelsschiedsgerichte mit Sitz in der EU* (Tübingen: Mohr Siebeck, 2019).

**1149.** The question of the applicability of the Rome I Regulation to commercial arbitration is highly controversial. The starting point is Article 1(2)(e) of the Rome I Regulation, with its exception for arbitration and choice of court agreements. Both have their own regimes, for example, regarding arbitration in the New York UN Convention on the Recognition and Enforcement of Foreign Arbitral Awards.[15] For choice of court agreements there is a specific rule in Article 25 Brussels Ibis Regulation.[16] Even though the respective regulatory framework does not contain a comprehensive set of rules for the PIL of arbitration and choice of court agreements,[17] the exception in the Rome I Regulation seems well-founded, as it helps avoid regulatory conflicts between the different legal regimes.

**1150.** However, the question of the applicability of the Rome I Regulation in the arbitral proceedings itself is quite different. No one doubts that the Rome I Regulation applies to proceedings before state courts, even given the exception contained in Article 1(2)(e) Rome I Regulation for choice of court agreements. And yet, precisely this argumentation is used for arbitration proceedings as a whole: Hence, the applicability of the Rome Regulations is widely rejected here.[18] By contrast, a narrow understanding of the aforementioned exception in the Rome I Regulation also appears possible, as this would bolster the harmonisation intended by this legislative instrument. Consequently, specific conflict-of-law rules in domestic law pertaining to the choice of law in arbitration would be superseded in this regard.[19] If one were to subscribe to this view, the Rome I Regulation would also apply in arbitration proceedings.

---

15 Of 10 June 1958, BGBl. II 1961, p. 122; cf. OLG Hamm SchiedsVZ 2014, 38; BGH IPRax 2016, 63.

16 Cf. already above at paras. 1453 ff.

17 There is a tendency to apply Article V(1) lit. a of the New York Convention by analogy; cf. e.g. BGH IPRax 2021, 544 paras. 48 ff. For an opposing view cf. Stürner/Wendelstein, *IPRax* 2014, 473. On the law applicable to choice-of-court clauses cf. below at paras. 1455 ff.

18 Cf. J. von Hein, in R. Wilhelmi/M. Stürner, *Post-M&A-Schiedsverfahren. Recht und Rechtsfindung jenseits gesetzlichen Rechts* (Wiesbaden: Springer, 2019), p. 121; Wolff, in Gössl e.a., *Politik und Internationales Privatrecht*, 2017, p. 53; Hausmann, in *Festschrift für von Hoffmann*, 2011, p. 971.

19 Mankowski, *Interessenpolitik und europäisches Kollisionsrecht*, 2011, pp. 60 ff.; id., in *Festschrift für von Hoffmann*, 2011, p. 1012; id., *RIW* 2018, 1; McGuire, *SchiedsVZ* 2011, 257; Ulfat, in Gössl e.a., *Politik und Internationales Privatrecht*, 2017, p. 37.

## 2. TREATY LAW TO TRUMP PIL

References: J. Basedow, 'Internationales Einheitsprivatrecht im Zeitalter der Globalisierung', *RabelsZ* 81 (2017), 1.

**1151.** The existence of harmonising international conventions makes the operation of PIL superfluous as far as the harmonisation extends.

### *a) UN Sales Convention*

**1152.** The Vienna Sales Convention[20] regulates its scope of application in Article 1 ff. CISG. Therefore, it supersedes national regulations in its scope of application and also makes any recourse to the conflict of laws of the respective forum and also to national substantive law unnecessary. According to its Article 25, the Rome I Regulation does not prejudice the application of international conventions to which one or more Member States are parties and which lay down conflict-of-laws rules relating to contractual obligations.[21] Hence, the Rome I Regulation applies only to the extent that the CISG contains a gap. Whether and to what extent such a gap exists depends on the UN Sales Convention itself. A general distinction may be made between 'internal' and 'external' gaps: Internal gaps can be found within the material scope of the CISG; they are to be filled by the uniform law itself. Examples include a party's lack of will in cases of a successive exchange of offer and acceptance. This option does not exist for external gaps, i.e. legal questions that lie outside the scope of the CISG. Since the CISG does not claim to regulate this, the general rules apply, so that, as usual, the domestic law that is designated by the relevant conflict-of-laws rules applies. Examples are, in particular, questions of limitation of actions, the amount of interest, set-off,[22] and effects of contracts in rem or assignment.

**1153.** If the conditions for application are fulfilled, the CISG applies ipso iure. The parties may, however, waive it in whole or in part, even with retroactive effect (Article 6 CISG). However, this must be done in a sufficiently clear manner, for example, by referring to the sales law of the French code civil or the Polish Kodeks cywilny. By contrast, the clause 'German law shall apply', for example, does not amount to an exclusion of the CISG, since the CISG is also German law, providing a special regime for international commercial sales contracts.

---

20 Cf. above at paras. 92 ff., 1081.

21 This is, of course, not undisputed, cf. the references in von Hein, in Rauscher (ed.), *Europäisches Zivilprozess- und Kollisionsrecht*, 5th ed. 2023, Art. 25 Rom I-VO paras. 5 ff.

22 The situation is different, however, for so-called intra-Convention offsetting, which is subject to the CISG, cf. BGHZ 202, 258.

### b) *EU Sales Law*

**1154.** Similar to the CISG, if it existed, a uniform EU sales law would also take precedence over EU conflict-of-laws rules. Recital 14 of the Rome I Regulation was supposed to act as a kind of 'placeholder' in this respect.[23] Barely two years after the Rome I Regulation entered into force, the EU Commission presented, on 11 October 2011, the proposal for a Regulation on a Common European Sales Law (CESL).[24] In addition to sales contracts, the provision of digital content and related services were also to be covered; this related in particular, but not only, to consumer contracts. The Common European Sales Law was designed as an optional instrument. It was, therefore, intended only to apply if the parties chose it in the first place. Thus, it left the validity of other European legal acts unaffected. At the same time, it left the respective autonomous domestic sales law regimes untouched. However, the relationship of this proposed regulation to the conflict of laws was problematic.[25] This is because, from the Commission's point of view and in contrast to the CISG, it did not amount to uniform law but only a '2nd sales law regime', which was supposed to stand alongside the respective Member State's sales law. Therefore, the conflict-of-laws rules could not be displaced and would continue to apply to the choice of the CESL. The desired uniformity would have been significantly diminished if, for example, the special connection of Article 6 Rome I Regulation had applied. This is exactly what the Commission's proposal wanted to prevent (see Recitals 10 and 12 of the CESL). However, severe doubts remained as to the viability of that approach. Due to massive criticism both from political and academic stakeholders, the Commission announced in late 2015 that it no longer wished to maintain the CESL proposal in this form.[26] This means that the European uniform law approach is (for the time being) off the table.

## 3. STRUCTURE

**1155.** The core of the Rome I Regulation is Chapter II (uniform conflict-of-laws rules). Here, in addition to the choice of law (Article 3 Rome

---

23 Cf. the analysis in Herresthal, in Langenbucher, *Europäisches Privat- und Wirtschaftsrecht*, §2 paras. 3 ff.

24 COM(2011) 635 final; cf. Herresthal, in Langenbucher, *Europäisches Privat- und Wirtschaftsrecht*, §2 paras. 6 ff.

25 For more details, see the contributions in M. Gebauer (ed.), *Gemeinsames Europäisches Kaufrecht – Anwendungsbereich und kollisionsrechtliche Einbettung* (Munich: Sellier, 2013); Stürner, *GPR* 2011, 237.

26 Commission Work Programme 2015 – A New Start of 16 December 2014, COM(2014) 910 final, Annex II No 60 reads: 'Modified proposal in order to fully unleash the potential of e-commerce in the Digital Single Market.'

I Regulation) and the general determination of the contract statute in the case of an objective connection (Article 4 Rome I Regulation), which does not contain a unitary connection, there are numerous special conflict-of-laws rules (including Article 6 Rome I Regulation for consumer contracts,[27] Article 7 Rome I Regulation for insurance contracts and Article 8 Rome I Regulation for individual employment contracts). This is followed by general provisions on legal transactions (agreement and substantive validity, Article 10 Rome I Regulation; form, Article 11 Rome I Regulation; legal capacity and capacity to contract, Article 13 Rome I Regulation) as well as the determination of the scope of the law applicable (Article 12 Rome I Regulation). At the end of the chapter, rules on assignment (Articles 14 and 15 Rome I Regulation), multiple liability (Article 16 Rome I Regulation), set-off (Article 17 Rome I Regulation) and burden of proof (Article 18 Rome I Regulation) can be found. Chapter III contains other provisions, including the public policy exception (Article 21 Rome I Regulation), definitions (Articles 19 and 21 Rome I Regulation) and the exclusion of renvoi (Article 20 Rome I Regulation).

## III. CHOICE OF LAW

References: J. Böhle, 'Die Abwahl zwingenden Rechts vor staatlichen Gerichten in Inlandsfällen', *ZEuP* 2019, 72.

### 1. PRINCIPLES AND SUBJECT MATTER

**1156.** The freedom of choice of law according to Article 3 Rome I Regulation runs parallel to the contractual freedom in substantive law. However, it 'replaces' the entire legal system regarding the respective legal relationship, including, in principle, the rules that cannot be derogated from.[28] Special provisions regarding the choice of law exist for consumer contracts (Article 6(2) Rome II Regulation)[29] and for transport, insurance and employment contracts.[30] The freedom of choice of law granted in Article 3 Rome I Regulation is not intended to be merely a fallback option[31] but rather 'one of the cornerstones of the system

[27] Cf. below at paras. 1181 ff.
[28] For exceptions see below at para. 1164.
[29] Cf. below at paras. 1194 ff., 1175.
[30] Cf. below at para. 1201.
[31] Cf. G. Kegel/K. Schurig, *Internationales Privatrecht*, 9th ed. (Munich: Beck, 2004), §18 I 1c (p. 653).

of conflict-of-law rules in matters of contractual obligations' (Recital 11 Rome I Regulation).[32] EU PIL rules thus adopt a basically globally recognised principle.[33] In the Rome I Regulation, the subjective connecting factors of Article 3 takes precedence over the objective ones in Article 4. This follows from the matter's nature and is also explicitly regulated in Article 4(1) Rome I Regulation.

**1157.** Since the choice of law is free, in principle, any law is available. This includes the choice of a neutral law to which neither the contractual relationship nor the parties nor the circumstances of the contract have any connection. Often, such a choice is the result of a compromise between the contracting parties. The choice of Swiss law, for example, is not uncommon.[34] One concession must be made: Only 'state-made' law is eligible.[35] A choice of a non-governmental set of rules (such as the UNIDROIT Principles[36]) would not lead to a complete superseding of the otherwise applicable state law. The same is true for a choice of the 'Lex Mercatoria' or the like: In such cases, the legal system is not 'exchanged'; rather, the party's agreement merely works on a substantive level as it only replaces the dispositive law of the legal system designated in the context of the objective connection (Articles 4 et seq. Rome I Regulation).

**1158.** In arbitration proceedings, there might be a greater degree of freedom for the parties.[37] However, there is a certain risk that decisions relating such a contract will be made by state courts, for example, if the arbitration clause is ineffective or void. In this case, the law applicable according to Articles 4 et seq. of the Rome I Regulation will apply. This means that the choice of law can only supersede the dispositive law of the legal system thus invoked and not the mandatory law, i.e. it only affects substantive law and not conflict of laws.

---

32 On the rationale behind party autonomy Arnold, in Arnold, *Grundfragen des Europäischen Kollisionsrechts*, 2016, p. 23; Maultzsch, in von Hein/Rühl (eds.), *Kohärenz im Internationalen Privat- und Verfahrensrecht der Europäischen Union*, 2016, p. 153; Maultzsch, *RabelsZ* 75 (2011), 60; Kroll-Ludwigs, *Die Rolle der Parteiautonomie im europäischen Kollisionsrecht*, 2013, pp. 148 ff.

33 Overview in von Bar/Mankowski, *Internationales Privatrecht*, Volume 1: Allgemeine Lehren, 2nd ed. 2003, pp. 592 ff.

34 This is often accompanied by a corresponding jurisdiction or arbitration agreement, cf. below at paras. 1453 ff.

35 On that point Martiny, in *Münchener Kommentar zum BGB*, 9th ed. 2025, Art. 3 Rom I paras. 29 ff.; Mankowski, in Schmidt-Kessel, *Der Gemeinsame Referenzrahmen*, 2009, p. 389, 394 ff.; Magnus, *IPRax* 2010, 27, 33; more openly Leible/Wilke, in *Festschrift für Kronke*, 2020, p. 296.

36 Cf. above at para. 105.

37 On the question whether or not arbitral tribunals are bound by the Rome I Regulation, cf. already above at para. 1150.

## 2. THE CHOICE OF A LEGAL SYSTEM UNDER CONFLICT-OF-LAWS RULES

### a) *The Parties' Common Intention*

**1159.** The decisive factor for the choice of law is the common intention of the parties. This choice must be made expressly or clearly demonstrated by the terms of the contract or the circumstances of the case, as states Article 3(1) Rome I Regulation. The implied choice of law thus addressed has the same weight as an explicit choice of law. If a real intention cannot be determined with the necessary certainty, the choice of law is void, and an objective connecting factor comes into play according to Articles 4 et seq. of the Rome I Regulation.

### b) *Explicit Choice of Law*

**1160.** It is irrelevant whether the choice of law is made in the context of an individual agreement or as a choice of law clause in general terms and conditions, even if it is made subsequently (Article 3(2) Rome I Regulation). It must contain a clear agreement on the chosen law.

### c) *Implied Choice of Law*

**1161.** In practice, cases of a tacit choice of law are more problematic. Although Article 3(1) Rome I Regulation requires an unambiguous choice, the circumstances of the case must also be taken into account. Since a hypothetical intention of the parties is not sufficient, the indications in favour of certain laws must have so much weight that it can be concluded from them that the parties were conscious concerning their choice. In particular, the fact that the contract contains a choice of court agreement may serve as an indicator for an initial implied choice of law (Recital 12 Rome I Regulation). However, this does not automatically result in favour of the choice of law, as choice of court and choice of law agreements do have different functions.[38] The same applies to an agreement to an arbitration clause: It usually only has an indicative effect as to the question of choice of law if an institutional arbitral tribunal is chosen at a given place.

**1162.** In addition, a corresponding intention to choose the law can also be distinguished from further indicative conduct of the parties, for example, in the use of forms based on a certain legal system or other references to provisions

[38] Cf. Stürner, in Erman, *BGB Kommentar*, 17th ed. 2023, Art. 3 Rom I-VO para. 15.

of a legal system.[39] Due to the requirement of unambiguousness, an overall consideration of the parties' behaviour is usually required, which includes elements such as the language, the common habitual residence, or the currency used.

**1163.** The parties' subsequent conduct, especially during the proceedings, may also indicate a corresponding intention to choose the law. If the parties in court proceedings agree on the existence of claims under the Spanish Código civil, this may indicate a subsequent choice of law in favour of Spanish law.[40] This applies in any case if there is a corresponding awareness of the declaration so that an erroneous or unreasonable citation of Spanish legal norms, for example through an unreflected submission on Spanish law despite an obvious reference to a foreign country, is not to be regarded as the exercise of a choice of law.[41]

## 3. LIMITS TO THE CHOICE OF LAW

**1164.** The party autonomy thus granted is delimited, firstly, by overriding mandatory provision of the law of the forum (Article 9(1) Rome I Regulation).[42] Secondly, as explained above, the parties may also choose a neutral law that has no genuine connections to the case. Here, however, it is not possible to deviate from any mandatory rules of the chosen law (Article 3(3) Rome I Regulation or Article 3(4) Rome I Regulation for internal market cases and in the case of a choice of a third country's law). As a result, only a substantive choice of law is possible here. In light of the paramount importance of party autonomy, however, a generous approach towards the cross-border character of a contractual relationship seems appropriate.[43]

## 4. THE LAW APPLICABLE TO THE CHOICE OF LAW AGREEMENT

**1165.** The choice of law agreement is a contract independent of, and to be distinguished from, the main contract. Consequently, the choice of law

39 Cf. RGZ 95, 164, 165 f.; BGH JZ 1963, 167; BGH NJW 1997, 399; BGH NJW 2001, 1936; BGH NJW 2013, 308.
40 Cf. Mansel, *ZVglRWiss* 86 (1987), 1, 11.
41 Cf. OLG Köln NJW 1987, 1151, 1152; BGH NJW 1993, 1126.
42 Cf. below at paras. 1265. On the significance of the freedom of choice of law for the restriction of fundamental freedoms Herresthal, in Langenbucher, *Europäisches Privat- und Wirtschaftsrecht*, §2 paras. 71 ff.
43 See Böhle, *ZEuP* 2019, 72, 79 ff.; on the applicability of Article 3(3) Rome I Regulation to interest rate swap contracts, cf. Dias, *ZEuP* 2019, 615.

agreement must be validly concluded between the parties. As to the formation and validity of the parties' agreement regarding the applicable law, Articles 10, 11 and 13 of the Rome I Regulation apply (Article 3(5) of the Rome I Regulation). Therefore, the validity of a possible choice of law depends on the law that would (hypothetically) be applicable to the contract, were it to be considered valid. According to Article 10(2) Rome I Regulation, the law of the habitual residence of a party is also to be applied in addition to the contract law if the party claims that it did not consent to the contract and that it would be inequitable in the circumstances of the case to assess the legal effects of its conduct solely according to the contract law.

## IV. OBJECTIVE CONNECTION

References: C. Okoli, *Place of Performance. A Comparative Analysis* (London: Bloomsbury Publishing, 2020); F. Ferrari, 'From Rome to Rome via Brussels: Remarks on the Law Applicable to Contractual Obligations Absent a Choice by the Parties (Article 4 of the Rome I Regulation)', *RabelsZ* 73 (2009), 750; M.F. Müller, 'Objektive Anknüpfungsmomente für Schuldverhältnisse im europäischen IPR und IZVR', in J. von Hein/G. Rühl (eds.), *Kohärenz im Internationalen Privat- und Verfahrensrecht der Europäischen Union* (Tübingen: Mohr Siebeck, 2016), p. 243.

### 1. TAXONOMY OF CONTRACT TYPES

**1166.** If the parties have not made an effective choice of law, the law applicable to the contract must be determined objectively. If none of the specific contract types regulated in Articles 5 to 8 Rome I Regulation come into play,[44] Article 4 Rome I Regulation applies.

#### *a) Overview*

**1167.** Article 4(1) Rome I Regulation distinguishes between different types of contracts that occur particularly frequently, such as the purchase of movable goods (lit. a), service contracts (lit. b)[45] or rent/lease contracts (lit. c). In these cases, the contract has the closest connection to the state in which the party obliged to perform the characteristic service has his habitual residence at the time of the conclusion of the contract. The decisive factor is, therefore, not the

---

[44] Cf. below at paras. 1201 ff.

[45] According to the interpretation of the CJEU, this is to be understood as an obligation to perform a certain activity for remuneration, cf. CJEU, 8 May 2019, Case C-25/18, *Kerr/Postnov*, ECLI:EU:C:2019:376, paras. 36 ff.; CJEU, 3 October 2019, Case C-272/18, *TVP*, ECLI:EU:C:2019:827, para. 46.

place of performance of the respective obligation but the place of residence (or place of establishment, as the case may be) of the debtor of the characteristic performance. In other words, the performance of that party who does not owe the remuneration, gives the contract its distinct characteristics.[46] Note that the connecting factor in PIL differs from procedural law: Here, the special head of jurisdiction in Article 7 no. 1 Brussels Ibis Regulation is based on the place of performance.[47]

**1168.** If the subject matter of the contract is a right in rem in immovable property or a right to use immovable property, the law of the state in which the property is situated is applicable (*lex rei sitae*, Article 4(1)(c) Rome I Regulation). This applies, for example, to the purchase and rental of real estate, but not to the construction contract, which is to be regarded as a service contract – hence, Article 4(1)(b) Rome I Regulation is applicable.[48]

**1169.** Article 4(2) Rome I Regulation designates, as a presumption, the law of the habitual residence of the contracting party who provides the characteristic performance for contracts that are not to be classified under the contract types of the first paragraph or, as mixed contracts, fall under more than one of the contract types listed in lit. a to h. If, based on the individual circumstances of a certain case, the resulting connection does not appear to be fitting, the exception clause of Article 4(3) Rome I Regulation applies. It may only be referred to if the contract is 'manifestly more closely connected' to a country other than the one determined according to the first two paragraphs can be established. Finally, Article 4(4) Rome I Regulation has the function of a catch-all provision that covers contracts which, due to their structure, cannot be classified under para. 1 or para. 2 and are therefore not covered by para. 3 (with priority over para. 4).

### *b) Contracts for the Sale of Movable Property*

**1170.** Article 4(1)(a) Rome I Regulation basically covers all types of sales of movables, including consumer sales contracts, unless they fall under Article 6 Rome I Regulation.[49] Within the scope of application of the UN Sales Convention, the connecting factors of the Rome I Regulation do not apply insofar as the Convention applies as uniform law pursuant to Article 1(1)(a) CISG[50] or if, pursuant to Article 1(1)(b) CISG, conflict-of-laws rules lead to the application

46 On the principle of characteristic performance C. Wendelstein, *Kollisionsrechtliche Probleme der Telemedizin* (Tübingen: Mohr Siebeck, 2012), pp. 242 ff.

47 Arguing in favour of the use of this connecting criterion also in the context of cross-border trade contracts, therefore C. Okoli, *Place of Performance. A Comparative Analysis*, 2020.

48 On the broad understanding of the notion of services already above para. 1173.

49 Cf. below at para. 1181.

50 Cf. above at paras. 1151 ff.

of the law on the sale of goods of a contracting state. This primacy of the CISG applies, in principle, also in the case of a choice of law agreement, provided that it refers to the law of a state which has enacted the UN Sales Convention. However, sometimes, based on an interpretation of the contract, the common intention of the parties can be inferred that the CISG should be waived according to its Article 6. Only where the CISG has (external) gaps (e.g. concerning the statute of limitations, the amount of interest, set-off or assignment), the law invoked under conflict of laws must be used to fill the gap.[51]

**1171.** Outside the CISG's scope of application, Article 4(1)(a) Rome I Regulation refers to the law of the seller's habitual residence, i.e. the law of the seller's principal place of business or other place of business in the case of business transactions. This determines the law of the contract as the law of obligations that applies to the sales contract; the performance by transfer of ownership, on the other hand, is not governed by the Rome I Regulation (but normally by the *lex rei sitae*, as regulated by the applicable domestic PIL).

**1172.** The Rome I Regulation does not contain a separate definition for the habitual residence of the seller. If the seller is a natural person who does not act commercially, their 'de facto centre of main interests' is the habitual residence; if, on the other hand, the seller acts commercially or is a legal person or other commercial company, Article 19 Rome I Regulation applies, so that the place of business or the principal place of business or branch that they have at the time of conclusion of the contract must be considered (Article 19(3) Rome I Regulation). In cases where the conclusion of the contract and the performance by payment and transfer of ownership takes place at the same place and at the same time, Article 4(3) Rome I Regulation usually applies, as the connection to the place of conclusion clearly dominates.[52]

### *c) Service Contracts*

**1173.** For service contracts, Article 4(1)(b) Rome I Regulation designates the law of the state in which the 'service provider' has his habitual residence as the proper law. As some legal systems have a rather narrow concept of the term 'service', it is important to stress that this notion is to be interpreted autonomously. The term relates to services within the meaning of Articles 56 and 57(1) TFEU and the freedom to provide services regulated in the Services Directive so that contracts for commercial or freelance work are covered, whether for payment or free of charge. However, this only applies insofar as there are no

---

51 Cf. para. 1152.

52 Stürner, in Erman, *BGB Kommentar*, 17th ed. 2023, Art. 4 Rom I-VO para. 12; Thorn, in Grüneberg, *BGB Kommentar*, 84th ed. 2025, Art. 4 Rom I-VO paras. 6, 29.

other specific provisions in Article 4(1) Rome I Regulation or in Articles 5 to 8 Rome I Regulation. Thus, distribution contracts fall under Article 4(1)(f) Rome I Regulation, franchise contracts under lit. e, financial instrument contracts under lit. h, financial services contracts with consumers under Article 6 Rome I Regulation, transport contracts under Article 5 Rome I Regulation, individual employment contracts under Article 8 Rome I Regulation and insurance contracts possibly under Article 7 Rome I Regulation, otherwise under lit. b.[53]

### d) *Property-Related Contracts*

**1174.** In the absence of a choice of law under Article 4(1)(c) Rome I Regulation, contracts that concern the acquisition or transfer of a right in rem in an immovable object (land or a right equivalent to land, e.g. heritable building rights), e.g. sales contracts, gifts, or property development contract, are governed by the law of the place where the immovable property is located as this constitutes the law with the closest connection. The same applies to contracts concerning a right to use the property (rental and lease contracts, time-share contracts), which do not relate to a right in rem. Land acquisition or use or encumbrance must be the essential purpose of the contract so that, for example, a construction and repair contract[54] or a property management contract[55] do not fall under lit. c.

**1175.** The application of the *lex rei sitae* is justified by the close factual connection of the contract with the legal fate of the immovable property, which is generally determined by the *lex rei sitae*. Mandatory provisions of the tenancy law of the forum may prevail over a foreign tenancy statute for an object located in that state as overriding mandatory provisions (Article 9(1) Rome I Regulation), provided that don't already take precedence according to Article 3(3) Rome I Regulation. Article 4(1)(c) Rome I Regulation does not apply to a right in rem but only to the respective contractual relationship; in this respect, too, the *lex rei sitae* applies.

## 2. SUBSIDIARY CONNECTION

**1176.** If the applicable law cannot be determined via Article 4(1) Rome I Regulation because either none of the items is fulfilled or several are fulfilled simultaneously, the subsidiary general connection in Article 4(2) Rome I Regulation applies. It is based on the habitual residence of the party required

---

53 Cf. Stürner, in Erman, *BGB Kommentar*, 17th ed. 2023, Art. 4 Rom I-VO paras. 14 ff.

54 BGH RIW 1999, 456.

55 Magnus, in Staudinger, *BGB Kommentar* (2021), Art. 4 Rom I-VO para. 382.

to carry out the characteristic performance of the contract.[56] This is based on the insight that it should be the specific nature of the respective contractual relationship that determines the applicable law and not external and rather coincidental circumstances such as the place of conclusion of the contract. The subsidiary connection in Article 4(2) Rome I Regulation covers all contractual obligations for which a characteristic performance can be determined. It is relevant, for example, in the case of contracts for the sale of a business (M&A deals),[57] the donation or rental of movable property or also in the case of surety or licence agreements.[58]

**1177.** The characteristic performance of a contract against payment is not the monetary performance but the performance in kind or activity due under the specific type of contract, e.g. the landlord's performance in the case of a tenancy agreement. In the case of contracts without remuneration, the main performance of the party obliged to perform (e.g., a loan), and, in the case of unilateral obligations, the debtor's performance (e.g. the guarantor's performance) is considered the characteristic performance. Article 19 Rome I Regulation can be used to determine the habitual residence of the party providing the service, which becomes decisive in this way.

### 3. FALLBACK RULE

**1178.** If the individual contract lacks a characteristic performance obligation, as is the case with an exchange contract, the subsidiary connecting rule fails; for such cases, a catch-all provision exists in Article 4(4) Rome I Regulation. For such contractual relationships, the applicable law is to be determined according to the criterion of the closest connection by an overall weighing of the case's connections with a legal system, for example, by nationality, habitual residence, location, purposes, place of conclusion of contract, appearance in public or necessity of the involvement of public authorities. Whether the law thus found leads to the validity of the contract or not should be of no significance since the principle of *favor contractus* – unlike in Article 11(1) Rome I Regulation – does not play a role in this context.

---

56 Cf. BGH NJW 1987, 1141.

57 See Thorn, in Rauscher (ed.), *Europäisches Zivilprozess- und Kollisionsrecht*, 5th ed. 2023, Art. 4 Rom I-VO para. 89.

58 Cf. Thorn, in Rauscher (ed.), *Europäisches Zivilprozess- und Kollisionsrecht*, 5th ed. 2023, Art. 4 Rom I-VO paras. 90, 104 ff.

### 4. EXCEPTION CLAUSE

**1179.** Article 4(3) Rome I Regulation contains an exception clause for cases where the contract has an obviously closer connection to another state, i.e., if the reference to the habitual residence does not invoke the most relevant law (e.g. transactions against immediate cash payment).[59] The circumstances which should be considered in this respect include the relationship to other contractual relationships. It remains uncertain whether the common habitual residence of the parties in a country other than that which one of the connecting factors points to is sufficient for a closer connection.[60] Circumstances such as place of conclusion, contractual language and currency should be decisive.

**1180.** The regulatory system of Article 4 Rome I Regulation, however, precludes overriding the result established by paragraph 4 by applying the escape clause of paragraph 3 in a special case: A 'manifestly more close connection' than the 'closest connection' required for paragraph 4 cannot be reasonably argued for if para. 4 is applied correctly.

## V. THE CONSUMER CONTRACT

References: M. Dietrich, *Die situative Anwendung von Art. 17 Brüssel Ia-VO und Art. 6 Rom I-VO. Eine Untersuchung des kollisions- und zuständigkeitsrechtlichen Verbraucherschutzes unter Berücksichtigung US-amerikanischer Grundsätze* (Cham: Springer, 2020); G. Rühl, 'Consumer Protection in Choice of Law', (2011) 44 *Cornell Int'l L.J.* 569; G. Rühl, 'Die rechtsaktübergreifende Auslegung im europäischen Internationalen Privatrecht: Art. 6 der Rom I-VO und die Rechtsprechung des EuGH zu Art. 15 Brüssel I-VO', *GPR* 2013, 122; B. Scraback, 'Ökonomische Analyse des Verbraucherschutzes im Internationalen Privat- und Zivilverfahrensrecht', *GPR* 2017, 234.

### 1. OBJECTIVE CONNECTION

#### *a) Purpose of Protection*

**1181.** In globalised markets, national borders are hardly a barrier to commercial activities. This is particularly true for the EU's domestic market but often also for providers from third countries. From the consumer's point of view,

59 The escape clause is not applicable if the law applicable to the contract was determined via Article 4(4) Rome I Regulation, as the closest connection has already materialised.

60 Cf. e.g. BGH NJW 2015, 2581 (the case is now covered by the Matrimonial Property Regulation, cf. Stürner, in Erman, *BGB Kommentar*, 17th ed. 2023, Art. 27 EuGüVO para. 3).

it is often difficult to distinguish whether a contract has a foreign connection or not, especially in the case of contracts initiated or concluded via the internet. A problem can arise here if consumers do not encounter the level of protection they are familiar with in domestic transactions because the law of the provider applies. Of course, this is not the case for every foreign transaction. If, for example, a consumer goes abroad to make a purchase or request services, there is in itself no reason to subject the contract to be concluded or the contract concluded to a different law than that to which it is subject under the general rules (Articles 3 and 4 Rome I Regulation).

**1182.** Article 6 Rome I Regulation contains a special provision for consumers who are classified as particularly worthy of protection for the reasons mentioned. For them, the law of their habitual residence continues to apply, provided that the trader either carries out their professional or commercial activity in the consumer's state of residence (Article 6(1)(a) Rome I Regulation) or at least directs their activity to that state (Article 6(1)(b) Rome I Regulation). The second alternative, in particular, is very far-reaching.

**1183.** In principle, all types of contracts are covered, except for contracts of carriage and insurance contracts, insofar as they are governed by Articles 5 and 7 Rome I Regulation;[61] further exceptions can be found in Article 6(4) Rome I Regulation. This excludes, for example, contracts for the provision of services that must be provided exclusively in a state other than the state of the consumer's habitual residence (lit. b, e.g. hotel accommodation abroad, teaching courses abroad, language classes, etc.). The reference to foreign law is so strong here that the privileged treatment of consumers is not necessarily warranted.

### *b) Factual Requirements*

**1184.** For the application of consumer law, the existence of one of the two contract modalities covered by Article 6(1)(a) or (b) Rome I Regulation is necessary. These are intended to limit the application of the law of the consumer's habitual residence to situations where the consumer appears to require the protection of the legal system with which they are familiar because mutual trust is assumed (see Recital 25 Rome I Regulation). This is usually the case if the trader carries out professional or commercial activities in the state of the consumer's habitual residence.

---

61 Cf. paras. 1201 ff.

### aa) Business Activity in the State of the Consumer's Habitual Residence

**1185.** Lit. a requires the exercise of a typical sales or other business activity in the state of the consumer's habitual residence. This may be the case, for example, by making an explicit offer or advertising in that country.[62] Furthermore, the consumer must perform the legal acts necessary for the conclusion of the contract in that state, e.g. by accepting the offer. It is sufficient to send the offer to the state of the consumer's habitual residence; the receipt of the offer may also occur outside that state. Lit. a is also fulfilled by other business establishments in the state of the consumer's habitual residence.

### bb) Directing the Business Activity Towards the State of the Consumer's Habitual Residence

**1186.** The legislator deliberately designed lit. b to be of an extensive nature (Recital 25 Rome I Regulation). The trader does not need to exercise their activity in the state of the consumer's habitual residence (this is covered by lit. a), but rather, it is sufficient for the contract to be concluded so that it can be attributed to the trader's activity. 'Directing' refers to business activities (i.e. advertising activity) which are also directed in some way towards the state of the consumer's habitual residence ('direct by any means', '*diriger par tout moyen*'), with the aim of concluding and performing a contract.[63] In terms of content, the requirements in lit. b are lesser than in lit. a, even if the two alternatives are, from a systematic point of view, of equal rank. However, the trader must be the first to make contact with the consumer. If the 'initial contact' is made by the latter, lit. b does not apply.[64] As a general rule, the intention to direct one's activity to the consumer's state exists if the trader advertises there; in this respect, the medium (press, radio and television, mail, e-mail, social media) is of no primary importance.

**1187.** For the interpretation of the concept of 'directing', the case law of the CJEU on consumer jurisdiction in the Brussels I Regulation can be considered (cf. Recital 24 Rome I Regulation). According to the decision in the *Pammer/Alpenhof* case,[65] it has to be examined 'whether, before the conclusion of any contract with the consumer, it is apparent from [...] the trader's overall

62 BGHZ 167, 83, 89 f.

63 Martiny, in *Münchener Kommentar zum BGB*, 9th ed. 2025, Art. 6 Rom I-VO paras. 43 ff.; Magnus, in Staudinger, *BGB Kommentar* (2021), Art. 6 Rom I-VO para. 112; Mankowski, *IPRax* 2009, 238 f.

64 Cf. BGH NJW 2009, 298: the tourist approached the trader of his own free will; cf. also OLG Stuttgart IPRax 2016, 601 para. 40.

65 CJEU, 7 December 2010, Joined Cases C-585/08 and C-144/09, *Pammer/Hotel Alpenhof*, ECLI:EU:C:2010:740, paras. 92 f.

activity that the trader was envisaging doing business with consumers domiciled in one or more Member States, including the Member State of that consumer's domicile, in the sense that it was minded to conclude a contract with them. The following matters, the list of which is not exhaustive, are capable of constituting evidence from which it may be concluded that the trader's activity is directed to the Member State of the consumer's domicile, namely the international nature of the activity, mention of itineraries from other Member States for going to the place where the trader is established, use of a language or a currency other than the language or currency generally used in the Member State in which the trader is established with the possibility of making and confirming the reservation in that other language, mention of telephone numbers with an international code, outlay of expenditure on an internet referencing service in order to facilitate access to the trader's site or that of its intermediary by consumers domiciled in other Member States, use of a top-level domain name other than that of the Member State in which the trader is established, and mention of an international clientele composed of customers domiciled in various Member States.'[66] None of these characteristics are individually sufficient to fulfil the criterion of 'directing'. Rather, it depends on whether, during an overall consideration of the circumstances of the case, the trader's intention to conclude contracts with consumers domiciled in a certain state becomes apparent. The fact that the contract was not concluded through distance selling is irrelevant.[67]

**1188.** As a result, it might be difficult for businesses not to direct their activity practically worldwide if they use an English-language homepage. In these cases, an explicit 'disclaimer' and its consistent handling is probably necessary; this can be realised, for example, by not taking into account orders from consumers with habitual residence in one of the 'excluded' states, as far as this is possible without violating the prohibition of discrimination (Article 18 TFEU).

#### cc) In Particular: The Effects of the Geo-Blocking Regulation

**1189.** Seemingly contrary to the extension of the concept of 'directing', as developed by the CJEU, is also Regulation (EU) 2018/302, the so-called Geo-blocking Regulation.[68] According to Article 3(1) Geo-blocking Regulation, a provider is prohibited from blocking or restricting, by technical means or otherwise, a customer's access to the provider's online user interface on the grounds of the customer's nationality, place of residence or place of

---

[66] CJEU, 7 December 2010, Joined Cases C-585/08 and C-144/09, *Pammer/Hotel Alpenhof*, ECLI:EU:C:2010:740, para. 93.

[67] Cf. CJEU, 6 September 2012, Case C-190/11, *Mühlleitner*, ECLI:EU:C:2012:542, paras. 32 ff.

[68] On their private law aspects Hoffmann/Bombe, *EuZW* 2020, 131; on PIL issues Hoffmann, *JZ* 2018, 918; Martiny, in *Festschrift für Kronke*, 2020, p. 351.

establishment. According to Article 4(1) Geo-blocking Regulation, a provider may not apply different general terms and conditions for access to goods or services for reasons of the customer's nationality, place of residence or place of establishment under certain conditions. Finally, Article 5(1) Geo-blocking Regulation prohibits providers from applying different terms and conditions for a payment transaction within the framework of the payment methods it accepts based on the customer's nationality, place of residence or establishment, the location of the payment account, the place of establishment of the payment service provider or the place of issue of the payment instrument within the Union. However, Article 1(6) Geo-blocking Regulation explicitly clarifies that these requirements do not lead to a different assessment of the term 'directing' within the meaning of Article 6(1)(b) Rome I Regulation: Compliance with the requirements of Articles 3 to 5 of the Geo-blocking Regulation does not in itself warrant the conclusion that the trader is directing their activities towards the consumer state.

**1190.** The inherent contradiction cannot be resolved for all cases: If one takes the 'rule of interpretation' of the Geo-blocking Regulation seriously, this is likely to lead to consumer protection restrictions under the conflict of laws in some cases. However, if one grants priority to Article 6 Rome I Regulation, which has been done up to now, a trader's orientation towards the requirements of Articles 3 to 5 of the Geo-blocking Regulation often means that the requirements for 'directing' commercial or professional activities towards the consumer state are fulfilled. The chronological sequence of the two regulations speaks quite clearly in favour of the rule contained in Article 1(6) Geo-blocking Regulation.[69] The potential restriction of consumer protection that this implies may be justified as a general approach. It must be lamented, however, that it is not disclosed as such.[70]

### dd) Causality

**1191.** Finally, it is very controversial whether Article 6(1) Rome I Regulation also applies if the trader has directed his activity towards the consumer's country of domicile, but the conclusion of the contract has come about independently of this, for example, because the consumer has not taken note of the company's

---

69 Kohler (*ZEuP* 2020, 253, 262) sees the interpretation rule of Article 1(6) Geo-blocking Regulation as a mere 'precautionary measure' against an even broader interpretation of the concept of directing of the trader's activity by the CJEU.

70 Critical of this, also with reference to the basis of competence (Article 81(2) rather than Article 114 TFEU), Kohler, *ZEuP* 2020, 253, 259 ff.; cf. Martiny, in *Festschrift für Kronke*, 2020, pp. 351, 356 ff.; Hoffmann, *JZ* 2018, 918, 922 ff. For more details on the problem area, see also Dietrich, *Die situative Anwendung von Art. 17 Brüssel Ia-VO und Art. 6 Rom I-VO*, 2020, pp. 137 ff.

website at all. In this case, with regard to the conclusion of the contract, there is no causal link of directing the trader's activity towards the country of the consumer's domicile and the conclusion of the contract. But does this exclude the consumer protection at all?

**1192.** With respect to jurisdiction over consumer contracts, the CJEU has denied such a causality requirement.[71] The Court pointed to the wording of Article 15(1)(c) of the Brussels I Regulation, which does not mention any such causality. Moreover, the purpose of consumer protecting of the provision would be limited by a causality requirement, especially since difficult issues relating proof of causality would arise. However, the Court went on, causality could be a factor to be taken into account in the context of the criterion of 'directing' of the business activity.[72]

**1193.** As opposed to this view, it can be argued[73] that this leads to an unjustified preferential treatment of consumers who, without being 'attracted' by the trader, travels to the country where the trader has his seat of business on his own accord and concludes a contract there just like a citizen of that state. To avoid evidentiary problems, a presumption of the existence of causality could be set up.[74] In support of this approach, Recital 25 Rome I Regulation may be cited, which openly postulates the causality requirement for the context of Article 6(1) Rome I Regulation. Clearly, however, this would run counter to the plea of parallel interpretation of Rome I and Brussels Regulation, as spelled out in Recital 24 Rome I Regulation, as this would lead to a diverging interpretation of both legal acts.[75]

## 2. CHOICE OF LAW AND THE MOST FAVOURABLE SOLUTION

**1194.** According to Article 6(2) Rome II Regulation, a choice of law is also possible for consumer contracts. Exactly how the regulation of the choice of law for consumer contracts should be structured was controversial until the end of the legislative process. Initially, the European Commission and many of the Member States demanded that the choice of law for consumer contracts ought to be abolished altogether. Germany, Luxembourg and parts of the European Parliament, in particular, did not agree with this. They were

---

71 CJEU, 17 October 2013, Case C-218/12, *Emrek*, ECLI:EU:C:2013:666.

72 CJEU, 17 October 2013, Case C-218/12, *Emrek*, ECLI:EU:C:2013:666, para. 26. This is a circular argument, since one may only speak of a causal link between the directing of the trader's activity towards the consumer state and conclusion of the contract.

73 BGH EuZW 2012, 236.

74 Critical also Klöpfer/Wendelstein, *JZ* 2014, 298; Rühl, *IPRax* 2014, 41.

75 Cf. below at paras. 1397 ff.

concerned about a fair balance of the interests of consumers and entrepreneurs. Small and medium-sized enterprises, in particular, generally do not have a legal department. If the choice of law had been abolished in this area, they would have been burdened too much, as in that case the consumer's domestic law would have applied to every consumer contract. However, the possibility of choice of law in consumer contracts is not self-evident. Swiss law, for example, stipulates that a choice of law is ineffective in contracts with consumers (Article 120(2) Swiss Act on PIL). This is because the choice of law usually leads to the application of a legal system that is less favourable to the consumer.

**1195.** The Rome I Regulation did not choose this radical path. Rather, Article 6(2) Rome I Regulation was created as a compromise. For the consumer's benefit, however, the choice of law is subject to the condition that it does not deprive them of the protection that would be granted by mandatory provisions of the otherwise applicable law. A determination of the most favourable solution must therefore be made between the provisions of the chosen law and the provisions of the law actually applicable (i.e. according to Article 6(1) Rome I Regulation).[76]

**1196.** This comparison is to be carried out concerning non-dispositive consumer protection rules of the state of the consumer's habitual residence. This therefore concerns all rules of a contractual nature (conclusion of contract, binding nature, content of contract and review of content) in which either explicit consumer protection is regulated. This also includes rules of the general law of obligations, such as creditor-favouring rules on the burden of proof, mandatory provisions of the law on travel contracts, also rules of judge-made law, but not mandatory provisions that pursue other objectives (e.g. foreign trade or foreign exchange law objectives); these can, however, be applied if necessary as overriding mandatory provisions under Article 9 Rome I Regulation.[77] If the consumer-protective content of the chosen contract law falls short of the standard of the country of the habitual residence of the consumer, the special conflict-of-laws rule of Article 6(2) Rome I Regulation applies in favour of the more favourable law of the consumer's state of residence. It only applies insofar as the *lex causae* falls short of the more favourable consumer domicile law.

**1197.** According to Article 6(2) Rome I Regulation, the trader can also include a choice of law clause in favour of the law of their seat in their standard terms.[78]

---

[76] For an example cf. Stürner, in Langenbucher, *Europäisches Privat- und Wirtschaftsrecht*, §8 paras. 47 f.

[77] Cf. below at paras. 1265 ff.

[78] On the control of jurisdiction and arbitration agreements in GTC Mäsch, in Langenbucher, *Europäisches Privat- und Wirtschaftsrecht*, §9 paras. 47 ff.; cf. also Eichel, *IPRax* 2016, 305.

Their validity depends, first of all, on whether they do not violate rules on general terms and conditions. According to Article 3(5), 10(1) Rome I Regulation, this is based on the hypothetical contract law, i.e. the law of the seat of the trader. It is disputed whether or not already at this stage a comparison as to the most favoured solution should also be made. Such a comparison, however, would likely contradict the fact that Article 6(2) Rome I Regulation only protects consumers concerning the result of the choice of law but does not place the choice of law itself under any caveat of favourability; rather, it is subjected as a whole to the regime of Article 3 Rome I Regulation.[79] Also, Article 10(2) Rome I Regulation already contains a special protective provision.

**1198.** However, the CJEU found deficits concerning the clarity and transparency of a choice of law clause given the 'consumer's weak position vis-à-vis the seller or supplier with respect in particular to their level of knowledge'.[80] Unfairness of the choice-of-law clause within the meaning of Article 3(1) and (5) of the Unfair Terms Directive is, therefore, possible 'in so far as it leads the consumer into error by giving him the impression that only the law of that Member State applies to the contract, without informing him that under Article 6(2) of the Rome I Regulation they also enjoy the protection of the mandatory provisions of the law that would be applicable in the absence of that term'.[81] As a result, the choice-of-law clause must generally indicate that the consumer, pursuant to Article 6(2) Rome I Regulation also enjoys the protection of the mandatory rules of their state of residence in any case.

**1199.** It is doubtful whether a choice-of-law clause such as 'The contract shall be governed by the mandatory provisions of the country in which the customer habitually resides. In all other respects, Luxembourg law shall apply' would satisfy the requirements of Article 5 Unfair Terms Directive, namely that a clause must be drafted in plain, intelligible language. According to the standards of the CJEU, this may not necessarily be the case, as the favourability principle of Article 6(2) of the Rome I Regulation must be made explicit.

**1200.** However, the CJEU decision is not likely to be beneficial to the consumer – they will practically never take note of the choice of law agreement anyway

---

79 Thorn, in Grüneberg, *BGB Kommentar*, 84th ed. 2025, Art. 3 Rom I para. 9; Pfeiffer, *IPRax* 2015, 320, 322; contra BGH IPRax 2013, 557 para. 33; critically Pfeiffer, *LMK* 2013, 343552.

80 CJEU, 28 July 2016, Case C-191/15, *Amazon*, ECLI:EU:C:2016:612, para. 68; cf. W.-H. Roth, *IPRax* 2017, 449; Rühl, *Common Market Law Review* 2018, 201; P. Huber, in *Festschrift für Kronke*, 2020, p. 215.

81 CJEU, 28 July 2016, Case C-191/15, *Amazon*, ECLI:EU:C:2016:612, para. 71; likewise CJEU, 3 October 2019, Case C-272/18, *TVP*, ECLI:EU:C:2019:827, paras. 55 ff.

('rational disinterest').[82] Thus, for example, it seems to be irrelevant from the consumer's point of view whether or not the choice of law clause in an airline's general terms and conditions contains a reference to the fact that, according to Article 5(2) Rome I Regulation, not the law of any country may be chosen.[83]

# VI. SPECIFIC CONFLICT-OF-LAWS RULES FOR CONTRACTS OF CARRIAGE, INSURANCE AND EMPLOYMENT CONTRACTS

## 1. TRANSPORT CONTRACTS

**1201.** Article 5 Rome I Regulation regulates the conflict of laws of the contract of carriage. Paragraph 1 contains a connection to the habitual residence of the carrier for the contract of carriage of goods, paragraph 2 regulates the contract of carriage of passengers, for which, in principle and for their protection, the habitual residence of the passenger (person to be transported) is decisive, and secondly, the connection to the habitual residence of the carrier (and thus to the place of the characteristic performance). A choice of law is possible in accordance with lit. a-e.

**1202.** In the absence of a choice of law, the exception clause of paragraph 3 subjects the contract to the law of the country with which the contract has an obviously closer connection than to the law invoked. Insofar as they are not to be treated as consumer contracts or as package travel contracts within the meaning of Article 6(4)(b) Rome I Regulation, contracts of carriage do not fall under Article 6 Rome I Regulation.

## 2. INSURANCE CONTRACTS

**1203.** Article 7 Rome I Regulation contains another special conflict-of-laws rule for insurance contracts. It draws up a fundamental distinction between large risks and reinsurance risks on the one hand and mass risks on the other. For the former, the applicable law is determined by the general conflict-of-laws rules of Articles 3 and 4 Rome I Regulation; only for the latter does Article 7

---

82 In detail Mankowski, *IPRax* 2019, 208.

83 Against a corresponding obligation also OLG Frankfurt IPRax 2019, 241 paras. 26 ff. A referral to the CJEU by the AG Nuremberg (RRa 2019, 36; CJEU, Case C-701/18, *Geld-für-Flug GmbH ./. Ryanair Ltd.*, OJ 2019 C 72/16) on the question of the form of the choice of law clauses has been resolved due to a settlement agreement between the parties.

Rome I Regulation apply. Paragraph 1 of the Rome I Regulation regulates the scope of application for directly insured large risks located within and outside the EU and the EEA. Paragraph 2 allows a choice of law for large risks in the sense of Article 3 Rome I Regulation and prescribes the law of the insurer's habitual residence as a secondary connection if an effective choice of law is lacking. Paragraph 3 allows only a limited choice of law concerning the law of the location of the risk or regarding the law of the habitual residence, in part also concerning the nationality of the policyholder, for certain risks, such as life insurance, damage insurance and liability insurance. Furthermore, the law of the location of the risk is decisive in the event of a lack of choice of law. Para. 4 applies to compulsory insurance. Para. 5 regulates the case of risks spread over several Member States, para. 6 regulates the location of the risk.

## 3. EMPLOYMENT CONTRACTS

**1204.** Finally, the law applicable to the employment contract and the employment relationship is also subject to a special rule prescribed in Article 8 Rome I Regulation. This rule safeguards the interests of the employee as the 'weaker party' in the employment relationship. The law of the employment contract can also be determined through a choice of law pursuant to Article 3 Rome I Regulation. Structured similarly to Article 6(2) Rome I Regulation, para. 1 seeks to prevent the employees from being deprived of the protection afforded to them by the mandatory provisions of the law that would be applicable following the objective connections of the employment contract in the absence of a choice of law pursuant to para. 2 (see Recital 35 Rome I Regulation). They remain applicable, in principle, based on a so-called favourability comparison, even if a freely chosen contractual law applies.

**1205.** Paragraphs 2 and 3 contain a tiered regulation of objective references, which can take effect without a choice of law within the meaning of paragraph 1. Paragraphs 2 and 3 provide for a different objective connecting factor for two typical groups of employment contracts with a foreign connection. Paragraph 2 refers to the usual place of work, the law of which continues to apply even in the case of temporary posting, but the rule also contains further differentiations. Paragraph 3 concerns employees with changing assignments abroad. In the interest of avoiding an ongoing change of applicable laws, the law of the place of the employer's establishment, i.e. the *lex loci contractus*, generally applies. Paragraph 4 reverts to the principle of the closest connection in an escape clause modelled after Article 4(3) Rome I Regulation, which applies in the case of a closer connection to a state other than the one whose law is referred to in paragraphs 2 or 3.

# VII. A CONFLICT-OF-LAWS REGIME FOR SMART CONTRACTS

References: M. Lehmann, 'Digital assets and smart contracts', in M.M. Fogt (ed.), *Private International Law in an Era of Change* (Cheltenham: Edward Elgar Publishing, 2024), p. 81; B.Y. Ripley, 'The law applicable to (digital) transfer of digital assets: the transfer of cryptocurrencies via blockchains', in M.M. Fogt (ed.), *Private International Law in an Era of Change* (Cheltenham: Edward Elgar Publishing, 2024), p. 127; G. Rühl, 'Smart Contracts und anwendbares Recht', in T. Brägelmann/M. Kaulartz (eds.), *Smart Contracts* (Munich: C.H. Beck, 2019), p. 147.

**1206.** So-called smart contracts are a fairly new phenomenon. Their novelty lies in the fact that they consist of certain contractual obligations and framework conditions that are fed into software, which then uses other data sources to recognise events that trigger the specified legal consequences.[84] If blockchain technology is used, such contracts could be considered to have a cross-border element per se, as they have practically worldwide points of contact.[85] This view is not compelling if one considers the blockchain a purely technical medium for perpetuating information that does not give the contract any special character. The following account departs from the assumption, that a cross-border element beyond that is present.

## 1. A LEX DIGITALIS FOR SMART CONTRACTS?

**1207.** Some authors argue that smart contracts are subject to their own regulatory regime. This is best reflected by the slogan: 'Code is law!'[86] Taken at face value, this would mean that the instructions contained in the software would be valid in their own right and take precedence over the applicable law, and, indeed, over PIL.[87] It is true that in the seemingly borderless internet, a spatial-horizontal assignment to a state's legal system is difficult. This is mirrored, for example, by the difficulties in determining international jurisdiction and the applicable law in tort actions for violations of personality rights via social networks.[88] With respect to the software that executes the smart contract, any

84 For a definition cf. above para. 997.

85 See G. Rühl, in T.H. Brägelmann/M. Kaulartz, *Smart Contracts* (Munich: C.H. Beck, 2019), pp. 147, 150, 154.

86 Athanassiou, European Central Bank Working Paper Series No 16 (October 2017), pp. 38 ff.

87 Cf. Savelyev, (2017) 26(2) Information and Communications Technology Law 116.

88 Cf. CJEU, 25 October 2011, Joined Cases C-509/09 and C-161/10, *eDate Advertising/Martinez*, ECLI:EU:C:2011:685; cf. the overview in Stürner, in Erman, *BGB Kommentar*, 17th ed. 2023, Art. 40 EGBGB paras. 18 ff.

localisation is indeed difficult because its code – to stay in the classic terminology of PIL – 'has its seat everywhere and nowhere'.[89]

**1208.** It is settled that conflict-of-laws rules only apply if and to the extent that there is no overriding uniform law. This also applies regarding the Rome I Regulation: It grants priority to the UN Sales Convention insofar as the latter is not called upon to apply under conflict-of-laws rules, but applies *ipso iure* if the substantive requirements of Article 1 CISG are met.[90] The supremacy of the UN Sales Convention is accepted under conflict of laws, because the conflict between different legal systems that is constitutive for PIL no longer exists. However, this connection only applies to state law.[91] The Rome I Regulation does not consider non-governmental rules to be uniform laws in the sense mentioned. Even a corresponding party-autonomous agreement cannot help overcome this deficit.[92] If the parties agree that their contract is governed by the UNIDROIT Principles of International Commercial Contracts (PICC), this clause only has significance within the scope of what is permissible under the applicable legal system. The *lex mercatoria*, therefore, does not supersede the conflict of laws.[93]

**1209.** The same applies to the so-called *lex sportiva*: The world of professional sports – maybe even more than cross-border commercial transactions – has a massive interest in not being subjected to a state's law. This is already shown by the existence of the Court of Arbitration for Sport (CAS) in Lausanne, Switzerland, which decides on disputes between professional athletes and federations and is only subject to limited control by the Swiss Federal Supreme Court. Some argue that its judgments, together with the relevant statutes, such as those of the IOC or FIFA, form a legal order of their own like the *lex mercatoria* and should be eligible to apply under conflict of laws.[94] However, here, too, scepticism is warranted: The regulatory network of the *lex sportiva* can be described as patchy at best. The case of the German ice speed skater Claudia Pechstein has furthered this scepticism: The suspicion that the sports federations may promote inequality weighs too heavily.[95]

---

89 P. Vigna/M. Casey, The Age of Cryptocurrency: How Bitcoin and Digital Money Are Challenging the Global Economic Order (New York: St. Martin's Press, 2015), p. 66.

90 Cf. above at paras. 1143, 1151 ff.

91 Above at para. 1157.

92 The more openly drafted Article 3(2) of the original draft of the Rome I Regulation did not find its way into the adopted version, COM (2005) 650 final. Cf. Schinkels, *GPR* 2007, 106 (in favour of choice of the UNIDROIT Principles).

93 On the possibly differing assessment in the context of arbitration proceedings cf. above paras. 1149 f.

94 Cf. de Oliveira, *Int Sports Law J* (2017), 101; J. Adolphsen, in C. Bumke/A. Röthel, *Privates Recht* (Tübingen: Mohr Siebeck, 2012), p. 93.

95 In its decision in the *Pechstein* case (BGHZ 210, 292), the BGH considered the arbitration clause contained in the athletes' agreement to be effective and thus strengthened the

**1210.** A fortiori, these considerations must also apply to a lex digitalis of whatever form it takes.[96] An independent law of the internet beyond national legal systems has developed even to a lesser extent than in the fields of international business or sports.[97] The premise that smart contracts are designed to be forgery-proof and that legal regulations are therefore superfluous from the outset may not be beyond doubt: One may point to the attack on the crowdfunding vehicle 'The DAO' in the summer of 2016, in which hackers used a gap in the Ethereum blockchain[98] to divert considerable sums of the cryptocurrency Ether. Contrary to the dogma of the immutability of the blockchain, this transaction was reversed.[99] This case, which has created fuzz all the way up to the US Securities and Exchange Commission (SEC), illustrates that 'code' is ultimately made by humans and, therefore, prone to error. If legally significant consequences are intended and implemented through it, this must also be subject to legal rules. In other words, the blockchain does not create a legal vacuum.[100]

**1211.** The fact that 'the computer protocols underlying decentralised networks […] make transactions over any assets possible, […] allow machines to dispose of funds autonomously, and […] give people worldwide the ability to set binding rules for cooperation – without the involvement of intermediaries such as lawyers, accountants, banks, courts, or even without being based on a specific legal system',[101] as is claimed, is unlikely to be true in general terms.

**1212.** If one returns to the idea of 'code is law', this can, at best, be considered significant to the extent that it refers to purely factual circumstances. The agreements laid down in the code can, at most, have the substantive effects granted

autonomy of the sports associations. In contrast, the OLG Munich (JZ 2015, 355) as the lower court assumed that the arbitration clause was null and void due to market abuse (sec. 19 GWB). Apparently, the BGH did not want to initiate such a radical departure from the previous practice.

96 Calliess, *Zeitschrift für Rechtssoziologie*, 2002, Vol. 23(2), pp. 185, 188.

97 ICANN's conflict resolution procedure alone, which is cited as evidence of the autonomy of the lex digitalis, may be an example of the self-regulation of the Internet and the emergence of a global civil constitution from the perspective of legal sociology, see G. Teubner, *Globale Zivilverfassungen. Alternativen zu einer staatszentrierten Verfassungstheorie*, Kursbuch (Universitätsbibliothek Johann Christian Senckenberg, 2004), Heft 155: Neue Rechtsordnungen, p. 81. But in terms of contract law, it offers little support for a uniform law of any kind that would apply transnationally to internet contracts and thus make conflict of laws superfluous.

98 On this Allen, *ERCL* 2018, 307, 339 f.

99 Such occurrences can lead to a 'hard fork', i.e. a split-off of the cryptocurrency. This is what happened with Bitcoin Cash and Bitcoin Gold. Cf. Langenbucher, *AcP* 218 (2018), 385, 403 f.

100 Athanassiou, European Central Bank Working Paper Series No 16 (October 2017), pp 38 ff.; Fries, *AnwBl* 2018, 86, 87; Martiny, *IPRax* 2018, 553, 559 at note 109.

101 Glatz, in Blocher/Heckmann/Zech, DGRI Jahrbuch 2016, 2017, p. 81, citing D.R.G. Wood, 'Ethereum: A Secure Decentralised Generalised Transaction Ledger', 2013, http://gavwood.com/paper.pdf.

to them by the respective contract law. If one thus assumes that the contractual agreements, insofar as they are automated and 'self-executing', regulate the relevant legal relations between the parties completely and conclusively, and thus no legal enforcement by external bodies is necessary, such a statement would indeed be correct. However, this hardly differs from the otherwise valid assumption that contracts regulate the parties' contractual relations within the scope of what is legally permissible, superseding dispositive law. As Article 1103 of the French code civil states in an emblematic fashion:[102] '*Les conventions légalement formées tiennent lieu de loi à ceux qui les ont faites*.' The question of state law and state enforcement thus becomes factually irrelevant, but not legally.

## 2. THE APPLICATION OF THE ROME I REGULATION

**1213.** Article 1 Rome I Regulation states that the Regulation applies to contractual obligations in civil and commercial matters. Company law issues are excluded from the scope of application (Article 1(2)(f) Rome I Regulation). It could at least be considered that the blockchain network as a whole is to be regarded as a company,[103] so the Rome I Regulation would not apply. This idea could be based on the multipolar character of the network: This could prove to be characteristic of the entire smart contract, as its mechanisms of validation and perpetuation are constitutive of the entire agreement.

**1214.** However, such a classification is rather far-fetched. The criterion of a voluntary obligation entered into by the parties is of central importance for the applicability of the Rome I Regulation.[104] The smart contract is based precisely on this: Even if certain legal consequences are to occur automatically and a corresponding code is recorded in the blockchain network for this purpose, it is precisely the party agreement that proves to be formative and not, for example, the validation mode with the help of distributed ledger technology: This, ultimately, only has an information technology content and not so much a legal content. At most, legal constructions such as Initial Coin Offerings, which are processed via so-called Decentralised Autonomous Organisations (DAO), may qualify as corporations.[105]

---

102 Cf. above at para. 19.

103 Zimmermann, *IPRax* 2018, 566, 567 f.

104 Cf. above at para. 1145.

105 On this Zimmermann, *IPRax* 2018, 566, 567 ff. (who, however, in the absence of a suitable connecting factor such as the registered office, place of incorporation or incorporation of the company, wants to connect to the respective individual transaction in an accessory manner); Langenbucher, *AcP* 218 (2018), 385; S. Voshgmir, *Blockchains, Smart Contracts und das Dezentrale Web* (Berlin: Technologiestiftung Berlin, 2016), p. 26 (available at https://www.technologiestiftung-berlin.de/fileadmin/daten/media/publikationen/170130_BlockchainStudie.pdf).

## 3. THE CHARACTERISATION OF SMART CONTRACTS

**1215.** In the case of smart contracts, a legal distinction can be made between respective obligations and the performance thereof.[106] The fact that the performance of a contractual agreement – the opening of a door lock, the ordering of new milk or the debiting of Bitcoins as a contractual penalty for default on the part of the other party – is completely automated does not change the fact that in the legal sense, it is the level of performance that is involved.[107] From the perspective of the Rome I Regulation, such transactions belong to the law applicable to the contract as a whole (Article 12 Rome I Regulation).

**1216.** Approaches that split the smart contract into a 'smart' and an 'analogue' part, in the sense that the 'smart' part runs alongside the analogue part, but does not replace it, should be rejected.[108] Such a distinction is not relevant for the classification under the conflict of laws. The Rome I Regulation refers to the hypothetical contract law for the legal assessment of the conclusion of a contract (Article 10 Rome I Regulation). Regardless of how the conclusion of a contract via a blockchain network is assessed from a factual point of view,[109] a single legal regime applies from the perspective of conflict of laws.[110] Thus, with regard to the respective classification, the content of the smart contract is decisive.

## 4. CHOICE OF LAW

**1217.** As usual, a choice of law agreement takes precedence (Article 3 Rome I Regulation). This includes the application of Article 3(3) and (4) Rome I Regulation; the (intended) establishment of the contract in the blockchain as such is not sufficient to give the contract a cross-border dimension.

**1218.** It is a different issue whether the choice of law can also be made by third parties. Some authors argue that the operator of a platform through which the

---

106 For a (probably) different view, cf. Glatz, in Blocher/Heckmann/Zech, DGRI Jahrbuch 2016, 2017, p. 81.

107 Reference to the blurring difference between executory and executed contract also by Werbach/Cornell, (2017) 67 *Duke Law Review* 313, 335.

108 Martiny, *IPRax* 2018, 553, 555; for Austria Smets/Kapeller, *ÖJZ* 2018, 293.

109 It regularly appears preferable to examine the prerequisites of the conclusion of the contract 'analogously'; the feed into the blockchain network then functions as pure execution comparable to documentation; also Bertram, *MDR* 2018, 1416, 1419 f. The submission and receipt of a declaration of intent with the help of the blockchain network, on the other hand, are difficult to depict in legal terms, cf. Heckelmann, *NJW* 2018, 504, 505 f.

110 The legally relevant contract (as a consensus of will) is thus considered independently of its documentation (in the blockchain, on paper or otherwise), Allen, *ERCL* 2018, 307, 329.

smart contract is to be processed,[111] should have the mandate to agree on a choice of law. Others make the case for legislation to oblige the platform operators to choose certain legal systems (only), which then serve as the grounds for the choice of law of the parties joining the platform.[112] Admittedly, this can only become relevant in a few narrowly defined areas, and even there, only for platform operators subject to respective jurisdiction, such as the EU. It also remains unclear what purpose this restriction of the party's freedom of choice of law is supposed to serve. A concurrence of code (i.e. contract performance provisions) and law[113] is, after all, only required if the code violates overriding mandatory provisions of the *lex fori* (Article 3(3) or Article 9(1) Rome I Regulation). In many cases, it may not be possible to determine beforehand the legal system that decides over the characterisation of overriding mandatory provisions. At best, an exclusive place of jurisdiction might be agreed on by the parties. Which jurisdiction that might by and large follows from the interests of the parties, which, in turn, cannot be determined in an abstract manner and imposed on the platform operator as a regulatory duty. The better reasons, therefore, still speak in favour of not regulating the choice of law. This has nothing to do with the question of whether or not non-state law[114] can be chosen:[115] Code is not 'law', not even non-state law. The Code can only create rules within the framework set out by the dispositive part of the law invoked in each case.

## 5. OBJECTIVE CONNECTING FACTORS

**1219.** If, on the other hand, no such agreement is made, the law applicable to a smart contract must be determined objectively. The Rome I Regulation provides different connecting factors depending on the type of contract. In general, the domicile of the party providing the performance that is characteristic of the respective contract is chosen as the connecting factor. For example, in the case of a smart rental contract via an online platform, the law of the landlord is designated (Article 4(1)(b) Rome I Regulation).

### *a) Starting Point*

**1220.** The localisation of the smart contract is thus carried out outside the spatially intangible blockchain technology and is oriented towards the analogue

111 E.g. Ethereum, cf. above at para. 1000.
112 Kuntz, *AcP* 220 (2020), 51, 82 ff. referring to Directive 98/26/EC.
113 In that sense Kuntz, *AcP* 220 (2020), 51, 82; Paech, *Mod. L. Rev.* 80 (2016), 1073, 1102.
114 Cf. para. 1157.
115 In that sense, however, Kuntz, *AcP* 220 (2020), 51, 86.

world.[116] The 'smart', i.e. automated, performance of the contract or sanction for breach of duty is a 'performance' within the meaning of Article 12(1)(b) Rome I Regulation or an ancillary duty securing performance.

*b) Cryptocurrency Contracts*

**1221.** However, the determination of a connecting factor is more difficult if the exchange of performances itself is directed towards digital transactions. In many cases, so-called cryptocurrencies, such as Bitcoins or Ether, are exchanged or acquired within the framework of smart contracts. The mere fact that such virtual payment units are used does not eliminate the contractual qualification. Bitcoins and similar phenomena are generally not tradable securities, so the Rome I Regulation is also applicable to transactions related to them (Article 1(2)(d) Rome I Regulation).[117]

aa) Counter-Performance in Cryptocurrency

**1222.** In a contract where the counter-performance is provided as a cryptocurrency, it is debatable whether the regular connecting factors of Article 4(1) Rome I Regulation are to be applied or – as the consideration is not to be provided in monetary form – the subsidiary connecting factor of Article 4(2) Rome II Regulation or even the exception clause of Article 4(4) Rome I Regulation. If one classifies such contracts as an exchange,[118] then the latter is obvious.[119] However, there are good reasons for applying the more precise subsidiary connecting factor: According to the latter, reference is made to the domicile of the party that provides the performance characteristic of the contract. Usually, this will not be the obligation to transfer Bitcoins.[120]

bb) Cryptocurrency as Main Performance

**1223.** If, on the other hand, a contract for the (derivative) acquisition of Bitcoins or other virtual currency units in exchange for money is the subject matter, then the classification as a sales contract under conflict of laws should be ruled out in any case, since it is not about an obligation to transfer movable property (Article 4(1)(a) Rome I Regulation).[121] In this respect, the subsidiary connection in Article 4(2) Rome I Regulation is less important. It could be argued

[116] Cf. Zimmermann, *IPRax* 2018, 566, 568.
[117] Martiny, *IPRax* 2018, 553, 558, 560.
[118] Langenbucher, *AcP* 218 (2018), 385.
[119] Cf. Martiny, *IPRax* 2018, 553, 558, 561.
[120] In the case of contract concluded via an intermediary platform, however, the law applicable to the platform itself may be considered the designated law, cf. Martiny, *IPRax* 2018, 552, 560 f.
[121] The application of the CISG should also be ruled out for this reason, Martiny, *IPRax* 2018, 553, 561.

that the party owing the cryptocurrency provides the performance characteristic for the contract since it is not classified as money.[122]

cc) Cryptocurrency as Payment for Cryptocurrency

**1224.** The situation would be different again in the case of an exchange of two virtual currencies (e.g. Bitcoin against Ether): Here, only the escape clause of Article 4(4) Rome I Regulation remains. In this case, the applicable law must be determined by considering and weighing of all circumstances according to the principle of the closest connection.

## 6. THE LAW APPLICABLE TO THE FORM OF THE CONTRACT

**1225.** No special features apply concerning the law applicable to formal validity:[123] It is true that, because of the ubiquity of the blockchain, the lex loci actus (Article 11(1) Rome I Regulation) might be considered indeterminable. However, this view would disregard the fact that the unalterable documentation of the contractual programme in the blockchain is not the legally relevant form. Rather, the various formal requirements – such as written form or notarial certification – cannot be represented and fulfilled in the blockchain, so compliance with them must always occur outside the network.[124]

## 7. VIRTUAL SECURITIES

**1226.** Virtual collateral is widely used in smart contracts. This in itself does not eliminate the contractual qualification. However, the legal classification of the collateral itself must be considered differently. On the one hand, a classification as movable or immovable property can be considered. This cannot be discussed in depth here.[125]

## 8. DISRUPTION OF PERFORMANCE

**1227.** By definition, disruptions in performing the contractual obligations should not actually occur in the case of smart contracts. However, cases are

122 Martiny, *IPRax* 2018, 552, 561.

123 Cf. below at paras. 1244 ff.

124 Heckelmann, *NJW* 2018, 504, 507; Bertram, *MDR* 2018, 1416, 1418. The only dispute is whether the smart contract can comply with the text form (e.g. sec. 126b German Civil Code), cf. Heckelmann, *NJW* 2018, 504, 507 as opposed to Bertram, *MDR* 2018, 1416, 1418 f.

125 More on this issue in Martiny, *IPRax* 2018, 552, 556 ff.

conceivable in which the applicable legal system denies the contract's validity as a whole, for example, due to a violation of a legal prohibition or morality. If, for example, the 'smart rental contract' stipulates that the door lock will be locked automatically if the tenant is in default, the legal system will likely refuse to recognise this agreement – on whatever basis.[126] The resulting claims of the tenant, which are initially directed to the access to the flat, but also to changing the code in the blockchain so that such a breach of contract does not occur in the future, can be qualified contractually.

**1228.** Cases in which the error lies in the software are different again. This can be due to an error in the code ('bug') or also to the manipulative influence of third parties. Of course, a combination of both factors is also possible. The events surrounding the aforementioned case of The DAO show that such scenarios are quite real.

**1229.** However, an added block in the blockchain, once verified, proves to be unchangeable by its very nature and also by the underlying expectation of the participants in the blockchain network. Errors are excluded by definition. Technically, a change of the chain of blocks should only be possible if a programme code, however changed, is added to the blockchain. But what are the grounds for such a claim?

**1230.** A distinction must certainly be made between claims against the contracting party, i.e., performance modalities which are also subject to the law applicable to the contract (Article12(1) Rome I Regulation), and claims against manipulative third parties, which are likely to classify as unjust enrichment or torts and, as such, are subject to the Rome II Regulation. In this respect, it should be noted that difficulties might arise with regard to the determination of the relevant place of damage.

## VIII. PRE-CONTRACTUAL LIABILITY IN THE CONFLICT OF LAWS

References: C. Gomille, 'Die Informationshaftung im europäischen Kollisionsrecht', *JZ* 2017, 289.

**1231.** In contrast to notably German law, liability arising from *culpa in contrahendo* is explicitly considered a non-contractual obligation in EU PIL and

126 On 'digital ownership' Kuschel, *AcP* 220 (2020), 98.

thus placed in the Rome II Regulation. The Regulation thus follows the case law of the CJEU relating to the place of the jurisdiction on torts within Article 7 no. 2 Brussels Ibis Regulation, which considers the claim arising from *culpa in contrahendo* to be a tortious if a contract was not concluded.[127] However, Article 12(1) Rome II Regulation provides for an ancillary reference to the (hypothetical) contract law. Only if this cannot be determined may the case be classified as pertaining to tort law (Article 12(2) Rome II Regulation).

**1232.** According to Recital 30 Rome II Regulation, *culpa in contrahendo* is a concept that is autonomous of the Regulation and covers the breach of duties of disclosure, the breaking off of contractual negotiations and also the liability of administrators and the personal liability of representatives. Breaches of general duties of protection are not included, as these fall under Article 4(1) Rome II Regulation. Based on an autonomous interpretation of EU law, only breaches of duties of care that are related to the conclusion of the contract are to be classified as *culpa in contrahendo*. By contrast, breaches of commercial duties that only occur on the occasion of the conclusion of the contract are subject to the general rule of Article 4 Rome II Regulation.[128]

**1233.** In the context of Article 12 Rome II, another differentiation must be made that relates to the individual items that have been damaged. According to Recital 30 Rome II Regulation, bodily harm does not fall under Article 12 Rome II Regulation, but under the general rule on tort law in Article 4 Rome II Regulation. Thus, the applicable law is determined by the place where the damage occurred, which ought to be understood as the place where the violation of the legal interest occurred. However, the escape clause in Article 4(3) Rome II Regulation must be taken into account here: There could be a much closer connection to the (hypothetical) contract statute or the statute of *culpa in contrahendo*. However, the wording of Article 4(3) Rome II Regulation seems to speak against an ancillary connection to the contract since it did not yet exist at the time of the tort; rather, it related only to the initiation phase.

**1234.** However, it is more difficult to answer the follow-up question of whether an ancillary reference to the *culpa in contrahendo* (Article 12 Rome II Regulation) must be made according to Article 4(3) Rome II Regulation. This would at least not be excluded by the wording of Article 4(3) Rome II Regulation, since the provision, in principle, permits this with regard to all types of legal relationships.

---

127 CJEU, 17 September 2002, Case C-334/00, *Tacconi*, ECLI:EU:C:2002:499.

128 Thorn, in Grüneberg, *BGB Kommentar*, 84th ed. 2025, Art. 12 Rom II para. 2.

However, such an ancillary reference via Article 12(1) Rome II Regulation would, in the majority of cases, ultimately lead to a qualification of tort law as a mere appendix to contract law. Such a result is precisely not supposed to be possible according to the wording of Article 4(3) Rome II Regulation ('pre-existing'). Moreover, this approach would counteract the European legislator's intention to apply Article 4 Rome II Regulation instead of Article 12 Rome II Regulation to personal injuries.[129] In the end, better reasons speak against an ancillary connection to the law governing the *culpa in contrahendo*.

**1235.** Concerning damages to property in the contract's initiation phase, the question of their classification also arises. It has to be examined whether such claims are subject to the law governing the *culpa in contrahendo* (Article 12 Rome II Regulation) or the law governing torts (Article 4 Rome II Regulation). Looking at Recital 30 Rome II Regulation, claims for damages to an object are not excluded from the law governing the *culpa in contrahendo*. However, it is highly questionable whether this means that they fall under Article 12 Rome II Regulation. Ultimately, the decisive factor must be the type of interest protected. If only the interest in the corporal integrity is to be protected, a classification as exclusively tortious and thus an allocation to Article 4 Rome II Regulation seems appropriate and in line with the interests at stake.[130]

## IX. THE SCOPE OF THE LAW APPLICABLE TO CONTRACTS

**1236.** In principle, the law applicable to contracts determined according to Articles 3 to 8 Rome I Regulation (the *lex causae*) applies to a contract 'from the cradle to the grave' (to quote Gerhard Kegel), i.e. from its formation to its performance (see Articles 10, 12 and 14 Rome I Regulation). These rules also apply where substantive uniform law (e.g., the CISG) is incomplete in this respect, and subsidiary law applicable to contracts must therefore be determined. Article 12 Rome I Regulation lists by way of example ('in particular') the areas in which the law applicable to contracts applies. Pre-contractual obligations (*culpa in contrahendo*), however, as discussed, remain outside: They are not subject to the Rome I Regulation (Article 1(2)(i) Rome I Regulation) but are governed by Article 12 Rome II Regulation.[131]

---

129 Recital 30 Rome II Regulation.

130 Lüttringhaus, *RIW* 2008, 193, 197; similar also von Hein, *VersR* 2007, 440, 450; von Hein, *GPR* 2007, 54, 59; G. Wagner, *IPRax* 2008, 1, 13; C. Wendelstein, *Kollisionsrechtliche Probleme der Telemedizin* (Tübingen: Mohr Siebeck, 2012), p. 163.

131 Cf. above at paras. 1231 ff.

**1237.** The law applicable to contracts applies to the interpretation of the contract (Article 12(1)(a) Rome I Regulation). It also applies to the performance of the obligations created by the contract (Article 12(1)(b) Rome I Regulation). With regard to the manner of performance and the measures to be taken by the creditor in the event of defective performance (so-called performance modalities, e.g., in the case of rules on business hours, public holidays, on obligations to examine and give notice of defects and on the obligation to keep unaccepted goods), the law of the state in which the performance (actually) takes place must be taken into account (Article 12(2) Rome I Regulation). This does not translate to a constant necessity of application but rather to an application in cases where (e.g. due to the local connection) the application of the local law appears to be sensible.[132] Independent acts of performance are subject to their own law, e.g. the transfer of ownership is subject to the *lex rei sitae*.

**1238.** The law applicable to contracts also covers the legal consequences (e.g. withdrawal or claims for damages) of the complete or partial non-fulfilment of these obligations, including the assessment of damages (Article 12(1)(c) Rome I Regulation). This includes, in particular, the prerequisites (reminder, deadlines, effectiveness of exclusions of liability, fault) and consequences (including default interest) of default (breach of duty, impossibility, delay, frustration of contract) and warranty law.

**1239.** The law applicable to contracts applies to the various types of extinction of obligations as well as the statute of limitations (always to be qualified as a substantive, not a procedural issue) (time limit, interruption) and the consequences of the expiry of the time limit (Article 12(1)(d) Rome I Regulation). Finally, the law applicable to contracts applies to the consequences of the nullity of the contract (Article 12(1)(e) Rome I Regulation), e.g. due to illegality or immorality. Note that Article 12(1)(e) Rome I Regulation takes precedence over Article 10(1) Rome II Regulation.

**1240.** The law applicable to contracts also includes statutory presumptions and the burden of proof, Articles 1(3) and 18 Rome I Regulation. In contrast, the admissibility of certain types or means of evidence in a given civil proceeding is subject to the rules of forum law.

---

132 Magnus, in Staudinger, *BGB Kommentar* (2021), Art. 12 Rom I-VO para. 91.

# X. GENERAL ASPECTS OF CONTRACTUAL RELATIONSHIPS

## 1. LEGAL CAPACITY AND CAPACITY TO ACT

**1241.** The Rome I Regulation does not contain specific conflict-of-laws rules on legal capacity and the capacity to conclude a contract, as this continues to be determined by domestic law. However, Article 13 Rome I Regulation contains an exception to this, which is owed to the protection of the parties' justified expectations: It concerns contracts concluded between persons who are in the same country. Here, a natural person who would have capacity under the law of that country may invoke his incapacity resulting from the law of another country, but only if the other party to the contract was aware of that incapacity at the time of the conclusion of the contract or was not aware thereof as a result of negligence.

## 2. CONCLUSION OF CONTRACT

**1242.** The formation of the (main) contract (e.g. a loan contract) is governed by the law that would be applicable if the contract were, in fact, effective (Article 10 Rome I Regulation). This concerns declarations of intent and the conformity of the contractual offer and acceptance. It also includes grounds for nullity (e.g. immorality) and avoidance due to defects of intention. Pre-contractual elements (e.g. a binding effect of the offer) are also covered. For the choice of law contract, i.e., the agreement on the applicable law, Article 3(5) Rome I Regulation refers to this regulation, meaning it declares the (designated) *lex causae* applicable.

**1243.** If the circumstances show that it would not be justified to determine the effect of a party's conduct according to the law designated in Article 10(1) Rome I Regulation (the law applicable to the contract), said party may (cumulatively) invoke the law of the state of his habitual residence for the claim that he did not consent to the contract (Article 10(2) Rome I Regulation). What is meant here is the legally binding declaratory value of silence following a contractual offer, in particular in response to a letter of confirmation. The consumer's right to withdrawal, however, does not belong here. it is subject to the law applicable to the contract determined according to Article 6 Rome I Regulation.

## 3. THE LAW APPLICABLE TO THE FORM OF THE CONTRACT

**1244.** Article 11 Rome I Regulation provides for a specific conflict-of-laws rule on the law applicable to the form of the contract.

### a) Legal Sources

**1245.** The form of the legal transaction is partly regulated by uniform substantive rules. This is, in particular, the case in the UN Sales Convention. In this respect, according to Article 11 CISG, freedom of form applies as a general principle. Only Article 11 Rome I Regulation applies to the form of contractual obligations. Paragraph 4 contains a special provision for the form of consumer transactions.

### b) Basic Assumptions

**1246.** The law applicable to formal validity determines whether written form or notarial deed is required and whether the lack of form can be remedied. In particular, this relates to the purpose of ensuring the authenticity of declarations. It is often difficult to distinguish formal and evidentiary requirements; the latter are subject to the lex fori. For example, according to French law, a notarial or signed contract (‘*par écrit sous signature privée ou authentique*’) must be drawn up for transactions in private relationships (not in commercial matters) with a value of 1500 euros or more. Testimonial evidence is, in principle, not admissible.[133] Such provisions, which exclude testimonial evidence above a certain business value, are classified as substantive law. They must, therefore, also be observed in the forum state if they are part of the *lex causae* and lex loci actus.

### c) Commercial Transactions and Local Form

**1247.** According to Article 11(1) Rome I Regulation, a legal transaction is formally valid if it meets the formal requirements of the law applicable to the respective legal relationship (the *lex causae*) or the law of the state in which it is carried out (the lex loci actus). This is an alternative reference, meaning that the validity of the form is favoured (the *favor negotii*). The *lex causae* is the law determined according to the provisions of the Rome I Regulation. If, for example, the sale of a foreign property is subject to German law, the form requirement contained in sec. 311b(1) German Civil Code, which makes a notarial deed necessary, applies; this includes the possibility of remedying failures to comply with this form.

**1248.** It is sufficient to observe the law of the place of conclusion, i.e. the local form. Article 11(1) Rome I Regulation refers directly to the respective substantive provisions. As a basic rule, the local form is of equal rank to the

133 Article 1359 Code civil, modified by Ordonnance n° 2016-131 du 10 février 2016, to be read in connection with décret n° 80-533 du 15 juillet 1980 pris pour l'application de l'article 1341 du Code civil.

contract's form, i.e. it is sufficient, in principle, even if it is less restrictive than the contract's form.

#### d) *Distance Selling*

**1249.** If a contract is concluded between persons in different states, this is called a distance contract. According to Article 11(2) Rome I Regulation, such a contract is formally valid if it fulfils the formal requirements of the law applicable to the legal relationship forming its subject matter (*lex causae*) or the law of one of these states. There are thus – in accordance with the favourability principle – two places of conclusion and two laws applicable to the form of the contract.

#### e) *Agency*

**1250.** If the contract is concluded through an agent, the state where the agent is located is decisive when applying paragraphs 1 and 2 of Article 11 Rome I Regulation (Article 11(2) Rome I Regulation).

#### f) *Contracts on Rights in Rem, Use of Land*

**1251.** Contracts which concern a right in rem in immovable property or a right to use immovable property are subject to the mandatory formal requirements of the state in which the immovable property is situated, insofar as these are applicable under the law of that state irrespective of the place where the contract was concluded and of the law to which it is subject (Article 11(5) Rome I Regulation).

## 4. AGENCY

**1252.** The conflict-of-laws rules on agency are not regulated in the Rome I Regulation (Article 1(2)(g) Rome I Regulation). Autonomous national law applies. However, the exception only extends to the power of attorney and its effects vis-à-vis third parties and the prerequisites and effects of a power of attorney on a prima facie basis. The basic contractual relationship between the principal or represented party and the representative, however, is determined according to Articles 3 et seq. Rome I Regulation.

## 5. SET-OFF

**1253.** Article 17 Rome I Regulation contains a separate rule for set-off: If the claims are subject to different legal systems, set-off is governed by the law of the claim against which the set-off is made, because this claim is to be lapsed (passive claim). The law governing set-off is, therefore, the law governing the principal claim.

**1254.** In the absence of a more specific provision, these principles also apply in the realm of the UN Sales Convention, which does not contain any express provisions on set-off. Accordingly, it is decisive whether the question concerns 'matters governed by this Convention' (Article 7(2) CISG), which is to be decided primarily by recourse to the general principles underlying the CISG (so-called 'internal gap'), or whether there is rather an 'external gap', which is always to be filled by the autonomous national law invoked under conflict-of-laws rules. So far, the prevailing opinion has argued for the latter. However, the German Federal Supreme Court has adopted the view that the CISG applies at least for the set-off of (monetary) claims arising from the same contractual relationship, while the set-off should otherwise be assessed according to the respective applicable non-uniform (national) law.[134] This is justified by the legal idea underlying the provisions in Articles 88(3) and 84(2) CISG and the principle of concurrent payment, which is, inter alia, enshrined in Articles 58(1) and 81(2) CISG. Consequently, a set-off of such claims is permitted, provided they are exclusively subject to the CISG and are directed towards monetary payment (intra-Convention set-off). Thus, the opposing, mutual pecuniary claims are extinguished by set-off insofar as they correspond in amount; conflict-of-laws rules do not apply.

**1255.** The admissibility and procedural effects of set-off in proceedings are determined by the *lex fori*,[135] in insolvency proceedings by the insolvency statute (Article 7(2)(d) European Insolvency Regulation). Here, too, the substantive requirements of set-off are determined by the statute of set-off invoked under Article 17 Rome I Regulation.[136]

## 6. ASSIGNMENT

References: T. Frech, *Die Drittwirkung der Forderungsabtretung im internationalen Privatrecht* (Tübingen: Mohr Siebeck, 2024); L. Hübner, 'Die Drittwirkungen der Abtretung im IPR. Ein weiterer Schritt zur Fortentwicklung des Europäischen Kollisionsrechts', *ZEuP* 2019, 41; H. Labonté, *Forderungsabtretung International. Art. 14 Rom I-Verordnung und seine Reform* (Tübingen: Mohr Siebeck, 2016); S. Leible/M. Müller, 'Die Anknüpfung der Drittwirkung der Forderungsabtretung nach der Rom I-Verordnung', *IPRax* 2012,

[134] BGHZ 202, 258, cf. P. Huber, *IPRax* 2017, 268; Stürner, *JURA (JK)* 2015, p. 311.
[135] BGHZ 38, 254, 258; BGHZ 60, 85, 87.
[136] BGHZ 201, 252; cf. Wendelstein, *IPRax* 2016, 572.

491; C. Wendland, 'Abtretungen und Verbraucherschutz unter der Rom I-Verordnung – Zessionsbedingte Neuanknüpfung von Verbrauchervertragsforderungen?', *ZVglRWiss* 118 (2019), 422.

**1256.** The PIL of assignment has been regulated extensively in Articles 14 to 16 Rome I Regulation. Article 14 Rome I Regulation determines the law applicable to assignments and regulates the problems associated with the transfer of claims by legal transactions. This includes every type of transfer of claims, including assignments by way of security, as well as the transfer of liens and security interests in claims (Article 14(3) Rome I Regulation).[137] Legal subrogation is governed by Article 15 Rome I Regulation. Finally, Article 16 Rome I Regulation essentially regulates the PIL of joint and several recourses for both forms of assignment. Accordingly, the law of the debtor's obligation enforcing the recourse against the creditor is the statute of recourse.

**1257.** Article 14(1) Rome I Regulation determines the law of the relationship between the old and the new creditor as the contract law underlying this transfer agreement (Articles 3 et seq. Rome I Regulation). This law governs not only the causal transaction, i.e. the purchase of the claim, but also the transfer, i.e. the assignment itself. However, it follows from Recital 38 Rome I Regulation that the law of the transfer determined by Articles 3 et seq. only covers this contractual relationship between the old and new creditor, i.e. whether there is an effective sale of the claim, how it is to be fulfilled and how the assignment is carried out, given that it represents an execution of the causal transaction of the claim.

**1258.** Whether and what effect the transfer of the claim between the old and new creditor has vis-à-vis third parties is not expressly regulated in Article 14 Rome I Regulation. From the CJEU's point of view, the provision cannot be applied by analogy, as, according to the Court, an unintended loophole does not exist.[138] The question is significant for the effect of global assignments and multiple assignments vis-à-vis affected third parties. If it is a question of the protection of third parties, which is not covered by the provision of Article 14 Rome I Regulation (which refers to new creditors, old creditors and debtors), the first thing to consider is the effect of the assignment, third party protection can then be measured against this. The transfer is initiated by the assignor so that their conduct is important regarding the connecting factors at play. Translated into a connecting principle, this means that the law of the assignor's habitual

[137] The assumption of a debt, on the other hand, is not covered by Article 14 Rome I Regulation; cf. Stürner, in Erman, *BGB Kommentar*, 17th ed. 2023, Art. 14 Rom I-VO paras. 11 ff.

[138] CJEU, 9 October 2019, Case C-548/18, *BGL BNP Paribas*, ECLI:EU:C:2019:848, paras. 24 ff.

residence at the time of the act of transfer/declaration of transfer with the effect of a disposition is generally decisive for the statute of assignment.[139]

**1259.** The proposal for a Regulation on the law applicable to third-party effects of assignments of claims[140] provides in its Article 4 for uniform conflict-of-laws rules for the effects of a transfer of a claim on third parties. The rule invokes the law of the assignor's habitual residence. In exceptional cases, such as claims arising from a financial instrument, the law of the assigned claim applies. In the case of securitisation, the assignor and assignee may choose the law of the assigned claim as the law applicable to the third-party effect of the assignment of the claim.[141] The outcome of the current legislative process is currently still open.

## XI. QUESTIONS OF THE GENERAL PART OF PIL

### 1. EXCLUSION OF RENVOI

**1260.** All references in the Rome I Regulation are references to substantive rules (Article 20 Rome I Regulation): This means that the PIL of the relevant law is not concerned; any renvoi is excluded. This represents a general approach in EU conflict of laws; only the Succession Regulation contains a differentiated approach.[142] Within the Member States, the exclusion of renvoi is self-evident: Within a uniform conflict-of-laws system such as the Rome I Regulation, there a renvoi does not work as the connecting factors are by definition the same for all.

**1261.** However, since the Rome I Regulation has a universal application (Article 2 Rome I Regulation) and, therefore, may also refer to legal systems outside of the EU, the exclusion of renvoi also applies to references to third-state law. This reduces complexity, as legal practice does not have to take foreign conflict-of-laws rules into account.[143] However, this also means that a lack of clarity in the conflict-of-laws system must be accepted; also, it amounts to a departure from the ideal of international uniformity:[144] Any consideration of the conflict-of-laws assessment of a third state's law is omitted. Even if one considers that the legal figure of the renvoi is somehow emblematic of the

139 In detail *Mankowski*, *NIPR* 2018, 26; similarly also Kieninger, *NJW* 2019, 3353.
140 COM(2018) 96.
141 On the proposal Hemler, *GPR* 2018, 185; Müller, *EuZW* 2018, 522; Hübner, *ZEuP* 2019, 41; Einsele, *IPRax* 2019, 477; for a comparative account cf. Frech, *Die Drittwirkung der Forderungsabtretung im internationalen Privatrecht*, 2024.
142 Article 34 Sucession Regulation.
143 Cf. above at paras. 1080 ff, 1128 ff.
144 Cf. Nietner, *Internationaler Entscheidungseinklang im europäischen Kollisionsrecht*, 2016.

overly sophistication of PIL,[145] the almost complete rejection reflects a general tendency in EU conflict of laws towards Eurocentrism.

## 2. STATES WITH MORE THAN ONE LEGAL SYSTEM

**1262.** Some states combine several partial legal systems within their territory. Concerning such multi-jurisdictional states, the applicability of the partial legal systems in relation to each other must be clarified. Article 22(1) Rome I Regulation directly invokes the respective partial legal order; the possibly existing interlocal conflict of laws therefore plays no role. This applies both to the choice of law of the law applicable to the contract and to its objective references. If the parties subject their contract to English law, for example, only this partial legal system applies from the outset. If the contract is governed by Articles 4 et seq. Rome I Regulation, the conflict-of-laws rule of Article 4(1)(b) Rome I Regulation leads directly to the law of New York in the case of a contract for work and services concluded with a contractor from New York.

## 3. PRELIMINARY QUESTIONS

References: C.C. Bernitt, *Die Anknüpfung von Vorfragen im europäischen Kollisionsrecht* (Tübingen: Mohr Siebeck, 2010); S.L. Gössl, 'Die Vorfrage im Internationalen Privatrecht der EU', *ZfRV* 2011, 65; D. Solomon, 'Die Anknüpfung von Vorfragen im Europäischen Internationalen Privatrecht', in *Festschrift für Spellenberg* (Munich: Sellier, 2010), p. 355.

**1263.** German conflict-of-laws doctrine distinguishes between main and preliminary questions: The classification of legal questions under the conflict of laws (main question) can depend on the connection of a incidental legal relationship (preliminary question). In principle, there are two possible ways to solve the problem of the preliminary question: On the one hand, the law that is applicable to the main question could also be used to solve the preliminary question. On the other hand, the law applicable to the preliminary question could be determined independently from the main question, i.e., once again, according to the PIL of the *lex fori*. For the first solution, the advantage of international uniformity is often brought forward. The second, on the other hand, guarantees internal uniformity of the reference in the domestic legal system: the preliminary issue can, after all, become important in different contexts (law

---

[145] The dispute about the meaningfulness of the renvoi cannot be traced here. Radical rejection of the legal figure in Mäsch, in Arnold, *Grundfragen des Europäischen Kollisionsrechts*, 2016, p. 55; for an opposing position cf. Solomon, in *Liber Amicorum Schurig*, 2012, p. 237.

of succession, maintenance, descent, etc.). For this reason, the latter approach seems generally preferable.[146]

**1264.** The EU conflict-of-laws regulations rarely position themselves with respect to this issue; only the Rome III Regulation deals with the preliminary question. Recital 10 of this Regulation states: 'Preliminary questions such as legal capacity and the validity of the marriage, and matters such as the effects of divorce or legal separation on property, name, parental responsibility, maintenance obligations or any other ancillary measures should be determined by the conflict-of-laws rules applicable in the participating Member State concerned.' This favours an independent treatment of preliminary questions. On the one hand, this seems preferable for reasons of systemic justice within the EU, and on the other hand, because in the case of a dependent reference, the material scope of application of the respective regulation would be extended in an unacceptable manner. In this respect, it can also be assumed that the conflict-of-laws rules in EU regulations generally aim to solve the preliminary question independently.[147] Therefore, also those preliminary questions which may arise in connection with contracts must be treated independently.

## 4. OVERRIDING MANDATORY PROVISIONS

References: J. Fetsch, *Eingriffsnormen und EG-Vertrag: die Pflicht zur Anwendung der Eingriffsnormen anderer EG-Staaten* (Tübingen: Mohr Siebeck, 2001); S. Franq, 'Public Policy and Overriding Mandatory Rules as Mirrors of the EU System of Thought and Integration: On the 'Europeanness' of Exceptions and Oddities', in J. von Hein/ E.-M. Kieninger/G. Rühl (eds.), *How European is European Private International Law? Sources, Court Practice, Academic Discourse* (Cambridge: Intersentia, 2019), p. 305; P. Hauser, *Eingriffsnormen in der Rom I-Verordnung* (Tübingen: Mohr Siebeck, 2012); A. Hemler, *Die Methodik der 'Eingriffsnorm' im modernen Kollisionsrecht. Zugleich ein Beitrag zum Internationalen Öffentlichen Recht und zur Natur des ordre public* (Tübingen: Mohr Siebeck, 2019); A. Köhler, *Eingriffsnormen – Der 'unfertige Teil' des europäischen IPR* (Tübingen: Mohr Siebeck, 2013); J.D. Lüttringhaus, 'Eingriffsnormen im internationalen Unionsprivat- und Prozessrecht: Von Ingmar zu Unamar', IPRax 2014, 146; F. Maultzsch, 'Forumsfremde Eingriffsnormen im Schuldvertragsrecht zwischen Macht- und Wertedenken', in *Festschrift für Kronke* (Bielefeld: Gieseking, 2020), p. 363; M.F. Müller,

[146] For Germany cf. BGHZ 43, 213, 218 ff.; G. Kegel/K. Schurig, *Internationales Privatrecht*, 9th ed. (Munich: Beck, 2004), §9 II (pp. 376 ff.); Stürner, in Erman, *BGB Kommentar*, 17th ed. 2023, Vor Art. 3 EGBGB para. 63.

[147] Bernitt, *Die Anknüpfung von Vorfragen im europäischen Kollisionsrecht*, 2010, pp. 145 ff. (on the Rome II Regulation); Gössl, *ZfRV* 2011, 65, 68 ff.; Nehne, *Methodik und allgemeine Lehren des europäischen Internationalen Privatrechts*, 2012, pp. 203 ff.; Wilke, *A Conceptual Analysis of European Private International Law*, 2019, pp. 121 ff.; BGH NJW-RR 2015, 302 para. 12; in that sense also CJEU, 28 July 2016, Case C-191/15, *Amazon*, ECLI:EU:C:2016:612, para. 49.

'Internationale Anwendbarkeit des handelsvertreterrechtlichen Ausgleichsanspruchs – Vom Intervall Ingmar und Unamar zum Dreiklang mit Agro', *GPR* 2017, 203; O. Remien, 'Variationen zum Thema Eingriffsnormen nach Art. 9 Rom I-VO und Art. 16 Rom II-VO unter Berücksichtigung neuerer Rechtsprechung zu Art. 7 Römer Übereinkommen', in *Festschrift für von Hoffmann* (Bielefeld: Giesekig, 2011), p. 334; M. Renner, 'Ordre public und Eingriffsnormen: Konvergenzen und Divergenzen zwischen IPR und IZVR', in J. von Hein/G. Rühl (eds.), *Kohärenz im Internationalen Privat- und Verfahrensrecht der Europäischen Union* (Tübingen: Mohr Siebeck, 2016), p. 359; B. Rentsch, 'Krisenbewältigung durch Kollisionsrecht – Eingriffsnormen als integraler Bestandteil des europäischen Internationalen Privatrechts', in J. Bauerschmidt/B. Fassbender *et al.* (eds.), *Konstitutionalisierung in Zeiten globaler Krisen* (Baden-Baden: Nomos, 2015), p. 255; G. Rühl, 'Commercial agents, minimum harmonization and overriding mandatory provisions in the European Union: Unamar', (2016) *Common Market Law Review*, 209; M.-P. Weller/A. Schulz, 'Political Private International Law: How European are Overriding Mandatory Provisions and Public Policy Exceptions?', J. in von Hein/ M.-E. Kieninger/G. Rühl (eds.), *How European is European Private International Law? Sources, Court Practice, Academic Discourse* (Cambridge: Intersentia, 2019), p. 285.

#### *a) Domestic Overriding Mandatory Provisions*

**1265.** The system of conflict-of-laws rules is, to a certain extent, disturbed by the supremacy of so-called 'overriding mandatory provisions' ('*lois de police*'; '*Eingriffsnormen*').[148] These are provisions of the forum state which, irrespective of the law applicable to a contract under conflict of laws, apply to the facts of the case in an overriding mandatory manner without regard to the otherwise applicable law. To qualify as overriding mandatory provision, it is not sufficient that a rule is simply mandatory, i.e. not dispositive: such 'simple' mandatory rules do not supersede the deviating law applicable to contracts. Rather, a clear intention that the rule should apply no matter where the choice of law leads to must exist as well. This is expressed in the definition in Article 9(1) Rome I Regulation. It is based on the *Arblade* decision of the CJEU.[149]

#### aa) Overriding Mandatory Provisions of the *Lex Fori*

**1266.** The origin of the rule, whether it is of a public or private law nature, is irrelevant. First and foremost, the intention of the legislator as to the international application of a provision must be determined based on the wording of the provision. Other criteria of interpretation, in particular the purpose of the provision, must also be applied. Rules stemming from private law must also serve a supra-individual purpose. Hence, the compensation claim

[148] Cf. below at para. 1273.

[149] CJEU, 23 November 1999, Joined Cases C-369/96 and C-376/96, *Arblade*, ECLI:EU:C:1999:575, para. 30.

of the commercial agent based on the Commercial Agents Directive, albeit private law in nature, may qualify as overriding mandatory provision.[150]

**1267.** It is doubtful whether private law consumer protection regulations or the provisions on the protection of tenants in residential buildings may be classified as overriding mandatory provisions. The answer is arguably to the negative as the main thrust of these rules pertains to the protection of the individual.[151] This appears reasonable, especially since there is usually a sufficient level of protection via Article 6 Rome I Regulation.[152] These special references would be circumvented if domestic consumer law were to be applied via Article 9 Rome I Regulation in cases where these strict requirements are not met.

**1268.** If the rule does not have the quality of an overriding mandatory provision in this sense, its regulatory purpose can still form part of the domestic state's public policy. However, these are very rare cases: If the quality of an overriding mandatory provision is rejected, this can be seen as an indication that public policy is not affected. This results from the definition in Article 9(1) Rome I Regulation, which can be seen as a positive definition of public policy.[153]

**1269.** The decisive factor is own assessment of the respective Member State's law. EU law itself has only set a rather loose framework in Article 9(1) Rome I Regulation (and likewise in Article 16 Rome II Regulation). The limit of the Member States' freedom to regulate is reached only if the regulation's practical effectiveness (*effet utile*) is impaired by a rather sweeping qualification of sets of rules as overriding mandatory provisions.[154] For example, a regulation that would make an entire area (such as the parent company's liability within a supply chain) exclusively subject to domestic law by considering all of them overriding mandatory provisions would probably not be compatible with the principle of effectiveness.[155]

bb) Limits Stemming from Directive Law

**1270.** Whether an overriding mandatory character can also be derived from EU directives without their own conflict-of-laws rule is disputed. The hierarchy

150 Cf. CJEU, 9 November 2000, Case C-381/98, *Ingmar*, ECLI:EU:C:2000:605.
151 Cf. e.g. BGH NJW 2006, 762.
152 Above at para. 1181.
153 For details see Stürner, in *BeckOGK-BGB* (1 November 2024), Art. 6 EGBGB paras. 67 ff., 140 f.
154 On the need for a narrow interpretation of Article 9(1) Rome I Regulation cf. below at para. 1273.
155 But things are different with the introduction of a specific obligation under EU law to that extent, cf. above at paras. 1115 f.

of rules alone cannot be decisive in this regard, as directives always require transposition (Article 288(3) TFEU).[156] Thus, the origin of the consumer-protective right of withdrawal from EU directive law cannot justify its classification as an overriding mandatory provision vis-à-vis third-country law since the directive is, in any case, not primarily aimed at contracts with third-country nationals.

**1271.** Concerning the commercial agent's right to compensation, which is provided for in Article 17(2) of the Commercial Agents Directive, the CJEU ruled in the *Ingmar* case that it was of an overriding mandatory character and justified this on the grounds of the protection of the commercial agent, equality of competition and the case's 'strong Community connection'.[157] As a result, this assessment led to a preference for EU directive law over a third state's (in the case: Californian) law chosen by the parties, although the choice of this law could well have found its justification in the principal's seat in California.[158] Greater caution is therefore required in EU internal matters, as the CJEU later ruled in the *Unamar* case; this applies in any case if the provisions of the Commercial Agents Directive have also been correctly transposed in the chosen law. However, even then, the *lex fori* can provide for an increased level of protection through an excessive transposition,[159] which would have to be clarified by interpreting the provisions in question.[160]

cc) Enforcement

**1272.** According to Article 9(2) Rome I Regulation, the overriding mandatory provisions of the *lex fori* defined in this way remain unaffected by the Regulation with regard to their application, i.e., they are applied even if the applicable contract law is not forum law. In case of doubt, whether the application of the rule to the specific facts is necessary is to be decided if the application is not explicitly prescribed or results from the ratio of the provision by an overall consideration and weighing taking into account the domestic relevance[161] and the importance and weight of the interests protected by the rule.[162]

---

156 Cf. above at paras. 308 ff.

157 CJEU, 9 November 2000, Case C-381/98, *Ingmar*, ECLI:EU:C:2000:605, para. 21; CJEU, 17 October 2013, Case C-184/12, *Unamar*, ECLI:EU:C:2013:663, para. 40.

158 In the opposite constellation – commercial agent's seat in a third country, principal's seat in an EU country – there is, however, no obligation on the part of the Member States to extend the protection of the Commercial Agents Directive to this extent, CJEU, 16 February 2017, Case C-507/15, *Agro*, ECLI:EU:C:2017:129, paras. 33 f.

159 Cf. above at paras. 366 ff.

160 CJEU, 17 October 2013, Case C-184/12, *Unamar*, ECLI:EU:C:2013:663, paras. 50 ff.; Rühl, *CMLRev* 2016, 209.

161 Cf. BGHZ 123, 391; BGH NJW 1997, 1699.

162 BGH NJW 2006, 762.

**1273.** There is a dispute regarding the doctrinal character of the overriding mandatory rules. This is mainly because PIL and conflict of laws regarding substantive public law come into contact here.[163] Whether or not Article 9 Rome I Regulation has an independent conflict-of-laws content is judged differently. This is widely denied.[164] Most commentators consider the provision as merely being a 'door-opener'. The opposing view, however, sees conflict-of-laws content in the fact that the exception from the law applicable to the contract only applies under the conditions standardised in paragraph 1.[165] The differences are not as great as they may seem. Ultimately, it is about creating special conflict-of-laws rules that are legitimised by Article 9(1) and (2) Rome I Regulation and, in derogation from the rules, invoke individual provisions of forum law. These provisions can be located purely in the Union[166] or at least partly in the respective national law.[167] In any case, their formation must not undermine the *effet utile* of the Rome I Regulation. The CJEU has repeatedly pointed out that Article 9 Rome I Regulation must be interpreted narrowly as an exception provision.[168]

*b) Foreign Overriding Mandatory Provisions*

**1274.** The relevance of foreign overriding mandatory provisions is regulated in Article 9(3) Rome I Regulation. This rule allows for the 'taking into account' of mandatory rules of a foreign state if they, as provisions of the state in which the obligations created by the contract are to be performed or have been performed, make the performance of the contract unlawful. According to Article 9(3) Rome I Regulation, the courts of the forum state have the power to consider and weigh the overall situation, which includes a prognosis of consequences, when deciding whether and how to apply or not to apply these foreign rules. This allows for flexible handling of foreign overriding mandatory provisions; based on this, the fulfilment of unlawful contractual provisions and a corresponding demand for fulfilment by a contracting party can be countered.

**1275.** In this respect, the concept of third-state overriding mandatory provisions does not differ from that of the *lex fori*. Their legal effect, which is to be measured according to the law of the state enacting them, must at least

---

163 On this amply Hemler, *Die Methodik der 'Eingriffsnorm' im modernen Kollisionsrecht*, 2019, pp. 61 ff.

164 E.g. Mansel, in *Festschrift für W.-H. Roth* (Munich: C.H. Beck, 2015), pp. 377, 378 f.

165 Maultzsch, in *BeckOGK-BGB* (1 December 2024), Art. 9 Rom I-VO paras. 7 ff.

166 In that sense Hemler, *Die Methodik der 'Eingriffsnorm' im modernen Kollisionsrecht*, 2019, pp. 191 ff.

167 Maultzsch, in *BeckOGK-BGB* (1 December 2024), Art. 9 Rom I-VO para. 11.

168 Cf. CJEU, 17 October 2013, Case C-184/12, *Unamar*, ECLI:EU:C:2013:663, para. 49 (still referring to the old law); CJEU, 18 October 2016, Case C-135/15, *Nikiforidis*, ECLI:EU:C:2016:774, para. 44.

make a contract's performance unlawful, e.g. in the case of import and export prohibitions. Their effect must be assessed according to the circumstances at the place of the legal or also the de facto performance[169] since only at the latter place may the rule be given effect. The legal consequence is, first of all, the unlawfulness of the performance, i.e., it may be prohibited, provided it has not yet happened, with the further consequence that the ramifications of non-performance according to the relevant law applicable to the contract (Article 12(1)(c) Rome I Regulation) arise (impossibility of performance with the consequences following from the applicable law for the counter-performance and the other party) or that the consequences arising according to Article 12(1)(e) Rome I Regulation, i.e., nullity of the contract, arise.

**1276.** Whether the overriding mandatory provisions of the foreign state are given domestic effect must be established by the court of the forum state in a balancing exercise (Article 9(3), first sentence: 'may'; second sentence requires balancing). However, this is not a matter of mere discretion. Rather, a decision is to be made on the basis of the balancing process which must include all relevant aspects (objective of the mandatory rule, severity of the infringement, etc.).[170]

**1277.** From a systematic point of view, this gives rise to a specific conflicts rule enabling the application of the foreign overriding provision. Article 9(3) Rome I Regulation prescribes the basic prerequisite for applying a foreign mandatory rule, i.e. its close connection to the facts of the case and the fundamental harmony of interests and values from the perspective of the mandatory rule's state and the forum state.[171] Further differentiation within the meaning of sentence 2 is possible concerning the individual types and manifestations of foreign mandatory rules. For example, it may be stated that export and import bans for reasons of species protection, the protection of cultural property or rules based on the goal of peacekeeping are generally more likely to be accepted and applied than corresponding bans that have been set based on economic policy, foreign policy or judicial policy of the state that issued the overriding mandatory provision.[172] This is doubtful, for example, in the case of regulations that were obviously enacted to protect individuals, even if macroeconomic interests behind them also exist, as was partly the case with the legislative decrees enacted in Italy in response to the Covid crisis in March 2020 (e.g. 'Heal Italy.): Here, for example, it was decreed with an explicit international intention that an obligation to perform under a package travel contract is deemed impossible if it affects a person affected by COVID-19; payments already made, for example,

---

169 Mankowski, *IHR* 2008, 133, 147.

170 Cf. also BAGE 159, 69.

171 In that sense for Switzerland Article 19 IPRG; cf. Vischer, *RabelsZ* 53 (1989), 438, 452 ff.

172 Cf. Thorn, in Grüneberg, *BGB Kommentar*, 84th ed. 2025, Art. 9 Rom I-VO para. 13.

were to be refunded.[173] The situation will likely differ if such regulations impose export bans concerning urgently needed medical devices.[174]

**1278.** A case decided by the Frankfurt Regional Court[175] and Higher Regional Court[176] is also instructive: The Boycott Law no. 21/1964 of the State of Kuwait prohibits Kuwaiti citizens from concluding and executing contracts with citizens of the State of Israel. With reference to this prohibition, Kuwait Airways refused to transport an Israeli citizen residing in Germany from Frankfurt to Bangkok with a stopover in Kuwait despite a valid transport contract. Hence, he demanded performance, alternatively compensation for damages.[177]

**1279.** First of all, German law applies to the contract in the case of an objective connection pursuant to Article 5(2) subpara. 1 var. 1 Rome I Regulation.[178] However, the claim for carriage resulting from the contract validly concluded thereafter could be extinguished due to impossibility (sec. 275(1) German Civil Code). First of all, the aspect of legal impossibility could come into consideration, because the transport was prohibited by the Kuwaiti Boycott Law. For this to be the case, however, it would have to apply to the case at all. This, in turn, could only be realised by means of Article 9(3) Rome I Regulation. In order to do so, the Boycott Law would first have to be regarded a foreign overriding mandatory provision; furthermore, Kuwait would have to be regarded as the place of performance within the meaning of Article 9(3) Rome I Regulation; and finally, it would have to be examined whether the discretion existing within the framework of the rule could be exercised to apply Kuwaiti law at all, which does not seem to be tolerable from the German point of view. While the first point can still be clarified quite easily if the standards developed above are applied, the second is more difficult; the application of the Boycott Law must fail, however, in any case with regard to the third point.

**1280.** The Frankfurt Higher Regional Court argued that a place of performance within the meaning of Article 9(3) Rome I Regulation could be established by the stopover in Kuwait: A 'de facto performance' had taken place there or had

---

173 Article 28 Decreto-legge, 2.3.2020, no 9, Misure urgenti di sostegno per famiglie, lavoratori e imprese connesse all'emergenza epidemiologica da COVID-19, Gazzetta Ufficiale, Serie Generale no. 53 del 2.3.2020.

174 Weller/Lieberknecht/Habrich, *NJW* 2020, 1017.

175 LG Frankfurt JZ 2018, 153 paras. 47 ff.; case notes by Mörsdorf, *JZ* 2018, 156; Freitag, *NJW* 2018, 430.

176 OLG Frankfurt NJW 2018, 3591.

177 On the underlying (also) political agenda of the lawsuit cf. Mankowski, *RIW* 2019, 180, 181.

178 In casu, an implied choice of law seems to have been made in the process by mutual reference to German law, cf. OLG Frankfurt NJW 2018, 3591 para. 20.

at least been intended.[179] However, the discretion standardised in Article 9(3) Rome I Regulation was correctly exercised to the effect that the Boycott Law was not applied. On the one hand, this Act was exclusively meant to apply throughout Kuwaiti territory, and thus differed from a UN embargo, which was based on a general international consensus.[180] Secondly, however, the fact that the law ultimately pursued discriminatory goals by declaring agreements with persons of Israeli nationality illegal is a decisive argument against taking the law into account. This is diametrically opposed to the EU-wide recognised ideal of non-discrimination based on nationality (Article 18 TFEU and Article 21(2) CFR) and, at least indirectly, also national and ethnic origin (Article 21(1) CFR), as it is highly likely that the law covers people of Jewish descent.[181] Consideration of the Boycott Law as a third-state overriding mandatory provision is therefore out of the question.

**1281.** However, at least factually, the Boycott Law implies that the flight cannot be carried out as booked. In all likelihood, an insurmountable obstacle to performance would stand in the way of the transport since the customs authorities of the state of Kuwait would refuse the plaintiff passage when he would change planes, making the performance impossible.[182] The Kuwaiti Boycott Law thus gains validity through the back door of substantive law, although consideration via Article 9(3) Rome I Regulation, as seen, had to be ruled out.[183] Whether this is possible can be assessed differently.

**1282.** According to the wording of Article 9(3) Rome I Regulation ('... in so far as those ...'), the rule intends to regulate conclusively when foreign overriding mandatory provisions can be applied.[184] The CJEU clarified this in the *Nikiforidis* case, as otherwise, the principle of legal certainty and predictability of the references (as postulated in Recital 16 Rome I Regulation) would be jeopardised.[185] However, a question that must be separated from this is whether third-state overriding mandatory rules can be taken into account at the level of

---

179 OLG Frankfurt NJW 2018, 3591 para. 34.

180 OLG Frankfurt NJW 2018, 3591 paras. 37 f.

181 OLG Frankfurt NJW 2018, 3591 paras. 39 ff.

182 OLG Frankfurt NJW 2018, 3591 paras. 44 ff.; likewise OLG München NJW-RR 2020, 1061.

183 Whether any difference results from the fact that the carrier is a state-owned enterprise is rather controversial, see Freitag, *NJW* 2018, 430, 433 (the Kuwaiti standard of intervention does not represent an external obstacle to performance for the carrier; the conduct of the sole shareholder Kuwait, which controls it, is to be attributed to the carrier because the state of Kuwait is not allowed to derive advantages under private law from the form of organisation that it can freely choose). However, the Frankfurt Higher Regional Court did not follow this line of argument (NJW 2018, 3591 paras. 50 ff.).

184 On this point Thorn, in Grüneberg, *BGB Kommentar*, 84th ed. 2025, Art. 9 Rom I-VO para. 14; Freitag, *IPRax* 1998, 109, 115; LG Hamburg RIW 2015, 458.

185 CJEU, 18 October 2016, Case C-135/15, *Nikiforidis*, ECLI:EU:C:2016:774, paras. 46 ff.

substantive law as factual circumstances (local data). Indeed, this makes sense: Article 9(3) Rome I Regulation does not prevent this, as the regulatory content of the Rome I Regulation is limited to conflict of laws and is not intended to harmonise substantive law.[186] In this respect, the solution of the Higher Regional Court of Frankfurt in the Kuwait case is in line with the requirements of the Rome I Regulation.

## 5. THE PUBLIC POLICY EXCEPTION

References: A. Engel, 'The ECHR in the German Legal System', in M. Fornasier/ M.G. Stanzione (eds.), *The European Convention on Human Rights and its Impact on National Private Law. A Comparative Perspective* (Cambridge: Intersentia, 2023), p. 11; S. Franq, 'Public Policy and Overriding Mandatory Rules as Mirrors of the EU System of Thought and Integration: On the "Europeanness" of Exceptions and Oddities', in J. von Hein/E.-M. Kieninger/G. Rühl (eds.), *How European is European Private International Law? Sources, Court Practice, Academic Discourse* (Cambridge: Intersentia, 2019), p. 305; H. Grosser, 'Der ordre public-Vorbehalt im Europäischen Kollisionsrecht', *BLJ* 2008, 9; G. Reichelt, 'Zur Kodifikation des Europäischen Kollisionsrechts – am Beispiel des ordre public', in Reichelt (ed.), *Europäisches Gemeinschaftsrecht und IPR – Ein Beitrag zur Kodifikation der allgemeinen Grundsätze des Europäischen Kollisionsrechtes* (Vienna: Manz, 2007), p. 5; K. Siehr, 'Der ordre public im Zeichen der Europäischen Integration', in *Festschrift für von Hoffmann* (Bielefeld: Gieseking, 2011), p. 424; M. Stürner, 'Europäisierung des (Kollisions-)Rechts und nationaler ordre public', in *Festschrift für von Hoffmann* (Bielefeld: Gieseking, 2011), p. 463; M. Stürner, 'Der ordre public im Europäischen Kollisionsrecht', in S. Arnold (ed.), *Grundfragen des Europäischen Kollisionsrechts* (Tübingen: Mohr Siebeck, 2016), p. 87; I. Thoma, *Die Europäisierung und die Vergemeinschaftung des nationalen ordre public* (Tübingen: Mohr Siebeck, 2007); M.-P. Weller/A. Schulz, 'Political Private International Law: How European are Overriding Mandatory Provisions and Public Policy Exceptions?', in J. von Hein/E.-M. Kieninger/ G. Rühl (eds.), *How European is European Private International Law? Sources, Court Practice, Academic Discourse* (Cambridge: Intersentia, 2019), p. 285.

### a) *Content and Purpose*

**1283.** The goal of the public policy exception is to prevent legal consequences incompatible with fundamental legal principles of the *lex fori* and that would arise as a result of the application of foreign law designated under conflict-of-laws rules. The foreign rule in question, on which the incriminated legal consequence is based, then remains inapplicable. The reservation of public policy thus

[186] As ruled in CJEU, 18 October 2016, Case C-135/15, *Nikiforidis*, ECLI:EU:C:2016:774, paras. 51 ff.

serves as a 'safety net' in the system of conflict-of-laws references. The Rome I Regulation, like the other EU Regulations on PIL, is no exception.

**1284.** The public policy exception protects the public interests of the state of the court, not the interests of the parties. Recital 37 Rome I Regulation, also explicitly states this. Contrary to the ambiguous wording ('may'), there is, therefore, no discretion with regard to its application. The public policy exception must always be considered ex officio,[187] even if the party invoking its application has a burden of proof concerning the relevant facts.

**1285.** Article 21 Rome I Regulation only applies in cases where the result of an application of foreign law would lead to an obvious incompatibility with domestic public policy. Under no circumstances should the provision be misunderstood as a general escape clause that could be used to correct connections that are perceived as inappropriate. There are separate provisions on this, such as Article 4(3) Rome I Regulation.[188] In particular, overriding mandatory provisions (Article 9 Rome I Regulation) must also be considered before applying the public policy exception.[189]

**1286.** Article 21 Rome I Regulation is an open provision, meaning that it has to be concretised.[190] In court practise, the formula has emerged that a violation occurs if 'the result of the application of the foreign law contradicts the basic ideas of the regulations of the forum and the concepts of justice contained in them to such an extent that it appears unacceptable according to domestic ideas'.[191] According to the clear wording of Article 21 Rome I Regulation, what matters is the public policy of the forum state. Even if the Rome I Regulation is, in principle, to be interpreted autonomously, no European concept of public policy was created (yet).[192]

**1287.** Nevertheless, there is a clear influence of European law in two ways: On the one hand, it can be noted that the fundamental values of the forum legal system are influenced or even superseded by European values (positive function of European values). This applies, for example, to the ECHR or the Charter of

---

187 Stürner, in Erman, *BGB Kommentar*, 17th ed. 2023, Art. 21 Rom I-VO para. 2b; Martiny, in *Münchener Kommentar zum BGB*, 9th ed. 2025, Art. 21 Rom I-VO para. 2; Magnus, in Staudinger, *BGB Kommentar* (2021), Art. 21 Rom I-VO para. 23.

188 Cf. above at paras. 1179 ff.

189 On the interplay between the public policy exception and other conflict-of-laws rules see generally Stürner, in *BeckOGK-BGB* (1 November 2024), Art. 6 EGBGB paras. 140 ff.

190 Cf. Stürner, in *BeckOGK-BGB* (1 November 2024), Art. 6 EGBGB paras. 182 ff.

191 Cf. e.g. BGHZ 50, 370, 375; BGH NJW 1979, 488, 489; BGHZ 75, 32, 43; BGHZ 104, 240, 243; BGH NJW-RR 2000, 1372; BGHZ 147, 178 para. 45; BGHZ 118, 312, 330.

192 Cf. Stürner, in *BeckOGK-BGB* (1 November 2024), Art. 6 EGBGB paras. 174, 202 ff.

Fundamental Rights. In this respect, one can speak of a Europeanisation of public policy.[193] On the other hand, European values may also serve as barriers to national public policy (negative function of European values): The application of the public policy exception, specified by applying national standards, must, therefore, not lead to these European values being impaired.[194] It follows from this that violations of public policy can also be considered when applying Member State law. However, some restraint is necessary in this respect: If the law is applied correctly, the common legal convictions and the validity of the ECHR and the Charter of Fundamental Rights mean that the application of the public policy exception is, in fact, only very rarely conceivable.

### b) *Consequences of a Violation*

**1288.** If domestic public policy is violated, this entails the inapplicability of the rule from which the offending legal consequence follows for the specific case. This does not mean, however, that the reference to foreign law should be entirely invalid.[195] From the outset, the public policy exception is directed only against the result of the application in the specific case; there cannot and must not be any abstract scrutiny of the applicable law. If, however, the reference ought to remain, other ways must be found to obtain a basis for a decision. Here, the principle of the least possible interference with foreign law applies: If possible, the reference should only be corrected to the extent necessary to prevent the violation of public policy of the forum.[196] Ultimately, the postulate of the *effet utile* of the Rome I Regulation also argues in favour of this.

**1289.** If the result is only objectionable in a single point, the foreign rule is excluded from its domestic application, but in all other respects, the reference must still be followed, and the foreign *lex causae* must be applied. The gap created by applying the public policy exception is thus filled primarily with foreign law.[197] The case is to be decided under the hypothetical assumption that the rule that leads to the objectionable result from the perspective of the forum state remains unapplied.[198] This can be done, for example, by going back

---

[193] Engel, in Fornasier/Stanzione (eds.), *The European Convention on Human Rights and its Impact on National Private Law*, 2023, pp. 17 ff.; Stürner, in *Festschrift für von Hoffmann*, 2011, pp. 463, 464 ff., 473 ff.; Magnus, in Staudinger, *BGB Kommentar* (2021), Art. 21 Rom I-VO paras. 13 f.

[194] Cf. CJEU, 28 March 2000, Case C-7/98, *Krombach/Bamberski*, ECLI:EU:C:2000:164 (on the public policy exception in the field of recognition of judgments).

[195] Magnus, in Staudinger, *BGB Kommentar* (2021), Art. 21 Rom I-VO para. 30.

[196] Schwung, *RabelsZ* 49 (1985), 407; Magnus, in Staudinger, *BGB Kommentar* (2021), Art. 21 Rom I-VO para. 30.

[197] Stürner, in Erman, BGB Kommentar, 17th ed. 2023, Art. 21 Rom I-VO para. 2; Magnus, in Staudinger, B*GB Kommentar* (2021), Art. 21 Rom I-VO paras. 30 f.

[198] Magnus, in Staudinger, *BGB Kommentar* (2021), Art. 21 Rom I-VO para. 30.

to the general rule on which the incriminated provision is based. Alternatively, the provision in question can be 'reduced to preserve its validity'. This can be considered in particular when it comes to legal consequences to be determined quantitatively, such as the award of damages: If 'punitive damages' are to be awarded according to the *lex causae*, public policy requires a reduction of the damages awarded to an amount that just seems appropriate under the law of the forum, and not to the amount that would be awarded under that law.[199] If such a solution is impossible, a substitute law will be applied. As a rule, this will be the *lex fori*. There are no special features in this respect either.[200]

### c) *Specific Examples*

**1290.** In the area of contract law, breaches of public policy are very rare.[201] This is mainly due to the fact that the differences between the individual legal systems are less pronounced than, for example, in family or succession law.

**1291.** Some examples from German case law: The prohibition of abuse of rights is part of public policy.[202] If a legal system does not provide for the possibility to oppose the enforcement of a claim by raising the defence of abuse, this may constitute a violation of public policy.[203] Likewise, the right to avoid a contractual obligation in the case of relevant defects of will may be considered part of the public policy.[204] However, there is no infringement if the *lex causae* merely imposes stricter requirements on the challenge for fraud.[205] It may amount to a violation of public policy if a suretyship concluded under foreign law entails a grossly excessive obligation for the guarantor.[206]

---

199 Cf. BGHZ 44, 183 paras. 37 ff. and Article 26 Rom II-VO with Recital No 32.

200 Cf. Stürner, in *BeckOGK-BGB* (1 November 2024), Art. 6 EGBGB paras. 286 ff.

201 In general, on the shrinking importance of the public policy exception Stürner, in *BeckOGK-BGB* (1 November 2024), Art. 6 EGBGB paras. 66 ff.

202 LG Frankfurt IPRax 1981, 165, 167 with, however, a rather sweeping conflict-of-laws test (see Horn, *IPRax* 1981, 149, 154); Goerke, *Kollisionsrechtliche Probleme internationaler Garantien*, 1982, pp. 124 f.; cf. also Swiss Bundesgericht SZIER 2003, 259, 263.

203 Likewise SozG Stuttgart FamRZ 1992, 234, 235 with regard to forfeiture; Magnus, in Staudinger, *BGB Kommentar* (2021), Art. 21 Rom I-VO para. 26; Martiny, in *Münchener Kommentar zum BGB*, 9th ed. 2025, Art. 21 Rom I-VO para. 4; for a more restrictive approach cf. Hohloch, in *Festschrift für Frank*, 2008, pp. 141, 157 f.

204 RG IPRspr. 1928 Nr. 10; Wahl, *RabelsZ* 3 (1929), 775, 788 f.; left open by LAG Düsseldorf RIW 1987, 61; cf. also Magnus, in Staudinger, *BGB Kommentar* (2021), Art. 21 Rom I-VO para. 26.

205 RG IPRspr. 1933 Nr. 16.

206 Cf. BGHZ 118, 312 para. 61; Dörner, in *FS Sandrock*, 2000, pp. 205, 215.

# PART FOUR

# EUROPEAN CONTRACT LAW IN CONTEXT

# §33. COHERENCE AND SYSTEM BUILDING IN EUROPEAN CONTRACT LAW

## CONTENTS

References: S. Grundmann (ed.), *Systembildung und Systemlücken in Kerngebieten des Europäischen Privatrechts – Gesellschaftsrecht, Arbeitsrecht, Schuldvertragsrecht* (Tübingen: Mohr Siebeck, 2000); P. Letto-Vanamo/J.M. Smits (eds.), *Coherence and Fragmentation in European Private Law* (Munich: Sellier, 2012); H.W. Micklitz, 'The (Un)-Systematics of (Private) Law as an Element of European Culture', in G. Helleringer/K. Purnhagen (eds.), *Towards a European Legal Culture* (Munich/Oxford/Baden-Baden: C.H. Beck/Hart/Nomos, 2014), pp. 81 ff.; K. Riesenhuber, *System und Prinzipien des Europäischen Vertragsrechts* (Berlin: De Gruyter, 2003); G. Rühl, 'Bessere und intelligente Rechtsetzung: Die Evaluation von Verordnungen zum Internationalen Privat- und Verfahrensrecht', *ZVglRWiss* 115 (2016), 499; T. Wilhelmsson, *Free Movement of Legal Ideas. Towards a Dynamic Europeanisation of Private Law* (London: Bloomsbury Publishing, 2024).

# I. THE FRAGMENTARY APPROACH TO HARMONISATION

**1292.** This fourth part attempts to bring together what has previously been presented with a primary focus on individual issues. The principle of limited conferral of powers, which underlies the European Treaties, originates in the principle of subsidiarity and thus ultimately draws its legitimacy from the sovereignty of the Member States. This leads to a plethora of individual regulations, which, for their part, are in many cases not sufficiently coordinated with each other. But how much substantive coherence is to be demanded? Must we go so far as to understand EU private law as a (for the time being still: incomplete) system, despite its lacunae?

## 1. A 'POINTILLISTIC' PAINTING

**1293.** It has already been pointed out that the TFEU contains no legislative powers to harmonise private law.[1] Even if the internal market clause (Article 114 TFEU), especially in conjunction with the idea of consumer protection (Article 169 TFEU), would certainly permit far-reaching steps, the European legislation has progressed rather cautiously over the decades, i.e. through selective legal harmonisation in those places that were considered particularly significant for the functioning of the internal market. In many cases, different

[1] Cf. above at paras. 209 ff.

Directorates-General of the Commission inspired the legislative projects related to private law, which is reflected in their different style and content. Quite a few projects were stopped in the Council or shrunk to a less ambitious level.

**1294.** The result of this is a fragmentary[2] or pointillistic[3] structure, which, as such, was not necessarily designed with coherence in mind. There is no lack of metaphorical descriptions: European legal acts in the field of private law, for example, were described as 'islands in the sea of national law'[4] which, with increasing harmonisation, is becoming an 'archipelago of European consumer law'[5] joint together and even 'a more or less coherent terra firma'.[6] These descriptions do not in themselves paint a primarily negative picture: islands in the sea seem positive at first, archipelagos even more so. If one adds the allusions to the style of pointillism, which was influenced by post-impressionist artists such as Seurat, Signac or Pissarro, the sum of the individual points seems to result in an appreciable painting if the viewer is sufficiently detached. However, such a conclusion would be deceptive, given the predominance of critical tones towards the fragmentary approach to regulation.[7]

## 2. CRITICISM

**1295.** The criticism of this approach can be summarised as follows: A legal order, however much it may still be in the making, must avoid internal contradictions as far as possible. This is based, on the one hand, on the principle of equality, but on the other hand, also on the principle of legal certainty and predictability, which is certainly of great importance in the internal market.

**1296.** The Commission itself was and is well aware of these shortcomings. In a summary of the criticism voiced by the so-called stakeholders, in the 2003 Action Plan it stated the following:[8]

**1297.** 'Another criticism concerned the coexistence of two different legislative approaches in one and the same directive. This could lead to inconsistencies within the system of the directive itself. An example mentioned concerned the

---

2 Ulmer, *JZ* 1992, 1, 6.

3 Kötz, *RabelsZ* 50 (1986), 1, 5; Riesenhuber, *System und Prinzipien des Europäischen Vertragsrechts*, 2003, pp. 55 ff.; Leible, *NJW* 2008, 2558, 2559.

4 Rittner, *JZ* 1995, 849, 851.

5 Basedow, *AcP* 200 (2000), 445, 453.

6 Busch, *euvr* 2013, 48.

7 E.g. Honsell, *ZIP* 2008, 621, 622 f.

8 Communication from the Commission to the European Parliament and the Council – A more coherent European Contract Law – An Action Plan, COM(2003) 68 final, at No 18.

differentiation between the approaches to the applicable law on marketing and contracts in the Directive on electronic commerce. The inconsistency within the system of the Directive could also have consequences for the national implementation law. An example, which was mentioned, is the coexistence in the Commercial Agents Directive of both the concept of 'indemnity' and the concept of 'compensation', where a Member State in its implementation had not opted for one concept but taken over both. According to the relevant contributions, this leads to a lack of legal certainty in commercial and legal practice. Other criticisms mentioned by many contributors were formulated in the context of the use of abstract legal terms in Directives. These include fundamental terms like 'contract', 'damage' or more specific terms like 'equitable remuneration', 'fraudulent use' or 'durable medium'.

**1298.** Such a system will lose acceptance in legal practice in the long run. It must therefore be the goal of the EU's legislative bodies to find ways to make the rules more coherent. This applies first and foremost to the EU Commission, on which the TFEU confers the monopoly on legislative initiatives.

## II. ATTEMPTS AT MORE COHERENT RULE-MAKING

**1299.** Thus, since the turn of the century, there have been repeated attempts to replace the fragmentary approach with a more systematic one. To stay in the picture: Is EU private law really on its way to becoming a '*terra firma*'[9]? Mainly three approaches may be distinguished: (1) positive harmonisation that does not only intervene selectively ('horizontal harmonisation'), (2) internal improvement of coherence ('toolbox approach') and (3) optional harmonisation. The greatest challenge is probably to harmonise the various legal acts in such a way that there remain no internal contradictions and inconsistencies. This applies in particular where new legal acts do not repeal older ones but merely cast a new regulatory layer on top of them. The 2011 Proposal for a Common European Sales Law shows what implications such legislation can have.

### 1. HORIZONTAL HARMONISATION

**1300.** In October 2008, the Commission presented a draft directive on consumer rights,[10] the aim of which was 'to achieve a real business-to-consumer internal market striking the right balance between a high level of consumer

[9] Busch, *euvr* 2013, 48.
[10] COM(2008) 614 final.

protection and the competitiveness of enterprises, while ensuring respect of the principle of subsidiarity'.[11] The draft directive merged four existing directives that can be counted as part of the core area of the consumer protection acquis: The Doorstep Selling Directive,[12] the Unfair Terms Directive,[13] the Distance Selling Directive,[14] and the Consumer Sales Directive.[15] By means of a so-called horizontal instrument, inconsistencies between these legal acts should be eliminated, regulatory gaps filled and common aspects regulated systematically.[16]

**1301.** The Commission's main criticism of the current legal situation was the continuing fragmentation of the law despite the harmonisation already achieved through the four directives mentioned. The reason for this was the concept of minimum harmonisation that had been pursued until then. The result is that businesses still have to comply with different legal provisions when offering goods and services in the internal market, which is a factor that makes cross-border trade more expensive and is likely to hinder it in the long term.[17]

**1302.** The so-called horizontal approach of the proposal was meant to bring about a considerable simplification of the acquis in consumer protection by merging the four directives mentioned above. This was done by systematically regulating common features and eliminating overlaps and inconsistencies. From the Commission's point of view, such commonalities concerned, for example, definitions, central pre-contractual information duties as well as individual provisions on the contractual aspects of sales contracts.[18]

**1303.** The failure of this horizontal approach[19] had less to do with the fact that the Commission's regulatory concern was met with fundamental criticism. Rather, the combination with the principle of full harmonisation implemented in the Directive Proposal appeared unacceptable from the perspective of the Member States.[20]

---

11 COM(2008) 614 final, p. 2.
12 Directive 85/577/EEC on contracts concluded away from business premises of 20 December 1985, OJ L 372/31.
13 Directive 93/13/EEC on unfair terms in consumer contracts of 5 April 1993, OJ L 95/29.
14 Directive 97/7/EC on the conclusion of distance contracts of 20 May 1997, OJ L 144/19.
15 Directive 1999/44/EC on the sale of consumer goods and associated guarantees of 25 May 1999, OJ L 171/12.
16 COM(2008) 614 final, p. 3.
17 Thus, the Green Paper 'The Review of the Consumer Acquis', COM(2006) 744 final, p. 7 pointed out that only 19% of retail companies in the EU trade with and advertise in at least one other Member State.
18 COM(2008) 614 final, p. 10.
19 Cf. above at paras. 127 ff.
20 Cf. Stürner, in Stürner (ed.), *Vollharmonisierung im Verbraucherrecht?*, 2010, p. 3.

## 2. TOOLBOX APPROACH

**1304.** The second line of development is almost parallel. It sought to achieve greater coherence less by positively setting standards and more through indirect instructions to legal policy actors. The central instrument was supposed to be the so-called Common Frame of Reference, 'a non-binding set of fundamental principles, definitions and model rules to be used by the lawmakers at Union level to ensure greater coherence and quality in the lawmaking process', as stated in the Stockholm Programme of the European Council.[21] On the one hand, the EU legislator could thus fall back on uniformly formulated definitions for every harmonisation measure. In addition, entire legal acts could be drafted based on an already existing set of rules such as the DCFR – the image of the 'toolbox' is derived from this.[22] However, it would then be correct to speak of a legal DIY store since the DCFR is conceived more as a reservoir of building blocks for legal instruments and thus has the function of a repository of standards.[23] However, this concept also failed to gain acceptance, which was not exclusively due to the quality of the DCFR.[24]

## 3. OPTIONAL HARMONISATION

**1305.** Finally, attempts at more coherent rulemaking can also be observed where legal acts do not supersede autonomous national law but provide new rules that are optionally available to those who want to base their legal relationships on them.

### *a) In the Field of Procedural Law*

**1306.** In European procedural law, optional regulations have become somewhat widespread. The European Small Claims Regulation (Article 1 and Recital 8 European Small Claims Regulation) and the European Order for Payment Procedure Regulation (Article 1(2) European Order for Payment Procedure Regulation) are particularly worth mentioning here. Even though Article 288(2) TFEU prescribes the direct applicability of regulations, it is nevertheless up to the claimant to initiate the European Small Claims Procedure according to Article 4(1) European Small Claims Regulation, to recover the sum due in the traditional way according to the provisions of the autonomous

---

21 Of 10–11 December 2009 (Doc. No 17024/09, p. 33).

22 Von Bar/Clive/Schulte-Nölke, *DCFR 2008 Interim Edition*, Introduction No 76.

23 Ernst, *AcP* 208 (2008), 248, 277; Herresthal, in Langenbucher, *Europäisches Privat- und Wirtschaftsrecht*, §2 para. 4.

24 On the fate of the DCFR cf. above at paras. 120 ff.

national procedural law (vertical optionality) or to choose another European form of procedure or enforcement (horizontal optionality). This optionality can be seen as a characteristic of a newer generation of procedural regulations. The European Small Claims Regulation thus follows the same pattern as the European Order for Payment Procedure Regulation and the European Enforcement Order Regulation, which entered into force a few years earlier.

**1307.** This optionality has the advantage of being less invasive vis-à-vis the interests of the Member States. This has a political and legal dimension, given that Article 81 TFEU refers exclusively to cross-border judicial cooperation. Hence, it does not seem to be beyond doubt, whether this competence would also cover purely national proceedings. In any case, the regulatory scope of the Member States is not directly restricted by optional instruments; their competence to create parallel regulations continues to exist. However, a certain incentive to adapt exists insofar as the competing national laws may come under a certain pressure as the acceptance of an optional instrument increases among the parties to economic transactions. Thus, the creation of optional instruments may serve as a blueprint for autonomous implementation at the Member State level.

*b) Within Substantive Private Law*

**1308.** The creation of such 'optional instruments' is not limited to the area of judicial cooperation. In company law, for example, supranational company forms have been created with the European Economic Interest Grouping (EEIG), the Societas Europaea (European Company, EC) and the Societas Cooperativa Europaea (European Cooperative Company, ECC), which do not affect the existence of the traditional company forms in the law of the Member States, i.e. they do not create a binding uniform company law.

**1309.** The proposal for a Common European Sales Law[25] also adopts this regulatory technique. The idea of optionality has thus arrived in the core area of private law, namely contract law. The fact that this proposal was not pursued further for political reasons[26] does not fundamentally contradict the attractiveness of this harmonisation model in terms of legal policy.

---

[25] Proposal for a Regulation of the European Parliament and of the Council on a Common European Sales Law of 11 October2011, COM (2011) 635 final.

[26] Commission Work Programme 2015: A New Start, of 16 December2014, COM(2014) 910 final, Annex II at No 60.

## 4. THE INTERPLAY BETWEEN EU INSTRUMENTS: THE EXAMPLE OF THE CESL

**1310.** If implemented, the proposal for a CESL would have created a second track of European consumer contract law. This is because the CESL would have left both the existing autonomous national sales law and the consumer acquis untouched. The relationship between these two harmonisation tracks must be clarified:[27] The starting point for the proposal for a CESL was the Commission's endeavour to consolidate four key directives in the field of consumer law and recast them in a fully harmonising directive.[28] This attempt has largely failed: the Consumer Rights Directive, which entered into force in October 2011,[29] is limited to regulating withdrawal and information obligations for consumer distance and off-premises contracts. Nevertheless, certain overlaps exist with the CESL proposal since this also regulates these issues.

### a) *The Influence of the Directive Acquis on the CESL*

**1311.** According to the Commission Communication of 11 October 2011 accompanying the proposed Regulation, the proposed Regulation is 'a complementary approach to that found in the existing acquis in the field of consumer protection. In the first instance, it incorporates and is consistent with those measures'.[30] This results in at least two important ramifications: On the one hand, the existing acquis and the CESL should run parallel. On the other hand, the previous jurisprudence of the CJEU would thus gain significance for those parts of the CESL that are taken from the acquis.

### b) *Similarities with the Consumer Acquis*

**1312.** Mandatory law should be the exception in a legal system based on the principle of private autonomy.[31] This is all the more true as private autonomy is also recognised in European private law.[32] Article 1(1) CESL and Recital 30

---

[27] Cf. Stürner, in Schulte-Nölke/Zoll/Jansen/Schulze, *Der Entwurf für ein optionales europäisches Kaufrecht*, 2012, p. 47; Zöchling-Jud, *AcP* 212 (2012), 550.

[28] Cf. the contributions in Stürner (ed.), Vollharmonisierung im Europäischen Verbraucherrecht?, 2010.

[29] Above at paras. 1300 ff., 127 ff.

[30] Communication from the Commission of 11 October 2011, COM(2011) 636 final, p. 12.

[31] On the role of mandatory law in the consumer acquis G. Wagner, in Eidenmüller/Faust/Grigoleit/Jansen/Wagner/Zimmermann, *Revision des Verbraucher-acquis*, 2011, p. 1.

[32] This follows from Article 16 GR Charter, cf. e.g. M. Ruffert, in C. Calliess/M. Ruffert, *EUV/AEUV*, 6th ed. (Munich: C.H. Beck, 2022), Art. 16 EU-GRCharta para. 2; Riesenhuber, *EU-Vertragsrecht*, 2013, §2 para. 20.

of the CESL Regulation also clearly state this.[33] However, consumer contract law consists predominantly of mandatory regulations, which is also true for the CESL. The interests of businesses and consumers must nevertheless be balanced in a meaningful way:[34] If the CESL contained fewer mandatory provisions, the costs reduced in this way could be passed on to the consumer by lowering prices. Politically, however, such a design is likely to be unacceptable; there is a risk that consumer protection associations would issue blanket warnings against the choice of such an optional sales law. It would hardly be compatible with the previous harmonisation approaches in consumer law if the trader could 'buy' a lower level of protection from the consumer in this way.[35]

**1313.** The CESL proposal explicitly states for each individual set of rules which provisions are to be mandatory as an exception to the fundamentally dispositive nature of each provision (Article 1(2) CESL). What is remarkable about this is that even those rules that serve to protect the consumer are not generally described as mandatory at this point. Rather, the CESL specifies in each case which parts cannot be waived to the consumer's detriment. According to Recital 30 of the CESL Regulation, this is intended to highlight the exceptional nature of mandatory provisions. This is partly done chapter by chapter, such as for the pre-contractual information obligations in Article 22 CESL[36] or for unreasonable general terms and conditions in Article 81 CESL.[37] Often, however, the mandatory nature of certain provisions is prescribed in the respective rule.[38] According to Article 47 of the CESL, the provisions in Chapter 4 on the right of withdrawal should also be mandatory for consumer contracts. Overall, as far as can be seen, the level of consumer protection should not be lowered at any point compared to the acquis.

---

33 The Commission's Communication of 11 October 2011 also makes this clear, COM(2011) 636 final, p. 8.

34 Cf. P. Lagarde, in R. Schulze/H. Schulte-Nölke, *European Private Law - Current Status and Perspectives* (Munich: Sellier, 2011), pp. 277 f.

35 For an optional right of withdrawal in distance selling transactions G. Wagner, in Eidenmüller/Faust/Grigoleit/Jansen/Wagner/Zimmermann, *Revision des Verbraucher-acquis*, 2011, pp. 1, 29 f. as well as Eidenmüller, in Eidenmüller/Faust/Grigoleit/Jansen/Wagner/Zimmermann, *Revision des Verbraucher-acquis*, 2011, pp. 109, 134 ff.

36 Article 22 CESL is semi-mandatory; likewise Article 27, Article 47 and - with restrictions - Article 108 CESL proposal.

37 The rules on unfair contract terms are also mandatory for contracts not involving consumers. Further examples of a chapter-by-chapter exclusion of negotiability can be found in Article 171 CESL proposal for late payment by traders and in Article 177 CESL proposal for the rules on rescission in consumer contracts.

38 'In relations between a trader and a consumer the parties may not, to the detriment of the consumer, exclude the application of this Article or derogate from or vary its effects.' Cf. e.g. Articles 10(6), 28(3), 29(4), 64(2), 69(4), 71(2), 72(4), 75(4), 77(2), 92(3), 99(4), 101(2), 102(5), 105(5), 135(4), 142(5), 148(5), 150(3), 158(3), 167(5) and 186(5) CESL proposal.

**1314.** In some areas of the CESL proposal, the consumer's position was even strengthened: For example, the withdrawal period for the consumer is now uniformly standardised as fourteen days (Article 42 CESL); the Doorstep Selling Directive had only specified seven days as a minimum.[39] Concerning remedies, it was noteworthy that the proposed regulation postulated a free choice of the consumer between available remedies.[40] The Consumer Sales Directive, on the other hand, sets out a priority of supplementary performance, with the prerequisite of the expiry of the deadline in Article 3(3) and (5). However, a corresponding provision was missing in the CESL proposal; Article 114(2) CESL restricts the right to terminate the contract by rescission only in the case of an insignificant defect. Finally, another example can be found concerning the consumer's remedies in case of a defect: If the consumer demands supplementary performance in case of a non-conforming performance,[41] they should have the right to choose between repair and replacement, as under Article 3(3) CSD.[42] According to Article 111(2) of the CESL, the seller must provide subsequent performance within a reasonable period of time; however, this period may not exceed 30 days. However, according to the Consumer Sales Directive, subsequent performance after more than one month would still be reasonable under certain circumstances.[43]

### c) *The Relationship with the Consumer Rights Directive*

**1315.** To the extent that the Consumer Rights Directive contains fully harmonising provisions, i.e., in particular, in the area of information duties and rights of withdrawal, but also concerning the 'other consumer rights' in Chapter IV concerning delivery and the transfer of risk, an optional CESL could contain provisions deviating from these.[44] In general, a problem regarding the

39 Article 5(1) Doorstep Selling Directive. On other changes in this area Lehmann, *GPR* 2011, 218, 223.

40 Emphasising this, the Commission Communication of 11 October 2011, COM(2011) 636 final, p. 11.

41 The term 'supplementary performance' does not appear in the CESL. Rather, Article 110 of the CESL speaks of the 'performance of seller's obligations', which also 'includes the remedying free of charge of a performance which is not in conformity with the contract'.

42 Article 111 CESL proposal refers to 'repair and replacement' – probably without differences in content.

43 Further examples are the catalogues of unfair terms in Articles 84, 85 CESL proposal, which protect the consumer more extensively than the merely indicative list in the Annex to the Terms Directive, as well as the regulation of damages in Articles 159 ff. CESL proposal, which has so far not been covered by the Consumer Sales Directive – a corresponding obligation of the seller can thus only arise from the law of the Member State applicable to the facts of the case. The obligation to pay interest on arrears was not previously regulated for consumer contracts in the Directive, cf. Article 168 CESL proposal and Lehmann, *GPR* 2011, 218, 224.

44 But cf. Article 25 CRD, according to which consumers cannot waive the protection granted by the Directive.

EU's legislative powers could arise from the parallel design of the regulations:[45] Insofar, as the areas mentioned are already fully harmonised by the Consumer Rights Directive, it does not appear to be absolutely necessary for the realisation of the internal market within the meaning of Article 114 TFEU to bring another parallel legislative instrument into force with the CESL. This is because the harmonisation of rules in the internal market sought by the EU would already have been achieved in these areas.[46] Here, it would depend on whether, for Article 114 TFEU, the legal act is considered as a whole, and its role for the internal market is determined at the global level, or whether individual parts of it can also be subjected to an isolated consideration. The Commission has apparently taken the former position.[47]

#### d) *Beyond Consumer Protection*

**1316.** In the case of contracts without consumer participation, it seems reasonable and necessary to provide for a far-reaching dispositive nature of the rules of the optional sales law. This is exactly what has happened: The basic rule of Article 1(2) CESL applies, according to which all provisions are dispositive unless their mandatory application is explicitly prescribed. In the B2B area, only a few provisions are expressly mandatory, such as the scrutiny of unfair GTC in Article 86 in conjunction with Article 81 CESL[48] or the provisions on liability for late payment in Articles 168 et seq. CESL.[49] Also, the remedies for fraud, threats and unfair exploitation cannot be excluded, Article 56(1) CESL.[50]

#### e) *The Relationship between CESL and CISG*

**1317.** Finally, the relationship of the CESL proposal to the existing international uniform sales law in the form of the CISG was also problematic. The Vienna Sales Convention is designed as a substantive uniform law for contracts between companies. According to Article 1 CISG, it is applicable *ipso iure* in all contracting states as soon as the conditions for application are met.[51] In this respect, there

---

45 Cf. above at paras. 133 ff.

46 Cf. Vogenauer, *ERCL* 2010, 143, 176.

47 This problem would have been avoided by the IMCO proposal to adopt the CESL as a directive and to exclude those parts that are already regulated in the Consumer Rights Directive (above at paras. 138 ff).

48 Here, the standard of review is less strict compared to B2C contracts.

49 In particular, the non-dispositive obligation of the parties to conduct pre-contractual negotiations in accordance with the principle of good faith, Article 27(2) Feasibility Study, has not made it to the final version of the CESL proposal.

50 However, in the B2B area, remedies due to mistake are dispositive, Article 56(2) CESL proposal *e contrario*.

51 For a comparison of the material scope of application of the CISG and the CESL, cf. Hellwege, *IHR* 2012, 180.

may be some kind of competition with the CESL in certain constellations.[52] According to Recital 25 of the draft CESL Regulation, the choice of the CESL under Article 8 of the CESL Regulation should, at the same time, mean that the Vienna Sales Convention is no longer applicable (Article 6 CISG).[53] However, it seems more plausible than this substantive solution to base this precedence on a conflict-of-laws approach by which the CESL is seen as a conflict-of-laws instrument in the sense of Article 25(2) Rome I Regulation (or Article 28(2) Rome II Regulation), at least in purely internal cases:[54] According to this rules, the Rome Regulation 'shall, as between Member States, take precedence over conventions concluded exclusively between two or more of them in so far as such conventions concern matters governed by this Regulation'.

## III. SYSTEM BUILDING THROUGH THE APPLICATION OF LAWS ACROSS LEGAL ACTS

References: T. Ackermann, 'Sektorielles EU-Recht und allgemeine Privatrechtssystematik', *ZEuP* 2018, 741; E.B. Crawford/J.M. Carruthers, 'Connection and coherence between and among european instruments in the private international law of obligations', *ICLQ* 63 (2014), 1; J.D. Lüttringhaus, 'Übergreifende Begrifflichkeiten im europäischen Zivilverfahrens- und Kollisionsrecht. Grund und Grenzen der rechtsaktsübergreifenden Auslegung, dargestellt am Beispiel vertraglicher und außervertraglicher Schuldverhältnisse', *RabelsZ* 77 (2013), 31; G. Rühl, 'Die rechtsaktsübergreifende Auslegung im europäischen Internationalen Privatrecht: Art. 6 der Rom I-VO und die Rechtsprechung des EuGH zu Art. 15 Brüssel I-VO', *GPR* 2013, 122; F.M. Wilke, 'Dimensions of coherence in EU conflict-of-law rules', *J. Priv. Int'l Law* 2020, 163.

### 1. FUNDAMENTALS

**1318.** At least from the point of view of most continental legal academics, legal orders should be comprehensive, systematic, and coherent. Given that system-building through legislation is often hardly feasible, especially for political reasons, the question arises as to what role legal practice plays in the endeavour to achieve a coherent application of the law following the principle of equality. This concerns, first and foremost, the CJEU, which has the exclusive

[52] On the respective advantages and disadvantages Hellwege, *IHR* 2012, 221; cf. also the contributions in U. Magnus (ed.), *CISG vs. Regional Sales Law Unification* (Munich: Sellier, 2012).

[53] Critical Hesselink, *ERPL* 2012, 195, 201 f. (ultra vires, as the CISG itself determines when a deselection is valid). On a positive note Staudenmayer, *NJW* 2011, 3491, 3495.

[54] On constellations involving third countries, cf. Mansel, *WM* 2012, 1253, 1265.

right to interpret EU law.[55] However, the courts of the Member States are also responsible for the correct application of primary and secondary law ('decentralised application'). This is primarily expressed in the fact that courts, as public authorities, must ensure the effective enforcement of the provisions of EU law within the scope of their competencies;[56] this results, in particular, in the obligation to apply national laws in conformity with the directives. However, the practical effectiveness (*effet utile*) of EU law as a whole must be ensured, not just with regards to individual provisions. In this respect, the Member States' courts also bear responsibility regarding the overall system of Union law.

**1319.** From the perspective of German jurisprudence, it may seem obvious to use the concepts and categories established here as a yardstick for EU private law. Grundmann[57] and Riesenhuber,[58] in particular, have undertaken to demonstrate the beginnings of a system in directive law. Following Canaris,[59] in particular, a distinction is usually made between the external and the internal system: The former characterises the formal structure of a legal order; in this respect, aspects that establish further order are, in particular, the various sources of law and their subdivisions. The latter refers to the uniformity and consistency of the substantive rules of a legal system. Other legal systems, especially those of common law, make no such claims from the outset. The classic quote by Oliver Wendell Holmes, Jr. puts it succinctly: 'The life of the law has not been logic: it has been experience.'[60] Since EU law is, on the one hand, fragmentary in nature and, on the other, committed to many legal traditions, the claim to interpret legal acts, especially secondary law, along the lines of an internal system seems difficult to achieve[61] and perhaps not at all appropriate.[62]

## 2. AN 'INTERNAL SYSTEM' OF EU LAW?

**1320.** According to the case law of the CJEU, the interpretation of an EU legal act must be based on the entire body of Union law; 'every provision of Community law must be placed in its context and interpreted in the light of the

---

55 Cf. paras. 326 f., 1377 ff.

56 Cf. CJEU, 19 January 2010, Case C-555/07, *Kücükdeveci*, ECLI:EU:C:2010:21, para. 47 with references on previous case law.

57 Grundmann (ed.), *Systembildung und Systemlücken in Kerngebieten des Europäischen Privatrechts*, 2000.

58 Riesenhuber, *System und Prinzipien des Europäischen Vertragsrechts*, 2003.

59 C.-W. Canaris, *Systemdenken und Systembegriff in der Jurisprudenz, entwickelt am Beispiel des deutschen Privatrechts*, 2nd ed. (Berlin: Duncker & Humblot, 1983), pp. 24 ff.

60 O.W. Holmes, *The Common Law* (Boston: Little, Brown & Co., 1881), p. 1.

61 From the perspective of the sociology of law, see the contributions in Helleringer/Purnhagen (eds.), *Towards a European Legal Culture*, 2014.

62 Decidedly Ackermann, *ZEuP* 2018, 741, 768, 779.

provisions of Community law as a whole [...]'.[63] However, the intensity of the systematic interpretation thus addressed depends essentially on the degree of harmonisation in the relevant area of law. In European labour law, for example, approaches towards an internal system can be observed.[64] This is a minimum requirement for a systematic interpretation across legal acts. The harmonisation of laws in the internal market has, so far, been sector-specific; the EU legislator has also pursued different regulatory purposes in the various legal acts; the lack of coordination between them has often been criticised. The attempt to create a common frame of reference for European contract law must be considered a failure. For example, systems thinking in European private law is not yet very strongly developed.[65] Therefore, to interpret or specify a legal concept contained in a directive, another secondary legal act cannot be used indiscriminately.[66]

**1321.** It must be examined for each individual area to what extent parallels exist between legal acts that support a systematic interpretation. To use the above-mentioned metaphor again: Individual legislative islands cannot be combined into a uniform legal territory by way of systematic interpretation; they are usually not based on a coherent 'inner system'. As Thomas Ackermann puts it:[67] 'Sector-specific regulations of Union law are the natural enemy of the general private law system.' However, if there is already a set of islands or even an archipelago of secondary law which, in terms of content, share the same objective (such as consumer protection), the postulate of the CJEU quoted at the beginning, according to which the entire body of EU law must be taken into account when interpreting any legal act, applies.

**1322.** This is quite clear, for example, in those cases in which the EU legislator has already coordinated the content of two or more pieces of secondary legislation. Such is the case, e.g., with respect to the Digital Content Directive and the Sale of Goods Directive. Moreover, the CRD, to which these two legal acts refer, must be included in this kind of systematic interpretation. However, inconsistencies are already apparent here, for example, concerning the concept of the consumer.[68] The systematic argument is less problematic here if it is only used as a fallback position. Thus, in order to clarify whether the consumer-protecting right of withdrawal contained in the Doorstep Selling Directive[69] covers linked

[63] CJEU, 6 October 1982, Case 283/81, *CILFIT*, ECLI:EU:C:1982:335, para. 20.
[64] Cf. K. Riesenhuber, *European Employment Law*, 2nd ed. (Cambridge: Intersentia, 2021), §1 para. 44.
[65] Likewise Langenbucher/Donath, in Langenbucher, *Europäisches Privat- und Wirtschaftsrecht*, §1 para. 11; Ackermann, *ZEuP* 2018, 741, 745 ff.
[66] Grigoleit, *AcP* 210 (2010), 354, 395 ff.; Höpfner/Rüthers, *AcP* 209 (2009), 1, 12 f.
[67] Ackermann, *ZEuP* 2018, 741, 758.
[68] Cf. below at paras. 1332 ff.
[69] Repealed by the CSD; cf. above at paras. 607 ff.

contracts, the CJEU referred to the Consumer Credit Directive,[70] which also aims to protect consumers. Since it contains provisions on linked contracts, but the Doorstep Selling Directive does not, it follows by implication that a provision to that effect was not intended in the latter directive.[71]

**1323.** Such coexistence proves to be far more challenging where consumer law is not or merely partly the main regulatory subject. Particularly in the area of PIL and international civil procedure, problematic cases arise quite regularly. The Brussels Ibis Regulation and the Rome Regulations are to be interpreted uniformly (Recital 7 Rome I Regulation and Rome II Regulation).[72] Therefore, claims arising from pre-contractual obligations (*culpa in contrahendo*), which must be classified as torts, can fall under the jurisdiction of the consumer contract according to Article 17 Brussels Ibis Regulation in order to establish a coherent interpretation between PIL and international civil procedure law.[73]

**1324.** However, even if comparable provisions exist, such systematic interpretation is not always possible. One example is the question of whether the specific consumer protection provisions regulated in Articles 17 to 19 Brussels Ibis or in Article 6 Rome I Regulation presuppose causality between 'directing' entrepreneurial activity towards the country of domicile of the consumer and the conclusion of the contract.[74] In other cases, the CJEU has explicitly chosen different ways of interpretation, for example, concerning the jurisdiction on tort claims in Article 7 no. 2 Brussels Ibis Regulation, which is not necessarily coherent with the corresponding concept of the Rome II Regulation.[75]

**1325.** Due to the different regulatory contexts, is it possible only in rare cases to transfer interpretive results from substantive consumer law to PIL and international civil procedural law. Thus, the CJEU has refused to transfer the case law on the obligation of courts to carry out an ex officio review concerning unfair terms in consumer contracts[76] to the Brussels Ibis Regulation. The question arose in the context of the certificate of enforceability under Articles 42 and 53 of the Brussels Ibis Regulation, which is issued without an examination on the merits. The national court asked whether the court entrusted with

---

70 Cf. above at paras. 1004 ff.

71 CJEU, 25 October 2005, Case C-350/03, *Schulte/Badenia*, ECLI:EU:C:2005:637, para. 76.

72 Cf. Crawford/Carruthers, *ICLQ* 63 (2014), 1; Lüttringhaus, *RabelsZ* 77 (2013), 31; Rühl, *GPR* 2013, 122; Wilke, *J. Priv. Int'l Law* 2020, 163.

73 CJEU, 2 April 2020, Case C-500/18, *Reliantco*, ECLI:EU:C:2020:264, para. 72.

74 Cf. above at para. 1191.

75 CJEU, 16 January 2014, Case C-45/12, *Kainz*, ECLI:EU:C:2013:390, para. 20, cf. below at para. 1330.

76 Cf. e.g. CJEU, 14 June 2012, Case C-618/10, *Banco Español de Crédito*, ECLI:EU:C:2012:349, paras. 39, 41 and 43; see below at paras. 1374 ff.

issuing the certificate could or even had to inform the defendant, who is also a consumer, of a possible infringement of the rules of jurisdiction on consumer claims and, thus, of the possibility of an objection to recognition within the meaning of Article 45(1)(e) Brussels Ibis Regulation. Even if the comparison with the law on the scrutiny of standard terms seems to be valid at first glance given that consumer protection is pursued in both legal acts, the CJEU rightly emphasised the differences that, ultimately, prevent such a transfer: The Brussels Ibis Regulation has its own mechanisms through which consumer protection is realised; an extension through judge-made law may not be considered in this respect.[77]

**1326.** On the other hand, the CJEU used the provisions of the Package Travel Directive[78] to interpret the notion of a 'contract which, for an inclusive price, provides for a combination of travel and accommodation' in Article 15(3) Brussels I Regulation. Since the Brussels I Regulation – and likewise Article 17 Brussels Ibis Regulation – does not directly refer to this legal act, the CJEU offered the following line of arguments: First, the court referred to the parallel provision in Article 6(4)(b) Rome I Regulation. Then, the court argued that the principle of uniform interpretation of both legal acts also applies to the concept of package travel. However, the Rome I Regulation also directly refers to Directive 90/314/EEC, so the assumption of a procedural context and the reference to the Package Travel Directive was rather obvious in the first place.[79]

**1327.** Such a uniform interpretation becomes more difficult when there are no interrelated regulatory complexes. For example, the CJEU dealt with the question of whether the classification of a person as a 'retail client' within the meaning of Article 4(1)(12) of Directive 2004/39 on markets in financial instruments could possibly have repercussions on their consumer status under Article 17 of the Brussels Ibis Regulation or Article 2(b) of Directive 2004/39. In principle, this was denied: Since autonomous criteria exist for the concept of the consumer concerning each legal act, recourse to other legal concepts is unnecessary in this respect.[80] This also shows that, even from the outset, EU private law does not even claim to be coherent throughout its realm: At best, this category plays a role in certain regulatory contexts.

---

77 CJEU, 4 September 2019, Case C-347/18, *Salvoni*, ECLI:EU:C:2019:661, paras. 40 ff.

78 For the Package Travel Directive cf. above at para. 1023.

79 CJEU, 7 October 2010, Joined Cases C-585/08 and C-144/09, *Pammer/Hotel Alpenhof*, ECLI:EU:C:2010:740, paras. 38 ff.

80 CJEU, 2 April 2020, Case C-500/18, *Reliantco*, ECLI:EU:C:2020:264, paras. 55 f.

## 3. UNIFORM SYSTEM CONCEPTS IN PIL AND EU PRIVATE LAW?

**1328.** Although harmonisation is quite advanced, system coherence is still the exception rather than the rule, despite many pleas to this effect by the legislator. This is especially true if one includes private international law and procedural law in addition to substantive private law to provide the full picture of EU private law.[81]

### a) *The Ideal of a Uniform Interpretation: Theory and Practice*

**1329.** Recital 7 to the Rome I Regulation[82] aims at a synchronisation of the material fields of application to the Brussels I Regulation.[83] Thus, as just explained, the CJEU has interpreted Article 15(3) Brussels I Regulation in light of the identical term found in Article 6(4)(b) Rome I Regulation.[84]

**1330.** However, this does not apply without restriction: The provisions of the Brussels I Regulation are by no means always to be interpreted in light of the provisions of the Rome I Regulation. According to a decision of the CJEU, the desired coherence between the legal acts 'cannot, in any event, lead to the provisions of Regulation no 44/2001 being interpreted in a manner which is unconnected to the scheme and objectives pursued by that regulation'.[85] In the respective case, this concerned the interpretation of the place of jurisdiction on torts (today: Article 7 no. 2 Brussels Ibis Regulation) with regard to product liability claims. The CJEU ruled that only the place where the product's manufacturer is located could be considered to give rise to jurisdiction, as the court in question was particularly close to the relevant factual issues. A comparison to the conflict-of-laws connection in Article 5(1) Rome I Regulation, which, in lit. b – subsidiarily, but nevertheless – also invokes the law of the place of the relevant market, was not drawn,[86] as the respective interests of the law on jurisdiction differed from those of the PIL. Indeed, uniformity of interpretation regarding international jurisdiction and applicable law does not have to be achieved at any cost. However, localisation at the place where the

---

81 Cf. Schaub, *JZ* 2005, 328.
82 Likewise Recitals 17 and 24 of the Rome I Regulation and Recital 7 of the Rome II Regulation.
83 Surprisingly, there is no corresponding Recital in the Brussels Ibis Regulation.
84 Cf. above at para. 1326.
85 CJEU, 16 January 14, Case C-45/13, *Kainz*, ECLI:EU:C:2013:390, para. 20.
86 Critical therefore Freitag, *LMK* 2014, 355576.

defective product was put on the market would not have been far-fetched, not least with recourse to the rationale underlying Article 5(1) Rome II Regulation.

**1331.** This relationship between international jurisdiction and applicable law becomes evident in the case of consumer protection laws.[87] In this respect, it has already been explained that Recital 25 Rome I Regulation requires causality between the direction of the entrepreneurial activity and the conclusion of the contract in order to apply the special protection regime of Article 6 Rome I Regulation. However, the CJEU decided that the parallel problem regarding the head of jurisdiction for consumer cases in Article 17 of the Brussels Ibis Regulation, which largely uses identical terminology, does not depend on causality.[88] There was no reference to the Rome I Regulation in the judgment in question. An interpretation of Article 6(1) of the Rome I Regulation that is coherent with these requirements, as demanded by Recital 24 of the Rome I Regulation, can only be achieved by abandoning the causality requirement postulated in Recital 25 of the Rome I Regulation.[89]

*b) The Concept of the Consumer*

**1332.** Many of the EU's legal acts in the field of private law are at least also addressed to consumers. The concept of the consumer used in such legal acts is to be interpreted in an autonomous manner. It depends on the specific situation of the conclusion of the contract: The contract must not have been concluded for professional or commercial purposes.[90] Contracts with mixed purposes pose difficulties in this respect. If, for example, a teacher buys a notebook that is to be used for preparing lessons as well as for private correspondence, the question arises as to whether the protective mechanisms contained in the Consumer Rights Directive apply. According to Recital 17 CRD, it is sufficient for contracts with a dual purpose ('dual use') that the commercial purpose is not dominant. Moreover, the Directive – which is otherwise fully harmonising – opens up the possibility for the Member States to use a more extensive consumer concept than the Consumer Rights Directive, in particular, to include certain legal persons (such as ideal associations).[91]

**1333.** In the context of procedural law (Article 17 Brussels Ibis Regulation), however, the CJEU interprets the term 'consumer' in a rather restrictive manner.

---

87 In detail Rühl, *GPR* 2013, 122.

88 CJEU, 17 October 2013, Case C-218/12, *Emrek*, ECLI:EU:C:2013:666; cf. above at paras. 1324, 1445.

89 Critical therefore Klöpfer/Wendelstein, *JZ* 2014, 298.

90 On the notion of consumer cf. above at paras. 31 ff.

91 Recital No. 13 CRD.

It only covers contracts concluded by individuals to meet their own needs for private consumption. This condition is not met in the case of contracts the purpose of which is a professional or commercial activity, even if such activity is only intended for the future. The reason is that even if such an activity is only to be taken up in the future does not change its professional or commercial nature. Start-ups thus do not benefit from the advantages of such a forum at their seat of (intended) business.[92] In the case of mixed contracts, an object of the contract intended for a purpose that is partly professional and partly unrelated to professional or commercial activity is not a consumer contract. This must be judged differently if the professional or commercial purpose is so secondary that it plays only a very minor role in the overall context of the transaction.[93]

**1334.** In turn, it seems very questionable whether the concept of consumer of the Brussels Ibis Regulation or the Consumer Rights Directive should apply to Article 6(1) Rome I Regulation. If one stresses the idea of coherence between the Rome I Regulation and the Brussels Ibis Regulation, as already described, the Brussels Ibis Regulation should prevail.[94] On the other hand, however, the idea of consumer protection under conflict of laws would speak for a solution which favours the Rome I-Regulation, which in any case does not make a restrictive interpretation appear attractive.[95] Thus, there is no uniform consumer concept in EU secondary law. The specific contract, together with its EU legal context, is decisive.

### *c) The Contract*

**1335.** Another core concept of EU private law is that of the contract. It has already been mentioned that, in the context of the jurisdiction of the place of performance in Article 7 no. 1 lit. a Brussels Ibis Regulation, the CJEU defines the contract as an obligation that the parties entered into voluntarily.[96] The Consumer Rights Directive confines itself to defining individual contract types (sales contract, service contract, distance contract, etc.),[97] but remains silent on the contract itself. The delimitation of the individual contract types

92 CJEU, 3 July 1997, Case C-269/95, *Benincasa*, ECLI:EU:C:1997:337.

93 CJEU, 20 January 2005, Case C-464/01, *Gruber*, ECLI:EU:C:2005:32, paras. 32 f.

94 Above at para. 1329.

95 Cf. S. Segger-Piening/O. Remien, in H. Prütting/G. Wegen/G. Weinreich, *BGB Kommentar*, 19th ed. (Hürth: Luchterhand, 2024), Art. 6 Rom I para. 5 with further references.

96 CJEU, 17 June 1992, Case C-26/91, *Handte*, ECLI:EU:C:1992:268, para. 15; CJEU, 14 March 2013, Case C-419/11, *Česká spořitelna*, ECLI:EU:C:2013:165, para. 47; CJEU, 18 July 2013, Case C-147/12, *ÖFAB*, ECLI:EU:C:2013:490, para. 33; CJEU, 21 April 2016, Case C-572/14, *Austro-Mechana*, ECLI:EU:C:2016:286, para. 36; CJEU, 8 May 2019, Case C-25/18, *Kerr/Postnov*, ECLI:EU:C:2019:376, para. 25.

97 Article 2 Nos. 5–8 CRD.

already poses difficulties here. According to Article 2 no. 6 CRD, a service contract is 'any contract other than a sales contract under which the trader supplies or undertakes to supply a service to the consumer and the consumer pays or undertakes to pay the price thereof'. Without further justification, the CJEU reduced this to a shortened definition: Any contract that is not a sales contract is a contract for services.[98] According to the principles outlined above, these concepts should have no direct relevance for PIL and international civil procedural law: There is a separate system in place that implements a regulatory plan specific to each of these areas.

**1336.** The proposal for a directive on certain aspects of the online sale of goods (Distance Selling Directive),[99] for example, shows how little EU private law pay attention to developing overarching concepts.[100] In Article 2(h) of the draft Directive on Distance Selling, the contract was defined as an agreement 'intended to give rise to obligations or other legal effects'. This is based on Article 2(a) CESL, which has the same content. The Distance Selling Directive proposal, which was much narrower than the Consumer Rights Directive, was much more far-reaching without substantive justification.

**1337.** Certainly, this concept of the contract would have been binding only regarding the scope of the Directive, i.e. for the distance selling. Nevertheless, it would have had an enormous spill-over effect since the Member States would have had to rely precisely on this contract concept when transposing the Directive. Since it would have been obvious not to use a different contract concept outside the scope of the Directive, this could have led to discrepancies with other EU legal acts.[101] The version of the Sale of Goods Directive that has now been adopted has not incorporated this broad contract concept for good reasons.[102] In this respect, too, the definition remains sector-specific.

---

98 CJEU, 12 March 2020, Case C-583/18, *Verbraucherzentrale Berlin*, ECLI:EU:C:2020:199, para. 23.

99 Proposal for a Directive of the European Parliament and of the Council on certain aspects of contract law applicable to online and other distance marketing of goods, COM(2015) 635 final.

100 Cf. Kähler, in Arnold, *Grundlagen eines europäischen Vertragsrechts*, 2014, p. 79.

101 However, for concurrence of the concept of consumer contract in the European enforcement order regulation and the Brussels Ibis Regulation CJEU, 5 December 2013, Case C-508/12, *Vapenik*, ECLI:EU:C:2013:790 (no application to C2C contracts); critically Klöpfer/Ramić, *GPR* 2014, 107; Stadler, *IPRax* 2015, 203.

102 Cf. above at para. 834.

## 4. USE OF FURTHER INSTRUMENTS FOR SYSTEMATIC INTERPRETATION?

**1338.** It has already been mentioned that individual Advocates General have referred to the DCFR and the PECL in their Opinions.[103] Methodologically, this is unproblematic as long as a the purely academic character of these instruments is clearly mentioned from the outset.[104] The use of formal sources of law of non-EU origin, such as the Vienna Sales Convention, is, from a strict point of view, inadmissible.[105] At most, these can be considered to elucidate the genesis of a given provision.[106] After all, all EU Member States are now also contracting states to the CISG: the United Kingdom has left the EU, and Portugal declared its accession to the CISG on 7 August 2020.

# IV. A COMMON EUROPEAN METHODOLOGY?

References: C. Baldus/T. Raff, 'Unionsrechtliche Überformung mitgliedstaatlicher Methodik?', *GPR* 2016, 71; T. Coendet, *Rechtsvergleichende Argumentation. Phänomenologie der Veränderung im rechtlichen Diskurs* (Tübingen: Mohr Siebeck, 2012); H. Fleischer, 'Europäische Methodenlehre: Stand und Perspektiven', *RabelsZ* 75 (2011), 700; F. Gómez, 'The Harmonization of Contract Law through European Rules: a Law and Economics Perspective', *ERCL* 2008, 89; Grundmann, '"Inter-Instrumental-Interpretation". Systembildung durch Auslegung im Europäischen Unionsrecht', *RabelsZ* 75 (2011), 882; M. Grünberger, 'Responsive Rechtsdogmatik – Eine Skizze', *AcP* 219 (2019), 924; T. Henninger, *Europäisches Privatrecht und Methode* (Tübingen: Mohr Siebeck, 2009), pp. 323 ff.; F. Kainer, 'Privatrecht zwischen Richtlinien und Grundrechten – Zu den Grenzen richtlinienkonformer Auslegung und horizontalen Richtlinienwirkungen', *GPR* 2016, 262; E.A. Kramer, 'Die Methode bestimmt den Inhalt: eine weiterhin offene Grundsatzfrage des Unionsrechts', *GPR* 2015, 262; E.A. Kramer, 'Replik zu Riesenhuber, Methodendivergenzen ertragen', *GPR* 2016, 210; H.P. Mansel, 'Rechtsvergleichung und europäische Rechtseinheit', *JZ* 1991, 529; S.A.E. Martens, *Methodenlehre des Unionsrechts* (Tübingen: Mohr Siebeck, 2013); S.A.E. Martens, 'Methodenfragen und die Behandlung von Grundlagenstörungen im Europäischen Privatrecht', *ZEuP* 2017, 600; S. Pötters/R. Christensen, 'Das Unionsrecht als Hybridform zwischen case law und

---

103 Cf. e.g. AG Trstenjak, Opinion of 11 June 2008, Case C-275/07, *Commission/Italy*, para. 90 on the ancillary nature of interest to the principal claim; here a reference is made to Article III.-3:708(1) DCFR. Cf. also Basedow, *AcP* 210 (2010), 157, 185 note 103.

104 But see Martinek, in *Staudinger-Eckpfeiler* (2011), Teil A para. 111.

105 But see CJEU, 25 February 2010, Case C-381/08, *Car Trim*, ECLI:EU:C:2010:90, paras. 36 ff.: Article 3(1) CISG is an 'indication, therefore, that the fact that the goods to be delivered are to be manufactured or produced beforehand does not alter the classification of the contract at issue as a sales contract'.

106 On the close relationship of the Consumer Sales Directive to the CISG para. 840.

Gesetzesrecht', *JZ* 2012, 289; K. Riesenhuber (ed.), *European Legal Methodology*, 2nd ed. (Cambridge: Intersentia, 2021); K. Riesenhuber, 'Auf dem Weg zu einem europäischen Privatrecht', in K.J. Hopt/D. Tzouganatos (eds.), *Das Europäische Wirtschaftsrecht vor neuen Herausforderungen* (Tübingen: Mohr Siebeck, 2014), p. 183; K. Riesenhuber, 'Methodendivergenzen ertragen!', *GPR* 2016, 158; K. Riesenhuber, 'Neue Methode und Dogmatik eines Rechts der Digitalisierung?', *AcP* 219 (2019), 892; W.H. Roth, 'Europäische Verfassung und europäische Methodenlehre', *RabelsZ* 75 (2011), 787; M. Stürner, 'Common Law, Civil Law und Europäisches Privatrecht. Zur Angleichung methodischer Grundsätze in den Gemeinschaftsrechtsordnungen', in A. Tietze/M. McGuire *e.a.* (eds.), *Europäisches Privatrecht – Über die Verknüpfung von nationalem und Gemeinschaftsrecht, Jahrbuch Junger Zivilrechtswissenschaftler 2004* (Stuttgart: Boorberg, 2005), p. 79; C. Wendehorst, 'Methodennormen in kontinentaleuropäischen Kodifikationen', *RabelsZ* 75 (2011), 730.

## 1. METHODOLOGY AS A NATIONAL DOMAIN?

**1339.** It has already been said that the case law of the CJEU, in principle, does not prescribe certain national methodological approaches.[107] The courts of the Member States must indeed do everything possible to apply the law to ensure the practical effectiveness of EU law. However, the limit of the obligation to apply the law in conformity with the directives is the respective national approach towards methodology: If that approach does not allow for the further development of law *contra legem* in conformity with a given directive, EU law does not impose an obligation to change this approach. This may be criticised for a number of reasons.[108] However, the approach of the CJEU can be justified by the autonomy of the Member States and, thus, the postulate of sovereignty.

**1340.** Another issue is the question of which method is the right one. This is true even for the Member States' laws. E.g. in Germany, after many decades in which the doctrine of methodology was essentially oriented towards Savigny's classical canons of methods,[109] the recent past has seen a plethora of alternative approaches. Above all, interpretation in conformity with the constitution and application of the law in conformity with the directives can be regarded as new sub-types of a systematic-teleological interpretation.[110] However, they are also characterised by the assumption that law is ultimately a self-contained (autopoietic[111]) system characterised by coherence and absence of contradictions.

107 Cf. above at paras. 357 ff.
108 Cf. again the controversy in Kramer, *GPR* 2015, 262; Riesenhuber, *GPR* 2016, 158; Kramer, *GPR* 2016, 210.
109 Cf. above at para. 346.
110 Cf. above at para. 348.
111 To use a term coined by the system theory: N. Luhmann, *Das Recht der Gesellschaft* (Frankfurt am Main: Suhrkamp, 1993), pp. 538 ff.; G. Teubner, *Recht als autopoietisches System* (Frankfurt am Main: Suhrkamp, 1989).

It has already been shown that, concerning EU private law, there are doubts as to whether this claim can be fulfilled.[112] Against this backdrop, calls are being made for a more open approach, which can go in the direction of an orientation towards the practical consequences, such as the economic analysis of law does,[113] or at least take into account extra-legal factors.[114]

**1341.** This debate cannot be developed any further here.[115] However, one may at least assume that, despite its incompleteness, a certain degree of systems thinking is also inherent in EU private law. Even if this is still far from forming an 'internal' system in the sense described above, it primarily constitutes the reference system itself, which is decisive for legal interpretation.[116] This is not to say that contextual, extra-legal perspectives cannot be included in the hermeneutic process. However, this an approach presupposes that such perspectives must at least be reflected in each provision in question.

## 2. SPONTANEOUS METHODOLOGICAL HARMONISATION?

**1342.** Nevertheless, there are indications of further convergence of national methodological approaches beyond the requirements of EU law. In this respect, one could speak of spontaneous methodological harmonisation in Europe.[117]

### a) *Convergence of Common Law and Civil Law*

**1343.** Comparative lawyers are familiar with the fact that different legal systems usually find similar solutions to comparable problems. This is increasingly true with respect to English common law and continental civil law; these are the key sources that European private law continues to draw from. Therefore, the thesis of the slow convergence of the two systems has often been advocated in comparative law.[118] This was proven above all for substantive law. In this

112 Cf. above at paras. 1320 ff.

113 Cf. above at paras. 341 ff.

114 The term 'responsive approach' ('*responsive Rechtsdogmatik*') has been coined by Grünberger, *AcP* 219 (2019), 924.

115 A methodology based on the reasoning (of judgements) is advocated by S.A.E. Martens, *Methodenlehre des Unionsrechts* (Tübingen: Mohr Siebeck, 2013), pp. 72 ff., 294 ff.

116 On this 'strictly legal point of view' cf. Riesenhuber, *AcP* 219 (2019), 892; Lobinger, *AcP* 216 (2016), 28; Using the example of the transposition of the CSD into the German Civil Code, also Lobinger, *GPR* 2008, 262.

117 The following draws on Stürner, in *Jahrbuch Junger Zivilrechtswissenschaftler* (Stuttgart: Bohrberg, 2004), p. 79.

118 J.H. Merryman, in M. Cappelletti (ed.), *New Perspectives for a Common Law of Europe* (Leyden/London: Stijhoff, 1978) (= *The Loneliness of the Comparative Lawyer* (The Hague: Kluwer, 1999), pp. 17 ff.; Glenn, (1993) Rev.int.dr.comp. 559 ff.; M. Reimann, in M. Reimann

respect, one could mention, for example, the relaxation of the English doctrine of privity of contract and the acceptance of cases where a contract might also have legal effects vis-à-vis third parties.[119] However, it can also be demonstrated in procedural law and likewise in the area of legal methodology.

aa) Legislation

**1344.** Perhaps the most remarkable convergence of common law and continental law may be witnessed in an area that has been affected by private law harmonisation only indirectly: procedural law. The differences in the structure of civil procedural laws could not have been greater: The adversary system of the common law stood for a strict rule of party presentation; litigation was regarded as a kind of private property of the parties.[120] The role of the judge was limited to that of a neutral and detached observer who determines a winner in the battle of the parties, which Lord Denning once described as follows: 'In litigation as in war. If one side makes a mistake, the other can take advantage of it. No holds are barred.'[121] The principle of orality was so strong that every document referred to by the parties had to be read out during trial.[122]

**1345.** On the continent, social conceptions of civil proceedings dominated in various forms, with the judge as the central figure determining the progress of the trial and the lawyers as more passive participants. To Anglo-American commentators, this distribution of tasks has traditionally been so alien that it has been repeatedly described as 'inquisitorial'.[123]

(ed.), *The Reception of Continental Ideas in the Common Law World 1820–1920* (Stuttgart: Duncker & Humblot, 1993), pp. 7 ff.; B.S. Markesinis, in B.S. Markesinis (ed.), *The Gradual Convergence* (Oxford: Clarendon Press, 1994), pp. 1, 2, 20, 30 ff.; M. Vranken, *Fundamentals of European Civil Law* (Sydney: Federation Press, 1997), pp. 212 ff.; more cautiously Kötz, *ZEuP* 1998, 493, 500 ff. Against this trend, however, Legrand, 45 *ICLQ* 1996, 52, 55 ff.; Legrand, 60 MLR 1997, 44. For more references cf. J.M. Smits, *The Making of European Private Law* (Antwerp: Intersentia, 2002), pp. 103 f. From an American perspective, on the other hand, English law has been said to be moving primarily in the direction of US common law, cf. Levitsky, 42 (1994) *Am.J.Comp.L.* 347, 380.

119 Since the enactment of the Contracts (Rights of Third Parties) Act 1999, the contract for the benefit of third parties has been part of English law, which is now on a par with the civil law jurisdictions, which all know this construction, cf. Palmer, *ERPL* 11 (2003), 8, 10 and W. Lorenz, in B.S. Markesinis (ed.), ibid., pp. 65, 72 ff. Even before that, case law recognised protective effects of a contract vis-à-vis third parties, cf. *White* v. *Jones* [1995] 2 WLR 187, HL.

120 J.I.H. Jacob, *The Fabric of English Civil Justice* (London: Stevens, 1987), p. 8.

121 *Burmah Oil Co. Ltd.* v. *Governor and Co. of the Bank of England* [1979] 1 WLR 473, 484 (CA).

122 J.I.H. Jacob, *The Fabric of English Civil Justice* (London: Stevens, 1987), 19 f.

123 Cf. Kötz, in *Festschrift für Zajtay* (Tübingen: Mohr Siebeck, 1982), pp. 277, 280 ff. In principle, however, it is rather uncontroversial that German civil procedure is also an adversary system., cf. Stürner, *ZVglRWiss* 99 (2000), 310, 329 f. with further references.

**1346.** In England, the Civil Procedure Rules (CPR),[124] designed under the leadership of Lord Woolf and enacted in 1999, curtailed the traditional adversary system by giving the court responsibility for the progress of the proceedings and, to that end, vesting it with wide-ranging trial management power.[125] 'Ultimate responsibility for the control of litigation must move from the litigants and their legal advisors to the court', as Lord *Woolf* succinctly writes.[126] The principle of orality was also restricted; the parties must now extensively prepare the proceedings in writing.[127] For proceedings up to an amount of 15,000 pounds, the costs are already determined before the start of the proceedings based on a fixed fee system.[128]

**1347.** What is even more important, however, is that the reform of the civil procedure was put in place by means of a codification.[129] The CPR do not only summarise the previous rules but herald a radical change of style. Besides, it strives at internal coherency. Moreover, the CPR are preceded by general principles that the courts must consider when interpreting the provisions and exercising discretion. This is, of course, nothing entirely new: the common law has been familiar with general principles of law since the early times. It has already been mentioned that these principles are slowly emerging from many individual decisions. What is downright revolutionary, however, is the fact that the procedural maxims of the CPR are not only a consolidation of the previously established case law. In particular, the principle of proportionality, hitherto unknown to English procedural law in this form, has been decreed by legislation, i.e. top-down.[130] In other words, it has not been developed organically by the courts. i.e. bottom-up.

bb) Approach in Style and Methodology

**1348.** This seems to represent a change that goes deeper than, for example, the recognition of third-party effects of contracts. The English Parliament is increasingly pushing the former protagonists of lawmaking, the judiciary, out of their creative responsibility through a denser network of formal laws. Now, with

---

124 On the CPR cf. Sobich, *JZ* 1999, 775; Stürner, *ZVglRWiss* 99 (2000), 310; Greger, *JZ* 2002, 1020, 1026 ff.; N. Andrews, *On Civil Processes*, 2nd ed. (Cambridge: Intersentia, 2019), paras. 1.08 ff., 2.01 ff.

125 Case management, rule 3.1 CPR. Cf. N. Andrews, ibid., paras. 9.01 ff.

126 Access to Justice Final Report, 1996, p. 14. Judge Lightmant's assessment is similar: 'The judges are the masters now.' (1998) 17 *CJQ* 373, 389.

127 Pre-action protocols, statements of case, skeleton arguments und trial bundles. Cf. Dreymüller, *ZVglRWiss* 101 (2002), 471, 474 ff.

128 For the fast track: rule 46.2 (1) CPR.

129 Cf. rule 1.1 (1) CPR; Stürner, *ZVglRWiss* 103 (2004), 349, 352 ff.

130 In detail Stürner, *ZVglRWiss* 103 (2004), 349, 366 ff.

the Civil Procedure Rules, the judges have to apply provisions that are designed as a codification, contain general clauses and are, thus, obviously oriented towards the deductive method of finding the law characteristic of civil law. For the existence and development of European private law, it can be inferred from this that the 'harmonisation bottom-up' continues to progress, namely in the area of lawmaking and the application of the law.

### (1) Changes in Lawmaking

**1349.** If the comprehensive regulation of an area of law in a systematically structured code was identified as the main characteristic of lawmaking in civil law, this finding must be put into perspective. Throughout Europe, the major codifications were getting increasingly less important, which was referred to under the term 'decodification'.[131] E.g. in Germany, one of the heartlands of codification, the Civil Code has long since ceased to regulate all parts of civil law. Essential areas, especially consumer protection law, were outsourced in the second half of the last century and laid down in secondary legislation. A wave of re-codification in 2001 has tried to change this,[132] but it cannot disguise the fact, that most other European countries have departed from the ideal of an overarching codification in civil law.

**1350.** Conversely, lawmaking by precedent in the original form of common law has proven incapable of providing sufficient legal certainty when new legal problems arose, so legislative activity became imperative. Guido Calabresi, therefore, spoke of a 'statutorification' of common law with regard to US law.[133]

### (2) Changes Regarding the Application of the Law

**1351.** The approach towards the application of the law has also changed in both legal systems. Most notable is the liberalisation of interpretative methodology in English common law.[134] The reason for the long-practised, interpretation-related formalism lies in the great importance of the principle

---

131 The term was coined by N. Irti, *L'età della decodificazione*, 3rd ed. (Milan: Giuffrè, 1989). On the ageing of codifications Wieacker, in *Festschrift für Boehmer* (Bonn: L. Röhrscheid Verlag, 1954), pp. 34, 47 ff.; Kübler, *JZ* 1969, 645; Kötz, 50 *MLR* 1987, 1 ff.; K. Schmidt, *Die Zukunft der Kodifikationsidee* (Heidelberg: C.F. Müller, 1985), pp. 13 ff., 47 ff.

132 The effect of which has been rather doubtful, cf. e.g. Lando, *RabelsZ* 67 (2003), 231, 244 f. ('labyrinth of provisions'); Dauner-Lieb, *NJW* 2004, 1431, 1432.

133 G. Calabresi, *A Common Law for the Age of Statutes* (Cambridge (MA): Harvard University Press, 1982), p. 1.

134 Cf. S. Vogenauer, *Die Auslegung von Gesetzen in England und auf dem Kontinent* (Tübingen: Mohr Siebeck, 2001), pp. 665 ff.

of parliamentary sovereignty. According to the classical understanding of the constitution, as stated by Dicey, there are no limits to the legislative competence of parliament.[135] Once an area of the law has been regulated by statute, a court can no longer decide to deviate from it. Traditionally, therefore, interpretation always strictly adhered to the wording of a provision.[136] Any extensive interpretation was considered to be 'legislation'[137] and would be tantamount to a violation of parliamentary sovereignty.[138]

**1352.** In recent decades, it has been realised – not least due to Lord *Denning's* constant impulses – that an interpretation must also be based on the meaning and purpose of the law.[139] This development was accelerated by the accession of the United Kingdom to the European Communities in 1973: The interpretation of directives, just like the interpretation of the standards transposing them, must not be limited to an interpretation of the wording; rather, the principle of interpretation in conformity with EU law applies.[140] Lord *Denning* justified this approach with remarkable pragmatism: 'Just as in Rome, you should do as Rome does. In the European Community, you should do as the European Court does.'[141]

---

135 A.V. Dicey, *Law of the Constitution*, 1st ed. (London: MacMillan, 1885), pp. 39 f. writes: 'The principle of parliamentary sovereignty means neither more nor less than this, namely, that Parliament [...] has, under the English constitution, the right to make or unmake any law whatever; and, further, that no person or body is recognised by the law of England as having a right to override or set aside the legislation of Parliament.'

136 Literal interpretation, cf. K. Zweigert/H. Kötz, *Introduction to Comparative Law*, 3rd ed. (Oxford: Clarendon Press, 1996), §18 III; W. Fikentscher, *Methoden des Rechts in vergleichender Darstellung*, Volume II (Tübingen: Mohr Siebeck, 1975), pp. 111 ff.; B. Bankowski/N. MacCormick, in N. MacCormick/R.S. Summers, *Interpreting Statutes* (London: Routledge, 1991), pp. 359, 365 ff. On the other traditional methods of interpretation golden rule and mischief rule S. Vogenauer, *Die Auslegung von Gesetzen in England und auf dem Kontinent* (Tübingen: Mohr Siebeck, 2001), pp. 676 ff., 863 ff.

137 Cf. *James Buchanan & Co. Ltd.* v. *Babco Forwarding and Shipping (UK) Ltd.* [1978] AC 141, 156 (HL), where Viscount Dilhorne said: 'I know of no authority for the proposition that one consequence of this country joining the European Economic Community is that the courts of this country should now abandon principles as to construction long established in our law. The courts have rightly refused to encroach on the province of Parliament and *have refused to engage in legislation.*' [italics added].

138 Cf. Everling, *RabelsZ* 50 (1986), 193, 209; Levitsky, 42 (1994) *Am.J.Comp.L.* 347, 349 ff.

139 Purposive approach, cf. *Carter* v. *Bradbeer* [1975] 1 WLR 1204, 1206 f., HL (Lord Diplock); *James Buchanan & Co. Ltd.* v. *Babco Forwarding and Shipping (UK) Ltd.* [1977] QB 208, 213 f., CA (Lord Denning); but cf. the appellate decision by the House of Lords, *James Buchanan & Co. Ltd.* v. *Babco Forwarding and Shipping (UK) Ltd.* [1978] AC 141.

140 Cf. CJEU, 13 November 1990, Case C-106/89, *Marleasing*, ECLI:EU:C:1990:395.

141 *James Buchanan & Co. Ltd.* v. *Babco Forwarding and Shipping (UK) Ltd.* [1977] QB 208, 214 (CA).

**1353.** Finally, in 1992, the last fortification of genuine British interpretative formalism fell: The exclusionary rule. In the famous *Pepper v. Hart* decision,[142] the House of Lords, for the first time, allowed the use of parliamentary records, the so-called Hansards, as a source of interpretation in the context of historical interpretation. This step had become almost unavoidable after case law had recognised that a consultation of the legislative history of the respective secondary legislation was mandatory for any interpretation in conformity with the directive.[143]

cc) Methods of Finding the Law

**1354.** If one looks at the methods of finding the law, one notices a gradual adoption of approaches that are actually alien to the English system. The common law judge has to get used to a deductive approach, the continental legal practitioner to the inductive one.

**1355.** The ever-increasing number of laws and, in particular, the fact that the directives to be transposed into national law mostly follow the civil law approach and contain general clauses means that legal practitioners trained in common law jurisdictions are increasingly getting familiar with the deductive method. The reform of English procedural law shows that a systematic structure and the use of general clauses and general principles of interpretation have also become integral parts of purely national legal matters. It will take time for this change to be fully internalised. Judges still seem to have to remind themselves with every judgment that a new era has dawned in which 'overriding principles' are to be observed and no longer old case law.[144]

**1356.** Conversely, in continental legal orders, the role of the judge as a substitute legislator in private law is increasingly important.[145] Regardless of the formal validity of the doctrine of binding precedent, in a system that operates with general clauses, the precedent for legal practice is maybe even more important than the rule itself. This is very clearly reflected in the practical work of a judge or lawyer. Almost every judgement handed down by the superior courts is published in specialised journals; systematic databases make it possible to search

---

142 *Pepper (Inspector of Taxes)* v. *Hart* [1992] 3 WLR 1032. Cf. S. Vogenauer, *Die Auslegung von Gesetzen in England und auf dem Kontinent* (Tübingen: Mohr Siebeck, 2001), pp. 969 ff.

143 *Pickstone* v. *Freemans plc* [1989] 1 AC 66, 112, 121 f. In *Pepper* v. *Hart* the decision was called 'a major inroad on the exclusionary rule', [1992] 3 WLR 1032, 1052 f. (Lord Browne-Wilkinson).

144 Cf. Stürner, *ZVglRWiss* 103 (2004), 349, 356 ff.

145 Cf. K.P. Berger, *The Creeping Codification of the Lex Mercatoria* (The Hague/London/Boston: Kluwer Law International, 1999), pp. 95 ff.; E.A. Kramer, in H.-D. Assmann/G. Brüggemeier/R. Sethe (eds.), *Unterschiedliche Rechtskulturen – Konvergenz des Rechtsdenkens* (Baden-Baden: Nomos, 2001), pp. 31, 36 ff.

by keywords. Lately, AI generators even provide fully-fledged legal arguments. Which practising lawyer, therefore, who is trying to solve an intricate legal problem, will not begin their deliberations by searching to see whether the case has already been decided rather than deduct the solution from the provisions of the codification? The courts proceed similarly. As a general rule, they do not deviate from established case law. The German Federal Court of Justice once formulated this as follows: 'A departure from the continuity of the case law can only be accepted as an exception if there are clearly overriding or even plainly compelling reasons for doing so.'[146]

**1357.** As a rule, lower-instance courts follow the case law of the higher or supreme courts; deviation from this may oblige the lower-instance courts to allow for the decision to be appealed.[147] For lawyers, knowledge of, and compliance with, the case law of the higher and supreme courts is essential for avoiding liability risks: According to the German Federal Supreme Court, a lawyer is liable for errors based on ignorance of the case law.[148] Therefore, as a matter of principle, they must orient themselves on the case law of the highest courts and may rely on its continuation.[149] One can, therefore, speak with good reason of a persuasive authority, or a de facto binding effect,[150] of the judgments of the higher courts in continental law,[151] which only permit a deviation for compelling factual reasons.[152] One such objective reason – and this brings us back to the common law – is, of course, the lack of comparability of the case's facts with the previous authorities. In legal practice, therefore, an inductive method similar to that of common law dominates in civil law systems. The technique of distinguishing just as well as the concepts of *ratio decidendi* and *obiter dictum*, should, therefore, be familiar to every practitioner on the continent.

**1358.** Admittedly it is true that the idea of the legal order as a coherent system is still rather alien to common law, as Lord Porter put it: 'The Common Law is a historical development rather than a logical whole, and the fact that a particular doctrine does not logically accord with another or others is no ground for its rejection.'[153] Nevertheless, the preceding remarks lead to the conclusion that

---

146 BGHZ (GrS) 85, 64, 66. Cf. also K. Langenbucher, *Die Entwicklung und Auslegung von Richterrecht* (Munich: Beck, 1996), pp. 106 ff., 126 ff. and Krebs, *AcP* 195 (1995), 171, 182 ff.

147 Sec. 511(2) no 2, (4) (*Berufung*) and sec. 543(2) (*Revision*) of the German Code of Civil Procedure.

148 BGH NJW 1983, 1665; BGH NJW-RR 1993, 243, 245; BGH NJW 2001, 675, 678.

149 BGH NJW 1993, 3323, 3324.

150 Cf. Olzen, *JZ* 1985, 155, 157.

151 Honsell, in Staudinger, *BGB Kommentar* (2018), Einl. BGB paras. 224 ff.

152 Honsell, in Staudinger, *BGB Kommentar* (2018), Einl. BGB para. 229; *Krebs, AcP* 195 (1995), 171, 182 ff.; K.P. Berger, *The Creeping Codification of the Lex Mercatoria* (The Hague/London/Boston: Kluwer Law International, 1999), p. 94.

153 *Best v. Samuel Fox & Co. Ltd.* (1952) AC 716, 727, HL (Lord Porter).

common law and civil law also converge when it comes to legal methodology.[154] This remains important for the development of the law even after Brexit.[155]

### *b) The Contribution of Methodology to the Harmonisation of EU Private Law*

**1359.** This insight raises the question of whether there is also a genuinely European methodology as a substrate or catalyst of this convergence. This relates exclusively to the approximation of non-harmonised law. In the area of harmonised law, there is a duty to interpret EU law in conformity with the directives. In the area of a partially harmonised field of law, there is a standard for harmonising interpretation. The indications of a gradual convergence of style and method in common law and civil law, as described above, and the increasing harmonisation efforts at a European level, but above all the emergence of the Consumer Sales Directive, drew the attention of academia to the development of a European methodology from around the mid-1990s onwards. Even though this impetus has clearly waned since the political failure of the DCFR at the latest, the discussion has never subsided.[156]

#### aa) Starting Point

**1360.** The calls for a uniform European methodology[157] as a fundament for the further development of a European unification of private law[158] find additional legitimacy in this convergence. This methodology must be grounded in the recognition of comparative law as an independent methodological instrument that enables a 'euro-friendly' or 'internationally acceptable' interpretation[159] or a 'comparative approach'.[160] What all these views have in common is that international coherence of judgements is already achieved in substantive law. Further down the road this culminates in a call for a transnational system of

---

154 Cf. S. Vogenauer, *Die Auslegung von Gesetzen in England und auf dem Kontinent* (Tübingen: Mohr Siebeck, 2001), pp. 1295 ff.; J.M. Smits, *The Making of European Private Law* (Antwerp: Intersentia, 2002), pp. 94 ff.; J. Taupitz, *Europäische Rechtsvereinheitlichung heute und morgen* (Tübingen: Mohr Siebeck, 1993), §6; *Lordi*, (2002) 22 *Journal of Law and Commerce*, 1, 5; Martens, *ZEuP* 2017, 600, 601 (Common law and civil law each combine deductive and inductive approaches).

155 Cf. above at paras. 157 ff.

156 Cf. above at paras. 18 ff.

157 Schulze, *ZfRV* 1997, 183, 192 ff.; Berger, *ZEuP* 2001, 4, 12 ff.; Flessner, *JZ* 2002, 14, 16 ff.; Hahn, *ZfRV* 2003, 163; G. Brüggemeier, in H.-D. Assmann/G. Brüggemeier/R. Sethe (eds.), *Unterschiedliche Rechtskulturen – Konvergenz des Rechtsdenkens* (Baden-Baden: Nomos, 2001), pp. 1, 7 f.

158 Berger, *ZEuP* 2001, 4, 6 f.

159 Odersky, *ZEuP* 1994, 1, 2 ff.; von Bar, *ZfRV* 1994, 221, 230 f.; Berger, *ZEuP* 2001, 4, 12 ff.; cf. also Gruber, *ZVglRWiss* 101 (2002), 38, 40 ff.

160 Flessner, *JZ* 2002, 14, 18 ff.

precedents stemming from the general principle of equality under European law as a methodological starting point.[161]

bb) Objections

**1361.** Even if such a transnational doctrine of precedents as a component of a common European methodological approach certainly follows a certain internal logic, some limitations remain, particularly because an obligation for a comparative methodology in the area of non-harmonised law is not required by EU law.[162]

**1362.** First of all, comparative interpretation is not yet really accepted on either side of the Channel. English judges seem to be more open to it than their continental colleagues. This applies, at least, to the comparative use of the law of other common law states. In the recent past, legal observations across the Channel were, in fact, undertaken, for example, in *White v. Jones*, in which Lord Goff reported in detail on the experience with contractual third-party effects in other countries.[163] As a common law system, however, comparative law in England comes into play less with respect to interpretation than in the judicial development of the law; in this respect, the House of Lords (or, respectively, the Supreme Court), in particular, has been regularly inspired by comparative law.[164] The Swiss Federal Supreme Court also excels in comparative law work, not least due to the 'insularity' of Switzerland and the resulting increased pressure to adapt.

**1363.** As a methodological instrument in its own right, comparative law is not wholeheartedly recognised, at least in Germany. In court practise, it still

---

161 Berger, *ZEuP* 2001, 4, 24 ff.; I. Klöckner, *Grenzüberschreitende Bindung an zivilgerichtliche Präjudizien* (Tübingen: Mohr Siebeck, 2006); Henninger, *Europäisches Privatrecht und Methode*, 2009, pp. 357 ff.

162 Cf. CJEU, 17 July 1997, Case C-28/95, *Leur-Bloem*, ECLI:EU:C:1997:369, paras. 32 f.; CJEU, 17 October 2013, Case C-184/12, *Unamar*, ECLI:EU:C:2013:663, para. 31; W.-H. Roth, in *Festgabe 50 Jahre Bundesgerichtshof*, Volume II (Munich: C.H. Beck, 2000), pp. 847, 865 f.; Mayer/Schürnbrand, *JZ* 2004, 545, 548 ff.

163 [1995] 2 WLR 187, 194 f. 201 ff. Cf. further *Woolwich Equitable Building Society* v. *Inland Revenue Commissioners* [1993] AC 70, 174 ff., HL; *McFarlane* v. *Tayside Health Board* [1999] 4 All ER 961, 975 f., HL; *Greatorex* v. *Greatorex* [2000] 1 WLR 1970, QBD, or *Fairchild* v. *Glenhaven Funeral Services Ltd.* [2002] 3 All ER 305, 327 f., HL (Lord Bingham). For further references, cf. von Bar, *ZfRV* 1994, 221, 231 and E. Örücü, in U. Drobnig/J.H.M. van Erp (eds.), *The Use of Comparative Law by the Courts* (The Hague: Kluwer Law International, 1999), pp. 253 ff.

164 Stoll, *RabelsZ* 68 (2004), 541, 543 f. rightly points out that in a case-law system a more 'unbiased' development of the law is possible.

plays hardly any role.[165] This is not least due to practical reasons because it is not only the judges at the courts of instance who lack comparative law routine, access to legal sources and, above all, the necessary time to refer to foreign legal systems to solve a legal problem.[166] It is to be feared that the superficial use of comparative law arguments will do more harm than good if it is done without the necessary in-depth knowledge of the respective legal system.[167] The seamless incorporation of a foreign precedent into one's system will also likely cause difficulties. According to German understanding, there is only an obligation to use comparative arguments in specific cases, e.g. when it comes to classification in private international law, i.e. the question of whether a foreign legal institution falls within the scope of a German conflict-of-laws rule,[168] or in the context of the interpretation of uniform transnational law.[169]

**1364.** There is also no agreement on the methodological foundation of comparative law as an independent method of statutory interpretation.[170] This disagreement already starts with the question of which legal systems must be used for a serious comparison.[171] One can cautiously argue that a consensus exists insofar as comparative arguments are, in any case, not harmful.[172]

**1365.** The missing link so far seems to be a robust point of reference for the uniform interpretation of national law and, thus, the justification for a transnational doctrine of precedent. Neither the PECL nor the DCFR are suitable for this: Only a democratically legitimised, binding set of rules at the European level can serve as a joint standard for a comparative interpretation.[173]

---

165 Cf. Kötz, in *Festgabe 50 Jahre Bundesgerichtshof*, Volume II, 2000, pp. 825 ff.; Gruber, *ZVglRWiss* 101 (2002), 38 ff.; U. Drobnig, in U. Drobnig/J.H.M. van Erp (eds.), *The Use of Comparative Law by the Courts* (The Hague: Kluwer Law International, 1999), pp. 127 ff.; *id.*, *RabelsZ* 50 (1986), 610, 612 ff.; B.S. Markesinis, *Comparative Law in the Courtroom and Classroom: The Story of the Last Thirty-Five Years (Oxford: Hart Publishing, 2003-*. For comparative influences in the case law of the CJEU cf. Everling, *RabelsZ* 50 (1986), 193, 211; Rodríguez Iglesias, *NJW* 1999, 1, 6 ff.

166 Zweigert, *RabelsZ* 15 (1949/50), 5, 18; Behrens, *RabelsZ* 50 (1986), 19, 27; even the proponents of a European methodology admit this, cf. von Bar, *ZfRV* 1994, 221, 231; Schulze, *ZfRV* 1997, 183, 196; Berger, *ZEuP* 2001, 4, 13.

167 Cf. Rösler, *JuS* 1999, 1186, 1189.

168 Cf. Rabel, *RabelsZ* 5 (1931), 241; Drobnig, *RabelsZ* 50 (1986), 610, 613; G. Kegel/K. Schurig, *Internationales Privatrecht*, 9th ed. (Munich: Beck, 2004), pp. 343 ff.; BGHZ 47, 324, 332.

169 Cf. Kötz, in *Festgabe 50 Jahre Bundesgerichtshof*, Volume II, 2000, pp. 825, 828 f.; Mansel, *JZ* 1991, 529, 531.

170 Cf. E. Örücü, in A. Harding/E. Örücü (eds.), *Comparative Law in the 21st Century* (London: Kluwer Academic, 2002), pp. 1 ff.; Micklitz, *ZEuP* 1998, 253, 268.

171 Cf. Berger, *ZEuP* 2001, 4, 13; Zweigert/H. Kötz, *Introduction to Comparative Law*, 3rd ed. (Oxford: Clarendon Press, 1996), §3 IV.

172 Cf. Drobnig, *RabelsZ* 50 (1986), 610, 627.

173 Riesenhuber also points out this weakness of the Principles (in *Europäisches Vertragsrecht*, 2nd ed. 2006, para. 57). Similarly Schulze, *ZfRV* 1997, 183, 197 ('no normative basis'). In

The principle of equality under European law prohibits unequal treatment of essentially identical facts, but only in such fields of law which have already been harmonised.[174] Any comparative approach to methodology going beyond a mere sidenote, must therefore be limited to that part of national law that has already been harmonised.

**1366.** If, in a legal dispute, the decision of a court from another Member State on a functionally comparable legal problem is available, this judgment does not amount to an authoritative line of reasoning. However, the court is, of course, free to consider suggestions from other legal systems within its framework of permissible interpretation and further development of its own law.[175]

general W. van Gerven, in A. Harding/E. Örücü (eds.), *Comparative Law in the 21st Century* (London: Kluwer Academic, 2002), pp. 155, 170 ff.

174 Also conceded by Berger, *ZEuP* 2001, 4, 24.

175 Cf. Odersky, *ZEuP* 1994, 1, 2; W.-H. Roth, in *Festgabe 50 Jahre Bundesgerichtshof*, Volume II, 2000, pp. 847, 887 f. The same is true for overshooting transposition of directives, cf. Mayer/Schürnbrand, *JZ* 2004, 545, 550 (on this issue cf. above at paras. 374 ff.).

# §34. THE ROLE OF THE COURTS IN ENFORCING EU LAW

## CONTENTS

References: J. Basedow, *EU Private Law. Anatomy of a Growing Legal Order* (Cambridge: Intersentia, 2021), p. 539; T. von Danwitz, 'Die Aufgabe des Gerichtshofes bei der Entfaltung des europäischen Zivil- und Zivilverfahrensrechts', *ZEuP* 2010, 463; C.N.K. Franklin (ed.), *The Effectiveness and Application of EU and EEA Law in National Courts* (Cambridge: Intersentia, 2018); B. Gsell/W. Hau (eds.), *Zivilgerichtsbarkeit und Europäisches Justizsystem* (Tübingen: Mohr Siebeck, 2012); B. Hess, *Europäisches Zivilprozessrecht*, 2nd ed. (Berlin: De Gruyter, 2020), §12; M. Jestaedt, 'Der "Europäische Verfassungsgerichtsverbund" in (Verfahrenskenn-)Zahlen Die Arbeitslast von BVerfG, EuGH und EGMR im Vergleich', *JZ* 2011, 872; J. Raitio, 'European Union Law and Comparative Law', in J.M. Smits/J. Husa/C. Valcke/M. Narciso (eds.), *Elgar Encyclopedia of Comparative Law* (Cheltenham: Edward Elgar Publishing, 2023), p. 78; H. Rösler, *Europäische Gerichtsbarkeit auf dem Gebiet des Zivilrechts* (Tübingen: Mohr Siebeck, 2012); C. Toader, 'Europan Contract Law in the EU Court of Justice's Case Law', in S. Grundmann/M. Grochowski (eds.), *European Contract Law and the Creation of Norms* (Cambridge: Intersentia, 2021), p. 255.

# I. THE IMPORTANCE OF ENFORCEMENT FOR SUBJECTIVE LEGAL POSITIONS

**1367.** After describing how the EU can influence Member State law in the area of contract law and the extent to which the EU has already made use of these possibilities or intends to do so, the question will now be addressed as to how a bearer of rights conferred to him under EU law can enforce these rights in court. It would amount to a major deficiency if a right entailed no remedy (at least in case of violation) – the legal system would probably lack any practical effect. Even if one cannot always accurately predict the outcome of judicial decisions, since, according to a saying, 'in court and on the high seas one is in God's hands', which is apparently also known in Luxembourg,[1] EU procedural law created robust structures that are designed to facilitate cross-border enforcement of claims.

**1368.** Legal redress at the level of European contract law has two tracks: On the one hand, relief is provided by European courts, in particular by the CJEU,[2] and, on the other hand, by national courts, which must apply European law or national law with European roots. According to the established case law of the CJEU, the task of each Member State court within its jurisdiction is to ensure the full effectiveness of the provisions of EU law and to protect the rights that it confers on EU citizens.[3]

**1369.** Particularly in the field of contract law, legal redress by the respective national courts is of utmost importance since the contracting parties in this area of law usually cannot sue directly before the European courts. Such a possibility only exists if decisions within the meaning of Article 288(4) TFEU are involved. However, since the EU's activities in contract law are predominantly legislative rather than executive, there are generally no decisions of the European institutions that address the contracting parties, so there is rarely a reason and an opportunity to bring a direct action before the European courts. According

---

1 AG Bobek, Conclusions of 19 October 2017, Case C-470/16 – *North East Pylon Pressure Campaign*, ECLI:EU:C:2017:781, para. 90 with note 41: 'In conclusion, the separation or dividing up being proposed is to my mind conceptually odd. It would not only be additionally laborious for national judges to deal with costs applications, but, above all, it would generate unpredictability for litigants, thus potentially discouraging them from bringing any environmental claim at all. There is indeed the (I understand originally German) saying that "in court and on the high seas, one is in the hands of God". ["Vor Gericht und auf hoher See ist man in Gottes Hand."] But I would assume that the effort of this Court, as, for that matter, of any other court, is to prove that saying wrong, not to confirm it.'

2 The contribution of the Court of First Instance towards European contract law is almost neglectable.

3 CJEU, 15 October 1987, Case 222/86, *Unectef*, ECLI:EU:C:1987:442; CJEU, 19 November 1991, Case C-6/90, *Francovich*, ECLI:EU:C:1991:428.

to Article 263(4) TFEU, natural and legal persons have only limited options to attack legal acts of the EU. Disputes in the field of European contract law are, therefore, predominantly brought before national courts. If questions of the validity and interpretation of European law become relevant to a decision in such proceedings, the respective national court may (or must, as the case may be) refer these questions to the CJEU for a preliminary ruling in accordance with Article 267 TFEU. This preliminary ruling procedure is, therefore, at least indirectly important for the protection of individual rights.[4]

## II. DOMESTIC PROCEDURAL LAW

References: A. Beka, *The Active Role of Courts in Consumer Litigation. Applying EU Law of the National Courts' Own Motion* (Cambridge: Intersentia, 2018)

### 1. STARTING POINT

**1370.** Since the EU does not have a fully developed court system, its effectiveness hinges on decentralised enforcement. In this respect, the courts of the Member States are primarily responsible for the implementation of EU law, and the CJEU is limited to its role as guardian of the Treaties and dwells on the monopoly of binding interpretation,[5] the latter being driven by requests of the Member States' courts in the for of preliminary proceedings under Article 267 TFEU. In this respect, one can speak of a cooperative relationship between the courts of the Member States and the CJEU,[6] even if this term obscures the fact that the mutual cooperation for the achievement of a common goal that this refers to takes place on very different levels and thus has a strong hierarchical character.

### 2. THE ROLE OF DOMESTIC PROCEDURAL LAW

**1371.** Since EU law is based on the principle of decentralised enforcement, implementation is carried out by the Member State courts and their autonomous national procedural laws. However, according to the case law of the CJEU,

4 J. Schwarze/N. Wunderlich, in J. Schwarze, *EU-Kommentar*, 4th ed. (Baden-Baden/Vienna/Basel: Nomos/Facultas/Helbing Lichtenhahn, 2019), Art. 267 AEUV para. 5; B.W. Wegener, in C. Calliess/M. Ruffert, *EUV/AEUV*, 6th ed. (Munich: C.H. Beck, 2022), Art. 267 AEUV para. 1.

5 CJEU, 4 July 2006, Case C-212/04, *Adeneler*, ECLI:EU:C:2006:443, para. 40.

6 B.W. Wegener, in C. Calliess/M. Ruffert, *EUV/AEUV*, 6th ed. (Munich: C.H. Beck, 2022), Art. 267 AEUV para. 1.

limits exist whenever the peculiarities of the respective procedural law would jeopardise the practical effectiveness of an EU legal act.

### a) *Procedural Autonomy*

**1372.** EU law respects the procedural autonomy of the Member States. This means that no specific procedural regime applies to cases related to EU law.[7] Depending on its design, this can lead to differences in the enforcement in the Member States. This can lead to problems, for example, in the area of consumer law, if the EU's mandatory protection regime has no counterpart in the procedural law of a Member State insofar as the principle of party-presentation applies there, which does not take into account the typically weaker position of the consumer.

**1373.** The postulate of the practical effectiveness of EU law applies not only to a specific regulatory context but to the entire legal system of a Member State. Consequently, national procedural law can also stand in the way of the practical effectiveness of the law of directives and regulations.[8]

### b) *Examination Ex Officio Instead of Principle of Party-Presentation?*

**1374.** Such conflicts arise in particular where the principle of party-presentation applies under the Member State's procedural law or where the court has only limited power to examine the case. The latter is the case, for example, in proceedings for an order for payment: here, in many systems it suffices for the claimant to submit an arguable, or conclusive, case.

**1375.** The CJEU had already been asked several times whether a duty of the national courts arose from the Unfair Terms Directive to examine ex officio the unfairness of clauses in consumer contracts during proceedings on an order for payment conducted under the respective autonomous national law. The CJEU answered in the affirmative. The relevant decisions concerned proceedings that had already entered the adversarial phase due to an objection or opposition.[9] In

---

[7] J. Schwarze/N. Wunderlich, in J. Schwarze, *EU-Kommentar*, 4th ed. (Baden-Baden/Vienna/Basel: Nomos/Facultas/Helbing Lichtenhahn, 2019), Art. 267 AEUV para. 4; Rösler, *Europäische Gerichtsbarkeit auf dem Gebiet des Zivilrechts*, 2012, pp. 230 ff.

[8] On the restriction of the principle of procedural autonomy of Member States by the principles of effectiveness and equivalence Rösler, *Europäische Gerichtsbarkeit auf dem Gebiet des Zivilrechts*, 2012, pp. 235 f.

[9] *CJEU, 4 June 2009, Case C-243/08, Pannon GSM*, ECLI:EU:C:2009:350, para. 32 (choice-of-court agreement in mobile phone contract); CJEU, 9 November 2010, Case C-137/08, *VB Pénzügyi Lízing Zrt.*, ECLI:EU:C:2010:659, para. 56 (choice-of-court agreement in loan contract).

the *Banesto* case, the CJEU found that an obligation to examine the content of the order for payment proceedings did indeed exist. This applies at least if the court 'has all the legal and factual elements necessary [for the review of content]'.[10] This should also apply to appeal proceedings when the violation of the Directive is raised there for the first time.[11] However, this ex officio examination only extends to those clauses which are directly related to the subject matter of the dispute.[12]

**1376.** In general, the ex officio investigation of a breach of EU consumer protection rules may be required by EU law.[13] Thus, the CJEU has ruled on the CSD that the court must consider a reduction of the price on its own motion if the contract cannot be terminated due to the minor nature of the defect, even if the consumer has not applied for a reduction and, according to the procedural law of forum law, no longer can claim it.[14] This judgment, however, was instigated by a distinct feature of Spanish procedural law; a generalisation does not seem appropriate.[15]

## III. ENSURING UNIFORMITY OF INTERPRETATION

### 1. PRELIMINARY RULING PROCEDURE BEFORE THE CJEU

References: A. Bruns, 'Die Revision zum Europäischen Gerichtshof in Zivilsachen – akademische Zukunftsvision oder Gebot europäischer Justizgewährleistung?', *JZ* 2011, 325; S. Clavora/T. Garber (eds.), *Das Vorabentscheidungsverfahren in der Zivilgerichtsbarkeit* (Vienna: NWV Verlag, 2014); B. Gsell/W. Hau (eds.), *Zivilgerichtsbarkeit und Europäisches Justizsystem* (Tübingen: Mohr Siebeck, 2012); H.J. Hellwig, 'Kritisches zur Kontrolle der Pflicht zur Vorlage an den EuGH', in *Festschrift für Müller-Graff* (Baden-Baden: Nomos, 2015), p. 416; J. Kühling/S. Drechsler, 'Alles "acte clair"? – Die Vorlage an den EuGH als Chance', *NJW* 2017, 2950; A. Piekenbrock, 'Vorlagen an den EuGH nach Art. 267 AEUV im Privatrecht', *EuR* 2011, 317; K. Riesenhuber, 'Aspekte der Fehlerkultur im Europarecht. Zusammenwirken von EuGH und nationalen Gerichten', *IWRZ* 2018, 243; H. Rösler, *Europäische Gerichtsbarkeit auf dem Gebiet des Zivilrechts* (Tübingen: Mohr Siebeck, 2012), pp. 70 ff., 165 ff..

---

10 CJEU, 14 June 2012, Case C-618/10, *Banco Español de Crédito*, ECLI:EU:C:2012:349; on that Stürner, *ZEuP* 2013, 671.

11 CJEU, 30 May 2013, Case C-397/11, *Jőrös*, ECLI:EU:C:2013:340.

12 CJEU, 11 March 2020, Case C-511/17, *Lintner*, ECLI:EU:C:2020:188, paras. 30 ff.

13 Cf. the references given in CJEU, 21 April 2016, Case C-377/14, *Radlinger*, ECLI:EU:C:2016:283, para. 62. On the Consumer Credit Directive also CJEU, 5 March 2020, Case C-679/18, *OPR-Finance*, ECLI:EU:C:2020:167, paras. 18 ff.; cf. above at paras. 672 ff.

14 CJEU, 3 October 2013, Case C-32/12, *Autociba*, ECLI:EU:C:2013:637, paras. 34 ff.

15 In detail Kern, *Festschrift für Müller-Graff*, 2015, p. 400. For an account of various types of cases cf. Beka, *The Active Role of Courts in Consumer Litigation*, 2018.

### a) *Functions of the Preliminary Ruling Procedure under Article 267 TFEU; Monopoly on Interpretation*

**1377.** The preliminary ruling procedure under Article 267 TFEU is the most important procedure before the CJEU in practice. In 2022, of 806 cases brought before the court, 546 were references for a preliminary ruling, corresponding to a share of around 68%.[16] However, even irrespective of these figures, it can be stated that the preliminary ruling procedure occupies a prominent position, as the central statements of the Court of Justice on the legal nature, interpretation and supremacy of EU law are regularly made within the framework of this procedure.[17]

**1378.** The high practical relevance of the preliminary ruling procedure also results from its function: Large parts of European treaty law are directly applicable in the Member States. This applies particularly to secondary EU laws, namely regulations (Article 288(2) TFEU) and decisions (Article 288(4) TFEU). Directives can also have a direct effect in the Member States under certain conditions.[18] From the point of view of the respective Member State court, this means that, in certain cases, it has to apply not only national but also EU law provisions or standards with Union law origin.

**1379.** In order to assist the respective national court in answering the legal questions relevant to the decision but also to ensure a uniform interpretation and application of EU law in the Member States,[19] Article 267 TFEU establishes a preliminary ruling procedure before the CJEU to secure its interpretation monopoly. In addition to this function, the preliminary ruling procedure is also indirectly intended to ensure the effective enforcement of individual rights under EU law.[20] This possibility of indirect legal redress by way of the preliminary ruling procedure as an interlocutory mechanism is of immense importance for EU citizens, especially in the area of contract law. In this respect, the preliminary ruling procedure has a certain focus on protecting individual rights. However, citizens do not have an enforceable right to a referral to the CJEU. Rather, they

---

16 Cf. the Annual Report – The Year in Review 2022, p. 29, available at https://curia.europa.eu/panorama/2022/en/.

17 B. Schima, *Das Vorabentscheidungsverfahren vor dem EuGH*, 2nd ed. (Vienna/Münster: Manz/C.H. Beck, 2004), pp. 1 f. On the workload in general, cf. also Rösler, *Europäische Gerichtsbarkeit auf dem Gebiet des Zivilrechts*, 2012, pp. 70 ff.

18 Cf. above at paras. 386 ff.

19 CJEU, 16 January 1974, Case 166/73, *Rheinmühlen-Düsseldorf*, ECLI:EU:C:1974:3, para. 2.

20 A. Haratsch/C. Koenig/M. Pechstein, *Europarecht*, 13th ed. (Tübingen: Mohr Siebeck, 2023), para. 584; J. Schwarze/N. Wunderlich, in J. Schwarze, *EU-Kommentar*, 4th ed. (Baden-Baden/Vienna/Basel: Nomos/Facultas/Helbing Lichtenhahn, 2019), Art. 267 AEUV para. 5; B.W. Wegener, in C. Calliess/M. Ruffert, *EUV/AEUV*, 6th ed. (Munich: C.H. Beck, 2022), Art. 267 AEUV para. 1.

may request a preliminary ruling, but they can enforce it to a limited extent only.[21] In this respect, it is possible to speak of a review of the application of the law of the Member States regarding its conformity with EU law on the occasion of an individual dispute.

### *b) Designation of the Preliminary Ruling Procedure as an Interim Procedure*

**1380.** Within the framework of the preliminary ruling procedure, the CJEU does not act as a European Court of Appeal in disguise. Rather, the preliminary ruling procedure is designed as a judicial cooperation mechanism that does not give the parties control over the proceedings. The preliminary ruling procedure begins before a court of a Member State, reaches the CJEU in a kind of intermediate proceedings and finally ends before the court of the Member State. The respective national court suspends or interrupts the legal dispute, formulates the legal question that has arisen in an abstract manner and transmits it to the CJEU. The CJEU is limited to answering the question that the court referred to it. The actual application of EU law to the individual case and, above all, the interpretation and application of national private and procedural laws remain exclusively for the national court.[22]

**1381.** The preliminary ruling procedure is governed by Articles 93 to 118 of the Rules of Procedure of the Court of Justice.[23] The language of the proceedings is the language of the national court that referred the matter to the CJEU (Article 37(3) of the Rules of Procedure of the Court of Justice). The procedure, which is initially in writing, is not adversarial; all parties make their submissions and statements in parallel.[24] Pursuant to Article 96(2) of the Rules of Procedure of the Court of Justice, an oral hearing usually follows.[25]

### *c) Submission Requirements*

**1382.** The requirements for referrals have only been regulated to a small extent in the TFEU. Essentially, however, they result from the case law of the CJEU. First of all, the CJEU must have jurisdiction;[26] in principle, this is the case in the area of contract law. However, a delimitation problem may arise with regard to

21 Cf. Bruns, *JZ* 2011, 325, 331 ff. See below at paras. 1406 ff.

22 CJEU, 22 November 2005, Case C-144/04, *Mangold*, ECLI:EU:C:2005:709, paras. 32 ff.

23 On the main changes since 2012 Dittert, *EuZW* 2013, 726; Berrisch, *EuZW* 2013, 881 ff.

24 J. Schwarze/N. Wunderlich, in J. Schwarze, *EU-Kommentar*, 4th ed. (Baden-Baden/Vienna/Basel: Nomos/Facultas/Helbing Lichtenhahn, 2019), Art. 267 AEUV para. 59.

25 For exceptions cf. J. Schwarze/N. Wunderlich, in J. Schwarze, *EU-Kommentar*, ibid., Art. 267 AEUV para. 62.

26 A. Haratsch/C. Koenig/M. Pechstein, *Europarecht*, 13th ed. (Tübingen: Mohr Siebeck, 2023), para. 585; M. Herdegen, *Europarecht*, 24th ed. (Munich: C.H. Beck, 2023), §9 para. 26.

the action for annulment under Article 263(4) TFEU since the latter is subject to a time limit of two months under Article 263(6) TFEU, in contrast to the preliminary proceedings. According to the case law of the CJEU, the two-month time limit of Article 263(6) TFEU may not be circumvented if the action for annulment is or was obviously admissible.[27]

### d) *Content of the Preliminary Ruling Procedure*

References: M. Niestedt, in B. Gsell/W. Hau, *Zivilgerichtsbarkeit und Europäisches Justizsystem* (Tübingen: Mohr Siebeck, 2012), p. 22; A. Obert, 'Neues vom acte clair – Übersicht über ältere und aktuelle Rechtsprechung des EuGH', *GPR* 2019, 206.

#### aa) The Subject Matter

**1383.** Pursuant to Article 267(1) TFEU, the CJEU shall give rulings on the interpretation of the Treaties (lit. a) and the validity and interpretation of acts of the institutions (Article 13 TFEU), bodies, offices or agencies of the Union (lit. b) within the framework of the preliminary ruling proceedings. Treaties within the meaning of Article 267(1)(a) TFEU are the provisions of the TEU and the TFEU, including their annexes and protocols, including any amendments, and the accession treaties with the new Member States.[28] 'Acts of the institutions of the Union' within the meaning of Article 267(1)(b) TFEU refers to the entire secondary legislation of the EU. Restrictions result only from the limitation of the CJEU's jurisdiction by Articles 275 and 276 TFEU.[29] Furthermore, questions on the interpretation of all legal acts mentioned in Article 288(1) TFEU, i.e. on regulations, directives, decisions, recommendations and opinions, may be submitted insofar as they produce legal effects. In contrast, in principle, provisions of domestic law cannot be the subject of a preliminary ruling.[30] Referring courts frequently ask whether national legislation is compatible with EU law. Here, too, the CJEU's decision-making power is limited to the interpretation of EU law itself;[31] in these cases, the CJEU regularly rephrases the question put to it so that

---

27 CJEU, 9 March 1994, Case C-188/92, *Textilwerke Deggendorf*, ECLI:EU:C:1994:90. On the case cf. Niestedt, in Gsell/Hau, *Zivilgerichtsbarkeit und Europäisches Justizsystem*, 2012, p. 17; Hau, in Gsell/Hau, *Zivilgerichtsbarkeit und Europäisches Justizsystem*, 2012, p. 83.

28 J. Schwarze/N. Wunderlich, in J. Schwarze, *EU-Kommentar*, 4th ed. (Baden-Baden/Vienna/Basel: Nomos/Facultas/Helbing Lichtenhahn, 2019), Art. 267 AEUV paras. 9 f.

29 B.W. Wegener, in C. Calliess/M. Ruffert, *EUV/AEUV*, 6th ed. (Munich: C.H. Beck, 2022), Art. 267 AEUV para. 10.

30 This is consistent case law, cf. CJEU, 19 March 1964, Case 75/63, *Unger*, ECLI:EU:C:1964:19; CJEU, 12 October 1993, Case C-37/92, *Vanacker und Lesage*, ECLI:EU:C:1993:836, para. 7; CJEU, 19 September 2006, Case C-506/04, *Wilson*, ECLI:EU:C:2006:587, para. 34.

31 B.W. Wegener, in C. Calliess/M. Ruffert, *EUV/AEUV*, 6th ed. (Munich: C.H. Beck, 2022), Art. 267 AEUV para. 6.

misunderstandings are avoided.[32] The application of EU law, as interpreted by the CJEU, also remains the sole responsibility of the national courts.[33]

**1384.** Due to the legal force of the CJEU's judgments, its decisions are not a suitable subject for an action for annulment. However, it is unclear whether CJEU judgments themselves may at least be the subject of further proceedings for a preliminary ruling if the findings of the court appear to be insufficient or need further clarification.[34]

#### bb) Parties Entitled and Obliged to Submit

**1385.** According to Article 267 (2)–(4) TFEU, only the courts of the Member States are entitled or obliged to make submissions.[35] In this respect, it is irrelevant whether the courts are lower or higher instance courts. Differences result from this only for the question of whether there is an obligation to refer or only an entitlement to refer.[36] Submissions by the parties, by public authorities and by courts of third countries or international organisations are thus excluded. The term 'court' is to be interpreted autonomously.[37] According to the case law of the CJEU, for an institution to qualify as a court, it must be established by law, its jurisdiction must be of a permanent and compulsory nature, and it must give potentially final judgments in a dispute based on a procedure governed by the rule of law and carried out independently.[38] However, according to the more

---

[32] CJEU, 15 July 1964, Case 6/64, *Costa/E.N.E.L.*, ECLI:EU:C:1964:66. This is introduced with formulations such as 'The referring court's first question is essentially whether …' or similar.

[33] CJEU, 27 March 1963, Cases 28 to 30/62, *Da Costa*, ECLI:EU:C:1963:6.

[34] Affirmatively J. Schwarze/N. Wunderlich, in J. Schwarze, *EU-Kommentar*, 4th ed. (Baden-Baden/Vienna/Basel: Nomos/Facultas/Helbing Lichtenhahn, 2019), Art. 267 AEUV para. 11; for an opposing view, cf. B.W. Wegener, in C. Calliess/M. Ruffert, *EUV/AEUV*, 6th ed. (Munich: C.H. Beck, 2022), Art. 267 AEUV para. 10.

[35] On the concept of 'court', see the referral decision of Landgericht Erfurt of 24 June 2020, C-276/20: There, the independence and impartiality of German courts in connection with the so-called diesel emissions scandal and a (presumed) political influence was considered so doubtful that a corresponding question for a preliminary ruling was formulated.

[36] Heiderhoff, *Europäisches Privatrecht*, 6th ed. (Heidelberg: C.F. Müller, 2023), paras. 141 ff.

[37] CJEU, 30 March 1993, Case C-24/92, *Corbiau*, ECLI:EU:C:1993:118, para. 15; M. Pechstein/N. Görlitz, in *Frankfurter Kommentar zu EUV, GRC, AEUV*, 2nd ed. (Tübingen: Mohr Siebeck, 2023), Art. 267 AEUV para. 38.

[38] Cf. CJEU, 30 June 1966, Case 61/65, *Vaassen-Göbbels*, ECLI:EU:C:1966:39; CJEU, 11 June 1987, Case 14/86, *Pretore di Salò/X*, ECLI:EU:C:1987:275, para. 7; CJEU, 17 October 1989, Case C-109/88, *Danfoss*, ECLI:EU:C:1989:383, paras. 7 f.; CJEU, 27 April 1994, Case C-393/92, *Almelo*, ECLI:EU:C:1994:171, paras. 21 ff.; CJEU, 19 October 1995, Case C-111/94, *Job Centre*, ECLI:EU:C:1995:340, para. 9; CJEU, 29 November 2001, Case C-17/00, *De Coster*, ECLI:EU:C:2001:651, paras. 10 and 12; CJEU, 21 March 2000, C-110 to 147/98, *Gabalfrisa*, ECLI:EU:C:2000:145, para. 33; CJEU, 30 May 2002, Case C-516/99, *Walter Schmid*, ECLI:EU:C:2002:313, paras. 34–44; CJEU, 27 April 2006, Case C-96/04, *Niebüll*, ECLI:EU:C:2006:254, para. 12–16.

recent case law of the CJEU, a contentious procedure is not (or no longer) a prerequisite.[39] The courts dealing with private law disputes – on which the focus of interest lies here – are therefore entitled to make submissions.

**1386.** While courts of lower instances are, in principle, not obliged to refer cases to the CJEU,[40] a final instance court, i.e. a court 'against whose decisions there is no judicial remedy under national law', must refer, pursuant to Article 267(3) TFEU, if a question of validity or interpretation of EU law arises in the legal dispute. The exception previously existing under Article 68(1) TEC (old version) concerning legal acts in the area of judicial cooperation based on Article 65 TEC (old version) (now Article 81 TFEU) – here, only the court of last instance was allowed to refer[41] – was abolished by the Treaty of Lisbon.

**1387.** How Article 267(3) TFEU ought to be understood is disputed. Since this relates to an interpretation of EU law, this must be determined by autonomous interpretation. In essence, there are two opposing views regarding this issue: According to one interpretation, the decisive factor is which court is the last possible instance following an abstract assessment.[42] According to the opposing view, the decisive factor is whether the respective court is the last possible instance for the parties in concreto.[43] The wording of Article 267(3) TFEU is not very helpful in this respect, as the quoted part allows for both understandings.[44] However, the fact that a review is only possible in every procedure in which Union law is applied if a court that is obliged to make a referral can be reached speaks in favour of a concrete approach.[45] This is desirable, especially due to the function of the preliminary ruling procedure to ensure a uniform interpretation and application of EU law. The CJEU also seems to lean towards this approach. In the *Costa/E.N.E.L.* decision, for example, the court stated that 'national courts against whose decisions, as in the present case, there is no judicial remedy'

---

39 CJEU, 17 May 1994, Case C-18/93, *Corsica Ferries*, ECLI:EU:C:1994:195, para. 12; CJEU, 19 October 1995, Case C-111/94, *Job Centre*, ECLI:EU:C:1995:340, para. 9.

40 According to the case law of the CJEU, an exception is supposed to exist if the cognising court has doubts about the validity of the EU standard that is relevant for the decision, cf. CJEU, 22 October 1987, Case 314/85, *Foto-Frost*, ECLI:EU:C:1987:452.

41 Critical of this because of curtailing judicial remedies: Hess, *RabelsZ* 66 (2002), 471, 488 ff.

42 Cf. e.g. A. Bleckmann, *Europarecht*, 6th ed. (Cologne: Heymann, 1997), para. 921; M.A. Dauses, *Das Vorabentscheidungsverfahren nach Artikel 177 EG-Vertrag*, 2nd ed. (Munich: C.H. Beck, 1995), p. 111.

43 Heiderhoff, *Europäisches Privatrecht*, para. 143; Hess, *Europäisches Zivilprozessrecht*, 2nd ed. 2020, §12 para. 26; Schima, *Das Vorabentscheidungsverfahren vor dem EuGH*, 2nd ed. 2004, pp. 59 f.; Piekenbrock, *EuR* 2011, 317, 334.

44 But see Hess, *Europäisches Zivilprozessrecht*, 2nd ed. 2020, §12 para. 26 with note 109, according to which a concrete approach is already to be decisive according to the wording.

45 Schima, *Das Vorabentscheidungsverfahren vor dem EuGH*, 2nd ed. 2004, p. 59.

are obliged to ask for a preliminary ruling.[46] Even from such a point of view, however, it is possible for a court of first instance or an appellate court to pass on the responsibility to fulfil the duty of submitting the case to the CJEU by giving leave to an appeal, if so required by the relevant procedural law.

cc) No Submission in Irrelevant Cases

**1388.** According to Article 267(2) TFEU, a court of a Member State is only entitled or obliged to refer a question to the CJEU if the decision on the respective issue is relevant to the case's final outcome.[47] Behind this restriction of the preliminary ruling procedure is the fact that the CJEU should not preoccupy itself with merely hypothetical questions. This would oppose not only procedural economy but also the purpose of the preliminary ruling procedure. As explained, it aims to ensure a uniform interpretation and application of EU law and thus to safeguard the administration of justice. This purpose cannot justify an extension of the preliminary ruling procedure to hypothetical questions.[48]

**1389.** In principle, 'it is for the national court hearing the case, within whose jurisdiction the judicial decision to be given falls, alone to assess, in the light of the specific features of the case, both the need for a preliminary ruling to enable it to give judgment and the relevance of the questions referred to the Court'.[49] Otherwise, the CJEU would have to examine the relevance of the question based on the respective *lex causae*, which would not appear to be appropriate and would also not correspond to Article 267 TFEU: The CJEU does not interpret national law; the national courts have exclusive jurisdiction for this.[50] Only in cases where the question for a preliminary ruling is obviously irrelevant does the CJEU reject the reference by a Member State court as inadmissible for lack of necessity.[51] However, a decision by the CJEU is still considered necessary

---

46 CJEU, 15 July 1964, Case 6/64, *Costa/E.N.E.L.*, ECLI:EU:C:1964:66; even more clearly CJEU, 4 June 2002, Case C-99/00, *Lyckeskog*, ECLI:EU:C:2002:329, paras. 14 ff.

47 M. Pechstein/N. Görlitz, in *Frankfurter Kommentar zu EUV, GRC, AEUV*, 2nd ed. (Tübingen: Mohr Siebeck, 2023), Art. 267 AEUV para. 54.

48 Cf. CJEU, 26 March 2020, Case C-66/19, *JC*, ECLI:EU:C:2020:242, para. 30; CJEU, 3 July 2019, Case C-242/18, *UniCredit Leasing*, ECLI:EU:C:2019:558, para. 46; CJEU, 4 July 2006, Case C-212/04, *Adeneler*, ECLI:EU:C:2006:443, para. 42; CJEU, 22 November 2005, Case C-144/04, *Mangold*, ECLI:EU:C:2005:709, para. 36; CJEU, 22 November 1978, Case 93/78, *Mattheus/Doego*, ECLI:EU:C:1978:206.

49 Such a constantly recurring formula, cf. e.g. CJEU, 18 October 1990, Joined Cases C-297/88 and C-197/89, *Dzodzi*, ECLI:EU:C:1990:360, paras. 33 f.; CJEU, 13 March 2001, Case C-379/98, *PreussenElektra*, ECLI:EU:C:2001:160, para. 38.

50 CJEU, 26 March 2020, Case C-66/19, *JC*, ECLI:EU:C:2020:242, para. 31; CJEU, 3 July 2019, Case C-242/18, *UniCredit Leasing*, ECLI:EU:C:2019:558, para. 47; CJEU, 16 February 2017, Case C-507/15, *Agro*, ECLI:EU:C:2017:129, para. 23.

51 CJEU, 24 March 2011, Case C-194/10, *Robert Nicolaus Abt*, ECLI:EU:C:2011:182, para. 21; CJEU, 14 June 2012, Case C-618/10, *Banco Español de Crédito*, ECLI:EU:C:2012:349, para. 79.

within the meaning of Article 267(2) TFEU if there are mere doubts regarding the interpretation and/or the validity of a potentially relevant EU provision.

dd) Exceptions to the Submission Requirement under the *Acte Clair* Doctrine

**1390.** According to the case law of the CJEU, a court of last resort is not obliged to ask for a preliminary ruling, despite the relevance of the question, 'where previous decisions of the Court have already dealt with the point of law in question'[52] or if the answer to the question is obvious.[53] According to the CJEU, the latter is only the case if the question is 'so obvious as to leave no scope for any reasonable doubt'. The German Federal Supreme Court, in particular, has already resorted to the *acte clair* doctrine on several occasions in order to avoid a referral that appeared, as such, at least arguable.[54]

**1391.** This exemption from the obligation to ask for a preliminary rule makes sense, as in these cases, there is no threat of differing interpretations of EU law in the various Member States.[55] Often, however, the problem will arise that the national courts will assume that the legal question is obvious without actually knowing the exact legal situation (in terms of EU law!). The assessment of an *acte clair* requires a precise examination of different language versions of Union law as well as comprehensive knowledge of the entire legal order of the EU, including the relevant questions of interpretation.[56] Additional difficulties are caused by the fact that, strictly speaking, not only the relevant language version of a legal act of the EU may be used for interpretation in order to determine the obviousness. Rather, according to the case law of the CJEU, it is necessary to take into account all 24 official languages.[57] Moreover, the CJEU often determines the meaning of a directive or a regulation according to evaluative principles of comparative law, which a national court can hardly ever manage.[58]

**1392.** In general, a tendency can be observed that final instance courts – probably convinced of the correctness of their interpretative result – often shy away from submitting a question that appears relevant to the decision. Instead,

---

52 CJEU, 6 October 1982, Case 283/81, *CILFIT*, ECLI:EU:C:1982:335, para. 14.

53 CJEU, 6 October 1982, Case 283/81, *CILFIT*, ECLI:EU:C:1982:335. A critique of this doctrine can be found in Hess, *RabelsZ* 66 (2002), 471, 493 ff. (who makes the case for a limitation of the obligation to submit to fundamental questions).

54 BGH NJW 2005, 1045; BGHZ 110, 47, 68 ff.

55 Piekenbrock, *EuR* 2011, 317, 336, who advocates a restrictive interpretation of Article 267 TFEU.

56 Kühling/Drechsler, *NJW* 2017, 2950, 2952.

57 Cf. CJEU, 17 July 1997, Case C-219/95, *Ferriere Nord*, ECLI:EU:C:1997:375, para. 15; CJEU, 6 October 1982, Case 283/81, *CILFIT*, ECLI:EU:C:1982:335, paras. 16 ff.

58 On this criticism Hess, *Europäisches Zivilprozessrecht*, 2nd ed. 2020, §12 paras. 27 ff.

they give detailed reasons for the 'obvious' correctness of their interpretative result, so that the question arises, based on the scope of the argumentation alone, as to whether the result can really be considered be obvious.[59]

## 2. SPECIFIC ISSUES

### a) *Preliminary Ruling with Respect to National Law which Continues to Apply after Entry into Force of Directive*

**1393.** Sometimes Member State law as it stands already complies with an upcoming directive. Hence, that state will not have to change its law in transposition of the directive.[60] After the entry into force of the directive, however, the respective national provisions are within the realm of EU law, so that the obligation to refer an issue to the CJEU described above also exists with respect to that law. In principle, it is left to the Member States to decide how to comply with their obligation under Article 288(3) TFEU to transpose EU directives.[61] It is, therefore, not a mandatory prerequisite for Article 267 TFEU that the question arises in connection with laws that were passed to transpose the directive.

### b) *Preliminary Ruling in the Event of Excessive Transposition of Directives*

References: B. Gsell, in B. Gsell/W. Hau, *Zivilgerichtsbarkeit und Europäisches Justizsystem* (Tübingen: Mohr Siebeck, 2012), p. 123.

**1394.** The question of whether a preliminary ruling is also possible concerning questions of interpretation that arise with regard to an excessive transposition of a directive may be answered differently. Should a Member State extend the directive's provisions beyond its (substantive, temporal, or personal) scope of application,[62] from the perspective of EU law, the framework of Article 288(3) TFEU has been exceeded. It could therefore be argued that the preliminary ruling procedure must also be ruled out since it is ultimately only a matter of interpreting Member State law. However, in principle, the CJEU allows for a referral if the question concerns the interpretation of EU law in cases where the facts in question do not fall under EU law and, therefore, solely within the competence of the Member States but where these EU provisions nevertheless

---

59 Heitsch, *EuGRZ* 1997, 461; Kühling/Drechsler, *NJW* 2017, 2950, 2953. Furthermore, there is also a divergence in the frequency of referrals with regard to the individual Member States., cf. Rösler, *Europäische Gerichtsbarkeit auf dem Gebiet des Zivilrechts*, 2012, pp. 165 ff.

60 Cf. paras. 317 ff. above.

61 On the transposition of directives through general clauses above at paras. 317 ff.

62 On issues of admissibility cf. above at paras. 366 ff.

apply by virtue of a designation in national law on those EU norms.[63] In these cases, the decision on the interpretation of the directive must be directly relevant to the resolution of the national dispute.[64] Some authors remain more sceptical in this respect[65] but the prevailing opinion argues rightly in favour of the referral.[66]

**1395.** What is more, practical considerations speak for this: How should the CJEU verify whether the question of interpretation arises within or outside the scope of the Directive? In many cases, it would depend on the wording of the national court's question whether it actually relates to a legal field that the directive aimed to cover or not. Ultimately, it is a question of the relevance of the legal question at stake for a decision: If the answer to a question that arises regarding an excessive transposition of directives is left to the courts of the Member States, the consequence is plain simple: The decision on this is, in principle, left to the referring court. From the perspective of the Member State's legal order, the question remains significant irrespective of whether it arises within or outside the scope of application of the directive.

**1396.** From the perspective of EU law, there is also an interest in the uniform application of the law – otherwise, there would be a risk of inconsistent interpretation practices in the individual Member States' laws. Finally, the EU's interest in a uniform application of the provisions and concepts adopted from EU law exists irrespective of the conditions under which they are to be applied in order to prevent future differences in interpretation.[67]

### *c) Questions Relating to General Clauses Contained in Directives*

References: M. Stürner, in C. von Bar/A. Wudarski, *Deutschland und Polen in der Europäischen Rechtsgemeinschaft* (Munich: Sellier, 2011), p. 65.

---

63 CJEU, 26 March 2020, Case C-66/19, *JC*, ECLI:EU:C:2020:242, para. 28; CJEU, 12 July 2012, Case C-602/10, *Volksbank România*, ECLI:EU:C:2012:443, para. 86; CJEU, 7 January 2003, Case C-306/99, *BIAO*, ECLI:EU:C:2003:3, paras. 88 ff.; CJEU, 17 July 1997, Case C-28/95, *Leur-Bloem*, ECLI:EU:C:1997:369, paras. 30 ff.

64 CJEU, 18 October 1990, Joined Cases C-297/88 and C-197/89, *Dzodzi*, ECLI:EU:C:1990:360, para. 37; CJEU, 17 July 1997, Case C-130/95, *Giloy*, ECLI:EU:C:1997:372, paras. 22 ff.

65 Habersack/Mayer, *JZ* 1999, 913; W.-H. Roth, in *Festschrift für Drobnig* (Tübingen: Mohr Siebeck, 1998), p. 135; M. Franzen, *Privatrechtsangleichung durch die Europäische Gemeinschaft* (Berlin: De Gruyter, 1999), p. 536.

66 Drexl, in *Festschrift für Heldrich* (Munich: C.H. Beck, 2005), pp. 67, 83 ff.; Hess, *RabelsZ* 66 (2002), 471, 484 ff.; Heiderhoff, *Europäisches Privatrecht*, paras. 175; cf. also Gsell, in Gsell/Hau, *Zivilgerichtsbarkeit und Europäisches Justizsystem*, 2012, pp. 123, 136 ff.

67 CJEU, 26 March 2020, Case C-66/19, *JC*, ECLI:EU:C:2020:242, para. 29; CJEU, 19 October 2017, Case C-303/16, *Solar Electric Martinique*, ECLI:EU:C:2017:773, para. 26; CJEU, 17 October 2013, Case C-184/12, *Unamar*, ECLI:EU:C:2013:663, para. 31; CJEU, 17 July 1997, Case C-28/95, *Leur-Bloem*, ECLI:EU:C:1997:369, paras. 27, 32; CJEU, 17 July 1997, Case C-130/95, *Giloy*, ECLI:EU:C:1997:372, para. 28.

**1397.** It is particularly challenging to answer the question of whether the courts of the Member States have a duty or right to ask for a preliminary ruling in cases where a directive contains general clauses or broadly construed legal terms. If a directive contains a general clause, one could argue that it simply cannot be applied at all without thorough interpretation.[68] The same problem arises regarding indeterminate legal concepts, as such provisions also require further specification before they can be applied. As a result of the need for interpretation, the question in which cases an obligation to ask for a preliminary ruling exists is essential. A prominent example of a general clause contained in a private law directive is Article 3 of the Unfair Terms Directive.[69]

**1398.** One may assume at the outset that all questions and doubts regarding the interpretation of general clauses such as Article 3 of that Directive trigger the obligation to ask for a preliminary ruling.[70] In contrast, an opposing view seeks to limit the workload of the CJEU brought about by such a broad and open approach.[71] One commentator has argued that the CJEU should not be called upon because it lacks the competence to specify general clauses:[72] The legal form of the directive gives the Member State legislators a certain leeway in implementation. The respective legislators of the Member States could and were allowed to make use of this by creating a more specific provision than the provision of the Directive or by simply transforming the general clause of the Directive into Member State law and leaving its interpretation to the courts. Regardless of the path taken by the respective national legislator, the leeway in implementation must not be eliminated by granting the CJEU jurisdiction to interpret general clauses.[73] This applies above all if the general clause is contained in a minimum harmonising directive and the question of interpretation arises in a framework that goes beyond the required level of protection: In this case, there is, in any case, no obligation to refer the matter to the Court.[74]

---

68 Cf. A. Röthel, *Normkonkretisierung im Privatrecht* (Tübingen: Mohr Siebeck, 2004), pp. 353 ff.

69 On clause control cf. above at paras. 654 ff.

70 Coester, in *Festschrift für Heinrichs*, 1998, pp. 99, 104; J. Basedow, *Nationale Justiz und Europäisches Privatrecht. Eine Vernetzungsaufgabe* (Heidelberg: C.F. Müller, 2003), pp. 9 f.; Müller-Graff, *Gemeinsames Privatrecht in der Europäischen Gemeinschaft*, 2nd ed. 1999, pp. 9, 64; Coester-Waltjen, *JURA* 1997, 272, 275.

71 The German Federal Supreme Court also seems to assume that ultimately there is no obligation to submit a case, cf. BGH NZM 2004, 734; BGH NJW-RR 1998, 1661, 1662. Against that M. Habersack, in P. Ulmer/H.D. Brandner/H.E. Hensen, *AGB-Recht*, 13th ed. (Cologne: Otto Schmidt, 2022), Einl. paras. 99 ff.; Ulmer, *BB* 1998, 1865 ('setback into the EC legal stone age').

72 W.-H. Roth, in *Festschrift für Drobnig*, 1998, p. 135.

73 W.-H. Roth, in *Festschrift für Drobnig*, 1998, pp. 135, 141 ff.

74 Heiderhoff, *Europäisches Privatrecht*, para. 162.

**1399.** It is also a matter of controversy whether the *acte claire* doctrine imposes restrictions on the obligation to submit general clauses to the CJEU. Some commentators deny that.[75] Others argue in favour of a limitation to refer such questions to the CJEU as *acte clair* if the directive concerned neatly defines its scope of application and the purpose of the general clause clearly emerges from it, such as Article 3(1) Unfair Terms Directive does.[76]

**1400.** The CJEU itself acts very cautiously in this respect: In principle, it leaves the interpretation of general clauses to the courts of the Member States.[77] Only in cases where a clause is per se unfair, irrespective of the contract's other provisions, does the CJEU itself intervene and declare the clause invalid.[78] As a rule, the CJEU itself does not control standard terms.[79] The aim is to define the criteria for a review of the standard of control in an abstract manner, but to leave the application of these criteria in individual cases in the hands of the respective national court.

**1401.** As a rule, the Court of Justice does not have the power to review contractual clauses. Rather, this task is, in principle, the sole responsibility of the respective national courts. Correspondingly, regarding the application of general clauses contained in directives, the national courts only have a duty or a right to ask for a preliminary ruling insofar as the interpretation of the general clause is at stake. The limitation of the CJEU's competence follows from the Unfair Terms Directive itself. The decisive standard of review for determining unfairness is the question of whether and to what extent the respective contractual term deviates from the respective *lex causae*. Thus, it is not at all the issue of whether Article 3(1) of the Directive can be interpreted autonomously, detached from the respective law to be applied, based on a standard of good faith to be determined in whatever way. Rather, it must be examined in each case to what extent the contractual clause deviates from the content and model of the law to be applied as designed by the national legislator. It is always necessary for the assumption of unfairness that the term deviates so clearly from the respective *lex causae* (to the detriment of the consumer) that the deviation appears to be contrary to good faith.[80]

---

75 A. Röthel, *Normkonkretisierung im Privatrecht* (Tübingen: Mohr Siebeck, 2004), 2004, p. 384.

76 Heiderhoff, *Europäisches Privatrecht*, para. 163.

77 CJEU, 1 April 2004, Case C-237/02, *Freiburger Kommunalbauten*, ECLI:EU:C:2004:209, paras. 21 ff.

78 CJEU, 27 June 2000, Joined Cases C-240/98 to C-244/98, *Océano*, ECLI:EU:C:2000:346, paras. 21 ff.; CJEU, 1 April 2004, Case C-237/02, *Freiburger Kommunalbauten*, ECLI:EU:C:2004:209, para. 23.

79 *CJEU, 4 June 2009, Case C-243/08, Pannon GSM*, ECLI:EU:C:2009:350, para. 42; CJEU, 9 November 2010, Case C-137/08, *VB Pénzügyi Lízing Zrt.*, ECLI:EU:C:2010:659, paras. 43 f. Cf. below at paras. 657 ff.

80 A. Stadler, in O. Jauernig, *BGB Kommentar*, 19th ed. (Munich: C.H. Beck, 2023), §307 para. 10.

**1402.** It follows from this that, in order to determine the unfairness of a contractual term, a comparison of the clause with the applicable national law must always be made. Note that the CJEU may not undertake such comparisons, as the issue here is less one of interpreting the law but rather of applying it.[81] Such a comparison is no longer about the interpretation of the directive and, thus, about an interpretation of EU law reserved for the CJEU but about the interpretation and application of the applicable national law.[82] In this respect, the CJEU does not have jurisdiction in the first place. As a result, due to the distribution of work between the CJEU and the national courts, the CJEU can only define abstract criteria for a review of standard terms, while the case-specific application of these criteria and the subsequent rejection of the contractual term as unfair is carried out by the national courts.[83]

**1403.** Hence, the CJEU can or must always be asked for a preliminary ruling if it is about a question of interpretation. A submission to the CJEU must not be made if the issue relates to the application of the law.

**1404.** Before a review of the content of a contract can even begin, it is necessary to abstractly determine which legal interests or concerns are to be included in the respective consideration. Subsequently, these interests must be weighed, and in this way, an abstract standard must be determined. Only after these steps were undertaken can one determine in each individual case, which fundamentally relevant circumstances characterise the dispute to be decided and what weight they have in the light of any possible additional circumstances. As a result, the court can assess which interests predominate in the individual case.

**1405.** If one considers the interplay of the balancing exercise just outlined, the concept of the distribution of competences between state courts and the Court of Justice becomes clear. The boundary between the interpretation and application of the law runs along the border between abstract and specific parts of the weighing process. The determination of this boundary must be carried out separately for each legal act.[84] As a side note, it should be pointed out that an autonomous interpretation of Article 3(1) of the Directive appears to be very

---

81 Heiderhoff, *Europäisches Privatrecht*, para. 169.

82 CJEU, 1 April 2004, Case C-237/02, *Freiburger Kommunalbauten*, ECLI:EU:C:2004:209, paras. 21 f.

83 This was also the conclusion of the *CJEU, 4 June 2009, Case C-243/08, Pannon GSM*, ECLI:EU:C:2009:350, para. 42; CJEU, 9 November 2010, Case C-137/08, *VB Pénzügyi Lízing Zrt.*, ECLI:EU:C:2010:659, paras. 43 f.

84 Möslein/Röthel, in Riesenhuber, *European Legal Methodology*, §11 paras. 12 ff.; Heiderhoff, *Europäisches Privatrecht*, para. 168.

difficult in the current state of EU contract law, as there is no dispositive law available to date that could fill out the concept of unfairness.[85]

## 3. REMEDIES AGAINST FAILURE TO INITIATE PRELIMINARY RULING

**1406.** As outlined above, the parties have no right to initiate a preliminary ruling procedure in civil proceedings. However, the question arises as to what the consequences of a breach of the duty to submit a case are. Remedies under national civil procedural law will not be discussed here in detail. Some systems see the CJEU as integral part of the national court system, so that an appeal may lie against an unjustified decision of a court of first instance not to put a relevant issue to the CJEU.

### *a) Enforcing Rights before the CJEU*

**1407.** It doubtful whether the CJEU is competent to decide questions of violations of Article 267 TFEU. First of all, infringement proceedings pursuant to Article 19(3)(a) TEU and Article 258 TFEU may be considered. However, these cannot be initiated by the parties. Only the Commission – in the case of a supervisory action (Article 258(2) TFEU) – or another Member State – in the case of a state action (Article 259 TFEU) – can initiate infringement proceedings.

**1408.** Another possibility is an action for failure to act against the Commission pursuant to Article 19(3)(a) TEU, Article 265 TFEU. However, with the action due to a failure to act, the parties would be seeking the performance of an action (namely, the initiation of infringement proceedings) which would not (according to the standards of Article 263(4) TFEU) affect them directly and individually. Therefore, the action for failure to act already lacks an admissible cause of action. Moreover, the Commission would also not be obliged to initiate infringement proceedings, as follows from the wording of Article 258(2) TFEU ('may'). Rather, it has discretionary powers within the framework of its task to ensure the application of EU law (Article 17(1) TEU).

### *b) Individual Complaints to the ECtHR*

**1409.** Finally, an individual complaint to the European Court of Human Rights under Articles 34 and 35 ECHR should be considered. However, Article 35(1) ECHR requires the exhaustion of all domestic remedies, which also includes

[85] Cf. paras. 657 ff.

constitutional complaints, if available under national law. It is possible that the violation of the obligation to ask for a preliminary ruling under Article 267(3) TFEU constitutes a violation of the right to a fair trial guaranteed in Article 6(1) ECHR. However, a violation will only be pertinent in cases of arbitrary failure to submit the case, otherwise an individual complaint will have no chance of success.

## 4. REFORM OF THE EU COURT SYSTEM

References: B. Hess, 'Die Zukunft des Vorabentscheidungsverfahrens nach Art. 19 EUV und Art. 267 AEUV', in B. Gsell/W. Hau (eds.), *Zivilgerichtsbarkeit und Europäisches Justizsystem* (Tübingen: Mohr Siebeck, 2012), p. 181; T. Riehm, 'Pro und Contra Europäisches Fachgericht für Privatrecht', in B. Gsell/W. Hau (eds.), *Zivilgerichtsbarkeit und Europäisches Justizsystem* (Tübingen: Mohr Siebeck, 2012), p. 203; H. Rösler, *Europäische Gerichtsbarkeit auf dem Gebiet des Zivilrechts* (Tübingen: Mohr Siebeck, 2012), pp. 275 ff.

**1410.** The current, limited function of the CJEU as an interpretative instance and intra-EU constitutional court already brings the court to the limits of its capacity. A possible further development of European private law from a 'pointillistic' patchwork to an overarching, systematic body of rules would have massive effects on the cooperation between Member State courts and the CJEU. If, for example, the CJEU were to acquire powers of interpretation in this area through the enactment of an instrument on European contract law, this would inevitably lead to a fundamental reform of the court system. This is because the preliminary ruling procedure would not be able to channel the expected flood of questions of interpretation to be clarified in a meaningful way.[86] The system of the preliminary ruling procedure is obviously not set up for such an extensive jurisdiction of the CJEU.[87] From the perspective of the citizens, the situation would appear equally unsatisfactory: Since the clarification of a legal issue cannot be forced in preliminary ruling proceedings, judicial remedy would remain incomplete.[88]

**1411.** The CJEU currently has neither the capacity nor the necessary legal specialisation to be a supreme private law court.[89] A reform of the European court system would have to address two major points: First, the establishment

---

86 Basedow, *AcP* 210 (2010), 157, 192 f.; Rösler, *Europäische Gerichtsbarkeit auf dem Gebiet des Zivilrechts*, 2012, pp. 165 ff.

87 Cf. already Kohler, *ZEuP* 1995, 482; Remien, *RabelsZ* 66 (2002), 503, 528–529, who emphasize the limited suitability of the CJEU to clarify private law matters.

88 Along these lines also Basedow, *AcP* 210 (2010), 157, 193.

89 Jansen, *ZEuP* 2010, 69, 101; Basedow, *AcP* 210 (2010), 157, 189–193.

of possibly decentralised lower instance courts or at least specialised chambers with jurisdiction for civil and commercial law, antitrust law or state aid law, for example, should be considered.[90] Some support for this approach is provided by Article 257 TFEU, which contains a competence to establish specialised courts 'to hear and determine at first instance certain classes of action or proceeding brought in specific areas'. The CJEU would also have to be embedded in a European court system in order to guarantee adequate legal protection. More restrictive admissibility conditions that go beyond the *acte clair* doctrine[91] are also repeatedly discussed.[92]

**1412.** This idea is by no means new. The division of the US court system into federal courts and state courts is repeatedly mentioned, and a possible model function for the reform of European jurisdiction is emphasised.[93] European courts would then have jurisdiction, analogous to the US federal question doctrine, for cases in which European law is decisive.[94] This would certainly involve many challenges, ranging from the fundamental question of the court's jurisdiction to organisational details such as the location of such courts and their staffing.[95]

## IV. EUROPEAN LAW OF CIVIL PROCEDURE

References: B. Hess, *Europäisches Zivilprozessrecht*, 2nd ed. (Berlin: De Gruyter, 2020), §6; B. Hess, 'Digital judicial cooperation in the area of freedom, security and justice: the judicial cooperation in civil matters', in M.M. Fogt (ed.), *Private International Law in an Era of Change* (Cheltenham: Edward Elgar Publishing), 2024, p. 161; M. Stürner, 'Die justizielle Zusammenarbeit im Privatrecht in der EU', *JURA* 2015, 813.

**1413.** Procedural law serves to enforce legal positions granted by substantive law. Even if EU law does not have a specific procedural code for the realisation of claims originating in EU law,[96] there is a whole series of legal acts that deal with the (cross-border) enforcement of claims without being limited to substantive EU law itself.

---

90 Rösler, *Europäische Gerichtsbarkeit auf dem Gebiet des Zivilrechts*, 2012, pp. 366 ff., 387 ff. In contrast, see the proposal by G. Hirsch, *ZRP* 2000, 57, 59, who has advocated the establishment of 'European senates' at the highest national courts.

91 Cf. above at paras. 1390 ff.

92 Cf. Rösler, *Europäische Gerichtsbarkeit auf dem Gebiet des Zivilrechts*, 2012, pp. 315 ff.

93 Cf. e.g. Rehm, in *Festschrift für Heldrich* (Munich: C.H. Beck, 2005), pp. 955, 967 ff.

94 Sceptically G. Wagner, *ZEuP* 2008, 6, 21.

95 Rehm, in *Festschrift für Heldrich* (Munich: C.H. Beck, 2005), pp. 955, 970.

96 Cf. above at paras. 1367 ff.

**1414.** However, there are also EU civil procedure laws that serve precisely to implement EU law: One example is the EU Injunctions Directive[97] which helps enhance the enforcement of the prohibition of unfair terms as set out by the Unfair Terms Directive.[98] These kinds of procedural laws that accompany other substantive rules are also being discussed concerning EU antitrust law. Here, this relates primarily to instruments of collective redress.[99]

## 1. BASICS

**1415.** Efficient judicial cooperation in cross-border cases is of considerable importance in the internal market. Article 81(1) TFEU, therefore, formulates the mandate to develop judicial cooperation in civil matters with cross-border implications. The fundamental freedoms require the removal of obstacles to cross-border trade in goods and services and the free movement of persons and capital. One aspect of this is the enforcement of rights through court proceedings. For example, obstacles in the law of the Member States that make it more difficult for nationals of other Member States to sue before domestic courts may constitute an impairment of fundamental freedoms. This can, for example, concern obstacles to bringing an action before the courts, such as the requirement of a security deposit by a claimant domiciled abroad for the costs of proceedings at the request of the defendant if the action was dismissed. The CJEU considered this a violation of primary law as far as other EU Member States were concerned.[100]

**1416.** In the context of Article 81 TFEU, however, it is not so much a matter of removing obstacles to cross-border legal transactions contained in the Member States' legal systems, but conversely of actively facilitating cooperation through the adoption of corresponding legal acts. One of the first regulations in the area

[97] Directive 2009/22/EC of the European Parliament and of the Council of 23 April 2009 on injunctions for the protection of consumers' interests, OJ 2009 L 110/30. Cf. Riesenhuber, *EU-Vertragsrecht*, 2013, §10 para. 46.

[98] The scope of application of which should be enlarged, cf. the Proposal for a Directive of the European Parliament and of the Council on representative actions for the protection of the collective interests of consumers, and repealing Directive 2009/22/EC, COM/2018/184 final.

[99] Cf. the White Paper of the EU-Commission on 'Damages actions for breach of the EC antitrust rules' of 2 April 2008, COM(2008) 165 final, pp. 4 ff.; Commission Recommendation of 11 June 2013 on 'common principles for injunctive and compensatory collective redress mechanisms in the Member States concerning violations of rights granted under Union Law', 2013/396/EU.

[100] CJEU, 1 July 1993, Case C-20/92, *Hubbard*, ECLI:EU:C:1993:280 and CJEU, 7 April 2011, C-291/09, *Guarnieri*, ECLI:EU:C:2011:217; cf. also CJEU, 10 February 1994, Case C-398/92, *Hatrex*, ECLI:EU:C:1994:52 on attachment in rem and CJEU, 19 December 2012, Case C-325/11, *Alder*, ECLI:EU:C:2012:824 on fictitious service in the case of service abroad (cf. the case note in Stürner, *ZZP* 126 [2013], 137).

of judicial cooperation, the Brussels I Regulation,[101] contains, first and foremost, detailed rules on jurisdiction. In this way, parallel jurisdictional competences that may exist in the laws of the various Member States, which may lead to simultaneous actions regarding the same case, are replaced by uniform rules, thus limiting so-called forum shopping. Furthermore, the Brussels I Regulation contains provisions on the recognition and enforcement of judgments in other Member States. This aspect is also crucial for the internal market. If, for example, a seller residing in France has successfully brought an action regarding the payment of the purchase price against a buyer residing in Germany, this verdict is of little use if it cannot also be enforced in Germany since most of the buyer's assets might be located (exclusively) there. In particular, the Brussels I Regulation enshrines the principle that each Member State recognises and, in principle, enforces judgments from other Member States, although the explicit declaration of enforceability (the exequatur) is no longer required under the recast version of the Brussels I Regulation, sometimes referred to as Brussels Ibis Regulation,[102] and enforcement can only be refused in exceptional cases, namely if the debtor can assert grounds for a refusal of the recognition in a special procedure.

**1417.** Article 81(2) TFEU exhaustively lists the legislative powers of the EU.[103] A legal act may also be based on several competence titles contained in para. (2). Harmonisation measures in the field of substantive private law can still only be based on the general internal market competence of Article 114 TFEU.[104] Pursuant to Article 81 TFEU, reasons beyond the internal market can, in principle, also speak in favour of an approximation in private law matters at the European level. However, in these cases, too, due to the general principle of subsidiarity of Article 5(1) in conjunction with Article 3 TEU, Article 69 TFEU must be applied. According to Article 3 TEU, which Article 69 TFEU emphasises in particular within the context of judicial cooperation, the necessity of harmonisation must be established.[105] The most important competencies

---

101 Council Regulation (EC) No 44/2001 of 22 December 2000 on jurisdiction and the recognition and enforcement of judgments in civil and commercial matters, OJ 2001 L 12/1.

102 Regulation (EU) No 1215/2012 of the European Parliament and of the Council of 12 December 2012 on jurisdiction and the recognition and enforcement of judgments in civil and commercial matters (recast), OJ 2012 L 351/1.

103 S. Leible, in R. Streinz, *EUV/AEUV*, 3rd ed. (Munich: C.H. Beck, 2018), Art. 81 AEUV para. 19; M. Rossi, in C. Calliess/M. Ruffert, *EUV/AEUV*, 6th ed. (Munich: C.H. Beck, 2022), Art. 81 AEUV para. 7; Frenz, *JURA* 2012, 701, 704; differently Hess, in E. Grabitz/M. Hilf/M. Nettesheim, *Das Recht der Europäischen Union* (Stand: September 2010), Art. 81 AEUV para. 38.

104 Cf. M. Rossi, in C. Calliess/M. Ruffert, *EUV/AEUV*, 6th ed. (Munich: C.H. Beck, 2022), Art. 81 AEUV para. 15.

105 BVerfGE 123, 167, 415 (Lisbon Treaty Case); Rosenau/Petrus, in C.W. Vedder/W. Heintschel von Heinegg, *Europäisches Unionsrecht*, 2nd ed. (Baden-Baden: Nomos, 2018), Art. 81 AEUV para. 7.

are presented below.[106] Of paramount importance for European contract law is the question of the enforcement of contractual claims. The relevant rules on international jurisdiction are also presented in an overview.

## 2. HARMONISATION OF RULES ON CROSS-BORDER CIVIL PROCEEDINGS

### a) *Effective Legal Redress*

**1418.** It is of vital importance to the area of freedom, security and justice, also emphasised by Article 47 CFR and Article 67(4) TFEU, that all citizens have effective access to justice. Based on Article 81(2)(e) TFEU, several measures have already been taken to achieve this goal.

**1419.** The first measure concerns the so-called Legal Aid Directive.[107] This guarantees natural persons that the legal aid standard applicable under their domestic law also applies in cross-border disputes. Although the country-of-origin principle implemented here does not lead to an approximation of legal aid standards in the Member States, it does allow for cross-border participation in proceedings without any possible disadvantages of the respective *lex fori* regarding the status of the foreign party.

**1420.** The second measure is not so much aimed at creating such procedural minimum standards but rather at providing information on the procedural rules existing in the Member States. To facilitate access to justice, the European Judicial Network in civil and commercial matters[108] and the European Judicial Atlas[109] have been set up. The Judicial Atlas provides information on the court systems of the Member States in all official languages of the EU. It also contains forms needed for the cross-border enforcement of claims or that can be used for communication between judicial authorities of the different Member States.

---

106 For more details cf. Stürner, in *Frankfurter Kommentar zu EUV, GRC, AEUV*, 2nd ed. (Tübingen: Mohr Siebeck, 2023), Art. 81 AEUV paras. 23 ff.

107 Council Directive 2002/8/EC of 27 January 2003 to improve access to justice in cross-border disputes by establishing minimum common rules relating to legal aid for such disputes, OJ 2003 L 26/41.

108 Cf. https://e-justice.europa.eu/topics/trainings-judicial-networks-and-agencies/european-judicial-network-civil-and-commercial-matters_en.

109 Cf. https://e-justice.europa.eu/topics/taking-legal-action/european-judicial-atlas-civil-matters_en.

### b) *Responsibilities and Avoidance of Competence Conflicts*

**1421.** A core area of judicial cooperation concerns a court's international jurisdiction for civil proceedings. This relates to the distribution of judicial competencies between the Member States. In this regard, Article 81(2)(c) TFEU contains legislative powers for the approximation of laws. It is in the interest of legal transactions in the internal market to have a transparent and predictable system of jurisdiction in place in order to prevent multiple and parallel proceedings as far as possible. In this regard, there are regulations for jurisdiction as well as for recognition and enforcement in civil and commercial matters in the Brussels Ibis Regulation, for matrimonial matters in the Brussels IIter Regulation,[110] for cross-border insolvency proceedings in the (recast) European Insolvency Regulation,[111] for maintenance proceedings[112] in the European Maintenance Regulation, concerning the area of succession and inheritance matters in the European Succession Regulation,[113] as well as for matrimonial property law in the European Matrimonial Property Regime Regulation[114] and the European Property of Registered Partnerships Regime Regulation.[115] These regulations are, therefore, not about any cooperation between courts in the true sense of the word; instead, they establish in abstract terms before which court actions may be brought in the areas mentioned. However, this by no means opens up an exclusive forum in a given Member State for each and every case.

**1422.** The general rule is that jurisdiction always lies with the court of the defendant's domicile (actor sequitur forum rei); this also applies to contractual claims, Article 4(1) in conjunction with Articles 62 and 63 Brussels Ibis Regulation. In addition, there is a whole series of further special heads of jurisdiction, which

---

110 Council Regulation (EU) 2019/1111 of 25 June 2019 on jurisdiction, the recognition and enforcement of decisions in matrimonial matters and the matters of parental responsibility, and on international child abduction (recast).

111 Regulation (EU) 2015/848 of the European Parliament and of the Council of 20 May 2015 on insolvency proceedings (recast), OJ 2015 L 141/19.

112 Council Regulation (EC) No 4/2009 of 18 December 2008 on jurisdiction, applicable law, recognition and enforcement of decisions and cooperation in matters relating to maintenance obligations, OJ 2009 L 7/1.

113 Regulation (EU) No 650/2012 of the European Parliament and of the Council of 4 July 2012 on jurisdiction, applicable law, recognition and enforcement of decisions and acceptance and enforcement of authentic instruments in matters of succession and on the creation of a European Certificate of Succession, OJ 2012 L 201/107.

114 Council Regulation (EU) 2016/1103 of 24 June 2016 implementing enhanced cooperation in the area of jurisdiction, applicable law and the recognition and enforcement of decisions in matters of matrimonial property regimes, OJ 2016 L 183/1.

115 Council Regulation (EU) 2016/1104 of 24 June 2016 implementing enhanced cooperation in the area of jurisdiction, applicable law and the recognition and enforcement of decisions in matters of the property consequences of registered partnerships, OJ 2016 L 183/30.

reflect the diversity of the legal contexts and the unique features of the legal relationships concerned. This applies, for example, in contractual disputes according to Article 7 no. 2 Brussels Ibis Regulation: Following this provision, a court has international jurisdiction at the place of performance.[116] In cases of disputes between consumers and traders, under certain conditions, there is even a semi-mandatory special head of jurisdiction at the consumer's place of residence according to Articles 17 et seq. Brussels Ibis Regulation.[117] Still, other heads of jurisdictions deviate from the jurisdiction at the domicile for reasons of proximity to the subject matter. For example, actions concerning rights in rem in immovable property must be brought exclusively before the court where the immovable property in question is located (Article 24 no. 1 Brussels Ibis Regulation). Furthermore, the parties may agree on the competent court within the framework of a so-called prorogation according to Article 25 Brussels Ibis Regulation.

**1423.** It may well happen that two or even more competent courts may be considered for the same set of facts and that an action is also brought in all of these jurisdictions. In these cases, the need for coordination of parallel proceedings arises. The Brussels Ibis Regulation, like other relevant regulations, therefore, contains provisions intended to resolve conflicts of jurisdiction. In the interest of clarity and predictability, all legal acts are based on a strict principle of priority (Article 29 Brussels Ibis Regulation). This has the consequence that the court seised later cannot itself decide on its competence but must stay the proceedings until the court first seised has rendered a corresponding decision, which in turn has a binding effect on the second court.

**1424.** This principle of priority can be exploited in such a way that a party fearing legal action might bring a corresponding counterclaim (such as a negative declaratory action to the effect that the claim to be asserted does not exist) in a jurisdiction known for their slow proceedings. Such actions, vividly referred to as Italian (or formerly also Belgian) torpedoes since these states were typically chosen for the preventive action, can block any later action of the opponent for a considerable time. In this respect, the CJEU ruled out the objection of abuse of rights.[118] Because of this unsatisfactory result, the recast version of the Brussels I Regulation modified the strict principle of priority, at least in the case of a choice of court agreement. It now grants the chosen court priority of jurisdiction: the court first seised must stay the proceedings until the chosen court has decided on its jurisdiction (Article 31(2) Brussels Ibis Regulation).

---

116 See below at paras. 1432 ff.

117 See below at paras. 1440 ff.

118 CJEU, 9 December 2003, Case C-116/02, *Gasser*, ECLI:EU:C:2003:657.

### c) *Recognition and Enforcement of Judgments between Member States*

**1425.** The recognition and enforcement of judgments between the Member States is one of the central areas of judicial cooperation, as it is directly aimed at implementing said principle, which is mentioned in Article 67(4) TFEU and repeated by Article 81(1) TFEU. Several regulations have already been adopted based on Article 81(2)(a) TFEU (or its predecessor, Article 65(a), third para. EC). These legal acts generally lead to a facilitation of litigation in cross-border disputes and to an acceleration of the proceedings as a whole. In many cases, it is still of considerable importance for the parties whether enforcement is also possible in other Member States. Obstacles in this regard will likely deter a claimant from bringing their claim to court in the first place since a judgment is useless if it cannot be enforced (or only with considerable effort). Article 81(2)(a) TFEU, therefore, creates legislative powers to harmonise the law in this area.

**1426.** The rationale behind this legislative competence is the principle of recognition, which is also prominently mentioned in Article 81(1) TFEU. A whole series of legal acts contain corresponding regulations, first and foremost the Brussels Ibis Regulation. However, these 'first generation' regulations implement the recognition principle only with certain restrictions: Thus, based on the Brussels I Regulation in force until 10 January 2015, a special procedure had to be carried out in the Member State in which enforcement was to take place with the aim of declaring the foreign judgment enforceable (so-called exequatur proceedings). In this procedure, the debtor could raise certain objections against the enforcement, for example, that they had not been granted a fair hearing in the state of judgment or that the recognition and enforcement violated the forum state's public policy. The 'second generation' of civil procedure Regulations, however, waived the exequatur requirement. First, in 2004, the European Enforcement Order Regulation[119] created an EU-wide freedom of movement for court decisions on uncontested claims under certain preconditions. The European Order for Payment Procedure Regulation,[120] the European Small Claims Regulation,[121] and – with restrictions – the European Maintenance Regulation as well as the European Succession Regulation also follow a similar approach. The Regulation on Mutual Recognition of Protection Measures in Civil Matters[122] also abolished exequatur proceedings. The Brussels

119 Regulation (EC) No 805/2004 of the European Parliament and of the Council of 21 April 2004 creating a European Enforcement Order for uncontested claims, OJ 2004 L 143/15.

120 Regulation (EC) No 1896/2006 of the European Parliament and of the Council of 12 December 2006 creating a European order for payment procedure, OJ 2006 L 399/1.

121 Regulation (EC) No 861/2007 of the European Parliament and of the Council of 11 July 2007 establishing a European Small Claims Procedure, OJ 2007 L 199/1.

122 Regulation (EU) No 606/2013 of the European Parliament and of the Council of 12 June 2013 on mutual recognition of protection measures in civil matters, OJ 2013 L 181/4.

Ibis Regulation, which has been applicable since 10 January 2015, also no longer has an exequatur procedure. The complete abolition of the grounds for a refusal of recognition, which was initially planned by the Commission,[123] failed for political reasons. Although the recast version of the Brussels I Regulation has abolished the exequatur procedure, the existing grounds for refusal of recognition have been fully retained.[124] These grounds must be raised in separate proceedings upon a corresponding application by the debtor.[125]

**1427.** Several 'second generation' legal acts are optional, i.e. the creditor has, for example, the right to choose whether to initiate a European order for payment procedure or to resort to the corresponding procedure under the respective national law.[126] The difference, however, becomes apparent concerning the enforcement in other Member States: Whereas a European order for payment procedure culminates in an order which is enforceable throughout Europe without any further intermediate steps (cf. Article 19 European Order for Payment Procedure Regulation), an order for payment procedure carried out according to national law still needed a declaration of enforceability that had to be obtained in an exequatur procedure in every Member State in which enforcement was to be carried out – at least until now. The abolition of this procedure in the Brussels Ibis Regulation has now levelled the difference between the two procedures; nevertheless, the risk remains that the debtor will try to prevent enforcement with the action as to Article 46 Brussels Ibis Regulation.

*d) General Harmonisation Competence for Civil Proceedings*

**1428.** Furthermore, the EU's competence to remove obstacles to the proper functioning of civil proceedings in the EU and to promote the compatibility of the rules of civil procedure applicable in the Member States must be considered (Article 81(2)(f) TFEU). From a neutral perspective, a very far-reaching power to harmonise the procedural rights of all Member States could be derived from the provision's wording, for the proper functioning of civil proceedings mentioned therein could ultimately only be realised based on a uniform European procedural law. Only if every Member State court had to apply identical procedural rules would all conceivable obstacles to the proper functioning of proceedings be excluded beyond possible divergences of interpretation.

---

123 Proposal for a Regulation of the European Parliament and of the Council on jurisdiction and the recognition and enforcement of judgments in civil and commercial matters, COM (2010) 748 final.

124 Cf. Cadet, *EuZW* 2013, 218; Pohl, *IPRax* 2013, 109; Domej, *RabelsZ* 78 (2014), 508; Stürner, *DGVZ* 2016, 215.

125 Cf. Articles 46 ff. and Article 45 Brüssel Ibis Regulation.

126 On the optionality of such legal acts Stürner, in *Enzyklopädie Europarecht*, Volume 3, 2nd ed. 2021, §23 paras. 14 ff.

**1429.** However, there is widespread agreement that harmonisation must be limited to cross-border proceedings[127] so that the legal provisions of the Member States applicable to purely domestic proceedings cannot be affected. Accordingly, the legal acts of the 'second generation', particularly the European Enforcement Order Regulation, the European Order for Payment Procedure Regulation and the European Small Claims Regulation, only contain procedural provisions concerning cross-border disputes. Nevertheless, this development will be significant for common standards of European civil procedure since, although the legal acts mentioned are only of sectoral significance, they contain, at least in a fairly sketchy form, the blueprint of a civil procedure and could thus serve as a model for a future European instrument in the area of procedural law. As such, they may also serve as a model for the Member State legislators in possible reforms of their own procedural laws and thus facilitate autonomous harmonisation.[128]

## 3. IN PARTICULAR: HEADS OF JURISDICTION FOR CONTRACTUAL CLAIMS

### a) *Applicability of the Brussels Ibis Regulation*

**1430.** The Brussels Ibis Regulation applies to civil and commercial matters (Article 1(1) Brussels Ibis Regulation).[129] This concept is to be interpreted autonomously,[130] but a sometimes incoherent case law has developed based on the delimitation criteria developed by the CJEU.[131] Thus, a case may be excluded from the scope of application of the Regulation because of the nature of the legal relations between the parties or because of the subject matter of the dispute. Article 1(2) Brussels Ibis Regulation contains a catalogue of exceptions concerning, for example, matrimonial or status matters. The Regulation applies to all Member States except Denmark (Recital 41 Brussels Ibis Regulation). By contrast Ireland participates in the Regulation (Recital 40 Brussels Ibis Regulation). After Brexit, the Regulation no longer applies to the United Kingdom.[132] In principle, the defendant must be domiciled in the territory of a

127 Hess, *Europäisches Zivilprozessrecht*, 2nd ed. 2020, §2 para. 26; Stürner, in *Frankfurter Kommentar zu EUV, GRC, AEUV*, 2nd ed. (Tübingen: Mohr Siebeck, 2023), Art. 81 AEUV paras. 17 ff.

128 Stürner, in *Enzyklopädie Europarecht*, Volume 3, 2nd ed. 2021, §23 paras. 103 f.

129 On the scope of application of the Brussels Ibis Regulation Stürner, *ZVglRWiss* 119 (2020), 143.

130 CJEU, 14 October 1976, Case 29/76, *LTU/Eurocontrol*, ECLI:EU:C:1976:137.

131 Cf. J. Kropholler/J. von Hein, *Europäisches Zivilprozessrecht*, 9th ed. (Frankfurt am Main: Verlag Recht und Wirtschaft, 2011), Art. 1 EuGVVO paras. 6–10.

132 Cf. above at paras. 153 ff.

Member State (Articles 4–6 Brussels Ibis Regulation). For companies and legal persons, several criteria are deemed to be sufficient, namely domicile, head office or principal place of business (Article 63 Brussels Ibis Regulation). Otherwise, the domestic rules on international jurisdiction of the Member State concerned apply (Article 6(2) Brussels Ibis Regulation). Note, however, that if one of the conditions mentioned in Article 6(1) Brussels Ibis Regulation are fulfilled, the defendant's domicile is irrelevant. This concerns, in particular, consumer disputes (Article 18(1) Brussels Ibis Regulation), cases of exclusive international jurisdiction (Article 24 Brussels Ibis Regulation) and choice of court agreements (Article 25 Brussels Ibis Regulation).

#### *b) General Place of Jurisdiction*

**1431.** Persons domiciled in a Member State shall be sued in the courts of that Member State, irrespective of their nationality (Article 4(1) Brussels Ibis Regulation). They can only be sued in the courts of another Member State under the special conditions of Articles 7 et seq. Brussels Ibis Regulation (Article 5(1) Brussels Ibis Regulation).

#### *c) Jurisdiction at the Place of Performance*

##### aa) The Systematic Structure of Article 7 no. 1 Brussels Ibis Regulation

**1432.** Such a special head of jurisdiction, which deviates from the standard rule (defendant's domicile), is established by Article 7 no. 1 Brussels Ibis Regulation. If its requirements are met, the plaintiff has the right to choose between the general and the specific jurisdiction.[133]

**1433.** Article 7 no. 1 Brussels Ibis Regulation presupposes a contractual claim. This is defined by the CJEU as an obligation entered into voluntarily. In this respect, the cause of action and not the identity of the parties is decisive.[134] Moreover, a chain of interrelated voluntary obligations is sufficient. Hence, Article 7 no. 1 Brussels Ibis Regulation is relevant for a passenger's action against the operating air carrier for compensation, even if no contract was concluded between these parties and the flight operated by the air carrier was provided for

---

[133] Cf. A. Stadler, in H.-J. Musielak/W. Voit (eds.), *ZPO Kommentar*, 21th ed. (Munich: Verlag Franz Vahlen, 2024), Vor Art. 7 Brüssel Ia-VO; R. Geimer, in R. Geimer/R.A. Schütze, *Europäisches Zivilverfahrensrecht*, 4th ed. 2020, Art. 7 EuGVVO para. 4.

[134] Cf. CJEU, 7 March 2018, Joined Cases C-274/16, C-447/16 and C-448/16, *flightright*, ECLI:EU:C:2018:160, para. 61.

in a package travel contract concluded with a third party which also included accommodation.[135]

**1434.** The system of Article 7 no. 1 Brussels Ibis Regulation prescribes a subdivision into sales and service contracts (lit. b) and other contracts (lit. a). For the former, the place of performance is determined autonomously by the Regulation. First of all, the place chosen in the contract is decisive. In the absence of such a choice, the place of performance is the place where the buyer has actually received the goods and has or should have had actual control over them.[136] This leads to a uniform place of jurisdiction for all contractual obligations.

**1435.** For all other types of contracts, the provision of lit. a applies due to the reference in lit. c. The place of performance is not determined autonomously but based on the applicable law (the *lex causae*).[137] Thus, a licence agreement is not subject to lit. b, but to lit. c in conjunction with lit. a.[138] One may lament that, within the same paragraph, there are two fundamentally different ways of determining the place of performance. No changes were made to this during the revision of the Brussels I Regulation. Lit. a continues to apply if the place of performance is outside the Member States. In this case, too, the *lex causae* must be applied.

**1436.** The substantive rules that determine the place of performance have been standardised partially. In particular, Article 57 CISG may apply to claims for the price. According to this provision, the price is to be paid at the seller's place of business. For other matters, Article 31 CISG determines the place of performance. Outside its scope of application, e.g. under German law, the place of performance is the debtor's seat (sec. 269 German Civil Code). In some other legal systems (England, Italy, the Netherlands), the place of performance is at the creditor's seat.

**1437.** Agreements regarding the place of performance are also possible and effective within the framework of Article 7 no. 1 Brussels Ibis Regulation. They

---

135 CJEU, 26 March 2020, Case C-215/18, *Primera Air Scandinavia*, ECLI: ECLI:EU:C:2020:235, paras. 39 ff. However, this is not the case for the consumer court pursuant to Article 17-19 Brussels Ibis Regulation, which presupposes a contractual relationship between the plaintiff consumer and the defendant entrepreneur (CJEU, C-215/18, paras. 57 ff.).

136 CJEU, 25 February 2010, Case C-381/08, *Car Trim*, ECLI:EU:C:2010:90, para. 59.

137 *CJEU*, 6 October 1976, Case 12/76, *Tessili*, ECLI:EU:C:1976:133, paras. 13 ff.; CJEU, 15 January 1987, case 286/85, *Shenavai*, ECLI:EU:C:1987:154, para. 7; CJEU, 29 June 1994, Case 288/92, *Custom Made Commercial*, ECLI:EU:C:1994:268, para. 26; CJEU, 28 September 1999, Case C-440/97, *Concorde*, ECLI:EU:C:1999:456, para. 13.

138 CJEU, 23 April 2009, Case C-533/07, *Falco Privatstiftung*, ECLI:EU:C:2009:257.

can be made explicitly or tacitly; there are no special formal requirements. The CJEU initially allowed such agreements without limitations[139] but then restricted them to the effect that there must be a specific reference to the contract.[140] Consequently, abstract agreements on the place of performance are only effective if the formal requirements for choice of court agreements in Article 25 Brussels Ibis Regulation[141] are met. An abstract agreement on the place of performance in this sense is thus (also) classified as a procedural matter.[142]

### bb) Determining the Place of Performance: Problematic Cases

**1438.** The demarcation between the two types of contracts regulated in Article 7 no. 1 Brussels Ibis Regulation is problematic, especially in the case of contracts for the delivery of goods to be manufactured or produced: According to the case law of the CJEU, it is the contract's characteristic performance that matters; if it consists in the delivery of an object, it is about the sale of a movable object. If the goods are manufactured or produced first, the interpretation must be based on EU law and the CISG. If the seller manufactures the raw material from which the goods are to be made, this also amounts to a contract for the supply of movable goods if the buyer makes certain specifications for its procurement, processing or delivery. In addition, the fact that the seller is liable for the quality and conformity of the goods with the contract may speak in favour of a contract for the sale of movable goods. If the performance is characterised by delivery to a place other than the place of performance, the place determined in the contract as the place of delivery is decisive. In the absence of such a provision, the relevant location is the place where the buyer actually took over the goods and had or should have had actual control over them. This interpretation avoids further recourse to the *lex causae* and has the advantage of a simple and foreseeable determination of the place of performance.[143]

**1439.** Furthermore, there is the issue of how to treat services provided in several Member States. For actions for compensation under the Air Passenger Rights Regulation, the court at the place of departure or arrival has – at the choice of the claimant – jurisdiction. By contrast, there is no jurisdiction at the head office of the airline provider.[144] This constellation is also of practical importance in commercial agency contracts. Here, too, lit. a does not apply. Rather, according to the case law of the CJEU, the place of the primary provision of

---

139 CJEU, 17 January 1980, Case 56/79, *Zelger/Salinitri*, ECLI:EU:C:1980:15, para. 4.
140 CJEU, 20 February 1997, Case C-106/95, *MSG*, ECLI:EU:C:1997:70, paras. 31 ff.
141 Cf. below at paras. 1453 ff.
142 Cf. Stürner, *GPR* 2013, 305, 311 f.
143 CJEU, 25 February 2010, Case C-381/08, *Car Trim*, ECLI:EU:C:2010:90, paras. 53 ff.
144 CJEU, 9 July 2009, Case C-204/08, *Rehder*, ECLI:EU:C:2009:439.

services must be considered.[145] The court's jurisdiction in that place then relates to all actions arising out of the contract and not only to that part which is performed in that Member State. Alternatively, the place where the service provider has actually carried out the majority of its activities for the performance of the contract is to be used, provided that the provision of the services at that place is not contrary to the parties' intentions as stipulated by the terms of the contract. In addition, the CJEU considers factual aspects of the case, particularly the time spent at these locations and the importance of the activities carried out there. Subsidiary jurisdiction exists at the service provider's domicile.

#### d) *Jurisdiction for Consumer Contracts*

##### aa) Content

**1440.** In court proceedings, the consumer – like the employee and the insurance policyholder – is generally considered to be the weaker party (Recital 18 Brussels Ibis Regulation). Therefore, consumers hold a privileged position as spelled out in Articles 17 to 19 Brussels Ibis Regulation. The prerequisite – in contrast to the more extensive jurisdiction at the place of performance in Article 7 no. 1 Brussels Ibis Regulation[146] – is the existence of a contractual relationship between the consumer and the (defendant-)trader.[147] However, it does not necessarily follow from this that this head of jurisdiction by any means serves to enforce contractual claims only.[148]

**1441.** The notion of consumer must be interpreted autonomously. It depends on the specific situation at the conclusion of the contract: It must not have been concluded for professional or commercial purposes. According to the case law of the CJEU, if the claim is assigned, the assignee does not benefit from the consumer jurisdiction even if they are themselves a consumer.[149] The rationale behind this is that the jurisdiction under Article 17 Brussels Ibis Regulation intends to protect the consumer only with regard to the individual contract or claims resulting from it.[150] It is not necessary that the consumer acts in a particular way under this contract, e.g. showing a specific lack of professional expertise.[151] Consequently, it does not matter whether a private investor has carried out transactions worth millions of euros in limit orders speculating

---

145 CJEU, 11 March 2010, Case C-19/09, *Wood Floor Solutions*, ECLI:EU:C:2010:137.

146 Cf. above at para. 1433.

147 CJEU, 26 March 2020, Case C-215/18, *Primera Air Scandinavia*, ECLI: ECLI:EU:C:2020:235, paras. 57 ff.

148 Cf. below at paras. 1447 ff.

149 CJEU, 25 January 2018, Case C-498/16, *Schrems/Facebook*, ECLI:EU:C:2018:37, paras. 45 ff.

150 Stürner/Wendelstein, *JZ* 2018, 1083, 1090 f.

151 CJEU, 3 October 2019, Case C-208/18, *Petruchová*, ECLI:EU:C:2019:825, para. 58.

on a fall in the price of petrol, whether these transactions were particularly risky, whether the consumer had special knowledge or experience in the field of financial instruments or whether they carried out the transactions within a relatively short period of time.[152] Irrespective of this, corporations are never consumers; even start-ups do not benefit from the favourable place of jurisdiction.[153]

**1442.** If the purpose of a contract is partly professional and partly not related to professional or commercial activity (so-called dual-use transaction), it does not fall under the rules on consumer jurisdiction. An exception will be made only if the professional purpose is so marginal that it plays only a minor role in the overall context of the transaction.[154] Likewise, where the customer has behaved in a way that their contractual partner could rightly gain the impression that they are acting for professional or commercial purposes, the transaction does not fall under Articles 17 to 19 Brussels Ibis Regulation.

bb) Material Scope of Application and 'Direction' of Commercial Activities

**1443.** Hence, if the subject matter of a claim is a contract or claims arising from a contract concluded by a person for a purpose which is not attributable to that person's trade, business or profession, jurisdiction is determined in accordance with Article 17 Brussels Ibis Regulation. This is provided that it concerns the purchase of movable goods on instalment credit terms (lit. a) or a loan repayable in instalments or another credit transaction intended to finance a purchase of such goods (lit. b). In all other cases, Article 17 to 19 Brussels Ibis Regulation apply if the trader pursues a professional or commercial activity in the consumer's country of residence or directs such activity by any means to that Member State or several States, including that Member State, and the contract falls within the scope of this activity (lit. c).[155]

**1444.** Difficulties arise primarily concerning lit. c. The CJEU has ruled that the decisive criterion is whether the trader has already expressed their intention to establish business relations with consumers of one or more other Member States, including the consumer's Member State of residence, before the actual conclusion of the contract. This may be indicated, for example, by the international nature of the trader's activities, the provision of directions from

---

152 CJEU, 2 April 2020, Case C-500/18, *Reliantco*, ECLI:EU:C:2020:264, paras. 53 f.

153 CJEU, 3 July 1997, Case C-269/95, *Benincasa*, ECLI:EU:C:1997:337, para. 17.

154 CJEU, 20 January 2005, Case C-464/01, *Gruber*, ECLI:EU:C:2005:32, paras. 32 f. For a diverging point of view in substantive law cf. above at paras. 36, 1332 f.

155 The question of whether the cross-border dimension must already exist at the time of the conclusion of the contract or only when the action is brought, for example because the consumer has moved to another Member State in the meantime, is still open.

other Member States to the place where the trader is established, or the use of a language or currency other than that commonly used in the Member State where the trader is established, or the possibility of booking and confirming the booking in that other language.[156] In any case, it does not matter whether the contract was concluded by means of distant selling.[157]

**1445.** Finally, it is irrelevant for the consumer jurisdiction that the trader has directed his business activities towards the state of the consumer's domicile, but the conclusion of the contract has come about independently from this (e.g. because the consumer has not taken note of the company's website in the first place). In this case, there is no causal link between the 'direction' of the business activity of the trader towards the country of the consumer's domicile and the conclusion of the contract. Nevertheless, the CJEU does not consider this factor as being at all relevant.[158]

cc) Consequence: Favourable Head of Jurisdictional

**1446.** If the conditions of Article 17 Brussels Ibis Regulation are met, the action of a consumer against the trader may be brought either before the courts of the Member State in the territory of which this contracting party is domiciled or before the court of the place where the consumer is domiciled (Article 18(1) Brussels Ibis Regulation). The trader's action against the consumer can only be brought before the courts of the Member State in the territory of which the consumer is domiciled (Article 18(2) Brussels Ibis Regulation). If the consumer's contracting partner is not domiciled in a Member State but has a branch, agency or other establishment in a Member State, they shall be treated for disputes arising out of its operation as if they were domiciled in the territory of that State (Article 17(2) Brussels Ibis Regulation).

*e) The Difference Regarding the Place of Jurisdiction for Torts*

**1447.** For tort claims, Article 7 no. 2 Brussels Ibis Regulation provides for a separate head of jurisdiction. An action may be brought before the court of the place where the harmful event occurred or is likely to occur. According to the case law of the CJEU, the claimant may choose between the place of action and the place of success,[159] which allows forum shopping to a certain extent. The

156 CJEU, 7 December 2010, Joined Cases C-585/08 and C-144/09, *Pammer/Hotel Alpenhof*, ECLI:EU:C:2010:740.

157 CJEU, 6 September 2012, Case C-190/11, *Mühlleitner*, ECLI:EU:C:2012:542.

158 CJEU, 17 October 2013, Case C-218/12, *Emrek*, ECLI:EU:C:2013:666; for a critical comment cf. Klöpfer/Wendelstein, *JZ* 2014, 298.

159 CJEU, 30 November 1976, Case 21/76, *Bier/Mines de Potasse d'Alsace*, ECLI:EU:C:1976:166; CJEU, 16 July 2009, Case C-189/08, *Zuid-Chemie BV*, ECLI:EU:C:2009:475.

question is whether breaches of contract, in particular, can be regarded as torts in this sense. From the CJEU's perspective, the heads of jurisdiction regarding delictual and contractual claims are mutually exclusive.[160] Such was the position e.g. in the *Brogsitter* case for an action for civil liability under sec. 823(2) German Civil Code in connection with the relevant law on unfair competition. Even though this claim would be seen as delictual under German law, it was held that it nevertheless relates to a 'contract' within the meaning of Article 7 no. 1 lit. a Brussels Ibis Regulation. This is because 'the conduct complained of may be considered a breach of contract, which may be established by taking into account the purpose of the contract'.[161]

**1448.** From the CJEU's point of view, an interpretation of the contract must appear indispensable to clarify whether the conduct in question is lawful.[162] This is the case if the relief sought relates to a claim for compensation; in this respect, its cause may reasonably be seen in a breach of the rights and obligations under the contract so that its consideration would be mandatory for the court's decision.[163] According to these criteria, claims against a social network due to data protection violations in connection with a private user account, for example, must also be classified as torts since these result directly from statutory provisions and thus, the content of the terms of use has no direct relevance for their existence and content.[164]

**1449.** However, the CJEU does not consistently follow this line of reasoning: If a consumer bases their action on tort law, it should nevertheless fall under Articles 17 to 19 Brussels Ibis Regulation if it is inextricably linked to a contract concluded between the consumer and the trader.[165] At least this is what the CJEU ruled in the case of liability due to deficient pre-contractual information. The *Reliantco* decision concerned a 'retail client' who had concluded a contract with the defendant on financial contracts and sued for damages after a total loss of the investment sum – almost two million euros.[166] The consumer, who is generally seen as vulnerable, cannot be expected to sue in several different courts with regard to claims that are inextricably linked.[167] In this respect, the CJEU emphasised that a contract must be concluded in order to benefit from consumer

[160] CJEU, 13 March 2014, Case C-548/12, *Brogsitter*, ECLI:EU:C:2014:148, para. 20.
[161] CJEU, 13 March 2014, Case C-548/12, *Brogsitter*, ECLI:EU:C:2014:148, para. 24.
[162] CJEU, 13 March 2014, Case C-548/12, *Brogsitter*, ECLI:EU:C:2014:148, para. 25.
[163] Cf. Wendelstein, *ZEuP* 2015, 624.
[164] Stürner/Wendelstein, *JZ* 2018, 1083, 1085 ff. In the decision *Schrems II* (CJEU, 25 January 2018, Case C-498/16, *Schrems/Facebook*, ECLI:EU:C:2018:37) the CJEU admittedly only dealt with the consumer jurisdiction, albeit without problematising this.
[165] CJEU, 2 April 2020, Case C-500/18, *Reliantco*, ECLI:EU:C:2020:264, paras. 67 ff.
[166] Cf. CJEU, 2 April 2020, Case C-500/18, *Reliantco*, ECLI:EU:C:2020:264, paras. 24 ff.
[167] CJEU, 2 April 2020, Case C-500/18, *Reliantco*, ECLI:EU:C:2020:264, para. 63.

jurisdiction. However, the fact that the asserted claim based on pre-contractual liability falls under the Rome II Regulation and thus cannot be classified as a contract, does not constitute an obstacle: According to Article 12(1) of the Rome II Regulation, the law applicable to a pre-contractual obligation shall be the law that applies to the contract or that would have been applicable to it had it been entered into.[168] Consequently, this 'ancillary competence' for actions based on pre-contractual liability strengthens the coherence between the Brussels Ibis Regulation on the one hand and the Rome II Regulation on the other since the intended contract is decisive for both.[169]

**1450.** However, this last argument is only partially conclusive: Coherence between the two legal acts is hardly promoted by the decision; rather, this relates to the harmony between international jurisdiction and applicable law. This aspect, in turn, is not extraordinarily important for civil and commercial matters – unlike, for example, for the area of the European Succession Regulation[170] – that it could be used as decisive interest for legal interpretation.[171] Apart from this, it appears to require clarification when a tort claim is so 'inextricably' linked to the contract that it qualifies for the jurisdiction on consumer claims.[172] According to settled case-law, Article 17 of the Brussels Ibis Regulation is to be interpreted narrowly as an exceptional provision.[173] The provision applies to 'matters relating to a contract'. The CJEU states that this rule 'applies only in so far as the action at issue concerns a contract concluded between a consumer and a seller or supplier'.[174] This might be explained with the more open formulations in other language versions ('*wenn ein Vertrag oder Ansprüche aus einem Vertrag den Gegenstand des Verfahrens bilden*' or '*en matière de contrat*'). However, it does not explain why the CJEU wants to allow such 'ancillary actions' in this particular constellation since this was rejected in other cases – for example, in the *Brogsitter* decision. The *Reliantco* ruling does not refer to this line of case law at any point. According to this judgment, the court must examine whether an interpretation of the contract appears indispensable to clarify the existence of the claims asserted. However, this cannot be assumed to be the case in the constellation at hand: The pre-contractual obligations the defendant supposedly infringed stem from legal (and not contractual) duties and would exist even if the contract was not concluded. Thus, the consumer jurisdiction would not have been applicable following the *Brogsitter* principles but only the jurisdiction on

168 CJEU, 2 April 2020, Case C-500/18, *Reliantco*, ECLI:EU:C:2020:264, para. 71.
169 CJEU, 2 April 2020, Case C-500/18, *Reliantco*, ECLI:EU:C:2020:264, para. 72.
170 Recital No. 27 of the Succession Regulation.
171 Cf. Dutta, in *Festschrift für Kronke*, 2020, p. 51.
172 The German Federal Supreme Court operates with similar terminology, cf. BGHZ 187, 156 para. 23; BGHZ 190, 28 paras. 32, 43.
173 Cf. CJEU, 20 January 2005, Case C-464/01, *Gruber*, ECLI:EU:C:2005:32, para. 32.
174 CJEU, 2 April 2020, Case C-500/18, *Reliantco*, ECLI:EU:C:2020:264, para. 60.

torts in Article 7 no. 2 Brussels Ibis Regulation. Overall, the impression remains of a not always consistent, piecemeal approach, in which consumer protection considerations are only partly relevant.

### *f) Exclusive Jurisdiction*

**1451.** Article 24 Brussels Ibis Regulation lists some cases of exclusive jurisdictions. These exist regardless of the defendant's domicile. In the field of contractual claims, the jurisdiction in rem as set out in Article 24 no. 1 Brussels Ibis Regulation is of particular importance. According to this provision, the courts of the Member State in which the immovable property is located have jurisdiction over actions concerning rights in rem in immovable property and the rent or lease of immovable property. An action for the removal or omission of an impairment of a right in rem does not fall under Article 24 no. 1 Brussels Ibis Regulation.[175]

**1452.** According to the CJEU, that exclusive jurisdiction covers all disputes concerning the obligations of the landlord and tenant under a rental contract, in particular, the existence or interpretation of rental contracts, their duration, the rent and ancillary costs. This does not include claims that only indirectly relate to the use of a holiday home; this relates, in particular, to claims for a loss of holiday enjoyment and travel expenses.[176] In a departure from this case law, in the revision the Brussels I Regulation, an exception was inserted in Article 24 no. 1 Brussels Ibis Regulation: According to this provision, the courts of the Member State in which the defendant is domiciled also are competent regarding actions concerning the lease of immovable property for temporary private use for a maximum of six consecutive months, provided that the tenant is a natural person and the owner and the tenant are both domiciled in the same Member State. If the dispute is a consumer dispute, Article 24 no. 1 Brussels Ibis Regulation must be construed narrowly.

### *g) Choice of Court Agreements*

#### aa) Legal Nature and Applicable Law

**1453.** Party autonomy exists not only in substantive law and conflict of laws but also in European civil procedure law.[177] Article 25 of the Brussels Ibis Regulation,

---

[175] But possibly under Article 7 no. 2 Brussels Ibis Regulation, cf. CJEU, 18 May 2006, Case C-343/04, *Land Oberösterreich./. ČEZ*, ECLI:EU:C:2006:330.

[176] CJEU, 15 January 1985, Case 241/83, *Rösler/Rottwinkel*, ECLI:EU:C:1985:6.

[177] In addition, the parties (at least in B2B constellations) are free to achieve a complete derogation of state courts for certain disputes by agreeing on an arbitration clause. Article 1(2)(d) Brussels Ibis Regulation contains an exception for arbitration.

therefore, allows the conclusion of contracts on a court's jurisdiction, by which an otherwise existing jurisdiction can be excluded (derogation), and, what is more, another court can be declared competent (prorogation). Both might have an exclusive effect if the parties decide accordingly (Article 25(1) Brussels Ibis Regulation). The prorogated court must examine its jurisdiction ex officio. If the case is brought before a non-prorogated court, the defendant must object due to the choice of court agreement. Otherwise, there is a risk that this court becomes competent if the defendant enters an appearance (Article 26 Brussels Ibis Regulation).

**1454.** As already mentioned, the rationale behind choice-of-court agreements is private autonomy. However, such agreements bear certain risks. In most cases, the party with the stronger negotiating power will opt for a forum that is generally more favourable to their interests. For the other party, the 'away game' involved can entail considerable disadvantages: The proceedings will be conducted before a possibly distant, foreign court, applying unfamiliar procedural law; additional costs will be incurred through foreign trial lawyers; the time and costs involved in participating in the foreign proceedings will be high. Therefore, it must be ensured that the parties are aware of the consequences of the choice-of-court agreement. The Brussels Ibis Regulation sets up formal and substantive requirements to that end.

**1455.** The predominant view is that the choice-of-court agreement is to be considered a procedural agreement, as it only has procedural effects.[178] However, some commentators claim that, especially concerning pre-litigation prorogations, that an agreement on jurisdiction has no effect if neither party invokes it. Consequently, they see a choice-of-court agreement as a substantive contract on procedural relations.[179] Regardless of that, both viewpoints agree that the conclusion, i.e. concerning possible defects of will, is governed by substantive law.[180] As follows from Article 25(1) of the Brussels Ibis Regulation (' …, unless the agreement is null and void as to its substantive validity under the law of that Member State'), the *lex fori prorogati* is the designated law. This formulation is linked to the solution of the Hague Convention on Jurisdiction of 2005, which also refers to the *lex fori prorogati* in its Article 5(1).[181]

178 L. Rosenberg/K.H. Schwab/P. Gottwald, *Zivilprozessrecht*, 18th ed. (Munich: C.H. Beck, 2018), §37 para. 2; Schultzky, in R. Zöller, *ZPO Kommentar*, 35th ed. (Cologne: Otto Schmidt, 2024), §38 para. 4; G. Wagner, *Prozessverträge* (Tübingen: Mohr Siebeck, 1998), pp. 346 ff., with further references.

179 BGHZ 49, 384, 386 f.

180 For an overview cf. J. Heinig, *Grenzen von Gerichtsstandsvereinbarungen im Europäischen Zivilprozessrecht* (Jena: JWV, 2010), pp. 75 ff.

181 Cf. M. Weller, *ZZPInt* 19 (2014), 251, 259 ff.

**1456.** According to Recital 20 of the Brussels Ibis Regulation, this reference also includes foreign conflict-of-laws rules. However, the solution, which is to be applauded in principle, is not without pitfalls, as the Rome I Regulation, which is at present governing the subject matter, excludes choice-of-court agreements from its scope of application in Article 1(2)(e). Consequently, the autonomous national PIL of the Member State the courts of which have been prorogated applies. Real progress could only be achieved if the scope of application of the Rome I Regulation were extended to the substantive side of choice-of-court agreements. It was also rightly pointed out that even a prorogation statute unified in this way would have a relatively narrow scope of application since partial questions such as legal capacity and representation are still treated independently anyway, and European conflict of laws does not (currently) provide a uniform choice-of-law rule for these issues.[182] The form, admissibility and procedural effects, however, are governed by the relevant procedural law, i.e. the *lex fori*, here Article 25 Brussels Ibis Regulation.

**1457.** Jurisdiction agreements may be entered into in conjunction with a (main) contract or separately. According to Article 25(5) Brussels Ibis Regulation, the choice-of-court agreement remains legally independent, so that it is not affected by any invalidity of the main contract. As a result, an aggrieved party must challenge the contract's validity before the prorogated court.

bb) Conditions for Effectiveness According to Article 25 Brussels Ibis Regulation

**1458.** According to the previous version of the Brussels I Regulation, at least one party had to have her seat or residence in the territory of a Member State (Article 23(1) Brussels I Regulation). The recast version explicitly waives this condition ('regardless of their domicile'). This is intended to increase the attractiveness of the courts of the Member States for parties from third countries as well.[183] In any case, the jurisdiction of the courts of a Member State must be agreed on. In addition, a cross-border dimension is required, albeit not necessarily to any Member State (Recital 8 Brussels Ibis Regulation).[184]

**1459.** Article 25 Brussels Ibis Regulation requires a sufficiently specific 'agreement' of the parties. This is an autonomous concept.[185] In principle, a choice of court agreement can be entered into for a dispute that has already

---

182 Gebauer, in *Festschrift für von Hoffmann*, 2011, pp. 577, 585 ff.

183 Cf. U. Magnus, in *Festschrift für von Hoffmann*, 2011, pp. 664, 672 f.; M. Weller, *ZZPInt* 19 (2014), 251, 254 ff.

184 CJEU, 1 March 2005, Case C-281/02, *Owusu/Jackson*, ECLI:EU:C:2005:120.

185 Cf. CJEU, 16 March 1999, Case C-159/97, *Trasporti Castelletti*, ECLI:EU:C:1999:142, para. 17.

arisen or for any disputes that may arise in the future, provided that the legal relationship on which it is based is sufficiently specific. However, this does not apply to the contracts mentioned in Article 25(4) Brussels Ibis Regulation, according to which the special requirements of Articles 15 (insurance matters), 19 (consumer matters) and 23 (employment contracts) Brussels Ibis Regulation, which only permit subsequent agreements on jurisdiction, must be observed, as well as the exclusive jurisdictions of Article 24 Brussels Ibis Regulation, which cannot be waived.

**1460.** The formal requirements set out in Article 25(1) and (2) Brussels Ibis Regulation pursue a warning function due to the potential disadvantages that a choice of court agreement may have for one of the parties; they are intended to ensure that the required agreement of the parties actually exists. The provision contains – depending on the will of the parties – a cascade of requirements regarding form. In principle, the written form is required (lit. a alt. 1). In this respect, the reference to GTC is sufficient if this is contained in the text of the contract. The same is true where a reference is made to an offer containing the clause. By contrast, a mere reproduction on the back of business paper or invoice is insufficient. Alternatively, the so-called semi-written form (lit. a alt. 2), i.e. the oral agreement with written confirmation, is sufficient. Here, a prior agreement of will is therefore required; this can then be confirmed (unilaterally) in writing by each party. In particular, it is not necessary for the defendant (who is disadvantaged by the regulation!) to confirm the agreement on the place of jurisdiction. In both cases, the electronic form is equivalent to the written form (Article 25(2) Brussels Ibis Regulation).

**1461.** Furthermore, an agreement in a form that corresponds to the parties' usual commercial practice is sufficient (Article 25(1) Brussels Ibis Regulation). This, however, presupposes an actual practice. The purpose of the provision is to simplify the requirement of the written form requirement set up in lit. a. In particular, it is intended to make it easier to include jurisdiction clauses in the absence of ongoing business relationships. Finally, the agreement may also be concluded in a form corresponding to a commercial custom prevailing in this particular sector of business, provided the parties were aware of this custom and that it is, in fact, generally accepted in that business sector (Article 25(1) Brussels Ibis Regulation). One party's silence following a confirmation letter that introduces a choice-of-court agreement for the first time may suffice here.[186] The agreement of the parties is presumed in lit. c – in this respect, there is a difference to the semi-written form requirement according to lit. a: There, the parties' agreement must be explicit.

186 Cf. Stürner, *ZEuP* 2012, 353.

# §35. STATE LIABILITY FOR INFRINGEMENTS OF EU LAW

## CONTENTS



References: M. Breuer, *Staatshaftung für judikatives Unrecht. Eine Untersuchung zum deutschen Recht, zum Europa- und Völkerrecht* (Tübingen: Mohr Siebeck, 2011); D. Tietjen, *Das System eines gemeinschaftsrechtlichen Staatshaftungsrechts* (Berlin: Duncker & Humblot, 2010).

## I. BASIC POINTS

**1462.** State liability is a vital part of the effective protection of rights in all legal systems. First, if the state does not comply with its obligations, there must be a remedy for aggrieved citizens to enforce those obligations in courts of law.

However, this may not be sufficient in all cases. It may happen that the state cannot fulfil its obligation any longer: In the context of European private law, this refers, above all, to incorrect or omitted transpositions of EU directives, provided that a party lost a case because of that.

**1463.** Since a direct horizontal effect of a directive between private parties is ruled out,[1] the courts must, first and foremost, try to apply and interpret the law in conformity with the directive. In doing so, the courts must try to comply with the requirements of the directive using the methodology of their legal system. However, there is no obligation to go beyond this and, for example, to develop the law in conformity with the directives where this would not be permissible in purely national situations.[2] Hence, there may be cases where the obligation to transpose and follow EU law is not fully observed. The obvious solution of a horizontal direct application of the directive encounters – at least from the CJEU's point of view – fundamental concerns, as this would be to the detriment of the other party: That party should be rightfully be in a position to rely on her legal position following from the Member State's law. Consequently, the only possible redress will be offered by the state liability claim under EU law.

**1464.** Two addressees of said liability are conceivable in this regard: The EU itself, or the Member States. The former is rarely relevant in the context of private law since it is mostly the Member States that act vis-à-vis the citizens through the decentralised enforcement of EU law. However, with Article 340 TFEU, an explicit provision on liability exists in this respect, whereas such grounds for state liability claims against the Member States must be determined in the respective national laws – if necessary, by developing it in conformity with EU law.

## II. LIABILITY OF THE EU

**1465.** State liability claims against the EU itself are explicitly regulated in Article 340 TFEU. The provision distinguishes between contractual and non-contractual liability claims.

### 1. CONTRACTUAL LIABILITY OF THE EU

**1466.** Article 340(1) TFEU establishes the liability of the EU and its institutions for breaches of contractual obligations. The legal capacity of the EU stems from

1 Cf. above at paras. 392 ff.
2 Cf. above at paras. 355 ff.

Article 47 and Article 335 TFEU.[3] The liability claim is governed by the law of the country which is also applicable to the contract in question; this is determined in accordance with the Rome I Regulation.[4] Following the common practice of the EU institutions, the applicable law is generally chosen when the contract is concluded.[5]

**1467.** Claims arising from unauthorised representation, *culpa in contrahendo* and unjust enrichment are not subject to contractual liability pursuant to Article 340(1) TFEU; the respective dispute on the classification of these matters has been clarified in the Rome II Regulation.[6]

## 2. NON-CONTRACTUAL LIABILITY OF THE EU

**1468.** The non-contractual liability of the EU covers non-contractual damages caused by EU institutions or officials that arise during the performance of their duties. Its prerequisites result from Article 340(2) TFEU.[7] Institutions, in this sense, are all those mentioned in Article 13(1) TEU and all other institutions based on EU primary law and acting on behalf of the EU;[8] staff, in this sense, are all officials, employees and workers of the EU.[9] The liability is extended to damages caused during the performance of official duties where the conduct giving rise to the damage is directly connected with the performance of EU tasks.[10] The action must also be unlawful; according to the case law of the CJEU, this requires a sufficiently qualified infringement of a provision, which must be designed (also) to protect individuals.[11] The EU shall not be liable for lawful conduct.[12]

---

3 J.P. Terhechte, in *Frankfurter Kommentar zu EUV, GRC, AEUV*, 2nd ed. (Tübingen: Mohr Siebeck, 2023), Art. 340 AEUV para. 12.

4 W. Berg, in J. Schwarze, *EU-Kommentar*, 4th ed. (Baden-Baden/Vienna/Basel: Nomos/Facultas/Helbing Lichtenhahn, 2019), Art. 340 AEUV para. 6.

5 Cf. e.g. CJEU, 1 June 1995, Case C-42/94, *Heidemji Advies*, ECLI:EU:C:1995:163, para. 5; M. Ruffert, in C. Calliess/M. Ruffert, *EUV/AEUV*, 6th ed. (Munich: C.H. Beck, 2022), Art. 340 AEUV para. 4.

6 W. Berg, in JJ. Schwarze, *EU-Kommentar*, 4th ed. (Baden-Baden/Vienna/Basel: Nomos/Facultas/Helbing Lichtenhahn, 2019), Art. 340 AEUV para. 6.

7 Cf. CJEU, 28 April 1971, Case C-4/69, *Lütticke*, ECLI:EU:C:1971:40.

8 CJEU, 2 December 1992, Case C-370/89, *Etroy*, ECLI:EU:C:1993:202, para. 16.

9 M. Böhm, in R. Schulze/A. Janssen/S. Kadelbach (eds.), *Europarecht – Handbuch für die deutsche Rechtspraxis*, 4th ed. (Baden-Baden: Nomos, 2020), §12 para. 13.

10 CJEU, 10 July 1969, Case C-9/69, *Sayag*, ECLI:EU:C:1969:37, para. 5/11; J.P. Terhechte, in *Frankfurter Kommentar zu EUV, GRC, AEUV*, 2nd ed. (Tübingen: Mohr Siebeck, 2023), Art. 340 AEUV para. 20.

11 CJEU, 10 December 2002, Case C-312/00, *Camar und Tico*, ECLI:EU:C:2002:736, para. 53.

12 CJEU, 9 September 2008, Joined Cases C-120/06 P and 121/06 P, *FIAMM*, ECLI:EU:C:2008:476, paras. 175 f.; on possible future developments W. Berg, in J. Schwarze, *EU-Kommentar*, 4th ed. (Baden-Baden/Vienna/Basel: Nomos/Facultas/Helbing Lichtenhahn, 2019), Art. 340 AEUV para. 52.

**1469.** The claimant must have suffered actual damages; he bears the burden of proof for this.[13] Regarding the calculation of damages, a comparison must be made of the economic situation before and after the event giving rise to the damage.[14] A direct causal connection between the violation of the respective rule and the damage is required.[15] Fault, or negligence, on the other hand, is not a prerequisite for a claim.[16]

## III. LIABILITY OF THE MEMBER STATES

**1470.** In the EU's system of decentralised law enforcement, the liability of the Member States is of greater practical importance. This is all the more true for private law matters.

### 1. RATIONALE

**1471.** Since a horizontal direct effect is ruled out in the case of directives that have not been transposed properly (or, indeed, not at all), aggrieved individuals must be compensated. This is the main objective of the state liability claim.[17] According to the CJEU, it is rooted in the nature of the European Treaties that a Member State must be liable for damages caused to individuals following breaches of Community law that are attributable to Member States.[18] In general, liability is based on the practical effectiveness of EU law (the effet utile) and the loyalty principle under Article 4(3) TEU. Articles 288 and 340 TFEU and Article 19(1) subpara. 2 TEU may also be cited in this context.[19] Ultimately, as there is no explicit legal basis for such claims, the legal basis of the state liability is judge-made law.[20]

---

13 CJEU, 2 December 1971, Case C-5/71, *Schöppenstedt*, ECLI:EU:C:1971:116, para. 9.

14 Cf. the calculation given in CJEU, 4 October 1979, Case C-238/78, *Ireks-Arkady*, ECLI:EU:C:1979:226, para. 13.

15 CJEU, 10 December 2002, Case C-312/00 P, *Camar und Tico*, ECLI:EU:C:2002:736, para. 53; Court of First Instance, 18 September 1995, Case T-168/94, *Blackspur*, ECLI:EU:T:1995:170, para. 40.

16 M. Böhm, in R. Schulze/A. Janssen/S. Kadelbach (eds.), *Europarecht – Handbuch für die deutsche Rechtspraxis*, 4th ed. (Baden-Baden: Nomos, 2020), §12 para. 43.

17 Cf. e.g. Kling, *JURA* 2005, 298.

18 The seminal judgment is CJEU, 19 November 1991, Case C-6/90, *Francovich*, ECLI:EU:C:1991:428.

19 CJEU, 5 March 1996, Joined Cases C-46/93 and C-48/93, *Brasserie du pêcheur/Factortame*, ECLI:EU:C:1996:79, para. 27.

20 F. Ossenbühl/M. Cornils, *Staatshaftungsrecht*, 6th ed. (Munich: C.H. Beck, 2013), pp. 597 ff.; Breuer, *Staatshaftung für judikatives Unrecht*, 2011, p. 382; Tietjen, *Das System eines gemeinschaftsrechtlichen Staatshaftungsrechts*, 2010, pp. 118 ff.

## 2. PREREQUISITES

**1472.** According to the established case law of the CJEU, the following conditions must be met for the Member State to be liable for breaches of EU law:[21]

- Infringement of a provision of EU law by a Member State, for example, due to an incomplete transposition of a directive (infringement of Article 288(3) TFEU). In this context, it is irrelevant which organ of the state concerned caused the infringement.[22] In many cases, this will regard acts or omissions of the executive branch. However, also acts of the legislator[23] or even the judiciary[24] can trigger liability.
- The violated rule of EU law must intend to confer determinable rights on individuals. It is sufficient if the protected group of persons can be determined by interpretation.
- The infringement must be sufficiently severe:[25] This is the case if the acting institution has manifestly and substantially exceeded the limits set determined by EU law.
- The infringement must have been the cause of the damage.

**1473.** The limitation in time of the state liability claim under EU law is governed by the respective applicable national law. A limitation period of three years is appropriate, as it does not appear likely to make the exercise of the rights conferred by the EU legal order practically impossible or excessively difficult.[26] A Member State may rely on the expiry of a limitation period which is reasonable in that sense against an action brought by an individual in order to preserve rights under a directive even if it has failed to transpose the directive correctly, provided that its conduct has not caused the action to be brought after it became time-barred.[27]

---

21 Cf. A. Haratsch/C. Koenig/M. Pechstein, *Europarecht*, 13th ed. (Tübingen: Mohr Siebeck, 2023), paras. 649 ff.

22 CJEU, 5 March 1996, Joined Cases C-46/93 and C-48/93, *Brasserie du pêcheur/Factortame*, ECLI:EU:C:1996:79, para. 32; CJEU, 30 September 2003, Case C-224/01, *Köbler*, ECLI:EU:C:2003:513, para. 31.

23 CJEU, 8 October 1996, Cases C-178/94 *e.a.*, *Dillenkofer*, ECLI:EU:C:1996:375; CJEU, 15 June 1999, Case C-140/97, *Rechberger*, ECLI:EU:C:1999:306.

24 CJEU, 30 September 2003, Case C-224/01, *Köbler*, ECLI:EU:C:2003:513; Breuer, *Staatshaftung für judikatives Unrecht*, 2011.

25 CJEU, 5 March 1996, Joined Cases C-46/93 and C-48/93, *Brasserie du Pêcheur/Factortame*, ECLI:EU:C:1996:79, para. 51 ff.

26 CJEU, 24 March 2009, Case C-445/06, *Danske Slagterier*, ECLI:EU:C:2009:178, para. 32.

27 CJEU, 19 May 2011, Case C-452/09, *Iaia*, ECLI:EU:C:2011:323.

## 3. RELEVANT FIELDS OF PRIVATE LAW

**1474.** The state liability claim concerning private law matters primarily relates to cases where a qualified infringement of an EU rule that aims to harmonise private laws between EU Member States exists. The main categories are failures to transpose a directive, or insufficiently transposed directives, which (also) concern the legal positions between private parties.[28]

### a) *Infringement of Primary Law*

**1475.** However, liability claims for the violation of primary law are also conceivable. According to the CJEU, provisions of primary EU law may also contain actionable private rights.[29] A violation of fundamental EU rights, e.g. the right to property, might be an option in this respect.[30] However, as a general rule, primary remedies must be used first and foremost before damages can be claimed.[31]

### b) *Deficits During Legislative Implementation of the Directive*

**1476.** Concerning the liability for deficiencies in the implementation of directives, three main groups of cases have emerged: total lack of implementation, late implementation and incomplete implementation.

#### aa) Lack of Implementation

**1477.** In the case of the implementation of directives, a manifest and substantial infringement within the meaning of the above criteria exists if the directive has not been transposed at all.[32] This is probably the most straightforward case of a violation of EU law.

#### bb) Late Implementation

**1478.** Late implementation ultimately only represents a temporary infringement of EU law. The difference to a total failure to implement becomes apparent when it comes to assessing damages: If, following an established breach of EU law, a

---

28 Müller-Graff, in Gebauer/Teichmann, *Enzyklopädie Europarecht*, Volume 6: European Private and Corporate Law, 2nd ed. 2022, §2 para. 26.

29 CJEU, 5 March 1996, Joined Cases C-46/93 and C-48/93, *Brasserie du pêcheur/Factortame*, ECLI:EU:C:1996:79, paras. 20 ff.

30 CJEU, 14 January 1987, Case 281/84, *Zuckerfabrik Bedburg*, ECLI:EU:C:1987:3, paras. 25 ff.

31 Tietjen, *Das System eines gemeinschaftsrechtlichen Staatshaftungsrechts*, 2010, pp. 188 f.

32 CJEU, 23 May 1996, Case C-5/94, *Hedley Lomas*, ECLI:EU:C:1996:205, para. 31.

directive is transposed and applied retroactively, this is generally sufficient to compensate for the damage; the claim is then limited to the losses incurred precisely because of the late transposition.[33]

### cc) Incomplete Implementation

**1479.** It is most difficult if the Member State has transposed the directive but has not done so in a way that meets all EU law requirements. Because of the regulatory autonomy that Article 288(3) TFEU confers on the Member States, such infringements are not rare, especially in private law. Concerning the existence of a qualified infringement, the decisive factors are the definiteness and clarity of the infringed norm, the scope of the discretion granted, the intentionality of the infringement and the excusability of a possible legal error.[34]

**1480.** There is no infringement if an EU directive merely contains a catalogue of exemplary clauses which the Member States' legislator may or may not implement at its discretion.[35] Here, the realisation of the objective of a directive represents the outer framework of the implementation choices.[36] However, there is an infringement if the contents of a directive with vast discretionary powers are to be made accessible to the general public in any case however the state thinks fit,[37] but the legislator fails to fulfil this obligation.

**1481.** In the context of EU private law, such a duty to provide information on the content of the directive to the public may exist where a directive is intended to confer private rights on individuals.[38] The non-binding parts of the directive may thus be relevant in the context of an interpretation in conformity with EU law, irrespective of the absence of an obligation to transpose those parts. However, such a vague obligation publicise the transposition norms does not constitute an obligation of the Member States, which means that, at best, a marginal negligence of the legislator can be established.[39] Therefore, the infringement is not sufficiently severe. The same applies if the Member State assumed and was entitled to assume that it had transposed the directive correctly.[40]

---

33 CJEU, 10 July 1997, Case C-373/95, *Maso/INPS*, ECLI:EU:C:1997:353, para. 41.
34 CJEU, 4 July 2000, Case C-424/97, *Haim*, ECLI:EU:C:2000:357, para. 43; Herresthal, in Langenbucher, *Europäisches Privat- und Wirtschaftsrecht*, §2 para. 127.
35 CJEU, 7 May 2002, Case C-478/99, *Commission/Sweden*, ECLI:EU:C:2002:281, paras. 20 f.
36 CJEU, 17 June 1999, Case C-336/97, *Commission/Italy*, ECLI:EU:C:1999:314, para. 19.
37 CJEU, 7 May 2002, Case C-478/99, *Commission/Sweden*, ECLI:EU:C:2002:281, para. 22.
38 CJEU, 10 May 2001, Case C-144/99, *Commission/Netherlands*, ECLI:EU:C:2001:257, para. 17.
39 Herresthal, in Langenbucher, *Europäisches Privat- und Wirtschaftsrecht*, §2 para. 127.
40 Heiderhoff, *Europäisches Privatrecht*, para. 95.

### c) *Mistakes by the Judiciary*

References: M. Breuer, *Staatshaftung für judikatives Unrecht. Eine Untersuchung zum deutschen Recht, zum Europa- und Völkerrecht* (Tübingen: Mohr Siebeck, 2011); M. Stürner, 'Staatshaftung für judikatives Unrecht, Anmerkung zu EuGH v. 30.9.2003 – Rs. C-224/01 (*Köbler*)', *ERPL* 2005, 426.

#### aa) Basic Points

**1482.** With the decision in *Köbler ./. Austria*, the CJEU has continued its previous case law on the liability of Member States for infringements of Community law by their institutions. If, according to the *Francovich*,[41] *Brasserie du Pêcheur/Factortame*[42] and *Hedley Lomas*[43] judgments, it had previously been established that a Member State was liable for actions of its executive and legislative bodies that were contrary to Community law, it was still open whether this also applied to mistakes by the judiciary.[44] The CJEU has – not surprisingly[45] – extended this Europhile and integration-friendly case-law to acts of Member State courts. It has, in principle, established the liability of Member States for infringements of Community law by final instance courts.

##### (1) Undermining the Effects of Res Judicata?

**1483.** It has been argued against Member State liability for violations of EU law by the judiciary that the possibility of an action for state liability might undermine the *res iudicata* effect of decisions of courts of last instance. In the *Köbler* decision, the CJEU relied on a rather formal reasoning, according to which the original proceedings and the subsequent state liability action had different subject matters; this also usually results from the fact that the parties are not identical.

**1484.** Of course, a successful state liability action does not affect the validity of the court's decision of the last instance. However, if – as in the *Köbler* case – the initial claim was for payment of a sum of money, a successful state liability action does de facto lead to the legal consequence initially sought but were rejected by the final court decision. The CJEU thus somehow postulates a 'tolerate and

41 CJEU, 19 November 1991, Case C-6/90, *Francovich*, ECLI:EU:C:1991:428.

42 CJEU, 5 March 1996, Joined Cases C-46/93 and C-48/93, *Brasserie du Pêcheur/Factortame*, ECLI:EU:C:1996:79.

43 CJEU, 23 May 1996, Case C-5/94, *Hedley Lomas*, ECLI:EU:C:1996:205.

44 Cf. Kremer, *NJW* 2004, 480 with further references.

45 Already in the judgement *Brasserie du Pêcheur/Factortame* (CJEU, 5 March 1996, Joined Cases C-46/93 and C-48/93, ECLI:EU:C:1996:79, para. 32), the CJEU had emphasised that it could not matter which national institution had committed the infringement.

liquidate' approach under EU law, according to which the decision contrary to EU law must be accepted, but compensation can be claimed under certain circumstances.

### (2) Weakening the Authority of the Court?

**1485.** In view of this, concerns have been expressed – especially from English commentators – that the possibility of a legal remedy against decisions contrary to EU law would weaken the authority of the court of the last instance and impair the independence of the judges.[46] The CJEU rightly rejected this. The existence of a court of appeal shows that a correction mechanism for wrongful judgements is accepted in all legal systems and in no way weakens the courts' authority.[47] This is true also to courts of the last instance.[48] Problems can only arise if the state liability claim is designed in a way as to effectively establish another appellate instance under EU law and thus counteracts the domestic system of legal remedies. However, the Member States have a certain leeway in this respect.

### (3) Arguments under EU Law for Judicial State Liability

**1486.** Despite all criticism, the liability for violations of EU law by the judiciary proves to be a necessary consequence of the loyalty principle; it is also an essential part of the EU Member States' legal traditions.[49] According to the European Court of Human Rights case law, the ECHR parties may also be obliged to pay damages under Article 41 ECHR if a decision of a court of the last instance has violated a fundamental right.[50] Nevertheless, this is not entirely comparable because, in the ECHR, the claim for liability for violations of fundamental rights was explicitly laid down, while this is not the case in EU primary law. When the CJEU ruled in favour of liability for judicial injustice in the *Köbler* case, it was about the determination of Member State obligations through the *interpretation* of primary law; the corresponding case law of the ECtHR, on the other hand, concerned the *application* of an international treaty.[51]

---

46 On this Wattel, *CMLRev* 41 (2004), 177, 180 ff., who fears an avalanche of lawsuits.

47 Cf. A. Voßkuhle, *Rechtsschutz gegen den Richter* (Munich: C.H. Beck, 1993), pp. 168 ff., 276 f.

48 In that sense also Wegener, *EuR* 2002, 785, 792 f.; Wegener, *EuR* 2004, 84, 88.

49 In detail Breuer, *Staatshaftung für judikatives Unrecht*, 2011, pp. 406 ff.

50 European Court of Human Rights, 21 March 2000, ECHR 2000, 108 (*Dulaurans ./. Frankreich*), concerning an alleged violation of the right to a fair trial under Article 6(1) ECHR by a decision of the French Cour de cassation. In the *Köbler* judgment, the CJEU explicitly refers to this decision in para. 49.

51 Wegener, *EuR* 2004, 84, 86 f.

### bb) Types of Cases

**1487.** In the case of failure to consider an EU provision or CJEU case law during the application of the law, an exceptionally qualified, i.e. flagrant, infringement by the judiciary is required, which the CJEU itself considers to be an exceptional case.[52] It must not be inferred from this that a statutory limitation of liability to intentional and grossly negligent but nevertheless obvious infringements would be permissible.[53]

**1488.** If, however, the case is about consequential errors in a final, legally binding judgment due to a legislative infringement of EU law, this amounts, from a purely formal point of view, to an infringement by the legislator, which, however, is inevitably reflected in the judgment by the court's application of the relevant law in relevant cases. The CJEU considers this an infringement by the court since individuals must have the possibility of asserting their subjective rights by recourse to the state after all judicial remedies have been exhausted.[54]

**1489.** There are no grounds for a state liability claim under EU law if a national court acts *contra legem* (i.e. against national law) based on the methodological principles of the development of the law in conformity with a directive:[55] The court does not run counter to the requirements of EU law. At most, it could be considered whether a violation of national law could be grounded in the fact that the court has arbitrarily acted, in disregard of the national methodological doctrine, *contra legem*. Such a claim, however, would be outside the realm of the EU liability claim.

### cc) Design in National Law

#### (1) Procedural Autonomy of the Member States

**1490.** In principle, the Member States also have procedural autonomy with regard to the form of the state liability claim for judicial injustice. However, this is limited by the principle of equivalence: The state liability claim under EU law may not be more restrictive than a corresponding claim under national law.[56] Liability claims are, in principle, limited to judgements of the court of the last

---

52 CJEU, 30 September 2003, Case C-224/01, *Köbler*, ECLI:EU:C:2003:513, paras. 53–56.

53 CJEU, 13 June 2006, Case C-173/03, *Traghetti del Mediterraneo*, ECLI:EU:C:2006:391, para. 46.

54 CJEU, 30 September 2003, Case C-224/01, *Köbler*, ECLI:EU:C:2003:513, para. 34.

55 In favour Schinkels, *JZ* 2011, 394, 398; critical Heiderhoff, *Europäisches Privatrecht*, para. 98.

56 CJEU, 26 January 2010, Case C-118/08, *Transportes Urbanos*, ECLI:EU:C:2010:39.

instance: First, the affected party must seek redress in the court of appeal;[57] the priority of primary remedies over actions for damages applies.[58]

(2) Jurisdiction

**1491.** The question of jurisdiction for the state liability claim is left to the national legal systems.[59] In German law, for instance, the Regional Court has jurisdiction for public liability claims (Article 34 German Basic Law in conjunction with sec. 40(2) German Code of Administrative Court Procedure, sec. 71(2) no. 2 German Courts Constitution Act). As a consequence, this court, which has normally jurisdiction to adjudicate first instance cases, has to decide whether the German Federal Administrative Court or the German Federal Supreme Court could have realised that a certain legal question should have been submitted to the CJEU. However, this circumstance can hardly be avoided. Since the German legislature has expressly provided for it, there is no reason to change the jurisdiction precisely for the state liability claim under European law.

(3) Intra-Judicial Correction?

**1492.** By contrast, it would be at least conceivable to establish an intra-judicial remedy that allows for judicial self-correction in order to avoid state liability actions for violation of Community law altogether.[60] E.g. German law has introduced such a possibility in the case of violations of the fundamental right to be heard by decisions that cannot be appealed (sec. 321a of the German Code of Civil Procedure). There are good arguments for applying this provision by analogy to all cases of violation of fundamental procedural rights.[61] The arbitrary violation of the obligation to make a reference pursuant to Article 267(3) TFEU by a court of last instance means, according to the German understanding, a violation of the principle of the statutory judge (Article 101(1) German Basic Law).[62] An intra-judicial correction of the violation of the law could, at least in cases such as *Köbler*, in which the violation is ultimately based on the violation of

57 CJEU, 30 September 2003, Case C-224/01, *Köbler*, ECLI:EU:C:2003:513, para. 34.

58 M. Ruffert, in C. Calliess/M. Ruffert, *EUV/AEUV*, 6th ed. (Munich: C.H. Beck, 2022), Art. 340 AEUV para. 52.

59 However, this did not prevent the CJEU from deciding on the prerequisites of the state liability claim in the *Köbler* case itself. For a critique, cf. von Danwitz, *JZ* 2004, 301, 303.

60 Cf. Stürner, *ERPL* 2005, 426.

61 Among those who advocate the application of sec. 321a of the code of civil procedure to other cases of violation of fundamental procedural rights are e.g. G. Vollkommer, *Der ablehnbare Richter* (Tübingen: Mohr Siebeck, 2002), pp. 343 ff.; Lipp, *NJW* 2002, 1700, 1702; H.-F. Müller, *NJW* 2002, 2743, 2747; for an opposing view cf. e.g. Voßkuhle, *NJW* 2003, 2193, 2199.

62 Cf. BVerfGE 73, 339, 366 ff. (Solange II); BVerfG JZ 2001, 923, 924.

the obligation to refer the question at stake to the CJEU,[63] prevent a subsequent state liability action. At any rate, *de lege ferenda*, a legislative correction would be welcome.

*d) Mistakes by the Executive Branch*

**1493.** Finally, there is also liability for violations of EU law by the executive branch. In principle, this presupposes that the acting official has a margin of discretion in their decision.[64] This concerns both breaches during the application of properly transposed law in breach of EU law and the application of national law in breach of EU law.[65]

*e) No Liability of Private Parties for Breaches of EU Law*

**1494.** EU law obligations are primarily directed towards the Member States. In principle, private individuals cannot derive any legal position from directives vis-à-vis other private individuals.[66] Hence, no private party can be accused of having enforced a legal position based on Member State law that has been transposed and applied contrary to EU law. The liability claim under EU law does not apply to private individuals; the intended sanctionatory character only regards to Member States.[67]

**1495.** Of course, this is not the case for those provisions of EU law that are directly applicable between private parties. Thus, a company may be liable if it has harmed others through prohibited price agreements contrary to Article 101 TFEU.[68]

---

63 The CJEU (30 September 2003, Case C-224/01, *Köbler*, ECLI:EU:C:2003:513, para. 102) primarily regarded the right to free movement of workers and relevant secondary law as the standards protecting the individual. However, the violation of the obligation under Article 267 TFEU to refer an issue to the CJEU plays an important role in the assessment of obviousness.

64 J.P. Terhechte, in *Frankfurter Kommentar zu EUV, GRC, AEUV*, 2nd ed. (Tübingen: Mohr Siebeck, 2023), Art. 340 AEUV para. 53.

65 CJEU, 22 June 1989, Case 103/88, *Fratelli Costanzo*, ECLI:EU:C:1989:256, paras. 32 ff.; CJEU, 20 March 1997, Case C-24/95, *Alcan*, ECLI:EU:C:1997:163; CJEU, 23 May 1996, Case C-5/94, *Hedley Lomas*, ECLI:EU:C:1996:205, paras. 24 ff.

66 Cf. at paras. 392 ff. above.

67 M. Ruffert, in C. Calliess/M. Ruffert, *EUV/AEUV*, 6th ed. (Munich: C.H. Beck, 2022), Art. 340 AEUV para. 52.

68 W. Berg, in J. Schwarze, *EU-Kommentar*, 4th ed. (Baden-Baden/Vienna/Basel: Nomos/Facultas/Helbing Lichtenhahn, 2019), Art. 340 AEUV paras. 105 ff.

# §36. ALTERNATIVE DISPUTE RESOLUTION

## CONTENTS



References: M. Fries, *Verbraucherrechtsdurchsetzung* (Tübingen: Mohr Siebeck, 2016); F. Hidding, *Zugang zum Recht für Verbraucher* (Berlin: Duncker & Humblot, 2019); J. Kotzur, *Die außergerichtliche Realisierung grenzüberschreitender Verbraucherforderungen. Eine rechtsvergleichende Untersuchung zur Bedeutung der Verbraucherschlichtung* (Tübingen: Mohr Siebeck, 2018); G. Rühl, 'Alternative and Online Dispute Resolution for Cross-Border Consumer Contracts: a Critical Evaluation of the European Legislature's Recent Efforts to Boost Competitiveness and Growth in the Internal Market', (2015) *J Consum Policy* 38:431; M. Schmidt-Kessel (ed.), *Alternative Streitschlichtung. Die Umsetzung der ADR-Richtlinie in Deutschland* (Jena: JWV, 2015); M. Stürner, 'ADR and Adjudication by State Courts: Competitors or Complements?', *GPR* 2014, 122; M. Stürner/F. Gascón Inchausti/R. Caponi (eds.), *The Role of Consumer ADR in the Administration of Justice. New Trends in Access to Justice under EU Directive 2013/11* (Munich: Sellier, 2015); M. Stürner, 'Wahrung oder Durchsetzung von Verbraucherrechten? Zur Rolle der Verbraucherstreitbeilegung im europäischen Justizraum', in T. Hörnle/C. Möllers/G. Wagner (eds.), *Gerichte und ihre Äquivalente* (Baden-Baden: Nomos, 2020), p. 73.

## I. POLICY CONSIDERATIONS

**1496.** When it comes to consumer claims, there are often practical obstacles to legal action:[1] legal proceedings are expensive; especially in the case of low sums

[1] Cf. the analysis in Fries, *Verbraucherrechtsdurchsetzung*, 2016, pp. 30 ff.; cf. also Hau, *ZZP* 129 (2016), 133. The following is partly based on Stürner, in Hörnle/Möllers/Wagner (eds.), *Gerichte und ihre Äquivalente*, 2020, p. 73.

in dispute, the monetary risks incurred can hence easily exceed the sum at stake. Besides, proceedings may linger for a long time, even if they produce a favourable result. In general, consumers rarely appear in court and shy away from the complexity of the system. There is also often a feeling of inferiority vis-à-vis the supposedly stronger entrepreneur. All that has been known for a long time and has already led to legislative activity at the European level.[2] However, since it is based on Article 81(1) TFEU, such activity is essentially limited to cross-border proceedings:[3] the EU's legislative powers as a matter of principle do not permit intervention in the civil procedural laws of the Member States. The TFEU, therefore, does not provide a sufficient basis for a reform of the judicial systems in the Member States, with respect to which there is still considerable room for improvement.

**1497.** Therefore, at first glance, it is unsurprising that the EU has turned to promoting out-of-court dispute resolution in consumer cases. The goal is comprehensive, low-threshold access to alternative dispute resolution mechanisms. But is this also about access to justice, or is it just about balancing interests? A popular critique of alternative dispute resolution is that it promotes dispute resolution at any cost without necessarily considering the legal soundness of the parties' positions. *Hazel Genn* has put it succinctly as follows:[4] 'The outcome of mediation is not about *just* settlement, it is *just about settlement*.' While it is true that, in practice, going to court may be considered to be the ultima ratio, one should not draw the counter-inference that any kind of alternative dispute resolution is preferable[5] to court proceedings.[6]

**1498.** Admittedly, there is a whole range of alternative forms of dispute resolution, and this kind of criticism is not likely to apply to all of them equally. The ADR mechanisms that have been established for many years throughout Europe, for example, in the insurance or banking sector, are mostly characterised by an obligation laid down in the respective procedural rules to abide by the law as it stands when adjudicating cases.[7] However, a dilemma becomes apparent at this point: A respect for the rule of law is desirable even for ADR mechanisms.

---

2 Particular mention should be made of the jurisdiction for consumer disputes in Articles 17 to 19 Brussels Ibis Regulation (cf. above at paras. 1440 ff.).

3 On the leeway left by this term, cf. Stürner, in *Frankfurter Kommentar zu EUV, GRC, AEUV*, 2nd ed. (Tübingen: Mohr Siebeck, 2023), Art. 81 AEUV paras. 17 f.

4 H. Genn, *Judging Civil Justice* (Cambridge: Cambridge University Press, 2009), p. 117.

5 Here, reference is frequently made to BVerfG NJW-RR 2007, 1073, 1074, cf. e.g. Hirsch, in *Festschrift für E. Lorenz* (Karlsruhe: VVW, 2014), pp. 159, 173. For a critique of this approach, cf. R. Stürner, *ZZP* 127 (2014), 271, 325 with note 261; H. Roth, *DRiZ* 2015, 24, 27; Leipold, in *Festschrift für Klamaris* (Athens: Sakkoulas Publications, 2016), pp. 443, 455 ff.

6 Cf. Fiss, (1984) 93 *Yale L.J.* 1073 ('Against Settlement'); cf. also Eidenmüller/Engel, (2014) 29 *Ohio St. J. Disp. Resol.* 261, 287 ff. ('Against False Settlement'); Caponi, *RabelsZ* 79 (2015), 117, 122.

7 Cf. below at paras. 1512 ff.

However, by sticking to more or less rigid procedural and substantive rules, the desirable flexibility in the process of adjudication is lost. Consequently, the closer alternative dispute resolution resembles traditional legal approaches and procedures, the more it merely mimics the judiciary. But does this not make it a competitor, a 'second-class procedure similar to the judiciary'?[8] Does it even set an 'ADR trap' for the consumer[9]? In any case, the label 'parallel universe' has been used by both opponents[10] and supporters[11] of consumer ADR.

## II. DEVELOPMENT

**1499.** In a Green Paper of the EU Commission of 16 November 1993 entitled 'access of consumers to justice and the settlement of consumer disputes in the single market'[12] the need to strengthen out-of-court dispute resolution mechanisms in consumer law was pointed out already.[13] The Paper referred to the idea of '"alternative" justice'[14] and the 'creation of voluntary arbitration systems, either at sectoral or regional level',[15] which should be explored following the example of the Dutch *Geschillencommissie*. This was followed later by the 'Action plan on consumer access to justice and the settlement of consumer disputes in the internal market',[16] which already focused on promoting out-of-court procedures – in addition to improving access to justice.[17]

### 1. NON-BINDING RECOMMENDATIONS

**1500.** Subsequently, in 1998, the Commission presented a recommendation on principles applicable to out-of-court settlements of consumer disputes.[18] It concerned only those procedures 'which, no matter what they are called, lead to the settling of a dispute through the active intervention of a third party, who proposes or imposes a solution' and thus did not aim to regulate 'procedures that merely involve an attempt to bring the parties together to convince them to find

8 H. Roth, *JZ* 2013, 637, 642 (marked there as polemic); *id.*, *DRiZ* 2015, 24 ('second-class consumer protection').
9 Eidenmüller/Engel, *ZIP* 2013, 1704.
10 H. Roth, *JZ* 2013, 637, 644.
11 Hirsch, *NJW* 2013, 2088, 2089.
12 COM(1993) 576 final, with references to previous initiatives.
13 COM(1993) 576 final, pp. 82 ff.
14 COM(1993) 576 final, p. 83.
15 COM(1993) 576 final, p. 86.
16 COM(1996) 13 final of 14 February 1996.
17 COM(1996) 13 final, pp. 13 ff.
18 Commission Recommendation 98/257/EC of 30 March 1998 on the principles applicable to the bodies responsible for out-of-court settlement of consumer disputes, OJ 1998 L 115/31.

a solution by common consent'.[19] The latter type of dispute settlement was then addressed in another recommendation from 2001.[20]

**1501.** In line with this different objective, the principles contained in both recommendations also differ in some details, although not fundamentally. Both documents are, due to their legal nature, non-binding (Article 288(5) TFEU). They aim to simplify the implementation of out-of-court procedures for the settlement of consumer disputes. Despite their gradually different objectives, both recommendations essentially focus on the independence of the person or body involved in the dispute resolution in order to ensure an impartial decision.

## 2. BINDING STANDARDS FOR CONSUMER ADR

**1502.** Then, in November 2011, the Commission presented the proposal for a Directive on Alternative Dispute Resolution for Consumer Disputes[21] (hereinafter: ADR Directive). This paper proposed the introduction of a legal framework for out-of-court dispute resolution for consumer contracts for goods and services.[22] In contrast to the two Recommendations of 1998 and 2001, the directive is a binding legal act which must be transposed into national law by the Member States (Article 288(3) TFEU). The proposal for a directive includes both dispute resolution models that were introduced in the Recommendations. The proposal for an ADR Directive was flanked by the proposal for a Regulation on consumer ODR[23] (hereinafter: ODR Regulation).

**1503.** In order to justify the necessity of the proposed legal acts, the Commission refers in the proposals, among other things, to a Eurobarometer study from 2011, which shows that almost every other consumer in Europe would not take legal action regarding a sum at stake of up to 500 euros.[24] At the same time, in 2010, more than 20% of European consumers felt they had proper cause to complain about a product or service they bought.[25] However,

---

19 See the Recitals of Recommendation 98/257/EC.

20 Commission Recommendation 2001/310/EC of 4 April 2001 on the principles for out-of-court bodies involved in the consensual resolution of consumer disputes., OJ 2001 L 109/56.

21 Proposal of 29 November 2011 for a Directive of the European Parliament and of the Council on alternative dispute resolution for consumer disputes and amending Regulation (EC) No 2006/2004 and Directive 2009/22/EC (Directive on consumer ADR), COM(2011) 793 final.

22 On the proposals Isermann/Berlin, *VuR* 2012, 47; Berlin/Creutzfeldt-Banda, *ZKM* 2012, 57; Becklein, *GPR* 2012, 232; Deutlmoser/Engel, *MMR* 2012, 433; Davies, *euvr* 2012, 63.

23 Proposal of 29 November 2011 for a Regulation of the European Parliament and of the Council on the online settlement of consumer disputes (Online Dispute Resolution Regulation), COM(2011) 794 final.

24 43%: Consumer Empowerment Survey, Eurobarometer No 342, 2010, p. 217.

25 21%: Consumer Empowerment Survey, Eurobarometer No 342, 2010, p. 169.

only 16% of them took action by resorting to a consumer organisation or a public body or court. The Commission wanted to counteract this by providing simple and inexpensive ways of resolving disputes (Recitals 2 and 6 of the proposed ADR Directive). The Commission hoped that this would strengthen consumer confidence in the internal market and stimulate growth (Recital 4 to the proposed ADR Directive).

**1504.** The Council gave its opinion on the proposals in a paper in May 2012;[26] the Internal Market Committee of the European Parliament in June 2012.[27] In May 2013, both legal acts were adopted: The Directive on Alternative Dispute Resolution for Consumer Disputes[28] and the Regulation on Online Dispute Resolution for Consumer Disputes.[29]

**1505.** While the two proposals were mainly discussed among experts,[30] the ADR Directive, in particular, triggered a sometimes heated discussion in legal academia about the role of consumer arbitration in the rule of law after its entry into force.[31] On a political level, the usefulness of consumer ADR as such, however, was not questioned, but at the same time, at least in Germany, the Directive was implemented with as few adjustments as possible.

## III. MAIN OBJECTIVES OF THE ADR DIRECTIVE

### 1. COMPREHENSIVE ACCESS TO ADR FOR CONSUMERS

**1506.** The ADR Directive aims to give consumers access to dispute resolution bodies for the purpose of resolving disputes with traders. Article 5 of the ADR Directive, therefore, obliges the Member States to ensure that all disputes falling within the scope of the Directive, i.e. contractual claims of consumers against

---

26 Council document (General Approach) of 30 May 2012 No 10622/12.

27 Draft report of the Internal Market Committee from 18 April 2012, IMCO Document No PE487.749v01 (Rapporteur: Louis Grech).

28 Directive 2013/11/EU of the European Parliament and of the Council of 21 May 2013 on alternative dispute resolution for consumer disputes and amending Regulation (EC) No 2006/2004 and Directive 2009/22/EC (Directive on consumer ADR), OJ 2013 L 165/63.

29 Regulation (EU) No 524/2013 of the European Parliament and of the Council of 21 May 2013 on online dispute resolution for consumer disputes and amending Regulation (EC) No 2006/2004 and Directive 2009/22/EC (Regulation on consumer ODR), OJ 2013 L 165/1.

30 Cf. the references provided in para. 1502.

31 Cf. e.g. Hirsch, *NJW* 2013, 2088; Hirsch, in *Festschrift für E. Lorenz* (Karlsruhe: VVW, 2014), p. 159; H. Roth, *JZ* 2013, 637; Eidenmüller/Engel, *ZIP* 2013, 1704; G. Wagner, *ZKM* 2013, 104; *id.*, *CML Rev.* 51 (2014), 165; Rühl, *RIW* 2013, 737; *id.*, ZRP 2014, 8; *id.*, *ZZP* 127 (2014), 61; Meller-Hannich/Höland/Krausbeck, *ZEuP* 2014, 8 as well as the contributions in Stürner/ Gascón Inchausti/Caponi (eds.), *The Role of Consumer ADR in the Administration of Justice*, 2015.

traders in the area of sales and service law, can be submitted to a dispute resolution body meeting the minimum requirements of the Directive.[32] This applies in any case if the trader involved has their registered office in the territory of this Member State. For the Member States, this results in the obligation to create a nationwide and cross-sectoral network of such dispute resolution bodies,[33] or, at least, to ensure that existing institutions meet the standards of the Directive.

## 2. STRENGTHENING THE INTERNAL MARKET

**1507.** By thus ensuring access to simple, fast and inexpensive dispute resolution mechanisms, the Directive aims at strengthening consumer confidence in the internal market[34] and at the same time seeks to increase the interest of the consumers to buy goods and demand services across borders.[35] The Commission considers the rules on alternative dispute resolution 'as one of the twelve levers to boost growth and strengthen confidence in the single market'.[36]

**1508.** These formulations primarily serve to justify the EU's legislative power to adopt both legal acts since, from the Commission's point of view, these are not instruments of judicial cooperation according to Article 81 TFEU, but rather measures to promote the internal market within the meaning of Article 114 TFEU. This seems doubtful this for various reasons:[37] One might refer to the primacy of Article 81 TFEU, which is limited to cross-border situations, and paragraph 2 lit. g of which considers the development of alternative methods for the settlement of disputes of the Union to be a part of the field of judicial cooperation.[38] This could be understood as a violation of the subsidiarity principle of Article 5 TEU.[39] Furthermore, one might doubt whether the Directive will improve the internal market's functioning.[40] The latter remains to be seen.

---

32 Article 5(1) ADR Directive as well as Recital 26: '[...] Member States' responsibility to ensure full coverage by and access to ADR entities'. See previously the Green Paper on 'Access of Consumers to Justice and the Settlement of Consumer Disputes in the Single Market', COM(1993) 576 final and the 'Action Plan on Consumer Access to Justice and the Settlement of Consumer Disputes in the Single Market', COM(1996) 13 final.

33 As explicitly stated in the Commission's explanatory memorandum, COM(2011) 793 final, p. 4.

34 Recitals 4, 11 and 15 ADR Directive.

35 Recital 6 ADR Directive.

36 Communication of 13 April 2011 entitled 'Single Market Act – Twelve levers to boost growth and strengthen confidence – "Working together to create302 new growth"', repeated in Recital No 9 ADR Directive.

37 In detail Rühl, in *Festschrift für Wulf-Henning Roth* (Munich: C.H. Beck, 2015), p. 459.

38 Eidenmüller/Engel, *ZIP* 2013, 1704, 1706 f.; Engel, *NJW* 2015, 1633, 1634.

39 H. Roth, *JZ* 2013, 637, 642.

40 Meller-Hannich/Höland/Krausbeck, *ZEuP* 2014, 8, 16; J. Davies, in B. Hess/M. Bergström/E. Storskrubb (eds.), *EU Civil Justice – Current Issues and Future Outlook* (Oxford: Hart Publishing, 2016), p. 36.

The Commission's prerogative of assessment is, in any case, quite extensive; the CJEU intervenes basically never on grounds of lack of competence.[41] No Member State has brought an action for annulment. The subsidiarity complaint of the German Federal Council[42] and some other parliaments did not reach the required quorum.

## 3. CONSUMER ADR AS A VOLUNTARY MECHANISM

**1509.** However, the access to dispute resolution facilities thus guaranteed for consumers is not necessarily matched by a right to have a dispute resolved in that way: For the trader, participation is also voluntary from a European perspective: the Directive expressly grants traders the right to refuse alternative dispute resolution (Recital 49 of the ADR Directive). This type of dispute resolution is, therefore, by no means comparable to the right of access to justice.[43]

**1510.** The Directive itself also points out the danger that, because of this voluntary nature, the entire ADR system will run dry, and thus, the primary purpose of improving the internal market might not be achieved. It explicitly calls on Member States to '[encourage] traders as far as possible to participate in [alternative dispute resolution] procedures' (Recital 49 ADR Directive). This can be done by making participation in ADR compulsory for traders under national law or 'subject to incentives or sanctions'.

**1511.** However, e.g. the German legislator has not crossed this golden bridge.[44] Admittedly, there are no compelling reasons against compulsory participation in out-of-court dispute resolution proceedings.[45] Nevertheless, the voluntariness of participation appears to be essential for the acceptance of a possible decision proposal, and indeed of ADR as a whole. Experience with compulsory arbitration in Italy,[46] for example, shows that entrepreneurs predominantly treat

---

41 For an exception CJEU, 5 October 2000, Case C-376/98, *Germany/Parliament and Council*, ECLI:EU:C:2000:544, paras. 84 ff. (Annulment of the Tobacco Advertising Directive).

42 BR-Drucks. 772/11 (Resolution).

43 On the issue Greger, in *Festschrift für Klamaris* (Athens: Sakkoulas Publications, 2016), p. 319; Storskrubb, *ERPL* 2016, 7.

44 The legal situation is different in England, where the unwillingness to conduct mediation proceedings can be accompanied by cost disadvantages in court proceedings (cf. rule 1.4(2)(e) CPR). Critically H. Genn, *Why the Privatisation of Civil Justice is a Rule of Law Issue*, 36th F.A. Mann Lecture, 2012, pp. 12 ff.; cf. also Stürner, *ZVglRWiss* 103 (2004), 349, 364.

45 Eidenmüller, *JZ* 2015, 539, 544 f., who, however, rejects a statutory duty to conduct arbitration for B2C disputes due to the extensive protection of the consumer under substantive law. On the legal assessment of arbitration clauses in such cases Eidenmüller/Engel, *ZZP* 128 (2015), 149, 156 ff.

46 Cf. CJEU, 14 June 2017, Case C-75/16, *Menini und Rampanelli*, ECLI:EU:C:2017:457; Kramme, *GPR* 2018, 83.

the imposed dispute resolution procedure in a dilatory manner.[47] The failure of compulsory conciliation in Germany in selected areas can also be cited as a negative example. The goal of speedy dispute resolution is thus turned into the opposite.[48]

**1512.** The evolution of ADR in Germany, which has been very successful in specific sectors, shows that the principle of voluntariness can certainly be combined with the legal policy goal of a broad societal impact. One example is the insurance ombudsman scheme (*Versicherungsombudsmann*), which has been conducting out-of-court dispute resolution in the private insurance sector for twenty years now.[49] It is an association under private law supported by the participating insurance companies and the German Insurance Association. According to its own data, more than 95% of the German insurance market in the private customer business is represented by the *Versicherungsombudsmann*.[50]

**1513.** However, the foundation of the association took place not merely out of altruistic motives. The background was the implementation of the Insurance Mediation Directive,[51] the aim of which is to promote the out-of-court settlement of disputes in the interest of policyholders. In implementation of these requirements, sec. 214 German Insurance Contract Act enables the recognition of conciliation bodies organised under private law in insurance matters. Complaints to the insurance ombudsman can only be made by consumers and only against an insurer that is a member of the *Versicherungsombudsmann* association.[52]

---

47 F. Padovini, in *Jahrbuch für Italienisches Recht*, Volume 29 (Heidelberg: C.F. Müller, 2016), p. 47.

48 Swiss law is different, however, and Articles 197 ff. Code of civil procedure provide for a compulsory attempt at conciliation for many proceedings.

49 The establishment took place on 1 October 2001. Detailed information can be found at www.versicherungsombudsmann.de; cf. Hirsch, *VuR* 2010, 298; I. Benöhr/C. Hodges/N. Creutzfeldt-Banda, in C. Hodges/I. Benöhr/N. Creutzfeldt-Banda (eds.), *Consumer ADR in Europe* (London: Bloomsbury Publishing, 2012), pp. 90 ff.

50 Cf. http://www.versicherungsombudsmann.de/Navigationsbaum/WirUeberUns/StellungDerMitglieder/index.html.

51 Directive 2002/92/EC of the European Parliament and of the Council of 9 December 2002 on insurance mediation, OJ 2003 L 9/3; Article 11 of the Directive requires Member States to promote the establishment of adequate and effective complaints and redress procedures for the out-of-court settlement of disputes between insurance intermediaries and customers, this can be done by using existing bodies.

52 The limitation of the possible respondents is explained by the structure of this institution and has apparently not yet led to problems in practice, cf. D. Looschelders, in *Münchener Kommentar zum VVG*, 3rd ed. (Munich: C.H. Beck, 2024), §214 VVG para. 13. But see Römer, *NVersZ* 2002, 289, 290: The parent company, for example, could be a member. However, this does not necessarily mean that all subsidiaries are members. In case of doubt, the ombudsman should then ask the parent company how the declaration of membership should be interpreted, instead of rejecting the complaint as inadmissible.

**1514.** A similar development can be observed in the field of air passenger transport. The German Act on ADR in Air Transport in has been in force since 1 November 2013.[53] According to this law, dispute settlement is to be carried out primarily by conciliation boards organised under private law and supported by the air carriers. The law sets certain minimum standards for these procedures. If companies do not set up their own voluntary private conciliation bodies, they will be submitted to subsidiary official conciliation at the Federal Office of Justice. In this way, all consumer claims in the air transport sector (e.g. due to delay, overbooking or loss of luggage) up to a value at stake of 5,000 euros are to be subject to a basically free ADR scheme. As a reaction to this development, all German and numerous international airlines joined the dispute settlement board for public passenger transport (*Schlichtungsstelle für den öffentlichen Personenverkehr*[54]) on 1 November 2013.

## 4. NO BINDING FORCE OF THE OUTCOME OF CONSUMER ADR

**1515.** The ADR Directive does not comment on what result is to be achieved within the framework of dispute settlement. However, it allows Member States to establish or maintain competent arbitration boards to issue a binding decision (Article 2(4) ADR Directive) – such a binding effect may also be unilateral for the trader only. It is probably this option that appears preferable from the perspective of the Directive in order not to unduly restrict the consumer's right of access to justice.

**1516.** Thus, the proceedings do not have to end with a decision that is binding with regard to one or both parties. The ADR procedures covered by the Directive thus include a mere attempt at conciliation, as in mediation, but also a settlement proposal by the dispute resolution body or even a decision that binds one or both parties. The ADR Directive obviously assumes that the dispute resolution body has no decision-making power. Furthermore, not only the participation in the procedure itself but also the acceptance of a possible settlement proposal submitted to the parties at the end of the procedure is not subject to any constraints. If just one of the parties is not satisfied with the proposal, the ADR ends without a result.[55]

---

53 Of 11 June 2013, BGBl. I, p. 1545.

54 Later the name was changed to Schlichtungsstelle Reise & Verkehr e.V.

55 On the *res iudicata* effects of settlements in consumer ADR: Stürner, in *Festschrift für Klamaris* (Athens: Sakkoulas Publications, 2016), p. 791.

## 5. CROSS-BORDER CONSUMER ADR

**1517.** A major criticism of the ADR Directive concerns the regulation of cross-border constellations.[56] It should be at the centre of the regulatory interest since the raison d'être of the Directive, the improvement of the functioning of the internal market, is decisively based on increasing the attractiveness of ADR, especially with respect to cross-border contracts. However, the ADR Directive is characterised by an almost total lack of regulation in this respect.[57] Instead, it assumes free competition between different ADR bodies in the internal market. This can make access to ADR, which is held in such high regard by the ADR Directive, much more difficult, especially in the case of cross-border consumer contracts. A privilege for consumers (as it exists concerning judicial proceedings in Articles 17 and 18 Brussels Ibis Regulation) does not exist. However, the trader will usually not get involved in out-of-court dispute settlement procedures that ought to take place outside their state of domicile. In any case, the Member States' responsibility to ensure that conciliation bodies are established throughout the country is limited to disputes with traders who have their registered office in that Member State (Article 5(1) ADR Directive).

**1518.** It seems that under the ADR Directive the situation for the consumer is much less favourable as compared to judicial redress.[58] Even though this certainly has less severe consequences because the arbitration procedure is usually conducted in writing and there are no additional costs for the consumer, arbitration procedures conducted abroad often leave the consumer at a disadvantage with regard to language requirements and potential differences in the cultural setting. The ODR Regulation can hardly provide a remedy to this disadvantage. The online dispute resolution platform ('ODR platform') created by it only acts as a broker; it is not established to conduct cross-border ADR itself.[59]

# IV. CONFLICTING OBJECTIVES: EASY ACCESS VS. HIGH STANDARDS OF PROTECTION

**1519.** Thus, it is obvious that the ADR Directive tries to solve an almost insoluble conflict of objectives: On the one hand, the threshold to accessing

56 Cf. Rühl, *RIW* 2013, 737; J. Kotzur, in Stürner/Gascón Inchausti/Caponi (eds.), *The Role of Consumer ADR in the Administration of Justice*, 2015, p. 59; Gössl, *RIW* 2016, 473.

57 On issues of conflict of laws Wiese, in *Festschrift für Kronke*, 2020, p. 633.

58 Presentation of the problem and proposed solution for this in J. Kotzur, *Die außergerichtliche Realisierung grenzüberschreitender Verbraucherforderungen*, 2018, pp. 117 ff.

59 On this point J. Kotzur, *VuR* 2015, 243.

ADR mechanisms should be as low as possible to make out-of-court settlement for consumer cases in the internal market as attractive as possible. Consequently, consumer ADR is characterised by a low degree of formalisation, the absence of a lawyer, no cost risks on the consumer's side and a short duration of proceedings. On the other hand, ADR should also strive to achieve high standards in legal terms, and it should be fair, possibly observing the rule of law, conducted by independent and impartial persons with possibly extensive legal knowledge and a maximum of transparency. In this context, the decision on how much emphasis should be placed on the former or on the latter has been left open for the Member States. The question of what role substantive consumer law should play in dispute resolution is of decisive importance in resolving those conflicting objectives: Does the legal standard set by EU consumer law merely represent one of several parameters that are taken into account in the procedure, or does it – as in court proceedings – have a strictly binding effect?

## V. ROUGH JUSTICE?

**1520.** The ADR Directive appears to mirror the fact that consumer law seems to have become so complicated that it overburdens consumers and the judiciary alike. For the Commission, the remedy to this problem does not seem to lie in a new approach to substantive law or procedural law (keyword are: reduction of 'information overload', collective redress, small claims procedures or cross-border enforcement of claims). Rather, with the entry into force of the ADR Directive, the enforcement of the standards set by consumer law is more or less waived in favour of a mere approximation towards these standards in the framework of consumer ADR schemes. In an area of freedom, security and justice, such an approach is somewhat disconcerting – all the more so when one realises that the problem is homemade: After all, consumer law, the complexity of which justifies the need for the ADR Directive, also originates from Brussels.

# INDEX

*The index entries refer to paragraph numbers*

# IUS COMMUNITATIS SERIES

Published titles within the series:

1. Stefan Grundmann, *European Company Law. Organization, Finance and Capital Markets*, 2nd edn., Cambridge-Antwerp-Portland, Intersentia, 2012
   ISBN 978-1-78068-019-4
2. André Klip, *European Criminal Law. An Integrative Approach*, 3rd edn., Cambridge-Antwerp-Portland, Intersentia, 2016
   ISBN 978-1-78068-270-9
3. Pieter Boeles, Maarten den Heijer, Gerrie Lodder and Kees Wouters, *European Migration Law*, 2nd edn., Cambridge-Antwerp-Portland, Intersentia, 2014
   ISBN 978-1-78068-155-9
4. Karl Riesenhuber, *European Employment Law*, Cambridge-Antwerp-Portland, Intersentia, 2012
   ISBN 978-1-78068-080-4
5. Norbert Reich, Hans-Wolfgang Micklitz, Peter Rott and Klaus Tonner, *European Consumer Law*, 2nd edn., Cambridge-Antwerp-Portland, Intersentia, 2014
   ISBN 978-1-78068-086-6
6. Frans Pennings, *European Social Security Law*, 6th edn., Cambridge-Antwerp-Portland, Intersentia, 2015
   ISBN 978-1-78068-276-1
7. Karl Riesenhuber, *European Legal Methodology*, 2nd edn., Cambridge-Antwerp-Portland, Intersentia, 2021
   ISBN 978-1-83970-136-8

www.ingramcontent.com/pod-product-compliance
Ingram Content Group UK Ltd.
Pitfield, Milton Keynes, MK11 3LW, UK
UKHW051906290926
8980IPUK00017B/1787